Colonial Families of the United States of America

IN WHICH IS GIVEN THE HISTORY, GENEALOGY AND
ARMORIAL BEARINGS OF COLONIAL FAMILIES WHO
SETTLED IN THE AMERICAN COLONIES FROM THE
TIME OF THE SETTLEMENT OF JAMESTOWN,
13TH MAY, 1607,
TO THE BATTLE OF LEXINGTON, 19TH APRIL, 1775

EDITED BY
NELSON OSGOOD RHOADES

MEMBER OF THE

Society of Mayflower Descendants, New England Historic-Genealogical
Society, New York Genealogical and Biographical Society, National
Historical Society, Valley Forge Historical Society, California
Genealogical Society, National Genealogical Society, Utah
Genealogical Society, Society Sons of the Revolution,
Society of Colonial Wars, Order of Washington,
Order of Founders and Patriots of
America, etc.

(George Norbury Mackenzie, deceased, was the founder
and publisher of the first six volumes of this work.)

VOLUME VII

Baltimore
GENEALOGICAL PUBLISHING COMPANY
1966

Originally Published
Baltimore, 1920

Library of Congress Catalog Card No. 66-18423

Colonial Families of the
United States of America

In Kingdoms, the first foundation, or plantation, is of more noble dignity and merit than all that followeth.—*Lord Bacon.*

He lives with his ancestry, and he lives with his posterity; to both does he consider himself involved in deep responsibilities.—*Washington Irving.*

Colonial Families of the United States of America

Ahles

ROBERT LAWRENCE AHLES of "Whitehall," East Williston, New York; *b.* 14th August, 1878, at Bayside, Long Island, New York; *m.* 12th November, 1902, at Washington, District of Columbia, Helen Wilmer KEMPER, *b.* 11th February, 1879, at Port Republic, Virginia, dau. of Fontaine Llewellyn and Sarah B. (BROWN) KEMPER, of White Hall, Virginia.

ISSUE

I. Lydia Bell, *b.* 25th September, 1909.

ROBERT LAWRENCE AHLES was educated at Mount Pleasant Academy, Ossining, New York; is President of the Sweet Steel Company of Williamsport, Pennsylvania.

Lineage

The patronymic of this family is of great antiquity, having originated with the Latins. Several members of the family of LAWRENCE have held and still hold responsible and distinguished stations, as well in the church and civil service, as in the army and navy of the British Empire; and many branches, also, have intermarried with the clergy and nobility. The first ancestors of this family, of which we have any knowledge, was Sir Robert LAWRENCE, of Ashton Hall, in Lancashire, England. It may perhaps be interesting to this family to know that there is a marriage between a grandson of this gentleman and the WASHINGTON family; Sir James LAWRENCE and Matilda WASHINGTON, in the reign of Henry III. Lawrence WASHINGTON purchased the property at Mount Vernon about 1743, after his return from the expedition to Carthagena, where he had served under the celebrated Admiral VERNON, and in honor of whom he named his country seat. General WASHINGTON inherited Mount Vernon from his half-brother Lawrence WASHINGTON, with whom he was a favorite. Lawrence WASHINGTON died at the early age of thirty-four years, and was interred in the old vault on his estate. Sir Robert LAWRENCE accompanied Richard Coeur de Lion in his famous expedition to Palestine, where he signalized himself in the memorable siege of St. Jean d'Acre, in 1119, by being the first to plant the banner of the cross on the battlements of that town, for which he received the honors of knighthood from King Richard, and also a coat of arms (this coat of arms is still preserved, impressed on the seal appended to a document of William LAWRENCE, 1680, and also Richard LAWRENCE, 1711, preserved in the Surrogate's Office, New York City) at the same time. After this the family became eminent in England, so much so, that Sir John LAWRENCE, the ninth in lineal descent from the above Sir Robert LAWRENCE, possessed thirty-four manors, the revenue of which amounted, in 1491, to £6000 sterling per annum. Having, however, killed a gentleman-usher of King Henry VII, he was outlawed and died in exile in France, issueless, when Ashton Hall and his other estates passed, by royal decree, to his relatives, Lord MONTEAGLE and GERARD. Henry LAWRENCE, one of the patentees of land on the Connecticut River, granted in 1635, and who, with Lords SAY and SELE and Lord BROOKE, Sir Arthur HASSELRIGG, Richard SALTONSTALL, George FENWICK, and Henry DARLEY commissioned John WINTHROP, Jr., as governor over this territory, with the following instructions: "To provide able men for making fortifications and building houses at the mouth of the Connecticut River, and the harbor adjoining; first, for their own present accommodation, and then such houses as may receive men of quality, which latter houses we would have to be builded within the fort." This was the same expedition in which Lion GARDINER was appointed chief engineer. The above individuals intended to accompany John WINTHROP, Jr., to America, but were prevented by a decree of Charles I. The above Henry LAWRENCE was of some considerable distinction in England during CROMWELL's time. He was born in the year 1600, entered a fellow-commoner at Emanuel College, Cambridge, 1622, retired to Holland to escape the persecution of bishops and their courts; was Member of Parliament for Westmoreland in 1641, but withdrew when the life of the king began to be in jeopardy from the independents. In a curious old pamphlet printed in the year 1661, entitled, "The mystery of the good old cause is briefly unfolded in a catalogue of the members of the late Long Parliament that held office, both civil and military, contrary to the self denying ordinance," is the following pastage: "Henry LAWRENCE, a Member of the Long Parliament, fell off at the murder of his majesty, for which the Protector, with great zeal, declared that a neutral spirit was more to be abhorred than a cavalier spirit, and that such men as he were not fit to be used in such a day as that, when God was cutting down kingship root and branch." Yet he came into play again, and contributed much to the setting up of the Protector, for which worthy service he was made and continued Lord President of the Protector's Council, being also one of the Lords of the other House. In 1646, he published, at Amsterdam, his book, entitled, "Book of our Communion and Warre with Angels," and a "Treatise on Baptism" the same year. He married Amy, dau. of Sir Edward PEYTON, Baronet, of Iselham, in Cambridgeshire. He leased his estates at St. Ives, from the year 1631 to 1635, to Oliver CROMWELL, to whom he was second cousin. He was twice returned as Member of Parliament for Hertfordshire, in 1653 and 1654; and once for Colchester borough in Essex, in 1656; his son Henry representing Caernarvonshire the same year. He was President of the Council in 1656, and gazetted as "Lord of the Other

House" in December, 1657. He proclaimed, after the death of CROMWELL, his son Richard as his successor. In a Harleian manuscript, No. 1460, there is a drawing of all the ensigns and trophies won in battle by Oliver, which is dedicated to his councillors, and ornamented with their arms; amongst these are those of Henry LAWRENCE the Lord President. The motto "Nil Admirari," appears to have been assumed by the President during the revolutionary troubles, probably on his being made a Councillor. A picture of the President is inserted in Clarendon's history of the rebellion. His gravestone, not yet effaced, is in the chapel of St. Margaret's, alias Thele in Hertfordshire. There may be clearly traced on it the arms, viz.: a cross, raguly gules, the crest, a fish's tail or demidolphin. A letter directed by him to Sir Simon D'EWES, is sealed with a small red seal, cross ragguly gules, the same crest, and a Lion in the Chief, as borne by the ST. IVES family. While the Dutch were prosecuting their settlements on Long Island and in New York, the English settlers slowly infused themselves among the Dutch population of the island; among which were three brothers, John, William and Thomas LAWRENCE ancestors of a numerous and enterprising family in this country. These three brothers, as well as the above Henry LAWRENCE, were all descended from John LAWRENCE, who died in 1538, and was buried in the Abbey of Ramsay in corroboration of the relationship between Henry LAWRENCE and the above named brothers, we find on the seals appended to their wills, now on file at New York, and on old plate still possessed by their descendants, the same crest and arms as those upon the tomb of the lord president.

A John LAWRENCE was Chief Burger of St. Albans in 1553 and Mayor in 1567 and 1575 and may have been the father of William LAWRENCE, with whom the proven pedigree of this family begins. This William LAWRENCE of St. Albans, Hertfordshire, England, *m.* 25th November, 1559, Katerin BEAUMONT.

ISSUE

I. JOHN, *bapt.* 12th January, 1561–1562, of whom later.
II. Elizabeth, *bapt.* 16th September, 1572.
III. Thomas, who *m.* 5th November, 1589, Marie WILKINSON.

JOHN LAWRENCE of St. Albans, England; *bapt.* 12th January, 1561–1562; *m.* (firstly) wife's name not given; *m.* (secondly) 25th January, 1586–1587, Margaret ROBERTES.

ISSUE BY FIRST MARRIAGE

I. William, *bapt.* 4th December, 1580.
II. Edward, *bapt.* 18th June, 1582.

ISSUE BY SECOND MARRIAGE

I. Richard, *bapt.* 26th July, 1587.
II. THOMAS, *bapt.* 2d Feb., 1588–1589, of whom later.

THOMAS LAWRENCE, *bapt.* 2d February, 1588–1589; probably Chief Burger of St. Albans in 1622; *d.* 20th March, 1624–1625; *m.* 23d October, 1609, Joane ANTERBUS, dau. of Walter and Jane (ARNOLDE) ANTERBUS.

ISSUE

I. Joane, *bapt.* 29th August, 1610; *d.* 31st August, 1610.
II. Jane, *bapt.* 18th December, 1614; *m.* George GIDDINGS.
III. Marie, *bapt.* 17th November, 1616; *d.* 28th November, 1616.
IV. John, *bapt.* 26th July 6, 1618; emigrated in 1635, in the *Planter*, Nicholas TRAVIS, master, in company with Governor John WINTHROP, Jr., and landed at Plymouth, Massachusetts, 1635; he removed from thence to Ipswich, where, after residing some time, he removed to Long Island. He became, in 1644, one of the patentees of Hempstead, on that island, under grant from the Dutch governor, KIEFT. He, together with his brother William, and sixteen others, in the following year, obtained the patent of Flushing from the same governor, and were also among those to whom the confirmatory patent was issued by Governor NICOLL, 16th February, 1666, to wit: John LAWRENCE, Alderman of the City of New York; Richard CORNHILL, Justice of the Peace; Charles BRIDGES, William LAWRENCE, Robert TERRY, William NOBLE, John FFOVBUSH, Elias DOUGHTY, Robert FFIELD, EDMUND FFARINGTON, John MASTON, Anthony FFIELD, Philip UDALL, Thomas STYLES, Benjamin FFIELD, William PIDGEON, John ADAMS, John HINCKMAN, Nicholas PARCELL, Tobias FFEEKS, and John BOWNE patentees for, and in behalf of themselves and their associates, the freeholders, inhabitants of the town of Flushing, their heirs, successors and assigns, forever, all that certain town in the North Riding of Yorkshire, upon Long Island, called by the name of Flushing, situate, lying and being on the north side of the said island; which said town hath a certain tract of land belonging thereto, and bounded westward, beginning at the mouth of a creek, and from thence including a certain neck of land called Tew's Neck, to run eastward as far as Matthew Garrison's Bay, from the head or middle whereof a line is to be run south-east, in length about three miles, and about two miles in breadth, as the land hath been surveyed and laid out by virtue of an order made at the general meeting held at Hempstead, in the month of March, 1665; and that there be the same latitude in breadth on the south side as on the north, to run in two direct lines southward, to the middle of the hills, to the bounds between the said towns of Flushing and Jamaica." He must have attained some eminence in the Massachusetts Colony before removing to New Amsterdam, as Governor ENDICOTT writes, 15th September, 1658, specially commending him; 16th November, 1644, we find him as one of the original corporators of "The Great Plains" (after-

ward Hempstead, Long Island) and 10th October, 1645, of Flushing, 1st February, 1648, he is one of the committee asking that a minister shall be settled at Flushing; in 1658 removed to New Amsterdam and engaged in business there; 23rd July of that year, the Council inquires concerning "goods removed from the house of Cornelis STEENWYCK by John LAURENS an English merchant." He owned a small trading vessel called the *Adventure*, with which he traded up the Hudson to Albany and on both sides of Long Island. He was very successful in his affairs, became a Burgher of the City and gained the good will of the Dutch. Governor STUYVESANT, speaking of him, 10th June, 1664, as "well affected to the Dutch;" 29th May, 1664, he buys a negro for 345 florins. In October, 1663, with two others, is sent as a Commissioner to the General Assembly at Hartford, Connecticut; 1st March, 1664-1665, he is Attorney for Flushing in a boundary dispute. After the capture of the province by the English he is one of the first Aldermen (appointed, 12th June, 1665, holding office until 1667, and again 1670-1672; the latter year he is elected Mayor; 18th August, 1673, "the Burgomasters and Schepens resolve that the mace, gowns, and city seal of the late Mayor, John LAWRENCE, be brought in, and the late Mayor reappearing delivers up his gown or cloak, with the city seal and mace." 1st November, 1673, is one of three guardians of the estate of Richard MORRIS, brother of Colonel Lewis MORRIS. In the Dutch recapture of the city, in 1673, his house was not plundered. 19th February, 1674, in a valuation of the best and most affluent inhabitants of New Amsterdam, John LAWRENCE has 10,000 florins, Holland currency, only ten others having as much or more. Is again Alderman of New York in 1680, and until 1684. 29th September, 1683, he has at Flushing "1 male, 12 acres upland, 10 of meadowes, 1 horse, 5 cowes, 6 young cattle, 1 pig, and is taxed 7 shills. 5d." The same year has at Newtown "10 acres of lande, 4 cowes, and 3 three-year olds." In 1664, is appointed a member of the Governor's Council. The same year he has, in New York City, a house of the first class, and property valued at £2,000, on the west side of Pearl Street, called the Water Side, between Wall and William Streets, and a house of the fourth class, and property valued at £750, on the west side of Pearl Street, between Franklin Square and Wall Street. In 1687 is Alderman of the East Ward of New York. 20th August, 1689, appointed a Justice of the Peace for New York City; 26th March, 1690, he is one of the Special Commission to try Jacob LEISLER and his confederates after their unsuccessful revolution, and as such signs and seals LEISLER's commitment. A facsimile of his signature will be found in Gen. J. Grant WILSON's "Memorial History of New York." 27th March, 1691, with Col. Richard TOWNLEY, who had married his brother's widow, he is re-appointed to the Governor's Council, and the same year is again Mayor of New York. 20th April, 1693, he is one of the Justices of the Supreme Court of the Colony. 28th September 1698, Governor BELLOMONT writes that "he has suspended from the Council Colonel BAYARD, Colonel MONVIELLE, Colonel WILLET, and Mr. LAWRENCE, because they were always resty and perverse in everything that I proposed for the King's service, tho' such sycophants as to comply with Colonel FLETCHER in all parts of his corrupt administration," while the third head of the bill of complaint against the Governor, dated 11th March, 1700, declares that "upon frivolous pretences he suspended ten of the most considerable for estates and parts and experience in busynesse (Mr. LAWRENCE named amongst them) and placed six of the Leislerian faction in their room." 21st October, 1698, as further excuse for his action the Governor writes he is superannuated, being eighty-two years of age. His will, proved 7th January, 1689–1699, recorded Liber 5, p. 346, names "his dau., Martha, widdow of Thomas SNOWSELL (deceased above seventeen years ago), his sons, John and Thomas, daughters, Martha as aforesaid, Susanna, wife of Gabriel MONBEILLE, his dau., WITHINGHAM's children, and his son Joseph's dau." and states that he was a patentee in Hempstead and Flushing and the only survivor in both. He has given to every one of his children a considerable part of his estate, they being all of full age and marriageable. Ends: "Soe I pray God bless them as my children, and make them his children, by faith and love in Christ Jesus. Amen." His wife, Susanna and Gabriel MONVEILLE are executors. He *m.* Susanna (surname not given), who survived him.

ISSUE

1. JOHN, in several papers called his eldest son, of whom presently.
2. Joseph, said to have *d.*, leaving a dau.; *d.* young; there is no trace of him outside the mention in his father's will.
3. Thomas, may possibly be the Thomas LAWRENCE taxed at Flushing, 9th October, 1675, on thirty-two acres, and is said to have *d.* unmarried.
4. Martha, *m.* (license dated 22d August 1675), Thomas SNOWSELL, who *d.s.p.*, in 1682.
5. Susanna, *m.* (firstly), license 25th January, 1676–1677, Gabriel MINVIELLE, or MONVIELE, Mayor of New York and Member of the Governor's Council; made his will 8th March, 1697–1698; proved, 1st October, 1702; Executors, Robert LIVINGSTON and John BARBARIE, his nephew; he leaves his wife, "All his servants, household stuff, silver plate, gold chains, pearls, dyamonds, gold rings and other jewels;" the rest of the estate to his nephews and nieces. She

m. (secondly) by license dated 22d December, 1702, William SMITH, Alderman of New York, and *d. s. p.*

6. Mary, *m.* William WHITTINGHAME; graduated at Harvard University, in 1660, and had a dau. Mary, of some literary culture, a liberal benefactor of Harvard and Yale Colleges; *m.* Gordon SALTONSTALL, Governor of Connecticut, and *d.* in 1730. See a notice in Knapp's "Female Biography," p. 453.

v. Thomas of St. Albans, England; *bapt.* there 8th March, 1619–1620. He appears to have emigrated after the rest of the family, but the date is not known. He obtained possession of a tract of a land in Newtown, on Long Island, being mentioned as patentees in the patent of that town, granted by Governor DONGAN, in 1689. Thomas subsequently purchased the whole of Hell Gate Neck, then consisting of several valuable farms, extending along the East River, from Hell Gate Cove to Bowery Bay. On receiving the news of the Revolution in England, of 1668, and of the removal of Sir Edmund ANDROS as Governor of Massachusetts, the family of Thomas became decided actors in assisting the principles which had prompted his departure from England. Many persons in Queens, however, as well as Suffolk County, were not disposed to second the popular feeling which had vacated the offices at the city of New York, and placed LEISLER at the head of affairs. Not discouraged at the lukewarmness of his neighbors, Thomas LAWRENCE, though far advanced in years, accepted the command of the forces of Queens County. William, one of his sons, was appointed one of the Committee of Safety, by whom the government of the Colony was for a time assumed, and soon after, one of the Council of the Province; an office which he subsequently held from 1702 to 1706, under a commission from Queen Ann. John LAWRENCE; another of the sons of Thomas, had the command of the troop of horse of the county assigned to him, with his brother Daniel as Cornet. John was soon afterwards appointed High Sheriff of the county, to which place he was also chosen in 1698. Among the meagre records which are left of LEISLER's times, is the entry of an order to Maj. Thomas LAWRENCE, dated 29th July, 1690, "to press seventy men, horse and foot, as he shall think fit; and horses and provisions; and dispatch them to Southold for the defence and protection of their Majesties' subjects there." The misconception or obstinacy, whichever it was, that influenced LEISLER in delaying to surrender the fort at New York to Governor SLAUGHTER on his arrival, involved all the members of his council in the consequences of this omission; and William LAWRENCE with the rest of them, were seized and committed, on a charge of high treason. John LAWRENCE, his uncle, who, from the caution of age, or a disapprobation of the violence of some of LEISLER's proceedings, had never countenanced his elevation, was appointed on the commission with Sir Thomas ROBINSON, Col. William SMITH, and others, to try those political offenders. These proceedings do not appear, however, to have interrupted the mutual confidence and affection of the uncle and nephew. The descendants of Thomas LAWRENCE (being the Newtown branch of the family) are very numerous, residing in Connecticut, New York, New Jersey, and other states of the Union. He died at Newtown in July, 1704, leaving five sons, and one daughter. The first notice we find speaks of him as being at New Haven, 24th August, 1651, with money of Governor STUYVESANT'S to which the New England authorities laid claim and arrested him. After his release he joins with his brothers in the patent of Middleburgh, afterward Newtown, Long Island, in 1655, and appears to have settled there; on 10th July, 1662, being owner of two lots. 23d August, 1665, he receives license, as Capt. Thomas LAWRENCE, to purchase of the Indians "Round Island near Helgate," about eight or nine acres of land. This purchase is disputed by William HALLETT, in 1667, but confirmed by the Governor. 14th March, 1669-1670, he is one of the road surveyors at Newtown. In September, 1675, he has at Newtown 40 acres of land, 2 horses, 4 oxen, 8 cows, 12 younger cattle and 8 swine. Three years later he has 4 persons, 40 acres, 10 horses, 2 oxen, 8 cows, 22 younger cattle, 20 sheep and 12 swine. December, 1677, he has a patent of Anneke Jans's farm on Hellgate Neck. 16th February, 1689-1690 he is spoken of as Maj. Thomas LAWRENCE of Queen's County, on 24th December, of that year, having been commissioned by Jacob LEISLER as Major of Horse for the Company. This branch of the family adhered to the cause of LEISLER. William LAWRENCE was one of the Committee of Safety. John and Daniel had commissions in the Company militia from the rebel Governor. His first wife's name is unknown. 9th November, 1692, Thomas LAWRENCE, widower, of Newtown, has a license to marry Mary FERGUSON. His will was made 5th February, 1703; proved 25th April, 1703 (Liber 7, pp. 134, 135). He leaves "his son Thomas the great neck of land with the island, his wife Mary, the third part of his movable estate, his son Johnathan (sic) that lot of land which was (illegible) the house he now lives in; to his sons William and Johnathan the piece of Salt Medow bought of Robert Beacham, to son Daniel, Trains Medows, names also his grandchild Elizabeth Saunders and four sons—Thomas, William, John and Johnathan." Spells his surname LAWRANCE. 27th January, 1704-1705, Mary, his widow, complains of ill-treatment at the hands of William LAWRENCE, her stepson. 5th, 10th, and 17th February, there are further depositions in the case, and 3d April, she complains also against John, his brother. By his first wife, Major LAWRENCE had issue (the order of birth is uncertain, but probably was):

1. Thomas, for whose descendants see Thomas LAWRENCE's Genealogy of the family (1858), pp. 84-87.
2. WILLIAM, of whom presently.
3. John.
4. Johnathan, see LAWRENCE Genealogy for his issue.
5. Daniel, commissioned Cornet of a Troop of Horse by Governor Bellomont; his issue, if any, is unknown.
6. Elizabeth, *m.* by license dated 26th July, 1683, John SAUNDERS, and had a dau. ELIZABETH, living in 1703.

VI. WILLIAM C., 27th July 1622; of whom later.
VII. MARIE, *bapt.* 10th April, 1635.

CAPTAIN WILLIAM LAWRENCE of Flushing, New York; *b.* in St. Albans, Hertfordshire, England; *bapt.* there 27th July, 1622; he embarked, together with his brother John, in the ship *Planter*, in 1635 for America. He was in 1645, in the twenty-second year of his age, associated with him as one of the patentees of Flushing, on Long Island, in which town he resided during the remainder of his life. His correspondence, during the years 1642-1643, with Governor STUYVESANT, may be found among the archives at Albany, and are ably written, evincing his energy and decision of character, and are evidently the production of a man of superior mind and liberal education. He was the largest landed proprietor at Flushing. He resided upon Lawrence's or Tew's Neck (so called), of which he was the owner, and seemed to have been a gentleman of affluence, his sword, plate and personals alone being valued at £4,430, sterling (see inventory of his estate, on file in the Surrogate's Office, City of New York, recorded in 1680, in Liber No. 22, page 24.) He was a Magistrate under the Dutch government at Flushing, in 1655, and also held, under the English government, a military commission. He was also in the magistracy of the North Riding of Yorkshire, on Long Island. His first wife's name is unknown; he *m.* (secondly), marriage license 4th March, 1664, Elizabeth SMITH, *b.* Smithstown, New York, *d.* 1712, in Elizabeth Town, New Jersey, dau. of Richard SMITH of Nessequack; she *m.* (secondly) Sir Philip CARTERET, Governor of New Jersey, and being a woman of more than ordinary endowments and strength of mind, she was entrusted with the affairs of the colony during her husband's absence in Europe, and in the title to some of the acts of that period, it is stated that they were "passed under the administration of Lady Elizabeth CARTERET." Sir Philip founded Elizabethtown, in New Jersey, giving it her name. Sir Philip *d.* in 1682 leaving the whole of his estate, situate in the Province of East New Jersey to his wife Elizabeth and her heirs forever, appointing the said Elizabeth his sole executrix. His widow afterwards *m.* Col. Richard TOWNLEY, the eighth son of Nicholas TOWNLEY of Littleton, about twelve miles from London. The said Col. Richard TOWNLEY came over in the suite of Lord Effingham HOWARD, Governor of Virginia, in the year 1683 and settled in Elizabethtown. Colonel Richard was one of the Privy Council of Deputy Governor Neil CAMPBELL in 1686.

ISSUE

I. William, Major, a member of the Committee of Safety, then on the Commission dated 16th August, 1689, appointing Capt. Jacob LEISLER Commander-in-Chief of the Province; 14th December, 1689, was a member of LEISLER'S Council; *m.* by license dated 1st June, 1680, Deborah SMITH, dau. of Richard SMITH, a patentee of Smithtown, on Long Island.

II. John, Member of the Council, 10th August, 1702; *d.* before 21st February, 1714–1715; *m.* Elizabeth CORNELL, *b.* 1662, dau. of Richard CORNELL; had issue.

ISSUE BY SECOND MARRIAGE

I. Mary, *b.* 1665; *d.* in New York, 13th April, 1713; *m.* (firstly) in 1682–1683, James EMOTT, Secretary of the Province of New Jersey; Clerk of the Council in 1683; Deputy Secretary, 1684; Captain-Lieutenant of a Foot Company at Perth Amboy, 11th December, 1686; he was counsel for the celebrated pirate, Capt. Richard KIDD; he left his widow with four sons and a fortune of £2,000; she *m.* (secondly) in 1714, Rev. Edward VAUGHAN, who *d.* 12th October, 1747, Missionary for the Society of the Propagation of the Gospel at Elizabeth.

II. JOSEPH, *b.* circa 1666, of whom later.

III. Thomas, *b.* 1668; *d.* 26th October, 1687.

IV. Richard, *m.*, license dated 24th September, 1699, Charity CLARKE, dau. of Thomas CLARKE or CLARKE, Gentleman.

V. Samuel, *b.* 1672; *d.* 16th August, 1687.

VI. Sarah, *m.* James TILLETT.

VII. James, of whom nothing is known.

JOSEPH LAWRENCE, *b.* about 1666, 10th September, 1684; was commissioned an Ensign in the New York Provincial troops. 14th March, 1685–1686, there is a capias against him recorded, for a debt of £2,000. In 1701 he signs a petition of the inhabitants of East Jersey, addressed to the King, and does the same again in 1717, with his brother Richard, also John BOWNE, John and Benjamin LAWRENCE. In 1698 he is recorded at Flushing, with his wife Mary and children, Richard and Thomas. 8th December, 1754, he made his will, proved 18th April, 1759, recorded Liber 22, p. 7. Mentions his wife, his sons Richard and John, and dau. Elizabeth BOWNE, Sarah LAWRENCE, Hanna MOLYNEX, and Abigail FORBES. Unvarying family tradition marries him to a Mary TOWNLEY, who was probably a dau. of his mother's third husband, Col. Richard TOWNLEY, of New Jersey. There appears to be no legal proof of his wife's name, and the early records of the first Presbyterian Church of Elizabeth where the marriage was probably performed, have been destroyed. In this connection it may be well to note, that even though it were proven Mrs. LAWRENCE was a dau. of Colonel TOWNLEY, that would not make her descendants heirs of any great English estate, for two good and sufficient reasons: first, Colonel TOWNLEY was eighth son of a younger branch of the family and the elder line TOWNELEY, of Towneley, has never lacked direct male heirs until 1879, when the three daughters and co-heiresses of Col. Charles TOWNELEY, elder brother of Col. John TOWNELEY, the last male, carried the property into the families of their respective husbands, Lord NORREYS, Lord LENNOX, and Lord O'HAGAN. A second reason why there is no English fortune for her heirs, is the non-existence of any such enormous unclaimed sums of money in the possession of the British Court of Chancery, or the Bank of England, and the passage of an act in 1869 by Parliament which escheated to the Crown all unclaimed funds which had been in Chancery for over sixteen years, in all only £2,327,823. Joseph and Mary (TOWNELEY?) LAWRENCE, had issue:

I. RICHARD, *b.* about 1691, of whom later.
II. Thomas, living at Flushing in 1698, but not mentioned in his father's will.
III. Elizabeth, *m.* John BOWNE.
IV. John, *b.* in 1703; removed to Newport, Rhode Island, and *d.* 10th November, 1781; among his descendants were Joseph LAWRENCE, *b.* 1729, founded the insurance business in Rhode Island. His son, Thomas LAWRENCE, *b.* 21st May, 1792, was the author of the "Lawrence Genealogy," printed in 1858. The LAWRENCE family of Hudson, New York. Laura GARDINIER, *m.* Theodore S. FAY, *b.* in 1809; United States Minister to Switzerland; author of "Norman Leslie," "Hoboken," etc., and Eugene LAWRENCE, *b.* 4th October, 1823, author of "Lives of the British Historians," etc.; *d.* unmarried.
V. Sarah, unmarried in 1754.
VI. Hannah, *m.* Moses MOLYNEUX, of Westchester.

ISSUE

1. Mary MOLYNEUX, *b.* 26th March, 1723.
2. Joseph MOLYNEUX, *b.* 5th September, 1724.

VII. Abigail, *m.* Major Alexander FORBES, of the British Army, from whom descends the present James PARKER, of Perth Amboy, New Jersey.

RICHARD LAWRENCE of Flushing, Long Island, New York; *b.* circa 1691; *d.* 1781, in Flushing, New York; *m.* 6th April, 1717, Hannah BOWNE, *b.* 30th March, 1697, dau. of Samuel BOWNE, a minister among the Friends, who *m.* at the Meeting House at the Falls of the Delaware, 4th August, 1691, Mary BECKET, an English lady who came over with William PENN in 1682 and whose father Captain BECKET was said to have been killed fighting under the Duke of Marlboro, and Eleanor PERCY, his wife of Northumberland County, England.

ISSUE

I. Mary, *b.* 2d April, 1718; *m.* Edward BURLING.
II. Elizabeth, *b.* 15th June, 1719; *m.* John EMBREE; had issue.
III. Joseph, *b.* 10th September, 1721; *d.* young.
IV. Caleb, *b.* 10th February, 1723–1724; *m.* 7th June, 1754, Sarah BURLING, dau. of James and Elizabeth BURLING.
V. Hannah, *b.* 2d April, 1726; *m.* Abraham WILLETT.
VI. Liddya, *b.* 29th September, 1728; *m.* 1745, Stevanus HUNT.
VII. John, *b.* 31st January, 1730–1731; *d.* 9th February same year.
VIII. John, again, *b.* 22d January, 1731–1732; *d.* 26th July, 1794, in New York City; *m.* 13th August, 1755, Ann BURLING, who *d.* 14th February, 1821.
IX. Effingham, *b.* 6th June, 1734–1735; *d.* 1806, Captain of the ship *Lord Dunmore* in 1771; 9th June, 1773, carried General GAGE and others to England; removed to London and became an eminent merchant there; *m.* Catherine FARMER; removed after his marriage to London and was appointed to the command of a British frigate and became one of the corporation of the elder brethren of the Trinity House, London; he resided at Tower Hill.
X. Norris, *b.* 6th January, 1737–1738, *m.* (license 6th January, 1765) Ann PELL, dau. of Caleb and Mary (FERRIS) PELL.
XI. JOSEPH, *b.* 23d August, 1741, of whom below.

JOSEPH LAWRENCE, of Flushing, Long Island, New York; *b.* 23d August, 1741; *d.* 1781; inherited under his father's will the estate of "Bayside;" *m.* Phoebe TOWNSEND (license dated 17th March, 1764), dau. of Henry TOWNSEND of Oyster Bay, Long Island.

ISSUE

I. Elizabeth, *b.* 1765; *m.* Silus TITUS; had issue.
II. HENRY, *b.* 22d April, 1767, of whom later.
III. Phebe, *m.* Obadiah TOWNSEND.
IV. Richard, *m.* Betsey TALMAN.
V. Lydia, *m.* Anthony FRANKLIN.
VI. Abigail, *d.* unmarried.
VII. Effingham, was for several years first judge of the County of Queens; *m.* Anna TOWNSEND, dau. of Solomon TOWNSEND, *b.* in Oyster Bay, 1746, the eldest son of Samuel, who was fifth eldest son in line from the first John TOWNSEND.

HENRY LAWRENCE of Flushing, Long Island; *b.* 22d April, 1767; *d.* 11th February, 1824; *m.* (firstly) Harriet VAN WYCK, *b.* 25th February, 1771, *d.* 12th August, 1812; *m.* (secondly) Amy PEARSALL.

ISSUE (NO RECORD AS FROM WHICH MARRIAGE)

I. Cornelius W., *b.* 1791; a merchant of New York City; Member of Congress, Mayor of the City of New York; President of the Bank of the State of New York and subsequently Collector of the Port of New York; *m.* (firstly) Maria C. PRALL, dau. of Abraham PRALL; *m.* (secondly) Rachel A. HICKS, dau. of Willet HICKS; *m.* (thirdly) Lydia A. LAWRENCE, widow of Edward N. LAWRENCE.
II. Joseph, *d.* in infancy.
III. Joseph, again, *d.* in infancy.
IV. Joseph, again, *b.* 1797; was a merchant of New York City; President of the Bank of the State of New York for several years; Treasurer of the City of New York; President of the United States Trust Company; *m.* Rosetta TOWNSEND, dau. of Thomas S. TOWNSEND.
V. Richard, *m.* Sarah Ann DRAKE, dau of James DRAKE.
VI. This name is not given in record.
VII. Phoebe, unmarried.
VIII. CATHERINE H., of whom below.
IX. Harriet, *d.* unmarried.
X. Esther P., *m.* (firstly) William POST; *m.* (secondly) Greenville P. OSGOOD of Louisiana.

ISSUE

1. Jeanne Nicola, the Cantatrice.

CATHERINE H. LAWRENCE of "Bayside," Long Island, New York; *b.* there 19th January, 1807; *d,* there in 1880; *m.* there Robert Moore BELL, *b.* March, 1807, *d.* 1888, at Bayside.

ISSUE

I. Richard Moore BELL, *b.* 20th February, 1841, at Bayside, Long Island; *m.* 4th December, 1873, Julia Newbold BLACK, of New Jersey.

ISSUE

1. Henry Lawrence BELL, *m.* Lisa RIDGELY.
2. Lydia BELL, *m.* Charles M. GOULD.
3. Emily Newbold BELL, *m.* Harry HUTCHINSON.

II. Lydia Ann BELL, *b.* 2d April, 1845, at Bayside, Long Island; *d.* there 27th May, 1896; *m.* there 19th June, 1873, John William AHLES, *b.* there 13th July, 1845, *d.* there 18th August, 1915.

ISSUE

1. ROBERT LAWRENCE AHLES, *b.* 14th August, 1878, the subject of this memoir.
2. Gertrude F. AHLES.
3. Virginia AHLES.

Arms (LAWRENCE).—Argent, a cross raguley gules, on a chief of the second a lion passant guardant or.
Crest.—The tail and lower part of a fish erect and couped ppr.
Motto.—In cruce salus.
Residence.—East Williston, Nassau County, New York.
Clubs.—Riding Club, St. Nicholas, Turf and Field, Engineers Club, Racquet Club of Philadelphia.
Societies.—Colonial Wars, American Institute of Mining Engineers, American Iron and Steel Institute, Iron and Steel Institute of Great Britain.

Ahles-Bryant

JOHANNES BRYANT came from Amsterdam, Holland, and settled at Hackensack, New Jersey. His wife's name is not given.

ISSUE

I. Simeon, *m.* and had a family, many of the descendants of which are to be found in the Passaic Valley.
II. CORNELIUS, *d.* 1792, of whom below.

CORNELIUS BRYANT of Springfield, New Jersey; *d.* 1792; was *b.* at Hackensack; he built the first two houses erected at Springfield and Westfield, New Jersey; *m.* Hannah CARTERET, dau. of Capt. James CARTERET, some of whose descendants settled in Pennsylvania and who *m.* in 1671, Frances DELEVAL, dau. of the Mayor of New York. Captain CARTERET was the son of Sir George CARTERET, one of the Lord Proprietors of New Jersey, who *d.* 1679. Sir George was a loyal and gallant officer, who defended the Isle of Wight, Jersey, against the Long Parliament and was a court favorite of James II, his wife Dame Elizabeth CARTERET *d.* 1717.

ISSUE

1. John of Albany, New York, where in 1708 he commenced the manufacture of the first bricks made in Albany and continued same for thirty-five years; his business was called "Bryant's Business;" bricks were then sold by the pound; *m.* Ellen SPARLING.

ISSUE

1. Sarah, *m.* Angus McDUFFIE, of Albany, New York; had issue.
2. Hannah, *m.* Jacob ROSEBOOM; had issue.
3. Elizabeth, *m.* Jackson BIGELOW; had issue.
4. Mary, *m.* Capt. Henry H. BUCKBEE, of Albany, New York; had issue.
5. Ellen, *m.* (firstly) James BROWN; *m.* (secondly) Capt. William ELLIS, of Scotland.
6. Jane.
7. John.
8. George, *m.* three times; wives' names not given; had issue.

II. Phoebe, *m.* John BARTON, of Elizabeth Town, New Jersey.
III. Benjamin.
IV. ELIZABETH, *b.* 1768, of whom later.
V. Nancy, *m.* Cornelius MUMFORD, son of Capt. Jonathan MUMFORD, of New Providence, New Jersey.

ELIZABETH BRYANT of Elizabethtown, New Jersey; *b.* at Springfield, New Jersey, 1768; *d.* 26th June, 1845; *m.* (firstly) Jonathan BONNELL, of Chatham, New Jersey; *m.* (secondly) John BALLANTINE of Edinburgh, Scotland; *m.* (thirdly) Samuel WILLIAMS of Hackensack, New Jersey, who *d.s.p.*

ISSUE BY FIRST MARRIAGE

I. Jonathan BONNELL.
II. Charlotte BONNELL.

ISSUE BY SECOND MARRIAGE

I. Eliza H. BALLANTINE, *b.* 14th July, 1795, of whom later.

ELIZA H. BALLANTINE of Poughkeepsie, New York; *b.* 14th July, 1795; *d.* 8th August, 1856, at Newark, New Jersey; *m.* (firstly) 1814, John J. CHARRUAUD of France; *m.* (secondly) 23d September, 1832, Gerlando MARSIGLIA of Palermo, Sicily.

ISSUE BY FIRST MARRIAGE

I. John Henry CHARRUAUD, unmarried, lost on the steamer *Pacific*, 1856.
II. Pierre Eugene CHARRUAUD, *d.s.p.* July, 1885; *m.* Matilda J. ALLEN of New York.
III. ZOE PARINE CHARRUAUD, of whom later.
IV. Emma Serena CHARRUAUD, *m.* John F. LOHSE of Germany.
V. Frances Augusta CHARRUAUD, *m.* Juan BARCELO of Spain.
VI. Ada Geraldine CHARRUAUD, *m.* Horatio LEONARD of New York.

ISSUE BY SECOND MARRIAGE

I. Gerlando Antonio MARSIGLIA, *d.* in infancy.
II. Catherine Romano MARSIGLIA, *m.* Francis A. CLEVELAND, son of Eyra CLEVELAND of Elizabeth, New Jersey, a relative of President Grover CLEVELAND.

ZOE PARINE CHARRUAUD of Poughkeepsie, New York; *m.* George AHLES of Germany.

ISSUE

I. Zoe AHLES, *m.* Edward WALKER.
II. Emma AHLES, *m.* John LAWRENCE of Long Island.
III. JOHN WILLIAM AHLES, *b.* 13th July, 1845, of whom later.
IV. Fannie AHLES.
V. Clara AHLES, *m.* Charles RUSSELL.
VI. Georgia AHLES, *d.* in infancy.
VII. Evaline AHLES, *d.* in infancy.

JOHN WILLIAM AHLES, of Bayside, Long Island, New York; *b.* there 13th July, 1845; *d.* there 18th August, 1915; *m.* there 19th June, 1873, Lydia Ann BELL, *b.* there 2d April, 1845, *d.* there 27th May, 1896, dau. of Robert MOORE and Catherine (LAWRENCE) BELL.

ISSUE

I. ROBERT LAWRENCE AHLES, *b.* 14th August, 1878, the subject of this memoir.
II. Gertrude F. AHLES.
III. Virginia AHLES.

Akers

MATTHEW LOVE AKERS of Louisville, Kentucky; *b.* 10th September, 1866, in Floyd County, Indiana; *m.* 16th December, 1901, in Louisville, Kentucky, Frank GUTHRIE, *b.* 8th March, 1873, dau. of Benjamin Franklin GUTHRIE, *b.* 4th June, 1831, in Shelby County, Kentucky, *d.* 18th April, 1891, in Jefferson County, Kentucky, *m.* 1st December, 1852, Keziah Jane POLLARD, *b.* 20th August, 1831, in Henry County, Kentucky, *d.* 23d April, 1891.

ISSUE

I. Frank Guthrie, *b.* 9th December, 1902; student at St. Mark's, 1918.

MATTHEW LOVE AKERS was educated at public schools and by private tutoring; began railroad career with Pennsylvania Lines, West; afterwards with Chesapeake and Ohio Railway; is at present General Agent of that road at Louisville, Kentucky; also is Vice President Louisville and Jeffersonville Bridge and Railroad Company; was President Kentucky Horse Show, 1907-1908.

Lineage

SIMON AKERS, *b.* 2d June, 1730; *d.* in Clark County, Indiana, 19th March, 1819; emigrated from England to Virginia, then to Kentucky and Indiana (in 1812); was granted land in Warrant No. 4985, issued to him in Williamsburg, Virginia, 18th February, 1801, for three years' service in the Virginia Continental Line; *m.* Sarah MALONE, dau. of Stephen MALONE.

ISSUE

I. GEORGE, *b.* 30th March, 1791, of whom later.

GEORGE AKERS of Tarrant County, Texas; *b.* 30th March, 1791, at Augusta County, Virginia; *d.* 16th December, 1859, in Tarrant County, Texas; was a Justice of the Peace in Indiana for many years prior to 1832 when he removed to Texas; *m.* Nancy AKERS, dau. of Thomas and Millicent AKERS of Floyd County, Indiana.

ISSUE

I. HIRAM, *b.* 26th February, 1811, of whom below.

HIRAM AKERS of Clark County, Indiana; *b.* 26th February, 1811, in Shelby County, Kentucky; *d.* 22d May, 1856, in Clark County, Indiana; *m.* 10th October, 1833, Amelia GARRITSON, dau. of Washington and Millicent (TOMLIN) GARRITSON of Cape May County, New Jersey.

ISSUE

I. REASON LAWSON, *b.* 9th January, 1837, of whom below.

REASON LAWSON AKERS, Surgeon United States Army; *b.* 9th January, 1837, in Clark County, Indiana; *d.* there 23d November, 1878; served during Civil War from 1862–1865 as Surgeon in 144th Regiment, United States Volunteers; *m.* 28th September, 1865, Louisa Abraham MILLER, *b.* 13th August, 1847, dau. of Abraham and Louisa (OWEN) MILLER.

ISSUE

I. MATTHEW LOVE, *b.* 10th September, 1866, the subject of this memoir.
II. Owen Miller, *b.* 20th September, 1868.
III. Charles Lawson, *b.* 9th September, 1872.
IV. Minnie Caroline, *b.* 23d December, 1876.

Arms.—Argent on a bend sable, three acorns or, husked vert.
Crest.—A dove rising ppr. on the beak an acorn of the arms ppr.
Motto.—La Liberte.
Residences.—1028 Cherokee Road, Louisville, Kentucky, "Upland House," Hot Springs, Virginia.
Clubs.—Pendennis of Louisville and Westmoreland of Richmond, Virginia.
Societies.—Colonial Wars, Sons of the American Revolution.

Miller

ABRAHAM MILLER of Northampton County, Pennsylvania; *b.* in Holland; *d.* 1752 in Northampton County; emigrated from Holland to Northampton County (formerly a part of Bucks County) in 1740; was a large land owner, much of which he purchased from Richard PETERS; *m.* in Holland (wife's name is not given).

ISSUE

I. ABRAHAM, *b.* 1st April, 1735, of whom later.
II. Joseph.
III. Catherine.
IV. Salome.
V. Elizabeth.

CAPT. ABRAHAM MILLER of Southport (Elmira), New York; *b.* 1st April, 1735, in Holland; *d.* 25th July, 1815, in Tioga County, New York; removed to Southport, New York, from Mount Bethel, Pennsylvania, in the spring of 1788; served in French and Indian Wars as non-commissioned officer; member committee from Northampton County, December, 1774; recruiting officer at Easton, June, 1775; Captain of MILLER's Company of THOMPSON's Pennsylvania Rifle Battalion, 25th June, 1775; Captain of Pennsylvania Militia, 1776; member Constitutional Convention, 15th July, 1776; first Judge of Tioga County, New York, by appointment of Governor CLINTON 17th February, 1791; 27th October, 1788, had patent No. 113 for 1000 acres in the town of Southport; *m.* Winifrede McDOWELL, dau. of John McDOWELL of Hamilton Township, Northampton County, Pennsylvania.

ISSUE

I. JOHN, *b.* 1760, of whom later.
II. Jacob, served in his father's company during the Revolution.

JUDGE JOHN MILLER of Elmira, Tioga County, New York; *b.* 1760, in Northampton County, Pennsylvania; *d.* 13th April, 1833, in Tioga County, New York; was appointed first Judge 3d April, 1807, and held office until 31st March, 1810; was private in his father's company June, 1775, afterwards served in same company when it became part of First Pennsylvania Continental Line; member New York Assembly, 1804–1807; invested in Indiana lands and was member Indiana Legislature from Clark County, 1820–1821; *m.* Hannah BIRNEY.

ISSUE

I. ABRAHAM (only son), *b.* 9th April, 1787, of whom below.

ABRAHAM MILLER of Clark County, Indiana; *b.* 9th April, 1787, in Luzerne County, Pennsylvania; *d.* 22d April, 1867, in Clark County; served in the Black Hawk War and was wounded at the battle of Tippecanoe; member City Council, Jeffersonville, Clark County, Indiana, 1841–1844; served in United States naval forces on Ohio, Mississippi and Red Rivers, 1862–1865; honorably discharged by Admiral LEE at Mound City, Illinois, July, 1865; *m.* 24th August, 1842, Louisa OWEN, dau. of John and Rebecca (LOVE) OWEN of Jefferson County, Kentucky.

ISSUE

I. Louisa Abraham MILLER, *b.* 13th August, 1847; *m.* 28th September, 1865, Reason Lawson AKERS (see supra).

Arnold

GEORGE CARPENTER ARNOLD of Providence, Rhode Island; *b.* there 31st July, 1868; *m.* there 14th December, 1892, Flora Etta RICHARDS, *b.* 13th September, 1870, dau. of Isaac Pratt RICHARDS, *b.* June, 1834, *d.* July, 1913, *m.* Marietta NICHOLSON, *b.* January, 1838, *d.* 2d September, 1894.

ISSUE

I. Lincoln Richards, *b.* 15th October, 1893; Brown University Class of 1916; Delta Phi Fraternity; *m.* 1st May, 1920, Madeleine W. Webster, dau. John W. Webster.
II. Philip Rhodes, *b.* 4th March, 1895; Amherst College, class of 1918; Phi Delta Theta Fraternity; *m.* 28th June, 1919, Marian B. Harris, dau. of Fred A. W. Harris.
III. George Carpenter, *b.* 6th November, 1896; Darmouth College, class of 1918; Sigma Alpha Epsilon Fraternity; in Consular Office, Milan, Italy, 1920.

GEORGE CARPENTER ARNOLD was of the class of 1887, Episcopal Academy Cheshire, Connecticut; First Lieutenant Company C, First Regiment Infantry, Rhode Island Militia; for more than a quarter of a century he was engaged in the worsted yarn business, being New England Representative of the Highland and Bristol Worsted Mills and the Continental Worsted Mills, all of Philadelphia, Pennsylvania; retired from the mill business in 1912; now Treasurer and General Manager of the Arnold Real Estate Company of Providence; Vice-President of the Providence Realty Company, Director Central Real Estate Company; President and Treasurer Possnegansett Ice Company, Lakewood, Rhode Island; Treasurer Motor League of Rhode Island; Publisher of the "Arnold Genealogical Tree from 1100 A. D.," "The Numismatic Guide," copyright 1905–1907–1910–1911–1914–1920; Alliteration 1916, etc., elected Historian General National Society Sons American Revolution 21st May, 1918, and reelected at the Detroit Congress, 1919.

Lineage

WILLIAM ARNOLD, the founder of the American family, was of the eighteenth generation recorded of the family; he was *b.* 24th June, 1587; *m.* Christian PEAKE, dau. of Thomas PEAKE of Muchelney where all of his children were born. William ARNOLD set sail with his family 1st May, 1635, from Dartmouth, England, and arrived 24th June, 1635, in New England. He is mentioned in LINCOLN'S "History of Hingham, Massachusetts," as William ARNALL and as coming thither in 1635. He removed with his family 20th April, 1636, to Providence, Rhode Island, where he received grants of land from Roger WILLIAMS and his initials W. A. are second in the famous Initial deed of Roger WILLIAMS and became one of the original proprietors of Providence Plantations in 1636, the lands being purchased from the Indian Sachems, Conanicus and Miantonomi of Mooshansic, afterward called Providence. He was President of the four towns, Portsmouth, Newport, Providence and Warwick for five years and Governor of the Colony for ten years. This real estate was mostly in Providence, Pawtuxet and Warwick, Rhode Island, where he had houses and lived at his pleasure, being held in high esteem; he held various important offices of trust. One hundred and twenty acres of the original grant including a 27-acre Lake at Warwick, Rhode Island where 14,000 tons of ice is cut each winter is now owned by George Carpenter ARNOLD of Providence, Rhode Island (publisher of the "Arnold Genealogical Tree") and the ancestral house built in 1771 by his great, great, grandfather George ARNOLD is now (1918) used by him as a summer residence.

ISSUE

I. Elizabeth, b. 23d November, 1611; m. William CARPENTER.
II. STEPHEN, b. 22d December, 1622, of whom later.
III. Benedict, b. 21st December, 1615; d. 20th June, 1678; removed to Newport in 1653; chosen Assistant to manage the affairs of the Colony the following year; in 1657 he succeeded Roger WILLIAMS as Governor and continued in office to 1660; he was the wealthiest man in the Colony and by his acquaintance with the manners as well as the language of the Indians he became the most efficient auxiliary in all negotiations with them; he was also Governor from 1662 to 1666 and from 1669 to 1672 and from 1677 to 1678; m. 17th December, 1640, Damaris WESTCOTT, dau. of Stukeley WESTCOTT of Providence.

ISSUE

1. Benedict of Newport; b. 10th January, 1641; was Assistant from 1690 to 1695; Repersentative to the General Court in 1699; Captain; m. (firstly) 9th March, 1671, Mary TURNER; m. (secondly) Sarah MUMFORD.

ISSUE BY FIRST MARRIAGE

1[1]. Benedict of Newport, Rhode Island; Captain; m. there 8th November, 1733, Mrs. Hannah (WATERMAN) KING, widow of Abraham KING.

ISSUE

1[2]. Benedict, b. 15th August, 1738; d. 30th April, 1739.

2². Benedict, *b.* 3d January, 1740–1741, at Norwich, Connecticut; *d.* 14th June, 1801, at London, England; his services during the Colonial Wars and the American Revolution, attaining in the latter the rank of Major-General, and being placed in command of West Point, which he planned with Major John ANDRÉ of the English Army to betray to the British are too well known for detailed mention; *m.* (firstly) 27th February, 1767, Margaret MANSFIELD, who *d.* 19th June, 1775, dau. of Samuel MANSFIELD; *m.* (secondly) 8th April, 1779, Margaret SHIPPEN, who *d.* 24th August, 1804, dau. of Judge Edward SHIPPEN of Pennsylvania; she was regarded by English Society as the most beautiful woman of her time in England.

ISSUE BY FIRST MARRIAGE

1³. Benedict, *b.* 14th February, 1768; *d. s. p.* Jamaica, aged 27 years.
2³. Richard, *b.* 22d August, 1769; *d.* 9th December, 1847; *m.* 30th December, 1804, Margaret WEATHERHEAD, dau. of Samuel WEATHERHEAD of Augusta, Canada; had issue.
3³. Henry, *b.* 19th September, 1772; *d.* 8th December, 1825; *m.* 4th December, 1796, Hannah TEN EYCK, dau. of Richard TEN EYCK of New York; they had eleven children of whom only one survived infancy, viz.: Sophia, who *m.* ——— SILL of New York.

ISSUE BY SECOND MARRIAGE

1³. Edward Shippen, Lieutenant 6th Bengal of Cavalry and Paymaster at Multra; *d.* unmarried, 13th December, 1813, at Singapore, India.
2³. James Robertson, Lieutenant General; K. C. (Knight of the Crescent); K. H. (Knight of Hanover); *d. s. p.* 27th December, 1854; *m.* Virginia GOODRICH, *d.* 14th July, 1852, dau. of Bartlett GOODRICH, of Saling Grove, Essex, England.
3³. George, Lieutenant-Colonel 2d Bengal Cavalry; *d.* 1st November, 1828, in India; *m.* Ann Marten BROWN.

ISSUE

1⁴. George, *d.* circa 1865; *m.* a dau. of Sir Thomas SEATON, K. C. B.; left one daughter.
2⁴. Sophia Mary, *m.* Rev. Archer Wilmington INGRAM.

4³. William Fitch, *b.* in London, 25th June, 1794; *d.* 7th November, 1846; was Captain in the 17th Lancers and a Justice of the

2[4]. Peace for the County of Bucks; *m.* 19th May, 1819, Elizabeth Cecilia RUDDACH, only dau. of Alexander RUDDACH of the Island of Tobago, Captain in the Royal Navy.

ISSUE

1[4]. Edward Gladwin, *b.* 25th April, 1823; M. A. Oxford; was a clergyman of the Established Church of England and Rector of Great Massington, in Norfolk; *m.* 27th April, 1852, Lady Charlotte Georgiana CHALMONDELEY, oldest dau. of Lord Henry CHOLMONDELEY, later Marquis of CHOLMONDELEY.

ISSUE

1[5]. Edward Cholmondeley, *b.* 13th December, 1854; *d.* 27th November, 1873.
2[5]. William Henry, *b.* 23d March, 1856; Sub-Lieutenant in the Royal Navy.
3[5]. Charles Lowther, *b.* 28th December, 1859; an undergraduate of the University of Cambridge.
4[5]. Henry Abel, *b.* 5th April, 1861.
5[5]. Archer Seymour, *b.* 24th April, 1865.
6[5]. Herbert Tollemache, *b.* 5th April, 1867.
7[5]. George Hugh Bryant, *b.* 29th October, 1871.
8[5]. Marcia Elizabeth.
9[5]. Emma Charlotte Georgiana.
10[5]. Mabel Caroline Frances.
11[5]. Ada Caroline Margaret.

2[4]. William Trail, *b.* 23d October, 1826; Captain 4th (King's Own) Regiment, and killed 5th May, 1855 at Sebastopol; General Lord RAGLAN said of him "The loss of the services of the officer is greatly to be regretted. He has done his duty unremittingly, and in the most spirited manner throughout the operations of the siege."
3[4]. Margaret Steuart, *m.* Rev. Robert H. ROGERS.
4[4]. Elizabeth Sophia, *m.* Rev. Bryant BURGESS.
5[4]. Georgiana Phipps, *m.* Rev. John STEPHENSON.
6[4]. Louisa Russell, *m.* Rev. J. Cecil ROGERS.

5[3]. Sophia Matilda, *d.* 1828, *m.* Col. Pownall PHIPPS, Knight of Crescent, in the East India Company's Service and related to the Earl of MULGRAVE's family.

2. Caleb, *b.* 19th December, 1644; Captain and "practitioner of physic;" *m.* 10th June, 1666, Abigail WILBUR.
3. Josiah, *b.* 22d December, 1646; *m.* (firstly) Sarah MILLS; *m.* (secondly) Mary BRINLEY.
4. Damaris, *b.* 23d February, 1648; *m.* John BLISS, 24th January, 1666.
5. William, *b.* 21st Otcoberer, 1651; *d.* 23d October, 1651.
6. Penelope, *b.* 10th February, 1653; *m.* (firstly) Roger GOULDING, 1st January, 1672; *m.* (secondly) ———— CUTLER.
7. Oliver, *b.* 25th July, 1655 at Newport; *m.* Phebe COOK.
8. Godsgift, *b.* 27th August, 1658; *m.* Jireh BULL.
9. Freelove, *b.* 20th July, 1661; *m.* Edward PELHAM; his seven children gave him sixty-one grandchildren, his son Joseph with his two wives contributing eighteen, the sixteenth being named Content and the eighteenth Comfort.

IV. Joanna, *b.* 27th February, 1617; *m.* three times.

STEPHEN ARNOLD of Pawtuxet, Rhode Island; *b.* 22d December, 1622; *d.* 15th November, 1699; came with his father to New England and after residing some time in Providence, removed to Pawtuxet in 1638, where, and at other places in Rhode Island he had large landed property, a portion of which he called the "Coweset Purchase;" he divided among his sons in his life time. He became a man of wealth and was prominent in public affairs and filled important offices in the Colony. He was chosen Deputy-Governor in 1664 and Assistant in 1667. His will dated 2d June, 1698, was proved 12th December 1699; *m.* 24th November, 1646, Sarah SMITH, dau. of Edward SMITH of Rehoboth.

ISSUE

I. Esther, *b.* 22d September, 1647; *m.* ———— HAWKINS.
II. ISRAEL, *b.* 30th October, 1649, of whom later.
III. Stephen, *b.* 27th November, 1654.
IV. Elizabeth, *b.* 2d November, 1659; *d.* 5th June 1758; *m.* Peter GREENE, Deputy-Governor of Rhode Island.
V. Elisha, *b.* 18th February, 1662; *d.* March 24th, 1710; *m.* Susannah CARPENTER, dau. of William CARPENTER
VI. Sarah, *b.* 26th January, 1665; *m.* ———— CARPENTER.
VII. Phoebe, *b.* 9th November, 1671; *m.* 25th December, 1691, Benjamin SMITH.

ISRAEL ARNOLD of Providence, Rhode Island; *b.* 30th October, 1649; *d.* 15th September, 1717; resided in the south part of the ARNOLD Purchase in Pawtuxet; his achievements equaling those of his father Stephen; made his will 23d March, 1717; *m.* 16th April, 1677, Mary (BARKER) SMITH, dau. of James BARKER and widow of Elisha SMITH; he resided on Providence River, north of John GREENE.

ISSUE

I. Israel, *b.* 1678; *m.* Elizabeth SMITH, dau. of Benjamin SMITH.
II. William, *m.* Christine (surname not given).
III. James, *b.* 1689, of whom later.
IV. Elisha.
V. Barbary.
VI. Josiah.
VII. Joseph.

JAMES ARNOLD of Warwick, Rhode Island; *b.* 1689; *d.* 1777, *m.* 25th October, 1711, Elizabeth RHODES, dau. of Peleg RHODES; he was the recording clerk for the original Proprietors on a Plat made by William HOPKINS of land near Pawtuxet.

ISSUE

I. James, *b.* 1724, of whom later.
II. Sion, *m.* Sarah (surname not given).
III. Elizabeth, *m.* ——— FENNER.

JAMES ARNOLD of Warwick, Rhode Island; Signer Declaration of Independence of Rhode Island in 1776; *b.* 11th July, 1724; *d.* 6th January, 1793; *m.* 1744, Elizabeth ARNOLD, *b.* 24th September, 1724, *d.* 11th August, 1811, dau. of Philip ARNOLD, *b.* 12th February, 1693, son of Stephen ARNOLD, *b.* 27th November, 1654, who was the son of Stephen, son of William ARNOLD.

ISSUE

I. George, *b.* 1747, of whom later.
II. James, *b.* 1750; *d.* 1812; his silver mounted rapier is now (1918) in the possession of George Carpenter ARNOLD, of Providence, Rhode Island.
III. Philip, *b.* 15th May, 1754; *d.* 1824; *m.* Amy WATERMAN, *b.* 1757.
IV. Oliver, *m.* Susanna POTTER.
V. Moses, *m.* Sarah GREEN.

GEORGE ARNOLD of Warwick, Rhode Island; *b.* 1747; *d.* 1822; *m.* 5th December 1773, Ruth UTTER, *b.* 16th December, 1746; *d.* 8th March, 1836, dau. of Jebulon UTTER, founder of the Utter Manufacturing Cotton Company, Warwick, Rhode Island; *b.* 1725, *d.* 1802, *m.* 7th March, 1745.

ISSUE

I. Sally, *b.* 3d January, 1774; *d.* 1826; *m.* James RHODES, *b.* 1791, *d.* 6th December, 1818.

II. Waterman.
III. James Utter, *b*. 4th June, 1776, of whom later.
IV. Mary, *b*. 1778; *d*. 1791.
V George R., *b*. 21st October, 1781; *d*. 1872; *m*. Elizabeth Padelford, *b*. 17th July, 1789; *d*. 1840.

James Utter Arnold of Warwick, Rhode Island, *b*. 4th June, 1776, at Narragansett, in town of Warwick, Rhode Island; he became a man of large interests and later moved to Providence; *d*. 3d February, 1852; *m*. 5th May, 1798, Mehetabel Carpenter, *b*. 30th April, 1778, *d*. 5th January, 1864.

ISSUE

1. William Utter, *b*. 11th December, 1800; *d*. 9th August, 1887; he operated the Cotton Mills at Factory Pond, Warwick, and one at Liberty Mill, West Greenwich, Rhode Island; *m*. Phebe Ann Low, of Warwick, dau. of Samuel and Elizabeth (Holden) Low.

ISSUE

1. Samuel Low, *b*. 1820, *d*. 1837.
2. John Holden, *b*. 1828, *d*. 1866.
3. Mehetable, *d*. young.
4. William, U., *b*. 1838, *d*. 1839.
5. Elizabeth, *b*. 1836.
6. Mehetabel (again), *b*. 1823.
7. William James, *b*. 26th June, 1842; *m*. Abbie Stone, dau. of Daniel and Harriet (Chase) Stone.

II. George C., *b*. 1803
III. James O., *b*. 1806.

ISSUE

1[1]. Hettie F. Arnold. *b*. 26th September, 1870.
II. George Carpenter, *b*. 24th July, 1803, of whom later.
III. James Oliver, *b*. 21st January, 1806; *d*. 24th September, 1838.

George Carpenter Arnold of Providence, Rhode Island; *b*. 24th July, 1803 *d*. 5th August, 1884; his homestead, built 1830, is the present site of the Arnold Building, 124 Washington Street, Providence, Rhode Island, where George C. Arnold, his grandson, now has his office; *m*. 19th May, 1831, Phebe Rhodes, *b*. 18th December, 1810; *d*. 28th October, 1894, dau. of Col. William Rhodes of Pawtuxet, *b*. 11th February, 1782, *d*. 23d July, 1854, *m*. 20th February 1804, Sarah Arnold, *b*. 20th May, 1783, *d*. 25th September, 1843.

ISSUE

1. Sarah Rhodes, *b.* 2d March, 1832; *d.* 28th January, 1906; *m.* 24th December, 1851, Henry Thayer DROWNE of New York, *b.* 25th March, 1822, *d.* 10th December, 1897.

ISSUE

I. Henry Russell, *b.* 31st August, 1860, Secretary Sons of Revolution, New York.
II. William Penn Rhodes, *b.* 24th October, 1834; *d.* 24th September, 1858.
III. John Rice, *b.* 20th February, 1837; *d.* 31st July, 1861.
IV. WILLIAM RHODES, *b.* 21st June, 1839, of whom later.
V. George Jay, *b.* 7th November, 1845; *m.* 21st December, 1874, Mary E. W. BRAYTON.

WILLIAM RHODES ARNOLD of Providence, Rhode Island; *b.* 21st June, 1839; *d.* 2d July, 1912; *m.* 7th June, 1864, Sarah Hill CARPENTER, *b.* 5th July, 1843, dau. of Joseph and Emma Eliza (CLARKE) CARPENTER.

ISSUE

I. GEORGE CARPENTER, *b.* 31st July, 1868, the subject of this memoir.
II. Sarah Rhodes, *b.* 20th January, 1871; *d.* 20th November, 1876.
III. Edith Genevieve, *b.* 23d January, 1873; *d.* 12th November, 1876.
IV. William Rhodes, Jr., *b.* 23d March, 1879; *m.* 18th June, 1902, Clara Louise WRIGHT.

ISSUE

1. Mitchell Wright, *b.* 19th May, 1903.

Avery

CHARLES FRENCH AVERY of Newton, Middlesex County, Massachusetts; *b.* in New York City, 25th March, 1847; *m.* 12th November, 1877, Florence Adelaide TOPPING, *b.* 8th October, 1850, dau. of Henry J. and Mary Catherine (HOBART) TOPPING, of Orient, New York.

ISSUE

I. Elisha Lothrop, *b.* 19th January, 1879; *m.* 17th August, 1906, May Hepzebah URQUHART, *b.* 27th August, 1877, dau. of William and Judith (SPRAGUE) URQUHART.

ISSUE

1. Florence May, *b.* 26th March, 1908.

II. Charles Henry, *b.* 5th March, 1880; *m.* 18th June, 1912, Bertha BLANPIED, *d.s.p.* January, 1913, dau. of David and Bertha (SAWYER) BLANPIED.

III. Helen Ogden, *b.* 2d May, 1881, *m.* 22d. October, 1907, Frederick Henry BLAKE.

ISSUE

1. Avery Hobart BLAKE, *b.* 29th August, 1908.
2. Frederick Henry BLAKE, *b.* 22d November, 1910.
3. Charles Avery BLAKE, *b.* 4th February, 1913.
4. Dexter Barnes BLAKE, *b.* 22d September, 1914.

IV. Lester Hobart, *b.* 10th March, 1884; *d.* 25th May, 1905.
V. Florence Gladys, *b.* 25th January, 1888.

CHARLES FRENCH AVERY was educated in the Public Schools of New York City; entered in the wool trade as a boy, in March, 1862; started the wool business on own account 1st January, 1873, in New York. In 1884 removed business to Boston. Has supplied technical and statistical information to the United States Government. Ex-President of Boston Wool Trade Association; member of Newton School Board for five years; member Boston Board of Aldermen for three terms, part of which time was Chairman of Finance Committee; President Albemarle Golf Club of Newton. Appointed by Federal Reserve Board as Chairman of Liberty Loan Committee, securing subscriptions for $33,000,000 bonds.

Lineage

ROBERT AVERY, Yeoman, of Pill (now Pylle) Somerset, England; *b.* previous to 14th October, 1575, this being the date of the proving of his will; his wife evidently predeceased him as she was not mentioned in his will; he names the following children.

ISSUE

 I. WILLIAM, of whom later
 II. Richard.
 III. Thomas.

WILLIAM AVERY, of Congnesbury in Winterstoke Hundred, England; *d.* 1585; wife's name is unknown, he had, however, issue.

ISSUE

 I. ROBERT, of whom later.

ROBERT AVERY, lived in Wokingham, Berkshire, England; he was by trade a blacksmith; his will, found in the Diocese of Doctors Common, bears date of 30th March, 1642.

ISSUE

 I. WILLIAM, b. 1622, of whom later.
 II. Robert.
 III. Frances.

LIEUTENANT WILLIAM AVERY, M.D., of Dedham and Boston, Massachusetts; *b.* 1622, in England; *d.* 18th March, 1686, and his tombstone stands in King's Chapel burying ground, Boston; came to Dedham, Massachusetts, in 1650, bringing his wife Margaret, who *d.* 28th September, 1678, and three children from Barkham County, Berkshire, England. He is designated as Sergeant in 1669 and was a Deputy to the General Court, 1669, from Springfield; Lieutenant of Dedham County, 1673; Member of Ancient and Honorable Artillery Company; he was the earliest educated physician known to have taken up his life in Dedham; *m.* (secondly) Mrs. Mary (WOODMANSEY) TAPPING, dau. of Robert (probably) WOODMANSEY.

ISSUE

 I. Mary, *bapt.* 19th December, 1645, in England; *d.* 9th September, 1713; *m.* 5th November, 1666, James TISDALE; of Taunton, Massachusetts.
 II. William (Deacon), *bapt.* 27th October, 1647; *m.* (firstly) 21st September, 1673, Mary LANE, *d.* 11th October, 1681; *m.* (secondly) 29th August, 1682, Elizabeth WHITE, *d.* 3d October, 1690; *m.* (thirdly) 25th August, 1698, Mehitable (HINCKLEY) WORDEN, dau. of Gov. Thomas HINCKLEY and widow of Samuel WORDEN, *m.* 22d July, 1679, Sybil SPARHAWK, dau. of Secretary Nathanial and Patience (NEWMAN) SPARHAWK.

III. ROBERT, *bapt.* 7th December, 1649, of whom later.
IV. Jonathan, M.D., *b.* 26th May, 1653.
V. Rachel, *b.* 20th September, 1657.
VI. Hannah, *b.* 27th September, 1660.
VII. Ebenezer, *b.* 24th November, 1663; *d.* before 1683, as he is not mentioned in his father's will.

ENSIGN ROBERT AVERY, of Dedham, Masaachusetts; *bapt.* 7th December, 1647, in Barkham, Berks, England; *d.* 3d October, 1722; was ensign; *m.* Elizabeth LANE, *b.* circa 1665, *d.* 21st October, 1764, dau. Job and Sarah LANE of Malden.

ISSUE

I. Elizabeth, *b.* 21st December, 1677; *d.* 28th January, 1746-1747; *m.* 6th August, 1697; husband's name not given.
II. Rachel, *b.* 1st September, 1679; *d.* 1775; *m.* 14th May, 1702, Michael DWIGHT.
III. Robert, *b.* 28th November, 1681; killed by falling of tree, 21st August, 1723.
IV. JOHN, *b.* 4th February, 1684-1685, of whom later.
V. Jonathan, *b.* 20th January, 1694-1695; *m.* 1st February, 1721-1722, Lydia HEALEY.
VI. Abigail, *b.* 8th May, 1699.

REV. JOHN AVERY of Truro, Massachusetts; *b.* 4th February, 1684-1685; *bapt.* 27th April, 1686; *d.* 23d April, 1754, in the forty-fourth year of his ministry; was ordained 1st November, 1711, as pastor of the First Church in Truro; graduated Harvard College, 1706, and began his ministerial work in Truro soon after; *m.* (firstly) 23d November, 1710, Ruth LITTLE, *b.* 23d November, 1686, *d.* 1st October, 1732, dau. of Ephraim and Mary (STURDEVANT) LITTLE, of Marshfield and gr. gd. dau. of Mr. Richard WARREN who came in the *Mayflower* in 1620 (Ephraim LITTLE was the son of Thomas and Ann (WARREN) LITTLE, she the dau. of Richard WARREN), *m.* (secondly) 3d July, 1733, Ruth KNOWLES, of Eastham, gd. dau. of Hon. John FREEMAN, and gr. gd. dau. of Governor PRINCE; *m.* (thirdly) 24th June, 1748, Mrs. Mary ROTCH, widow of William ROTCH.

ISSUE BY FIRST MARRIAGE

I. John, *b.* 24th August, 1711; Harvard College, 1731; became "the Boston Merchant;" *m.* 13th June, 1734, Mary DEMING, of Boston, *d.* 2d December, 1763.
II. EPHRAIM, *b.* 22d April, 1713, of whom later.
III. Ruth, *b.* 26th July, 1715; *m.* Rev. Jonathan PARKER.
IV. Elizbeth, *b.* 5th March, 1716-1717; *m.* John DRAPER of Boston.
V. Robert, *b.* 26th May, 1719; removed to Lebanon, Connecticut.

vi. Job, *b.* 14th January, 1722–1723; inherited the homestead.
vii. Mary, *b.* 19th January, 1724–1725; *m.* ——— WEST.
viii. Abigail, *b.* 1st June, 1727; *m.* Elisha LOTHROP, Norwich, Connecticut.
ix. Ann, *b.* 6th July, 1729; *d.* 25th August, 1747.

REV. EPHRAIM AVERY, of Brooklyn, Connecticut; *b.* 22d April, 1713, in Truro, Massachusetts; *d.* 20th October, 1754; graduated from Harvard College, 1731; was the first minister ordained, 24th September, 1735, in Brooklyn, Connecticut; *m.* 21st September, 1738, Deborah LOTHROP, *b.* 9th January, 1716–1717, dau. of Samuel and Deborah (CROW) LOTHROP.

ISSUE

i. John, *b.* 14th July, 1739; *d.* 20th August, 1779; *m.* 26th June, 1769, Ruth SMITH, *b.* 5th May, 1741; *d.* 4th October, 1779, dau. of Jehiel and Kesia (WOOD) SMITH.
ii. EPHRAIM (twin), *b.* 13th April, 1741, of whom later.
iii. Samuel (twin), *b.* 13th April, 1741, *d.* soon.
iv. Samuel, *b.* 7th November, 1742; *m.* Mrs. Mary (FILLIS) ACKINCLOSS of Nova Scotia.
v. Elisha, *b.* 3d December, 1744; *m.* Emma PUTNAM.
vi. Elizabeth, *b.* 5th December, 1746; *m.* Rev. Aaron. PUTNAM.
vii. Septimus, *b.* 21st July, 1749; *d.* 10th October, 1754.
viii. Deborah, *b.* 5th July, 1751; *m.* Dr. Joseph BAKER.
ix. Ruth, *b.* 13th January, 1754; *m.* Dr. John Brewster HAMPTON.

REV. EPHRAIM AVERY, M.D., of Rye, New York; *b.* 13th April, 1741; *d.* 5th November, 1776; graduated from Yale, 1761; M.A. King's College, New York, 1767; went to England; was ordained Deacon Priest by Dr. HINCHMAN, Bishop of London, *m.* Hannah PLATT (?).

ISSUE

i. Hannah Platt, *b.* 16th April, 1763; *m.* Stephen BARRITT.
ii. Elizabeth Draper, *b.* 29th August, 1764; m. (firstly) ——— CHURCH, who *d.* in the West Indies.
iii. JOHN WILLIAM, *b.* 24th May, 1767, of whom later.
iv. Elisha Lothrop, *b.* 27th November, 1768.
v. Joseph Platt, *b.* 24th March, 1771.
vi. Deborah Putnam, *b.* 1st June, 1773.

JOHN WILLIAM AVERY of Stratford, Connecticut; *b.* 24th May, 1767; *d.* 1799; the family tradition is that he was a clergyman; *m.* Sarah FAIRCHILD of Stratford, Connecticut.

ISSUE

1. John William, *b.* 1794; in early life was lost at sea in the *Jeannette*.
11. Samuel Putnam, of New York City, *b.* January, 1797; *d.* of cholera, 1832; was proprietor of the hotel called "East River Mansion House;" *m.* 1st January, 1821, Hannah Ann PARK, *b.* 24th April, 1805, *d.* 26th June, 1888, dau. of Capt. Benjamin PARK, who *d.* 5th August, 1807, and whose tombstone is still standing in old Trinity Church Yard, New York City.
111. Sarah Elizabeth (Betsey) *m.* 1817, Ebenezer R. DUPIGNAC.
1v. ELISHA LOTHROP, *b.* 1799, of whom below.

ELISHA LOTHROP AVERY of Brooklyn, New York; *b.* 1799; *d.* in Brooklyn 3d August, 1879. Lost his father in early life, worked on a farm at ten or twelve years of age, and later was appointed to a cord wainer in New York City. Served his time and started a shoe store, as a manufacturer and dealer. He employed his leisure in study and had teachers in various branches, and eventually gave up his store and established a private school, which he conducted for a number of years, until appointed Principal of Grammar School No. 42, in Allen Street, New York. He accumulated quite a collection of philosophical instruments and lectured to the evening schools of New York City for several years. Resigning from his position in 1863, he opened a private school in Brooklyn for the preparation of young men for college and the Naval Academy. He was awarded a diploma by the American Institute for the invention of an instrument for decomposing water; *m.* (firstly) in 1822, Jane GUNNING, *d.* September, 1837; *m.* (secondly) 12th April, 1839, Sarah COIT, dau. of David COIT, of New London, Connecticut, who *m.* Sarah OGDEN, of Morristown, New Jersey.

ISSUE BY FIRST MARRIAGE

1. John William, *b.* 24th November, 1824; *d.* November, 1862.
11. Jane Gunning, *b.* 4th September, 1826; *d.* 9th November 1917.
111. Elisha Lothrop, *b.* 10th January, 1832; *d.* 10th May, 1882.

ISSUE BY SECOND MARRIAGE

1. Sarah Coit, *b.* 12th April, 1842; *m.* 25th December, 1865, Dr. J. Lester KEEP, *b.* 18th March, 1838; educated at Thetford Academy, Vermont, and at Dr. Russell's Collegiate Institute, New Haven, Connecticut; took a course at the Yale Medical College, and was graduated from the Hahnemann Medical College and Hospital in Philadelphia, in 1866; in 1867, he established the Gates Avenue Homeopathic Dispensary, in Brooklyn, and was Consulting Physician in the Brooklyn Homeopathic Dispensary, and a member of the Medical Staff of Brooklyn Homeopathic Society for a number of years; in 1868, he was commissioned

Surgeon of the 13th Regiment, National Guard, New York; in 1869, was promoted to position of Surgeon of the 5th Brigade; in 1880, to Surgeon of the 2d Division, National Guard, New York; in 1883, he was breveted Colonel for long and meritorious service; he was a member of many societies, medical and social; *d*. 30th September, 1916.

ISSUE

1. John S. Bassett KEEP, *b*. 20th October, 1866.
2. Jay Lester KEEP, *b*. 19th August, 1874; *d*. 25th August, 1875.
3. Ogden Avery KEEP, *b*. 18th November, 1878.
4. Marian Lavinia KEEP, *b*. 30th August, 1881; *m*. Charles Lewis MORSE.

II. Ogden, *b*. 1844; *d*. November, 1845.
III. CHARLES FRENCH, *b*. 25th March, 1847, the subject of this memoir.
IV. Harriet, *b*. 1850; *d*. October, 1852.

Arms.—Gules a chevron between three besants, or.
Crest.—Two lions gambs or, supporting a besant.
Motto.—Fidelis.
Residence.—Newton, Middlesex County, Massachusetts.
Clubs.—Newton Golf, Newton, Boston Art, and Traffic Club.
Societies.—Bostoman, Chamber of Commerce, Art Museum, Associate Metropolitan Museum of Art of New York, Society for Preservation of New England Antiquities, League to Enforce Peace; member Mayflower Society, Boston Chamber of Commerce, United States Chamber of Commerce, Boston Press Club, Archæological Society, Society for the Preservation of New England Antiquities.

Bain

ROBERT EDWARD MATHER BAIN of St. Louis, Missouri; *b.* 9th August, 1858, in Chicago, Illinois; *m.* 3d November, 1880, in St. Louis, Missouri, Mary VALLÉ, *b.* there 17th December, 1859, dau. of John Baptiste VALLÉ, *b.* 1827, at St. Genevieve, Missouri, *d.* 22d August, 1869, buried at St. Genevieve, *m.* 9th June, 1857, Lucie Mary DESLOGE, *b.* 8th June, 1836, living 1st May, 1918, dau. of Firmin René DESLOGE of Potosi, Missouri.

The VALLEÉ family is one of the oldest and best known of the early settlers of the Mississippi Valley. The name was originally spelled in the French manner, but was changed under the Spanish regime to accord to that form. The men of the family were among the earliest traders, at St. Louis, with the Indians west of the river and trading stations were maintained along the entire length of the Missouri River. The goods traded in were brought from the Eastern Colonies by way of wagons to the Ohio River, and thence by boats via the Ohio and Mississippi Rivers to St. Louis, then the chief trading station in the west.

ISSUE

I. Marie Zoé, *b.* 6th November, 1881; *m.* 12th October, 1910, Charles Bernard Raoul FITZ-WILLIAM of Trinidad, British West Indies, son of Charles FITZ-WILLIAM of Trinidad, British West Indies, and his wife Louise Delor WALKER of the same place.

ISSUE

1. Marie Louise FITZ-WILLIAM, *b.* 2d April, 1913.
2. Lucie Delor FITZ-WILLIAM, *b.* 20th June, 1914.
3. Charles Bernard Raoul, *b.* 24th January, 1916.

II. Catherine Louise, *b.* 5th May, 1884; *m.* 5th May, 1903, Elliott Chalmers BENNETT of St. Louis, Missouri, son of E. C. and Julia (CHITTENDEN) BENNETT.

ISSUE

1. Robert Chalmers BENNETT, *b.* 2d November, 1904.
2. Virginia Louise BENNETT, *b.* 25th July, 1906.
3. Theodora Valleé BENNETT, *b.* 19 January, 1908.
4. Vallé Chittenden BENNETT, *b.* 17th February, 1909.
5. Elliott Walter Mather BENNETT, *b.* 8th August, 1910.

III. George Valleé, b. 16th July, 1886; m. 28th April, 1915, Clara Louise GREGG, of Los Angeles, California, dau. of James Donald and Margaret (CAMPBELL) GREGG of St. Louis.

ISSUE

1. Margaret Louise, b. 21st March, 1916
2. George Valleé, Jr., b. 28th March, 1917.

IV. Marguerite Desloge, b. 28th February, 1890; m. 27th December, 1911, Charles Henry ADAMS, of New Orleans, Louisiana, son of C. H. and Marie (ZIEGLER) ADAMS.

ISSUE

1. Francis Valleé ADAMS, b. 23d March, 1913.
3. Marguerite Marie Adams, b. 17th April, 1914.
3. Charles Henry ADAMS, Jr., b. 8th May, 1916.
4. David Bain ADAMS, b. 26th February, 1918.
5. Andrew Robert Adams, b. 21st January, 1920.

V. Lucie Clara, b. 18th December, 1893; m. 2d December, 1914, at St. Louis, Missouri, John Bernard FURSTENBERG of Hutchinson, Kansas, son of Bernard C. and Barbara (RAUH) FÜRSTENBERG.

ISSUE

1. Mary Barbara FÜRSTENBERG, b. 8th September, 1915.
2. Lucie Anne FÜRSTENBERG, b. 12th September, 1916.
3. John Bernard FÜRSTENBERG, b. 26th June, 1919.

ROBERT EDWARD MATHER BAIN was a member of the Missouri House of Representatives 1883 to 1885. He is well known as an amateur photographer. Traveled during 1894 through Egypt, Palestine, Asia Minor, Greece and Italy for book illustrating purposes. Illustrated "Earthly Footsteps of the Man of Galilee," "Child's Bible," "A Romance of Palestine," and the "Self-Interpreting Bible," the last named having sold throughout the world. President of the St. Louis Photographic Club 1882 to 1902. Holds medals for photographic work, granted by American and foreign societies.

Lineage

The English progenitor of the MATHER family was Thomas MATHER of Lancashire, England, the father of John MATHER of Lancashire, who was the father of Richard MATHER, the immigrant ancestor of the MATHER family of America.

REV. RICHARD MATHER, the emigrant ancestor, b. 1596, at Lowten, Winwick Parish, of Toxteth Parish, England and of Dorchester, Massachusetts; d. 22d April, 1669, in Dorchester; he was noted for the vast number of his writings, some of which have been published by the Dorchester Antiquarian Society in 1850; *m.* (firstly) 29th September, 1624, Catherine HOLT, *d.* 1655, dau. of Edmund HOLT of Bury; *m.* (secondly) 26th August, 1656, Sarah (HANDRIDGE) (STORY) COTTON, who *d.* 27th May, 1676, she was the dau. of Richard HANDRIDGE of Boston, England, and widow firstly of William STORY and secondly of Rev. John COTTON.

ISSUE BY FIRST MARRIAGE

I. Rev. Samuel, *b.* 13th May, 1626; *d.* 29th October 1671; *m.* Miss STEVENS.
II. TIMOTHY, *b.* 1628, in Liverpool England, of whom later.
III. Rev. Nathaniel, *b.* 20th March, 1630; *d.* 26th July, 1697.
IV. Joseph. *b.* 1634.
V. Rev. Dr. Increase, *b.* 21st June, 1639; *d.* 23d August, 1723; settled in Boston; *m.* (firstly) 16th March, 1662, Marie COTTON, *b.* 15th February, 1642, *d.* 4th April, 1714, dau. of Rev. John COTTON; *m.* (secondly) Anna (LAKE) COTTON, dau. of Rev. John COTTON of New Hampshire.
VI. Rev. Eleazer, *b.* 13th May, 1639; *d.* 24th July, 1669; *m.* 29th September, 1659, Esther WARHAM, *b.* 1644, *d.* 10th February, 1736, dau. of Rev. John WARHAM of Northampton, Massachusetts.

TIMOTHY MATHER of Dorchester, Massachusetts; *b.* 1628 in Liverpool, England; *d.* 14th January 1684, at Dorchester; was the only son of the emigrant who grew up to manhood who was not a preacher, and is called "The Mather Farmer" of the early time, and settled in the town with his father. His brothers, Samuel and Nathaniel went back to Europe and were noted preachers. Eleazer was the first minister in Northampton, Massachusetts, where he *d.* the same year his father, Timothy MATHER, had a fall from his barn which resulted in his death at the age of fifth-six years; *m.* (firstly) 1650 (?), Catherine ATHERTON, dau. of Maj. Gen. Humphrey ATHERTON *m.* (secondly) 20th March, 1678-1679, Elizabeth WEEKS dau. of Amiel WEEKS. All persons by the name of MATHER who are descended from the New England MATHERS can be traced directly to Timothy MATHER.

ISSUE BY FIRST MARRIAGE

I. Rev. Samuel, *b.* 5th July, 1650; *d.* 18th March, 1728; Graduate of Harvard, 1671; one of the founders of Yale College; *m.* Hannah TREAT, dau. of Gov. Robert TREAT of Connecticut.
II. Richard, *b.* 22d December, 1653.
III. Catherine, *b.* 6th January, 1655-1656
IV. Nathaniel, *b.* 2d September, 1658.
V. Joseph, *b.* 25th May, 1661.
VI. ATHERTON, *b.* 4th October, 1663, of whom later.

ATHERTON MATHER of Suffield, Connecticut; *b.* 4th October, 1663, in Dorchester, Massachusetts; *d.* 9th November, 1734, in Suffield. Settled in Windsor, Connecticut and five of his children were born there. In 1712 he removed to Suffield, where the remainder of his children were born. He was a prominent and public spirited man; represented the town in Boston for four years in the General Court. His mother was the daughter of Gen. Humphrey ATHERTON of Dorchester, whose monument stands in close proximity to that of his grandfather Rev. Richard MATHER. *m.* (firstly) Rebecca STOUGHTON; *m.* (secondly) 24th October, 1705, Mary LAMB.

ISSUE

I. William, *b.* 2d March 1698.
II. Jerusha, *b.* 18th July, 1700.
III. Joshua, *b.* 26th November, 1706.
IV. RICHARD, *b.* 21st November, 1708, of whom later.
V. Mary, *b.* 2d March, 1711.
VI. Thomas, M.D., *b.* 5th April, 1713.
VII. Eliakim, *b.* 10th July, 1715.
VIII. Catherine, *b.* 5th January, 1717.

RICHARD MATHER of Windsor, Connecticut; *b.* 31st November, 1708, at Windsor, Connecticut; *m.* 21st March, 1733-1734, Lois BURBANK.

ISSUE

I. Charles, *b.* 20th February 1734.
II. Elisabeth, *b.* 22d December, 1738.
III. Elihu, *b.* 2d April, 1741.
IV. Zachariah, *b.* 22d September, 1743.
V. COTTON, *b.* 1746, of whom later.
VI. Lois.
VII. Mary.
VIII. Sarah.
IX. Lucinda.
X. Anna.

COTTON MATHER of Windsor, Connecticut; *b.* 1746; he married three times but the names of his wives or the date of his marriages are not given.

ISSUE

I. Cotton Smith, *b.* 1770
II. Philo.
III. Horace, *b.* 1775.
IV. Thomas.
V. CHARLES, *b.* 15th April, 1790, of whom later.
VI. John.
VII. Thersey.
VIII. Clarissac.

ix. Betsey N.
x. Sally.
xi. Zilpha.

CHARLES MATHER of Sugar Grove, Illinois; *b.* 15th April, 1790; *d.* 11th May, 1879; *m.* ———, Mary HARD.

ISSUE

i. Mary J., *b.* 15th September, 1814; *d.* 8th August, 1888; *m.* 3d April, 1841, H. B. DENSMORE.
ii. Caroline M., *b.* 8th August, 1816; *m.* 1848, George STEVENS.
iii. Cordelia, *b.* 26th May, 1818; *d.* 1842.
iv. Helen L., *b.* 9th July, 1820; *m.* 3d February, 1842, P. Y. BLISS.
v. Catherine L., *b.* 26th September, 1822; *m.* 15th September, 1851, Frank PARTRIDGE.
vi. Henry William, *b.* 26th September, 1824.
vii. Louise M., *b.* 29th March, 1827; *d.* 30th March, 1881; *m.* 4th November, 1850, Jacob BLACK.
viii. Solon Henry, *b.* 24th August, 1829, *m.* 1855, Mary RUSSELL.
ix. CLARA C., *b.* 13th July, 1832, of whom later.

CLARA C. MATHER, *b.* 13th July, 1832, at Sugar Grove, Illinois; *d.* 9th December, 1913, at St. Charles, Missouri; *m.* 5th November, 1857, George BAIN, of Chicago, Illinois, removed in 1864 to St. Louis where he held many prominent positions, *b.* 5th May, 1836, at Stirling, Scotland, *d.* 2d November, 1891, at St. Louis, Missouri, he and his wife are buried in Bellefontaine Cemetery, St. Louis, Missouri.

ISSUE

i. ROBERT EDWARD MATHER, *b.* 9th August, 1858, the subject of this memoir.
ii. Charlotte Louise, *b.* 25th July, 1860.
iii. George Grantham, *b.* 7th January, 1864.
iv. William Brown, *b.* 24th April, 1868; *d.* 20th April, 1878.
v. Walter Howard, *b.* 15th May, 1871; *d.* 2d September, 1895.
vi. Clara Lucie Vallé, *b.* 16th December, 1877; *m.* 1905, John Edgar HALLOWELL of Sandy Spring, Maryland.

Arms (Mather).—Ermine on a fesse wavy azure, three lions rampant or.
Crest.—A lion sejant or.   (This coat of arms is found in MS "Promptuarium Armourum" as the Arms of Wm. MATHER of Salop 1602),
Motto.—Virtus vera nobilitas est.
Residence.—3801 Flora Boulevard, St. Louis, Missouri.
Clubs.—Mercantile, Missouri Athletic Association, Automobile of St. Louis.
Societies.—Colonial Wars; Navy League of the United States, National Security, American Red Cross, Missouri Historical Society, National Geographic Society, Travellers Club of America.

Ball

DAVID CHARLES BALL of "DeVere Place," Baltimore County, near Ellicott City, Maryland; *b.* 4th April, 1844; *m.* 7th Novemger, 1867, Annie Clay DeVere, youngest child of Col. William and Sarah (Jones) DeVere, of "Windsor," Baltimore County, Maryland.

ISSUE

I. Eleanor DeVere, *m.* 6th June, 1893, Howard Stabler Milnor.

ISSUE

1. Eleanor DeVere Milnor, *b.* 23d July, 1903.
2. William Ball Milnor, *b.* 26th October, 1911.

II. Annie Boyd, *m.* Waldern Carey Nimmo, 2d December, 1896.

ISSUE

1. Ruth Natali Nimmo; B.A. Goucher College; *b.* 14th September, 1897.

III. Owen Lester.
IV. Elizabeth Rogers, *m.* 12th October, 1899, William Bull Stoddard of Boulder, Colorado, B.A. University of Colorado; Ph.D. Johns Hopkins University, Baltimore, Maryland.

ISSUE

1. Mary Carlton Stoddard, *b.* 7th November, 1900.
2. Eleanor DeVere Stoddard, *b.* 19th December, 1902.
3. William Bull Stoddard, Jr., *b.* 10th February, 1907.
4. David Farnum Stoddard, *b.* 13th October, 1908.

V. Rosalia Barrett.
VI. Mary Virginia, *m.* 16th October, 1907, T. Carroll Davis of Syracuse, New York.

ISSUE

1. Rosalia Ball Davis, *b.* 22d January, 1909.
2. T. Carroll Davis, Jr., *b.* 25th August, 1911.

VII. Albert Day (twin), *b.* 12th June, 1885.
VIII. Sara Jeannetta (twin), *b.* 12th June, 1885.

Lineage

This family derives its descent from Col. William BALL of Virginia, *b.* in England in 1615; *d.* November, 1680, in Millenbeck, Lancaster County, Virginia. He came from England with his family in 1650 and settled at the mouth of the Corotorcian River in Lancaster County. William BALL came from Virginia and settled in Annapolis, Maryland, and married there under most romantic circumstances, Sarah DORSEY, the ninth child of Nicholas DORSEY of "Huntington Quarter" and his wife Elizabeth (WORTHINGTON) DORSEY. According to tradition, she was engaged to marry a WORTHINGTON, a very wealthy gentleman, but she fell in love with William BALL of Annapolis while on a visit to that ancient burgh. William BALL, provided with a coach-and-four, drove to Elkridge one winter's night and went to Nicholas DORSEY's home according to agreement with his fair inamorata and carried her off like a knight errant of older days. Sarah climbed down a ladder from her bed-chamber and entered the coach provided by her lover. In her hasty flight she left one of her high heeled white slippers sticking in the snow bank, and this first led to the discovery of the elopement. Nicholas DORSEY, the irate father, pursued the lovers but when he caught up with them the next morning, he found that they had been quietly married. William BALL and his wife moved to Baltimore where they lived until their death.

ISSUE

1. William Dorsey, *b.* 1788; *d.* 30th July, 1863; *m.* (firstly) Miss ELDER; (*m.* (secondly) Elizabeth DORSEY, dau. of Michael of "Elioak" and Honor (HOWARD) DORSEY.

ISSUE BY FIRST MARRIAGE

1. William.

ISSUE BY SECOND MARRIAGE

1. Prudence Gough, *m.* John STORY.
2. Owen Dorsey, *b.* 17th February, 1817; *m.* Elizabeth Francis BOYD, dau. of David and Mary BOYD, of Frederick County, Maryland.

ISSUE

1[1]. William Edwin, *b.* 13th March, 1843, *m.* Mary JURDAN of Norfolk, Virginia.

ISSUE

1[2]. Charles.

2[1]. David Charles, *b.* 4th April, 1844; *m.* Annie Clay DeVERE, 7th November, 1867, the subject of this memoir.
3[1]. Elizabeth Prudence, *b.* 3d November, 1845; *m.* John William Hunter PORTER, of Portsmouth, Virginia.

ISSUE

1². John Ridgely PORTER, *m.* Augusta MAUPIN.

ISSUE

1³. Augusta Maupin PORTER.
2³. Sallie Macon PORTER.

2². Lieut. Hunter Ball PORTER.

4¹. Owen Dorsey, *b.* 31st December, 1846.
5¹. Albert Ritchie, *b.* 28th November, 1847; *m.* Jeannetta Wilkins MINTER, of Portsmouth, Virginia.
6¹. Helen Frances, *b.* 1st March, 1849; *d.* 1st July, 1895.
7¹. Mary Henrietta, *b.* 25th August, 1851; *d.* 20th July, 1917.
8¹. Catherine, *b.* 12th January, 1853; *d.* 18th March, 1855.
9¹. John Arthur, *b.* 17th September, 1854; *d.* 9th September, 1855.
10¹. Sarah Virginia, *b.* 17th August, 1856; *d.* 28th May, 1857.
11¹. Samuel Boyd, *b.* 21st September; *m.* Lula BLAIR, of St. Louis, Missouri.
12¹. Owen Davis, *b.* 30th March, 1861; *m.* Roberta FISHER, of Thomasville, Georgia, 16th September, 1904.

ISSUE

1². Alfred Harvey *m.* (firstly) Mary BARBEE, of Raleigh, North Carolina; *m.* (secondly) Mildred SAN SOUCI.

ISSUE BY FIRST MARRIAGE

1³. Edwin Barclay.
2³. George Fisher.

ISSUE BY SECOND MARRIAGE

1³. Constance Mildred.

2². Elizabeth Bruce, *m.* Ross NICKOLSON, of Fort Worth, Texas.

ISSUE

1³. Elizabeth Ross NICKOLSON.
2³. Roberta Bruce NICHOLSON.
3³. Thomas Ross NICKOLSON,
4³. Marie Ball NICKOLSON.

3². Alexis Smith, *m.* Richard Andrew JONES, of Norfolk, Virginia.

ISSUE

1³. Martha Alexis Jones.
2³. Richard Andrew Jones, Jr.

4². Raymond.
5². Robert Owen, of the "Norfolk Blues," United States Army.

3. John, b. 22d February, 1819.
4. Walter, b. 22d March, 1822; m. Ann Eliza Schminke.

ISSUE

1¹. George Henry, b. 20th April, 1844.
2¹. William Owen, b. 14th August, 1845.
3¹. Edwin Dorsey, b. 2d August, 1847.
4¹. Anne Virginia, b. 10th November, 1849.
5¹. Walter Summerfield, b. 29th February, 1852.
6¹. Elizabeth Dorsey, b. 12th January, 1854; m. James Raymond Boyce, 12th November, 1872.

ISSUE

1². James Raymond Boyce, m. Natalie Goffe.

ISSUE

1³. Raymond Boyce, Jr.
2³. Wallace Campbell Boyce.

2². Walter Ball Boyce.
3². Arthur Cauchoir Boyce, m. Edna Grandveaux.

ISSUE

1³. Elizabeth Boyce.

7¹. Henrietta Handy, b. 6th August, 1856; m. Geo. Medairy.
8¹. John Edwin, b. 24th October, 1858.
9¹. Charles Alexander, b. 2d December, 1860.
10¹. Ella, b. 10th September, 1865.

5. Alexander.
6. Summerfield.

11. Walter, b. 26th September, 1795; d. 25th September, 1863; m. Mary Ball, b. 12th January, 1794, d. 25th June, 1865.

ISSUE

1. Elizabeth Walker, *b.* 1818; *d.* 1838.
2. Eleanor, *b.* 30th May, 1821; *d.* December, 1909; *m.* James Aquilla Garrettson, 27th June, 1839.

ISSUE

1¹. Florence Garrettson, *m.* Henry Spooner.
2¹. Mary Elizabeth Garrettson, *m.* Henry Gotheal Evans.

ISSUE

1². Henry Ridgeley Evans, *m.* Florence Kirkpatrick.
2². Frank Garrettson Evans, *m.* firstly, Olivia Walter Cook; secondly Ella Warfield, of Gustavus.

ISSUE BY FIRST MARRIAGE

1³. Olivia Walter Evans.
2³. Henry Cotheal Evans, Captain, Third Artillery, 1st Division, U. S. A.
3³. Frank Garrettson Evans, Jr.

ISSUE BY SECOND MARRIAGE

1³. Gustavus Warfield Evans.
3². Helen Evans, *m.* Townsend Scott, III.

ISSUE

1³. Helen Townsend Scott.
2³. Gwendolyn Garrettson Scott.
3³. Townsend Scott, IV, Lieutenant Aviator, U. S. A.

4². Mary Garrettson Evans.
5². Marion Dorsey Evans.
6². Walter Dorsey Evans.
7². Florence Evans.
8². Ethlyn Evans.

3. Mary Louisa, *b.* 1824; *m.* John Randolphe Ridgely, *d.* 1896.

ISSUE

1¹. Rosa Ridgely, *m.* John Sherman Tapscott, of Baltimore.
2¹. Georgie Ridgely, *m.* Dr. Gavan.
3¹. Elizabeth Dorsey Ridgely.
4¹. Randolph Ridgely, Jr.

5¹. Mary Ball RIDGELY.
6¹. Frank RIDGELY.
7¹. Edith RIDGELY, *m.* William FISHER.
8¹. Florence RIDGELY, *m.* ———— COULTER.

ISSUE

1². Helen COULTER.

4. Walter, *b.* 1825; *m.* Eleanor Randall FORD, *d.* 1889.
5. Joshua Dorsey, *m.* Emily Ann COLE, of Massachusetts.

ISSUE

1¹. Arthur Dorsey.
2¹. Alice Worthington.

6. James McCabe, *m.* Fannie WALKER, of Florida.

III. Achsah, *m.* John ROBB, of Washington, D. C.
IV. Louisa, *m.* Charles KING, of Washington, D. C., *d.* 3d October, 1882.

ISSUE

1. Sarah Ann KING, *m.* Wm. T. MARSHALL.

ISSUE

1¹. Mary Graham MARSHALL.

V. John.
VI. Elizabeth, *m.* Lloyd WORTHINGTON, of Howard County, Maryland.
VII. Lloyd Dorsey, buried beside his mother and father in the BALL lot, Mount Olivet Cemtery.
VIII. Sarah Ann, *b.* 10th March, 1809; *m.* John D. WILSON, of Washington, D. C., *d.* 29th October, 1883.

1. William R. WILSON.
2. Louisa WILSON.
3. Marshall WILSON.
4. Hannah WILSON.

IX. Henrietta, *m.* Lieut. Levin HANDY, United States Navy.

Arms.—Argent a lion passant sable, on a chief of the second, three mulletts of the first.

Crest.—Out of the clouds ppr. a demi-lion rampant sable, powdered with stoiles argent, holding a globe ppr.

Motto.—Coelum qui tueri.

Residence.—DeVere Place, Ellicott City, Maryland.

Dorsey-Ball

EDWARD DORSEY, "The Immigrant," 1650.

In the Land Office of Annapolis, may be seen the following warrant which explains itself;

"Warrant MDCL, granted to Edward Dorsey of Anne Arundel County, for 200 acres of land, which he assigns as follows; as also 200 acres more, part of a warrant for 400 acres, granted John NORWOOD and the said Edward DORSEY, XXIII of February, MDCLI. Know of all men by these presents that I, Edward DORSEY, of the County of Anne Arundel, boatwright, have granted, bargained and sold, for a valuable consideration, already received, all my right, title, interest of and in a warrant for 200 acres, bearing date 1650, and also 200 acres more, being half a warrant of 400 acres—the one-half belonging to Captain NORWOOD, bearing the date 1651, both of which assigned to George Yate.—Edward DORSEY, Sealed." Signed in the presence of Cornelius HOWARD, John HOWARD, Oct. 22d, MDCLXVII (1667).

The name of the wife of "Edward DORSEY, The Immigrant" is unknown.

ISSUE

1. Col. Edward DORSEY, of "Major's Choice" was the heir-at-law of "Edward Dorsey, The Immigrant;" he *m.* (firstly) Sarah WYATT, dau. of Nicholas WYATT, the pioneer surveyor of the Severn; *m.* (secondly) Margaret LARKIN, dau. of John LARKIN, a wealthy land owner of the Patapsco, from whom Mrs. Potter PALMER, of Chicago, is a descendant. Col. Edward DORSEY inherited from his father the tract of land known as "Dorsey," which his widow, Margaret Larkin DORSEY, sold to John BLADEN in 1706. In 1681, he together with his brother Joshua, sold their right to "Hockley-in-the-Hole," to their youngest brother the Hon. John DORSEY. The other estates of Col. Edward DORSEY were "HOCKLEY," "Barnes Folly," "Major's Choice," "Long Reach at Elkridge" and "Long Reach." He moved from Annapolis to "Major's Choice," west of Waterloo and north of the Old Brick Church in Anne Arundel County, prior to 1700; he was at that time *m.* to Margaret LARKIN. From 1680 to 1705, Major DORSEY, as he was then titled, was in every movement looking to the development of the colony. From 1694 to 1696, he was Judge of the High Court of Chancery, during which time he was commissioned to hold the Great Seal. In 1694 he was a Member of the House of Burgesses for Anne Arundel County and from 1697 to his death in 1705, he was a member from Baltimore County (now Howard). His will is dated 1705.

ISSUE BY FIRST MARRIAGE

1. Joshua of "Major's Choice," *m.* in 1711, Ann RIDGLEY, dau. of Col. Henry and Katherine (GREENBURY) RIDGELEY of "Broome and Wardridge" (of Col. Henry RIDGELY of "Devonshire," England). Katherine GREENBURY, was the dau. of Col. Nicholas GREENBURY, Keeper of the Great Seal and Judge of the High Court of Chancery who came to this country on the good ship *Constant Friendship* in 1674.

ISSUE

1[1]. Henry of "Dorsey's Hills" and "Dorsey's Angles;" *b.* 8th November, 1712; *m.* Elizabeth WORTHINGTON, dau. of Thomas and Elizabeth (RIDGELY) WORTHINGTON.

ISSUE

1[2]. Joshua, *m.* Elizabeth HALL, dau. of the Rev. Henry HALL, of the Episcopal Church of West River (for issue, see HALL family).
2[2]. Thomas, *m.* Mary WARFIED, only dau. of Benjamine and Rebeckah (RIDGELY) WARFIELD of "Warfield's Range.'

ISSUE

1[3]. Elizabeth, *m.* Joshua WARFIELD, of "Warfield's Range."
2[3]. Rebecca, *m.* Capt. Vachel BURGESS.
3[3]. Mary Ridgeley, *m.* Philemon BURGESS.
4[3]. Benedict, *m.* Mararet WATKINS, dau. of Nicholas and Ariana (WORTHINGTON) WATKINS.

3[2]. Elizabeth, *m.* Elisha WARFIELD (of Benjamine).

ISSUE

1[3]. Mary WARFIELD, *m.* ———— FORD, of Kentucky.

ISSUE

1[4]. James FORD, *m.* Mary TRIMBLE, dau. of Justice Robert TRIMBLE, United States Supreme Court, a distinguished Kentuckian.

4[2]. Sarah, *m.* Benjamine DORSEY (of Patuxent John).
5[2]. Nicholas.
6[2]. Ariana, *m.* Beni. WARFIELD (of Seth), and lived upon "Warfield's Forest."

COLONIAL FAMILIES OF THE UNITED STATES

7². Ann, *m.* Davidge WARFIELD (of Azel).
8². Vachel.
9². Henry.
10². Charles.

2¹. Philemon, of "Brother's Partnership," b. 20th January, 1714; *m.* (firstly) Catherine RIDGELY, dau. of Col. Henry RIDGELY; *m.* (secondly) Rachel LAWRENCE, dau. of Levin LAWRENCE.

ISSUE BY FIRST MARRIAGE

1². Philemon, *m.* Ann (surname not given).

ISSUE

1³. Col. George, *m.* Rachel RIDGELY (of William RIDGELY Jr.).
2³. John, *m.* Miss STRINGER.

2². Ann, *m.* Capt. John DORSEY.
3². Elizabeth, *m.* William RIDGELY, of "White Wine and Claret."
4². Sarah, *m.* Vachel WARFIELD (of Benjamine and Rebeckah (RIDGELEY) WARFIELD.

ISSUE

1³. Lloyd WARFIELD.
2³. Philemon Dorsey WARFIELD.
3³. Greenbury WARFIELD.
4³. Joshua WARFIELD.
5³. Allen WARFIELD.
6³. Catherine WARFIELD, *m.* Lancelot LINTHICUM.

5². Catherine, *m.* Capt. Benj. WARFIELD (of Benjamine and Rebeckah (RIDGELY) WARFIELD.
6². Amelia, *m.* Samuel RIGGS (of John).

ISSUE BY SECOND MARRIAGE

1². Joshua, *m.* Janet KENNEDY, of Philadelphia.

ISSUE

1³. Elizabeth KENNEDY, *m.* Dr. JOHNSON.

2². Henrietta, *m.* William HOBBS (of Samuel).
3². Arianna, *m.* Samuel OWINGS (of Thomas).

3¹. Rachel, *b.* 6th July, 1717.
4¹. Elizabeth, *b.* 6th November, 1719-1720.
5¹. Joshua, *b.* 6th May, 1722-1723.
6¹. Nicholas, of "Huntington Quarter," *b.* 2d June, 1725; *m.* Elizabeth WORTHINGTON, dau. of John and Helen (HAMMOND) WORTHINGTON who was the dau. of Thomas and Mary (HEATH) HAMMOND.

ISSUE

1². Achsah.
2². Joshua, *m.* Henrietta HAMMOND.

ISSUE

1³. Sarah, *m.* Noah DORSEY (of Lloyd and Catherine (THOMPSON) DORSEY).

3². Lloyd, *m.* Catherine THOMPSON.

ISSUE

1³. Noah, *m.* Sarah DORSEY, dau. of Joshua an Henrietta (HAMMOND) DORSEY.

ISSUE

1⁴. Lloyd Egbert, *m.* Laura WORTHINGTON.

2³. Tristram Shandy, who held "Rich Neck and Riggs Hills."

4². Mary, *m.* Amos DORSEY (twin).
5². Ann, *m.* John WORTHINGTON (twin).
6². Lydia (?).
7². Elizabeth, *m.* Lieut. Joseph WARFIELD, of General SMALLWOOD's Battalion.
8². Nicholas Worthington, *m.* Rachael WARFIELD; removed to Seneca River.
9². Sarah, *b.* 1771; *d.* 23d October, 1828; *m.* William BALL, of Annapolis (see BALL family).
10². Henrietta, *m.* Judge Owen DORSEY, of Michael DORSEY the second, known as Michael of "Elioak" and his wife Honor (HOWARD) DORSEY.

ISSUE

1³. Elizabeth DORSEY, *m.* (firstly), ———— ADGATE; *m.* (secondly) Rev. Jas. HIGGINS.
2³. Edwin DORSEY.
3³. Owen DORSEY.
4³. Lorenzo DORSEY, *m.* Ann Hanson McKENNEY.

COLONIAL FAMILIES OF THE UNITED STATES 51

7[1]. Katherine, *b.* 21st December, 1727.
8[1]. Anna, *b.* 15th October, 1730; *m.* Col. HENRY RIDGELY, *d.* 1728; he was of "Montpelier" and was the son of Col. Henry and Elizabeth RIDGELY.

ISSUE

1[2]. Henry RIDGELY, a bachelor.
2[2]. Elizabeth RIDGELY, *m.* Dr. Charles Alexander WARFIELD.
3[2]. Polly RIDGELY, *m.* Thomas SAPPINGTON.
4[2]. Rachel RIDGELY, *m.* Jesse TYSON, near Laurel.
5[2]. Ann RIDGELY, *m.* Maj. Thomas SNOWDEN.

9[1]. Sarah, *b.* 27th May, 1733.
10[1]. Charles, of "Major's Choice," *b.* 11th November, 1736; he afterwards transferred this estate to his brother Joshua.

2. Samuel, of "Wyatt's Hills," exchanged his interests in "Major's Choice" and held the lands of his mother at "Wyatt's Hills," upon the Severn; he *m.* Jane DORSEY.

ISSUE

1[1]. Patience, *m.* Samuel HOWARD (of Philip) in 1740.

3. Nicholas, of "Long Reach at Elkridge."
4. Benjamine, of "Long Reach."
5. John, to whom was willed the remaining portion of "Long Reach" and who was known as "John of Col. Edward of Long Reach;" *b.* 1692; at sixteen years of age in 1708, *m.* Honor ELDER, heiress of John ELDER, a large landholder upon the Patapsco near Syksville. He was a member of Queen Caroline Parish and in its vestry. He took up "Dorsey's Grove" in Upper Howard, 1080 acres, extending from Glenelg to Glenwood. With his brother, Joshua, who *m.* Ann RIDGELEY, he took up "Brother's Partnership" in the neighborhood of Dayton and upon this he put his son Michael, the first. His adjoining tract, "Good Range," was also given to his son Michael.

ISSUE

1[1]. Michael, was known as "Michael of Good Range," *m.* Ruth TODD, dau. of Lancelot TODD, a descendant and heir of Capt. Thomas TODD, who owned the original site upon which Baltimore now is located. Lancelot TODD, was a brother of John TODD and occupied with him, pew number 20 in the Old Brick Church. He was always known as Lancelot TODD of "Altogether" and *m.* Elizabeth ROCKHOLD, dau. of Mary ROCKHOLD. It is said that Michael DORSEY and his wife Ruth (TODD) DORSEY, had daughters enough to fill a whole pew in the parish church.

ISSUE

1². Captain John, *m.* Ann DORSEY (of Philemon).

ISSUE

1³. Vachel, *m.* Ann POOLE.

ISSUE

1⁴. Harriet, *m.* Bazil CRAPSTER.

2³. Philemon.
3³. Michael.
4³. Ruth, *m.* Col. Gassaway WATKINS.
5³. Catherine, *m.* Charles WARFIELD (of John), of Fredericksburg.

2². Lancelot TODD, inherited "Altogether;" *m.* Sarah WARFIELD.

ISSUE

1³. Darius.

3². Elizabeth, *m.* Capt. John BURGESS.
4². Sarah, *m.* Richard BERRY.
5². Ruth, *m.* Ely DORSEY (of Edward and Sarah (TODD) DORSEY).
6². Honor Elder.
7². Ann Elder.
8². Lydia Talbott.
9². Michael, the second, of "Elioak;" *m.* his cousin, Honor HOWARD, who was the rich widow of three husbands, and after his marriage, moved to her estate at "Elioak." His wife was the youngest child of his father's sister (Sarah (DORSEY) HOWARD and her husband Henry HOWARD). Honor HOWARD was *m.* (firstly) Rezin WARFIELD with whom she lived at "White Hall," near Guilford and by whom she had three children; *m.* (secondl,y) John DAVIDGE, issue, two children; *m.* (thirdly), Joseph WILKINS. After her marriage to Michael DORSEY, the second, she returned to her homeplace at "Elioak."

COLONIAL FAMILIES OF THE UNITED STATES 53

ISSUE

1³. Elizabeth, *m.* William, DORSEY BALL, son of William and Sarah (DORSEY) BALL, dau. of Nicholas DORSEY of "Huntington Quarter," Annapolis Junction, and of whose marriage a detailed account is given in a previous section of this Chart; issue also previously stated.
2³. Jemime, *m.* Alexander WARFIELD, of Sam's Creek.
3³. Cecelia, *m.* Daniel DUNN.
4³. Honor, *m.* Joshua JONES.
5³. Judge Owen, *m.* Henrietta DORSEY, dau. of Nicholas DORSEY of "Huntington Quarter," Annapolis Junction; and sister to Sarah DORSEY who *m.* William BALL, of Annapolis, whose son William Dorsey BALL, *m.* Judge Owen DORSEY's sister, Elizabeth.

ISSUE

1⁴. Elizabeth, *m.* (firstly) ———— ADGATE; *m.* (secondly) Rev. Jas. HIGGINS.
2⁴. Edwin.
3⁴. Owen.
4⁴. Lorenzo, *m.* Ann Hanson McKENNEY.

ISSUE

1⁵. Louis.
2⁵. Clare, *m.* R. B. MOHUN.
3⁵. Angela, *m.* Major EASTMAN.
4⁵. Florence.
5⁵. Ella Loraine, who succeeded her mother in literary work.

6³. Michael, III, *m.* Amelia GREEN, dau. of Sarah (HOWARD) Nelson GREEN and her husband Maj. Richard GREEN. Amelia was Michael's first cousin, her mother, Sarah (HOWARD) Nelson GREEN, being a sister of his mother Honor (HOWARD) WARFIELD DAVIDGE WILKINS DORSEY.

2¹. Nathan, *m.* (firstly) Sophia (surname not given); *m.* (secondly) Ann OWINGS. He was located on the Old Frederick Road near Woodstock, upon "Ranters Ridge," Baltimore County; his homestead was known as "Waverly;" this Nathan or Nathaniel DORSEY was Secretary of the Society of the Cincinnati, after the Revolution.

ISSUE BY SECOND MARRIAGE

1^2. John.
2^2. Vachel, who lost a leg in the Revolution and from whom Dr. Nathaniel DORSEY is descended.
3^2. Edward, known as "Curly head Ned."
4^2. Dr. Samuel, who graduated from the University of Pennsylvania.
5^2. Priscilla, *m.* ——— REID.

3^1. Edward, *m.* "Betty GILLIS," dau. of Ezekiel and Mary (HILL) GILLIS; he was upon the Committee of Observation for Anne Arundel County in 1775 and built the brick house which stands upon the Sykesville Road.

ISSUE

1^2. Dr. Ezekiel John, *m.* Rebeckah MACCUBIN.
2^2. Edward, Jr., known as "Edward of Edward."

ISSUE

1^3. Robert.
2^3. Samuel, *m.* Mary GLENN.
3^3. Edward Hill, *m.* Julia Ann THOMAS.

3^2. Colonel Henry, *m.* Miss SMITHSON, a dau. of Mrs. FARNANDIS.
4^2. Joshua, *m.* Amelia GILLIS (of Henry and Agnes (BELT) GILLIS).

ISSUE

1^3. Edward.
2^3. Azekiel.
3^3. Mary Hill.
4^3. John.
5^3. Rebecca.
6^3. Ann.
7^3. James.
8^3. Elizabeth.
9^3. Matilda.
10^3. Harriet.
11^3. Clarissa.
12^3. Henry.

5^2. Betty, *m.* James VAN BIBBER.
6^2. Mary Hill, *m.* John WILKINS.

ISSUE

1³. Rebecca WILKINS, *m.* Howell WILLIAMS.

4¹. Vachel, *m.* Ruth DORSEY, dau. of Edward and Sarah (TODD) DORSEY.

ISSUE

1². Vachel, Jr., *m.* (firstly) Sarah NELSON, dau. of Burgess and Sarah (HOWARD) NELSON; *m.* (secondly) Elizabeth DORSEY, dau. of Joshua and Elizabeth (HALL) DORSEY.

ISSUE BY FIRST MARRIAGE

1³. Ruth.
2³. Marie.

ISSUE BY SECOND MARRIAGE

1³. Essex Ridley, late of "Hockley."
2³. Elizabeth Hall, *m.* Caleb DORSEY of "Hockley."
3³. Charles (Captain), killed in the battle of North Point.

2². Levin, who passed his estate through Edward, the executor of Mrs. Ruth DORSEY, his mother, to Nimrod DORSEY of Jefferson County, Kentucky, in 1814.

3². Edward, *m.* Susanna LAWRENCE (of Benjamine); he was known as "Fuzzy head Ned."

ISSUE

1³. Mary Ann, *m.* Bazil Nicholas HOBBS.
2³. Sally.
3³. Matilda.
4³. Elias.
5³. Levin Lawrence.
6³. Urith.
7³. Patience Lucker.
8³. Benjamin Lawrence.

4². Ruth, *m.* ———— OWINGS.

ISSUE

1³. Eliza OWINGS.

5². Joshua, *m.* Sarah HAMMOND, dau. of Rezin HAMMOND.

ISSUE

1³. Rezin Hammond.
2³. Nimrod, *m.* Matilda Dorsey, dau. of his Uncle Edward and Susannah (Lawrence) Dorsey.
3³. Mary, *m.* ———— Frost.

ISSUE

1⁴. Elizabeth Frost, *m.* ———— Childs.

6². Elias, *m.* (firstly) Susannah Snowden; *m.* (secondly) Mary Lawrence (of Benjamine).

ISSUE

1³. Mary.
2³. Ruth.

5¹. Honor, *m.* ———— Elder.

ISSUE

1². John Elder.

6¹. Hannah, *m.* Adams Barnes.

ISSUE

1². John Barnes.

7¹. Sarah, *m.* Henry Howard, son of Joseph Howard, and gd. son of Capt. Cornelius Howard who was representative from Anne Arundel County in the Legislative Assembly from 1671 to 1675. This Capt. Cornelius Howard was known as "Capt. Cornelius Howard of Howard's Heirship and Chance" and was the oldest son of Matthew Howard the First, who moved from Lower Norfolk, Virginia, together with his relative Edward Lloyd, in 1650, to the south side of the Severn settlements. Matthew Howard was a descendant of the "John Howard" who came to this country in 1621 and was killed by the Indians.

ISSUE

1². Dr. Ephraim Howard.
2². Dr. John Beale Howard.
3². Vachel Denton Howard, served in the Revolutionary War with Col. Richard Dorsey.

COLONIAL FAMILIES OF THE UNITED STATES 57

4². James HOWARD, executor of his father and his brother-in-law, Dr. Joshua WARFIELD, of Simpsonville.
5². Joshua HOWARD.
6². Sarah HOWARD, *m.* (firstly) Burgess NELSON of Montgomery County; *m.* (secondly) Maj. Richard GREEN of Montgomery County.

ISSUE BY FIRST MARRIAGE

1³. Henry NELSON.
2³. Benjamine NELSON.
3³. Racheal NELSON.
4³. Sarah NELSON, *m.* Vachel DORSEY (of Vachel) NELSON.
5³. Elizabeth NELSON, *m.* Charles GRIFFITH.

ISSUE BY SECOND MARRIAGE

1³. Ruth GREEN.
2³. Mary GREEN.
3³. Amelia GREEN, *m.* Michael DORSEY, III.

7². Rachel HOWARD, *m.* Dr. Joshua WARFIELD (of Alexander and Dinah (DAVIDGE) WARFIELD).

ISSUE

1³. Sarah WARFIELD.
2³. Dinah WARFIELD, *m.* Caleb DORSEY.
3³. Ruth WARFIELD, *m.* Richard OWINGS.
4³. Rachel WARFIELD, *m.* Nicholas WORTHINGTON DORSEY.

ISSUE

1⁴. Ezra DORSEY, of Texas.

5³. Lieut. Joseph WARFIELD, *m.* Elizabeth DORSEY, sister of Nicholas Worthington DORSEY.

8². Honor HOWARD, *m.* (firstly) Rezin WARFIELD (of Alexander) and lived at "White Hall" near Guilford, by whom she had three children; *m.* (secondly) in 1767, John DAVIDGE, by whom she had two children; *m.* (thirdly) in 1773, Joseph WILKINS and with him administered upon the estate of John DAVIDGE; *m.* (fourthly) Michael DORSEY, the second, youngest son of Michael DORSEY and Ruth (TODD) DORSEY. With her husband

Michael DORSEY she returned to her homeplace at "Elioak" and her husband was afterwards known as "Michael of Elioak." (Issue previously stated in this chart.)

8[1]. Susannah, *m.* Levin LAWRENCE.

ISSUE

1[2]. Benjamine LAWRENCE, *m.* a Mrs. Urith (RANDALL) OWINGS, dau. of Thomas and Hannah (BEALE) RANDALL.

ISSUE

1[3]. Levin LAWRENCE.
2[3]. Mary LAWRENCE.
3[3]. Susannah LAWRENCE.

9[1]. Ruth, *m.* (firstly) ——— LAWRENCE; *m.* (secondly) ——— TUMEY.

10[1]. Jemima, *m.* (firstly) Joseph HOBBS; *m.* (secondly) Charles ELDER.

ISSUE BY SECOND MARRIAGE

1. Lacon or Larkin, of "Hockley."
2. Charles.
3. Francis.
4. Edward, Jr., *m.* Phoebe TODD, who was supposed to be a relative of Ruth TODD who *m.* Michael DORSEY. This Phoebe (TODD) DORSEY afterwards became Mrs. Phoebe WILLIAMS and a western descendant says that her husband ——— WILLIAMS was the father of Gen. Otho Holland WILLIAMS.
5. Ann, *m.* John HAMMOND.

ISSUE

1[1]. Hannah Dorsey HAMMOND, *m.* John WELSH and from them are descended Gov. Edwin WARFIELD and Joshua WARFIELD, author of "Founders of Anne Arundel and Howard Counties."
2[1]. Ann HAMMOND, *m.* Francis DAVIS.

II. Joshua, was known as Joshua of "Hockley;" however in 1681 he transferred his right to "Hockley" to his brother John DORSEY and located at "Taunton;" *m.* Sarah RICHARDSON, dau. of Lawrence RICHARDSON who after the death of her husband Joshua DORSEY, *m.* Thomas BLACKWELL.

ISSUE BY FIRST MARRIAGE

1. Colonel Henry, *m.* Comfort STIMPSON, dau. of Thomas and Rachel STIMPSON.

    #### ISSUE

    1¹. John Hammond, of "Success," *m.* Frances WATKINS.
    2¹. Vincent, *m.* Sarah DAY.
    3¹. Captain Joshua, *m.* Flora FITZIMMONS.
    4¹. Greenbury, *m.* Mary BELT.
    5¹. Sarah.
    6¹. Venetia.

III. Hon. John, of "Hockley," came into possession of "Hockley" from his two brothers, Colonel Edward and Joshua, in 1681; in 1683 he *m.* Plesance ELY, who later took up a tract of land in Elkridge, which she names the "Isle of Ely."

ISSUE

1. Edward, *m.* Ruth (supposed to be the traditional Lady HILL, dau. of Captain Richard); this Ruth afterwards *m.* John GREENIFF and then John HOWARD (of John and Susannah HOWARD).

    #### ISSUE BY FIRST MARRIAGE

    1¹. Edward.
    2¹. "Patuxent" John, *m.* Elizabeth (surname not given).

2. Deborah, *m.* Charles RIDGELY.

    #### ISSUE

    1¹. Charles RIDGELY, of "White Wine and Claret;" he was the founder of the Ridgelys of "HAMPTON" and never lived upon his inheritance "White Wine and Claret."
    2¹. William RIDGELY, also of "White Wine and Claret."

3. Caleb, *b.* 1683; *m.* Elinor WARFIELD, dau. of Richard and Elinor (BROWNE) WARFIELD.

    #### ISSUE

    1¹. John.
    2¹. Bazil.
    3¹. Caleb of "Belmont."

4¹. Richard, "The Attorney."
5¹. Edward.
6¹. Thomas BEALE.
7¹. Sophia, *m*. Thomas GOUGH.
8¹. Achsah, *m*. Amos WOODWARD.
9¹. Samuel.

IV. Sarah (DORSEY or DARCY), so far as record discloses, was the only dau. of "Edward DORSEY, the Immigrant;" she *d*. 1692; *m*. Matthew HOWARD, the second (of Matthew and Ann HOWARD) and gd. son of John HOWARD who came to this country in 1621 and was killed by the Indians. Matthew HOWARD, the second, was Associate Judge of the County and upon the Committee of the Port of Entry.

ISSUE

1. John HOWARD, *m*. Susannah (surname not given).

ISSUE

1¹. Matthew HOWARD.
2¹. John HOWARD, *m*. Ruth (the traditional Lady HILL, supposed to be the dau. of Capt. Richard). She was first the widow of Edward DORSEY (of Hon. John and Plesance (ELY) DORSEY) and secondly widow of John GREENIFF.

ISSUE BY THIRD MARRIAGE

1². Abner HOWARD.
2. Matthew HOWARD.
3. Sarah HOWARD, *m*. (firstly) Capt. John WORTHINGTON, *b*. in England, 1650; *m*. (secondly) Capt. John BRICE, of Annapolis.

ISSUE BY FIRST MARRIAGE

1¹. Capt. John WORTHINGTON, *m*. Helen HEATH HAMMOND, dau. of Thomas and Mary (HEATH) HAMMOND. Thomas HAMMOND was the son of John and Mary (HOWARD) HAMMOND, this Mary (HOWARD) HAMMOND, being a sister of Capt. Cornelius, and Matthew HOWARD, the second, and dau. of MATTHEW the first.

ISSUE

1². William WORTHINGTON.
2². Charles WORTHINGTON.
3². Vachel WORTHINGTON.

4². Anne Worthington, *m.* Thomas Beale Dorsey.
5². Elizabeth Worthington, *m.* Nicholas Dorsey, of "Huntington Quarter," Annapolis Junction. (Issue previously stated in this Chart, see Ball line).
6². John Worthington, *m.* Susannah Hood.
7². Samuel Worthington, *m.* (firstly) Mary Tolley, dau. of Walter Tolley of Joppa; *m.* (secondly) Martha Garrettson.
8². Thomas Worthington.

2¹. Thomas Worthington, *b.* 1691.
3¹. William Worthington, *b.* 1694, *m.* Hannah Cromwell.

ISSUE

1². William Worthington.
2². John Worthington, *m.* Mary Todd.

4¹. Sarah Worthington, *b.* 1696.
5¹. Charles Worthington, *b.* 1701.

ISSUE BY SECOND MARRIAGE

1¹. Ann Brice, *m.* Vavhel Denton.
2¹. Rachel Brice, *m.* Philip Hammond, of Annapolis.
3². John Brice, Jr., *m.* Sarah Frisby, dau. of James and Ariana (Vanderheyden) Frisby. John Brice, Jr. was Judge of the Provincial Court.

Arms (Dorsey).—Azure a semil de crosses crosslet une three cenque foils argent.
Crest.—A bull sable horns and hoofs or.
Motto.—Un Dieu, un Roi.

Ballard

HARLAN HOGE BALLARD, A.M., of Pittsfield, Massachusetts; *b.* 26th May, 1853, in Athens, Ohio; *m.* 20th August, 1879, at Lenox, Massachusetts, Lucy Bishop PIKE, dau. of John Nicholas PIKE, of Newburyport, Massachusetts, and Lucy BISHOP, his wife, of Lenox, Massachusetts.

ISSUE

I. Harlan Hoge, *b.* 12th March, 1882; *m.* 18th June, 1908, Alice Whiting BARKER, dau. of Hon. James Madison BARKER.

ISSUE

1. Olive Barker, *b.* 4th July, 1913.

II. Elizabeth Bishop, *b.* 21st June, 1885; *m.* 28th February, 1911, Robert Thompson GAGE, of Cleveland, Ohio, who *d.* 21st December, 1916.

ISSUE

1. Elizabeth Bishop GAGE, *b.* 4th March, 1912.
2, Ruth Bulkley GAGE, *b.* 20th November, 1913.
3. Margaret Ballard GAGE, *b.* 9th March, 1915.
4. Robert Thompson GAGE, *b.* 29th April.

III. Lucy Bishop, *b.* 31st December, 1886.
IV. Margaret, *b.* 11th August, 1891; *d.* 16th July, 1893.

HARLAN HOGE BALLARD, A.B., of Williams College, 1874; Phi Beta Kappa of Williams; A.M. 1877; Principal of the Lenox Massachusetts High School, and Academy, 1874–1886; Librarian and Curator of the Berkshire Athenaeum and Museum, 1888; Founder and President of the Agassiz Association, 1875–1905; Author of "Three Kingdoms," 1896; World of Matter, 1892; Translation "Virgil's Aeneid," 1902–1911; Joint Author "American Plant Book," 1879; "Barnes' Readers" 1883, Adventures of a Librarian, 1920.

Lineage

The emigrant ancestor of this family was William BALLARD; *b.* in England circa 1617; *d.* July, 1689; was in Andover, Massachusetts, a husbandman, in 1644, freeman, 2d May, 1638; *m.* Grace (surname not given), who *d.* 27th April, 1694.

ISSUE

I. JOSEPH, of whom later.
II. William.
III. Sarah, *m.* 24th February, 1670, Henry HOLT.
IV. Elizabeth, *d.* 11th July, 1689; *m.* 11th November, 1668, William BLUNT.
V. John, *b.* 17th January, 1635.
VI. Hannah, *b.* 14th August, 1665; *m.* 20th September, 1681, John SPALDING.
VII. Lydia, *b.* 30th April, 1657; *m.* Joseph BUTTERFIELD.
VIII. Abigail.
IX. Ann, *m.* Samuel BUTTERFIELD.

ENSIGN JOSEPH BALLARD of Andover, Massachusetts; *d.* 1720; served as Constable, 1688; *m.* (firstly) 28th February, 1665, Elizabeth (surname not given), *d.* 27th July, 1692, dau. of Edward and Elizabeth (ADAMS) PHELPS; *m.* (secondly) 15th November, 1692, Rebecca (REA) STEVENS HORNE, *d.* 11th February, 1740, widow of Samuel STEVENS and Simon HORNE and dau. of Joshua and Sarah (WATERS) REA.

ISSUE BY FIRST MARRIAGE

I. Elizabeth, *m.* 13th September, 1689, George ABBOTT.
II. Joseph, *b.* 26th January, 1667.
III. Humphry.
IV. Ellenor, *b.* 24th August, 1672; *m.* 13th September, 1689, John JACKSON.
V. William, *b.* 3d December, 1674; *d.* 2d September, 1707.
VI. Hannah, *b.* 17th July, 1677.
VII. Dorothy, *b.* 8th November, 1679; *m.* Joseph GIBSON.
VIII. Hezekiah, *b.* 22d March, 1682.
IX. Uriah, *b.* 16th November, 1684.
X. Tabitha, *b.* 19th March, 1686; *d.* 30th March, 1687.
XI. Tabitha, *b.* 28th March, 1688; *d.* 24th February, 1691.

ISSUE BY SECOND MARRIAGE

I. Jeremiah, *b.* 29th March, 1697.
II. JOSIAH, *b.* 22d June, 1699, of whom below.

JOSIAH BALLARD of Andover, *b.* 22d June, 1699; *d.* 26th December, 1780; *m.* 7th August, 1721, Mary CHANDLER, *b.* 8th March, 1702, *d.* 3d April, 1779, dau. of Thomas and Mary (STEVENS) CHANDLER.

ISSUE

I. JOSIAH, *b.* 14th August, 1721, of whom later.
II. William, *b.* 2d October, 1723.
III. Mary, *b.* 29th December, 1725, *d.* 17th June, 1750; *m.* 7th June, 1744, William CHANDLER.

    IV. Lydia, *b.* 12th March, 1727, *d,* 6th July, 1779; *m.* Obadiah JOHNSON, Jr.
    V. James, *b.* 3d July, 1730.
    VI. Hannah, *b.* 3d January, 1732; *m.* 11th April, 1757, Isaac CHANDLER.
    VII. Sarah, *b.* 29th July, 1734; *m.* 25th May, 1756, Caleb DANA, Jr.
    VIII. Phebe, *b.* 25th July, 1738; *m.* James HOLT, Jr.
    IX. Dorothy, *b.* 24th June, 1741; *d.* 19th October, 1813; *m.* 11th December, 1760, Jeremiah LOVEJOY.
    X. Rebecca, *bapt.* 23d June, 1745; *m.* 5th February, 1767, William CLARK, he was buried 14th October, 1796.

DEACON JOSIAH BALLARD of Andover, Massachusetts; *b.* 14th August, 1721, at Andover, Massachusetts; *d.* 6th August, 1799, at Andover; *m.* (intention declared) 23d March, 1744, Sarah CARTER, *b.* 10th November, 1725, *d.* 31st March, 1799, dau. of Thomas and Ruth (PHELPS) CARTER.

ISSUE

    I. Sarah, *b.* 13th January, 1744.
    II. Sarah, *b.* 31st January, *d.* 1st February, 1745.
    III. Sarah, *b.* 30th November, 1747; *m.* 1st August, 1768, Samuel WILDER.
    IV. Josiah, *b.* 4th January, 1749; *d.* 17th September, 1771.
    V. Jeremiah, *b.* 9th March, 1752.
    VI. John, *b.* 19th January; *d.* February, 1755.
    VII. Mary, *b.* 28th January, 1756; *m.* 25th October, 1755, John PRESCOTT, Jr.
    VIII. James, *b.* 9th July, 1757.
    IX. John, *b.* 13th November, 1759.
    X. Thomas, *b.* 28th March, 1762.
    XI. WILLIAM, *b.* 23d March, 1764, of whom later.
    XII. Dolly, *bapt.* 20th August, 1767, *d.* 26th ———, 1795; *m.* 5th October, 1788, Jonas LANE.

CAPT. WILLIAM BALLARD of Lancaster, Massachusetts; *b.* there 23d March, 1764; *d.* there 25th May, 1842; commissioned in Charlemont, Massachusetts; *m.* 19th March, 1787, Elizabeth WHITNEY, *b.* 4th February, 1769, *d.* 7th December, 1857, dau. of Jonathan and Mary (WYMAN) WHITNEY, of Lancaster, Massachusetts.

ISSUE

    I. William, *b.* 1st November, 1787.
    II. Mary, *b.* 10th March, 1789, *d.* 23d August, 1874; *m.* Maj. James HAWKES.
    III. JOHN, *b.* 1st October, 1790, of whom later.
    IV. Otis, *b.* 10th October, 1792.
    V. Josiah, *b.* 30th August, 1794.
    VI. Jonas, *b.* 21st October, 1796.
    VII. Jonathan, *b.* 23d August, 1789.

VIII. Dorothy, *b.* 30th August, 1800; *m.* Edward TUCKER.
IX. Charles, *b*, 12th October, 1802; *m.* Adelaide FITCH.
X. James, *b.* 20th April, 1805.
XI. Eliza Whitney, *b.* 12th April, 1807; *m.* 6th May, 1830, Rev. Nathan ———; she *d.* 14th May, 1871.

JOHN BALLARD of Framingham, Massachusetts; *b.* 1st October, 1790, at Charlemont, Massachusetts; *d.* 23d August, 1880; *m.* 27th October, 1816, Pamelia BENNETT, *b.* 5th April, 1793, *d.* August, 1859, dau. of Joseph and Mary (Swift) BENNETT, of Lancaster, Massachusetts, who *d.* 12th December, 1883.

ISSUE

I. Otis, *b.* 6th October, 1817; *m.* 29th April, 1841, Emily PALMER, who *d.* 21st January, 1898
II. William, *b.* 8th September, 1819; *d.* in infancy.
III. Charles, *b.* 7th November, 1820; *m.* (firstly) Electa HAWKES; *m.* (secondly) Eunice HIBBARD, of Rowe, Massachusetts.
IV. ADDISON, *b.* 18th October, 1822, of whom later.
V. James, *b.* 18th July, 1824; *m.* Laura WALKER.
VI. Mary Swift, *b.* 8th June, 1827; *m.* Rev. William J. HOGE.
VII. William Whitney, *b.* 8th January, 1833; *d.* 1st May, 1854.
VIII. Elizabeth Whitney, *b.* 1st June, 1839; *d.* 1864; *m.* Rev. Edward WALKER.

REV. ADDISON BALLARD of Pittsfield, Massachusetts; *b.* 18th October, at Framington, Massachusetts; *d.* 2d December, 1914, at Pittsfield; *m.* 7th August, 1851, Julia Perkins PRATT, *b.* 27th March, 1828, at Athens, Ohio, *d.* 21st April, 1894, in New York City, dau. of Capt. David and Julia (PERKINS) PRATT, of Athens, Ohio.

ISSUE

I. HARLAN HOGE, *b.* 26th May, 1853, the subject of this memoir.
II. Winifred Pamelia, *b.* 16th January, 1860; *m.* Francis Clark BLAKE.
III. Julia Spaulding, *b.* 13th August, 1863; *d.* 13th January, 1871.

Arms.—Sable, a griffin segreant, ermine.
Crest.—A griffin's head erased ermine.
Motto.—Forti non ignavo.
Residence.—Pittsfield, Berkshire County, Massachusetts.
Clubs.—Park, Country, Monday Evening.
Societies.—Berkshire Historical (Secretary and Treasurer since 1888); Fellow of the American Association for the Advancement of Science; American Library Association; Massachusetts Library Club; Freemason (thirty-third degree); Royal Arcanum; Descendants of Founders of Norwich, Connecticut, etc.

Bell

JAMES EWELL BELL, M.D., *b.* 29th February, 1824, at Bridgtown in Northampton County, Virginia; *d.* 27th May, 1914; *m.* 4th December, 1851, Anne Virginia LAND, *b.* 25th October, 1832, *d.* 18th September, 1910, dau. of Edward Cannon and Elizabeth Smith (FOREMAN) LAND and gd. dau. of Capt. Peter LAND and Capt. Mitchell SMITH, officers from Norfolk and Princess Anne Counties, Virginia, in the War of 1812, ROBINSON's 8th Virginia Regiment and LEE's 95th Virginia Regiment, respectively.

ISSUE

I. Edward Land.
II. Charles Gibson.
III. Walter Land.
IV. Elizabeth Land.
V. Mary Bell, *b.* 4th June, 1860, Kempsville, Lynn Haven Parish, Princess Anne County, Virginia; *m.* 2d January, 1884, Matthew Johnston HEYER, *b.* 10th May, 1854, son of John C. and Margaret (JOHNSTON) HEYER, of Wilmington, North Carolina. Mrs. HEYER is a member of the following societies: First Families of Virginia, Daughters of the American Revolution, Daughters of 1812, Daughters of the Confederacy, Virginia Historical Association for the Preservation of Virginia Antiquities, Colonial Dames of the Seventeenth Century, Founders and Patriots of America, Order of the Crown.

ISSUE

1. Henry Yeatman HEYER, *b.* 20th September, 1884.
2. Mary Bell HEYER, *b.* 5th May, 1889.

VI. Maria Louisa.
VII. James Ernest.
VIII. Lelia.
IX. Ernestine.
X. William Keeling.
XI. Anne Virginia.
XII. Rosa.
XIII. Lilian.

JAMES EWELL BELL, M.D., was educated at St. Brides Academy, Norfolk County, Virginia, Brown University Providence, Rhode Island, Richmond College, Richmond, Virginia; assistant to Dr. Fitzalan BLACKWELL, Surgeon United States Navy; was stationed for two years in 1847 at Gosport Navy Yard, Portsmouth, Virginia; in 1861 organized a Company in Princess Anne County of which he was appointed Captain; after a year's service he resigned to become Surgeon; this company was merged with Company F, 6th Virginia Regiment, Mahone's Brigade, C. S. A.; later Dr. BELL was Sheriff of Princess Anne County, for eight years, 1869–1877; member of the Quarter Court, 1874, and five years later, School Trustee, covering a period of many years.

Lineage

SIR ROBERT BELL of Norfolk, England; *d.* 1577; he left sons and a widow who was the dau. and heiress of Edward BEAUPRE of Entwell. She subsequently married Sir John DODINGTON, Governor of the Tower of London, in the reign of Elizabeth, Member of the Privy Council and Governor of Gurnsey and Jersey under James I; his son, Edmund BELL *m.* Anne OSBORNE, dau. of Sir Peter OSBORNE; a son, Robert BELL was living in London in 1633 of Linne Street Ward, Agent for the Virginia Company 4th July, 1624; his will was probated 16th February, 1657; *m.* Alice COLSTON, dau. of Ralf COLSTON; a son, Robert BELL, in Virginia 1620, living in Northampton Co., 1623; a son Thomas BELL, *b.* 1618, came from London to Jamestown and was in Virginia 16th June, 1635, *d.* December, 1678; *m.* Mary NEAL, dau. of Capt. John NEAL, merchant and pioneer; commanded against the Indians April, 1644; Vestryman, May, 1636; Burgess for Accomac, 1639–1641; *d.* after 1644.

ISSUE

I. THOMAS, of whom later.
II. William, of Bell Haven, Virginia.
III. Robert, *d.* April, 1709; *m.* Tabitha SCARBOROUGH.
IV. Anthony, *m.* Abigail ROACH of Somerset County, Maryland.
V. George, *d.* October, 1723; *m.* Hannah BRICKHOUSE.
VI. Mary, *m.* ——— MADDOX.
VII. Elizabeth, *m.* Thomas GEBBINGS.

THOMAS BELL of Northampton, Virginia, *d.* 1715; *m.* Mary WATSON, dau. of Robert WATSON.

ISSUE

I. THOMAS (and others), of whom later.

THOMAS BELL of Accomac, Virginia; *d.* after 1715; *m.* Barbara Robins WISE, dau. of John and Hannah (SCARBOROUGH) WISE, and gd. dau. of Arthur ROBINS, 1694, all of Accomac County, Virginia. The WISES lived in West Devonshire, England, before 1066, whose seventh direct descendent was Sir William WISE, 1176, nearly related to John RUSSELL, first Earl of Bedford and Lord HUNSDON, first cousin to Queen Elizabeth. Sir William WISE was the progenitor of John WISE who came to Virginia, 1635, d. November, 1695. He was the ancestor of Gov. Henry A. WISE, of Virginia; he m. Hannah SCARBOROUGH, dau. of Capt. Edmund SCARBOROUGH. In the year 1400 the new Crest was added to the Arms of the WISE family.

ISSUE

I. George BELL, of whom later. (No record of other children.)

GEORGE BELL of Northampton County, Virginia; d. December, 1771; m. Leah (surname not given).

ISSUE

I. JOAB (and others), b. 1724, of whom later.

JOAB BELL of Northampton, Virginia, b. 1724; d. December, 1794; m. Kesiah (surname not given).

ISSUE

I. George (and others), b. 11th March, 1760, of whom later.

GEORGE BELL of Northampton County, b. 11th March, 1760; d. 25th April, 1834; served as a soldier during the Revolution in Capt. John BLAIR's Company, 9th Virginia Regiment; taken prisoner at Germantown, 4th October, 1777; m. (firstly) 25th December, 1795, his cousin Susanna BELL, who d. 1808, dau. of William and Elizabeth (SAVAGE) BELL; m. (secondly) Elizabeth SCOTT; William BELL served in Company 3, 3d Virginia Regiment, 1777, son of Capt. Robert BELL, who was commissioned Captain of the 9th Virginia Regiment, 16th April, 1776, taken prisoner at Germantown, October, 1777, and again a prisoner from January, 1783, to May, 1783.

ISSUE

I. SAVAGE, b. 15th December, 1796, of whom later.
II. Ewell, b. 25th June, 1799; d. 1817; unmarried.
III. Mary, b. 18th April, 1802; m. John GLEASON.

SAVAGE BELL of Northampton, Virginia, b. 15th December, 1795; d. 1864; m. 1822, Elizabeth Harmanson SPIERS, b. 4th August, 1797, d. 1st January, 1856, dau. of George and Elizabeth (HARMANSON) SPIERS of Accomac County, Virginia.

ISSUE

I. JAMES EWELL, b. 29th February, 1824, the subject of this memoir.

Arms.—A fesse ermine, between three bells argent, quartering argent on a bend azure, three crosses crosslet or, for Beaupre.
Crest.—A human heart, between two wings ppr.
Motto.—Forward, kind heart.
NOTE. The Eastern Shore of Virginia was originally the Kingdom of Accamake. Two counties were founded 1662, Accomac and Northampton, hence the seeming change of the settlers who occupied their original grants.

Waters

This family is traced to Middleham, Yorkshire, England. Arms, Crest, and Motto borne by the York Herald, 1377.

CAPT. EDWARD WATERS was in Virginia in 1608; *d.* 1630; was a member of the House of Burgesses; Lieutenant and Captain; *m.* Grace O'NEIL, she *m.* (secondly) Col. Obedience ROBINS of Northampton County; Burgess; their son,

COL. WILLIAM WATERS of Northampton County, Virginia, *b.* 1620; *d.* 1689; was member of the Assembly, Northampton County, Virginia, 1654–1660; Burgess, 1666–1676; Officer Colonial Army; Major, 1659; Colonel, 1676; Vestryman Hungar's Parish, Northampton County, 8th May, 1676.

Harmanson

THOMAS HARMANSON, Gentleman, a distinguished Lawyer of the Seventeenth century, of Virginia; was in Virginia 1622; *d.* there 1702; was a member of the House of Burgesses; *m.* Elizabeth (surname not given); their issue as follows:

 I. Thomas, *m.* Grace (surname not given).
 II. Colonel George, *m.* Elizabeth, dau. of Capt. Argall and Sarah (MICHAEL) YEARDLEY.
 III. Isabel, *m.* Col. William WATERS, son of Col. William WATERS.
 IV. William.
 V. Henry, *m.* Gertrude, dau. of Col. Southey LITTLETON and Elizabeth BOWMAN.
 VI. John, *m.* Susanna, dau. of John and Susanna (SAVAGE) KENDALL.
 VII. Alicia, *m.* Capt. Thomas SAVAGE, son of Capt. John SAVAGE and Mary ROBINS.

(Mary Bell HEYER is four times descended from Thomas HARMANSON through his children, George, John, Isabel and Alicia).

JOHN KENDALL HARMANSON, son of John and Susannah (KENDALL) HARMANSON *m.* Isabel HARMANSON, dau. of Col. George and Elizabeth (YEARDLEY) HARMANSON; their son Kendall, *m.* Anna. Their dau.

ELIZABETH HARMANSON *m.* 1784, George SPIERS; their dau.

ELIZABETH HARMANSON SPIERS, *m.* Savage BELL.

Littleton

The family of LYTTLETON has been of long standing in England, Worceshire, South-Lyttleton, where they had considerable possessions. They come in direct line from Thomas DE LUTTLETON, who m. Emma, dau. and heir of Sir Simon DE FRANKLEY, 1216. They quarter Arms with PLANTAGENET.

COL. NATHANIEL LITTLETON, of Virginia, 1622; was governor of Accomac, 1652; Member of Virginia House of Burgesses, Commander of Accomac, 1632; in Virginia, 1622; m. Anne SOUTHEY, dau. of Henry and Elizabeth SOUTHEY; their son

COL. SOUTHEY LITTLETON, b. 1645; d. September, 1679; was an officer in the Colonial Army; member of the House of Burgesses; served against the Indians and under Governor BERKELEY, Bacon's Rebellion; Justice and Sheriff in 1663; m. Elizabeth BOWMAN, dau. of Sir Edmund BOWMAN of England, who settled in Accomac, Virginia, for which County he was a Member of the House of Burgesses in 1663; their son

COL. NATHANIEL LITTLETON, d. 1703; was Sheriff, Justice, Colonel in the Colonial Army; m. Susanna WATERS, dau. of Col. William and Isabel (HARMANSON) WATERS; their dau.

ESTHER LITTLETON, m. 9th November, 1722, Thomas SAVAGE, son of Thomas and Alicia (HARMANSON) SAVAGE.

Savage

Of this ancient and noble family the first who came to these shores was THOMAS DE SAVAGE, who came from Normandy into England with the Army of the Conquerer, 1066; his name appears in the list of Normans who survived the battle of Hastings.

THOMAS SAVAGE, b. 1594; d. in Northampton County, 1627; immigrated to Virginia in 1607 from Cheshire, England, and lived among the Indians some years, was Ensign in the Indian Wars, 1624, and earlier, frequently employed against the Indians; given 9000 acres of land by Indian Chief Iomeesechemee, known as "Savage's Neck;" he m. Hannah TYNG; their only son

CAPT. JOHN SAVAGE of Savage's Neck, Northampton County, Virginia; b. 1624, d. 1678; was a Justice and Member of the Virginia House of Burgesses; m. (firstly) Ann ELKINGTON; m. (secondly) Mary ROBINS, dau. of Col. Obedience ROBINS. Member of the House of Burgesses and Commander of Accomac County, 1632.

CAPT. THOMAS SAVAGE of Savage's Neck, Virginia, d. June, 1728; served in the Indian Wars, m. 1702, Alicia HARMANSON.

CAPT. THOMAS SAVAGE of Savage's Neck, Virginia; Officer in Indian Wars; d. April, 1737; m. 9th November, 1722, Esther LITTLETON, dau. of Col. Nathanial and Susanna (WATERS) LITTLETON; their son

THOMAS SAVAGE of Northampton County, Virginia; d. after 19th December, 1795; enlisted in the Continental Army, 19th March, 1778; in Captain Adam WALLACE's Company, 5th Virginia Regiment; m. Elizabeth BELL, dau. of Ezekiel BELL, the son of George BELL, who was the son of Thomas BELL, I; their dau.

ELIZABETH SAVAGE *m.* her cousin William BELL, who served during the Revolution in the 3d Company, 9th Virginia Regiment, he was the son of Capt. Robert BELL, who was the son of Robert, the son of Thomas and Mary (NEALE) BELL, son of Robert.

Arms confirmed 16th September, 1614.

Scarborough

CAPT. EDMUND SCARBOROUGH of Virginia, *d.* 1635; was a Member of the House of Burgesses of Virginia, 1629; *m.* Hannah (surname not given).

ISSUE

I. Sir Charles.
II. EDMUND, of whom below.
III. Hannah, *m.* Col. John WISE.

COL. EDMUND SCARBOROUGH, *d.* 1671; Burgess for Northampton County, Virginia, 1642–1645, 1652–1655, 1660 and for Accomac, 1666; Speaker of the House of Burgesses of Virginia, 1645; High Sheriff of Accomac County, Virginia, 1660–1661; in command of the expedition against the Assateague Indians, 1659; Surveyor General of Virginia, 1655–1671; *m.* Mary CHARLETON, dau. of Stephen and Elizabeth CHARLETON. Col. Stephen CHARLETON commanded in Indian Massacre, 1644; Vestryman, 1635, Accomake; Burgess Northampton County, 1644–1645, 1652; *d.* 1653; he *m.* November 1653, Ann WEST, widow of Anthony WEST, Gentleman, of the family of Thomas WEST, Lords DE LA WARR, as shown by Arms on tomb of Maj. Charles WEST, his gr. gd. son, at Onancock, Northampton County, Virginia.

Anthony WEST, *d.* in Northampton County, 1652; this family was in England, 1207.

COL. CHARLES SCARBOROUGH, *d.* 1703; was a Member of the House of Burgesses, of Virginia; Justice; Commander-in-Chief of Accomac County, 1688–1691; *m.* Katharine WEST, dau. of Anthony WEST, who was in Virginia in 1622, their dau.

TABITHA SCARBOROUGH, *m.* Robert BELL, son of Thomas BELL, I, son of Robert.

Yeardley

SIR GEORGE YEARDLEY, Knight, *b.* 1577; *d.* 1627; in Virginia, 1609; Governor and Captain General of Virginia, 1619; *m.* Temperance FLOWERDEW (records give her name as Lady Temperance), dau. of Anthony FLOWERDEW, and niece of Baron Edward FLOWERDEW, County Norfolk, England. Sir George was a man of wealth and great personal wealth. He was descended from a Staffordshire family known as the Lords of Yeardley. He had served with distinction in Holland in the war against Spain. He was Deputy Governor of Virginia, 1616–17, Governor 1618–1621, again appointed Governor, 1626, and held the office until his death.

ISSUE

I. Argall.
II. Elizabeth.
III. Francis.

Their eldest son and heir

COL. ARGALL YEARDLEY, *b.* 1620; Member of Council of Virginia, 1643; *m.* 1649, dau. of John and Joan CUSTIS, early settlers in Northampton County, Virginia, ancestors of Daniel Park Custis, who *m.* Martha who later became the wife of Gen. George WASHINGTON.

ISSUE OF COL. ARGALL AND ANN (CUSTIS) YEARDLEY

I. ARGALL, of whom below.
II. Rose.
III. Henry.
IV. Frances, *m.* Col. Adam THOROWGOOD of Lynnhaven, Lower Norfolk, Virginia.

CAPT. ARGALL YEARDLEY, *d.* 1682; Member of Council of Virginia; *m.* Sarah MICHAEL, dau. of Capt. John and Elizabeth (THOROWGOOD) MICHAEL, dau. of Capt. Adam THOROWGOOD, *b.* 1603, *d.* 1640; their dau.

ELIZABETH YEARDLEY, *m.* Col. George HARMANSON, Member of the House of Burgesses of Virginia, 1722.

Flowerdew

JOHN FLOWERDEW, of Hathersett County, Norfolk; *m.* and had issue

EDWARD, a Baron of the Exchequer, *m.* Elizabeth, *d.s.p.* 31st March, 1586.

WILLIAM, brother and heir of Baron Edward FLOWERDEW, Edmund and others. William *m.* and had Anthony, *b.* 1557, *d.* 1620, heir of Baron Edward, and next heir to William, *m.* Martha (surname not given), she *m.* (secondly) Capt. Godfrey GARRETT; she *d.* 1626. Anthony FLOWERDEW, *b.* 1557, *d.* 1620, and Martha FLOWERDEW had a daughter who *m.* Thomas SHILTON, who *d.s.p.* 1620, son of Sir Thomas SHILTON, Knight, Stanley.

MARY FLOWERDEW, *m.* Dyonis ROSSINGHAM, son of Edmund ROSSINGHAM, Member of First General Assembly in Virginia, 1619.

TEMPERANCE FLOWERDEW in Virginia, 1608; *m.* 1618, Sir George YEARDLEY; after his death, 1627; she *m.* Francis WEST, son of Lord DE LA WARR, who succeeded her husband as Governor of Virginia, 1627; she *m.* Francis WEST, 1628, *d.* 1629. ("Virginia Magazine," Vol. 25, No. 2, April, 1917.)

Bell-Land

FRANCIS LAND, Gentleman, one of the earliest settlers of Lower Norfolk County, Virginia; came from England 1630; he was elected Church Warden of Lynn Haven Parish, 3d August, 1640; he was one of the largest land owners in this county, disposing of by his will, dated 15th April, 1654, one thousand and twenty acres of land to his two sons, Francis and Renatus, besides other valuable property; the name of his wife is not given.

RENATUS LAND, of Lynn Haven Parish, Norfolk County, Virginia; *d.* 1st May, 1681; *m.* Frances KEELING, dau. of Lieut. Thomas and Ann KEELING.

ISSUE

I. EDWARD (and others), *d.* 1722, of whom later.

EDWARD LAND of Lynn Haven Parish, Virginia, *d.* 1722; *m.* Elizabeth EDWARDS, dau. of John and Elizabeth EDWARDS.

ISSUE

I. EDWARD (and others), of whom later.

EDWARD LAND of Lynn Haven Parish, Virginia; *d.* February, 1774; *m.* Frances LANGLEY, dau. of James LANGLEY, of Norfolk, County.

ISSUE

I. JEREMIAH (and others), of whom later.

JEREMIAH LAND of Lynn Haven Parish, Virginia; *d.* January, 1805; *m.* Ann WOODHOUSE, *d.* after 1805, dau. of Maj. Jonathan and Mary WOODHOUSE.

ISSUE

I. PETER (and others), of whom later.

CAPT. PETER LAND of Lynn Haven Parish, Virginia; *d.* August, 1845; *m.* Elizabeth KEELING, *b.* 1764, *d.* 1808, dau. of William and Anne KEELING of Lynn Haven Parish, Princess Anne County.

ISSUE

I. Jeremiah, *d.* 25th March, 1832; unmarried.
II. William Keeling, *d.* 1834; *m.* Eliza Woodhouse STONE (?), 14th October, 1820.

  III. Littleton Waller Tazewell, *d.* 1859; unmarried.
  IV. Mary Woodhouse, *d.* November, 1876; *m.* 1830, her cousin, Thomas Stone LAND.
  V. Lovey, *m.* Thomas KEELING, her cousin, 27th January, 1823.
  VI. Eliza, *d.s.p.; m.* Henry WOODHOUSE.
  VII. Sarah.
  VIII. EDWARD CANNON, *b.* 1808, of whom later.

EDWARD CANNON LAND of Lynn Haven Parish, Virginia; *b.* 1808; *d.* 7th April, 1832; *m.* 1st August, 1827, Elizabeth (SMITH) FOREMAN, *b.* 1807, *d.* 6th October, 1837, dau. of Capt. Mitchell Smith and Olive WOODARD.

ISSUE

  I. Walter Scott.
  II. ANNE VIRGINIA, *b.* 25th October 1832, of whom later.

ANNE VIRGINIA LAND, *b.* 25th October, 1832; *d.* 18th September, 1910; *m.* December, 1851, James Ewell BELL, M.D., *b.* 29th February, 1824, *d.* 27th May, 1914. (See BELL.)

ISSUE

  I. Mary BELL, *b.* 4th June, 1860; *m.* 2d January, 1884, Matthew Johnston HEYER.

Arms. (LAND).—Gyronny of eight or and sable, a bend gules.
Crest.—A church environed with trees proper.

Woodhouse

Sir Henry was the son of Sir William who *m.* Elizabeth, dau. of Sir Philip CALTHORPE and Anne, dau. of Sir William BOLYNE. Sir Thomas BOLYNE, his son, was the father of Queen Ann BOLYNE and Mary who *m.* William CARY, their dau. Katherine CARY, *m.* Sir Francis KNOLLYS. She was first cousin to Queen Elizabeth; dau. Anne *m.* Thomas WEST, second Lord DE LA WARR; their son Francis WEST *m.* Lady Temperance YEARDLEY, 1628, in Virginia.

  At the present time, 1st May, 1896, after a lapse of two hundred and fifty-six years, three of the descendants of Henry WOODHOUSE, 1640, bearing his name are Vestrymen of the Eastern Shore Chapel, built 1754, Lynn Haven Parish, Princess Anne County, Virginia, namely, Judge John J. WOODHOUSE, Maj. Jonathan WOODHOUSE and Maj. John T. WOODHOUSE.

  CAPT. HENRY WOODHOUSE, *b.* 1607; *d.* 1655; son of Gov. Henry WOODHOUSE and gd. son of Sir Henry WOODHOUSE, of Waxham, County Norfolk, England, and his wife Ann BACON, dau. of Sir Nicholas BACON, came to Virginia and settled in Lower Norfolk County in 1637; was Burgess of that County from 1647 to 1652; Vestryman, Lynn Haven Parish, 1640; his son.

CAPT. WILLIAM WOODHOUSE, d. March, 1701; was a Captain in the Virginia Colonial Forces, 1700, in Princesse Anne County; his son.

CAPT. HENRY WOODHOUSE, d. December, 1743; in Colonial Army; m. Mary (surname not given), Princess Ann County; their son.

CAPT. WILLIAM WOODHOUSE, d. January, 1774; was a Church Warden of Lynn Haven Parish, 14th December, 1773; Military Officer 22d October, 1771; m. Pembroke THOROUGHGOOD, dau. of John THOROUGHGOOD, d. 1757; their son

MAJ. JONATHAN WOODHOUSE of Princess Anne County, Virginia; d. January, 1775; was an officer in the Colonial Army in 1775; m. Mary (surname not given); their dau.

ANN WOODHOUSE, m. Jeremiah LAND, who d. January, 1805.

Bray-Lawson

COL. ROBERT BRAY of Lower Norfolk County, Virginia; d. there June, 1681; rendered conspicuous service in Bacon's Rebellion; he was the son of Edward BRAY of New Bedfordshire, England; m. twice, the name of the first wife is not stated, but by the marriage he had a daughter who m. Thomas LAWSON; his second wife was Ann KEELING, who d.s.p., widow of Lieut. Thomas KEELING, who d. 1665.

THOMAS LAWSON, who m. the dau. of Col. Robert BRAY, was in Virginia in 1609; his son, Col. Anthony LAWSON, Member of the House of Burgesses of Virginia, his dau.

MARGARET LAWSON, m. Col. John THOROUGHGOOD.

Langley

CAPT. WILLIAM LANGLEY of Lower Norfolk County, Virginia, was in Virginia, 1625; d. 1675; m. Joyce (surname not given). Their son

CAPT. WILLIAM LANGLEY, d. 1718; Burgess in 1715 for Norfolk County; m. Margaret THELEBAL; their son, see Mason line.

NATHAN LANGLEY, d. November, 1742; m. Sarah (surname not given); d. 30th December, 1742; their son

JAMES LANGLEY of Norfolk County, Virginia; m. secondly 24th May, 1731, Sarah NICHOLSON, d. September, 1752; dau. of first marriage,

FRANCES LANGLEY, m. Edward LAND.

Mason

FRANCIS MASON of Lower Norfolk County, Virginia, in Virginia in 1613; d. 1648; County Lieutenant of Lower Norfolk, 1639, and same year Captain of the Royal Troops; Church Warden of Lynn Haven Parish, 1638; m. 1620, Alice (surname not given).

ISSUE

1. Elizabeth MASON, d. March, 1707; m. James THELEBAL, a Hugenot, Church Warden in Lower Norfolk, Elizabeth River Parish, in 1659.

Margaret THELEBAL, their dau., *m.* Capt. William LANGLEY, son of Capt. William and Joyce LANGLEY.

II. Col. Lemuel MASON, of Lower Norfolk County, Virginia; *d.* September, 1702; was Burgess, 1654 to 1692, and other years; *m.* Anne SEWELL, *d.* October, 1705, dau. of Henry SEWELL, also a Burgess for the same County, 1639.

Butt

ROBERT BUTT, *d.* 1676; settled in Lower Norfolk County, Virginia, in 1640; son of Joshua BUTT, of Warrington Hall, County Kent, England; *n.* Jane (surname not given); their son

THOMAS BUTT, *d.* after 1722; was Justice of Lower Norfolk County, February, 1637; he left a son

THOMAS BUTT of Butt's Road, Lower Norfolk County; *d.* June, 1764, Burgess, 1700; he left a dau.

OLIVE BUTT, *m.* (firstly) before 1785, William WOODARD, member of Captain MASSIE's Company, 6th Virginia Regiment, 1st September, 1776, Continental Army; *m.* (secondly) Thomas GRESHAM; *m.* (thirdly) 11th April, 1803, Dr. William HARDIGAN.

OLIVE WOODWARD, dau. of William and Olive (BUTT) WOODWARD, *b.* 3d May, 1785; *d.* 1856; *m.* (firstly) 1806, Capt. Mitchell SMITH, *b.* 1781, *d.* 1816, was Captain in LEE's 95th Virginia Regiment, 23d June, 1813; *m.* (secondly) George MARTIN. Capt. Mitchell SMITH was son of John SMITH Member of Troop from Norfolk County, Virginia, June, 1777, Revolutionary War.

ELIZABETH SMITH, *b.* 1807; *d.* 6th October, 1837, dau. of Capt. Mitchell and Olive (WOODWARD) SMITH; *m.* (firstly) 1822, Gen. Nehemiah FOREMAN; *m.* (secondly) 1st August, 1827, Edward Cannon LAND, who *d.* 7th April, 1832, son of Capt. Peter and Elizabeth (KEELING) LAND; *m.* (thirdly) Malachi WARDEN, who survived her.

ISSUE

1. Ann Virginia LAND,

Thoroughgood

ADAM THOROUGHGOOD, builder of the oldest Colonial home in America; Commander of a Royal Troop; Member of the King's Council; First Judge of Lower Norfolk, Virginia; *b.* 1602; *d.* 1641; came to Virginia in 1621; he was the son of William and Ann (EDWARDS) THOROUGHGOOD, who was the brother of Sir John and Sir Edward THOROUGHGOOD, of Gunsten, England. He *m.* Sarah OFFLEY, dau. of Robert OFFLEY, merchant of Grace Street, London, England, and his wife, Ann OSBORNE, dau. of Sir Edward OSBORNE, Knight, Lord Mayor of London, 1583, whose wife was Ann HEWITT, dau. of William HEWITT, Lord Mayor of London, 1559.

SARAH OFFLEY, *bapt.* 16th April, 1609; *m.* 18th July, 1627, at Saint Ann's, Black Friars, England, to Adam THOROUGHGOOD; they had one son Adam and three daughters: Ann, *m.* Job CHANLER, Maryland Councillor; Sarah OFFLEY, *m.* a Maryland Councillor; Elizabeth, *m.* Capt. John MICHAEL of Accomac, Virginia.

COL. ADAM THOROUGHGOOD of Lower Norfolk County, Virginia; *d.* March, 1686; was burgess, 10th October, 1665; *m.* Frances YEARDLEY, dau. of Argall YEARDLEY and Ann CUSTIS, and gd. dau. of Sir George YEARDLEY and Lady Temperance; their son,

COL. JOHN THOROUGHGOOD, Burgess of Lower Norfolk County, Virginia; *m.* Margaret LAWSON, dau. of Col. Anthony LAWSON and Mary GOOKIN, dau. of Capt. John and Sarah (OFFLEY) THOROUGHGOOD GOOKIN. Sarah (OFFLEY) GOOKIN, after the death of her second husband, Capt. John GOOKIN, *m.* (thirdly) Col. Francis YEARDLEY, youngest son of Sir George and Lady Temperance (WEST) YEARDLEY; no issue.

ANN THOROUGHGOOD, *d.* before 1771; dau. of Col. John and Margaret (LAWSON) THOROUGHGOOD *m.* Adam KEELING, who *d.* June, 1771; their dau.

ANN KEELING, *m.* her cousin William KEELING, who was Burgess 25th March, 1756–1758. She *d.* after 1768.

(Mary Bell HEYER is three times descended from Sarah OFFLEY, through her children: Col. Adam THOROUGHGOOD, ELIZABETH THOROUGHGOOD and Mary GOOKIN.)

Cock or Gookin

Arms granted 1199.

THOMAS GOOKIN of Kent, England; son of Arnold *Gookin; m.* 1538, Amy DURANT; their son,

JOHN GOOKIN, *m.* 25th October, 1566, Catherine DENNE; their son

DANIEL GOOKIN, came to Virginia in 1622, and founded the City of Newport News; *m.* 1609, Mary BYRD, dau. of Dr. Richard BYRD, Canon of Canterbury Cathedral, and gd. dau. of Dr. John MEYER, Bishop of Carlisle; their son,

CAPT. JOHN GOOKIN, of Lower Norfolk County, Virginia; *b.* 1613; *d.* 2d November, 1643; was commander of the County and Burgess, 29th March, 1643; *m.* Sarah (OFFLEY) THOROUGHGOOD, widow of Col. Adam THOROUGHGOOD, who was in Virginia in 1621; their dau.

MARY GOOKIN, *b.* 1641; *m.* (firstly) 1660, Capt. William MOSELEY, who *d.* 1671; *m.* (secondly) 1672, Col. Anthony LAWSON, by whom she had a dau., Margaret LAWSON.

SARAH OFFLEY is buried at the Lynn Haven Church, with her three husbands; COL. Adam THOROUGHGOOD, Capt. John GOOKIN, and Col. Francis YEARDLEY. The *Thoroughgood* and *Yeardley* Arms are on their tomb.

MARGARET LAWSON, dau. of Col. Anthony and Mary (GOOKIN) MOSELEY, *m.* her cousin, Col. John THOROUGHGOOD, who *d.* 1701, he was Burgess for his county; their dau.

ANN THOROUGHGOOD, *m.* Adam KEELING.

Keeling

A famous family from Worcestershire, England. William KEELING was the father of John KEELING, who was the father of Sir John KEELING, the Chief Justice of the King's Bench in 1665.

ENSIGN THOMAS KEELING, b. 1608; d. August, 1665; was living in Lower Norfolk County Virginia, in 1635; he was Church Warden in 1640; County Lieutenant, 2d December, 1659; m. Ann (surname not given).

ISSUE

  I. Frances, m. Renatus LAND.
 II. Alexander m. Grace (surname not given).
III. Anne, m. Henry WOODHOUSE.
 IV. ADAM, of whom below and others

CAPT. ADAM KEELING, d. 1683; m. Ann MARTIN, dau. of John MARTIN, Gentleman, who was in Jamestown, Virginia, 1607, d. Lynnhaven Parish, 1638, leaving a son Jonn, who was Church Warden in 1645, Burgess Lower Norfolk County, Virginia, 1651; m. and had dau. Ann, who m. Capt. Adam KEELING, Military Officer, son of Lieut. Thomas KEELING.

Benjamin

ADDISON BENJAMIN, *b.* 26th October, 1812, Jefferson, Maine; *d.* 4th March, 1887, North Whitefield, Maine. Addison BENJAMIN was the son of Benaiah BENJAMIN and Elizabeth NOYES, his wife. He lived and died on the old BENJAMIN homestead. For a while he was identified with lumbering and milling interests during the early days of that industry, in the vicinity of Ellsworth, Maine, and in the Kennebec River basin. Later he was in trade, conducting a general store. At the outbreak of the Civil War he enlisted in the Union Army. He served under several enlistments in the 19th and 31st Maine Regiments. Erskine Post, Grand Army of the Republic, of which he was a charter member, participated in the services at his funeral. He was a man of genial personality and helpful influence.

Lineage

JOHN BENJAMIN (circa 1598–1645), was the founder of the BENJAMIN family in America. He arrived with his family in Boston Harbor, Sunday evening, 16th September, 1632, on board the *Lion*, after a voyage of twelve weeks, being eight weeks from Lands End. His brother, Richard BENJAMIN, came with him on the *Lion* and settled in Southold, Long Island. In 1642 he was the largest landed proprietor in Newtowne, now Cambridge, Massachusetts. The will of John BENJAMIN was in the handwritng of Governor WINTHROP, who in his writings refers to the comfort and elegance of his residence in Cambridge. He *m.* 1619, Abigail EDDY, dau. of Rev. William EDDY (graduated M. A., Trinity in 1586), and Mary FOSTEN, his wife; their son,

JOHN BENJAMIN (circa 1620–1706), *m.* Lydia ALLEN; in 1664 he was of Hartford, Connecticut; *d.* in Watertown, Massachusetts; their son,

ABEL BENJAMIN (1668–1720); admitted to full communion 1697–1698; by his wife Abigail, he had several children; their son,

JONATHAN BENJAMIN (1697–1735), *m.* Susanna, dau. of Nathaniel and Susanna NORCROSS; their son,

ABEL BENJAMIN (1731–1758), a soldier in the French-Indian Wars; perished on the Expedition to Fort William Henry; *m.* Elizabeth NUTTING; their son,

JOHN BENJAMIN (1758–1814), *b.* in the year his father died. The service of seven years given by John BENJAMIN in the Continental Army, is fittingly commemorated by a tablet on the walls of the Washington Memorial Chapel at Valley Forge, Pennsylvania, the gift of his grand daughter, Mrs. PEARSON. He *m.* 1781, Jemima MILLS, who was descended from many early American emigrant ancestors; their son,

BENAIAH BENJAMIN (1791–1888), settled in Whitefield (originally Ballstown), Maine, and reclaimed his homestead from the wilderness. He m. Elizabeth NOYES, many of whose forebears and kinsmen were prominent in church and state in the Colonies and in England.

ISSUE

  I. ADDISON (1812–1887), the subject of this memoir.
 II. Ephraim Mellen (1814–1848); m. Meriam HUNT.
III. Hester Ann (1817–1892); m. William Washington HUNT.
 IV. Parson (1818–1833).
  V. Washburn (1820–1891); m. Helen Augusta TURNER.
 VI. Mary Elizabeth (1822–1845).
VII. Milton Noyes (1824–1897); m. Mary Ann MURPHY.
VIII. Lois Noyes (1826–1861). m. Guy LAMKIN.
 IX. Benaiah, Jr. (1829–1869).
  X. Catherine Emma (1831–1883); m. Miles Leroy BENNER.
 XI. Nancy Delia (1833–1917); m. William Henry PEARSON.
XII. John (1836–1857).

Arms.—Or, on a saltire, quarterly pierced, sable five annulets, counterchanged.
Crest.—On a chapeau, a flame of fire, all ppr.
Motto.—Poussez en avant.
NOTE.—The foregoing memoir was prepared and furnished by Mr. Arthur Emmons PEARSON, nephew of the late Mr. Addison BENJAMIN.

Benjamin

BENAIAH BENJAMIN, JR., b. 13th January, 1829, North Whitefield, Maine; d. 1st April, 1869, North Whitefield, Maine. BENAIAH BENJAMIN, Jr., was the son of Benaiah and Elizabeth (NOYES) BENJAMIN, and until 1852 he lived on the old homestead, when he went to Boston and became identified with the wholesale and retail shoe trade. He was there for about sixteen years, during which time, John BENJAMIN, his brother, was located in Boston in the same business. This brother was a young man of great promise through superior mental gifts, well directed and tireless industry, and genial personality; he d. in his twenty-first year. Benaiah BENJAMIN, Jr., was a man of unusually high mind and purpose, and the appeal of religion to him was significantly reflected in his words and acts, that caused his presence to be sought and his kindly coöperation invited. He d. in the house in which he was born, survived by his venerable parents.

Lineage

JOHN BENJAMIN (circa 1598-1645), the first of the line in America, sailed from Plymouth, England, in the ship, *Lion*, in June, 1632, with his wife Abigail and their children. She was the dau. of Rev. William EDDY, Vicar of St. Dunstan's Church, Cranbrook, County Kent, England. Governor WINTHROP in his writings refers to the home of Mr. BENJAMIN in Newtowne, now Cambridge, Massachusetts, in the following words: "Mr. BENJAMIN'S mansion was unsurpassed in elegance and comfort by any in the vicinity. It was the mansion of intelligence, religion and hospitality, visited by the clergy of all denominations, and by the literati at home and abroad." John BENJAMIN owned the largest homestall in Watertown in 1642; their son,

JOHN BENJAMIN (circa 1620-1706), lived the greater part of his life in Watertown, Massachusetts and d. there. He was in Hartford, Connecticut, in 1664 and shared in the establishment of their church. He m. Lydia ALLEN, dau. of William ALLEN, of Boston; their son,

ABEL BENJAMIN (1668-1720), was b. in Watertown, Massachusetts and was admitted to the church 6th February, 1697-1698. By his wife Abigail he had several children; their son,

JONATHAN BENJAMIN (1697-1735), m. Susanna, dau. of Nathaniel and Susanna NORCROSS and gd. dau. of Richard NORCROSS, the first schoolmaster mentioned in the records of Watertown, Massachusetts; their son,

ABEL BENJAMIN (1731-1758), was of a Company of Foot in His Majesty's service under Capt. Jonathan BROWN in Col. William WILLIAMS' Regiment which was raised by the Province of Massachusetts Bay for the reduction of Canada. Abel BENJAMIN perished on the Expedition to Fort William Henry. He *m.* Elizabeth NUTTING, whose gr. gd. father was killed by the Indians while defending his garrison house in Groton, Massachusetts; their son,

JOHN BENJAMIN (1758–1814), served in the Continental Army for seven years; he was in the Massachusetts Artillery Regiment of Colonel CRANE. His powder horn, carried throughout the war has been mounted on a silver base, suitably inscribed and presented to the Valley Forge Museum of American History by his gr. gd. son, Arthur Emmons PEARSON. His brother, Lieut. Samuel BENJAMIN, took the oath of fidelity at Valley Forge, 13th May, 1778; the document, witnessed by Baron DEKALB, is in the possession of his descendants. Martha BENJAMIN, dau. of Lieut. Samuel and Tabitha (LIVERMORE) BENJAMIN, *m.* Israel WASHBURN, and they were the progenitors of a family of pronounced ability who rendered distinguished services to the Union here and abroad. John BENJAMIN married in Needham, Massachusetts, 1781, Jemima MILLS, whose ancestry was identified with the history and development of Norfolk County; their son,

BENAIAH BENJAMIN (1791–1888), was *b.* in Roxbury, Massachusetts. His childhood was passed in Livermore, Maine. When nineteen years of age, he went with his father east from the Kennebec River and settled in North Whitefield, Maine. His brother, Jesse BENJAMIN, served in the War of 1812. Benaiah BENJAMIN *m.* Elizabeth NOYES, and they were blessed by a happy married life of sixty-seven years. She was descended from Rev. William NOYES of Choulderton Parish near Salisbury, England, through Nicholas NOYES, who landed at Parker River in Newbury, Massachusetts, in 1633.

ISSUE

I. Addison (1812–1887).
II. Ephraim Mellen (1814–1848); *m.* Meriam HUNT.
III. Hester Ann (1817–1892); *m.* William Washington HUNT.
IV. Parson (1818–1833).
V. Washburn (1820–1891); *m.* Helen Augusta TURNER.
VI. Mary Elizabeth (1822–1845).
VII. Milton Noyes (1824–1897); *m.* Mary Ann MURPHY.
VIII. Lois Noyes (1826–1861); *m.* Guy LAMKIN.
IX. BENAIAH, JR. (1829–1869); the subject of this memoir.
X. Catherine Emma (1831–1883); *m.* Miles Leroy BENNER.
XI. Nancy Delia (1833–1917); *m.* William Henry PEARSON.
XII. John (1836–1857).

Arms.—Or, on a saltire quarterly pierced, sable five annulets, counterchanged.
Crest.—On a chapeau, a flame of fire, all ppr.
Motto.—Poussez en avant.

NOTE.—The foregoing memoir was prepared and furnished by Mr. Arthur Emmons PEARSON, nephew of the late Mr. Benaiah BENJAMIN, Jr.

Benjamin

WASHBURN BENJAMIN, the son of Benaiah and Elizabeth (NOYES) BENJAMIN, *b.* 26th September, 1820, North Whitefield, Maine; *d.* 14th December, 1891, Gardiner-Maine; *m.* 3d October, 1867, Vassalboro, Maine, Helen Augusta TURNER, dau. of Samuel Williamson TURNER and Nancy Hall HOYT, his wife.

ISSUE

I. Mary Washburn BENJAMIN, *b.* 17th August, 1868, Vassalboro, Maine.

WASHBURN BENJAMIN, in his boyhood on the homestead, was blessed by the advantages of country life that laid the foundation of his robust health, that enabled him in later life, to participate effectively in his profession and in the life of the community in which he lived. As a youth he was an excellent scholar, especially in the classical branches. He was particularly proficient in Latin and Greek and he never ceased to maintain his interest in those two languages. He was educated at Kent's Hill, Readfield, Maine. He taught school for several years, for a part of the time in Camden, Maine. During this period he read law and was early admitted to the bar.

He built a residence on Brunswick Street, in Gardiner, Maine (1869), and lived there until his death in the year 1891. He became a member of Hermon Lodge, No. 32, Free and Accepted Masons, of Gardiner, Maine (1866); a member of Lebanon Royal Arch Chapter (1867), and a Knight Templar of Maine Commandery, No. 1 of Gardiner (1867). He was a man of sound judgment and conservative business ability, a stalwart personality, mentally and physically. He was intensely interested in horticulture and always worked in his garden, and was deeply interested in the production of any new variety of fruit and vegetable, and was successful in their propagation. His greatest pleasure was derived from books, and while he never published any work on philology, he was splendidly equipped to have undertaken such a work.

The estimate of Mr. BENJAMIN, as expressed in the resolutions of the Kennebec Bar, at the time of his death, most perfectly conveys the import and influence of his life.

"At a meeting of the Kennebec Bar held on the 17th December, 1891:

Voted: that Messrs. HEATH, SPEAR and L. TITCOMB be a committee to prepare resolutions relating to the decease of our late brother W. BENJAMIN.

"The committee previously appointed by L. TITCOMB, Esq., in behalf of the committee offered the following resolutions which were unanimously adopted.

Resolved: That the members of the Bar have heard with deep regret that Washburn BENJAMIN, Esq., who for forty years has been one of their most esteemed members, has departed this life.

Resolved: That during his long career as a lawyer and citizen, he has won respect for his integrity, admiration for his sense of justice and great kindness and affection for his unselfish nature. They unite with the citizens of Gardiner in sorrow for his demise and tender their profound sympathy to his bereaved family.

Resolved: That in token of our esteem for his memory we will attend his funeral and respectfully request the Superior Court now in session to adjourn for that purpose.

Resolved: That the Court be requested to order these resolutions to be entered upon its records by the Clerk, and that a copy thereof be transmitted to the family of the deceased by the Clerk of this Bar, and that a copy be furnished for publication.

Most respectfully transmitted,
(signed) H. W. TRUE,
Clerk."

Lineage

JOHN BENJAMIN (circa 1598–1645), England, Newtowne, now Cambridge and Watertown, in Massachusetts, founder of the BENJAMIN family in America; *m.* Abigail EDDY; their son

JOHN BENJAMIN (circa 1620–1706), of Watertown, Massachusetts, and sometime of Hartford, Connecticut; *m.* Lydia ALLEN; their son

ABEL BENJAMIN (1668–1720), of Watertown, Massachusetts, by his wife Abigail, had a son

JONATHAN BENJAMIN (1697–1735); *m.* Susanna NORCROSS; their son

ABEL BENJAMIN (1731–1758); *m.* Elizabeth NUTTING; their son

JOHN BENJAMIN (1758–1814); *m.* Jemima MILLS; their son

BENAIAH BENJAMIN (1791–1888); *m.* Elizabeth NOYES.

ISSUE

I. Addison (1812–1887).
II. Ephraim Mellen (1814–1848); *m.* Meriam HUNT.
III. Hester Ann (1817–1892); *m.* William Washington HUNT.
IV. Parson (1818–1833).
V. WASHBURN (1820–1891); the subject of this memoir.
VI. Mary Elizabeth (1822–1845).
VII. Milton Noyes (1824–1897); *m.* Mary Ann MURPHY.
VIII. Lois Noyes (1826–1861); *m.* Guy LAMKIN.
IX. Benaiah, Jr. (1829–1869).
X. Catherine Emma (1831–1883); *m.* Miles Leroy BENNER.
XI. Nancy Delia (1833–1917); *m.* William Henry PEARSON.
XII. John (1836–1857).

Arms.—Or, on a saltire quarterly pierced, sable five annulets, countercharged.
Crest.—On a chapeau, a flame of fire, all ppr.
Motto.—Poussez en avant.
Note.—The Benjamin, Noyes and Pearson memoirs in the several volumes of this work give extended reference to this lineage.

This memoir was prepared and furnished by Mr. Arthur Emmons Pearson, nephew of the late Washburn Benjamin, Esq.

Bourn

EX-GOVERNOR AUGUSTUS OSBORN BOURN, *b.* at Rhode Island, 1st October, 1834; *m.* 24th February, 1863, Elizabeth Roberts MORRILL, dau. of David C. MORRILL, of Dover, New Hampshire.

ISSUE

I. Augustus Osborn, *b.* 7th May, 1865.
II. George Osborn (twin), *b.* 6th January, 1874.
III. Elizabeth Roberts (twin) *b.* 6th January, 1874.
IV. Alice Mansfield Wentworth, *b.* 5th August, 1875.
V. Stephen Wentworth, *b.* 15th April, 1877.

THE HONORABLE AUGUSTUS OSBORN BOURN, was a member of the Rhode Island Senate, 1878–1883, and 1886–1888; Governor of Rhode Island, 1883–1885; United States Consul-General at Rome, 1889–1893.

Lineage

JARED BOURN of Boston and Roxbury, Massachusetts, and of Portsmouth, Rhode Island, granted land, and admitted to the Church in Boston, 22d April, 1634; admitted an inhabitant of Portsmouth, Rhode Island, 23d January, 1665; Deputy in the Colonial Legislature, 30th October, 1667; in charge of "BOURNS" garrison house, in Swanzy, Massachusetts, during King Phillip's War, *m.* Frances (name not given).

JARED BOURN of Swanzy, Massachusetts, living in 1680; *m.* Elizabeth BRAYTON dau. of Francis BRAYTON, and by her had issue.

FRANCIS BOURN (1693–1758), of Swanzy, Massachusettes, *b.* about 1693; *m.* 23d February, 1716, Charity WHEATON, dau. of John WHEATON; *d.* 1758, left issue.

STEPHEN BOURN (1724–1758), of Swanzy, Massachusettes; *b.* 25th October, 1724; *m.* 16th September, 1756, Charity CHASE, dau. of Elisha CHASE; *d.* 1758, left issue.

STEPHEN BOURN of Somerset, Massachusetts; *b.* 24th June, 1757; *d.* 5th November, 1822; *m.* 28th June, 1798, Deborah BOURN, *d.* 25th October, 1822, dau. of Francis BOURN; left issue.

GEORGE OSBORN BOURN of Providence, Rhode Island; *b.* 4th July, 1809; *d.* 17th August, 1859; *m.* 1st August, 1833, Huldah Battey EDDY, *d.* 8th September, 1892, dau. of Ezra EDDY; left issue.

AUGUSTUS OSBORN, *b.* 1st October, 1834, the subject of this memoir.

Residences.—Bristol, Rhode Island, and Providence, Rhode Island.

Bowie

THOMAS JOHN BOWIE, deceased, of "Grassland," near Annapolis Junction, Anne Arundel County, Maryland; *b.* 22d February, 1837; *d.* at "Grassland," 3d September, 1898; *m.* 26th May, 1870, Susannah ANDERSON, *b.* 27 April, 1850, at Laurel, Prince George County, Maryland, was co-heiress with her half brother, William Henry Harrison ANDERSON of her father, William ANDERSON of "Grassland," Anne Arundel County, Maryland, *b.* 30th August, 1797, Prince George County Maryland, *d.* 22d July, 1877, and his second wife, Sarah HALL, *b.* 27th February, 1811, Prince George County, Maryland, *d.* 1st May, 1875, *m.* 3d November, 1846, dau. of Richard Duckett HALL, *b.* 6th May, 1768, and Elizabeth PERKINS, *b.* 7th June, 1778 (see Hall Family, p. 229). William ANDERSON was of distinguished ancestry. He was the son of John and Sarah ANDERSON of Prince George's County, Maryland.

ISSUE

I. John, planter and man of public affairs; *b.* 21st January, 1871; educated at the Public Schools of Anne Arundel County, Millersville Academy and St. John's College Annapolis; Charter Member of the Benevolent and Protective Order of Elks, Annapolis, Maryland; member of the Third Order of Odd Fellows; *m.* 17th October, 1900, Ethel Frances COOK of Georgetown, District of Columbia, dau. of John George and Mary Eliza (MONROE) COOK, he resides at "Grassland," the old family homestead.

ISSUE

1. John, *b.* 8th April, 1902.
2. Susannah Frances, *b.* 8th December, 1904.
3. Henry Anderson, *b.* 30th June, 1908.
4. Robert Monroe, *b.* 3d March, 1911.

II. William, *b.* at "Grassland," near Annapolis Junction, Maryland, 6th May, 1872; he was educated at St. John's College, Annapolis, Maryland, Trinity College, Hartford, Connecticut, and at Lehigh University, South Bethlehem, Pennsylvania. He received the degree of B.S. and Sc.D.,M.A. from Trinity and of C.E. from Lehigh. He took an active part in athletics, having been a member of the Varsity base ball and foot ball teams at Trinity and of the base ball team at Lehigh. He entered the field corps of the United States Coast and Geodetic Survey in 1895 and for fourteen years was engaged in that organization upon various topographic, hydrographic and geodetic surveys in Alaska,

Porto Rico, Philippine Islands, and in many states of the Union. From 1909 to the present time, he has been in charge of the Division of Geodesy of the United States Coast and Geodetic Survey, Washington, D. C. He is the author of a number of publications of the Survey which give the results of research in geodesy. The most important of these are the "Texas-California Arc of Primary Triangulation," 1912; "Determination of Time, Longitude, Latitude and Azimuth," 1913; "Fourth General Adjustment of the Precise Level Net of the United States," 1914; and "Investigations of Gravity and Isostasy," 1917; and "Grid System for Progressive Maps in the United States", 1919. He has also contributed numerous articles on geodetic subjects to scientific and engineering journals. In 1917 he was commissioned by President Wilson a Hydrographic and Geodetic Engineer in the United States Coast and Geodetic Survey. In 1912 he was one of two delegates, representing the United States, at the conference held in Hamburg, Germany, of the International Geodetic Association. From 1916 until the time the United States entered the war, he was the representative of the United States on the Permanent Commission of that Association. In 1917 he was appointed by Secretary William C. Redfield as the representative of the Department of Commerce on the Military Mapping Committee, whose function was to coördinate the mapping work of those organizations of the Government carrying on such work. He was one of the representatives of the United States at the meeting of the International Research Council at Brussels, Belgium, in 1919. He was elected President, in 1919, of the Geodetic Section of the International Geodetic and Geophysical Union, and, in 1920, was elected Chairman of the American Geophysical Union. He is a Member of the American Association for the Advancement of Science, Fellow Association of American Geographers, National Geographic Society, American Society of Civil Engineers, Washington Society of Engineers (President, 1914), Washington Philosophical Society (Vice-President, 1912-1917), Washington Academy of Sciences (Vice President, 1914, Treasurer 1915-1918), Astronomic Society, Geological Society of America, Order of Washington, American Legion, American Officers of the Great War, Cosmos Club (Member Committee on Admissions 1916-1918), Delta Kappa Epsilon and Phi Beta Kappa college fraternities. From 1912 to 1917 he had charge of the summer course in practical astronomy and geodetic surveying of Columbia University, New York City, on 17th August, 1918, commissioned Major of Engineers, United States Army; and served in the Division of Military Mapping of the office of the Chief of Engineers until 28th February, 1919, whem he returned to his duties in the Coast and Geodetic Survey. *m.* 28th June, 1899, Elizabeth Taylor WATTLES, dau. of Henry Starr and Caroline (CLAGETT) WATTLES of Alexandria, Virginia.

ISSUE

1. William Tasker, *b.* 2d July, 1901; *d.* 20th July, 1901.
2. Clagett, *b.* 6th February, 1907.

III. Edward Hall, *b.* 29th May, 1874, at "Grassland" near Annapolis Junction, Maryland; was educated at the Millersville Academy, Millersville, Anne Arundel County, Maryland, and at St. John's College, Annapolis, Maryland. He entered the Meteorological branch of the United States Weather Bureau in December, 1891. He was assistant observer at Memphis, Tennessee, from 1891 to 1895 and at Montgomery, Alabama, from 1896 to 1898, observer at Dubuque, Iowa, from 1898 to 1901; Section Director at Galveston, Texas, from 1901 to 1903; Local Forecaster at St. Louis from 1903 to 1909 and from 1909 to 1917 was Official Forecaster at Washington, D. C. For some time he was the Chief of the Forecast Division. In June, 1913, he was appointed by the Secretary of Agriculture as Chairman of the Committee on Improvement of the Scientific, Technical and Business Activities of the Weather Bureau. He has served on many other special committees of the Weather Bureau to consider important official matters. In July, 1917, he was commissioned Major in the Signal Reserve Corps of the United States Army and in September of that year went to France and was appointed Commanding Officer of the Meteorological Division of the Signal Corps of the American Expeditionary Forces. He is the author of a number of papers on meteorological subjects. Some of the most important are: "Possible Method for Determining the Direction and Velocity of Storm Movement;" "Types of Storms in the United States and their Average Movements" (with R. H. Weightman); "Weather Forecasting in the United States" (author with others). He is an Honorary Member of the Aero Club of St. Louis, Missouri, Member of the Cosmos Club of Washington; Member of the Philosophical Society of Washington, and of the Washington Academy of Sciences; *m.* 12th December, 1895, Florence Clara HATCH of Oregon, Illinois, dau. of Rev. Alonzo Parry HATCH, *b.* 21st March, 1830; *d.* 19th September, 1899; and Clara MCKINSTRY, *b.* 16th October, 1837, *d.* 20th November, 1903.

ISSUE

1. Helen McKinstry, *b.* 7th September, 1898.
2. Margaret Lowndes, *b.* 20th November, 1903.
3. Susannah Anderson, *b.* 11th December, 1915.

IV. Henry Anderson, *b.* 27th June, 1875; *d.* 11th February, 1888.

v. Mary Tasker, *b.* 18th October, 1878; *m.* 27th September, 1905, NOAH ERNEST DORSEY, *b.* 15th March 1873, who was educated at County School 1881-1885; Friends' Elementary and High School, Baltimore, Maryland, 1885-1890; Johns Hopkins University, A.B., 1893; Fellow, 1896-1897; Ph.D., 1897; Student Assistant in Physics, 1893-1896; Assistant, 1897-1899; Associate, 1899-1901; Department of Agriculture, Bureau of Soils 1901-1903; Bureau of Standards, 1903-1912, 1913; Carnegie Institution of Washington, Research Associate Assigned to Department of Terrestrial Magnetism, 1912-1913; at present Physicist at Bureau of Standards; is a member of the following scientific societies: American Physical Society, Societe Francaise de Physique, American Association for the Advancement of Science, Fellow; Washington Academy of Sciences, Philosophical Society of Washington; is a member of the following clubs etc.: Phi Beta Kappa Society, Cosmos Club, Washington, D. C., Johns Hopkins Club and Washington Country Club.

THOMAS JOHN BOWIE was educated at private schools and at the Rockville Academy, and settled at Hyattsville, Maryland. Like his father he was a pronounced "Union Man" and when but twenty-five years of age was appointed by the Federal Government Deputy Provost Marshall for the northern part of Prince George County during the Civil War. He removed from Hyattsville shortly after the war to "The Wilderness," a farm owned by him in Anne Arundel County, near Annapolis Junction. Upon his marriage he removed to "Grassland," the adjoining farm, where he resided until his death. Took a great interest and active part in the public affairs of the County. Was a republican in politics and was a number of times nominated for office by his party. He was elected to the State Legislature in 1887. In 1888 his friends presented his name as a candidate for Congress but he retired in favor of Sydney MUDD, who secured election. Was long Worthy Master of his Masonic Lodge. Thomas John BOWIE numbers among his Maryland Colonial Ancestors Thomas GANTT, Sr., the emigrant, 1683; one of the Justices of the Quorum, and His Majesty's Justice of the Peace in 1689. Dr. Thomas GANTT, chairman of the Provincial Council in 1775, and a Member of the Association of Freeman the same year; he was a member of the Committee of Safety in 1774. Joseph BELT, who in 1725 patented Chevy Chase, Maryland, was a Justice of Prince George County, 1726-1728; Member of the House of Burgesses, 1725-1737; Lieutenant Colonel, 1725; Colonel, 1728; Member of Col. George BEALL'S Troop of Horse, 1748; one of the founders of Rock Creek Parrish in 1726. Col. Ninian BEALL, who in 1699 was made commander-in-chief of the Colonial forces of Maryland. Robert BROOKE, *b.* 1602; *d.* 1683; who came to Maryland in 1650; he was "Commander" of Charles County and had a seat in the Privy Council; in 1652 was made President of five Commissioners appointed for the government of the Colony of Maryland. Maj. Thomas BROOKE, *b.* 1632; *d.* 1676; in 1660 was commissioned Major of Colonial Forces and in 1661 led an expedition against the Indians. In 1673 he was elected a Member of the General Assembly. Col. Thomas BROOKE, *b.* 1660; *d.*

1730; was elected to the General Assembly a number of times, and was appointed a member of the Upper House; in 1720 was elected President of the Council, he was also a Justice of the Peace.

SUSANNAH (ANDERSON) BOWIE numbers among her Maryland Colonial Ancestors: Richard DUCKETT, Sr., first clerk of Queen Anne's Parish. Richard DUCKETT, Jr., an officer of the Maryland Militia in the Revolutionary War; a Gentleman Justice of the Peace and of the Quorum. Mareen DUVALL, a French Huguenot emigrant who settled in Anne Arundel County in 1659; he was appointed one of the Commissioners to survey and lay off towns and ports of entry in the Country; he was rewarded by the Province for service against the Nanticoke Indians in 1683. Rev. Henry HALL, who emigrated in 1698 and in that year was inducted as the first rector of St. James Parish, Anne Arundel Country; a few years later he was appointed to the office of "Commissary," the function of which was to represent the Bishop of London in the Colony. Benjamin HALL of Queen Anne's Parish; member of the Quorum for Prince George County 1750–1751. William HALL of Benjamin, Member of the Committee of Safety for Prince George County during the Revolutionary War. Major John WELSH, Justice in 1666; a Commissioner of Anne Arundel County in 1667 and from 1678 to 1679 High Sheriff of Anne Arundel County; d. possessed of seven thousand acres of land. Col. John WELSH, his son, one of the Board of Justices and County Commissioners of Anne Arundel County, 1726–1734; High Sheriff from 11th November 1732, to 27th June, 1733.

Lineage

The first of the name of BOWIE in Maryland, emigrated from Scotland according to the family tradition about the year 1705–1706; at the invitation of his maternal uncle, John SMITH, who, preceding him many years, had settled in the Patuxent River a few miles north of the present village of Nottingham. The first mention of John BOWIE is found in the will of John SMITH bearing date 23d September, 1707. John SMITH was in Maryland as early as 1671 as shown by the land records.

JOHN BOWIE, Sr., of Scotland; b. there 1688; d. in Maryland, 1759; emigrated to Maryland circa 1705; m. Mary MULLIKIN, circa December, 1707, dau. of James MULLIKIN of Scotland and settled near Nottingham, Prince George County, Maryland. James MULLIKIN lived upon his plantation in Prince George County called "The Level" and is said to have emigrated from Scotland about the middle of the seventeenth century; d. in 1715.

ISSUE

I. JOHN, b. 1708, of whom later.
II. Eleanor, b. 1709; was alive in 1776; m. (firstly) 1726, Benjamin BROOKE, had issue; m. (secondly) 1732, Edward CLAGETT, had issue; m. (thirdly) ——— SKINNER, d.s.p.

III. James, *b.* 1714; *d.* 1744; *m.* 1737, Martha, (surname not given); *d.* 1743; he received from his father a tract of land called "Craycroft's Right;" he left two daughters; his was the first BOWIE will ever recorded in Maryland.
IV. Allen, *b.* 1719; *d.* 1783; of Nottingham District, Prince George County, Maryland; *m.* Priscilla FINCH, widow of Capt. William FINCH, Mariner, who *d.* before 25th November, 1742; *m.* (secondly) Susan FRASER.
V. William, Captain, *b.* 1721, at Brookridge; *d.* 1791; *m.* circa 1745, Margaret SPRIGG, *b.* 20th April, 1726, dau. of Osborne and Elizabeth SPRIGG; had issue.
VI. Thomas, *b.* 1722; *m.* circa 1746, Esther SPRIGG, *b.* 15th February, 1730, *d.s.p.* 1740; *m*, (secondly) 1751, Hannah LEE, dau. of Philip and Elizabeth (LAWSON) LEE; had issue.
VII. Mary, *b.* 1726; her will was executed 27th March, 1792; *m.* circa 1745, William BEANS, Jr., of Upper Marlboro, Maryland, had issue.

JOHN BOWIE, JR., of "Thorpwood" Prince George County, Maryland; *b.* circa 1708; his will is dated 29th November, 1752; probated February, 1753; purchased in 1747 the plantation known as "The Hermitage" which is yet owned by his descendants; *m.* (firstly) circa 1729, Mary BEALL, dau. of William BEALL of same County; she *d.* 1733; *m.* (secondly) 18th December, Elizabeth POTTINGER; *b.* 1717, dau. of Dr. Robert and Ann (EVANS) POTTINGER (see Pottinger, Colonial Families, Vol. II); she *m.* (secondly) circa 1755, Thomas CRAMPHIN of Frederick County, Maryland.

ISSUE BY FIRST MARRIAGE

I. William, *b.* 1730; *d.* 1753; *m.* Rachel POTTINGER.
II. Mary, *b.* 1732; *m.* James MAGRUDER, Jr., *b.* 1721, *d.* 1773; had issue.

ISSUE BY SECOND MARRIAGE

I. ALLEN, Jr., *b.* 1737, of whom later.
II. James, *b.* circa 1739; living 1760, after which no mention is made of him in the county records, nor is he mentioned in the will of his maternal grandmother proven 1767; there is a tradition among some that he left Maryland upon attaining manhood and removed to South Carolina, and was probably the gd. father of Col. James BOWIE, hero of the Alamo, and Col. Rezin P. BOWIE; he is the only one of the Prince George County BOWIES whose record is uncertain.
III. Rev. John, *b.* circa 1744; went to Scotland and studied for the ministry at King's College, Aberdeen, thence to London, England, and on 28th July, 1771, was ordained a priest by the Bishop of London and licensed for Maryland; *m.* in Scotland, Margaret DALLAS, *b.* at Inverness, dau.

of Colonel DALLAS of the British Army, who *m.* a dau. of Lady and Lord Thomas HAMILTON who fell at the Battle of Culloden 1745; had issue.

IV. A posthumous child, unnamed, *d.* in infancy.

ALLEN BOWIE, JR., of "The Hermitage," Montgomery County, Maryland; *b.* near Upper Marlboro 1736–1737; *d.* 1803; was Captain in the 29th Battalion of the Maryland troops in the Revolutionary War; in 1774 and 1775 he was a Delegate to the Conventions held at Annapolis to protest against the Stamp Act and to devise means for resistance; was one of the leading patriots of his country during the American Revolution ("The Maryland Archives" record that Col. Allen BOWIE, Jr., of Montgomery County be reimbursed for expenses incurred in providing for the worth of his Regiment); *m.* 28th December, 1766, his stepsister Ruth CRAMPHIN, dau. of Thomas CRAMPHIN, Sr., and Mary JACKSON.

ISSUE

I. THOMAS, *b.* 22d December, 1767, of whom later.
II. John, M.D., *b.* 11th September, 1769; *d.* unmarried 17th February, 1825; graduated in medicine and resided at "The Hermitage" which he inherited; 7th July, 1808, was appointed by the Governor a Surgeon in Capt. B. M. PERRIE's Military Company, extra Battalion "Montgomery Guards;" participated in the War of 1812; elected to the State Legislature and nominated for United States Senator.
III. Elizabeth, *b.* 11th September, 1772; *d.* 23d November, 1840; *m.* 12th January, 1802, Thomas DAVIS, of Montgomery County, son of Ephraim DAVIS, of "Greenwood;" had issue.
IV. Mary, *b.* 27th October, 1774; *d.* unmarried 2d January, 1800.
V. Washington, Colonel, *b.* 12th August, 1776; *d.* 1825; in 1810 the *Annapolis Gazette* mentions "Col." Washington BOWIE as one of the wealthiest and most public-spirited citizens of Georgetown, District of Columbia, and is spoken of as "a merchant prince;" *m.* 1799, Margaret Crabb (JOHNS) CHEW, *b.* 1774, *d.* 22d July, 1840, dau. of Col. Thomas JOHNS of the Revolutionary Army and his wife Sarah HOLLYDAY, and widow of Rev. Thomas J. CHEW; had issue.
VI. Allen, *b.* 17th January, 1778; *d.* 7th August, 1782.
VII. Hannah, b. 28th September, 1780; *d.* 7th August, 1782.
VIII. Richard, *b.* 30th January, 1783; *d.* 27th March, 1801.

COL. THOMAS BOWIE of "War Park" near Bladensburg, Prince George County, Maryland; *b.* 22d December, 1767; *d.* 27th July, 1823, while on his knees in a Washington Church; 16th October, 1795, was elected to the State Legislature for Prince George County; 10th December, 1812, was appointed by the Governor a Justice of the Peace and Judge of the Orphans Court and again in 1814–1816; in all publications of that period he is unanimously spoken of as "Colonel;" *m.* 26th January,

1794, Margaret BELT, b. 1770, d. 2d January, 1814, dau. of Dr. Humphrey BELT, of Prince George County, Maryland, who served as a Captain during the Revolutionary War, m. Mary BROOKE (for BELT family, see Colonial Families, Vol. II).

ISSUE

I. Humphrey Belt, M.D., b. 20th July, 1796; graduated at Maryland Medical College, Baltimore, 1824; d. of consumption 8th June, 1828; unmarried.
II. Thomas J., b. 8th October, 1797; d. unmarried 9th October, 1827.
III. JOHN, b. 4th October, 1799, of whom later.
IV. Mary Ann, b. 12th March, 1802; m. 5th February, 1828, William D. CLAGETT, son of Joseph White CLAGETT; had issue.
V. George Washington, b. 11th April, 1804; d. 1870, in Georgetown, District of Columbia; m. 1827, Mary RAPINE, dau. of Daniel RAPINE, the fourth Mayor of Washington; had issue.
VI. Margaret Ruth, b. 15th March, 1806; d. 2d January, 1814.
VII. Richard Cramphin, b. 26th September, 1808; d. December, 1890; m. 1830, Martha Magdalene RAPINE, d. 16th December, 1863, dau. of Daniel RAPINE, Mayor of Washington, 1812; had issue.

JOHN BOWIE of Bladensburg and Hyattsville, Prince George County, Maryland; b. 14th October, 1799; d. 3d January, 1871; inherited his father's country home on the height of Bladensburg; a member of the Whig party he actively opposed "Secession;" was elected in 1861 as a Unionist Member of the State Legislature; during the Civil war entrusted by the Federal Government with matters of much importance and made a Provost Marshal; m. 19th November, 1833, Margaret Lowndes GANTT, d. 16th December, 1880, dau. of Levi and Harriet (LOWNDES) GANTT. Levi GANTT was the son of Dr. Thomas GANTT, who m. a Miss HILLEARY, served as a soldier during the Revolutionary War. Harriet LOWNDES was the dau. of Christopher LOWNDES who lived at "Blenheim," m. Elizabeth TASKER, dau. of Gov. Benjamin TASKER and his wife Ann BLADEN.

ISSUE

I. Amelia Gantt, b. 12th December, 1834; m. 1867, Dr. Charles M. B. HARRIS of Washington, D. C.

ISSUE
1. Anna Bowie HARRIS.
2. Charles Gantt HARRIS.
3. Thomas Cadwallader HARRIS.

II. THOMAS JOHN, b. 22d February, 1837, the subject of this memoir.

Arms.—Argent, on a bend sable, three buckles or.
Crest.—A demi lion azure, holding in the dexter paw a dagger.
Motto.—Quod non pro patria.
Residence (family).—"Grassland," Anne Arundel County, Maryland.

Breckinridge

CLIFTON RODES BRECKINRIDGE, diplomatist, of Fort Smith, Arkansas; *b.* at Lexington, Kentucky, 22d November, 1846; Member of Congress, 1883–1894; and United States Minister to Russia, 1894–1897; received a common school education and served as a private in the Confederate Army, and as midshipman in the Navy. At the close of the war attended Washington College for three years and subsequently became a cotton planter in Arkansas. Elected in 1882 to the 48th Congress from the State at large and was re-elected to the 49th and four succeeding Congresses; served 1883–1894; he resigned before the close of his term; United States Minister to Russia, 1894–1897; was a member of the Dawes Commission to the Five Civilized Tribes of the Indian Territory, 1900–1905; *m.* 21st November, 1876, Katherine Breckinridge CARSON, dau. of Doctor and Mrs. James Green CARSON, of the Parish of Carroll, Louisiana.

ISSUE

I. James Carson, *b.* 13th September, 1877; Lieutenant Colonel, United States Marine Corps.
II. Mary Carson, *b.* 17th February, 1881; *m.* (firstly) 1904, Henry Ruffner MORRISON, *d.* 1906; *m.* (secondly) 1912, Richard Ryan THOMPSON.

ISSUE

1. Breckinridge THOMPSON, *b.* 12th January, 1914; *d.* 23d January, 1918.
2. Mary Breckinridge THOMPSON, *d.* 8th July, 1916.

III. Susanna Preston Lees, *b.* 12th August, 1886; *m.* February, 1918, somewhere in France, Lieut. George DUNN, United States Artillery, Regulars.
IV. Clifton Rodes, *b.* 24th September, 1895; Lieutenant United States Army, Regulars.

Lineage

ALEXANDER BRECKINRIDGE of Orange County, Virginia; a Scottish covenanter who fled to America in the restoration of the STUARTS; at a court held for Orange County, 1740; came into Court and made oath that he imported himself, wife and children from Ireland to Philadelphia and thence into this Colony at his own charge, this is the first time of proving his and their rights in order to obain land which is ordered to be certified; *m.* Jane (surname not given).

ISSUE

1. ROBERT, *d*. 1772, of whom below.

LIEUT. ROBERT BRECKINRIDGE, of Botetourt County, Virginia; *b*. in Ireland, circa 1720-1725; *d*. 1772, at Fincastle in Botetourt County; took a prominent part in the French and Indian Wars; was Trustee for the new town of Staunton, 1796; *m*. 10th July, 1758, Lettica PRESTON, dau. of John and Elizabeth (PATTON) PRESTON, both Irish emigrants to Virginia, of Scottish descent.

ISSUE

I. JOHN, *b*. 2d December, 1760, of whom later.
II. James, *b*. in Virginia, 7th March, 1763; *d*. 9th August, 1846; Member of the General Assembly of Virginia, and a leader of the old Federal party in that body; represented the district of Botetourt in Congress, 1809-1817.

HON. JOHN BRECKINRIDGE of Cabell's Dale, Kentucky; *b*. near Staunton, Virginia, 2d December, 1760; *d*. 14th December, 1806; entered William and Mary College in 1778; elected a Member of the House of Delegates, 1780, when but nineteen years of age, and served there until 1785; admitted to the Bar, 1785; elected to the 3d Congress, 1793; removed to Kentucky, 1793; appointed Attorney General of the new State, 1795; at this time the Criminal Court of Kentucky prescribed death penalty to no less than one hundred and sixty crimes, juries could not be found to convict except in cases of aggravated criminalty and while in the legislature Mr. BRAINRIDGE secured a revision of the code so as to abolish the death penalty for all crimes except murder in the first degree; in 1799 he introduced into the Kentucky Legislature another bill that passed, affirming that "any State might nullify any act of Congress which it regarded as unconstitutional;" while the authorship of the original resolution is almost unanimously attributed to Thomas JEFFERSON it has been made clear that while the basis of the paper was from the hand of Mr. JEFFERSON, the most important portions were the work of Mr. BRECKINRIDGE, Member of the Legislature (serving as Speaker during his third and last term), 1707-1800; United States Senator, 1801-1805; United States Attorney General, 1805-1806; *m*. 28th June, 1785, Mary HOPKINS CABELL.

ISSUE

I. Letitia Preston, *b*. 22d June, 1786; *d*. 27th July, 1831; *m*. 24th October 1804, Alfred William GRAYSON, who *d*. 10th October, 1810, leaving issue; *m*. (secondly) 16th October, 1818, Col. Peter Buel PORTER, United States Secretary for War, 1828-1829; had issue.
II. JOSEPH CABELL, *b*. 24th July, 1788, of whom later.
III. Mary Ann, *b*. 1795; *m*. David CASTLEMAN.

IV. Rev. John, *b.* 4th, July, 1797; *d.* 4th August, 1841; a distinguished Presbyterian clergyman and controversalist; educated at Nassau Hall, Princeton, graduated, 1818; in 1841 president of Oglethorp College, Georgia.
V. Rev. Robert Jefferson, D.D., *b.* at Cabell's Dale, Kentucky, 8th March, 1800; *d.* 27th December, 1781, in Danville, Kentucky; President of Jefferson College, Pennsylvania, 1845–1847; removed to Lexington, Kentucky, 1847, and became pastor of the First Presbyterian Church there; *m.* 11th. March, 1823, Anna Sophonisba PRESTON, descendant of General CAMPBELL and Elizabeth HENRY, sister of Patrick HENRY.

ISSUE (AMONG OTHERS)

1. Gen. Joseph Cabell, *b.* 14th January, 1842, in Baltimore, Maryland; Inspector General, United States Army; served during the Civil War as artillery officer, promoted for gallantry at Battle of Mill Springs, Kentucky, when he served as Aide on General THOMAS' staff; was captured at Atlanta, Georgia, and brevetted for gallantry in action; promoted to the I. G. Department, 1881; *m.* 21st July, 1868, Louise Ludlow DUDLEY.

ISSUE

1[1]. Mary Dudley, *m.* Capt. John F. HINES, United States Navy; left issue.
2[1]. Joseph Cabell, United States Navy, *d.*
3[1]. Ethelbert Ludlow Dudley, *m.* (name not given); left issue.
4[1]. Lucien Scott, *m.* twice (wives' names not given).
5[1]. Lucy Hayes.
6[1]. Scott Dudley, *m.* (wife's name not given); left issue.
7[1]. Henry Skillman, Major, United States Army; *m.* (wife's name not given); left issue.
8[1]. Margaret Scott Skillman.
9[1]. John Preston.

VI. William Lewis, D.D., *b.* 22d July, 1803; President of Oakland College, Mississippi; *m.* (firstly) Frances C. PREVOST, dau. of Judge PREVOST, had issue; *m.* (secondly) Sarah TOMKINS, dau. of Judge Christopher TOMKINS, and widow of Dr. D. D. GARNETT.

JOSEPH CABELL BRECKINRIDGE, *b.* 24th July, 1788; *m.* Mary SMITH, dau. President Samuel SMITH, of Princeton University.

ISSUE

1. Frances Anne, *m.* 3d November, 1829, Rev. J. C. YOUNG, D.D., *d.* 2d November; left issue.
2. Caroline Lawrence, *m.* 31st October, 1832, Rev. J. J. BULLOCK, D.D., *d.* 4th November, 1867; left issue.

3. Mary Cabell, *m.* 1832, Dr. T. P. SATTERWAITE, *d.* 13th August, 1835; left issue.
4. JOHN CABELL, *b.* 21st June, 1821, of whom later.
5. Letitia Porter, *m.* 6th February, 1847, Charles Copeland PARKHILL, *d.s.p.* 15th May, 1862.

GEN. JOHN CABELL BRECKINRIDGE, *b.* at Cabell's Dale, Kentucky, 21st January, 1821; *d.* 17th May, 1875, at Lexington, Kentucky; Major in Kentucky Volunteers, 1847; serving in the war with Mexico; elected to Congress, 1851; and again 1853; Vice-President of United States, 1857–1861; United States Senator, 1861; appointed Brigadier-General in the Confederate States Army 1861, and Major-General, 1862; Secretary of War, 1865; at the Democratic Convention in Charleston, South Carolina, in 1860, he received seventy-two votes as a candidate for the Presidency of the United States against one hundred and eighty cast for Mr. LINCOLN, thirty-nine for John BELL and twelve for Stephen DOUGLASS. He took his seat in the United States Senate 4th March, 1861, where he announced the election of Abraham LINCOLN to the Presidency before both houses of Congress. Spurning a proposition made by Southern members that he should join in a plot to prevent the counting of the electoral vote, he left the Senate to join the Confederate Army. In September, 1861, he went to Richmond and was appointed a Brigadier-General, in the Army of the Confederacy and in 1862 Major-General and participated in many important engagements. In 1865 was appointed by President DAVIS, Secretary of War; assisted President DAVIS in his flight at the collapse of the Confederacy and himself escaped to England where he remained until 1868 when he returned to the United States and resumed the practice of law at Lexington, Kentucky, until his death; *m.* 12th December, 1843, Mary Cryene BURCH, dau. of Clifton Rodes BURCH.

ISSUE

1. Joseph Cabell, *b.* 29th December, 1844; *d.* 1906, served through the Civil War; *m.* 1st December, 1869, Sally Frances JOHNSON, dau. of the Hon. R. W. JOHNSON; had issue.

ISSUE

1. John Cabell, Captain, United States Reserves; *m.* Isabell GOODRICH.

ISSUE

1¹. Joseph Cabell.
2¹. Mary Marvin.
3¹. Charles David.
4¹. Robert.

2. Laura Johnson, *m.* John C. TEN EYCK.

ISSUE

1¹. Cabell Breckinridge TEN EYCK, *d.* January, 1918; Lieutenant United States Field Artillery, Regulars.
2¹. Julia TEN EYCK, *m.* Robert STODDARD, Lieutenant United States Field Artillery, Regulars.

ISSUE

1². Breckinridge Ten Eyck STODDARD, *b.* in Virginia, 1918.
3. Robert Johnson, *d.* in childhood.
4. Ben Johnson, Lieutenant United States Reserves; *m.* Helen STEELE.

II. CLIFTON RODES, *b.* 22d November, 1864, the subject of this memoir.
III. Frances, *b.* 21st June, 1848; *m.* 1879, John Andrew STEELE.

ISSUE

1. Anne VanderGraff STEELE, *m.* E. Waring WILSON.

ISSUE

1¹. John Steele WILSON, *d.* in infancy.
2¹. Frances Breckinridge WILSON.
3¹. Susanna Preston WILSON.

2. Frances Breckinridge STEELE, *m.* Maj. Jeter HORTON, United States Marine Corps.
3. Caroline Dupre STEELE, *m.* Joseph Coleman CARTER.

ISSUE

1¹. Joseph Coleman CARTER, Jr.
2¹. Sarah Fullerton CARTER.
3¹. Breckinridge CARTER, *d.* in infancy.

V. John Witherspoon Owen, *b.* 1850; *d.* 9th May, 1892; *m.* (firstly) Louise TEVIS, dau. of Lloyd TEVIS; *m.* (secondly) Harriet (surname not given).

ISSUE BY FIRST MARRIAGE

1. Lloyd Tevis, *d.*
2. Florence, *m.* Thomas Fermor HESKETH, of England.
3. John, *m.* Adelaide MURPHY.

ISSUE BY SECOND MARRIAGE

1. Elizabeth Lee, *m.* Joseph THOMAS.

ISSUE

1¹. Breckinridge THOMAS.

VI. Mary Desha, *b.* 1853; *m.* 1877, Anson MALTBY.

ISSUE

1. Marion MALTBY, a son, *d.* in infancy.
2. Frances MALTBY.
3. Mary Breckinridge MALTBY, *m.* (firstly) Ludwell Brooke ALEXANDER; *m.* (secondly) Kenneth KIRKELAND.

ISSUE

1¹. Ludwell Brook ALEXANDER, Jr.

4. Lees MALTBY, *d.* in infancy.
5. Elizabeth Marshall MALTBY.

Residence.—Fort Smith, Arkansas.
Clubs.—Honorary Member of the Cobden Club of London, Charter Member of League to Enforce Peace, Director Southern Commercial Congress.
Societies.—Sons of the American Revolution, Confederate Veterans Association.
Arms (BRECKINRIDGE).—Azure, three roses argent barbed vert, seeded or a pile of the last charged with a rose gules, also barbed of the third and seeded of the fourth.
Crest.—A pile gules charged with a rose as in the arms, between two wings azure.
Motto.—Virtute et industria.

Brent

DUNCAN KENNER BRENT, *b.* at New Orleans, Louisiana, 9th October, 1877; *m.* at Baltimore, Maryland, 5th December, 1900, Hally BROWN, dau. of Dr. Thomas Richardson and Hally BROWN, both of Baltimore, Maryland. The son of Dr. Thomas C. and Mary Elizabeth (HYNSON) BROWN. She dau. of John Kell Vallindengham and Mary (PENNIMAN) CARRINGTON, of Kent County, Maryland.

ISSUE

I. Joseph Lancaster, *b.* 30th June, 1903.
II. Duncan Kenner, *b.* 20th March, 1906.
III. Harriet Carrington, *b.* 23d August, 1913.

DUNCAN KENNER BRENT, A.B., Johns Hopkins University, 1898; LL.B., University of Maryland, 1900.

Lineage

According to Collinson

This family can trace its lineage through the English Gentry to the Norman Conquest when ODO DE BRENT was Lord of the Manor of Cosington, in Somersetshire, 1066–1087; his son's name is not known; his gd. son Jeffrey, had

NICHOLAS DE BRENT (wife's name not given), had

ROBERT DE BRENT, *m.* Millicent (surname unknown) and *d.* 46 Henry III, 1262; their son,

ROBERT, Knight, went to Gascony with Edward I, in 1277 and later to Scotland; *m.* Isabella DE MONTACUTE, dau. of Sir Simon DE MONTACUTE a Baron in 1300 whose arms, at the Siege of Falkirk, 1298, were: Quarterly, first and fourth, argent, three lozenges, conjoined, in fesse gules; second and third, azure, a gryphon segreant, or. This is one of the earliest examples of a quartered shield. With the first he sealed the Baron's Letter to the Pope in 1301, but at the Siege of Carlaverock, he used the gryphon only, which is supposed to have been the original DE MONTACUTE shield. On the Roll of Edward II, the name of Sir Robert DE BRENT appears, with a shield Gules, a gryphon segreant argent, which he evidently assumed from his marriage to Isabella DE MONTACUTE. He was Baron in Parliament and Knight of the Shire of Somerset; he also used a wivern on his shield and *d.* in 1309.

ISSUE

SIR ROBERT DE BRENT who lies buried on the North Side of the choir in Glastonbury Abbey; *m.* Clarissa DE LA FORD, dau. and heiress of Sir Adam DE LA FORD (or FFORDE) of Wiltshire, who bore at the Siege of Carlaverock, 1300, Azure, three lyonceaux rampant, two and one, crowned or. The Manor of Ford descended to his dau., the wife of Sir Robert DE BRENT.

ISSUE

I. SIR ROBERT, *d.* 1357, of whom later.
II. Sir John, of Charing, in Kent, founder of a family long prominent there.
III. Hawise, *m.* Hugh DE POPHAM.
IV. Joan, *m.* Thomas DENEBAND, the brother of her brother's wife, Elizabeth.

SIR ROBERT DE BRENT, *d.* 25 Edward III, 1357; Lord of the Manor of Cossington; *m.* Elizabeth Deneband, dau. of William Deneband.

ISSUE

I. SIR JOHN, of whom later.
II. Robert.

SIR JOHN BRENT of Cossington; *m.* Joan LE EYRE, dau. and heir of John Le Ayre.

ISSUE

I. JOHN, of whom later.
II. Hugh.

SIR JOHN BRENT, of Cossington, *m.* (firstly), Ida DE BEAUCHAMP, of Lillisdon, dau. of Sir John BEAUCHAMP of Lillisdon, Knight; *m.* (secondly) Joan LATIMER, dau. of Sir Robert LATIMER, Knight.

ISSUE BY FIRST MARRIAGE

I. Sir Robert, *m.* Joan HAREWELL, of Wooton, and *d.s.p.*
II. Joan, *m.* (firstly) Thomas HORSEY; *m.* (secondly) Thomas TRETHEKE of Tretheke.

ISSUE BY SECOND MARRIAGE

I. JOHN, of whom later.
II. Agnes, a nun.
III. Barbara.
IV. Thomasine.
V. William.
VI. Richard.

Sir John Brent, of Cossington; *d.* 22d August, 1524; a friend of Henry VIII, whom he entertained at his Manor of Wickins; *m.* (wife's name not given).

ISSUE

i. Robert, of whom later.
ii. John.
iii. Elizabeth, *m.* John Verney.

Sir Robert Brent, of Cossington; *d.v.p.*, 1508; *m.* (firstly) circa 1474, Margaret dau. of Hugh Malet of Currypool; *m.* (secondly) Joan (Malet) Crewkern, sister of his first wife; they were descendants of William Malet, Lord of Skepton Malet.

ISSUE BY FIRST MARRIAGE

1. John, of Goodwin's Bower, West Bagborough, Compton, Pauncefoot Roundfoot Hill, etc.; *b.* 1475; *d.* 1572; *m.* 1502, Maude Pauncefoot, dau. of Sir Walter Pauncefoot.

ISSUE

1. William, *b.* 1504; *m.* Lady Anne Stourton.

ISSUE

1^1. Richard, *d.* 1558.
2^1. Anne, *m.* Lord Thomas Pawlett.

2. John, *d.* 1557; *m.* (secondly) Mary Culpeper.

ISSUE

1^1. Stephen, who had issue.

ISSUE

1^2. John, *d.* 1610; his son, John *m.* (firstly) Winifred Arundel of Lanherne; *m.* (secondly) Mary Ludlow.
2^2. Anne.
3^2. Barbara, *m.* George Matthews.

2^1. Giles.
3^1. Margaret.
4^1. John.

3. John.
4. Agnes.
5. Richard.

II. ROBERT, of whom later.
III. Agnes, *b.* 1479; *m.* Giles HILL.

ROBERT BRENT, of Cossington; b. 1477, *d.* 1531; founded the BRENT family of Stoke and Admington; *m.* 1499, Margery COLCHESTER, dau. of George COLCHESTER, Esquire, Lord of Stoke and Admington, Warwickshire.

ISSUE

I. Richard, *d.v.p.*
II. WILLIAM, of whom later.
III. Nicholas. *b.* 1505; *d.* 1583; *m.* Elizabeth (surname not given).
IV. Thomas.
V. Helen.

SIR WILLIAM BRENT, of Cossington; *b.* 1503; *d.* 1595; *m.* Elizabeth WORTH and inherited, from his gd. father, Stoke and Admington.

ISSUE

I. RICHARD, of whom later.
II. Mary.
III. Elizabeth, *m.* John HAWTHEN.

SIR RICHARD BRENT, of Stoke and Admington; *d.v.p.* 1587; *m.* 1572, Mary HUGGERFORD, dau. of John and Katherine (HENNEAGE) HUGGERFORD.

ISSUE

I. RICHARD, of whom later.
II. Margaret, *m.* John FOWKE.
III. Catherine.
IV. Eleanor.
V. Anne.
VI. Mary, *m.* 8th August, 1598, Richard CATESBY.

SIR RICHARD BRENT, of Larke Stoke and Admington; *b.* 1573; *d.* 1652; he was Sheriff of Gloucester in 1614 and a subscriber to the building of the Bridge at Stratford-upon-Avon in 1618; *m.* in 1594, Elizabeth REED. dau. of Giles REED, Lord of Tusburie and Witten, by his wife, Katherine GREVILLE, dau. of Sir Fulke GREVILLE, of Millcote and Beauchamp's Court, by his wife, the Lady Elizabeth Willoughby DE BROKE.

ISSUE

I. Fulke, *d.s.p.* 1656; emigrated to Maryland, 1638; *m.* Cecilia (surname not given).
II. Richard, *bapt.* 7th November, 1596; *d.* 1671; *m.* 1622, Margaret, dau. of Sir John PESHELL, Baronet.

ISSUE

1. Robert, *d.* 1695; *m.* Catherine (surname not given).
2. Frances, *d.* 1656.
3. Mary, *d.* 1657.
4. Katherine, *b.* 1639.
5. Elizabeth, *d.* 1656.
6. Giles, *d.* 1665.
7. Margaret, *m.* Thomas BARTLETT.

III. William, *b.* 1600; *d.s.p.* 29th May, 1691; *m.* Barbara (surname not given).
IV. Margaret, *b.* 1601; *d.* 1671; famous as "Mistress Margaret BRENT of Maryland;" emigrated to Maryland, 1638.
V. Edward, *d.* unmarried.
VI. GEORGE, of whom later.
VII. Giles, *b.* 1606; *d.* 1671; Lieutenant-Governor of Maryland; Burgess; Member of the Council; Lord of Kent Fort Manor, etc. (see GILES-BRENT line).
VIII. Mary, *d.* unmarried, 1658; emigrated to Maryland, 1638.
IX. Catherine, *bapt.* 25th August, 1630; *d.* 1st November, 1640.
X. Elizabeth.
XI. Eleanor.
XII. Jane, *d.* 1680; *m.* Thomas CASSIE.
XIII. Anne, *b.* circa 1620; *bapt.* 7th August, 1637, at Ilmington, *d.* evidently before 1647; *m.* circa 1640, the Hon. Leonard CALVERT, First Governor of Maryland, second son of Sir George CALVERT, Lord Baltimore.

ISSUE

1. William CALVERT, Esquire, *b.* 1642; *d.* 1682; *m.* 1664, Elizabeth STONE, dau. of the Hon. William STONE, Governor of Maryland.

ISSUE

1[1]. George CALVERT, *b.* 1668; *d.* after 1739; *m.* Anne NOTTLEY.

ISSUE

1[2]. John, *b.* circa 1695; *d.* 1739; *m.* Elizabeth HARRISON, of Virginia.

ISSUE

1[3]. George, *b.* 1718; *d.* 1782; Member of the House of Burgesses from Prince William County, Virginia; Captain of Culpeper Company Militia; *m.* (firstly), Anne CRUPPER; *m.* (secondly) Mrs. Mary DEATHERAGE, née STROTHER.

ISSUE BY FIRST MARRIAGE

1⁴. John, *b.* 1742; *d.* 1790; Captain Continental Line; *m.*(firstly) Sarah BAILEY; *m.* (secondly) Hellen BAILEY, her sister, daus. of George and Hellen (NEWSOME) BAILEY, of "Hunting Ridge," Baltimore County, Md.

ISSUE BY SECOND MARRIAGE

1⁴. Elizabeth CALVERT, *b.* 1777; *d.* 1833; *m.* 1802, Joseph NICKLIN, V, Captain in War of 1812 (see NICKLIN, volume IV, and CALVERT, Volume VI).

2. Anne CALVERT, *m.* (firstly) Baker BROOKE; *m.* (secondly), her cousin, Henry BRENT, (q.v.); *m.* (thirdly) Richard MARSHAM and left many descendants.

GEORGE BRENT, of "Defford," Worcestershire, England; b. 1602; *d.* 1671; *m*, (firstly) Marianna PEYTON, dau. of Sir John PEYTON of Doddington, by his wife, Alice PEYTON, dau. of Sir John PEYTON of Isleham, *m.* (secondly) (name not given) *m.* (thirdly) (name not given).

ISSUE BY FIRST MARRIAGE

I. George, of whom later.
II. John, *d.* young.
III. Henry, *d.* 24th January, 1694; *m.* his cousin, Mrs. Anne (CALVERT) BROOKE (q.v.).
IV. William, *d.* unmarried.
V. Edward, *d.* young, while at College in Flanders.
VI. Robert, *d.* 19th January, 1696; *m.* Anne BAUGH.
VII. Anne, *m.* James CLIFTON.
VIII. Elizabeth, *d.* unmarried.
IX. Dorothy.
X. Mary, *m.* her cousin, Giles BRENT, Jr. (q.v.).
XI. Margaret, *d.* unmarried.
XII. Ursula, *m.* Charles UNFRAVILLE.

ISSUE BY SECOND MARRIAGE

I. Jane, *m.* Nathaniel SHRINE.

ISSUE BY THIRD MARRIAGE

I. Richard.

CAPT. GEORGE BRENT, Jr., *b.* 1641; *d.* 1699-1700; migrated to Virginia in 1660 and became Captain of Horse, 1667; Receiver General 2d May, 1683; Ranger General 10th July, 1690; Colonel in BACON'S Rebellion, etc.; he lived at "Woodstock." and also at "Brenton" and was agent for Lady CULPEPER and Lord FAIRFAX; *m.* (firstly) 1667, Elizabeth GREENE, dau. of William GREEN and niece of Sir William LAYTON, of England; *m.* (secondly) 27th March, 1687, Mrs. Mary (SEWELL) CHANDLER, dau. of Lady Baltimore (Jane Lowe SEWELL) by her first husband.

ISSUE BY FIRST MARRIAGE

I. George, *d.* 2d September, 1708.
II. Nicholas, *d.s.p.* 18th December, 1711; *m.* 10th April. 1711, Jane MUDD.
III. ROBERT, of whom later.
IV. Marianne, *d.* young.
V. Elizabeth, *d.* 6th November, 1719; *m.* 17th February, 1709, Thomas LANGMAN.
VI. Susannah, *m.* Raphael NEALE.
VII. Martha, *b.* 1678; *d.* 17th February, 1685.

ISSUE BY SECOND MARRIAGE

I. Clare, *d.* 10th March, 1689.
II. Henry, *d.* 24th December, 1709; *m.* Jane THOMPSON.
III. Mary, *d.* 17th December, 1715; *m.* Roswell NEALE.
IV. Martha, *d.* unmarried, 1715.

ROBERT BRENT, of "Woodstock," Stafford County, Virginia; *b.* 1672; *d.* 1721; *m.* 8th May, 1702, Susannah Seymour, dau. of Captain David SEYMOUR and gd. dau. of Gov. Florentius SEYMOUR of Bermuda, 1663-1668-1681, who *d.* 1681; he was also Councillor of State and Captain of Southampton Fort, 1661.

ISSUE

I. George, *b.* 1703; *d.* 1778, *m.* 1730, Catherine TRIMMINGHAM, of Bermuda.

ISSUE

1. Sarah, *d.s.p.*; *m.* George MASON, of "Gunston Hall."
2. Susannah, *m.* 15th September, 1756, John SUTHERLAND.
3. Robert, *d.* 1780; *m.* Anne CARROLL, sister of Archbishop CARROLL.

ISSUE

1[1]. George, *b.* 1762; *d.* 1804; Lieutenant in the Revolution; *m.* Mary FITZ-HUGH, of "Marmion."

2¹. Robert, *b.* 1764; *d.* 14th September. 1819; *m.* 1787, Mary YOUNG; he was the first Mayor of Washington.
3¹. John, *b.* 1766; *d.* 1813; *m.* Anne BRENT.
4¹. Daniel, *b.* 1768; *d.* 31st January, 1841; *m.* 13th April, 1813, Eliza WALSH.
5¹. Thomas, *d.* unmarried.
6¹. Eleanor, *d.* young.
7¹. Catherine, *m.* 1787, George DIGGS.
8¹. William, *b.* 1794; *d.* 16th December, 1848; *m* (firstly) 6th January, 1805, Catherine Walker JOHNSON; *m.* (secondly) April, 1825, Elizabeth NEALE.

4. Catherine, *d.* 1819; *m.* 1st October, 1754, James DOUGLAS.
5. Jane, *b.* 10th April, 1738; *m.* 10th February, 1775, Richard GRAHAM.
6. John, *d.* young.
7. Elizabeth, *d.* young, 1783.

II. ROBERT, of whom later.
III. Benjamin.
IV. Henry, *d.* 1769.
V. Elizabeth.
VI. Jane.
VII. Martha.
VIII. Susannah.

ROBERT BRENT, JR., of Virginia and Maryland, *b.* 1704, *d.* 4th February, 1750, in Maryland; *m.* 6th May, 1729, Mary WHARTON, dau. of Henry and Jane (DOYNE) WHARTON; the marriage is recorded in Durham Church, Trinity Parish, Charles County, Maryland.

ISSUE

I. Mary, *b.* 1st September, 1731; became a Carmelite nun.
II. ROBERT, *b.* 6th May, 1734, of whom later.
III. Jane, *b.* 2d January, 1736.
IV. George, *b.* 3d May, 1737; *d.* 16th December, 1754.
V. Susannah, *b.* 2d January, 1739; *d.* 4th March, 1739.
VI. Elizabeth, *b.* 4th March, 1740; *d.* 17th October, 1740.
VII. Nicholas, *b.* 1st November, 1741.
VIII. Francis, *b.* 7th July, 1745; *d.* 17th December, 1745.

ROBERT BRENT, III, of Charles County, Maryland; *b.* 6th May, 1734; *d.* 6th January, 1790; *m.* 5th October, 1756, Anna Maria PARNHAM.

ISSUE

1. Francis, *b.* 23d July, 1757; *d.* 13th May, 1758.
11. ROBERT, *b.* 17th June, 1759, of whom later.
111. Mary, *b.* 23d December, 1762; *d.* 8th September, 1815.
IV. Anna Maria, *b.* 4th January, 1765; *d.* 16th June, 1785.
v. Teresa, *b.* 3d May, 1767; *m.* Col. James FENWICK, *d.s.p.*
VI. Elinor, *b.* 11th February, 1770; *d.* 21st May, 1822; *m.* Francis DIGGES.
VII. James, *b.* 20th March, 1772.
VIII. Elizabeth, *b.* 13th June, 1774; *d.* 15th September, 1827.
IX. Frances Wharton, *b.* 7th November, 1776.

ROBERT BRENT, IV, of "Brentfield," Charles County, Maryland; *b.* 17th June, 1759; *d.* 1810; *m.* 23d February, 1783, Dorothy LEIGH, dau. of William and Dorothy (DOYNE) LEIGH.

ISSUE

1. WILLIAM LEIGH, *b.* 20th February, 1784, of whom later.
11. Anna Maria Parnham, *b.* 15th February, 1785; *m.* Joseph Thomas MITCHELL.

ISSUE

1. Joseph Thomas MITCHELL, Jr., *m.* (firstly) Caroline HORSEY; *m.* (secondly) Katherine KENT.
2. Louise MITCHELL.
3. Robert Brent MITCHELL.

111. George, *b.* 28th October, 1786; *m.* Matilda THOMAS.

WILLIAM LEIGH BRENT, of Maryland and Louisiana; *b.* 29th February, 1784; *d.* 3d July, 1848; Member of Congress from Louisiana, 1824–1826; *m.* 4th April, 1809, Maria FENWICK, dau. of James and Henrietta Maria (LANCASTER) FENWICK.

He was commissioned by President MADISON as Deputy Attorney General of the Territory of Orleans; practised law successfully in the Attakapas and in 1822 was elected as the Representative of Louisiana in Congress, that state being then entitled to only one Congressman; he was reelected in 1824 and 1826; he remained in Maryland and District of Columbia, practicing law and educating his children from 1826 to 1844, when he returned to Louisiana; his country residence, called "Pomonky," was on the Potomac River just above Indian Head.

ISSUE

1. Robert James, *b.* 12th May, 1811; *d.* 4th February, 1872; *m.* 1835, Matilda LAWRENCE, dau. of Upton and Elizabeth (HAGER) LAWRENCE.

ISSUE

1. Robert Fenwick.
2. Mary Hoke, *m*. William KEYSER, Vice-President of the Baltimore and Ohio Railroad.

ISSUE

1[1]. Robert Brent KEYSER.
2[1]. Matilda Lawrence KEYSER, *m*. 23d April, 1902, William Maurice MANLY.

ISSUE

1[2]. Keyser MANLY, *b*. July 12, 1903.

3[1]. William KEYSER.

3. Leila Lawrence, *m*. Dunbar HUNT.

ISSUE

1[1]. Anita Dunbar HUNT.

4. Emma Fenwick.
5. Ida Schreve.
6. Elizabeth Hager.

II. James Fenwick, *m*. Laura OVERTON.
III. Edward Watkins.
IV. Maria, *m*. Edward WATKINS.
V. Henrietta, *d.s.p.*
VI. William.
VII. Sarah Anne, *m*. Allen LUCE.
VIII. Edward Cole, *m*. Frances BAKER.
IX. Joseph LANCASTER, *b*. 30th November, 1826, of whom below.

JOSEPH LANCASTER, *b*. at "Pomonky," Charles County, Maryland, 30th November, 1826; studied law in Washington and in Louisiana and practiced law with his father, William Leigh BRENT, and later with his brother Edward C. BRENT in St. Martinsville, until 1850, when he went to California. There he became a leading lawyer in Los Angeles. Was twice Member of the State Legislature. He left California in 1861 to join the Confederate Army. Was arrested on the steamer along with Dr. William GIVIN and Mr. Calhoun BENHAM, by General SUMNER and imprisoned with his friends in Fort Lafayette. When released without parole, he ran the blockade into Virginia, joined General MAGRUDER, and served as major on his staff during the Peninsula Campaign and Seven Days battle around Richmond. Then ordered to report to Gen. Richard TAYLOR in Louisiana as Chief of

Artillery and Ordnance and was subsequently made Colonel of Artillery, an unusual rank at that time. When General TAYLOR left the Trans-Mississippi Department to take command on the other side of the Mississippi River, he made application to have some of his staff to go with him; among them Col. J. L. BRENT; however, the latter was not allowed to accompany General TAYLOR, but was retained in the Trans-Mississippi, and given the rank of Brigadier General. He commanded BRENT'S Brigade of Cavalry until the close of the War. He was one of the officers sent to New Oreans to negotiate the surrender of the Trans-Mississippi Department to the Federals. After his marriage he took charge of the extensive sugar plantation of his father-in-law, residing on Ashland plantation, Parish of Ascension. He represented that Parish for some years in the State Legislature. He was first President of the Louisiana State Agricultural Society and also of the Ascension Branch Sugar Planters Association. After the War he returned to Baltimore and practised law with his brother Robert J. Brent, an eminent lawyer.

At the breaking out of the Civil War he went South and offered his services to the Confederacy, and was Major on the staff of Gen. MAGRUDER, C.S.A.; Colonel of Artillery, C.S.A., 17th April, 1864, and promoted Brigadier-General October, 1864; 25th February, 1863, Major BRENT sank the United States ironclad gunboat *Indianola* on the Mississippi, while in command of the *Queen of the West* and the *Webb*, two ordinary river boats: Lieutenant General TAYLOR, C.S.A., paid the following tribute to General BRENT: "The esprit du corps of Major BRENT'S artillery was admirable, and his conduct and efficiency in action unsurpassed;" and in his history of those stirring times General TAYLOR speaks of the *Indianola* fight as "an action that for daring will bear comparison of any recorded of Nelson or Dundonald." He was one of the Governors of the University Club of Baltimore; Deputy Governor-General from Maryland of the Society of Colonial Wars, and Ex-President Maryland Society Sons American Revolution. He *m.* 1869 Frances Rosella KENNER, dau. of Duncan Farrar KENNER, and Anne Guilhelmine Nanine BRINGIER, his wife, both of Ascension Parish and New Orleans, Louisiana, by whom he had:

ISSUE

I. DUNCAN KENNER, *b.* 9th October, 1877, the subject of this memoir.
II. Nanine.

Arms.—Gules, a wyvern or.
Crest.—A wivern's head between two wings expanded or.
Motto.—Silento et diligentia.
Residence.—Ruxton, Baltimore County, Maryland.
Clubs.—Bachelors Cotillon, Baltimore Athletic, Baltimore Country, Green Spring Valley Hunt.
Societies.—Alpha Delta Phi Fraternity, Johns Hopkins Chapter.

The Giles Brent Line

GILES BRENT, SR., fifth son of Sir Richard and Elizabeth (REED) BRENT of Larke Stoke and Admington, England; *b.* in 1606 and *d.* in 1671, at his estate "Retirement," Westmoreland County, Virginia. He migrated to Maryland in 1638 with his brother, Fulke, and his sisters, Mary and Margaret. He was Deputy Governor of Maryland; Lieutenant-General of Militia; Lord of Kent Fort Manor; Member of the Council; of the House of Burgesses, etc., and his estates in Maryland and Virginia were enormous; he left Maryland in 1650 and went to Virginia; *m.* (firstly) circa 1650, the Princess Kitomagund dau. of the Emperor of Piscataway (she was adopted by Margaret BRENT, educated, baptized and given the name of Mary BRENT); *m.* (secondly) circa 1660, Mrs. Frances HARRISON, née WHITGREAVES, by which marriage there was no issue.

ISSUE BY FIRST MARRIAGE

I. Mary, *m.* John FITZHERBERT, and *d.s.p.*
II. GILES, of whom later.
III. Richard, *d.s.p.*
IV. Katherine, *m.* Richard MARSHAM, whose second wife was her cousin, Mrs. Ann Brooks BRENT, née CALVERT (q.v.) dau. of the Hon. Leonard CALVERT.
V. Henry, *d.* young.
VI. Margaret *d.* young.

GILES BRENT, JR., of "Retirement," Westmoreland County, Virginia; *b.* 1652; *d.* 2d September, 1679; *m.* 1671, his first cousin, Mary BRENT (q.v.) dau. of George and Marianna (PEYTON) BRENT, of "Defford."

ISSUE

I. Margaret, *b.* 1673; *m.* George PLOWDEN.

ISSUE

1. Edmund PLOWDEN, *m.* Henrietta SLYE.
2. Dorothy PLOWDEN, *m.* Col. James FENWICK.
3. Winnifred PLOWDEN.
4. George PLOWDEN, Jr., *d.* young.

II. Mary, *b.* 1675; *m.* John NUTWELL.
III. Giles, III, *b.* 1677; *d.* 1707; *m.* Jane CHANDLER, dau. of Col. William CHANDLER, *d.s.p.*
IV. WILLIAM, of whom later.

WILLIAM BRENT, of "Retirement;" *b.* 1679; *d.* 26th December, 1709; he also lived at "Richland" in Virginia and inherited the English Estates of the family, wherefore he migrated to England and died there; *m.* 12th May, 1709, Sarah GIBBONS, sister of Sir John GIBBONS, Member of Parliament.

ISSUE

I. WILLIAM, of whom later.

WILLIAM BRENT, JR., *b.* in England, 6th March, 1710; *d.* in Virginia, 17th August, 1742; he migrated to America with his mother in 1717 and became Justice, Member of the House of Burgesses, etc.; he lived at "Richland" and *m.* Eleanor CARROLL, dau. of Daniel and Eleanor (DARNALL) CARROLL of Maryland.

ISSUE

I. Anne, *d.* 1803; *m.* her cousin, Daniel CARROLL of "Duddington."
II. Eleanor, *m.* Clement HILL.
III. Richard, *d.* unmarried 30th December, 1814; Member of Congress, of the Senate, etc.
IV. DANIEL CARROLL, of whom later.
V. William, *d.s.p.*; Colonel of the Virginia Continental Line; *m.* Eliza Jacqueline AMBLER.

DANIEL CARROLL BRENT, *b.* 1759; *d.* 21st January, 1814; *m.* 3d January, 1782, Anne Fenton LEE, dau. of Thomas Ludwell and Mary (AYLETT) LEE.

ISSUE

I. WILLIAM, of whom later.
II. Thomas Ludwell Lee, *b.* 9th August, 1784.
III. Adelaide, *b.* 25th December, 1786.
IV. Eleanor, *b.* 11th October, 1787.
V. George Lee, *b.* August, 1793.
VI. Mary Aylett, *b.* 3d October, 1795.

WILLIAM BRENT, *b.* 13th January, 1783; *d.* 13th May, 1848; Member of the House of Delegates, Chargé de Affaires at Buenos Aires, etc.; *m.* 1810, his cousin, Winifred Beale LEE, dau. of Thomas Ludwell and Frances (CARTER) LEE, of "Cotton."

ISSUE

I. William.
II. Arthur Lee.
III. George Lee, Confederate States Army.
IV. THOMAS LEE, of whom later.

THOMAS LEE BRENT, *m.* 1835, Jane WILKINS; he graduated from West Point in 1835.

ISSUE

I. THOMAS LEE, *b.* 9th August, 1845, of whom later.
II. Winifred Lee, *m.* Dr. Henry F. LYSTER.
III. Eleanor, *m.* Gen. Orlando POE, United States Army.
IV. Mary, *m.* Lieutenant Orin GUROVITZ, United States Army.

THOMAS LEE BRENT, JR., *b.* 9th August, 1845; *d.* 24th May, 1880; *m.* 21st December, 1871, Flora DESHLER, dau. of David Wagner and Margaret (NASHEE) DESHLER. Thomas Lee BRENT, graduated at West Point, New York, 23d June, 1865, and by a singular coincidence received his appointment as Second Lieutenant and First Lieutenant, 18th Infantry, on same day, 23d June, 1865; served on garrison duty with 18th Infantry at Camp Thomas, Kentucky, October, 1865; frontier duty, Fort Lyon, Colorado, 1866; frontier duty, Fort Laramie, Dakota, 1866–1867; Fort McPherson, Nebraska, 1867; Fort Philip Kearney, 1867; Quartermaster 18th Infantry, 1867; Acting Assistant Adjutant General, Mountain District, 1867; went to relief Fort Philip Kearney; assigned to 3d Regiment Cavalry, January 1871, with rank of Captain, Company A, and served under General CROOK, Apache campaign; retired in 1876, on account of injuries honorably received while in discharge of duty.

ISSUE

I. Flora, *m.* 26th January, 1897, Thomas Benton HAMILTON, son of the late John HAMILTON, M.D., of Columbus.

ISSUE

1. Winifred Lee HAMILTON.
2. John Worden HAMILTON.
3. Flora Brent HAMILTON.

II. Winifred Eleanor, *m.* 5th April, 1899, Alexander William MACKENZIE of Columbus, Ohio; eldest son of the late R. Poyntz MACKENZIE, of Trinidad, British West Indies, Cadet of MACKENZIE of Gairloch and Lochend.

ISSUE

1. Margaret Louise MACKENZIE, *b.* Columbus, Ohio, 17th March, 1900.
2. Alexander Kenneth MACKENZIE, *b.* at La Pensee, Port of Spain, Trinidad, 30th March, 1905.

III. Thomas Ludlow Lee, *d.* in childhood.
IV. Marie Louise.

Descent of Elizabeth (Reed) Brent from Edward III

EDWARD III, King of England, *m.* Phillippa of Hainault.
THOMAS PLANTAGENET, Duke of Gloucester, *m.* Lady Alianore DE BOHUN.
The Princess ANNE PLANTAGENET, *m.* William BOURCHIER, Earl of Eu.
WILLIAM BOUCHIER, Knight of the Garter, *m.* Lady Margery BERNERS.
Lady JANE BOURCHIER, *m.* Henry NEVILLE of Latimer.
RICHARD DE NEVILLE, Lord Latimer, *m.* Anne STAFFORD of Grafton, who descended from Edward III, through John of Gaunt.
MARGARET DE NEVILLE, of Latimer, *m.* Edward Willoughby DE BROKE.
ELIZABETH WILLOUGHBY DE BROKE, *m.* Sir Fulke GREVILLE of Milcote.
KATHERINE GREVILLE, of Milcote, *m.* Giles REED, Lord of Tusburie and Witten.
ELIZABETH REED, of Tusburie and Witten, *m.* RICHARD BRENT, of Stoke and Admington.

Bringier

IGNACE BRANGIER, Judge, of Leniagne, in Auvergne, France, was the ancestor of the American family bearing the distinguished name. The name of his wife has not been handed down to us. Her son, *b.* in France, is

JEAN BRINGIER, also of Leniagne, Auvergne, France; *m.* in 1711, Marie DOURADOU of the family of Baron DOURADOU D'AUVERGNE, tenth. Louis XIV; their son

PIERRE BRINGIER DE LACADIERE, near Ambagne, in Provence, France; *m.* Agnes, ARNOUX; their son

MARIUS PONS BRANGIER, of Lacadiere; prior to the French Revolution, sold his estate "La Cadiere," near Marseilles, France, and with his young wife Marie Frances DURAND sailed from France, for the Island of Martinique; later he came to Louisiana. In Saint James Parish, which then bore the more grandiloquent title of "Paroisse St. Jacques Cote de Cabahanoce aux Accadiens," he acquired at different times, from 1785 to 1789, five adjoining plantations, these he threw into one; built a large and stately mansion and named the new habitation "La Maison Blanche," where hospitality was the prevailing spirit of both its master and mistress; their second son

MICHEL DOURADOU BRINGIER, *b.* at sea on 6th December, 1789, bought "White Hall" from the other BRINGIER heirs on the death of his father by act dated the 11th June, 1821. He *m.* Elizabeth Aglae DU BOURG. His marriage was also one "de convenance," and was brought about in this way, l'Abbe William DU BOURG, who had fled from Paris during the Reign of Terror, came on a visit to Louisiana, and forming a warm friendship for Mr. Marius BRINGIER, of "White Hall," proposed an alliance between their respective families. A niece of the Abbe then in a convent in Baltimore, became as a consequence contracted to Michel Douradou BRINGIER, younger son of Mr. Marius BRINGIER. She was a dau. of Pierre Francois DU BOURG, Sieur de Ste. Colombe, Chevalier de St. Louis, a brother of the Abbe. Her family were emigrés from France and San Domingo; having lost estates in both places by republican confiscation in the former country, and by negro devastation in the latter. Young Douradou BRINGIER proceeded to Baltimore. His fiancée (whom he had never seen except when, as a child, she had temporarily sojourned in New Orleans on her way from the West Indies to Baltimore) was brought out of the convent. She had reached the mature age of fourteen years. They were forthwith married by the abbé, the bride's uncle and god-father, Louis, surnamed "Le Beau Du Bourg" giving her away. Her miniature painted at the time shows a young maid of gentle face and great loveliness. As a marriage present, the "Hermitage" plantation, in Ascension Parish, was bestowed upon the young couple. The marriage in Baltimore took place on the 17th June, 1812. This was the year that war broke out between England and America, and we find a few years later, the young husband acting as a volunteer aid to General JACKSON on the field at Chalmette.

The Abbé Du Bourg, who had married them, had meantime become Administrator Apostolic of the Diocese of New Orleans, and, as students of Louisiana history know, it was he who welcomed JACKSON in the Place d'Armes (now Jackson Square) after the fight, and called on the General to ascribe the victory to divine providence, which the General, in a gracious reply, hastened to do. Just before the battle Mons. Du Bourg, in the chapel of Ursuline Convent (then situated on Ursuline and Chartres Streets), before a congregation of nuns and civilians, prepared to offer up a petition for divine aid to the American arms. The statue of "Our Lady of Prompt Succor" was placed upon the altar. As the cannon at Chalmette began to boom he entered upon the performance of his holy exercises. They were not yet concluded when a courier hastily entering the chapel announced the victory of the gallant defenders of the city. In commemoration of this event a "mass of thanksgiving," by permission granted by Pope Pius IX, is celebrated on the 8th of every January, in the Ursuline Convent. Mons. Du Bourg, a few months after the battle was consecrated first American Bishop of New Orleans. He *d.* in 1833, Archbishop of Besancon, France.

Michel Douradou BRINGIER in the 1830's acquired from Seaman FIELD, his brother-in-law, the place then and later known as "Melpomene," situated in Orleans Parish. This great edifice was latterly completely surrounded by city dwellings, and when the city was built up around, it occupied the center of a square formed by Carondelet, Baronne, Terpsichore and Melpomene Streets, but originally it had been built as a country house, the nearest dwellings or buildings being on Canal Street, then the upper boundary of New Orleans, and about a mile away. When as late as the 1830's New Orleans lay off in the distance. "Visiting the city" was the usual expression employed when any occupant of the place spoke of going to Canal Street or beyond. Carrollton was reached by long drives on country roads and under out-spreading forest trees.

Michel Daradou BRINGIER *d.* at Memphis, 13th March, 1847. He had built a family vault at Donaldsonville, and he was the first of the family to be buried in it. He was survived by three sons and six daughters. His eldest son was Marius Ste. Colombe BRINGIER of "White Hall" and "Houmas," *m.* his cousin, Augustine TUREAUD, and was father of Marius Ste. Colombe BRINGIER, Jr., his second son, succeeded to "The Hermitage," and *m.* his cousin Stella TUREAUED, leaving several daughters and four sons, Amedee, Trist, Browse and Du Bourg.

Michel Douradou BRINGIER's eldest daughter, *m.* Hore Browse TRIST, of Bowden plantation, kinsman and ward of Thomas JEFFERSON, and became mother of Nicholas Browse TRIST, Lieut. Julian Bringier TRIST, killed at the battle of Murfresboro; Nicholas Philip TRIST and Wilhelmine TRIST, who *m.* Col. Robert WOOD, nephew of Jefferson DAVIS and gd. son of President TAYLOR.

The second daughter of Michel Douradou BRINGIER, namely Louise, bestowed her hand upon Martin GORDON, Jr. to whom were born many daughters and an only son, Martin GORDON, who *d. vita patris.* Nanine, the third daughter, *m.* Duncan Farrar KENNER, Confederate States Congress, having issue, George KENNER and two daughters, the second of whom survives, Rosella, relict of Gen. Joseph Lancaster BRENT.

Aglea, the fourth daughter, *m.* her cousin, Benjamin TUREAUED, of Tezcuro, and left no male posterity. Myrthe, the fifth daughter, *m.* Gen. Dick, TAYLOR, of Fashion plantation, President TAYLOR's only son, and was survived by three daughters, two of whom intermarried with the STAUFFER family of New Orleans. The youngest daughter of Douradou BRINGIER, Octavie BRINGIER, became the wife of Gen. Allen THOMAS, of Dalton, Maryland; lately deceased, and one time United States Minister to Venezuela, their issue being four sons.

"White Hall" in the first half of the half century passed temporarily out of the possession of the BRINGIERS. It was sold to Gen. Wade HAMPTON, gd. father of Gen. Wade HAMPTON of Confederate fame, 1825, by Michel Douradou BRINGIER. On the 5th of February, 1848, it was repurchased from the heirs of General HAMPTON by Mme. Aglae Du Bourg BRINGIER, widow of the above mentioned Michel Daradou BRINGIER, and continued in the BRINGIER family (afterwards being the property of her son, Marius Ste. Colombe BRINGIER) until some years after the Civil War.

"Melpomene" on the death of Mme. Dubourg BRINGIER, in 1878, came into the hands of her son-in-law, Duncan F. KENNER, and not long afterwards the dwelling was demolished and the ground surrounding it was divided into lots, and now occupied by rows of modern city houses.

The following quaint account of "White Hall" is from the pen of Abbé DE LA SEICHARDIER, being here freely translated from the original French:

"On the borders of the Parishes of St. James and Ascension, seated picturesquely on the left bank of the great river, was the remarkable plantation of the BRINGIER family. The golden mark of luxury and opulence was stamped upon the place. One saw it in the decorative wrought-iron fence which inclosed the splendid plantation; in the tastefully laid out gardens and in the rare plants and exotic shrubs which they contained. It appeared in the fanciful scenery of a park stocked with game and in the lovely and spacious ponds filled with choice fish.

"Sadness was not supposed to enter this abode of delight. It was no doubt for this reason that the color scheme everywhere was white. The princely residence of the planter was white and so were all the dependencies of the place.

"White Hall" was in a constant state of animation. Visits succeeded visits and feasts succeeded feasts. It was the chosen rendezvous of fashion, of tourists and of strangers of renown . . . . . Jefferson College, St. Michel Convent, the post office clustered, so to speak, about 'BRINGIER la Maison Blanche.'

"The Villa absorbed the interest of the entire community, and was called the 'Capital of St. James.' But Solomon has said 'Vanity of vanities, all is vanity.' Time passed, and what remains of the delicious Creole abode, so hospitable and so charming in its various aspects? A shadow, a memory, a name. The boast of the banks of the Mechacebe (Mississippi) is no more. The nymphs and shouts of laughter are fled from this Eden, and the high weeds have conquered their former ground. Indeed, already the heedless 'settler' has arrived and erects here on all sides his tent where arose 'La Maison Blanche' in all its splendor.

"One day—about the year 1804, if my information is exact—Monsier DE MARIGNY, the emigrant of 1795, arrived at 'White Hall' on an unexpected visit. Three illustrious personages accompanied the old chevalier, the Count DE BEAUJOLAIX, the Duke DE MONTPENSIER and the Duke D'ORLEANS. The descendants of 'Monsieur,' brother of Louis XIV, were received with that unalloyed courtesy and frank hospitality which are a proverbial characteristic of the Louisianian. Fetes were given in their honor, which was most conspicuous among all was a great Indian chief shod in moccasins of beaver skin and wearing a mantle of the inner bark of the ash tree. He was the friendly Mico of the Houmas. The French princes did not omit to visit him in his savage hut. . . . ."

Bryan

JOSEPH BRYAN, Lawyer, Editor and Manufacturer, Philanthropist, of Virginia; b. 13th August, 1845, at "Eagle Point," Gloucester County, Virginia; d. 20th November, 1908, at his country seat "Laburnum," near Richmond, Virginia; m. 1st February, 1871, at "Brook Hill," Henrico County, Virginia, Isobel Lamont STEWART, b. 20th August, 1847, d. 11th September, 1910, dau. of John STEWART, of Rothesay, Scotland, b. 1st April 1806, d. 11th March, 1885, and his wife, Mary Amanda WILLIAMSON, b. 22d March, 1822, d. 20th November, 1910, dau. of Robert Carter WILLIAMSON.

ISSUE

I. John Stewart, of Richmond, Virginia; b. 23d October, 1871; President of the Richmond News Leader Company; m. 4th June, 1903, Anne Eliza Tennant, b. 19th February, 1875, dau. of David Brydon TENNANT, of Ayr, Scotland, and Willie Anne BUFFINGTON of Huntington, West Virginia.

ISSUE

1. Amanda Stewart, b. 13th July, 1904.
2. David Tennant, b. 3d August, 1906.
3. John Stewart, Jr., b. 11th March, 1911.

II. Robert Coalter, of Richmond, Virginia; b. 27th June, 1873; Professor of Surgery in the Medical College of Virginia; Major in the American and French Army Medical Corps; m. 17th October, 1914, Grace HAMILTON, dau. of Silas Marland HAMILTON, of Baltimore, Maryland, and Anne ADAMS, his wife, b. 24th October, 1883.

ISSUE

1. Jonathan, II, b. 9th July, 1915.
2. Robert Carter, b. 11th December, 1917.

III. Jonathan, of Rothesay, Henrico County, Virginia; b. 6th December, 1874; President of the Richmond Forgings Corporation, and also President of the Jefferson Realty Corporation; m. 1st June, 1911, Winifred DUFFY, b. 29th August, 1882, dau. of John and Sarah Jane (BILLINGS) DUFFY.

IV. Joseph St. George, Captain Aviation Supply Department; Manufacturer; b. 11th February, 1879; m. 15th April 1902, Emily Page KEMP, b. 15th April, 1879, dau. of Perrin and Louisa Richardson (SMITH) KEMP.

ISSUE

1. Joseph, III, *b.* 30th April, 1904.
2. Lamont Stewart, *b.* 24th July, 1910.

v. Thomas Pinckney, *b.* 24th October, 1882; *d.* 12th February, 1920; Lawyer and Lieutenant Commander United States Naval Reserve Force; *m.* 10th April, 1907, Helen McGill HAMILTON, *b.* 6th July, 1884, dau. of Alexander HAMILTON of Petersburg, Virginia, and his wife Helen McGill, *b.* 19th December, 1858, dau. of John McGill and Helen LEAVENWORTH.

ISSUE

1. Alexander Hamilton, *b.* 6th May, 1908.
2. Isobel Stewart, *b.* 24th October, 1909.
3. Helen McGill, *b.* 24th October, 1912.
4. Norma Stewart, *b.* 12th September, 1914.
5. Thomas Pinckney, Jr., *b.* 10th October, 1918.

JOSEPH BRYAN received his preliminary education at the Episcopal High School, near Alexandria, and under the preceptorship of private tutors, entering the University of Virginia in 1862. In 1863 his wrist was severely broken by a fall, and being temporarily unfitted for more active service, he took service in the nitre and mining bureau, and was assigned to duty in Pulaski County, southwest Virginia. In 1864 he got leave of absence and volunteered with the 2d Company, Richmond Howitzers, participating in the sanguinary conflict at Spottsylvania Court House. On the expiration of his leave he was obliged to report to his chief in Pulaski, but in October, 1864, he volunteered for more active service and joined MOUNTJOY'S Company of MOSBY'S Command. Soon after joining MOSBY he was wounded twice and went back to "Carysbrook," but his wounds soon healed, and from that time to the end he was in all the daring raids and hand-to-hand encounters of his brilliant cavalry leader. At the end of the war he gave every dollar he had to an impecunious comrade to enable him to return to Kentucky. Left penniless, he borrowed money and bought government mules in Washington, resold them to southern farmers to enable him to re-enter the University of Virginia, which he did in September, 1865, and pursued academic studies. In 1867 he entered the school of law of that institution. At the end of the session his money was exhausted and he was unable to return for his degree. Washington and Lee University gave him the degree of LL.D. in 1907. He was admitted to the bar of Virginia in 1867, and at once began practice at Palmyra, Fluvana County, but in 1870 settled in Richmond. Going about the practice of his profession with that keen and active interest that characterized his whole business life, in spite of the great prostration following the war, he became one of the most successful young men in the community, and within a few years so many large financial interests were confided to his management that gradually he relinquished active practice and entered upon his memorable career as a man of affairs. Apart from his mechanical and industrial activities, such as the Sloss-Sheffield Works, the Richmond Locomotive Works, afterwards acquired by the American Locomotive Company, and others of like kind, he was President of the Georgia Pacific Railway Company, which was built under his management, a director in the Southern Railway Company, and the New York Equitable Life Insurance Association, this latter at the express solicitation of Grover CLEVELAND, when chairman of the committee on re-organization. He was publisher of the Richmond *Times*, founded the *Evening Leader* which later became the *News-Leader*. He was a member of the Board of Visitors of the University of Virginia, trustee of the University Endowment Fund, President Virginia Historical Society, member Advisory Board Association for the Preservation of Virginia Antiquities, Vestryman of his Church in two parishes, member of the Standing Committee of the Diocese of Virginia, Delegate tri-annually from 1886 to 1907 to the General Convention of that Church, Trustee of the Episcopal Theological Seminary and High School of Virginia and a Director in the Jamestown Exposition, the chief management of which was twice pressed upon him and declined. He was prodigal in his liberality to religious welfare work, educational institutions, various charities, and especially to indigent Confederate soldiers. He believed in the righteousness of the "Lost Cause," yet strong and unwavering as was his conviction, with that sanity of vision and breadth of tolerance which characterized him in all things, he loyally accepted the results. It was mainly because of his belief that the various patriotic societies throughout the country were no mean agents in fostering the spirit of reconciliation that he joined the Society of Colonial Wars, of which he was President of the Virginia Chapter, Sons of the American Revolution and Society of the Cincinnati. He also took an active interest in the affairs of Phi Beta Kappa. Though an ardent churchman, he was free from anything savoring of ecclesiastical narrowness or sectarian prejudice. His hand was open to all creeds—to the Salvation Army and to negro evangelists. He assisted the Union Seminary (Presbyterian) to remove from Hampden-Sidney to Richmond, and ten days prior to his death he urged his fellow-citizens to completion of the endowment fund for Greater Richmond College (Baptist) to which he himself was a liberal contributor. It was largely through his influence that the Virginia Historical Society received as a gift the old residence of Robert E. LEE as a permanent home. He and Mrs. BRYAN gave to the Association for the Preservation of Virginia Antiquities a superb bronze statue of John SMITH, which was erected on Jamestown Island. Perhaps the proudest moment of his life was when he was able to buy back "Eagle Point," his boyhood home, which his father was obliged to sell immediately after the war. The story of his phenomenal success, his intuitive sagacity, quick, decisive action, his indomitable pluck and imperturbable nerve, his prodigious industry and intelligent alertness, his inflexible integrity, his absolute observance of the Golden Rule, his large-hearted generosity, his happy secret of winning the confidence and affection of men, his munificent unselfishness in furthering public enterprises, is an inspiration which has endured. JOSEPH BRYAN was one of the great men of his day. Though an aristocrat by instinct and heredity, the humblest artisan never felt him condescend, for, with high and low alike, he was always his natural self, and amid all sorts and conditions of men "bore himself at manhood's simple level." His dominating personal characteristics were his belief in righteousness and his love of his family and his mother state. He was saturated with the history and traditions of Virginia. His library comprises a priceless collection of Virginiana, which in point of completion and rareness stands unrivalled in any collection, public or private, in America. He had at his finger's end the entire history of the Old Dominion. Personally, he seemed to diffuse a sort of social sunshine wherever he might be, and in whatever company.

Lineage

The earliest ancestor of this American family was JOSEPH BRYAN who settled in South Carolina prior to 1697, at which time he owned lands there in Colleton County; *m.* previous to 1700 Janet COCHRAN.

ISSUE

I. Joseph, *b.* previous to 1700; *d.* 9th December, 1735 or 1736.
II. Hugh, *b.* 1699; *d.* 31st January, 1753.
III. Hannah, will probated 20th August, 1753.
IV. JONATHAN, *b.* 12th September, 1708, of whom below.

HON. JONATHAN BRYAN, of South Carolina and Georgia; *b.* 12th September, 1708; *d.* 9th March, 1788; was a man of marked influence in the Colonial and Revolutionary period of South Carolina and Georgia; assisted Oglethorpe in 1733 in selecting the site of Savannah, became a member of the King's Council in Georgia in 1754, and one of the first Justices of the Original General Court of the Colony appointed that same year; was a man of great piety and is mentioned by WHITEFIELD in his diary as one of his helpers in Georgia; took an active part in behalf of the rights of that Colony as early as 1769, and, continuing to do so, was in 1774 excluded from the King's Council of which he had for twenty years been a member; was elected a member of the Committee of Safety of Georgia, and in 1777 was a member of the Executive Council, and acting "as Vice-President and Commander in Chief of the State of Georgia, and ordinary of the same;" in January, 1779, he was captured by the British, heralded as "a notorious ring leader of rebellion," and imprisoned on Long Island until June, 1780; being exchanged, he, with his sons, engaged again in behalf of the independence of the Colony; he *d.* in 1788; owned plantations in South Carolina and also in Georgia; *m.* 13th October 1737, Mary WILLIAMSON, *b.* 23d March, 1722, *d.* 24th March, 1781, dau. of John and Mary (BOWER) WILLIAMSON. Jonathan BRYAN had eight sons of whom the fifth and the only one to leave issue was

ISSUE

V. JOSIAH, *b.* 22d August, 1746, of whom later.

JOSIAH BRYAN of "Nonchalance," Wilmington Island, Georgia; *b.* 22d August, 1746; *m.* 14th August, 1770, Elizabeth PENDARVIS, *b.* 23d May, 1755, dau. of Josiah PENDARVIS and his wife, Mary BEDON of South Carolina; he *d.* in the spring of 1774. [Elizabeth (PENDARVIS) BRYAN, his widow, *m.* a second time to John SCREVEN and had issue; she *d.* 4th April, 1804.]

ISSUE OF JOSIAH AND ELIZABETH BRYAN

I. JOSEPH, *b.* 18th August, 1773, only child, of whom below.

JOSEPH BRYAN, of "Nonchalance," Wilmington Island, Georgia; *b.* 18th August, 1773; *d.* 5th September, 1812; *m.* 5th April, 1805, Delia FORMAN, *b.* 4th March, 1788, *d.* 16th December, 1825, dau. of Gen. Thomas M. FORMAN of Maryland.

ISSUE

I. JOHN RANDOLPH, *b.* 23d March, 1806, of whom below.
II. H. Georgia.
III. Thomas Forman.
IV. Virginia.
V. Joseph.

JOHN RANDOLPH BRYAN, *b.* at "Nonchalance" on Wilmington Island, Georgia, 23d March, 1806; *d.* 13th September, 1887; spent much of his youth with John RANDOLPH of Roanoke, who wanted his namesake near him, and urged the better facilities for education in Virginia. He later entered Yale, spent seven years in the navy, from which he retired in 1831, and took up his residence at "Eagle Point," in Gloucester County, Virginia, and later at "Carysbrook," in Fluvanna County; *m.* 1830, Elizabeth Tucker COALTER, gd. dau. of St. George TUCKER, jurist and poet (see TUCKER, Vol. V, Colonial Families"), and related to the COALTERS, BLANDS and RANDOLPHS, and all that kinship that made up the leaders of the Old Dominion. He *m.* 27th January, 1830, Elizabeth Tucker COALTER, *b.* 25th June, 1805, *d.* 28th March, 1856, at Eagle Point, dau. of Judge John COALTER, of Augusta County, Virginia, *b.* 20th August, 1769, *d.* 2d February, 1838, and his wife Anne Frances Bland TUCKER, *b.* 26th September, 1779, *d.* 12th September, 1813.

ISSUE

I. JOSEPH, *b.* 13th August, 1845, the subject of this memoir.

Bulkeley

MORGAN GARDNER BULKELEY, Hartford, Connecticut; b. at East Haddam, Connecticut, 26th December, 1837; m. 11th February, 1885, Fannie (BRIGGS) HOUGHTON, of San Francisco, California, b. July 3rd, 1860, dau. of James Franklin and Caroline (SPARHAWK) HOUGHTON.

ISSUE

I. Morgan Gardner, b. 25th December, 1885; m. Ruth COLLINS.
II. Elinor Houghton, b. 7th April, 1893; m. John Avery INGERSOLL.
III. Houghton, b. 9th August, 1896, m. Margaret WHITTEMORE.

HON. MORGAN GARDNER BULKELEY received a high school education in Hartford, Connecticut; upon the outbreak of the Civil War he entered the Union Army, enlisting as a private in the 13th Regiment New York, serving in the Peninsular Campaign under Generals MANSFIELD and WEBER. After the war, removed to Hartford. Organized the United States Bank of Hartford, of which he was first President. In 1879 resigned to accept the presidency of the Aetna Life Insurance Company since which time he has been its President, to date (1918). Was connected with other leading financial institutions of the city. In 1875 was elected a Councilman, in 1876 an Alderman and in 1880 and four succeeding terms, Mayor of Hartford, serving from 1880 to 1888. Was elected on the Republican ticket, Governor of Connecticut in 1888 and held office for a second term under a constitutional provision from 1891–1893; there being no other choice by the electors and a dead lock in the Legislature. Governor of Connecticut 1889–1893. In 1891 he received in legislature caucus thirty-five votes as United States Senator; United States Senator from Connecticut 1905 to 1911. Delegate to Republican National Convention 1888–1896. Department Commander Grand Army of the Republic, 1894.

Lineage

THOMAS BULKELEY of Woore, Shropshire, England, descended from the ancient family of that name seated at Bulkeley, County Chester; m. Elizabeth GROSVENOR, dau. of Randle GROSVENOR.

ISSUE

I. Roland of Woore.
II. EDWARD, of whom later.

III. Margaret, *m.* Thomas SMITH.
IV. Catherine, *m.* George BAKER.
V. Ann, *m.* William GREENE.

EDWARD BULKELEY, 1620; D.D., Rector of Odell, County Bedford and Prebendary of Lichfield; one of the commissioners appointed by the Bishop of Lincoln for the "Levye of Armour in Bedfordshire" among the clergy 1608; *m.* Olive IRBY, of the County of Lincoln.

ISSUE

I. Nathaniel, *d.s.p.*
II. PETER, *b.* 31st January, 1583, of whom later.
III. Paul, *d.* at Cambridge.

REV. PETER BULKELEY, *b.* at Odell, County Bedford, England, 31st January, 1583; *d.* 9th March, 1659, at Concord, Massachusetts; graduated at St. John's College Cambridge, M.A. 1608; succeeded his father as Rector of Odell, 1620; ejected for non-conformity of Church ceremonies, 1634, by Archbishop LAUD; emigrated to America, 1635, settling at Cambridge; first settler and Minister of Concord, Massachusetts, 1635. His private collection of books was the nucleus of the library at Harvard College; he was the author of "The Gospel Covenant, or the Covenant of Grace Opened;" *m.* (firstly) Jane ALLEN, who *d.* 1626, dau. of Thomas ALLEN of Goldington, County Bedford; *m.* (secondly), 1634, Grace CHETWODE, who *d.* 21st April, 1669, dau. of Sir Richard CHETWODE.

ISSUE BY FIRST MARRIAGE

I. Edward, *b.* at Odell, 17th June, 1614; graduated at Harvard; succeeded his father as minister of Concord; *d.* 1696, leaving issue.
II. Mary, *b.* 24th August, 1615; *d* in infancy.
III. Thomas, *b.* 11th April, 1617.
IV. Nathaniel, *b.* 29th November, 1618; *d.* 1627.
V. John, *b.* 17th February, 1620.
VI. Mary, *b.* 1st November, 1621; *d.* in infancy.
VII. George, *b.* 17th May, 1623.
VIII. Daniel, *b.* 28th August, 1625.
IX. Jabez, *b.* 20th December, 1626; *d.* in infancy.
X. Joseph.
XI. William.

ISSUE BY SECOND MARRIAGE

I. Richard.
II. GERSHOM, *b.* 6th December, 1636, of whom later.
III. Eliza, *b.* 1638.
IV. Dorothy, *b.* 1640.

v. Peter, *b.* 12th June, 1643; Deputy of Concord, Massachusetts, 1673–1690; Speaker, 1676; Governor's Assistant, 1677–1685; *d.* 1688.

REV. GERSHOM BULKELEY, *b.* 6th December, 1636; *d.* 2d December, 1713; was a noted historian; second Minister of the Church at New London, Connecticut, 1661; removed to Wethersfield, 1667; appointed Surgeon in the Army in King Philip's War, 1675, and wounded in the fight at Deerfield; *m.* 26th October, 1659, Sarah CHAUNCY, dau. of Rev. Charles CHAUNCY, President of Harvard University.

ISSUE

I. Catherine, *b.* 1660; *m.* Richard TREAT.
II. JOHN, *b.* 1661, of whom later.
III. Dorothy, *b.* 1662; *m.* Thomas TREAT.
IV. Charles, *b.* 1663.
V. Peter, *b.* 1664; *m.* Rebecca TALCOTT.
VI. Edward, *d.* 27th August, 1748; *m.* Dorothy PRESCOTT, leaving issue.

REV. JOHN BULKELEY, of Colchester, Connecticut; *b.* 1661; graduated at Harvard, 1680; a distinguished scholar and divine; was first Minister and settler at Colchester; *m.* circa 1702, Patience PRENTICE, of New London, Connecticut.

ISSUE

I. JOHN, *b.* 1704, of whom later.
II. Gershom.
III. Charles (Major), *m.* Ann LATIMER, and had issue.
IV. Peter, *m.* and had issue.
V. Oliver, *m.* and had issue.
VI. Sarah, *m.* John TRUMBULL.
VII. Lucy, *m.* Elaphas LORD.
VIII. Patience, *m.* Ichabod LORD.
IX. Dorothy, *d.* unmarried.

HON. JOHN BULKELEY, of Colchester, Connecticut; *b.* 1704; *d.* 21st July, 1753; graduated at Yale, 1726; Judge of the Supreme Court of Connecticut; *m.* 29th October, 1738, Mary (ADAMS) GARDINER, dau. of Rev. Eliphalet ADAMS, and widow of Jonathan GARDINER.

ISSUE

I. Lydia, *bapt.* 28th October, 1739; *m.* 1761, Capt. Robert LATIMER.
II. Mary, *bapt.* 23d May, 1741; *m.* George B. HURLBUT.
III. ELIPHALET, *bapt.* 10th August, 1746, of whom later.
IV. Lucy, *bapt.* 27th August, 1749; *m.* Capt. John LAMB, of Groton, Connecticut; had issue.

Capt. ELIPHALET BULKELEY, of Colchester, Connecticut; *bapt.* 10th August, 1746; was Captain in the Revolutionary War; was in the Lexington alarm from Colchester; *m.* his cousin, Ann BULKELEY, dau. of Maj. Charles BULKELEY.

ISSUE

I. JOHN CHARLES, of whom later.
II. Jonathan, of Wilkesbarre; *m.* and left issue.
III. Eliphalet Adams, *d.* unmarried.
IV. Orlando, *d.s.p.*
V. Mary, *m.* ———— WORTHINGTON.
VI. Lydia Ann, *m.* Daniel WATROUS, of Colchester.
VII. Patience, *m.* ———— CHAPMAN.
VIII. Sarah Chauncey, *m.* ———— BOLTON.
IX. Frances, *m.* H. F. LAMB.
X. Julia, *m.* Stueben BUTLER.

JOHN CHARLES BULKELEY, of Colchester, Connecticut; was a farmer; *b.* there; *d.* there; *m.* there circa 1795, Sarah TAINTOR.

ISSUE

I. Charles Edwin, *m.* (firstly) Mary ISHAM; *m.* (secondly) Julia WORTHINGTON.
II. John Taintor, *m.* Clarissa BULKELEY, dau. of Elijah BULKELEY, of Colchester.
III. ELIPHALET ADAMS, *b.* 29th June, of whom later.

ELIPHALET ADAMS BULKELEY, *b.* at Colchester, Connecticut, 29th June, 1803; *d.* Hartford, Connecticut, 13th February, 1872; graduated at Yale, 1824; admitted to the Bar in Lebanon, Connecticut, Judge of the Probate Court and County Judge; was one of the founders of the Republican party in Connecticut; Member of the State Legislature and first Republican Speaker of the Connecticut General Assembly, 1857; State Senator for two years, 1840; Founder and First President of the Aetna Life Insurance Company of Hartford, and the Connecticut Mutual Life Insurance Company; *m.* Lydia Smith MORGAN.

ISSUE

I. Charles E., *d.* 1864. Captain 1st Connecticut Heavy Artillery.
II. MORGAN GARDNER, *b.* 26th December, 1837, the subject of this memoir.
III. William Henry, *b.* 2d March, 1840; Statesman; went to war as a private in 13th Regiment New York State Militia, in 1861, and the next year raised a company for the 56th New York Volunteers; was elected captain and served in General SMITH's Division until the regiment was

ordered home, during the New York draft riots, 1863; was a Member of the Common Council of Hartford for five years; Commissary General of Connecticut from 1879 to 1881; Lieutenant-Governor from 1881 to 1883, and State Commissioner to the Yorktown celebration 1881; founded Forest City, Potter County, South Dakota; he was President of the Forest City and Souix City Railroad and the Forest City Land and Improvement Company.

iv. Eliphalet.
v. Mary Morgan.

Residence.—100 Washington Street, Hartford, Connecticut.
Arms.—Sable, a chevron between three bull's heads, argent, armed or.
Crest.—Out of a ducal coronet or, a bull's head argent, armed of the first.
Motto.—Nec timera, nec timide.
Societies.—Colonial Wars, Society of Mayflower Descendants, Society of Cincinnati, Sons of the Revolution, Baronial Order of Runnemede, Loyal Legion, Grand Army Republic, Society War of 1812.

Bullitt

WILLIAM MARSHALL BULLITT, *b.* 4th March, 1873 at Louisville, Kentucky; *m.* 31st May, 1913, at Stockbridge, Massachusetts, Nora IASIGI, *b.* 23d August, 1881, at Boston, Massachusetts, dau. of Oscar and Amy Gore (WALKER) IASIGI.

ISSUE

I. Thomas Walker, *b.* 12th September, 1914, at "Clovercroft," Stockbridge, Massachusetts.
II. Nora Iasigi, *b.* 5th February, 1916, at Louisville, Kentucky.
III. Barbara Bullitt, *b.* 30th December, 1919, at Louisville, Ky.

WILLIAM MARSHALL BULLITT was educated in Louisville private schools; Lawrenceville School, New Jersey (Class 1890); B.S., Princeton University, 1894; LL.B., University of Louisville, 1895; Solicitor General of the United States 15th July, 1912 to 11th March, 1913, resigning at the close of the Taft administration; Counsel in various important cases in the Supreme Court of the United States, notably those involving the constitutionality of the War Time Prohibition Act, the Eighteenth Amendment, the Federal Farm Loan Act, the Income Tax Law as applied to the salaries of the President of the United States and the Federal Judges, the Newspaper Publicity Act, the Kentucky Insurance Premium Tax Act and the Anti-Removal Act; the "Cotton Corner," and the United States Shoe Machinery cases; in active practice especially in insurance, banking and general corporate matters; edited Bullitt's "Codes of Practice," 1899; Director and Member of Executive Committee, Fidelity and Columbia Trust Company; Director and Counsel, Citizens Union National Bank, Citizens Union Fourth Street Bank, Kentucky Title Company, Chairman Board of Public Safety of Louisville from November, 1907, until May, 1909, when he resigned; Delegate from state-at-large to the Republican National Conventions of 1908 and 1916; Republican nominee for the United States Senate in 1914 (defeated at election); active in organization of Plattsburg movement for military preparedness (1915–1918); Member of Executive Committee Military Training Camps Association, and chairman for Kentucky during the War; Major, American Red Cross, Deputy Commissioner for France 1918–1919. Mr. BULLITT descends from many distinguished ancestors, among whom are William RANDOLPH of Turkey Island, Virginia, Col. Gerard FOWKE, Capt. Randolph BRANDT, Dr. Gustavus BROWN, of Maryland; Col. John HENRY, Col. William CHRISTIAN, Maj. Thomas WALKER, Col. Joshua FRY, the Rev. James KEITH, and Col. Thomas MARSHALL, all of Virginia. Colonel FRY was *b.* in Somersetshire, England; educated at Oxford; commissioned Colonel and Commander-in-Chief of the Virginia forces in 1754; General WASHINGTON being Lieutenant-Colonel under him. Mr. BULLITT is the gr. gr. nephew of both Patrick HENRY and Chief Justice MARSHALL.

Lineage

JOSEPH BULLITT, the Huguenot ancestor of the BULLITT family in America, was one of the early settlers of Charles County, Maryland. He was *b.* prior to 1653, and it is believed that his father was born in the province of Languedoc, and left France as a young man to escape the persecutions which preceded and followed the Revocation of the Edict of Nantes. On 15th November, 1676, Joseph BULLITT witnessed the will of one Elizabeth LILLY in Charles County, Maryland (see Will Book 4, page 155, Land Office, Annapolis), and he purchased land near Port Tobacco, Charles County, Maryland, where he *d.* in March, 1692; he *m.* circa, 1685, Elizabeth BRANDT, *d.* in Maryland prior to March, 1694, when her will was probated, she was the dau. of Capt. Randolph BRANDT, *b.* in Barbadoes, West Indies, *d.* in Maryland, February, 1698.

ISSUE

I. Joseph, *b.* 8th February, 1688; *d.* 1709.
II. BENJAMIN, *b.* 28th April, 1693, of whom below.

BENJAMIN BULLITT, Gentleman; *b.* in Charles County, Maryland, 28th April, 1693; *d.* in Fauquier County, Virginia, 9th January, 1766; *m.* (firstly) 1737, Elizabeth HARRISON, she *d.* 1757, dau. of Hon. Thomas HARRISON, *b.* 1665, *d.* 1746, of "Chappawampsic," Stafford County, Virginia. Benjamin BULLITT was Justice of Prince William County, Virginia, in 1743.

ISSUE

I. Joseph, *b.* 1728; *d.* unmarried 1793.
II. Thomas, *b.* 1730; Captain of the 1st Virginia Regiment, French and Indian War, under command of General WASHINGTON, at that time a Colonel; visited the Falls of the Ohio as surveyor, 1773; *d.* unmarried in Fauquier County, Virginia, February, 1778.
III. Elizabeth, called "Seth" in her father's will; *b.* 1731; *d.* 1790; *m.* John COMBS; had issue.
IV. Benjamin, *b.* 1733; Lieutenant in the "Patriot Blues," commanded by SPOTSWOOD; killed, aged twenty, in an engagement with Indians, shortly after BRADDOCK'S defeat; unmarried.
V. CUTHBERT, *b.* 1740, of whom below.

HON. CUTHBERT BULLITT, *b.* 1740, in Fauquier County, Virginia; *d.* at "View Mount," Prince William County, Virginia, 27th August, 1791; studied law and practised in Prince William County; Delegate to Virginia Assembly, 1777 and 1787, and at one time Speaker of the House; Member of the Virginia Convention of 1775–1776–1778, and of Prince William County Committee of Safety; in 1777 appointed, with six others, Commissioner to ascertain loss by fire Norfolk, Virginia, sustained at hands of the British; elected 27th December, 1788, by joint ballot of the Senate and House of Delegates, Additional Judge of the General Court of Virginia; commissioned by Lord DUNMORE, in 1773, to survey land at the Falls of the Ohio with his brother, Capt. Thomas BULLITT, *m.* circa 1760, Helen SCOTT, *b.* in Overwharton Parish, Stafford County, Virginia, 7th June, 1739, *d.* in Prince William County, Virginia, 15th or 16th September, 1795, dau. of Rev. James SCOTT, *b.* Dipple Parish, Elgin, Scotland; *d.* at "Clermont," Prince William County, 1782; he *m.* 1738, Sarah BROWN, *b.* at "Rich Hill," Charles County, Maryland, 29th August, 1715; *d.* in Virginia. Sarah BROWN was sister of Dr. Gustavus Richard BROWN of "Rose Hill," who, with Dr. DICK and Dr. CRAIK attended WASHINGTON in his last illness.

ISSUE

I. ALEXANDER SCOTT, *b.* 1762, at Dumfries, Virginia, of whom later.
II. Thomas James, *b.* in Virginia; *d.* in Easton, Maryland, December, 1840; *m.* Mary Caile HARRISON, widow, of Baltimore, Maryland; had issue.
III. Frances, *m.* Capt. William GARRARD, of Stafford County, Virginia, and Bourbon County, Kentucky; had issue.
IV. Sarah, *m.* William BARNES, Justice of Prince William County, Virginia, 1793; had issue.
V. Helen Eleanor Grant, *d.* September, 1815; *m.* after 8th September, 1798, James HUIE, of Scotland, who settled in Dumfries County, Virginia, circa 1797; had issue.
VI. Sophia, *d.* unmarried December, 1803.

COL. ALEXANDER SCOTT BULLITT, *b.* at Dumfries, Virginia, 1762; *d.* at "Oxmoor," Jefferson County, Kentucky, 13th April, 1816; *m.* (firstly) October, 1785, Priscilla CHRISTIAN, *b.* in Virginia, circa 1770, *d.* at "Oxmoor," 11th November, 1806, dau. of Col. William CHRISTIAN, who emigrated to Kentucky, 1783-1784, and his wife, Anne (HENRY) CHRISTIAN sister of Patrick HENRY. Colonel BULLITT *m.* (secondly) Mary (CHURCHILL) PRATHER, widow; issue, Thomas James BULLITT and Mary, or "Polly" BULLITT, both *d.* young. Col. Alexander Scott BULLITT was member of Virginia House of Delegates, 1783; moved to Kentucky in 1783; commissioned by Patrick HENRY, Governor of Virginia, as major in the militia of Prince William County, 16th May, 1785; County Lieutenant of Jefferson County, 2d May, 1786; appointed one of the Trustees of Louisville by the Virginia Legislature; President of the Court-Martial, 21st March, 1787, which tried and convicted Col. Hugh McGARY; member of the Kentucky Convention at Danville, 1788; delegate to the Constitutional Convention, 1792, at Danville, and, with George NICHOLAS, drafted the first Constitution of Kentucky, which was then adopted; elected one of the forty electors on the first Tuesday in May, 1792; was then chosen one of the eleven State Senators and, upon the assembling of the first Kentucky Legislature at Lexington, 4th June, 1792, was elected Speaker of the Senate and re-elected for twelve successive years (1792-1804), when he retired from public life; President of the Constitutional Convention which met at Frankfort, 22d July, 1799, and framed the Second Constitution of Kentucky, that continued in force until 1850; elected 5-7th May, 1800, the first Lieutenant-Governor of the State.

ISSUE BY FIRST MARRIAGE

I. Annie Christian, *b.* 6th November, 1786; *d.* 10th May, 1828; *m.* 4th February, 1819, John HOWARD, widower; *b.* in Charles County, Maryland, 7th October, 1769; *d.* in Jefferson County, Kentucky, 25th June, 1843; had issue.

1. Alexander Scott Bullitt HOWARD, *b.* 24th October, 1819; *d.* 28th January, 1822.
2. William Bullitt HOWARD, *b.* 10th March, 1821; *d.* 1896; *m.* (firstly) Maria STROTHER, issue; *m.* (secondly), Mary Jones, had issue.
3. Helen HOWARD, *b.* 11th October, 1822; *d.* 10th December, 1841.
4. Annie Christian HOWARD, *b.* 1st February, 1825; *d.* 19th July, 1912; *m.* 13th October, 1842, Robert Graham COURTENAY, *b.* on the Irish Sea, 1813, *d.* in Louisville, Kentucky, 1st October, 1864.

1¹. Julia Christian COURTENAY, *b.* 8th January, 1844; *d.* 28th February, 1894; *m.* 5th December, 1866, Hector V. LOVING, *b.* 8th September, 1839, *d.* 27th March, 1913; had issue.
2¹. Henry COURTENAY, *b.* 10th January, 1846; *d.* 13th March, 1846.
3¹. Robert Martin COURTENAY, *b.* 28th November, 1848; *d.*, 6th July, 1851..
4¹. Thomas Anderson COURTENAY, *b.* 20th June, 1850; *m.* 30th January, 1877, Jane Short BUTLER, *b.* 25th April, 1853; had issue.
5¹. Helen Martin COURTENAY, *b.* 12th November, 1852.
6¹. Emma COURTENAY, *b.* 25th August, 1854.
7¹. Lewis Rogers COURTENAY, *b.* 23d May, 1857; *d.* 26th October, 1897; unmarried.
8¹. William Howard COURTENAY, C.E., *b.* 30th July, 1858; *m.* 27th April, 1893, Isabel Stevenson CLARK, *b.* 24th February, 1868.

ISSUE

1². Erskine Howard COURTENAY, C.E., *b.* 25th Aprll, 1895; Ensign United States Navy Reserve Force, 1918.
2². James Clark COURTENAY, C.E., *b.* 14th January 1897; United States Navy, (Aviation), 1918.

II. Cuthbert, *b.* 5th May, 1788; *d.* 23d February, 1854; *m.* Harriet WILLETT.

ISSUE

1. Henry Massie, M.D., *b.* 28th February, 1817; *d.* 5th February, 1880; *m.* (firstly) circa 1843; Julia ANDERSON, had issue; *m.* (secondly) 14th September, 1854, Sarah Crow PARADISE, widow, *b.* 30th April 1829, *d.* 2d December, 1901.

ISSUE BY FIRST MARRIAGE

1[1]. Virginia Anderson BULLITT, *b.* 5th January, 1844; *d.* 6th April, 1917; *m.* 1st December, 1869, John COOD.

ISSUE

1[2]. Helen Bullitt COOD, *b.* 2d November, 1870; *d.* 7th July, 1905; *m.* 3d January, 1895; Owen TYLER, *b.* 15th July, 1868.

ISSUE

1[3]. John Cood TYLER, Lieutenant United States Navy, *b.* 17th December, 1895; *m.* 3d April, 1918, Gertrude LYNN.
2[3]. Jane Owen TYLER, *b* 2d September, 1898.

2[1]. Helen Martin BULLITT, *b.* 9th August, 1848; *d.* 11th November, 1895; *m.* Philip Barbour BATE; no issue.

ISSUE BY SECOND MARRIAGE

1[1]. Elizabeth BULLITT, *b.* 16th June, 1855; *m.* 17th March, 1875, Charles William BUCK, *b.*, 17th March, 1849.

ISSUE

1[2]. Mamie BUCK, *b.* 30th April, 1877; *m.* 24th May, 1906; Vernon ROBINS, M.D., *b.* on Staten Island, New York, 14th June, 1872.
2[2]. Charles Neville BUCK, *b.* 15th April, 1879; *m.* 20th June, 1918, Margaret Field DE MOTTE, widow.

2[1]. Edward Crowe BULLITT, *b.* February, 1856.
3[1]. Julia BULLITT, *b.* 22d October, 1857; *m.* 21st January, 1891, Charles RAUTERBERG, *b.* 18th March, 1837, *d.* 24th July, 1913.

ISSUE

1[2]. Carl RAUTERBERG, Lieutenant United States Army, 1918; *b.* 23d March, 1892.
2[2]. Henry Bullitt RAUTERBERG, Sergeant United States Army, 1918; *b.* 6th October, 1893.
3[2]. Julia Bullitt RAUTERBERG, *b.* 30th October, 1894.

4[1]. Edith BULLITT, *b.* 27th February, 1861; *m.* 2d June, 1897, Hon. Charles Donald JACOB, *b.* 1st June, 1838; *d.* 25th December, 1898; no issue.

5¹. Annie Christian BULLITT, *b.* 4th March, 1863.
6¹. Henrietta BULLITT, *b,* 22d January, 1869.

2. Willett.
3. Cuthbert, M.D., *d.* in San Antonio, Texas; *m.* Helen WILLARD.

ISSUE

1¹. A. C. BULLITT.
2¹. Gordon BULLITT.
3¹. Samuel BULLITT.

4. Alexander Scott.
5. Ann Eliza, *m.* Lafayette FITZHUGH; had issue.
6. Harriet, *m.* John FITZHUGH; had issue.
7. William, *m.* Kate STEELE, widow; no issue.
8. Helen, *m.* Dr. LOWRY; had issue.
9. Priscilla, *m.* Archibald A. GORDON.

ISSUE

1¹. Harriet GORDON, *b.* 19th August, 1848; *d.* 22d January, 1909; *m.* 6th November, 1866, Logan Crittenden MURRAY.

ISSUE

1². Anna MURRAY, *b.* 15th October, 1867.
2². A. Gordon MURRAY, *b.* 11th February, 1870; *m.* 24th June, 1905, Grace STANTON.

ISSUE

1³. Archibald Gordon MURRAY, Jr., *b.* 1st May, 1910.

3². Illa MURRAY, *b.* 20th December, 1871.
4². Rosa MURRAY, *b.* 4th August, 1875; *d.* 24th January, 1895.

2¹. John GORDON, M.D.
3¹. Helen Martin GORDON, *m.* John ALMY; had issue.
4¹. Edward GORDON.
5¹. Archibald GORDON.
6¹. Fannie GORDON, *m.* Arthur MILLARD, deceased; had issue.

III. Helen Scott, "Aunt Key," *b.* 1790; *d.* 17th December, 1871; *m.* (firstly) Gen. Henry MASSIE, *b.* 1768, of Chillicothe, Ohio, and "Ridgeway," Jefferson County, Kentucky, where he *d.* in 1830, no issue; *m.*

(secondly) Col. John Lewis MARTIN, widower, b. Albemarle County, Virginia, 14th August, 1779; d. 17th October, 1854, no issue; m. (thirdly) Col. Marshall KEY, widower, b. 8th Sepember, 1783, d. 16th November, 1860, no issue.

IV. WILLIAM CHRISTIAN, b. 14th February, 1793, of whom below.

HON. WILLIAM CHRISTIAN BULLITT, b. 14th February, 1793; d. 28th August, 1877; m. 1st September, 1819, Mildred Ann FRY, b. in Albemarle County, Virginia, 9th July, 1798, d. in Louisville, Kentucky, 12th July, 1879, dau. of Joshua and Peacy (WALKER) FRY. He was admitted to the bar in Louisville, 1812, retiring from the practice of law in 1820; elected member of the Kentucky Constitutional Convention, 1849–1850.

ISSUE

1. Judge Joshua Fry, b. 22d February, 1821; d. 16th February, 1898; m. Elizabeth R. SMITH.

ISSUE

1. Alexander Scott BULLITT.
2. George Smith BULLITT.
3. Martha Bell BULLITT.
4. William Christian BULLITT.
5. Joshua Fry BULLITT; m. Margaret TALBOTT; had issue.
6. Charles Smith BULLITT.
7. Irene Smith BULLITT.
8. John Christian BULLITT; m. Frances WESTON; had issue.

ISSUE

1[1]. Henrietta Massie BULLITT, d. 1918; m. C. F. DEWEY; had issue.

9. James Bell, M.D., b. 1863; m. (firstly) 19th August, 1895 Clare Selby RALSTON, d. May, 1917; m. (secondly) 21st Sepember, 1918, Elizabeth SELBY.

ISSUE BY FIRST MARRIAGE

1[1]. Elizabeth BULLITT, b. 26th December, 1897.
2[2]. Ralston BULLITT, b. February, 1899.
3[2]. Minar Dixon BULLITT, b. 28th June, 1906.

II. Alexander Scott, b. 3d August, 1822; d. 3d February, 1840.
III. John Christian, b. 10th February, 1824; d. 25th August, 1902, at Paoli, near Philadelphia, Pennsylvania; m. in Louisville, Kentucky, 3d April, 1850, Therese Caldwell LANGHORNE, d. 1881.

ISSUE

1. Therese, *b.* 23d September, 1851, *m.* 27th October, 1874, John Woolston COLES, Surgeon United States Navy, *d.* April, 1895.

ISSUE

1[1]. Therese Pauline COLES, *b.* 26th June, 1884; *m.* 27th October, 1904, George Trotter TYLER, M.D.

ISSUE

1[2]. Elizabeth Therese TYLER, *b.* 1st January, 1907.

2. Anne, *b.* January, 1853; *d.* March, 1858.
3. Pauline, *b.* 1854; *d.* 18th September, 1866.
4. William Christian, *b.* 18th June, 1856; *m.* (firstly) 20th January, 1886, Emilie TATHAM, *d.* 27th October, 1886; *m.* (secondly) 4th June, 1889, Louisa Gross HORWITZ.

ISSUE BY FIRST MARRIAGE

1[1]. John Christian BULLITT, III, *b.* 27th October, 1886, *m.* (firstly) wife's name not given.

ISSUE BY SECOND MARRIAGE

1[1]. William Christian BULLITT, *b.* 25th January, 1891; *m.* Ernesta DRINKER.
2[1]. Orville BULLITT, *m.* Susan INGERSOLL.

5. John Christian, *b.* January, 1858; *d.* June, 1861.
6. Maurice Langhorne, *b.* March, 1859; *d.* 25th February, 1870.
7. Susan Dixon, *b.* March, 1860; *d.* July, 1861.
8. Julia Dunlap, *b.* 5th May, 1861; *d.* 1916; *m.* (firstly) 25th March, 1884, Frank M. DICK; *m.* (secondly) 9th March, 1896, A. Haller GROSS.

ISSUE BY FIRST MARRIAGE

1[1]. John Julian DICK, *b.* 22d January, 1886.
2[1]. Langhorne Bullitt DICK, *b.* 6th February, 1889.

ISSUE BY SECOND MARRIAGE

1[1]. Maria Rives GROSS, *b.* 15th October, 1898.

9. Logan McKnight, *b.* March, 1863; *m.* 4th November, 1889, Maria Stockton BROWN.

COLONIAL FAMILIES OF THE UNITED STATES 137

ISSUE

1[1]. Logan M. BULLITT, *b.* 25th November, 1890.
2[1]. Maria Stockton BULLITT, *b.* 3d August, 1893; *d.* 1913.
3[1]. Jean Christian BULLITT, *b.* 23d December, 1894.
4[1]. Richard Stockton BULLITT, *b.* April, 1896, killed in battle in France, 1918.

10. James Fry, D.D., *b.* 11th July, 1865; *m.* June, 1897, Margaret EMMONS.

ISSUE

1[1]. Martha Davis, *b.* 18th February, 1899.
2[1]. Margaret Emmons, *b.* December, 1901,
3[1]. Priscilla Christian, *b.* June, 1905.
4[1]. Jeanette Langhorne, *b.* September, 1908.

11. Helen Key, *b.* 27th February, 1867; *m.* June, 1886, Walter FURNESS.

ISSUE

1[1]. Helen Kate FURNESS, *b.* May, 1887; *m.* April, 1906, Wirt THOMPSON.

ISSUE

1[2]. Wirt Furness THOMPSON, *b.* 20th February, 1907.

2[1]. Fairman Rodgers FURNESS, *b.* 6th January, 1889.

12. John Christian, *b.* 30th November, 1871; *m.* Edna (surname not given).

IV. Martha Bell, *b.* 2d March, 1827; *d.* 26th October, 1847; *m.* Richard ALLISON, of Baltimore, Maryland.
V. Susan Peachy, *b.* 20th February, 1829; *d.* 25th July, 1907; *m.* Senator Archibald DIXON, widower.

ISSUE

1. Kate DIXON, *m.* David BURBANK; had issue.
2. William Bullitt DIXON, *m.* 28th December, 1897, Minna LOGAN.
3. Thomas Bullitt DIXON.

VI. David Bell, *b.* 15th December, 1830; *d.* 21st November, 1833.
VII. Helen Martin, *b.* 1st January, 1835; *d.* 29th March, 1896; *m.* 8th May, 1855, Henry CHENOWETH, M.D.

ISSUE

1. Mildred Ann CHENOWETH, *b.* 9th June, 1856; *m.* 4th October, 1877, John STITES, *b.* 9th October, 1850.

ISSUE

1[1]. Helen Chenoweth STITES, *b.* 6th March, 1879; *m.* 12th September, 1906, John Granville GILL.

ISSUE

1[2]. Mildred Ann GILL, *b.* 17th January, 1908.
2[2]. John Granville GILL, III, *b.* 22d November, 1909.
3[2]. Susan Barret GILL, *b.* 2d July, 1911.

2[1]. Mildred Bullitt STITES, *b.* 25th December, 1880; *m.* 17th September, 1907, Joseph Rowlett GANT.

ISSUE

1[2]. Elizabeth GANT, *b.* 6th August, 1909.
2[2]. John Stites GANT, *b.* 22d April, 1911.

3[1]. John Hunt STITES, *b.* 13th April, 1883; *m.* 15th May, 1912, Louise Parkhill PATTERSON.

ISSUE

1[2]. Sarah Parkhill STITES, *b.* 16th July, 1913.
2[2]. John STITES, *b.* 21st August, 1917, *d.* 25th January, 1918.

4[1]. Susie Barret STITES, *b.* 1st March, 1885; *d.* 11th November, 1902.
5[1]. Harry Pennington STITES, *b.* 15th January, 1887; *d.* 9th October, 1915.
6[1]. Elizabeth STITES, *b.* 18th August, 1889; *m.* 28th February, 1918, William Morton HANNAH, Jr.
7[1]. Francis Bell STITES, *b.* 18th August, 1891, United States Army, Aviation, 1918.
8[1]. Ann Lennox STITES, *b.* 27th December, 1892; *m.* 7th May, 1914, Charles William KARRAKER, M.D.

ISSUE

1[2]. Charles William KARRAKER, *b.* 29th November, 1915.
2[2]. Ann Chenoweth KARRAKER, *b.* 10th April, 1918.

9[1]. James Walker STITES, *b.* 25th November, 1897, United States Army, Aviation, 1918.

2. Fannie Bell CHENOWETH, *b.* 9th July, 1858.
3. Sue Bullitt CHENOWETH, *b.* 7th January, 1861; *m.* 28th February, 1884, Hugh L. BARRET, *b.* 16th May, 1850.
4. Henry Walker CHENOWETH, *b.* 11th August, 1873.
5. James Shreve CHENOWETH, M.D., *b.* 6th November, 1867; *m.* 6th February, 1894, Mary Thompson CREEL, *b.* 26th November, 1870.

ISSUE

1[1]. Nancy Creel CHENOWETH, *b.* 28th February, 1897; *m.* 11th March 1918, Alexander HEYBURN, *b.* 22d September, 1897.
2[1]. Helen Bullitt CHENOWETH, *b.* 21st April, 1909.

VIII. THOMAS WALKER, *b.* 17th May, 1838, of whom later.
IX. James Bell, *b.* 16th June, 1840; killed 4th July, 1863, in the Confederate Army.
X. Henry Massie, *b.* 9th November, 1842; *d.* 17th June, 1908; *m.* Mary L. FREDERICK; no issue.

THOMAS WALKER BULLITT, *b.* at "Oxmoor" near Louisville, Kentucky, 17th May, 1838; *d.* in Baltimore, Maryland, 3d March, 1910; *m.* 21st February, 1871, Annie Priscilla LOGAN, *b.* 26th April, 1847, dau. of Agatha Madison MARSHALL, and Judge Caleb WALLACE LOGAN, and gd. dau. of Judge William LOGAN, United States Senator in 1820, and the first male white child born in Kentucky. Mr. BULLITT was graduated from Center College, Danville, with degree of A.B., 1858; LL.B. University of Pennsylvania, 1861, admitted to Philadelphia bar same year; in 1862 joined the Confederate Army serving throughout the war; began practice of law in Louisville, 1865; member of Golf Club, Commercial Club, Filson Club, Lawyers Club, Country Club, Tavern Club and Conversation Club of Louisville; member of the University and Reform Clubs of New York; Director of Kentucky Title Company, Kentucky Title Savings Bank, the First National Bank, and Union National Bank; Founder of the Fidelity Trust Company (Louisville) the first trust company established west of the Alleghanies.

ISSUE

I. WILLIAM MARSHALL, *b.* 4th March, 1873, the subject of this memoir.
II. James Bell, M.D., *b.* 18th January, 1874, obtained his early education at the Rugby School, Louisville; received degrees of A.B., and A.M. from Washington and Lee University; degree of M.D., from University of Virginia; Demonstrator of Anatomy at same University, later was Professor in Medical Department of University of Mississippi and Uni-

versity of North Carolina; Captain, Medical Corps United States Army, in France, 1918; *m*. 30th May, 1901, Evelyn BRYAN, *b*. 28th January, 1874, dau. of John Randolph and Margaret Randolph (MINOR) BRYAN, both of Virginia.

ISSUE

1. Thomas Walker BULLITT, *b*. 30th November, 1903; *d*. June, 1905.
2. James Bell BULLITT, *b*. 8th April, 1906.
3. Margaret BULLITT, *b*. 9th August, 1908.

III. Agatha Marshall, *b*. 24th November 1875; *m*. 3d July, 1913, Herr Joseph GRABISCH.

ISSUE

1. Thomas Bullitt GRABISCH, *d*. in infancy.

IV. Alexander Scott, *b*. 23d January, 1877, was graduated from Louisville Male High School, 1894; A.B., Princeton University, 1898; LL.B., Louisville Law School, 1900; later took special course at Harvard Law School, appointed by the Governor in 1907, Sheriff of Jefferson County, Kentucky, for six months, serving an unexpired term; County Attorney Jefferson County, Kentucky, for eight years; elected in 1909, re-elected in 1913; Democratic Election Commissioner of Jefferson County, Kentucky, 1918; societies: Knight Templar in Masonic Order; Member of the Shrine; applied for aviation service, rejected account of being over age. Major United States Army, 1918–1920.
Clubs: Ivy Club (Princeton); Pendennis and River Valley (Louisville); *m*. 16th May, 1918, Dorothy Frances STIMSON, *b*. 5th February, 1892, dau. of Charles Douglass and Harriet (OVERTON) STIMSON.

V. Mildred Ann, *b*. 12th October, 1879; *d*. 16th April, 1889.

VI. Keith Logan, *b*. 18th February, 1881; LL.B. University of Louisville, 1905; President Louisville Bar Association 1918; member of Sigma Chi; clubs, Cornell Club (New York); River Valley, Pendennis and Country Club (Louisville); Candidate Field Artillery Central Officers Training School, Camp Zachary Taylor, Kentucky, October, 1918; *m*. 12th September, 1917, Dorothy TERRY, *b*. 24th February, 1892, dau. of Edward L. and Jane (FURTH) TERRY.

VII. John Christian, *b*. 31st March, 1883; *d*. 23d September, 1883.

VIII. Mirah Logan, *b*. 12th July, 1885, *m*. 13th April, 1910, William Howard RUSH.

Arms, Clubs and Societies of William Marshall Bullitt

Arms.—Azure, a chevron or between three plates.
Residence.—"Oxmoor," Jefferson County, Kentucky.

Societies.—Sons of the American Revolution, Maryland Historical Society and Virginia Historical Society.

Clubs.—Metropolitan, City Mid-day, National Republican Association of the Bar; Princeton (New York); Metropolitan, ChevyChase (Washington); Filson Club, Salmagundi, Pendennis, Country, Golf, and River Valley (Louisville).

Arms (RANDOLPH of Turkey Island, Virginia).—Gules on a cross or, five mullets, of the first.

Crest.—An antelope's head couped, holding in its mouth a stick or.

Motto.—Fari qual sentiat.

Arms (CHRISTIAN).—Azure, a demi-mascle, between three covered cups, or; crest, a unicorn's head, erased, argent, armed and gorged with a collar invecked or.

Motto.—Salus per Christum.

Arms (HENRY).—Per pale indented argent and gules, on the dexter side a rose of the second, a chief azure charged with a lion passant of the first.

Crest.—Out of a crown ppr. a demi-lion rampant argent, holding between the paws a ducal coronet or.

Motto.—Vincit veritas.

Arms (HARRISON, of Stafford County, Virginia).—Azure three demi-lions rampant or.

Crest.—A demi-lion rampant argent, holding a laurel branch vert.

Arms (FOWKE).—Vert a fleur-de-lis argent.

Crest.—A dexter arm embowed vested vert, cuffed argent; in the hand ppr an arrow or, feathered of the second, pheoned azure.

Motto.—Arma tuentur pacem.

Arms (MARSHALL of Ireland).—Gules, a cross between four (4) crescents argent.

Cabell

JAMES ALSTON CABELL, of "Point of York," Columbia, Virginia; *m.* 12th June, 1895, Ethel Hoyt SCOTT, of New York City, dau. of James and Antoinette (TAMS) SCOTT of New York City.

ISSUE

I. James Alston, *b.* 17th February, 1900, *d.* in infancy.
II. Ethel Alston.
III. Katherine Hamilton.
IV. Dorothy Temple.
V. Margery Wade, *d.* in infancy.

JAMES ALSTON CABELL, Lawyer, graduate of Richmond College and University of Virginia; Professor of Chemistry, Central University of Kentucky, 1876–1878; admitted to bar, 1879; elected to Richmond City Council, 1884; Member of Virginia Legislature, 1893–1897; Chairman of Virginia Commission on Uniformity of Legislation in United States, 1893-1902; took prominent part in framing Negotiable Instruments Act; Chairman of Commission on Uniform Insurance Legislation; Member of State Board Charities and Corrections, 1908–1912; revived Virginia Society of the Cincinnati and was first President of temporary organization 1889–1896; President of Virginia Society Sons of the Revolution, 1895–1901; Commander, Virginia Commandery Military Order Foreign Wars since 1899; Member of Executive Board of Virginia Historical Society, 1889–1893; Member of Advisory Board of Society for the Preservation of Virginia Antiquities; Governor of Society of Colonial Wars, Virginia, since 1913; President of Richmond Athletic Club, 1881–1887; Chairman of Jurisprudence Committee of Grand Lodge of Virginia and Editor of *Virginia Masonic Journal*, 1907–1910; elected Grand Master of Masons, 10th February, 1916; editor of the *Virginia University Magazine* when at the University; has written numerous scientific, historical and biographical papers.

Lineage

RICHARD CABELL of Cayford and Frome, in the County of Somerset, England; *b.* circa 1480; has various deeds from 1510 to 1528; *d.* in 1530, leaving issue.

RICHARD CABELL of Cayford and Frome; eldest son and heir; deeds from 1545 to 1557; buried 2d May, 1561; *m.* Thomasin (surname unknown) and had issue.

RICHARD CABELL of Cayford and Frome; eldest son and heir; in 1562 elected Member of Parliament for the Borough of Heytesbury in Wiltshire, which he represented from 11th January, 1563-1564 to 2d January, 1567-1568, and again 2d

April to 29th May, 1571; removed, circa 1575, to the Manor House of Brooke, in the Parish of Buckfastleigh, in the County of Devon, and *d.* 17th February, 1612–6; 3; Inq. p.m. 11 Jas., pt. 1, No. 37; will dated 28th August, 1610; probated 5th May, 1613; P. P. C., Capell 39; *m.* circa 1580, Susannah PETER, dau. of John PETER of Buckfastleigh, she *d.* 7th August 1597.

ISSUE

    I. RICHARD, *b.* 1582, of whom later.
    II. Samuel, *d.s.p.*, will dated 30th March, 1638, probated 6th June, 1638, P. P. C., Barrington 54.
    III. Bridget, *m.* Thomas MARTIN, of Totnes.
    IV. Susan, *m.* Thomas TURGIS, of Buckfastleigh.
    V. Anne, *m.* John HELE of Brooke.

RICHARD CABELL of Brooke, in the Parish of Buckfastleigh, in the County of Devon; *b.* 1582; *d.* 24th August, 1655; matriculated at Exeter College, Oxford, 12th December, 1600, aged eighteen; a student of the Middle Temple, 1604; held the Manor of Maynebow in Warnecombe, Somerset, in 1618; in 1620 gave in the pedigree of his family at the Heralds' Visitation of Devonshire; in 1649 compounded for his estates in the sum of £1430; *m.* Mary PRESTWOOD, dau. of George PRESTWOOD of Whetcombe Parish of North Huish, Devon, marriage license 4th December, 1618, Exeter.

ISSUE

    I. Richard, *b.* 1620; *d.* 1677; *m.* Elizabeth FOWELL; will dated 6th May, 1671; probated 9th March, 1677–1678, P. P. C., Eure 71.
    II. Samuel, *bapt.* 4th May, 1623; *d.s.p.* April, 1699; will dated 16th March 1698–1699; probated 22d April, 1699, P. P. C., Pett 55.
    III. George, *bapt.* 15th September, 1628; buried 8th March, 1631–1632.
    IV. WILLIAM, *bapt.* 4th January, 1630–1631, of whom later.
    V. John, *bapt.* 27th December, 1636, living in 1671.

WILLIAM CABELL, of "Bugley," *b.* 1630; *d.* September, 1704; removed, circa 1660, from Buckfastleigh to Bugley, near Warminster in the County of Wilts, and was buried at Warminster 4th September, 1704; *m.*, circa 1650, Mary (surname unknown) who survived him, and was buried at Warminster 5th December, 1704; her will, dated 29th September, 1704, recorded in the Court of the Archdeacon of Sarum.

ISSUE

    I. William, *d.* unmarried, December, 1734.
    II. Anthony, twice married but had no issue.
    III. Christopher, *bapt.* at Warminster 21st February, 1664–1665.
    IV. NICHOLAS, *bapt.* 29th May, 1667, of whom later.
    V. Elizabeth, *m.* ——— YEATMAN, and *d.* February, 1739–1740.

NICHOLAS CABELL of Warminster, b. May, 1667; d. 30th July, 1730; will dated 9th July, 1730; probated in the Court of the Archdeacon of Sarum 26th October, 1730; m. at Frome-Selwood, 15th November, 1697, Rachel HOOPER, dau. of George HOOPER, who survived him, and was buried 27th October, 1737.

ISSUE

I. William, b. 24th August, 1698; d. 8th December, 1698.
II. WILLIAM, b. 9th March, 1699–1700, of whom later.
III. Joanna, b. 6th February, 1702–1703; d. 2d July, 1728.
IV. Mary, b. 21st December, 1704; m. Christopher CARTER.
V. Joseph, b. 14th March, 1706–1707; d. 10th July, 1762.
VI. Elizabeth, b. 5th July, 1709; d. 12th October, 1709.
VII. Sarah, b. 26th December, 1710; buried 9th August, 1715.
VIII. Elizabeth, b. 30th January, 1712–1713; d. 1741; m. ——— DAVIS.
IX. Sarah, b. 6th August, 1715.

WILLIAM CABELL of "Warminster," in Virginia; b. 9th March, 1699–1700; d. 12th April, 1774; was graduated from the London Royal College of Surgery and Medicine, and served as a Surgeon in the English Navy; immigrated to Virginia in 1726 and settled in that portion of Henrico County which was sub-divided into Goochland in 1728; into Albemarle in 1745, and into Amherst in 1761 (and is now Nelson County); Under-Sheriff of Henrico, 1726; County Coroner for Goochland, 1729; Justice of the Peace for Goochland 1728–1745; served in the Indian Wars against the Tuscaroras or Monican Indians in 1730, and was Captain in the Goochland Militia in and before 1745; settled and christened the present "Warminster," Virginia, in 1742; Justice of the Peace for Albemarle, 1745–1761; Burgess for Albemarle for the sessions beginning 25th March, 1756; 20th September, 1756; 30th April, 1757, and 30th March, 1758; a resident of Amherst after 1761, and Burgess for Amherst for the sessions beginning 3d November, 1761; 14th January, 1762; 30th March, 1762; 2d November, 1762, 19th May, 1763; 12th January, 1764, 1st May, 1765, and October, 1765; m. (firstly) in 1726, Elizabeth BURKS, b. in 1705, d. 21st September, 1756, dau. of Samuel and Mary (DAVIS) BURKS of Hanover County, Virginia; m. (secondly) 30th Sepember, 1762, Margaret MEREDITH, by whom he had no issue.

ISSUE BY FIRST MARRIAGE

I. Mary, b. 13th February, 1727–1728; m. William HORSLEY, and had issue.
II. William, of Union Hill, b. 13th March, 1730; d. 23d March, 1798; Member of the House of Burgesses from Albemarle, 1757–1761; the first presiding Justice for the United States after the Declaration of Independence; chosen first Senator from the Eighth District and Member of Committee that prepared "the Declaration of Rights;" m. 1756, Margaret JORDAN, dau. of Col. Samuel and ——— JORDAN.

III. Joseph, *b.* 19th September, 1732; *d.* 1st March, 1798; Burgess from Buckingham, 1768–1771; Burgess from Amherst, 1774, Member of the Convention from Amherst, 1775–1776; Representative from Buckingham in the House of Delegates, 1780–1781; commanded the Buckingham County Militia during the Revolutionary War; *m.* 1752, Mary HOPKINS, *d.* 12th July, 1811, dau. of Dr. Arthur HOPKINS, left issue.

IV. John (Colonel) *b.* circa 1740; *d.* May, 1815; Sheriff of Buckingham County, 1774; Delegate from Buckingham County to the Convention, 1776; *m.* (firstly) 20th May, 1762, Paulina JORDAN, *d.* 31st July, 1781, dau. of Col. Samuel JORDAN and by her had issue; *m.* (secondly) 19th July, 1787, Elizabeth Brierton JONES, who *d.s.p.* 16th October, 1802.

V. George, *d.* young.

VI. NICHOLAS, *b.* 29th October, 1750, of whom later.

NICHOLAS CABELL of "Liberty Hall," Nelson County, Virginia, *b.* 29th October, 1750; *d.* 18th August, 1803; graduate of the College of William and Mary, 1771; Captain of the Amherst Minute Men, 1775; ordered out in May, 1776, and served till October, 1776, around Westham and Jamestown; Lieutenant-Colonel of Amherst Volunteers, 25th June, 1778; Colonel, September, 1780; served under LAFAYETTE in Virginia, April to November, 1781; taking part in siege at Yorktown; represented his county in the House of Delegates, 1783–1785; State Senator, 1785–1803; Member of the State Senate in the General Assembly, 1798; *m.* 16th April, 1772, Hannah CARRINGTON, *b.* 28th March, 1751, *d.* 7th August, 1817, dau. of Col. George and Anne (MAYO) CARRINGTON.

ISSUE

I. WILLIAM H., *b.* 16th December, 1772, of whom later.

II. George, *b.* 5th October, 1774; *m.* (firstly) 15th January, 1798, Susanna WYATT, *d.* July, 1817, and by her had issue; *m.* (secondly) Eliza Fitzhugh MAY, who *d.s.p.* 20th January, 1859.

III. Elizabeth, *b.* 5th May, 1776; *d.* 28th November, 1802; *m.* 11th July, 1793, Dr. William B. HARE; left issue.

IV. Joseph Carrington, *b.* 26th December, 1778; *d.* 5th February, 1856; *m.* 1st January, 1807, Mary Walker CARTER, dau. of George CARTER of Lancaster.

V. Nicholas, *b.* 24th December, 1780; *d.* 25th June, 1809; *m.* 20th October, 1802, Margaret Read VENABLE, *d.* 31st May, 1857, dau. of Samuel Woodson VENABLE, and by her had issue.

VI. Mary Anne, *b.* 2d January, 1783; *d.* 6th February, 1850; *m.* 3d May, 1804, Capt. Benjamin CARRINGTON, and left issue.

VII. Mayo Carrington, *b.* 25th August, 1784; *d.* in infancy.

VIII. Hannah, *b.* 27th March, 1786; *d.* 7th September, 1794.

IX. Heningham, *b.* 16th November, 1787; *d.* young.

X. Paul C., *b.* 8th May, 1791; *d.* in infancy.

Hon. William H. Cabell, of "Montevideo", *b.* at Boston Hill, Cumberland County, Virginia, 16th December, 1772; *d.* 12th January, 1853; a graduate of the College of William and Mary, 1793; Member of the Assembly, 1796–1798 and 1802–1805; Governor of Virginia from 1st December, 1805, to 1st December, 1808; Judge of the General Court, 1808–1811; Judge of Supreme Court of Appeals, 1811–1851, and the President of Supreme Court of Appeals, 1842–1851; *m.* (firstly) 9th April, 1795, Elizabeth Cabell, who *d.* 5th November, 1801, dau. of William and Margaret (Jordan) Cabell; *m.* (secondly) 11th March, 1805, Agnes Sarah Bell Gamble, *b.* 22d August, 1783, *d.* 15th February, 1863, dau. of Col. Robert and Catharine (Grattan) Gamble of Augusta County, Virginia, and, after 1790, of Richmond, Virginia.

ISSUE BY FIRST MARRIAGE

I. Nicholas Carrington, *b.* 9th February, 1796; *d.* unmarried 13th October, 1821.
II. Louisa Elizabeth, *b.* 19th February, 1798; *d.* 8th January, 1865; *m.* 23d May, 1820, Henry Carrington of Charlotte, *d.* 5th December, 1867; left issue.
III. Abraham Joseph, *b.* 24th April, 1800; *d.* October, 1831.

ISSUE BY SECOND MARRIAGE

I. Catharine Ann, *b.* 12th August, 1806; *d.* 12th October, 1807.
II. Emma Catharine, *b.* 10th March, 1808; *m.* 9th May, 1826, Paul S. Carrington, who *d.* 9th July, 1866; leaving issue.
III. Robert Gamble, of Richmond, Virginia; *b.* 9th December, 1809; *d.* 16th November, 1889; a graduate of the College of William and Mary, 1829; in Medicine of the University of Virginia, 1833, and of the College of Philadelphia; for years a practicing physician and Member of the Board of Aldermen and Common Council of Richmond, Virginia; *m.* 19th January, 1843, Margaret Sophia Caskie, *b.* 22d September, 1823, *d.* 3d July, 1867, dau. of James and Elizabeth (Pincham) Caskie, of Stewarton, Scotland.

ISSUE

1. James Caskie, *b.* 9th February, 1844; Nannie Enders; no issue.
2. William H., *b.* 13th November, 1845; killed at battle of Newmarket, 15th May, 1864.
3. Robert Gamble, *b.* 16th July, 1847; *m.* 14th November, 1877, Anne Harris Branch, *b.* 31st December, 1859, *d.* 14th February, 1915, dau. of James Read and Martha Louise (Patteson) Branch of Richmond, Virginia.
4. Edward Carrington, *b.* 4th January, 1850; *d.* 13th June, 1883; *m.* Isa Carrington; no issue.
5. Elizabeth Caskie, *b.* 1st May, 1851; *m.* Albert Ritchie.

COLONIAL FAMILIES OF THE UNITED STATES 147

ISSUE

1[1]. Albert Cabell RITCHIE, b. 29th August, 1876.

6. Arthur Grattan, b. 12th May, 1853; d. unmarried 19th June, 1906.
7. Agnes Bell, b. 18th November, 1856; m. John D. LOTTIER; no issue.
8. Henry Landon, b. 3d November, 1858; m. 27th April, 1897, Adah WYMOND.

ISSUE

1[1]. William Wymond, b. 2d April, 1898.
2[1]. Henry Landon, b. 23d July, 1903.
3[1]. Robert Gamble, b. 21st April, 1905.

9. Margaret Constance, b. 2d December, 1862; m. Boykin WRIGHT.

ISSUE

1[1]. Marguerite Cabell WRIGHT, b. 7th November, 1889; m. 25th November, 1914, James Frayer HILLMAN.
2[1]. Boykin Cabell WRIGHT, b. 20th September, 1891.
3[1]. Constance Cabell WRIGHT, b. 9th October, 1901.

IV. Elizabeth Hannah, b. 9th September, 1811; d.s.p., 7th November, 1892; m. 6th June, 1850, Judge William DANIEL, of Lynchburg, Virginia.
V. William Wirt, b. 1st November, 1813; d. unmarried.
VI. Edward Carrington, b. 5th February, 1816; one of the Delegates from Jefferson County to the Constitutional Convention, 1838; a Member of the United States House of Representatives, 1846; m. 5th November, 1850, Anna Maria WILCOX, dau. of Dr. Daniel P. WILCOX.

ISSUE

1. Ashley, b. 27th December, 1853; m. 19th October, 1881, Margaret HODGES, dau. of Dr. Aaron STRETCH, of Nashville, Tennessee; has issue.
2. William H., b. 29th December, 1857; d. 1889.
3. Florida, b. 17th September, 1857; d. 16th March, 1858.
4. Agnes Bell, b. 13th June, 1860; d. 10th November, 1860.
5. Elizabeth Crittenden, b. 13th June, 1860; m. 20th April, 1881, Benjamin F. GRAY, of St. Louis; has issue.
6. J. J. Crittenden, b. 10th January, 1863; d. 24th February, 1872.
7. Mary Hope, b. 25th January, 1867.

VII. John Grattan, *b.* 17th June, 1817; Lieutenant-Colonel of Cavalry in Confederate States Army; *m.* (firstly) 21st February, 1844, Sarah Marshall TANKERSLEY, of Richmond, who *d.* 15th March, 1855, leaving issue; *m.* (secondly) 9th June, 1869, Agnes C. COLES, dau. of Hon. Walter C. COLES, of Pittsylvania County, Virginia.

ISSUE

1. Walter Coles, *b.* 13th October, 1874.
2. Florence, *b.* 14th December, 1878.

VIII. HENRY COALTER, *b.* 14th November, 1820, of whom later.

HENRY COALTER CABELL, of Richmond, Virginia; *b.* 14th February, 1820; *d.* 31st January, 1889; Assistant Attorney General; Lieutenant-Colonel 1st Virginia Regiment of Artillery, Confederate States Army, 1861; Colonel, 1862; General, 1865; *m.* 1st May, 1850, Jane C. ALSTON, only child of Maj. James and Catherine (HAMILTON) ALSTON, of Abbeville, South Carolina.

ISSUE

I. JAMES ALSTON, the subject of this memoir.
II. Katherine Hamilton, *b.* Richmond, Virginia; Secretary of Female Humane Association of the City of Richmond; President since 1897 of the Colonial Dames of America in the State of Virginia; for two years Vice-President of National Society Colonial Dames of America, and President of that Society for twelve years, declining further reëlection at the National Council of 1914; was elected Honorary President of the National Society, and the Kate Cabell Cox Scholarship in American history was founded in her honor at the University of Virginia; President for three terms of the Woman's Club of Richmond; Vice President of Association for Preservation of Virginia Antiquities; Honorary President of Order of the Crown in America; Regent for South Carolina of the Confederate Memorial Literary Society; Chairman for Virginia of the Order of Descendants of Colonial Governors; Member and a former Vice-President of the George WASHINGTON Memorial Association; Member of First Families of Virginia, 1607-1620; Daughters of American Revolution; United Daughters of the Confederacy; Art Club, and Country Club of Richmond; Club of Colonial Dames, Washington, D. C., Richmond Society of the Archaeological Institute of America; Red Cross and many charitable and philanthropic Associations; Chairman for Richmond Second Liberty Loan; Vice-Chairman Woman's Committee, Council of National Defense, Virginia Division; *m.* (firstly) 1st February, 1882, Maj. Herbert Augustine CLAIBORNE, C.S.A., of Richmond, Virginia, lawyer, President Mutual Insurance Society of Virginia; *m.*

COLONIAL FAMILIES OF THE UNITED STATES 149

(secondly) 21st June, 1905, William Ruffin Cox, General Army Northern Virginia, of Penelo, North Carolina, Attorney-General, Judge of Superior Court, Member of Congress and Secretary of United States Senate.

ISSUE BY FIRST MARRIAGE

1. Jeanie Alston CLAIBORNE, *d.* young.
2. Herbert Augustine CLAIBORNE, *b.* 1886, Richmond, Virginia; graduated University of Virginia, Civil Engineer, 1908; for four years Engineer under the Isthmian Canal Commission in Panama, employed on Construction of Locks and Fortifications; practised profession for six years in Richmond, as member of Engineering and Contracting firm of SAVILLE and CLAIBORNE, recently employed as Engineers for the Government in the construction of Camp Lee, and Engineers for the Aviation Supply Depot, Richmond, Virginia; Lieutenant in the Signal Reserve Corps, Aviation Section; Member of American Society Civil Engineers; American Water Works Association; Member Society of the Cincinnati in the State of Virginia; Member Westmoreland Club.
3. Hamilton Cabell CLAIBORNE, *b.* 1889, Richmond, Virginia; educated at University of Virginia and George Washington University; in insurance business, Richmond, Virginia; entered United States Consular Service, 1915; served in Bradford, England, and Swansea, Wales, now (1918) serving in London; Member Commonwealth Club.

III. Henry Coalter, born in Richmond, Virginia, 11th December, 1858, graduated at United States Military Academy, West Point, 1883; Aide de Camp to Gen. John GIBBON, 1890; Military Secretary to the Governor-General and Captain and Adjutant-General in the Philippine Islands, Adjutant General of the 1st Division, 8th Army Corps and of General Loyd Wheaton's various commands, 1898–1899; Major, 1906; served on the General Staff of the Army, 1907–1911; Lieutenant Colonel, January, 1912; retired May, 1912; placed on active duty June, 1917; promoted Colonel and Adjutant-General January, 1918; Member of the Society of the Cincinnati in the State of Virginia and Sons of the American Revolution; *m.* 14th February, 1894, Emily Corbett FAILING, dau. of Henry and Emily (CORBETT) FAILING.

ISSUE

1. Henry Failing, *b.* 26th November, 1895; graduated at University of Virginia, B.A., 1917; appointed Second-Lieutenant from Fort Myer Training Camp, 1917; assigned to the 318th Infantry, 80th Division; promoted to 1st Lieutenant, January, 1918; served in the British

trenches in the Saint Mihiel offensive and in the Meuse-Argonne offensive; commanded Co. G-318 Infantry during all this service until incapacitated by wounds, in October, 1918; promoted Captain, served as Aid-de-Camp to the Commanding General 90th Division in the army of occupation of Germany until the return of his Division to the United States.

IV. Julian Mayo, *b.* 21st December, 1860; educated at the University of Virginia and graduated in Medicine in 1886; commissioned First Lieutenant and Assistant Surgeon, United States Army, April, 1887; served in South Dakota through the Sioux Campaign of 1890-1891; went to the Philippine Islands with Gen. Westley MERRITT in June, 1898, and served as Assistant to the Chief Surgeon, 8th Army Corps 1898-1899; went to South Africa with Lady Randolph CHURCHILL as Chief Surgeon Hospital ship *Maine* in 1889; was given the Natal Service (Boer War) Medal by the British Government; on active duty with the Army in Vera Cruz, Mexico from June to November, 1914; now (1918) on duty at Fort Myer, Virginia; is an hereditary member of the Society of the Cincinnati in the State of Virginia; was presented to Queen Victoria in Windsor Castle, December, 1899.

V. Clarence, *b.* in Richmond, Virginia; educated at University of Virginia and Harvard University; student and scholar; has spent most of his life in England and France.

VI. Alfred, *d.* in infancy.

Arms.—Sable, a horse upright argent, bitted and bridled or.
Crest.—An arm in armour embowed grasping a sword, all ppr.
Motto.—Impavide.
Residence.—"Point of Fork," Columbia, Virginia.
Clubs.—Richmond Athletic, Westmoreland, Albemarle, Powhatan Lakeside and Country.
Societies.—Colonial Wars, Cincinnati, Sons of the American Revolution, Military Order of Foreign Wars, Virginia Historical Society, Society for Preservation of Virginia Antiquities, American Historical Association, American Bar Association, Virginia State Bar Association.

Champlin

JOHN DENISON CHAMPLIN, III, of Kensington, Great Neck, Long Island, New York; *b.* 23d July, 1875, at Litchfield, Connecticut; *m.* 8th December, 1915, in New York City, Margery Howard BRIDGE, *b.* 29th September, 1886, dau. of James Howard BRIDGE of 1 West 67th Street, New York City, *b.* 8th May, 1862, in Manchester, Lancashire, England, *m.* Mary Ellen TAYLOR, *b.* 28th September, 1867, at Richmond, Natal, South Africa, *d.s.p.* 15th January, 1898.

JOHN DENISON CHAMPLIN, Jr., or III, was educated at Yale University, Sheffield Scientific School, Class of 1897; Manager Ling Asbestos Company mines, Province of Quebec, 1910; now with Fahnestock Electric Company, Long Island City.

Lineage

GEOFFREY CHAMPLIN settled in Aquidneck, now Rhode Island in 1638; he settled first at Pocasset (Portsmouth) on the north end of the Island, but removed the next year to Newport, at the south end; was admitted as an inhabitant of the Island, 24th November, 1638; and a Freeman, 14th September, 1640; in 1661 he removed with many others, to Misquamacut, (Westerly) in the Narragansett country, but returned to Newport in 1675, during King Philip's War and probably *d.* there; *m.* probably in Newport prior to 1650, but his wife's name has not been preserved.

ISSUE

I. Jeffrey, *b.* circa 1650; *d.* 1715 in Kingstown, Rhode Island; he was ancestor of Commodore Stephen CHAMPLIN, U.S.N., and of Dr. James Tift CHAMPLIN, President of Colby University.
II. WILLIAM, *b.* 1654, of whom later.
III. Christopher, *b.* 1656; *d.* 2d April, 1732; was the ancestor of George CHAMPLIN. Member of the Continental Congress and of Christopher Grant CHAMPLIN, United States Senator of Rhode Island in 1809.

WILLIAM CHAMPLIN, *b.* 1654 at Newport, Rhode Island; *d.* 1st December, 1715, at Westerly, Rhode Island; volunteered in 1675 and served in several campaigns both in the Narragansett and elsewhere; probably took part in the Great Swamp fight December, 1675, as he was one of the 185 volunteers who received in 1695 from the General Court of Connecticut for services in the War, the grant of six square miles, comprised in the present town of Voluntown; admitted Freeman at Westerly, 17th October, 1679; in 1684-1685, Member of the Town Council; in

1690 he was called Captain and was chosen one of the Deputies to represent Westerly in the First General Assembly summoned after Andros' deposition; *m.* at Westerly, Rhode Island, 1674, Mary BABCOCK, *d.* spring of 1747, dau. of Captain James and Sarah BABCOCK of Westerly.

ISSUE

I. Mary, *b.* 1675; *m.* in 1700, John BABCOCK, son of John and Mary (LAWTON) BABCOCK.
II. WILLIAM, *b.* 1677, of whom later.
III. Ann, *b.* 1678–1679; *m.* 19th January, 1698–1699, Samuel CLARKE, son of Joseph and Bethiah (HUBBARD) CLARKE.

WILLIAM CHAMPLIN, II, of Westerly, Rhode Island, *b.* circa 1677, at Newport, Rhode Island; *d.* 1746–1747, at Westerly; represented the town in the General Assembly in 1728, 1731, and 1732; was a large landholder; his will is dated 3d August, 1746; *m.* Mary CLARKE, *b.* 27th December, 1680, in Westerly, *d.* there 1760, gd. dau. of Joseph CLARKE of Westhorpe, Suffolk, England, and gd. niece of Dr. John CLARKE, one of the principal founders of Rhode Island.

ISSUE

I. WILLIAM, *b.* 31st May, 1702, of whom later.
II. Jeffrey, *b.* 6th March, 1704; *m.* 1724, Mary MAXON, dau. of Joseph and Tacy (BURDICK) MAXON.
III. Joseph, *b.* circa 1706; *m.* 1730, Deborah BURDICK, dau. of Samuel and Mary BURDICK.
IV. Samuel, *b.* circa 1708; *m.* 1735 Prudence THOMPSON, dau. of Capt. Isaac and Mary (HOLMES) THOMPSON, sister of Bridget THOMPSON.
V. Joshua, *b.* circa 1710; *m.* 11th June, 1730, Bridget THOMPSON.
VI. James, *b.* circa 1712; *m.* 15th January, 1734–1735, Prudence HALLAM, dau. of Amos and Phoebe (GREENMAN) HALLAM.
VI. Susanna, *b.* circa 1714; *m.* 1st November, 1742, Samuel STANTON, son of Samuel and Lois (COBB) STANTON.

WILLIAM CHAMPLIN, III, of Westerly, Rhode Island; *b.* there 31st May, 1702; *d.* there 14th April, 1774; in 1734–1736 was Ensign of the 1st Company of Westerly Infantry; representative from Westerly in the General Assembly in 1741–1742; *m.* 1st November, 1721, Sarah THOMPSON, *b.* there 3d March, 1703, dau. of Capt. Isaac and Mary (HOLMES) THOMPSON of Westerly.

ISSUE

I. Mary, *b.* 13th July, 1722; *m.* 9th August, 1738, Joseph STANTON, son of Joseph and Esther (GATHYP) STANTON.
II. Samuel, *b.* 6th October, 1724; *m.* 1744, Hannah GARDNER, dau. of Henry GARDNER.

III. Jeffrey, *b*. 30th September, 1726; *d*. young.
IV. Ann, *b*. 15th January, 1729; *m*. 1746, Joseph PENDLETON, son of Joseph and Sarah (WORDEN) PENDLETON.
V. WILLIAM, *b*. 14th August, 1731, of whom later.
VI. John, *b*. 30th September, 1733; *m*. (name unknown).
VII. Sarah, *b*. 5th March, 1735; *m*. 16th June, 1751, Sylvester PENDLETON, son of Joseph and Sarah (WORDEN) PENDLETON.
VIII. Oliver, *b*. 21st August, 1737; *d*. unmarried, 15th April, 1791.
IX. Anstis, *b*. 8th October, 1739; *m*. 1758, John DUNBAR.
X. Rowland, *b*. 8th January, 1741-1742; *m*. 21st December, 1763, Hannah STETSON.
XI. Eunice, *b*. 15th February, 1744; *m*. 24th August, 1764, Daniel LARKIN.

WILLIAM CHAMPLIN, IV, of Westerly, Rhode Island; *b*. there 14th August, 1731; *d*. there 17th October, 1798; in 1768 was Lieutenant of the 2d Company of Westerly Infantry and in 1776 was Captain of the 4th Company, 1st Newport County Regiment; was an ardent patriot durng the Revolutionary War; *m*. at Westerly, Rhode Island, Sarah PENDLETON, *b*. there 7th August, 1734, *d*. there 24th April, 1744, dau. of Joseph and Sarah (WORDEN) PENDLETON.

ISSUE

I. WILLIAM, V, *b*. 13th August, 1752, of whom later.
II. Anne, *b*. 19th May, 1754; *m*. 17th August, 1777, Dr. Isaac (surname not given), son of Maj. Edward ———.
III. Lucy, *b*. 17th May, 1756; *m*. 1783, Arnold CLARKE, son of Rev. Joshua and Hannah (COTTRELL) CLARKE.
IV. Deborah, *b*. 12th April, 1758; *m*. 21st November, 1779, Fones GREENE, son of Samuel and Elizabeth (MARSHALL) GREENE.
V. Pamelia, *b*. 5th June, 1760; *d*. unmarried, 8th November, 1809.
VI. Adam, *b*. 4th July, 1762; *m*. 21st March, 1793, Henrietta COGGSHALL.
VII. Lois, *b*. 27th July, 1764; *d*. unmarried, 22d October, 1855.
VIII. Sarah, *b*. 1st August, 1766; *m*. 17th May, 1795, Stephen WILCOX.
IX. Eunice, *b*. 18th September, 1768; *m*. 4th December, 1800, Thomas PARKE.
X. Elizabeth, *b*. 24th December, 1769; *m*. 2d April, 1796, William TILLINGHAST.
XI. Phoebe, *b*. 1st, 1772; *d*. unmarried, 22d August, 1791.
XII. Joseph, *b*. 7th October, 1774; *m*. Jane CARR.
XIII. Mary, *b*. 23d October, 1776; *d*. unmarried February, 1747.
XIV. Oliver, *b*. 6th June, 1778; *m*. Eunice Thruston MELVILLE.

WILLIAM CHAMPLIN, V, of Westerly, Rhode Island; *b*. there 13th August, 1752; *d*. there 31st August, 1803; lived in Newport until 1795, when he removed to South

Kingston; *m.* (firstly) 1780, Elizabeth WELLS, *b.* 14th January, 1758, at Hopkinton, Rhode Island, *d.* 1785–1786 at Newport, Rhode Island, dau. of James and Ruth (HANNAH) WELLS; *m.* (secondly) Margaret DREW, *d.* 28th September, 1830, dau. of Capt. James DREW.

ISSUE BY FIRST MARRIAGE

I. ISAAC, *b.* 20th November, 1781, of whom later.
II. James Wells, *b.* 20th March, 1784; lost at sea, 1810.

ISSUE BY SECOND MARRIAGE

I. Elizabeth, *b.* 4th October, 1787; *m.* 21st August, 1807, Col. Jedediah KNIGHT.
II. Margaret, *b.* 2d November, 1791; *m.* 18th March, 1810, Barker NOYES, son of Col. Joseph and Barbara (WELLS) NOYES.
III. William, *b.* 15th April, 1794.
IV. Sarah, *b.* 27th June, 1796.
V. John Drew, *b.* August, 1800; *d.* 31st August, 1803.

ISAAC CHAMPLIN, of Stonington, Connecticut; *b.* 20th November, 1781, at Newport, Rhode Island; *d.* 8th August, 1861, at Stonington, Connecticut; was a prominent merchant in Westerly; in 1811–1813 he was Brigade Quartermaster of the 3d Brigade of Washington County and in 1814–1817, Brigade Inspector with rank of Major; Representative in the General Assembly, 1819–1820, 1824–1825 and in 1830; removed to Stonington and was Postmaster under Jackson's Administration; *m.* 8th November, 1807, Mary DENISON, *b.* 14th October, 1787, at Stonington, Connecticut, *d.* 30th January, 1862, at Stonington, dau. of John and Edith (BROWN) DENISON.

ISSUE

I. Mary, *b.* and *d.* 12th August, 1808.
II. William, *b.* 3d October, 1809; *d.* 28th October, 1809.
III. JOHN DENISON, *b.* 5th December, 1810, of whom later.
IV. Mary Elizabeth, *b.* 2d November, 1813; *d.* 9th November, 1813.

JOHN DENISON CHAMPLIN, I, of New York City, *b.* 5th December, 1810, at Westerly, Rhode Island; *d.* 12th September, 1892, in New York City; *m.* (firstly) 12th September, 1831, Sylvia BOSTWICK, *b.* 5th December, 1810, at New Milford, Connecticut, *d.* 5th March, 1856, at Lexington, Kentucky, dau. of Joel and Mary (STONE) BOSTWICK; *m.* (secondly) 5th April, 1857, in St. Louis, Missouri, Nora CRUSMAN, *b.* 8th April, 1830, *d.* 2d June, 1882, dau. of Gen. Cornelius CRUSMAN of Clarksville, Tennessee.

ISSUE BY FIRST MARRIAGE

I. JOHN DENISON, b. 29th January, 1834, of whom later.
II. William Belden, b. 15th July, 1836; m, Mary A. BULLITT.
III. Caroline Brown, b. 4th February, 1839; m. John Lansing MACAULAY.
IV. Edward Elmore, b. 13th June, 1841; m. Esther SMITH.
V. Isabella, b. 20th October, 1843; d. 20th February, 1844.

JOHN DENISON CHAMPLIN, II, of New York City, b. 29th January, 1834, in Stonington, Connecticut; d. 8th January, 1915, in New York City. Was a graduate of the famous class of Yale, 1856, which counted among its members Chief Justices BREWER and BROWN and the Hon. Chauncey M. DEPEW. He was a lineal descendant of Rev. James NOYES, who served on Yale's first Board of Trustees. His preparatory training was at the Hopkins' Grammar School in New Haven. In college he was a member of the Brothers in Unity, Delta Kappa, Alpha Sigma Phi, Psi Upsilon and the Ariel Boat Club. Just before his death he was elected member of Wolf's Head. After graduation he studied law with Gideon H. HOLLISTER, B.A. 1840, in Litchfield, Connecticut, being admitted to the Bar there in 1859. He soon removed to Milwaukee, Wisconsin, and later removed to New York City, as a member of the firm of HOLLISTER, CROSS and CHAMPLIN. In 1864 he became Associate Editor of the Bridgeport, Connecticut, *Evening Standard* and a year later established *The Sentinel* in Litchfield. In 1869 he sold out *The Sentinel* and removed to New York City. In 1873 he edited "Fox's Mission to Russia." In April of the same year was chosen a member of the Staff of Revisers of "Appleton's American Cyclopedia" and for the next two years was one of the corps of editors. In 1879 he brought out "Young Folks' Cyclopedia of Common Things," "Young Folks' Catechism of Common Things," 1880, 1896; "Young Folks' Cyclopedia of Persons and Places," 1880, and 1899, 1911; "Young Folks' Astronomy," 1881; "Young Folks' History of War for the Union," 1881. In 1884 he went as the guest of Mr. Andrew CARNEGIE on a coaching trip through England and Scotland. After this trip he published his "Chronicles of the Coach," 1886. In 1890 with Arthur E. BOSTWICK the "Young Folks' Cyclopedia of Games and Sports" was published. In 1901 he issued his "Young Folks' Cyclopedia of Literature and Art." In 1905 the "Young Folks' Cyclopedia of Natural History." Mr. CHAMPLIN was the Editor of the "Cyclopedia of Painters and Paintings," 4 volumes, 1886-1888; "Cyclopedia of Music and Musicians," 3 volumes, 1888-1890. During 1892-1894 he was Associate Editor of the "Standard Dictionary" and in 1893 he was one of the three writers, with Rossiter JOHNSON and George Cary EGGLESTON selected by the Authors Club to edit "Liber Scriptorum," an unique volume containing contributions by more than a hundred members of the club, among them some of the most distinguished literary men in America and Europe. He was also a contributor of copyrighted articles in the "Encyclopedia Brittanica," he contributed the chapter on "Music of Two Centuries" for the "Memorial History" of New York and for a number of years wrote the art articles in "Appleton's

Annual Cyclopedia." In 1910 he edited the "Speeches and Orations of the Hon· Chauncey M. Depew," 8 volumes. In 1912 he compiled "One Hundred Allied Families of the Seventeenth Century in England and New England" and the same year "Anne Hutchinson; Her Life, Her Ancestry and Her Descendants;" these last two remain unpublished. *The Forum* and *The Popular Science Monthly*, as well as numerous other periodicals received many contributions from his pen. He was a member of the Century Association of New York, The Authors Club, the Barnard Club, the New York Genealogical and Biographical Society, the New England Historical Society, the Newport Historical Society, the Litchfield Historical Society. In 1886 he was a candidate on the Democratic ticket for the Connecticut State Senate; *m.* 8th October, 1873, Franka E. COLVOCORESSES, dau. of the late Capt. George M. COLVOCORESSES, U. S. N., and sister of the present Admiral George P. COLVOCORESSES, who was executive officer of the *Concord* at the battle of Manila Bay and chosen by Admiral DEWEY, to be the Executive Officer of the *Olympia* immediately after the action.

Arms.—Ermine, on a chief indented azure, three griffin's heads erased or.
Crest.—A griffin's head erased argent, ducally gorged or.
Residence.—Kensington, Great Neck, Long Island, New York.
Clubs.—Barnard, Theta Xi.
Societies.—Mayflower, Colonial Wars, Sons of the Revolution, Veteran Corps of Artillery of the State of New York, War of 1812, New York Genealogical and Biographical Society.

Conant

WILLIAM ALBERT CONANT, of Brookline, Massachusetts; *b.* 19th December, 1865; unmarried; was educated at Boston Public Schools and Massachusetts Institute of Technology; is engaged in the manufacture of rubber goods, under the title of W. H. CONANT Gossamer Rubber Company.

Lineage

JOHN CONANT, of Devonshire, England; *b.* there circa 1520; was the father of

RICHARD CONANT, who *m.* in England, 4th February, 1578, Agnes CLARKE, dau. of John CLARKE; he was church warden and one of the leading citizens of East Burleigh.

ISSUE

I. Rev. John, D.D., was Rector of Lymington, afterward Rector of Thomas à Becket, Salsbury, County Wilts; he preached a sermon by invitation 26th July, 1623, before the Commons, for which he received a vote of thanks; it was published by order of the Commons; it was on the "Woe and Weale of God's People;" he was one of the Assembly of Divines that put forth the Westminster catechism.

II. ROGER of Salem, *bapt.* 9th April, 1592, of whom later.

HON. ROGER CONANT, of Salem, Massachusetts; *bapt.* 9th April, 1592, in East Burleigh, Devonshire, England; *d.* 19th November, 1679, in Salem, Massachusetts; resided for a time in London and came from there on the ship *Ann*, arriving at Plymouth on July, 1623, with wife Sarah and son Caleb; he moved to Hull, thence to Gloucester in 1625 and from there with his small Gloucester Company to Salem, in 1626; he built the first house in Salem; was planter; Member of the General Court, 1634; Foreman of the Jury of General Trials; Justice of the Quarterly Court in Salem; prominent in all public affairs; one of the original members of the first church in Salem, 1637; was Governor of the Colony at Cape Ann, 1625–1626; and Salem, 1627–1629; *m.* in England, 11th November, 1618, Sarah HORTON.

ISSUE

I. Sarah, *bapt.* in London, England, 19th September, 1619; buried there 30th October, 1620.
II. Caleb, *bapt.* same place, 27th May, 1622.
III. Lot, *b.* circa 1624, of whom later.

  IV. Roger, *b.* 1626, the first white child *b.* in Salem.
  V. Sarah, *b.* circa 1628.
  VI. Joshua.
  VII. Mary.
  VIII. Elizabeth.
  IX. Exercise, *bapt.* 24th December, 1637; *d.* 28th April, 1722; *m.* Sarah (surname not given).

LOT CONANT, of Beverly, Massachusetts; *b.* circa 1624, Gloucester, Massachusetts; *d.* 29th September, 1648; Selectman, 1662; *m.* Elizabeth WALTON, *bapt.* in England, 27th October, 1629, *d.* 29th September, 1674, dau. of Rev. William WALTON.

ISSUE

  I. NATHANIEL, *b.* 28th July, 1650, of whom below.
  II. John, *b.* 15th December, 1652; *d.* 3d September, 1724; served in King Philip's War; *m.* 7th May, 1678, Bethiah MANSFIELD.
  III. Lot, *b.* 16th February, 1657–1658.
  IV. Elizabeth, *b.* 13th May, 1660.
  V. Mary, *b.* 14th July, 1662.
  VI. Martha, *b.* 15th August, 1664.
  VII. Sarah (twin), *b.* 19th February, 1666–1667.
  VIII. William (twin), *b.* 19th February, 1666–1667; *d.* at Bridgewater; will probated, 1754; *m.* before 1694, Mary WOODBURY, of Beverly.
  IX. Roger, *b.* 10th March, 1668–1669.
  X. Rebecca, *b.* 31st January, 1670–1671.

NATHANIEL CONANT, of Bridgewater, Massachusetts, *b.* 28th July, 1650; *d.* 1732; *m.* Hannah MANSFIELD.

ISSUE AMONG OTHERS

  I. LOT, *b.* 27th March, 1689, of whom below.

LOT CONANT, of Bridgewater, Massachusetts; *b.* there 27th March, 1689; *d.* June, 1774; *m.* Debach LOWELL, *d.* 15th September, 1773.

ISSUE AMONG OTHERS

  I. PHINEAS, *b.* 4th February, 1726–1727, of whom below.

PHINEAS CONANT, of Bridgewater, Massachusetts; *b.* there 4th February, 1726–1727; *d.* there 1798; *m.* Joanna PRATT.

ISSUE AMONG OTHERS

1. PHINEAS, *b.* 25th January, 1759, of whom below.

PHINEAS CONANT, of Bridgewater, Massachusetts; *b.* 25th January, 1759; *m.* Joanna WASHBURN.

ISSUE AMONG OTHERS

1. IRA, *b.* 1792, of whom below.

IRA CONANT, of Bridgewater, Massachusetts; *b.* there 1792; *m.* Lucy LEONARD.

ISSUE AMONG OTHERS

1. WILLIAM HENRY, *b.* 13th March, 1834, of whom below.

WILLIAM HENRY CONANT, of Bridgewater, Massachusetts; *b.* there, 13th March, 1834; *m.* 2d May, 1859, in Attleboro, Massachusetts, Isadora SHEPARDSON, *b.* 13th January, 1839, at Waterbury, Connecticut, *d.* 28th March, 1912, in Brookline, Massachusetts, dau. of George W. and Juliette (RICHARDS) SHEPHARDSON.

ISSUE

1. WILLIAM ALBERT, *b.* 19th December, 1865, in Boston, Massachusetts, the subject of the memoir.

Arms.—Gules, ten billets or, four, three, two, one.
Crest.—On a mount vert, a stag proper, sustaining in his dexter foot, an inescutcheon of the arms.
Motto.—Conanti Dabitur.
Residence.—82 Sewall Avenue, Brookline, Massachusetts.
Clubs.—Boston Athletic.
Societies.—Colonial Wars, Sons of the American Revolution.

Cooch

JOSEPH WILKINS COOCH, of Cooch's Bridge and Newark, Delaware; *b.* 23d June 1840, at Cooch's Bridge, Delaware; *d.* 26th March, 1917, at Newark, Delaware; *m.* 12th April, 1871, at Pencader Presbyterian Church, Glasgow, Delaware, Mary Evarts WEBB, *b.* 18th June, 1849, dau. of Rev. Edward WEBB, *b.* 15th December, 1819, at Lowestoft, England, *d.* on train near Lincoln University, Pennsylvania, 6th April, 1898, *m.* 30th September, 1845, Nancy Allyn FOOTE, *b.* 13th July, 1825, at Cayuga, New York, *d.* 20th January, 1902, at Oxford, Pennsylvania.

ISSUE

I. Caroline, *b.* 15th March, 1872; *m.* 20th October, 1897, William Smith SCHOOLFIELD, son of William M. and Emily (BARNES) SCHOOLFIELD, *b.* 4th September, 1861.

II. Francis Allyn, *b.* 25th November, 1873; *m.* 12th April, 1899, Mary Josephine LOGAN, dau. of Rev. William H. and Elizabeth (GREEN) LOGAN.

ISSUE

1. Francis Allyn, Jr., *b.* 30th December, 1899.
2. Richard Logan, *b.* 14th September, 1902.
3. Joseph Wilkins, II, *b.* 27th November, 1909.

III. Levi Griffith, *b.* 12th January, 1875; *d.* 14th January, 1875.

IV. Edward Webb, *b.* 17th January, 1876; *m.* 9th June, 1906, Eleanor Bedford WILKINS, *b.* 28th August, 1883, dau. of Dr. Joseph and Mary C. (RAWLINGS) WILKINS.

ISSUE

I. Thomas, *b.* 11th October, 1916.
II. Edward Allyn, *d.* 22nd March, 1920.

V. Levi Hollingsworth, *b.* 28th April, 1877; *d.* 23d June, 1918; *m.* 7th December, 1903, Marian Lawrence CLARK, *b.* 10th October, 1875, dau. of William Henry and Mary (HAINES) CLARK.

ISSUE

1. Margaret Hollingsworth, *b.* 16th September, 1905.
2. Phoebe Lawrence, *b.* 23d November, 1913.

COLONIAL FAMILIES OF THE UNITED STATES

JOSEPH WILKINS COOCH, *b.* Cooch's Bridge, Delaware; educated at Newark Academy and Delaware College; Member of State Senate from New Castle County, Delaware, sessions of 1878–1879 and 1880–1881; Colonel on Staff of Gov. John P. COCHRAN, 20th January, 1875; Register of Wills for New Castle County, Delaware; appointed 4th June, 1891, Trustee of the Poor from Pencader Hundred during the construction of the New Castle County Hospital and State (then County) Insane Asylum at Farnhurst; Jury Commissioner of New Castle County, Delaware, 30th March, 1907; Federal Jury Commissioner, District of Delaware at time of death; Member and Foreman of Grand Juries; Trustee of Newark Academy; Member of Hiram Lodge No. 25, Ancient Free and Accepted Masons, of Newark; Grand Receiver, Grand Lodge Ancient Order of United Workmen of Delaware; President of Farmers Trust Company of Newark; Director of Equitable Trust Company of Wilmington.

Lineage

COL. THOMAS COOCH, Sr., came to America from Hatfield, Hertford County, England, in 1746, and purchased Homestead at Cooch's Bridge, Delaware, 20th January, 1746; *d.* 16th November, 1788; was, in 1756, Captain in the French and Indian Wars; October, 1769, Commissioned by Lieutenant Gov. John PEN; a Judge of the Court of Common Pleas for New Castle County, Delaware; was 20th March, 1775, Colonel of Regiment for Lower Division of New Castle County, Delaware; *m.* in England, Sarah LOWEN, who *d.* October, 1784, sister of Francis LOWEN of Middlesex, England.

ISSUE

I. THOMAS, JR., *b.* in England, of whom later.
II. Frances Elizabeth, *m.* (firstly) John ARMITAGE; *m.* (secondly) John SIMONTON.

THOMAS COOCH, JR., of Cooch's Bridge; *b.* in England; *d.* February, 1785; served in Col. Samuel PATTERSON's Regiment, in the Revolution, of New Castle County, Delaware; *m.* (firstly) Sarah GRIFFITH, dau. of John and Jane RHYDDARCH, widow of Morgan ap RHYDDARCH, March, 1685–1686, GRIFFITH, and gd. dau. of John and Sarah GRIFFITH, immigrants in 1701; *m.* (secondly) Sarah WELSH, of Philadelphia.

ISSUE BY FIRST MARRIAGE

I. WILLIAM, *b.* 5th June, 1752, of whom later.
II. Elizabeth, *m.* Solomon MAXWELL.

ISSUE BY SECOND MARRIAGE

I. Thomas, III, *m.* (firstly), Hannah (surname not given); *m.* (secondly) Isabella (surname not given).
II. Francis Lowen, *b.* 1770; *d.* 1854; *m.* Elizabeth MARIS.

WILLIAM COOCH, of Cooch's Bridge, Delaware; *b.* 5th June, 1762; *d.* 25th September, 1837; ran away and enlisted as a privateer shortly after the battle of Cooch's Bridge, 3d September, 1777; was captured and taken to England, where he remained a prisoner until after the close of the Revolutionary War; Member of Delaware House of Representatives from New Castle County, October, 1795, to October, 1801; State Senate, 1804; *m.* 25th November, 1789, Margaret HOLLINGSWORTH, *b.* 7th December, 1766, *d.* 4th September, 1833, dau. of Zebulon and Mary (EVANS) HOLLINGSWORTH, of Elkton, Maryland.

ISSUE

I. Zebulon Hollingsworth, *b.* 11th September, 1790; *d.* 18th December, 1870; *m.* Ann HEIDE.
II. Thomas, *b.* 22d February, 1794; *d.* 25th September, 1804.
III. William, *b.* 20th September, 1796; *d.* 31st May, 1869; *m.* Tamar MILLER.
IV. LEVI GRIFFITH, *b.* 17th February, 1803, of whom later.

LEVI GRIFFITH COOCH, of Cooch's Bridge, Delaware; *b.* there 17th February, 1803; *d.* there 7th February, 1869; was a member of a mounted body of citizens who met the Marquis DE LAFAYETTE at the Pennsylvania-Delaware States line on the occasion of his visit to the United States in October, 1824, and acted as one of his escort during his triumphant passage through Delaware; was member of Delaware House of Representatives from New Castle County, Delaware, November, 1846, and November, 1848; *m.* 3d April, 1838, Sarah Conant WILKINS, *b.* 17th September, 1812, *d.* 8th May, 1900, dau. of Joseph and Mary C. (BEDFORD) WILKINS, of Baltimore, Maryland.

ISSUE

I. JOSEPH WILKINS, *b.* 23d June, 1840, the subject of this memoir.
II. Helen, *b.* 16th August, 1842; *d.* 25th October, 1918; *m.* 11th March, 1874, Rev. George J. PORTER, son of ——— PORTER and ——— RAE.

ISSUE

1. George Frederick PORTER, *b.* 3d March, 1876.
2. Gilbert Brackett PORTER, *b.* 21st June, 1878.

III. William, *b.* 6th January, 1845; *d.* 27th August, 1919; *m.* 14th May, 1874, Annie M. CURTIS, dau. of Frederick Augustus and Harriette (HOOKER) CURTIS.

ISSUE

1. Harriette, *b.* 16th February, 1875.
2. Helen, *b.* 21st June, 1877.

3. Eliza B., *b.* 29th December, 1878.
4. Nina, *b.* 20th August, 1883.
5. Sara, *b.* 20th October, 1886.

IV. Frank, *b.* 31st August, 1847; *d.* 8th December, 1848.
V. Zebulon Hollingsworth, *b.* 11th September, 1849; *d.* 3d February, 1918; *m.* 18th March, 1886, Nettie E. Dix, dau. of George Lewis and Avis M. (Wightman) Dix.

ISSUE

1. Lester Wilkins, *b.* 28th August, 1888.
2. Eleanor B., *b.* 30th December, 1889.
3. Thomas P., *b.* 26th November, 1892.

VI. Mary Bedford, *b.* 25th November, 1852; *m.* 8th October, 1873, **Samuel M. Donnell**, son of Andrew and Rosa (Mathewson) Donnell.

Arms.—A barry of ten, or and azure.
Crest.—An eagle displayed gules.
Residence.—Cooches Bridge and Newark, Delaware.
Societies.—Colonial Wars, Historical Society of Delaware.

Courtenay

WILLIAM HOWARD COURTENAY, of Louisville, Kentucky, *b.* there 30th July, 1858; *m.* 27th April, 1893, Isabel Stevenson CLARK, *b.* in Louisville, Kentucky, 24th February, 1868, dau. of James CLARK, *b.* in Scotland, 28th June, 1830, *d.* 25th April, 1902, in Louisville, Kentucky, *m.* 26th September, 1865, in Beith, Scotland, Jessie LA NAUZE, *b.* in India, 18th January, 1837, *d.* 19th November, 1908, in Louisville, Kentucky, dau. of Capt. George and Christiana (PARRY) LA NAUZE.

ISSUE

I. Erskine Howard, *b.* 25th April, 1895, was graduated from Louisville Male High School, 1913; Civil Engineer Rensselaer Polytechnic Institute, 1917; after graduation, Field Engineer, THOMPSON and BINGER, Inc; Junior Mechanical Expert, War and Gas Investigation, Bureau of Mines, Washington, D. C.; Ensign United States Naval Reserve Force, February, 1918; Delta Kappa Epsilon Fraternity; Society of Colonial Wars; Louisville, Country Club, Delta Kappa Epsilon Club, New York.

II. James Clark, *b.* 14th January, 1897, was graduated from Louisville Male High School, 1914; Senior, 1918 class, Rensselaer Polytechnic Institute, member Department Civil Engineering; Quartermaster, second class United States Navy, with the United States Naval Aviation Forces in France, May, 1918; Delta Kappa Epsilon Fraternity; Louisville Country Club, Society of Colonial Wars.

WILLIAM HOWARD COURTENAY, Civil Engineer, Rensselaer Polytechnic Institute, 1879; American Society Civil Engineers; Director, American Railway Engineering Association; at one time Director Alumni Association Rensselaer Polytechnic Institute; for some years past, and at present time, Chief Engineer of Louisville and Nashville Railroad Company.

Lineage

The COURTENAYS are one of the most illustrious families of the English nobility, and have intermarried with not a few of the Royal houses. They took a prominent part in the Crusades; and have had in GIBBON a brilliant historian. The family of COURTENAY took its name from the town of Courtenai, near Paris, about the time surnames came first to be used in France, shortly before the Norman Conquest. Sir Reginald DE COURTENAY came to England with the Duke of Normandy, afterwards Henry II of England, and Eleanor, his wife, in the year 1151, and married Hawise D'ABRINCIS, daughter of Robert D'ABRINCIS, and was succeeded by his eldest son, Robert DE COURTENAY as Feudal Baron of Okehampton, from whom descended the long and famous family of COURTENAY, Earls of Devon. It is from this COURTENAY that the COURTENAYS of Newry, Ireland, came down through a most distinguished line of English ancestors.

ATHON, the son of the Châtelain de Château Reynard, who in 1000, fortified the town of Courtenai, about fifty-six miles south from Paris, was the founder of the COURTENAY family.

ISSUE

1. JOSCELINE DE COURTENAI, 1065, m. Isabel DE MONTLHERRY, dau. of Milo de MONTLHERRY.

ISSUE

1. MILO DE COURTENAI, brother of Josceline, first Count of Edessa; founded Fountainjean and died there 1127; m. Ermengarde, dau. of Reginald, Comte DE NEVERS, gd. dau. of King Robert of France.

ISSUE

1. SIR REGINALD DE COURTENAI, went to the Holy Land, and to England with Queen Eleanor, who m. Henry II, Duke of Normandy, 1151, d. at Ford Abbey 27th September, 1194; m. (secondly) Hawisa D'AYNCOURT, "Lady of Okehampton," d. 31st July, 1219, dau. of Robert D'ABRINCIS or D'AVRANCHES, who, in 1173, m. Matilda (d. 1224) dau. of Adelina, m. Randolph AVENELL; Adelina was dau. of Adelicia, interred at Ford Abbey in 1142, and William D'ABRINCIS, "Nobile Viro;" Adelicia was dau. of Albreda, niece of the Conquerer, dau. of Richard LE GOS, Comte D'AVRANCHES, and Baldwin DE SAP. DE MOLIS, or BRIONIS, one of the Conqueror's Generals at Hastings, 1066, made by the Conqueror Baron of Okehampton, also called D'EXETER, from Castle of Exeter which he built.

ISSUE

1. ROBERT DE COURTENAY, "Baron of Okehampton," sixth Earl of Devon, dispossessed by Henry III; d. 28th July, 1242; buried at Tiverton; m. Mary DE REDVERS, youngest dau. and heir of William DE REDVERS, alias "DE VERONA."

ISSUE

1. SIR JOHN DE COURTENAY, fourth Baron of Oakhampton; d. May, 1273; m. Isabel DE VERE, d. 11th August, 1300; dau. of John DE VERE, seventh Earl of Oxford, Great Chamberlin of England, b. circa 1210; d. December, 1263, he married after February, 1223, Hawise, only dau. of Saire DE QUINCEY.

ISSUE

1. Sir Hugh de Courtenay Knight Baron of Okehampton; *b.* 25th March, 1250; *d.* 27th February, 1291; *m.* Alianora Despencer, dau. of Hugh Le Despencer, Earl of Winchester.

ISSUE

1. Sir Hugh de Courtenay, Baron of Okehampton, first Earl of Devon, (22d February, 1335); *m.* Agnes St. John, interred 27th June, 1340, dau. of Sir John St. John.

ISSUE

1. Sir Hugh de Courtenay, second Earl of Devon, Knight of the Garter; *d.* 2d May, 1377, and together with his Countess interred in the Cathedral of Exeter; *m.* Margaret de Bohun, dau. of Humphrey, Earl of Hereford and Essex, and Princess Elizabeth Plantagenet, dau. of Edward I, received Powderham Castle as her marriage portion.

ISSUE

1. Sir Philip Courtenay, *d.* 29th July, 1406; son of second Earl of Devon, ninth son of "Powderham;" Lord Lieutenant of Ireland from 1382 until 1384; *m.* Anne Wake, dau. of Sir Thomas Wake of Blyseworth.

ISSUE

1. Sir John Courtenay, of Powderham; ob. vit. pat. 1419, *m.* Agnes Champernowne, *d.* 1419, dau. of Alexander Champernowne of Dartington, and widow of Sir John Chudleigh.

ISSUE

1. Sir Philip Courtenay, of Powderham; *d.* 16th December, 1463; *m.* Elizabeth, dau. of Walter, Lord Hungerford.

ISSUE

1. Sir William Courtenay, of Powderham; *b.* 1428; *d.* September, 1485; interred at Powderham; brother of Peter Courtenay, Bishop of Winchester; *m.* Margaret, interred at Powderham; her will dated 1487, dau. of William, Lord Bonville, Knight of the Garter.

ISSUE

1. Sir William Courtenay, of Powderham; his will dated 8th September, 1511, proved 15th July, 1512; *m.* Cicely Cheney, dau. of Sir John Cheney of Pinhoe, Devon, and his wife, Elizabeth Hill.

ISSUE

1. SIR WILLIAM COURTENAY of Powderham; *d.* 24th November, 1535; *m.* (firstly) Margaret EDGECOMBE, dau. of Sir Robert EDGECOMBE.

ISSUE

1. SIR GEORGE COURTENAY, eldest son and heir apparent of Sir William COURTENAY, of Powderham; ob. vit. pat, *m.* 14th January, 1528, Katherine ST. LEGER, sole daughter of Sir George ST. LEGER.

ISSUE

1. SIR WILLIAM COURTENAY of Powderham; Knight, killed at battle of St. Quentine, 29th September, 1557; *m.* Elizabeth PAULET, dau. of John, Marquis of WINCHESTER.

ISSUE

1. SIR WILLIAM COURTENAY, of Powderham; *b.* May 1553; *d.* in London, 24th January, 1630; knighted in 1576; High Sheriff of Devonshire in 1581; *m.* (firstly) Elizabeth MANNERS, dau. of Henry MANNERS, Earl of Rutland, Knight of the Garter; in 1609 Sir William COURTENAY, settled on his fifth son, George Ouchtred COURTENAY, escheated lands he had acquired in Munster, Ireland.

ISSUE

1. FRANCIS COURTENAY, of Powderham; eldest surviving son of Sir William, succeeded to the Powderham estate; he was interred at Powderham, 5th June, 1638, aged sixty-two years; will dated 3d June, 1638; *m.* (secondly) Elizabeth SEYMOUR, interred at Powderham, 2d October, 1658, dau. of Sir Edward SEYMOUR, Baronet of "Berry," Pomeroy, and his second wife.

ISSUE

1. EDWARD, living in 1672, of whom later.

EDWARD COURTENAY, Captain, at Powderham; *bapt.* 17th July, 1631; according to an English record, he was living in 1672; *m.* 1661, Frances MOORE, of Drumbanagher; she having died intestate, administration of her goods was granted in Prerogative Court, Ireland, March, 1707–1708, to her children, Alice, Catherine, John, Henry, and Charles, *d.* 20th August, 1763, of whom later. Edward COURTENAY, had a gold frame glazed and prepared for the preservation of his royal genealogy, and also paid 100 pounds sterling to insure it from hazard of fire.

ISSUE

I. JOHN COURTENAY, of Lisburn; *m.* Miss SAVAGE of Ardes; had issue.

1. Hercules *b.* 15th October, 1736, near Newry and Belfast, Ireland; *d.* in Baltimore County, 20th August, 1816; landed in Philadelphia, Pennsylvania, 18th February, 1762, and came to Baltimore, Maryland, about 1769; Member of Vestry St. Paul's Church; Member of Committee of Safety, 1774; appointed Justice in 1774; authorized by Congress to sign bills of credit, 1776; Captain, 1st Pennsylvania Regular Artillery, in the Revolution; Town Commissioner, 1781–1785; Street Commissioner, 1792; Secretary Maryland Fire Insurance Company, 1796; first to institute in Baltimore the Insurance of Water Risks, similar to the United States Lloyds; President of the First Branch of the First Council, 1797, declined reelection; first ship built in Baltimore built, for and named for him; he was a property owner both in Baltimore and Baltimore County, and a slave-owner, freeing all of same by will in 1816; *m.* (firstly) in Hanover, Pennsylvania, 1774, Sarah DRURY, of Reading, Pennsylvania, *b.* 1st September, 1753, *d.* in Baltimore, 24th September, 1785; *m.* (secondly) in Old Swedes Church, Philadelphia, in 1790, Mary DRURY, sister of first wife, *b.* 20th October, 1748, *d.* in Baltimore County, 3d June, 1826, dau. of Edward and Sarah (MAUGRIDGE) DRURY, of Berks County, Pennsylvania.

ISSUE BY FIRST MARRIAGE

1^1. Henry, *d.* in infancy.
2^1. Henry, *b.* 20th October, 1776; *d.* in Baltimore County, 8th June, 1854; *m.* (firstly) 10th January, 1799, Isabella PURVIANCE, *b.* 4th June, 1779, *d.* 8th July, 1804, dau. of Samuel PURVIANCE, Jr., by his second wife, Catherine STEWART, of Baltimore; *m.* (secondly) 20th February, 1811, Elizabeth Isabella PURVIANCE, *b.* 16th October, 1770, *d. s. p.* in Baltimore, Maryland, 4th October, 1823, half-sister of first wife.

ISSUE BY FIRST MARRIAGE

1^2. David Stewart, *b.* 10th October, 1799; *d.* in Baltimore, 5th February, 1880; *m.* Elizabeth Dorsey HAWKINS, dau. of John and Elizabeth (DORSEY) HAWKINS of Baltimore.
2^2. Sarah Mary, *b.* 18th November, 1800; *d.* in Baltimore, 18th January, 1885.

3². Prof. Edward Henry Courtenay, A.M., LL.D., *b.* in Baltimore, 19th November, 1803, *d.* at the University of Virginia, 21st December, 1853, entered the Military Academy, West Point, as a cadet, 2d September, 1818, at about the age of fifteen years; graduated 1821, before he was eighteen years old; at the head of his class during most of the term of three years. Lieutenant Engineers, United States of America, 1821; Assistant Professor at Academy, 1821-1824; Professor at Academy, 1828-1834; Professor in University of Pennsylvania, 1834-1836; Civil Engineer in employ of United States Army, 1837-1842; Professor University of Virginia, 1842-1853. Author of works in use at United States Military Academy and various universities (see Register of United States Military Academy); *m.* (firstly) Harriet Whitehorne Rathbone of Newport, Rhode Island, who *d.* at the University of Virginia, 11th November 1844; *m.* (secondly) 7th July, 1846, Virginia Pleasants Howard, *b.* circa 10th March, 1815, *d.* at the University of Virginia, 16th May, 1853, dau. of Prof. Henry Howard of the University of Virginia.

ISSUE BY FIRST MARRIAGE

1³. Edward Henry, *d.* in infancy.
2³. Harriet Whitehorne, *d.* in infancy.
3³. Harriet Whitehorne, 2d, *d.* in infancy.
4³. Alexander Dallas Bache, *d.* in infancy.
5³. Unnamed.
6³. Unnamed.
7³. Unnamed.
8³. Sarah, *m.* Gen. Henry Brewerton, United States Army, Engineers.
9³. Catlyna Totten.
10³. Mary Isabella, *m.* Gen. Chauncey B. Reese, United States Army Engineers.
11³. Edward Henry, 3d, *b.* 11th April, 1842; *d.* in Washington, D. C., 3d June, 1902.

ISSUE BY SECOND MARRIAGE

1³. Henry Howard, *b.* 8th June, 1847; *m.* Carrie Lillian Hitchcock.
2³. Alexander Dallas Bache, *b.* 16th December, 1848; *m.* 3d September, 1881, Emma Virginia Dushane, *b.* 15th December, 1849, dau. of Col. Nathan Thomas Dushane, 1st Maryland Regiment, United States Volunteers, and Eliza Patterson, his wife, dau. of William and Eliza (Benson) Patterson.

ISSUE

1⁴. Edward Henry, IV, *b*. 23d February, 1883; *m*. 18th September, 1906, Elizabeth Cathcart (DOON), dau. of John Glasgow and Caroline (CATHCART) DOON.

ISSUE

1⁵. Hilda Doon, *b*. 2d July, 1907.
2⁵. Edward Henry, *b*. 5th December, 1909.

3³. David Stewart, *b*. 24th May, 1850.
4³. Marshall Howard, *b*. 24th April, 1853, *d*. at University of Virginia, 7th June, 1853.
5³. Hamilton Howard, *b*. 24th April, 1853; *d*. at University of Virginia, 7th June, 1853.

3¹. Mary, *b*. 20th January, 1778.
4¹. Edward, *b*. 2d June, 1780; lost at sea, 1803; was Supercargo of a vessel captured by the Algerians in the Mediterranean Sea.
5¹. William, *b*. 22d November, 1782; *d*. in Baltimore, 30th November, 1824; *m*. Hannah Maria WEATHERBURN.
6¹. Ann Boyd, *b*. 30th May, 1786; *d*. in infancy.

ISSUE BY SECOND MARRIAGE

1¹. Ann Boyd, *b*. 17th February, 1792; *d*. in Baltimore County, 5th June, 1878; *m*. Dr. Thomas Cradock RISTEAU.
2¹. John Skinner, *b*. 24th November, 1793; *d*. in Baltimore County, 9th March, 1827.

2. Conway.
3. Conrad.
4. Henry.
5. William.
6. Edward.

II. Henry, of Carlingford; *m*. 1734, Mary MAJOR.

ISSUE

1. Edward.
2. John, *b*. 1742; *d*. 1816; Member Parliament for Tamworth, 1781 to 1797; Member of Parliament for Appleby, 1797 to 1806; author of "Review of the Revolution."

3. William Major, Captain in Royal Navy; killed in action in 1793, while in command of the *Boston* frigate.

III. CHARLES, *d.* 20th August, 1763, of whom below.

CHARLES COURTENAY, of "Courtenay Hill," Newry; *d.* 20th August, 1763; Treasurer to the Turnpike-Road Trustees, from Newry to Armagh, February, 1754–1755, and January, 1763; *m.* 13th January, 1730, Mary (surname not given), who *d.* 8th May, 1757; only two sons, John and Edward, and one daughter, Anna Maria, survived the parents.

ISSUE

I. Anna Maria, *b.* 7th November, 1731; *m.* Jeremiah SEAVER, D.D., rector of Kilbroney; left issue.
II. James, *b.* 22d August, 1732.
III. JOHN, *b.* 17th November, 1733, of whom below.
IV. Margaret, *b.* 16th January, 1734.
V. Elizabeth, *b.* 20th October, 1736.
VI. Chichester, *b.* 22d February, 1737.
VII. Robert, *b.* 1740.
VIII. Edward, *b.* 7th October, 1741; *d.* 1787; *m.* 1765, Jane CARLILE, *b.* 1750, *d.* 1828, dau. of David CARLILE by his wife, Jane MEDILL.

ISSUE

1. Jane, *b.* 1766.
2. Charles Henry, of Southwark; *b.* 1768; *d.* 1809, *m.* Mary (surname not given).

ISSUE

1^1. Jane, *b.* 1801; *d.* 25th August, 1823.
2^1. Edward Henry, *b.* 1807, *d.* 3rd June, 1872; *m.* 29th October, 1835, Charlotte Jane IRVING; left issue.
3^1. Charles Henry, *b.* 1809; *d.* 5th September, 1827.

3. David, of Dundalk; Attorney; *b.* 1770; *d.* January, 1846; *m.* (wife's name not given).

ISSUE

1^1. David Carlile, M.A., D.D., *b.* 1800; *d.* 20th April, 1891.
2^1. Sarah Jane, *b.* 1801; *d.* 1871.

4. Edward, *b.* 9th September, 1771; came to the United States in 1791, and settled in Charleston, South Carolina, where he married.

ISSUE

1². Edward Smith, eldest son; *b.* 11th July, 1795; *d.* 5th October, 1857; *m.* Elizabeth Storer WADE.

ISSUE

1³. William Ashmead, *b.* in Charleston, South Carolina, 1830; *d.* in Columbia, South Carolina, 17th March, 1908; *m.* (wife's name not given), she *d.* January, 1917; left issue. Mr. COURTENAY was Captain, Washington Light Infantry; and several terms Mayor of Charleston; he had a record of remarkable public endeavor, and a career of fine achievements.

5. John, *b.* 1773; emigrated to America 1791, and settled in Savannah, Georgia.
6. Mary, *b.* 1775, *m.* Jacob TURNER.
7. Elizabeth, *b.* 1777; *m.* Thomas GREER.

IX. Henry, *b.* 1742.
X. Charles, *b.* 1744.
XI. Fortescue, *b.* 20th September, 1749.

JOHN COURTENAY, of "Courtenay Hill", Newry, *b.* 17th November, 1733; *d.* 28th May, 1798; *m.* 1764, Jane RHAMES, she *d.* 21st January, 1814.

ISSUE

1. Charles, *b.* 1765; *d.* 29th September, 1817.

ISSUE

1. John, *d.* 26th September, 1841 in France; *m.* 12th November, 1836, Catherine Sarah MURPHY; she *d.* 31st March, 1862, at Mentone, France.

II. Anne, *b.* 1767; *d.* 27th January, 1837; unmarried.
III. Edward, had one dau. Charlotte Mary, who *m.* Major MCNEALE.
IV. John Henry, *b.* at "Courtenay Hill," Newry, Ireland; *d.* in Illinois, circa 1824; *m.* (secondly) Maria GRAHAM, *b.* in England, *d.* in Illinois.

ISSUE

1. ROBERT GRAHAM, *b.* 1814, of whom later.
2. Emma, *b.* in Ireland, 1822; *d.* 26th October, 1872; *m.* James B. WILDER, *b.* in Maryland, 12th July, 1817, *d.* in Louisville, Kentucky, 16th May, 1888; left issue.

ROBERT GRAHAM COURTENAY, *b.* on the Irish Sea, circa 1813, *d.* in Louisville, Kentucky, 1st October, 1864, when very young came with his parents to America; upon their death, he went to reside with his maternal uncle, Robert GRAHAM, at Frankfort, Kentucky; at the age of fourteen he moved to Louisville, where he subsequently became a prominent man of affairs; member of the firm of Thomas ANDERSON and Company; Director in the Bank of Louisville, and Northern Bank of Kentucky at Lexington; Director of the Louisville and Frankfort, and Lexington and Frankfort Railroad Companies; Administrator of the John L. MARTIN estate, 1854; President of the Louisville Gas Company from November 1853 to 1st October, 1864; *m.* 13th October, 1842, Annie Christian HOWARD, *b.* 1st February, 1825; *d.* 19th July, 1912, and it is through this alliance that William Howard COURTENAY, traces his line back to many distinguished colonial ancestors, among whom are two Acting Governors of Maryland, namely, Commander Robert BROOKE and Col. Thomas BROOKE, the Rev. William WILKINSON, first minister of the Church of England, in the Province of Maryland; Gerard FOWKE, Colonel in Royalist Army and Knight of the Bedchamber to King Charles I of England. He descends also from Col. John HENRY, Judge Cuthbert BULLITT, and Col. William CHRISTIAN, all of Virginia.

ISSUE

1. Julia Christian, *b.* 8th January, 1844; *d.* 28th February, 1894; *m.* 5th December, 1866, Hector Voltaire LOVING, *b.* 8th September, 1839, *d.* 27th March, 1913.

    ### ISSUE

    1. Annie Courtenay LOVING, *b.* 10th November, 1867; *m.* 5th December, 1889, William Foote INGRAM.

        ### ISSUE

        1^1. Julian Courtenay INGRAM, *b.* 7th September, 1890.
        2^1. William Foote INGRAM, Jr., *b.* 30th September, 1893.
        3^1. Anita INGRAM, *b.* 18th December, 1895.
        4^1. Helen Courtenay INGRAM, *b.* 28th October, 1897.

    2. Ellen Quigley LOVING, *b.* 18th October, 1869; *d.* 16th July, 1870.
    3. Julia LOVING, *b.* 6th November, 1870; *m.* 13th September, 1892, Robert GEORGE, *b.* in Scotland, 2d February, 1853.

        ### ISSUE

        1^1. Julia Courtenay GEORGE, *b.* in Louisville, Kentucky, 24th July, 1896.
        2^1. Robert Clark GEORGE, *b.* in Minneapolis, Minnesota, 17th November, 1907.

4. William Voltaire LOVING, *b.* 1st March, 1872; *d.* 13th December, 1875.
5. Hector LOVING, *b.* 10th October, 1873; *m.* in San Francisco, California, 31st December, 1914, Katherine (MCKENNA) BROWN, widow.
6. Emma LOVING, *b.* 10th December, 1874.
7. Laura LOVING, *b.* 16th April, 1877; *m.* 22d October, 1903, Dwiggins Claude HARRIS, *b.* 21st November, 1877.

ISSUE

1^1. H. V. Loving HARRIS, *b.* 12th October, 1905.
2^1. Emma Nan HARRIS, *b.* 15th August, 1907.
3^1. Dwiggins Claude HARRIS, Jr. *b.* 27th December, 1908.

8. Robert Courtenay LOVING, M.D., Major United States Army; *b.* 16th July, 1878; *m.* 17th June, 1907, Anna Bella CASSEL.

ISSUE

1^1. Virginia LOVING, *b.* at West Point, New York, 17th February, 1909.
2^1. Dorothy LOVING, *b.* in Philadelphia, Pennsylvania, 7th May, 1910.
3^1. Helen LOVING, *b.* at Camp Connell, Samar, Philippine Islands, 17th December, 1911.
4^1. Mildred LOVING, *b.* in San Antonio, Texas, November, 1917.

II. Henry, *b.* 10th January, 1846; *d.* 13th March, 1846.
III. Robert Martin, *b.* 28th November, 1848; *d.* 6th July, 1851.
IV. Thomas Anderson, *b.* 20th June, 1850; *m.* 30th January, 1877, Jane Short BUTLER, *b.* 25th April, 1853.

ISSUE

1. Robert, *b.* 3d February, 1878.
2. Jane Short, *b.* 25th June, 1881; *m.* 30th January, 1906, Henry Samuel TYLER, *b.* 27th March, 1879.

ISSUE

1^1. Levi TYLER, *b.* 27th April, 1907; *d.* 27th June, 1909.
2^1. Thomas Courtenay TYLER, *b.* 20th June, 1909.
3^1. Caroline Atwood TYLER, *b.* 12th December, 1912; *d.* 25th July, 1914.
4^1. Henry Samuel TYLER, Jr., *b.* 13th March, 1917.

3. Thomas Anderson, Jr., *b.* 12th August, 1884.
4. Carl Butler, *b.* 22d October, 1885; *d.* 10th October, 1907.

5. Lewis Rogers (twin), *b.* 3d March, 1890.
6. William Howard, II (twin), *b.* 3d March, 1890.

v. Helen Martin, *b.* 12th November, 1852.
vi. Emma, *b.* 25th August, 1854.
vii. Lewis Rogers, *b.* 23d May, 1857; *d.* unmarried, 26th October, 1897.
viii. WILLIAM HOWARD, *b.* 30th July, 1858, the subject of this memoir.

Arms.—Quarterly 1st and 4th or; three torteaux, for COURTENAY; 2d and 3d or, a lion rampant, for REDVERS.
Crest.—A dolphin embowed ppr.
Motto.—Ubi lapsus quid feci.
Residence.—1110 Third Avenue, Louisville, Kentucky.
Clubs.—(Louisville) Engineers and Architects Club; Conversation Club.
Societies.—Order of Runnemede, American Society Civil Engineers, American Railway Engineering Association, National Geographic Society.

"*I shall pass through this world but once. Any good therefore that I can do, or any kindness that I can show to any human being, let me do it now. Let me not defer or neglect it, for I shall not pass this way again.*"—EDWARD COURTENAY, Earl of Devon.

Colonial Lineage

Howard

Arms.—Gules on a bend between six cross lets, fitchee argent, an escutcheon or, charged with a demi-lion rampant, pierced through the mouth with an arrow, within a double tressure, counter flory of the first.
Crest.—On a chapeau gules, turned up ermine, a lion statant gardant, with tail extended or.
Motto.—Desir na repos.

EDMUND HOWARD, "Gentleman," *b.* in England; *m.* in Somerset County, Maryland, 26th May, 1681, Margaret DENT, dau. of Thomas DENT, *b.* in Gisborough, England, circa 1630; *d.* in St. Mary's County, Maryland, 1676, and Rebecca WILKINSON, his wife; Justice of Somerset County, Maryland, 1689; Clerk of Charles County, Maryland, where he *d.* 1713; he was one of the earliest settlers of Maryland and was active in affairs civil and religious in that province.

ISSUE

1. Rebecca, *b.* February, 1682; *d.* 6th June, 1683.
11. William Stevens, *b.* 3d November, 1684; *m.* (firstly) Elizabeth (name not given), left issue. *m.* (secondly) Sarah BRISCOE, widow of Thomas TRUMAN; left issue.
111. George, *b.* 18th March, 1686.
IV. JOHN, *b.* 1688, of whom below.
v. Thomas, *b.* 5th September, 1690.
VI. Elizabeth, *d.* 1718.
VII. Edmund, *b.* 30th August, 1695.

JOHN HOWARD, *b.* in Somerset County, Maryland, 1688; *d.* in Charles County, Maryland, before 22nd March, 1742; *m.* in Prince George's County, Maryland, circa 1725, his first cousin, Rebecca BROOKE, *b.* in Prince George's County, Maryland, 1709 or 1710, *d.* in Charles County, Maryland, before 14th December, 1768, when her will was probated, dau. of Col. Thomas BROOKE, of Brookfield, Maryland, and Barbara DENT, his second wife, *b.* 1676, *d.* 1754; she was dau. of Thomas DENT, *b.* in Gisborough, England, circa 1630, *d.* in St. Mary's County, Maryland, 1676, who *m.* Rebecca WILKINSON, dau. of the Rev. William WILKINSON; she *m.* (secondly) Col. John ADDISON who emigrated to Maryland in 1667; *d.* during a visit to England, 1705.

ISSUE

1. Thomas HOWARD.
11. John HOWARD.
111. BAKER HOWARD, *b.* circa 1738, of whom later.
IV. Eleanor HOWARD, *m.* John DOUGLASS.
v. Elizabeth HOWARD, *m.* ——— STONE, before December, 1768.

BAKER HOWARD, *b.* circa 1738; was a resident of Charles County, Maryland, William and Mary Lower Hundred, 1775-1778; *d.* in Montgomery County, Maryland, August, 1790; *m.* (firstly) in Charles County, Maryland, Ann PHILLIPS, 6th April, 1761; *m.* (secondly) Ann SOLLERS.

ISSUE BY FIRST MARRIAGE

1. JOHN, *b.* 7th October, 1769, in Charles County, Maryland, of whom below.
11. Benjamin.
111. Hannah, *m.* James TRAILL, Jr., of Frederick County, Maryland; left issue.
IV. Rebecca.
v. Eleanor, *m.* 4th February, 1796, John Howard SIMMONS, who *m.* (firstly) his cousin Susannah HOWARD; had issue.
VI. Samuel Howard, *d.* unmarried, 4th February, 1797.

JOHN HOWARD, *b.* Charles County, Maryland, 7th October, 1769; *d.* in Jefferson County, Kentucky, 25th June, 1843; *m.* (firstly) in St. Mary's County, Maryland, 15th October, 1799, Mary LATIMER, *d.* 10th August, 1810, had issue; *m.* (secondly) in Jefferson County, Kentucky, 4th February, 1819, Annie Christian BULLITT, *b.* 6th November, 1786, *d.* 10th May, 1828, dau. of Priscilla CHRISTIAN, *b.* in Virginia about 1770, *d.* at "Oxmoor," Jefferson County, Kentucky, 11th November, 1806, *m.* October, 1785, Alexander Scott BULLITT, *b.* 1762, in Virginia, *d.* at "Oxmoor," Jefferson County, Kentucky, 13th April, 1816.

ISSUE BY SECOND MARRIAGE

I. Alexander Scott Bullitt, *b.* 24th October, 1819; *d.* 28th January, 1822.
II. William Bullitt, *b.* 10th March, 1821; *d.* circa 1896; *m.* (firstly) Maria STROTHER; had issue; *m.* (secondly) Mary JONES, had issue.
III. Helen, *b.* 11th October, 1822; *d.* 10th December, 1841.
IV. Annie Christian, *b.* 1st February, 1825; *d.* 19th July, 1912; *m.* 13th October, 1842; in Jefferson County, Kentucky, Robert Graham COURTENAY, *b.* on the Irish Sea, circa 1813, *d.* in Louisville, Kentucky, 1st October, 1864.

ISSUE

1. Julia COURTENAY, *b.* 8th January, 1844; *d.* 28th February, 1894; *m.* 5th December, 1866, Hector V. LOVING, *b.* 8th September, 1839, *d.* 27th March, 1913; had issue.
2. Henry COURTENAY, *b.* 10th January, 1846; *d.* 13th March, 1846.
3. Robert Martin COURTENAY, *b.* 28th November, 1848; *d.* 6th July, 1851.
4. Thomas Anderson COURTENAY, *b.* 20th June, 1850; *m.* 30th January, 1877, Jane Short BUTLER, *b.* 25th April, 1853; had issue.
5. Helen Martin COURTENAY, *b.* 12th November, 1852.
6. Emma COURTENAY, *b.* 25th August, 1854.
7. Lewis Rogers COURTENAY, *b.* 23d May, 1857; *d.* 26th October, 1897; unmarried.
8. William Howard COURTENAY, *b.* 30th July, 1858, the subject of this memoir.

Brooke

Arms.—Chequey or and azure, on a bend gules a lion passant of the first.

Crest.—A demi lion rampant, erased or.

COMMANDER ROBERT BROOKE, the emigrant ancestor of William Howard COURTENAY, the subject of this sketch, arrived in Maryland, 30th June, 1650, with his second wife, Mary MAINWARING, ten children and twenty-eight servants, all transported at his own cost. He was the son of Hon. Thomas BROOKE, and Susan FOSTER, and was *b.* in London, 3d June, 1602; *d.* 20th July, 1655, and is buried at Brooke Place Manor, Maryland; matriculated at Waldham College, Oxford, 28th April, 1618; B.A. 6th July, 1620; M.A. 23d April, 1624; Commission issued to him in London, 20th September, 1650, to erect a new County in Maryland, called Charles, of which he was constituted Commander; made Member of the Council the same day; Head of the Provisional Council under Cromwellian Government 29th March to 3d July, 1652, Acting Governor, 1652. Bozman says he was a Puritan, and Allen that he was a High Church Protestant; certain it is that he stood high in the confidence of the CROMWELL party; *m.* (firstly) 25th February, 1627, Mary BAKER, dau. of Thomas BAKER of Battel, Barrister at Law, and Mary ENGHAM, his wife, dau. of Sir Thomas ENGHAM, of Goodneston, Kent, she died in England, 1634; *m.* (secondly) Mary MAINWARING, *d.* 29th November, 1663, dau. of Roger MAINWARING, D.D., Dean of Worcester, and Bishop of St. Davids.

ISSUE BY FIRST MARRIAGE

I. Baker, *b.* 16th November, 1628; *d.* 1679; *m.* between 1664 and 1671, Ann CALVERT, dau. of Gov. Leonard CALVERT and Ann BRENT, sister of Mistress Margaret BRENT, of Maryland.
II. Mary, *b.* 19th February, 1630; *d.* in England.
III. THOMAS, *b.* in Battel, England, 23d June, 1632, of whom below.
IV. Barbara, *b.* 1634; *d.* in England.

THOMAS BROOKE, *b.* in Battel, England, 23d June, 1632; *d.* Calvert County, Maryland, 1676; will proved 29th December, 1676; arrived in Maryland with his father, 30th June, 1650; Major of Maryland Militia, 1660; Member of Assembly, 1663-1666 and 1671-1676; Burgess, 1666-1669; High Sheriff of Calvert County, 1666-1669; Presiding Justice, Mayor of Battle Creek, and one of the first vestrymen of St. Paul's Parish (Episcopal), Calvert County; *m.* circa 1658, Eleanor HATTON, *b.* in England, 1642, dau. of Richard and Margaret HATTON, and niece of Hon. Thomas HATTON, Secretary of the Province. Eleanor HATTON, widow of Maj.

Thomas BROOKE, *m.* (secondly) Col. Henry DARNALL, of Portland Manor, their daughter Mary DARNALL, at the age of fifteen, *m.* in 1693, Charles CARROLL, of Doughoregen Manor; their son Charles CARROLL, of Annapolis, and their gd. son Charles CARROLL, of Carrollton.

ISSUE

I. THOMAS, *b.* circa 1659, in Calvert County, Maryland, *d.* 7th January, 1730, in Prince George's County, Maryland, of whom later.
II. Robert, *b.* 24th October, 1663; *d.* 18th July, 1714.
III. Ignatius, *b.* 1670.
IV. Matthew.
V. Clement, of Prince George's County, Maryland; *b.* 1676; *d.* 1737; *m.* Jane SEWELL, daughter of Maj. Nicholas and Susannah (BURGESS) SEWELL.
VI. Mary, *m.* (firstly) Capt. James BOWLING, of St. Mary's County, Maryland, *d.* 1693; *m.* (secondly) Benjamin HALL, of Prince George's County, *d.* 1721; *m.* (thirdly) Henry WITHAM.
VII. Eleanor, *m.* (firstly) Phillip DARNALL, *d.* 1705, son of her stepfather, Col. Henry DARNALL, by a former marriage; *m.* (secondly) William DIGGES.

COL. THOMAS BROOKE, of Brookfield, Maryland; *b.* circa 1659, in Calvert County Maryland; *d.* 7th January, 1730, in Prince George's County; *m.* (firstly) Anne (surname not given), *d.* after 1687; *m.* (secondly) before 4th January, 1699, Barbara DENT, *b.* 1676, *d.* 1754, dau. of Thomas DENT, St. Mary's County, Maryland, and Rebecca WILKINSON, his wife, dau. of Rev. William WILKINSON, and Naomi (surname not given), his second wife. Col. Thomas BROOKE, was Colonel of Militia commissioned to treat with Piscataway Indians, 1697; Commissary General of the Province, 1701; Member of the Council, 1692–1701; and 1715–1724; Judge of the High Court of Admiralty, 1694; Deputy Secretary of Maryland, 1695; Acting Governor of the Province; President of the Council, 1720; he practically filled every office in the gift of the King, Queen and the Royal Governor; he was an active member of the Church of England, as shown by his will, probated 25th January, 1730–1731.

ISSUE BY SECOND MARRIAGE

I. Nathaniel.
II. John.
III. Benjamin.
IV. Jane, *d.* 1779; *m.* circa 1720, Alexander CONTEE, of Prince George's County, Maryland, who *d.* 24th December, 1740.
V. REBECCA, will dated 2d February, 1763, of whom below.
VI. Mary, *d.* 1758; *m.* Dr. Patrick SIM, of Prince George's County, Maryland, *d.* 24th October, 1740.

VII. Elizabeth, *m.* Col. George BEALL, *b.* 1695, *d.* 1780.
VIII. Lucy, *m.* Thomas HODGKIN.
IX. Baker.
X. Thomas, *b.* 1717; *d.* unmarried.

REBECCA BROOKE, will dated 2d February, 1763; probated in Charles County, Maryland, 14th December, 1768; *m.* her first cousin, John HOWARD, *b.* in Somerset County, Maryland, 1688, *d.* Charles County, Maryland, 1742, son of Edmund HOWARD, "Gentleman," and Margaret DENT, his wife, dau. of Thomas DENT, *b.* in Gisborough, England, circa 1630, *d.* in St. Mary's County, Maryland, 1676; who *m.* Rebecca WILKINSON, dau. of the Rev. William WILKINSON; she *m.* (secondly) Col. John ADDISON, who emigrated to Maryland in 1667; *d.* during a visit to England, 1705.

ISSUE

I. Thomas HOWARD.
II. John HOWARD.
III. BAKER HOWARD, *b.* circa 1738, of whom later.
IV. Eleanor HOWARD, *m.* John DOUGLASS.
V. Elizabeth HOWARD, *m.* ———— STONE, before December, 1768.

Arms Acquired by Courtenay Intermarriages

Arms (CHRISTIAN).—Azure, a demi-mascle, between three covered cups, or; crest, a unicorn's head, erased, argent, armed and gorged with a collar invecked or.
Motto.—Salus per Christum.

Arms (HENRY).—Per pale indented argent and gules, on the dexter side a rose of the second, a chief azure charged with a lion passant of the first.
Crest.—Out of a crown ppr. a demi-lion rampant argent, holding between the paws a ducal coronet or.
Motto.—Vincit veritas.

Arms (HARRISON; of Stafford County, Virginia).—Azure three demi-lions rampant or.
Crest.—A demi-lion rampant argent, holding a laurel branch vert.

Arms (FOWKE).—Vert a fleur-de-lis argent.
Crest.—A dexter arm embowed vested vert, cuffed argent; in the hand ppr. an arrow or, feathered of the second, pheoned azure.
Motto.—Arma tuentur pacem.

Dennis

ARTHUR WELLINGTON DENNIS, of Providence, Rhode Island, *b.* there 11th April, 1846; *m.* there 26th September, 1866, Annie Isabel SMITH, *b.* 11th July, 1846, dau. of Simri and Sarah F. (WHIPPLE) SMITH.

ISSUE

I. Hope Ann, *b.* 4th October, 1870.
II. John Rhodes, *b.* 8th May, 1877; *m.* 1st May, 1900, Bertha ROELOFS of Philadelphia.

ARTHUR WELLINGTON DENNIS was President of the City Council of Providence, 1888–1889; Speaker of Rhode Island House of Representatives, 1906; Lieutenant-Governor of Rhode Island, 1909; President International Braid Company of Providence; Deputy Governor General and Governor of Society of Colonial Wars in Rhode Island; President Rhode Island Society of Sons of the American Revolution.

Lineage

The ancestor of the family was Arthur DENNIS of Minehead, England; his son
CAPT. JOHN DENNIS, of Newport, Rhode Island, *b.* 1715, was lost at sea in 1756; *m.* Joanna BROWN, *bapt.* in Trinity Church, Newport in 1721; their son
ARTHUR DENNIS, of Swansea, Massachusetts, *m.* Elizabeth ROBINSON of the same town; their son
JOHN ROBINSON DENNIS, of Swansea, Massachusetts, *b.* 1800; *d.* 1846; *m.* Hope Ann RHODES, *b.* 1805, *d.* 1862, dau. of Charles RHODES, *b.* 19th December, 1780; *d.* 15th May, 1826, *m.* Nancy BROWN, *b.* 12th January, 1781, *d.* 17th June, 1857, the dau. of Abial and Hopestill BROWN.

ISSUE

I. ARTHUR WELLINGTON DENNIS, *b.* 11th April, 1846, the subject of the memoir.

Arms (DENNIS of England).—Azure, three leopards faces or, jessant-de-les, argent.
Crest.—A leopards head and neck couped ppr.
Residence.—Providence, Rhode Island.
Clubs.—West Side, Pomham, New York Yacht.
Societies.—Colonial Wars; Sons of the American Revolution; Calvary Commandery, Knight Templar, What Cheer Lodge, Ancient Free and Accepted Masons; thirty-second degree Mason.

Rhodes (Maternal Lineage)

The immigrant ancestor of the RHODES family was Zachariah RHODES, of Providence, Rhode Island; b. 1603; d. 1665; was Commissioner, 1658–1663; Deputy, 1659, 1661–1665; m. Joanna ARNOLD, dau. of William and Christian (PEAK) ARNOLD; their son

JOHN RHODES, of Providence, Rhode Island, b. 1658; d. 14th August, 1716; was Deputy to the Rhode Island Assembly, 1702–1704 and 1708; m. Waite WATERMAN, b. 1668, dau. of Resolved and Mercy (WILLIAMS) WATERMAN; Mercy WILLIAMS, b. 15th July, 1640; was the dau. of Roger and Mary (WARNARD) WILLIAMS. He was b. 1599, d. 1683, and served as Captain in King Philip's War; Assistant, 1647, et seq.; Governor of Rhode Island, 1654; Deputy, 1667.

MAJ. JOHN RHODES, of Warwick, Rhode Island; son of above, b. 20th November, 1691; d. 1776; Major of Colonial Troops; Deputy to the Rhode Island Assembly, 1742–1743; m. Catherine HOLDEN, d. 25th July, 1731, dau. of Charles and Catherine (GREENE) HOLDEN; he son of Randall and Frances (DUNGAN) HOLDEN.

CHARLES RHODES, of Providence, Rhode Island, son of Maj. John RHODES, b. 29th September, 1719; d. 1777; m. Deborah GREENE, dau. of Peter and Kezia (DAVIS) GREENE, the son of Peter, who was the son of Peter, the son of John who was the son of John and Joan (TATTERSALLE) GREENE.

CAPT. PETER RHODES, of Pawtucket, Rhode Island; son of Charles RHODES, b. 24th February, 1741; d. 1820; m. Esther ARNOLD, dau. of Simon and Lydia (GREENE) ARNOLD; he son of Israel, the son of Stephen, who was the son of William and Christian (PEAK) ARNOLD. The ARNOLDS their descent in an unbroken line in England to the eleventh century.

Capt. Charles RHODES, of Pawtucket, Rhode Island, son of Capt. Peter RHODES, b. 19th December, 1780, d. 15th May, 1826; m. Nancy BROWN, b. 12th January, 1781, d. 17th June, 1857, dau. of Abial (Abial-Captain John-Captain Joseph-John-John), and Hopestill BROWN; their daughter

Hope Ann RHODES, b. 4th March, 1805, d. 21st August, 1862; m. Capt. John Robinson DENNIS, b. 9th February, 1800, d. 3rd February, 1849; lost at sea; their son

Arthur Wellington DENNIS, b. 11th April, 1846, at Providence, Rhode Island; m. Annie Isabel SMITH; he is the subject of this memoir and the issue of his marriage is enumerated at the beginning of this sketch.

Arm.—(RHODES of Rhode Island).—Argent, two quarter foils slipped sable, a chief of the last.

Crest.—A wolf's head couped sable, collared argent.

Derby

LIEUTENANT-COLONEL GEORGE McCLELLAN DERBY, United States Army; *b.* at sea, Pacific Ocean, American ship, 1st November, 1856; *m.* (firstly), 6th November, 1878, in New York, Clara Matteson McGINNESS; *m.* (secondly) 4th November, 1904, at New Orleans, Louisiana, Bessie KIDDER, *b.* 3d January, 1884, dau. of Greer KIDDER of Wilmington, North Carolina, and Bessie Low, his wife, of New Orleans, Louisiana.

ISSUE

I. George Townsend, *b.* 14th January, 1905.
II. Roger Barton, *b.* 20th January, 1908.
III. Hollis Hasket, *b.* 30th June, 1911.
IV. Elizabeth Crowninshield, *b.* 27th September, 1917.

LIEUTENANT-COLONEL GEORGE MCCLELLAN DERBY was educated in private schools at Paris, Dresden and Lausanne, Switzerland, 1865–1871; Washington University, St. Louis, 1872–1873; Symonds Academy, Sing Sing, New York, 1873–1874; Graduate of United States Military Academy, 1878; United States Engineers School of Application, 1881; Appointed Second Lieutenant Engineers Corps, 14th June, 1878; First Lieutenant, 2d January, 1881; Captain, 7th April, 1888; Major, 5th July, 1898; Lieutenant-Colonel, Chief Engineers, United States Volunteers, 9th May, 1898; honorably discharged, 12th May, 1899; Lieutenant-Colonel United States Army, 5th May, 1906; on duty with battalion of United States Army, 1878–1881; Assistant to Gen. John NEWTON in local charge of works at Hell Gate, East River and other river and harbor work in New York and New Jersey, 1881–1889; instructor practical Military Engineering, United States Military Academy, 1889–1893; Assistant to Engineer Commissioner, District of Columbia, 1893–1894; in charge 4th District Mississippi River improvement; in Cuba during Santiago campaign and Chief Engineer 2d Army Corps, 1898; in charge of Louisville and Portland canal and other river and harbor work, Louisville, Kentucky, 1902–1903; in charge of reservoirs at headquarters of Mississippi in Minnesota, 1903–1906; retired at own request after thirty years service, 7th June, 1907.

Lineage

The emigrant ancestor of this family was Roger DERBY, the founder of the distinguished family of this name, who came from Topham, Derby, England; *d.* in Salem, 1698, to which town he removed in 1681; *m.* (firstly) 23d August, 1668, in England, Lucretia HINMAN, who *d.* 25th May, 1689; *m.* (secondly) Elizabeth (surname not given).

ISSUE BY FIRST MARRIAGE

 I. Charles, *b.* 27th July, 1669, in England; *d.* 8th October, 1690, in the crusade against Quebec.
 II. Experience, *b.* 18th December, 1671.
 III. Samuel, *b.* 24th November, 1673.
 IV. Roger, *b.* 1st January, 1675.
 V. John, *b.* 25th February, 1677.
 VI. RICHARD, *b.* 8th October, 1679, of whom below.
 VII. Lucretia, *b.* 17th August, 1681.
 VIII. Ebenezer, *b.* 9th July, 1683; *d.* at the age of five years.

ISSUE BY SECOND MARRIAGE

 I. Elizabeth, *b.* 14th March, 1692.
 II. Margaret, *b.* 10th December, 1695.
 III. Martha, *b.* 11th September, 1697; *m.* 1719, Joshua HICKS.

RICHARD DERBY, of Salem, Massachusetts; *b.* 8th October, 1679; *d.* 25th July, 1715; *m.* 25th February, 1702, Martha HASKET.

ISSUE

 I. John, *b.* 27th December, 1702.
 II. Mary, *b.* 9th January, 1702.
 III. RICHARD, *b.* 12th September, 1712, of whom below.

RICHARD DERBY, of Salem, Massachusetts; *m.* Mary HODGES.

ISSUE

 I. ELIAS HASKET, of whom below.

ELIAS HASKET DERBY, of Salem, Massachusetts; *m.* Elizabeth CROWNINSHIELD.

ISSUE

 I. JOHN, of whom below.

JOHN DERBY, of Salem, Massachusetts; *m.* Sallie BARTON.

ISSUE

 I. JOHN BARTON, of whom below.

JOHN BARTON DERBY, of Medfield, Massachusetts; *m.* Mary TOWNSEND.

ISSUE

1. GEORGE HORATIO, of whom below.

CAPT. GEORGE HORATIO DERBY, United States Army, of St. Louis, Missouri; Corps of Topographical Engineers, United States Army; *m.* Mary Angeline COONS.

ISSUE

1. GEORGE MCCLELLAN, *b.* 1st November, 1856, the subject of this memoir.

Doneghy

LIEUTENANT JOHN TEMPLEMAN DONEGHY, B.A., M.A., United States Army, of Macon, Missouri; *b.* 14th April, 1889, in La Plata, Missouri; Graduate of Smith Academy; of Washington University, St. Louis, Missouri, 1907; B.A., Yale, 1911; M.A., Yale, 1912; post graduate work, Chicago and Columbia Universities. Lieutenant DONEGHY went to St. Louis to reside October, 1914; accepted a position with the William R. COMPTON Bond Company as Advertising Manager, and continued with that firm until May, 1917, when he resigned to attend the First Officers' Training Camp at Fort Riley, Kansas. In January, 1917, he joined the Military Training Corps in St. Louis, and when war was declared with Germany was one of the first men in Missouri to volunteer for service. He was commissioned Second Lieutenant, 15th August, 1917, Field Artillery, Officers' Reserve Corps, and assigned to the 342d Field Artillery, 89th Division; re-commissioned First Lieutenant, 14th January, 1918; 25th February, 1918, was made Regimental Radio Officer. He attended the Detached School of Fire in Fort Sill, Oklahoma, from 23d April to 25th May. Before finishing this course he was recalled to Camp Funston, Kansas, to prepare for oversea service. With his Company, left Camp Funston 2d June, 1918, en route to Camp Mills, New York, where he remained until 26th or 27th June. The steamer on which he sailed, the *Justicia*, was torpedoed on its return trip. He landed in Liverpool, England, about 10th or 12th July, arrived in France 14th July, and was sent to the Artillery Camp de Souges, near Bordeaux, France. Sometime after 12th September he participated in the battles on the Western Front as Regimental Radio Officer on his Colonel's Staff; the 89th Division has been incorporated in the 3d Army, now one of the armies of occupation; Lieutenant DONEGHY is unmarried.

Lineage

CAPTAIN WILLIAM PEIRCE, the emigrant ancestor of the Westmoreland County, Virginia, family, *d.* in 1651; came to America with Sir Thomas GATES in the ship *Sea Venture*, in 1609; his wife Jane (surname not given) came in the *Blessing*, in 1610; in 1642 it was said of his home in Jamestown, that it was the "fairest in all Virginia;" Captain PEIRCE was one of the leading men of Virginia; Councillor, 1631–1648; in 1631 he was sixth in the Council of Sir John HARVEY and in 1646, Capt. William PEIRCE, Esquire, was second in standing in the Council; in 1623 was commissioned Lieutenant by Governor WYATT to go against the Indians; was Captain of the Governor's Guard in 1617; was a Member of the House of Burgesses from the incorporation of James City, besides filling many other important positions of responsibility and honor. His daughter Jane, *b.* 1620, was John ROLFE's third wife. "In 1625 John ROLFE's father-in-law, Capt. William PEIRCE owned Angelo, a negro woman, one of the first negroes brought to Virginia." She came in the *Treasurer* in 1619.

ISSUE

I. Jane, *b.* 1620, *m.* as his third wife, John ROLFE.
II. Thomas.
III. WILLIAM, *b.* 1632, of whom below.

COL. WILLIAM PEIRCE, *b.* in York County, Virginia, 1632; will probated 7th April, 1702; *d.* in Westmoreland County, Virginia, 1702; he settled on a grant of 300 acres of land at the junction of the Nomini and Peirce Creek, the latter so named for him; in 1666 he obtained a patent for 4310 acres in "The Forest;" here the family home was built and called "Level Green;" for a long time he was Major of Militia; Justice of the Quorum, 1668; Burgess, 1680, and Colonel the same year; his widow Sarah was living, in 1706, when she appeared in Court with reference to her gd. son, William PEIRCE, at school in care of his uncle, Col. Nathaniel POPE, in England.

ISSUE

I. JOHN, of whom later.
II. Sarah, *m.* Stanley GOWER, of Richmond County, Virginia.
III. Margaret, *m.* ——— GRAHAM.
IV. Mary, *m.* Edward ROWZIE, of Essex County.
V. Elizabeth, *m.* (firstly) Rozier BRIDGES; *m.* (secondly) Col. Nathaniel POPE, and 13th July, 1718, signed with him a deed for "Cliffe" to Thomas LEE, which later became the famous "Stratford" home of the LEES.

JOHN PEIRCE, of Virginia; *d.* before his father and only son mentioned in his will; *m.* Mary (surname not given).

ISSUE

I. WILLIAM, named in his gd. father's will as son of his deceased son John PEIRCE.

WILLIAM PEIRCE, of Virginia, *b.* in Westmoreland County, 1681; *d.* 1733; *m.* in Westmoreland County, 1716, Sibella THOMPSON, dau. of Thomas THOMPSON.

ISSUE

I. WILLIAM, II, *b.* 1717, of whom below.
II. Joseph, *b.* 1719; *d.* 5th June, 1798; *m.* Sarah Elliott RANSDALL, *b.* 1754, *d.* 20th September, 1783.

ISSUE

1. Sarah.
2. Mary.
3. Elizabeth.
4. Margaret.

WILLIAM PEIRCE, II, of Virginia; *b.* 1717; *d.* 1781; *m.* Ursula LOVELL, dau. of Robert LOVELL, whose will was probated in 1726 in Westmoreland County, Virginia.

ISSUE

I. WILLIAM, III, *d.* 1782, of whom below.
II. Jane, *m.* James TRIPLETT.
III. John Lovell, *m.* Mary Ann BERKLEY.

WILLIAM PEIRCE, III, of Virginia, *d.* 1782; his name, with that of his brother Joseph PEIRCE, appears on the 1766 "Famous Protest of Westmoreland Patriots" and he was one of the members of the "Committee of Safety;" *m.* Sarah (ALLAWAY) ARISS, who was living in 1792, she was the widow of Spencer ARISS, who was the gd. son of Nicholas SPENCER, Secretary of the Colony of Virginia and acting Governor in 1683. Elizabeth ARISS dau. of Spencer and Sarah (ALLAWAY) ARISS, *m.* Richard BUCKNER, of the well known Albany Estate situated on the creek called "BUCKNER."

ISSUE

I. Joseph.
II. ELLEN, of whom later.
III. Molly.
IV. Ursula, *m.* Churchill GORDON.

ELLEN PEIRCE, of Westmoreland County, Virginia, *m.* (firstly) ———— LAWSON; *m.* (secondly) 20th November, 1788, Capt. John TEMPLEMAN, *b.* 1758, *d.* near Danville, Kentucky, 1835.

ISSUE BY FIRST MARRIAGE

I. Ellen Lawson, *m.* 15th November, 1797, Stephen BAILEY.

ISSUE BY SECOND MARRIAGE

I. LUCY TEMPLEMAN, *b.* 1791, of whom below.
II. Polly TEMPLEMAN, *m.* Samuel WILSON.

LUCY TEMPLEMAN, of Virginia, *b.* 1791; *d.* near Danville, Kentucky, 1857; *m.* (firstly) ———— MOSS; *m.* (secondly) James DONEGHY, I, *b.* 1772, *d.* 1847, near Danville, Kentucky.

ISSUE BY FIRST MARRIAGE

I. Amelia Moss, *m.* Abraham Irvine.
II. Lucinda Moss, *m.* Gabriel Caldwell.

ISSUE BY SECOND MARRIAGE

I. Philip Doneghy.
II. Mary (Polly) Doneghy, *m.* Edward Hughes.
III. Ellen Peirce Doneghy, *m.* J. C. Maxwell, M.D.
IV. James Doneghy, II, of whom below.
V. John Templeman Doneghy, I, *m.* Media Burton.
VI. Sarah Doneghy, *m.* Nathaniel Wood.

James Doneghy, II, of Danville, Kentucky; *b.* 1827; *d.* 1862; *m.* Kate Bradshaw Campbell, *b.* 1830, *d.* 1913.

ISSUE

I. James Doneghy, III, *b.* 1850; *m.* (firstly) 1875, Anna Belle Coles; *m.* (secondly) 1916, Mrs. Jessie Murphy.
II. John Templeman Doneghy, II, *b*, Danville, Kentucky, 1852, of whom below.
III. Alexander Doneghy *b.* 1855; *m.* Martha Talbott Prewitt.
IV. Irvine Doneghy, *b.* 1857; *m.* Mattie Lee De France.
V. Herbert Doneghy, *b.* 1859; *m.* 30th September, 1890, Nannie Bertie Wooldridge.
VI. Hanson Weitman Doneghy, *b.* 1861; *m.* 10th January, 1900, Lucy Van Cleve.

John Templeman Doneghy, II, of Macon, Missouri; Banker and Capitalist; *b.* 1852, near Danville, Kentucky; came with his parents when a small child to Missouri and resided near Independence until 1873, when he settled at La Plata, Missouri, where he was engaged in mercantile and banking pursuits until 1900; in 1906 moved to Macon, Missouri; *m.* 20th May, 1885, Mary McKinley Craddock, *b.* Mexico, Missouri, 1864, dau. of Samuel and Mary (Atchison) Craddock.

ISSUE

I. John Templeman Doneghy, III, *b.* 14th April, 1889, the subject of this memoir.

Arms (Peirce).—Argent a fesse humettee gules between three ravens rising sable.
Crest.—A dove with an olive branch in its beak.
Motto.—Dixit et fecit.

Residence.—Oakleigh Place, Macon, Missouri.

Clubs.—University, Bondsmen, Advertising, all of St. Louis, Missouri.

Societies.—Colonial Wars; Zeta Psi; Sigma Xi; Member of Paleontological Society of America; Member of American Association for the Advancement of Science, Fellow American Geographical Society; Benevolent and Protective Order of Elks.

Ellegood

JOSHUA ATKINSON ELLEGOOD, M.D., *b.* 28th September, 1859, at Concord, Sussex County, Delaware; *m.* 19th November, 1884, at Laurel, Delaware, Marion DASHIELL, *b.* 19th November, 1863, dau. of William Winder DASHIELL, *b.* 9th December, 1823, at Laurel, Delaware, *d.* there 15th April, 1895, *m.* 26th June, 1854, Miranda WHEATLEY, *b.* there 24th April, 1834 (living May, 1918).

ISSUE

1. Claire Winder Dashiell, *b.* 27th December, 1886.

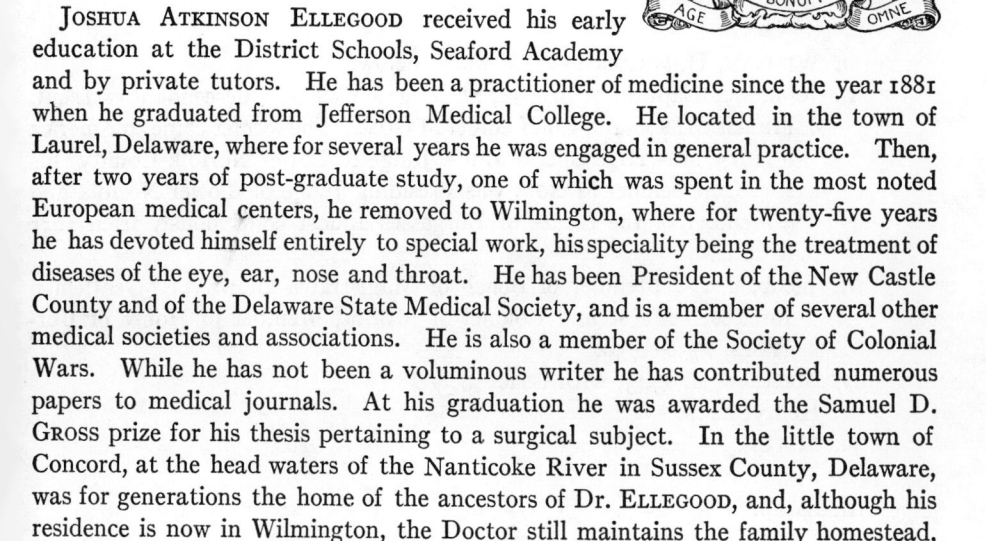

JOSHUA ATKINSON ELLEGOOD received his early education at the District Schools, Seaford Academy and by private tutors. He has been a practitioner of medicine since the year 1881 when he graduated from Jefferson Medical College. He located in the town of Laurel, Delaware, where for several years he was engaged in general practice. Then, after two years of post-graduate study, one of which was spent in the most noted European medical centers, he removed to Wilmington, where for twenty-five years he has devoted himself entirely to special work, his speciality being the treatment of diseases of the eye, ear, nose and throat. He has been President of the New Castle County and of the Delaware State Medical Society, and is a member of several other medical societies and associations. He is also a member of the Society of Colonial Wars. While he has not been a voluminous writer he has contributed numerous papers to medical journals. At his graduation he was awarded the Samuel D. GROSS prize for his thesis pertaining to a surgical subject. In the little town of Concord, at the head waters of the Nanticoke River in Sussex County, Delaware, was for generations the home of the ancestors of Dr. ELLEGOOD, and, although his residence is now in Wilmington, the Doctor still maintains the family homestead, where it is his pleasure to visit from time to time.

Lineage

The ancestor of this family was Thomas ELLEGOOD of Northampton County, Virginia; he was probably a descendant of Richard ELLEGOOD of Tostock Parish, Sussex County, England; he emigrated to America before 1658; *d.* 1689; *m.* (firstly) Mary FIELD, dau. of Henry FIELD; *m.* (secondly) Elizabeth (surname not given).

ISSUE BY FIRST MARRIAGE

I. Thomas, *d.* 1696.
II. Richard, *d.* 1716.

III. John, d. 1709; m. Ann RIDING, probably dau. of Thomas RIDING and Rose YEARDLEY, and gd. dau. of Sir George YEARDLEY.
IV. Henry, d. 1721.
V. Mazy.

ISSUE BY SECOND MARRIAGE

I. WILLIAM, b. circa 1680, of whom below.
II. Peter Norley, m. Margaret HARMONSON, s.d.p. 1746.

WILLIAM ELLEGOOD, I, b. circa 1680; m. Elizabeth (surname not given); d. Princess Anne County, Virginia, where he was a man of wealth and importance; he was appointed by King George II, a Justice and Tobacco Commissioner; he was a Church Warden and Vestryman in Lynnhaven Parish, and also a Captain of Militia.

ISSUE

I. WILLIAM, II, b. circa 1708, of whom below.
II. John, was Captain of Militia; m. Abigail MASON, a descendant of Lieut. Francis MASON and Col. Lemuel MASON. The former came to America in 1613; was High Sheriff and a Judge of Lower Norfolk County; his son, Col. Lemuel MASON, was Presiding Judge of Lower Norfolk and a member of the House of Burgesses almost continuously from 1655 to 1692.
III. Jacob, d.s.p.; Member of Bench of Magistrates known as "Gentlemen Justices;" Major and Colonel of Militia; Member of House of Burgesses, 1736–1750.
IV. Matthew, d. 1743, with issue.
V. Henry, d.s.p.
VI. Martha.
VII. Mary.
VIII. Sarah.

WILLIAM ELLEGOOD, II, of Northampton County, Virginia; b. circa 1708; d. Somerset County, Maryland; he moved first to Dorchester County, and then to Somerset County, Maryland; in 1760 he took up large tracts of land near the town of Concord, then in territory over which jurisdiction was claimed by Lord Baltimore; later in 1765, by the agreement between PENN and the Maryland Proprietor, it became a part of the State of Delaware; among other pieces of land, he took up one, in what is now Sussex County, Delaware, which was called "Isabelle's Choice;" a part of this land, referred to above, he sold to his son Robert ELLEGOOD, the gr. gd. father of Dr. Joshua A. ELLEGOOD; it is now in the possession of Dr. ELLEGOOD, having passed down to him through the succeeding generations; William ELLEGOOD II, m. before 1750, Mary COULBURN.

COLONIAL FAMILIES OF THE UNITED STATES

ISSUE

  I. John, *d.* 1777.
 II. William, *d.* 1776.
III. Thomas, *d.* 1822.
IV. ROBERT, *b.* 29th April, 1721, of whom below.
 V. Sarah.
VI. Elizabeth.

ROBERT ELLEGOOD, *b.* 29th April, 1752; *m.* Mary Brent ATKINSON, dau. of William B. ATKINSON and Mary Brent NUTTALL, 12th February, 1786; *d.* 1795; gr. gr. gd. dau. of Gen. Giles BRENT.

ISSUE

  I. William A., *b.* 27th May, 1787; *d.* 19th July, 1830.
 II. JOSHUA, *b.* 18th February, 1789, of whom below.
III. Sarah, *b.* 18th May, 1792; *d.* 7th April, 1833; *m.* Warren JEFFERSON.
IV. Thomas, *b.* 21st April, 1794; left issue.

JOSHUA ELLEGOOD, *b.* 18th February, 1789; *d.* 25th May, 1845; *m.* Ann Houston GRIFFITH, dau. of Col. Seth GRIFFITH.

ISSUE

   I. ROBERT GRIFFITH, *b.* 16th March, 1828, of whom below.
  II. Catharine G., *b.* 15th December, 1829.
 III. Ann Eliza, *b.* 26th October, 1831; living.
  IV. Mary Jane, *b.* 5th March, 1835; *d.* 18th July, 1879; has issue.
   V. William Thomas, *b.* 17th March, 1837; *d.* 4th December, 1867.
  VI. Sarah, *b.* 7th April, 1841.
 VII. Seth Griffith, *b.* 28th July, 1843; living.
VIII. Anna, *b.* 25th March, 1845; living.

ROBERT GRIFFITH ELLEGOOD, *b.* 16th March, 1828; *d.* 22d March, 1902; was educated at the District schools and Laurel Adademy; he studied medicine and graduated at the Pennsylvania Medical College at the age of twenty-four; his whole life was spent at Concord where for many years he was the leading citizen of the town; his judgment was sought and respected, not only in his immediate community but also in the political councils of the State; he was at one time a member of the State Legislature, and served three terms as State Auditor of Accounts; *m.* Elizabeth CANNON, *b.* 8th December, 1835, *d.* 12th April, 1897, dau. of Nutter and Margaret CANNON.

ISSUE

 I. JOSHUA ATKINSON, *b.* 28th September, 1859, the subject of this memoir.
II. Robert, *b.* 25th December, 1860; *m.* 6th November, 1893, Ida Horsey BENNEY, *b.* 1st May, 1871, *d.* 26th November, 1915.

ISSUE

1. Joshua Horsey, *b.* 24th September, 1894.
2. George Robert, *b.* 15th January, 1897; *m.* Hazell TURNER, 31st July, 1917.

ISSUE

1[1]. Robert Turner, *b.* 6th April, 1918.

III. Seth Griffith, *b.* 28th May, 1861; *m.* (firstly) 1884, Jennie (Mary Virginia) COBB, *b.* 2d March, 1855; *d.* 15th December, 1905; *m.* (secondly) 23d January, 1907, Anna Greenwood LAMBERT.

ISSUE

1. Robert R., *b.* 18th February, 1887.

DR. JOSHUA A. ELLEGOOD is a lineal descendant of Gen. Giles BRENT, whose sister Margaret BRENT was the first woman who ever claimed the right of suffrage in America. General BRENT was born in England about 1600, came to Maryland in 1638, served as Deputy Governor of Maryland, Treasurer of the Province of Maryland, and Member of the Assembly. He is also lineally descended from Col. William COULBOURN, who immigrated to Northampton County, Virginia, in 1651, and who was successively commissioned: Lieutentant, Captain, and Colonel of Militia by the Assembly of the Province of Maryland. Also of Captain Edmund SCARBOROUGH, who was *b.* at St. Martin's in the Fields, London, in 1588, and emigrated to Virginia in 1628; he was a Member of the first Board of Commissioners for the Plantation of Accomac, Justice of Peace, Member of the House of Burgesses, and a Captain in the Militia, organized for protection against the Indians. Also of Randall REVELL, who emigrated to America in 1633, who was a member of the General Assembly of Maryland from 1637 to 1642, and of the House of Burgesses in Virginia in 1661. Also of Samuel HANDY, who settled in Somerset County in 1664. Also of John NUTTHALL, who emigrated to Northampton County, Virginia, before 1643. Also of John LAWS, who emigrated to Somerset County, Virginia, before 1667. Also of John ALEXANDER who emigrated to Northampton County, Virginia, in 1639. He is descended from the Welsh family of GRIFFITH through Henry GRIFFITH, who received an original grant of land in Dorchester County, Maryland, in 1681; and from the Scotch family of HOUSTON, through Robert HOUSTON, who emigrated to Virginia in 1652.

The family named ELLEGOOD is of Anglo-Saxon derivation, from AETHELGEARD, which appears in tongues closely allied to the English as ELLEGAARD, or ELGERT, and has the meaning of "noble guardian." As is the case with names of ancient origin, the etymology varies, but as their name is by no means a common one, doubtless, all these families had a common ancestor.

The earliest English record of the name in approximately its present form, known to the biographer, is that of Simon ELGOOD, Burgess of the town of Bristol, who was buried in the chapel of St. Mary, in St. Thomas the Martyr, Bristol, and whose will dated 28th December, 1404, is on the record in the Prerogative Court of Canterbury; from that date on the name appears frequently in various Parishes with various slight changes until about 1575 when it is written ELLEGOOD in wills and baptismal records, a number of which are to be found in Hitcham and other Parishes in Southern England.

A petition to Parliament in 1649, now on file in the British Museum, discloses the fact that one Richard ELLEGOOD was an officer in CROMWELL'S army.

In the Parish of Tostock, County Suffolk, there is a record of the will of another Richard ELLEGOOD which was dated 23d October, 1632, proved at Bury St. Edmunds, 26th November, 1632, in which he bequeathed to his son Thomas property in the town of St. Edmunds.

While positive identifications of Thomas ELLEGOOD of Tostock as the emigrant to Virginia has not been effected, it is practically certain that he was from County Suffolk. It is also highly probable that the emigration of Thomas ELLEGOOD to America was caused by the political conditions which prevailed in England just prior to the downfall of the Commonwealth.

Arms.—Argent, a cross engrailed gules between four mullets azure, on a chief or, three damask roses of the second, seeded gold, barbed, vert.

Crest.—Two arms embowed in armour proper, holding in the hands a human heart gules, inflamed with a tower triple towered argent.

Motto.—Age bonum omne.

Residence.—1306 Delaware Avenue, Wilmington, Delaware.

Clubs.—Wilmington, Wilmington Country, Church, Rotary, Whist.

Societies.—New Castle County Medical Society; Delaware State Medical Society; American Medical Association; the American Academy of Ophthalmology, Rhinology, Ototogy, and Laryngology; American Laryngological, Rhinological and Otological Society; Member of Medical Advisory Board No. 1 of Delaware; Member "United States Public Service Reserve;" has had several degrees in the order of Masonry.

English

ALBERT JOHN ENGLISH, of Omaha, Nebraska; b. 21st February, 1886, at Yankton, South Dakota; was educated at Yankton Public Schools and by profession is an illuminating engineer. Appointed, 1907, First Lieutenant Infantry, South Dakota National Guards; 1917 Secret Service Nebraska State Council of Defense; 1918 Assigned to Officers' Training School, Camp Fremont, California.

Lineage

We cannot at this later period decide how the family name of ENGLISH originated but the ancient records of England known as the "Hundred Rolls" at an early date refers to "Walter LE ENGLEIS," the "Calendorium Inquisitorium Post Mortem" has a record of one "Richard LE ENGLEYS" and in some of the early writs of Parliament the name of "John LE ENGLISSHE" appears. However, the earliest record of the name to be found in Great Britain anywhere, and one which shows the family to have been in existence at a very early period is in the Parliamentary Roll of Arm for the Northern Counties of Northumberland and Cumberland for the year 1013, where the armory of 'Sire Joh'n LE ENGLEYS" is recorded as "de sable a lij lyounceus de argent." This armory: three lions argent on a sable shield, is the exact arms borne later by both the ENGLISH family of England and the INGLIS family of Scotland, which is strong evidence in support of the conclusion that the families had the same common origin and are possibly all descendants of this Sir John and that the name was originally "ENGLISH" and became "INGLIS" when transplanted later over the Border into Scotland, where it appeared in 1296 when Walter DE INGLIS, John DE INGLIS, Phillip DE INGLIS, etc., are mentioned as men of rank and property, following the time of the invasion and establishment of English authority in Scotland by King Edward I of England. It is noticeable that both families were originally located close to the border line between the two countries, showing another possible bond of relationship between them. Sir James ENGLISH of Craver, County Edinburgh, Scotland, gr. gr. gd. son of James INGLISH, a merchant burgess of Edinburgh at the time of the reformation (1520), was created by James II a baronet on 22d March, 1687, and d. in 1688; from him followed as baronets his son Sir John (2), Adam (3), John (4), Patrick (5), who d. in 1817, when the title became dormant. Another John LE ENGLEYS is reported as in the Parish of Lench in Worcestershire in 1327. (The marriage of Mary ENGLISH is recorded in this Parish, 25th October, 1345, to Francis GODFREE.) But the name does not appear again in the ancient records until 1375, when the seal of "Sir Richard ENGLISSCHE" with armorial bearings thereon appears attached to a deed made to him by the widow of Walter DE BEREFORD in connection with land rental at "North Petherton" (Pedarston), Somersetshire. The name next appeared of record in the northern counties of Westmoreland and Northumberland again where, the "Yorkshire Visitation" chronicles that "Isabella, daughter and heir of William ENGLISH of Appleby and Ashby, County Westmoreland, and of Brixworth, County Northampton, and his wife Ellen DAWNEY married Sir Nycholas HARRINGTON." The family later became a well established one in the County of Devon and branches of this Devonshire family located in the counties of Cumberland, Wilts and Kent. These families trace their origin directly to Cunnant ENGLISH, founder of this line, who *m.* Grace YARD of the YARD family of Bradley in Hants and Churchton Ferrers in Devonshire; following one of these branches from Cunnant ENGLISH down in a direct male line (most of whose names were Thomas) it seems not improbable that Thomas ENGLISH who came in the *Mayflower* may have come from this branch of the ENGLISH family.

CLEMENT ENGLISH, the first member of this branch of the family in America of whom we have authentic record, was *b.* in Salem, Massachusetts in 1646; *d.* 23d December, 1682, at Salem, where he was a merchant, and a man of consideration; family traditions claim him to have been a gd. son of Thomas ENGLISH, who came in the *Mayflower* and who *d.* at Plymouth, 1621; he *m.* 27th August, 1667, Mary WATERS, dau. of Richard WATERS, who emigrated to Salem, Massachusetts, in 1637, and was appointed, in 1667, Petitioner for Conciliation between the Colonial Government and the Crown.

ISSUE

1. BENJAMIN, *b.* 19th October, 1676, of whom below.

BENJAMIN ENGLISH, *b.* at Salem, Massachusetts, 19th October, 1676; *d.* 1725; *m.* (firstly) 8th January, 1699, Sarah WARD who *d.* 4th December, 1700; he moved to New Haven; *m.* (secondly), 23rd April, 1702, Rebecca BROWN, who brought into this family the strain of royal blood in direct descent from the earlier British Kings, including both the Anglo-Saxon line from Alfred the Great, and the Norman line from William the Conqueror down through King Henry III, whose son Edmond Plantagenet, married Queen Blanche, widow of King Henry of Navarre, whose grandfather was Louis VIII, of France, and great grandfather Alphonso IX, of Castile. Lady Plantagenet, the grand daughter of Prince Edmond and his wife Queen Blanche, married Richard Fitz-Alan, K. G., ninth Earl of Arundel, and their great, great granddaughter, Eleanor Fitz-Alan, married Sir Thomas Brown, of Beechwood Castle, treasurer of the household to King Kenry VI, whose great, great, great grandson, Francis Brown, *b.* at Waybird hall, County Brandon, Suffolk, in 1620, came to Salem and married in 1639, Mary Edwards. Their son Ebenezer Brown, *b.* there 1st July, 1647, married Hannah Vincent; they were the parents of Rebecca Brown, *b.* 1672, *d.* 6th May, 1768, aged 96 years.

ISSUE BY SECOND MARRIAGE

I. Sarah, *b.* 7th February, 1704; *m.* ——— S. BRADLEY.
II. BENJAMIN, *b.* 8th October, 1705, of whom below.
III. Mary, *b.* 10th February, 1707.
IV. Joseph, *b.* 2d February, 1709.
V. Clement, *b.* 1716; *d.* October, 1801.

BENJAMIN ENGLISH, of New Haven, Connecticut; *b.* 8th October, 1705, at New Haven, Connecticut; killed 3d July, 1779, by the bayonet of a Hessian soldier; was engaged for many years in the West India trade, being in command of a number of trading vessels; *m.* 24th September, 1735, Sarah DAYTON, dau. of Isaac and Elizabeth (TODD) DAYTON.

ISSUE

I. Sarah, *b.* 14th September, 1738; *d.* 28th September, 1794; *m.* William PLUYETT.
II. Abigail, *b.* 8th April, 1740; *d.* 30 November, 1795; *n.* Nathanial SPENCER.
III. BENJAMIN, *b.* 27th December, 1742, of whom below.
IV. Mary, *b.* 27th September, 1744; *d.* 27th October, 1794; *m.* David PHIPPS.
V. Hannah, *b.* 9th December, 1749; *m.* Daniel BROWN.

CAPT. BENJAMIN ENGLISH, of New Haven, Connecticut; *b.* 27th December, 1742; *d.* 19th April, 1809; *m.* 17th November, 1768, Abigail DOOLITTLE, dau. of Isaac and Sarah (TODD) DOOLITTLE) and gr. gd. dau. of Abraham DOOLITTLE, who fought in King Philip's War and was a Deputy for New Haven, 1668–1672; Isaac DOOLITTLE was appointed by the General Assembly in 1776 Inspector of Fire Arms; manufacturer of gun powder for the Revolutionary Government at his mills in New Haven.

ISSUE

I. ISAAC, *b.* 9th March, 1769, of whom below.
II. Benjamin, *b.* 5th January, 1770; lost at sea, October, 1809.
III. Sarah, *b.* 3d November, 1771; *d.* 26th March, 1843.
IV. John Todd, *b.* 3d August, 1773; *d.* 19th June, 1801.
V. Abigail, *b.* 13th February, 1776; *d.* 12th March, 1834; *m.* 29th August, 1802, Emanuel HOPKINS.
VI. Mary, *b.* 12th March, 1778; *d.* 13th December, 1845; *m.* 13th November, 1799, Roswell BROWN.
VII. Hannah Rebecca, *b.* January, 1780; *d.* 29th January, 1807; *m.* 7th December, 1799, Bertmel TUTTLE.
VIII. James, *b.* 26th July, 1784; *d.* 2d December, 1850; *m.* 29th March, 1807, Nancy GRISWOLD.
IX. Aaron, *b.* 25th November, 1786; *d.* 22d November, 1839; *m.* 9th August, 1823, Sarah HAYNES.

x. Eli, *b.* 9th March, 1789; *d.* January, 1853; *m.* 20th September, 1821, Emily STOCKING.
xi. Nathan Frederick, *b.* 9th April, 1792; lost at sea in brig *Arrow*, 1814.

ISAAC ENGLISH, of New Haven, Connecticut; *b.* there 9th March, 1769; *d.* there 7th October, 1826; *m.* there 26th July, 1807, Catherine ROSS, dau. of ———— ROSS.

ISSUE

I. William Frederick, *b.* 12th December, 1809; *d.* February, 1838.
II. NATHANIEL SPENCER, *b.* 10th December, 1811, of whom below.
III. Sarah Abigail, *b.* 16th October, 1814; *d.* 17th March, 1900; *m.* 23d April, 1845, Isaac PRYOR.
IV. Hannah Maria, *b.* 9th March, 1817; *d.* 22d December, 1846; *m.* 4th March, 1839, Maj. Benjamin M. PRESCOTT
V. Catherine, *b.* 16th December, 1817; *d.* 1st December, 1867.
VI. Julia, *b.* October, 1824; *d.* May, 1884; *m.* 23d March, 1844, Capt. George WARD.

NATHANIEL SPENCER ENGLISH, of New Haven, Connecticut; *b.* there 10th December, 1811; *d.* there 15th September, 1895; *m.* there 11th December, 1837, Hannah Burdick STANTON, a lineal descendant of Thomas STANTON, one of the founders of Stonington, Connecticut, who came from Virginia in 1635 and was appointed Interpreter General of the United Colonies for the Indian language; his mother was the dau. of Walter WASHINGTON of Sulgrave, Northamptonshire, England, and granddaughter of Robert WASHINGTON, the ancestor also of GEORGE WASHINGTON.

ISSUE

I. Sarah Maria, *b.* 13th September, 1838; *d.* 2d November, 1879; *m.* 13th May, 1862, Gen. John B. DENNIS.
II. William Spencer, *b.* 19th September, 1842; killed 16th July, 1864, at Drury's Bluff, Virginia, while serving in the Army of the James River.
III. EDMOND FRANKLIN, *b.* 2d May, 1844, of whom below.

MAJ. GEN. EDMOND FRANKLIN ENGLISH, of St. Helena Island, South Carolina; *b.* 2d May, 1844; *d.* 30th August, 1911; he enlisted in the 1st Connecticut Volunteer Cavalry when only seventeen years old and served in the Union Army during the entire Civil War, after which he was appointed military Aide to the Governor of South Carolina with the rank of Colonel; in 1905 he was commissioned by the Imperial Chinese Government, Major-General in the Chinese Army and invested by the Empress Dowager of China, with the order of the Double Dragon, first class; *m.* (firstly) 2d August, 1867, Jennie AUSTIN; *m.* (secondly) 12th April, 1883, Emily Cobby HEDGETHORN, *b.* 20th January, 1865, dau. of Rev. James HEDGETHORN, of Brighton, England.

ISSUE BY FIRST MARRIAGE

1. Mary Spencer, b. 29th November, 1868; d. 1st January, 1890; m. Arthur J. TUTTLE, of New Haven, Connecticut.

ISSUE

1. Philip English TUTTLE, b. 8th October, 1888; (now, 1918) in the United States Marine Corps.

ii. William Berney, b. 7th September, 1870; d. 10th September, 1870.

ISSUE BY SECOND MARRIAGE

1. Devereux York, b. 13th June, 1884.
ii. ALBERT JOHN, b. 21st February, 1886, the subject of this memoir.
iii. Franklin Edmond Stanton, b. 2d February, 1892.

Arms.—Sable, three lions rampant argent.
Crest.—Out of a ducal coronet or, a demi-lion rampant argent, with dexter paw on shield.
Motto.—Nobilis est ira leonis.
Residence.—823 South 35th Avenue, Omaha, Nebraska.
Clubs.—Carter Lake.
Societies.—Colonial Wars, Mayflower Descendants, Sons of the American Revolution, Sons of Veterans.

French

FRANCIS ORMOND FRENCH, deceased, A.B., LL.B., of New York and Newport, Rhode Island; *b.* in Chester, New Hampshire, 12th September, 1837; *d.* at Tuxedo Park, 26th February, 1893; fitted for college at Phillips Exeter Academy; Harvard College, graduate, A.B., 1857; LL.B., 1859; was Secretary of the Hasty Pudding Club, and class; was a pupil of James Lowell RUSSELL; appointed September, 1862, Deputy Naval Officer of Customs at Boston, and appointed, 1863, Deputy Collector of the Port; in 1865 entered the banking firm of Samuel A. WAY and Company, Boston; his paper upon the payment of the United States four per cents in gold coin was adopted by Secretary SHERMAN and circulated throughout Europe and the United States during the negotiations of these loans; later of the firm of FOTTE and FRENCH; represented the London firm of Jay Cook M'CULLOH and Company; Lawyer and Banker, admitted to the New York Bar May, 1860; Fourth President of the Manhattan Trust Company, 1888; President of the Harvard Club; Trustee of Phillips Exeter Academy; *m.* 5th March, 1861, ELLEN TUCK, dau. of Hon. Amos TUCK, Member of Congress, 1847–1853; Collector of the Port of Boston under President LINCOLN.

ISSUE

1. Amos Tuck, A.B., of Tuxedo Park, New York; *b.* in Boston, Massachusetts, 20th July, 1863; *m.* 2d December, 1885, in Newport, Rhode Island, Pauline LE ROY, *b.* 14th February, 1864, dau. of Stuyvesant and Pauline W. (BRIDGE) LE ROY of Newport, Rhode Island.

    ### ISSUE

    1. Pauline Le Roy, *b.* 30th November, 1886; *m.* 5th May, 1908, Samuel WAGSTAFF.
    2. Frances Ormond, *b.* 27th November, 1888, Petty Officer, United States Naval Reserves.
    3. Julia, *b.* 6th June, 1893; *m.* 8th August, 1911, John GERAGHTY.
    4. Stuyvesant Le Roy, *b.* 19th August, 1895; Lieutenant, United States Army.
    5. Edward Tuck, *b.* 3d May, 1899; Tank Corps, United States Army; *m.* 29th June, 1918, Miss Lillian HARRINGTON of Manchester, New Hampshire.
    6. Amos Tuck, *b.* 10th September, 1901.

II. Elizabeth Richardson (Lady CHEYLESMORE), *m*. 1892, Herbert Francis EATON, Third Baron CHEYLESMORE of 16 Prince's Gate, S. W. London, England, *b*. 25th June, 1848; Commander Royal Victorian Order, 1905; Knight Royal Victorian Order, 1909; former Colonel commanding Grenadier Guards; Member South Africa Compensation Committee, 1901; Mayor of Westminster, 1904–1905; Retired Major General of the Army; Justice of the Peace for Bucks and County London; a Deputy Lieutenant for Middlesex; Chairman of London County Council (Counsellor from St. George, Hanover Square Division); a Vice Chairman of the British Red Cross Society; Honorary Colonel 9th Battalion, County of London Regiment; Chairman Middlesex Army Association; a Knight of Grace of the Order of St. John of Jerusalem in England; owns the manor of Cheylesmore, Coventry, formerly possessed by Edward the Black Prince.

ISSUE

1. Hon. Francis Ormond Eaton, *b*. 19th June, 1893.
2. Hon. Herbert Edward Eaton, *b*. 1895.

III. Elsie, *m*. 11th January, 1901, Alfred Gwynne VANDERBILT, *b*. 20th October, 1877; A.B., Yale, 1889; murdered on the *Lusitania*, 1915; son of Cornelius and Alice Claypoole (GWYNNE) VANDERBILT; Alfred Gwynne VANDERBILT *m*. (secondly) Margaret (EMERSON) McKIM, dau. of Dr. Isaac EMERSON of Baltimore; she *m*. (thirdly) RAY BAKER, of Washington, D. C.

Lineage

EDWARD FRENCH of Salisbury, Massachusetts, *b*. in England; came to America in 1636; *d*. 28th December, 1674, with his wife Ann (surname unknown) and children, and settled at Ipswich, Massachusetts, of which he was one of the founders; in 1652 with the exception of two had the greatest estate of any one in Ipswich; removed in 1652 to that part of Salisbury which by change of boundaries of the Colony in 1741, became Southampton, New Hampshire.

ISSUE

I. Joseph, *b*. in England.
II. John, *m*. 23d March, 1659, Mary NOYES, dau. of Joseph NOYES.

ISSUE

1. John, *b*. 12th December, 1660.
2. Mary, *b*. 12th June, 1663.
3. Hannah, *b*. 9th August, 1669, *d*. in infancy.

4. Hannah, *m.* Jethro WHEELER of Rowley.
5. Samuel, *b.* 27th December, 1669.
6. Edward, *b.* 20th July, 1672.
7. Abigail, *b.* 6th May, 1675.
8. Nicholas, *b.* 28th October, 1677, *d.* 1698.
9. James, *b.* 15th August, 1679.
10. Timothy, *b.* 15th August, 1681.

III. Samuel, *m.* 1st June, 1664, Abigail BROWN.

ISSUE
1. Samuel.

IV. Philbrick, *m.* (firstly) 25th June, 1662, John WHITE of Haverhill; *m.* (secondly) 22d September 1669, Thomas PHILBRICK.

JOSEPH FRENCH, of Ipswich, *b.* in England, came to America with his father, in 1636; *m.* Susanna (surname unknown), who *d.* 16th February, 1688.

ISSUE
I. JOSEPH, *b.* 16th March, 1654.
II. Eliza, *b.* 5th November, 1655; *d.* 6th December, 1655.
III. Simon, *b.* 24th October, 1657.
IV. Ann, *b.* 10th March, 1659; *m.* 21st July, 1680, Richard LONG.
V. Edward, *b.* 14th May, 1663; *d.* 8th June, 1663.
VI. Edward, *b.* 6th April, 1667; *d.* 28th December, 1674.

JOSEPH FRENCH, of Salisbury, Massachusetts; *b.* 16th March, 1654; *d.* 14th December, 1683; *m.* 13th June, 1678, Sarah EASTMAN, dau. of Roger EASTMAN; she *m.* (secondly) 4th August, 1684, Soloman SHEPHERD.

ISSUE
I. JOSEPH, *b.* 26th March, 1679.
II. Timothy, *b.* 16th June, 1681.
III. Simon, *b.* 26th August, 1683.

JOSEPH FRENCH, of South Hampton, New Hampshire; *b.* in Salisbury, 26th March, 1679; *d.* 27th December, 1756; *m.* (wife's name not given).

ISSUE AMONG OTHERS
I. DANIEL, *b.* 21st August, 1708, of whom below.

DANIEL FRENCH, of South Hampton, New Hampshire; *b.* 21st August, 1708; *d.* 1st September, 1783; *m.* Sarah GOULD.

ISSUE AMONG OTHERS

1. GOULD, *b*. 17th September, 1741, of whom below.

GOULD FRENCH, of Epping, New Hampshire; *b*. 21st August, 1708; *d*. 12th May, 1823; fought in the Revolutionary War, *m*. 24th November, 1763, Dorothy WHITTIER.

ISSUE AMONG OTHERS

1. DANIEL, *b*. 22d February, 1769, of whom below.

DANIEL FRENCH, Lawyer, of Chester, New Hampshire; *b*. 22d February, 1769, *d*. 15th October, 1840; was Attorney-General of State of New Hampshire; *m*. (firstly) 15th September, 1799, Mercy BROWN, sister of Rev. Francis BROWN, President of Dartmouth College; *m*. (secondly) Sarah W. (FLAGG) BELL, widow.

ISSUE BY FIRST MARRIAGE AMONG OTHERS

1. BENJAMIN BROWN, *b*. 4th September, 1800, of whom below.

ISSUE BY SECOND MARRIAGE AMONG OTHERS

1. Henry Flagg, Jurist of Concord, Massachusetts; *b*. 14th August, 1813; *d*. 29th November, 1888; Justice of the Court of Common Pleas, 1855-1859; District Attorney for Suffolk County, Massachusetts, 1862-1865, appointed, 1876, by General GRANT, Second Assistant Secretary of the United States Treasury, and held office until 1885, when he returned to Concord; *m*. Anne RICHARDSON, dau. of Chief Justice W. H. RICHARDSON.

BENJAMIN BROWN FRENCH, Lawyer, of Chester, New Hampshire, and Washington, D. C.; *b*. in Chester, 4th September, 1800; *d*. in Washington, D. C., 12th August, 1870; educated at Dartmouth College; Graduate, A.M.; lived in Washington from 1833 to 1870; Commissioner of Public Buildings under President LINCOLN; President of the first company organized to construct a telegraph line between Washington and New York City; *m*. 12th January, 1825, Elizabeth RICHARDSON, dau. of Chief Justice W. H. RICHARDSON of New Hampshire.

ISSUE

1. FRANCIS ORMOND, *b*. 12th September, 1837, the subject of this memoir.

Arms.—Azure a chevron between three boars heads or.
Crest.—A boar's head erased cheque with five crosslets.
Motto.—Tuebor.

Fuller

HORACE FREDERICK FULLER, B.D., of Philadelphia, Pennsylvania; *b.* 17th February, 1865, at Washington, D. C.; *d.* 17th September, 1915, at Cedar Grove, Philadelphia; *m.* 7th June, 1904, Marion Graham NIMLET, *b.* 29th June, 1880, dau. of David Campbell NIMLET, *b.* 7th July, 1846, at Glasgow, Scotland, *d.* 11th November, 1912, at Philadelphia, *m.* 20th January, 1870, Mary Ann WHITAKER, of Cedar Grove, Pennsylvania, *b.* 6th March, 1845. David Campbell NIMLET, father-in-law of Horace Frederick FULLER, was the only son of David and Jean (CAMPBELL) NIMLET, *m.* 1st January, 1840, Glasgow, Scotland, and gd. son of Alexander and Elizabeth (MELVILLE) NIMLET. David Campbell NIMLET, was for many years senior member of the firm of William WHITAKER and Sons, founded in 1813, by Henry WHITAKER whose gr. gd. dau., Mary Ann WHITAKER, Mr. NIMLET married. David C. NIMLET was a Director of the First and Second National Banks, of the Fire Association of Philadelphia, the Camden Iron Works, and Arrott Steam Mills; he was a member of the Union League, the St. Andrew's Society, the Church Club, the Down Town Club, and for nearly thirty years, Vestryman and Accounting Warden of Trinity Church (Oxford) Philadelphia. The only surviving children of David C. and Mary NIMLET are Virginia CAMPBELL, *b.* 30th July, 1878, unmarried, and Marion GRAHAM, *b.* 29th June, 1880, widow of Mr. FULLER.

ISSUE

I. Melville Whitaker, *b.* 20th February, 1905.
II. Horace Neville, *b.* 28th December, 1906.
III. Virginia Weld, *b.* 18th January, 1912.

HORACE FREDERICK FULLER, graduated at the Philadelphia Divinity School of the Protestant Episcopal Church, 1888; Ordained, 1889, by Bishop WHITAKER, of Pennsylvania; successively in charge of Church of the Holy Comforter and old St. Paul's; from 1893–1903 Rector Trinity Church, Southwark; from 1903 to his death in 1915; Rector Trinity Church, Oxford, all of Philadelphia; Chairman Diocesan Convention's Committee on Charters; Chairman of Committee of Finance and Church Extension, Convocation of Germantown, and Overseer of Philadelphia Divinity School; Delegate to the Provincial Synod.

Lineage

The ancestor of the family was Edward FULLER, of Redenhall Parish, County of Norfolk, England; *bapt.* at Redenhall Church, 4th September, 1575, *d.* at Plymouth, between 11th January and 10th April, 1621; son of Robert FULLER; emigrated to America on the *Mayflower* in 1620, with his wife and son Samuel and Brother Dr. Samuel FULLER; settled in Plymouth; *m.* Ann (surname not given).

ISSUE

I. Matthew, *b.* 1603 (?), Redenhall, England, of whom later.
II. Samuel, *b.* about 1612, of whom later.

Matthew FULLER, *b.* 1603 (?); *d.* Barnstable, Massachusetts, August, 1678; *m.* Frances (surname unknown); emigrated to America and settled in Plymouth in 1640; represented Barnstable in the Colony Court in 1653; chairman of the Council of War, 1671; Surgeon-General of the Colony Troops, 1673; Captain of the Plymouth forces in King Philips War.

ISSUE

I. Mary, *b.* about 1625; *m.* 17th April, 1655, Ralph JONES, the Quaker of Barnstable; left issue.
II. Elizabeth, *m.* 22d April, 1652, Moses ROWLEY of Falmouth; left issue.
III. Samuel, *m.* Mary (surname not known).
IV. John, *m.* (firstly) Bethiah (surname unknown); *m.* (secondly) Hannah MORTON.
V. Anne, *m.* Samuel FULLER, her cousin, gd. son of Edward FULLER, of the *Mayflower*; left issue, of whom later.

SAMUEL FULLER, I, son of Edward and Ann FULLER, brother of Capt. Matthew FULLER, *b.* about 1612, in England; *d.* 31st October or 10th November, 1683, at Barnstable, Massachusetts; emigrated to America with his parents on the *Mayflower*, 1620; *m.* by Capt. Miles STANDISH, 8th or 18th April, 1635, Jane LATHROP, *bapt.* 29th September, 1614, *d.* between 1658–1683, dau. of Rev. John LATHROP. John LOTHROP was the second minister of the First Independent Church in England, and was imprisoned by Archbishop LAUD, came to America in 1634.

ISSUE

I. Hannah, *m.* 1st January, 1658–1659, Nicholas BONHAM; had issue.
II. SAMUEL, *bapt.* 11th February, 1637, of whom later.
III. Elizabeth, *m.* Joseph TAYLOR.
IV. Sarah, *bapt.* 1st August, 1641; *d.* 1651–1654.
V. Mary, *bapt.* 16th Jun, 1644; *d.* 1720; *m.* 18th November, 1674, Joseph WILLIAMS; had issue from whom descended Gen. John W. PHELPS, 1830–1870, and Hon. Hames H. PHELPS of Suffield, Connecticut, 1847–1893 and Ex-President William H. TAFT.

vi. Thomas, *b.* 18th May, 1651; *d.* young.
vii. Sarah, *b.* 10th December, 1654; *m.* ———— Crowe; had issue.
viii. John, *b.* circa 1656.

Samuel Fuller, II, of Barnstable, *bapt.* 11th February, 1637–1638; *m.* his cousin Anne Fuller, dau. of Capt. Matthew Fuller.

ISSUE

i. Barnabas, *b.* circa 1659; *m.* Elizabeth Young; had issue.
ii. Joseph, *b.* 1661; *m.* Thankful Blossom; had issue.
iii. Matthew, *b.* 1663, of whom later.
iv. Benjamin, *b.* 16th December, 1665.
v. Desire, *b.* 1667; *m.* 11th June, 1703, John Taylor.
vi. Sarah, *b.* circa 1669.

Matthew Fuller, *b.* circa 1663–1664, at Barnstable; *d.* before 1744 at Colchester; *m.* 25th February, 1692–1693, Patience Young, dau. of George Young of Scituate.

ISSUE

i. Anna, *b.* November, 1693; *m.* 17th October, 1717, Tristram Blush; had issue.
ii. Jonathan, *b.* October, 1696; *m.* Rebecca Parry.
iii. Content, *b.* February, 1698; *d.* 1754; *m.* (firstly) Benjamin Fuller, son of John Fuller, and gd. son of Samuel and Jane (Lathrop) Fuller; *m.* (secondly) 20th September, 1741, Deacon Nathanial Skinner.
iv. Jean, *b.* 1704, *d.* 1708.
v. David, *b.* 1706; *d.* young.
vi. Young, *b.* 1708, of whom later.
vii. Cornelius, *b.* 1710; *m.* Patience Chapell.
viii. Hannah, 1712, *m.* 1st November, 1733, Josiah Strong, Jr., of Colchester; had issue.

Young Fuller, *b.* 1708, in Barnstable; *d.* 17th June, 1796, at Ludlow, Massachusetts; *m.* 23d April, 1730, at Colchester, Jerusha Beebe, dau. of Jonathan Beebe.

ISSUE

i. Joshua, *b.* 9th September, 1731.
ii. David, *b.* 1733.
iii. Caleb, *b.* 1735, of whom later.
iv. Jerusha, *b.* 30th July, 1737, *m.* ———— Denslow.
v. Lydia, *bapt.* 13th December, 1741.
vi. Anne, *bapt.* 15th March, 1747.

CALEB FULLER, b. 1735, in Colchester, Connecticut; d. 20th August, 1815; graduated from Yale, 1758; received degree A.M., 1762; licensed to preach, 5th February, 1760; moved in 1790, from Middletown to Hanover, New Hampshire, where he was deacon of the church of Dartmouth College; m. 28th October, 1762, Hannah WELD, dau. of Rev. Habijah (Harvard, 1723), and Mary (Fox) WELD.

ISSUE

I. FREDERICK AUGUSTUS, b. 3d September, 1763, of whom later.
II. William, b. 6th November, 1764; d. 24th December, 1764.
III. Sophia, b. 29th March, 1766, d. 10th August, 1775.
IV. Rosina, b. 24th November, 1767; d. 11th July, 1861; m. Elam MARKHAM.
V. Caroline Matilda, b. 20th May, 1770; d. 26th June, 1823; m. 10th July, 1790, Rev. Benjamin CHAPMAN, A.M., Dartmouth; left issue.
VI. Thomas Weld, b. 20th April, 1773.
VII. Anna, b. 5th July, 1777; d. 10th March, 1841; m. Moses DAVIS; had issue.
VIII. Sophia, b. 20th March, 1779; m. M.D. HOPKINS.
IX. Henry Weld, b. 1st January, 1784; d. 29th January, 1841; m. 7th January, 1806, Esther GOULD, d. 26th July, 1866, from who descended Melville Weston FULLER (a gd. son), b. 1833, d. 1910, Chief Justice of the United States, 1888–1910.

FREDERICK AUGUSTUS FULLER, b. 3d September, 1763; buried 8th March, 1814; m. Anna BARRETT, d. at Terre Haute, Indiana, 31st August, 1828.

ISSUE

I. Mary, b. 14th December, 1782; d. 4th September, 1783.
II. HORACE, b. 20th March, 1785, of whom later.
III. Martha, b. 8th February, 1787; d. 17th January, 1873;
IV. Wilson, b. 16th February, 1789; d. 23d November, 1848.
V. Benjamin Chapman, b. 8th March, 1791; d. 4th January, 1858.
VI. Anna, b. 5th April, 1795; d. young.
VII. Anna, b. 23d July, 1796; d. February, 1836.
VIII. Cornelia Green, b. 31st October, 1801; d. 5th September, 1828.

HORACE FULLER, b. 20th March, 1785, at Wethersfield, Connecticut; d. 18th February, 1846, at Baltimore, Maryland; was for some years a sea-captain; m. (firstly) Nicea PATTERSON, in 1814, in Baltimore, she d. March, 1826; m. (secondly) in 1826, Emily NEVILLE, d. 19th November, 1838.

ISSUE BY SECOND MARRIAGE

I. Sarah, b. 12th September, 1827.
II. Cornelia, b. 27th March, 1830.

III. WILSON NEVILLE, *b.* 8th July, 1831, of whom later.
IV. Nicea, *b.* 8th April, 1832.
V. Benjamin Franklin, *b.* 8th December, 1834.
VI. Emma, *b.* 21st October, 1836.
VII. Sophia, *b.* 4th November, 1838.

WILSON NEVILLE FULLER, *b.* 8th July, 1831, in Baltimore, Maryland; *d.* 20th March, 1891, Washington, D. C.; *m.* (firstly) in Baltimore, 28th March, 1855, Susannah Mary MCDERMOTT, who *d.* in Washington, D. C., 8th November, 1874; *m.* (secondly) 25th November, 1880, Margaret J. CATHELL.

ISSUE BY FIRST MARRIAGE

I. HORACE FREDERICK, *b.* 17th February, 1865, the subject of this memoir.
II. Cornelia Annie, *b.* 27th June, 1867; *d.* 15th June, 1918, in Baltimore.
III. Wilson Neville, *b.* 17th March, 1870; *m.* 1905, at Alexandria, Virginia, Minnie J. JACKSON.

ISSUE

1. George Milton, *b.* 2d March, 1906.

IV. Joshua Riley, *b.* 31st October, 1872, *d.* in infancy.
V. Sarah Weld, *b.* 28th December, 1873; *d.* young.

ISSUE BY SECOND MARRIAGE

I. Benjamin Franklin, *b.* 17th January, 1884; *m.* 7th November, 1905, Ada C. SCHAEFFER.

ISSUE

1. Charles Francis, *b.* 3d January, 1907.
2. Benjamin Franklin, *b.* 11th December, 1913.

II. Margaret Emma, *b.* 20th June, 1887; *d.* 9th October, 1890.

Arms.—Argent, three bars gules, on a canton of the second, a castle or.
Crest.—A dexter arm embowed, vested argent, cuffed sable, holding in the hand proper, a sword of the first, hilt and pommel or.
Motto.—Semper Paratus.
Residence.—Cedar Grove, Olney, Philadelphia, Pennsylvania.
Clubs.—Friendly Sons of St. Patrick; the Union League of Philadelphia, Huntingdon Valley Country Club; Thirty-second Mason; Society of Colonial Wars; Mayflower Society; Order of Founders and Patriots.

Gay

EBEN HOWARD GAY of Boston, Massachusetts; *b.* 6th February, 1858, at Hingham, Massachusetts; *m.* 15th December, 1898, at Boston, Cornelia Spalding FANNING, *b.* 4th March, 1874, *d.s.p.*, 20th November, 1900, dau. of Charles Edward FANNING, *b.* 12th July, 1835, *d.* 12th June, 1889, *m.* November, 1872, Georgiana Frances WALKER, *b.* 17th December, 1854, *d.* 1902.

Eben Howard GAY was graduated from the English High School, Boston, in 1874, when he decided to follow banking as a life occupation. He established the original New York and Boston branches of the present banking-firm of HARRIS, FORBES and Company, and in 1890 founded the investment-house of E. H. GAY and Company. Acting as Fiscal Agents, the latter firm built the Adirondack Electric Power property, a hydroelectric company located on the upper waters of the Hudson River, which, through its concrete dam and power-house are converted into electrical energy, to be transmitted over its pole-lines to Albany, Troy, Schenectady and neighboring cities for light and power purposes.

An ardent devotee of archaeology, Mr. GAY erected in Boston in 1900 a Georgian house modeled upon the pure lines of the eighteenth century English home made famous by Sir Christopher WREN and contemporary architects. It was furnished throughout with original furniture of the period, chiefly of Chippendale origin, with marble fireplaces from old English manors, and was decorated with portraits by the English group of masters of that day and with antique Chinese porcelains, while the table appointments consisted entirely of contemporary English silver. This house furnished the inspiration for its builder's first serious literary work, "A Chippendale Romance" which was published in 1915 and contains illustrations of the interior and exterior, coupled with a relation of the writer's experiences, drawn both from fact and fancy, in collecting the antiquities which were grouped within its walls.

Immediately following the outbreak of the World War, Mr. GAY joined the 1st Motor Corps of the Massachusetts State Guard, a mobile body of troops which replaced in that Commonwealth the old 1st Corps of Cadets during their absence on the Western Front. In 1920 he was appointed Financial Adviser of the American Mutual Liability Insurance Company.

Lineage

JOHN GAY was one of a body of "spirited and determined men and women who in February, 1630, attended a meeting of the Puritans in the New Hospital, Plymouth, England, with the purpose of emigrating to the new world. This company was principally from the counties of Devon, Dorset and Somerset. They selected Gov. John WARREN and the Rev. John MAVERICK as their pastors. On 30th March, 1630 they embarked in the 400-ton ship *Mary and John*, Captain SQUEB (SQUEEB?). The number of the company was 140. After seventy days' sail they entered the harbor of Nantucket." *Pomeroy records.*

JOHN GAY settled first at Watertown, Massachusetts, and was a grantee in the Great Dividends and the Beaver Brook plowlands, owning altogether 40 acres. He was admitted Freeman 6th May, 1635. With others of Watertown he was one of the founders of the plantation at Dedham, his name appearing on the petition for incorporation, 6th September, 1636, and among the original proprietors of lands. He was one of the Selectmen, 1654. He *d.* 4th March, 1688. Joanna (surname not given) his wife, *d.* 14th August, 1691. She is said in family tradition to have been widow BALDWICKE before her marriage to John GAY. His will in the Suffolk records, dated 18th December, 1686, was proved 17th December, 1689, his wife Joanna and son John being the executors. His estate was valued in the inventory at £91-5s-8d.

ISSUE

I. Samuel, *b.* 10th March, 1639; *d.* 15th April, 1718.
II. Hezekiah, *b.* 3d July, 1640; *d.* 28th November, 1669.
III. NATHANIEL, *b.* 11th January, 1643, of whom later.
IV. Joanna, *b.* 23d March, 1645; *m.* (firstly) Nathl. WHITING, Jr.; *m.* (secondly) John WARE.
V. Eliezer, *b.* 25th June, 1647; *d.* 13th April, 1726.
VI. Abiel (twin), *b.* 23d April, 1649; *m.* Daniel HOWES, 23d February, 1677.
VII. Judith (twin), *b.* 23d April, 1649; *m.* John FULLER, 8th February, 1672.
VIII. John, *b.* 6th May, 1651; *d.* 19th November, 1731.
IX. Jonathan, *b.* 1st August, 1653.
X. Hannah, *b.* 16th October, 1656; *d.* 26th February, 1660.
XI. Elizabeth, *m.* Richard MARTIN, 1660.

NATHANIEL GAY, of Watertown, Massachusetts, *b.* 11th January, 1643; *d.* 20th February, 1712; admitted Freeman, 23d May, 1677; Selectman, 1704, and other years. His father left him a tract of land near Medfield, and confirmed a gift of lands in "Pecumtuck alies Derefeild in Hamsheir." His wife was Lydia LUSHER (dau. of Eleazor LUSHER). His will, dated 16th February, 1712 and proved 20th March, 1712, appoints his wife Lydia and sons Nathaniel and Lusher executors. In it he says: "Whereas I Have been att considerable expense in bringing up my son Ebenezer GAY fitt for, and in placeing him at Harvard College in Cambridge, where he now remains, I do appoint that ye charge of his further continuing there until the takeing of his first degree shall be payd and discharged out of my estate, which shall be reckoned and accounted unto him as his full share of my estate." His estate was valued in the inventory at £227-19s-6d. His wife Lydia *d.* 6th August, 1744, aged ninety-two.

ISSUE

1. Benjamin, *b.* 3d May, 1675; *d.* 1st August, 1675.
2. Nathaniel, *b.* 17th April, 1676; *d.* 1st May, 1676.
3. Mary, *b.* 30th March, 1677; *m.* Jabez POND, 11th January, 1699.
4. Lydia, *b.* 12th August, 1679; *m.* Thomas EATON, 5th October, 1697.
5. Nathaniel, *b.* 2d April, 1682; *d.* 25th May, 1750.
6. Lusher, *b.* 26th September, 1685; *d.* 18th October, 1769.
7. Joanna, 3d September, 1688; Ephraim WILSON, 19th December, 1706.
8. Benjamin, *b.* 20th April, 1691;
9. Abigail, *b.* 15th February, 1694.
10. EBENEZER, *b.* 15th August, 1696; of whom below.

REV. EBENEZER GAY, of Hingham, Massachusetts, *b.* 15th August, 1696; *d.* 18th March, 1787; graduated Harvard College, 1714; degree of D.D., Harvard College, 1785; preached at the First Parish Church of Hingham, Massachusetts, in 1717 and continued to be sole pastor there until his death, 8th March, 1787; lacking only a few months of seventy years. The ancient edifice which sheltered this memorable pastorate is one of the oldest churches in the United States still devoted to public worship. It was originally founded in 1635 and is familiarly known as the "Old Ship Church." "The honored Patriarch," says SAVAGE, "of our New England pulpit in that age." His religious views were broad and liberal, especially for that early period, and, together with the Rev. Mr. BRADSTREET of Charlestown, he was referred to by Governor BURNETT of their day as being "at the head of the clergy of New England in respect of erudition." Nineteen of his sermons and lectures were published at different times, the most celebrated being the one entitled "The Old Man's Calendar." He *m.* 3d November, 1719, Jerusha BRADFORD, dau. of Samuel and Hannah (ROGERS) BRADFORD.

ISSUE

1. Samuel, *b.* 15th January, 1721; *d.* 26th March, 1746.
2. Abigail, *b.* 8th September, 1722; *d.* 8th February, 1729.
3. Calvin, *b.* 14th September, 1724; *d.* 11th March, 1765.
4. MARTIN, *b.* 29th December, 1726, of whom later.
5. Abigail, *b.* 20th August, 1729; *d.* 7th April, 1804.
6. Celia, *b.* 13th August, 1731; *d.* 18th February, 1749.
7. Jotham, *b.* 11th April, 1733; *d.* 16th October, 1802.
8. Jerusha, *b.* 17th March, 1735; *d.* January, 1812; *m.* Rev. Simeon HOWARD, 29th November, 1790.
9. Ebenezer, *b.* 3d March, 1737; *d.* 3d July, 1738.
10. Persis, *b.* 2d November, 1739; *d.* 24th March, 1752.
11. Joanna, *b.* 23d November, 1741, *d.* 23d July, 1772.

CAPT. MARTIN GAY, *b.* 29th December, 1726; *d.* 3d February, 1809; he carried on the business of a brass founder in Union Street, Boston, and was also interested in shipping; he was a Deacon of the West Church, and Captain of the Ancient and Honorable Artillery Company; he was an addresser of Hutchinson in 1774, and of Gage in 1775; was proscribed and banished in 1778; he remained in Boston while the British were in possession, and left with them, March, 1776; he did not return to remain permanently until about November, 1792; during the war he lived in Nova Scotia and England; he *m.* (firstly) Mary PINCKNEY, 13th December, 1750; he *m.* (secondly) probably about 1770, Ruth ATKINS, who *d.* 12th September, 1810.

ISSUE

I. Celia, *m.* John BOYLE, 12th March, 1772.
II. Mary, *m.* Rev. Wm. BLACK, 1783.
III. Samuel, *b.* 1754; *d.* 21st January, 1847.
IV. Martin, *b.* 1760; *d.* 17th April, 1778.
V. Frances, *bapt.* April, 1763; *d.* 12th October, 1846; *m.* Dr. Isaac WINSLOW, 10th January, 1805.
VI. Pinckney, *bapt.* November, 1764; *d.* April, 1773.
VII. Ebenezer, *bapt.* 1766; *d.* young.
VIII. EBENEZER, *bapt.* 24th February, 1771; of whom later.
IX. Pinckney, *bapt.* 2d July, 1775; *d.* 16th July, 1775.

EBENEZER GAY, of Hingham, Massachusetts, *b.* 24th February, 1771; *d.* 11th February, 1842; graduated Harvard College, 1789; practised law for some years in Boston and afterwards at Hingham; Member of the State Senate; 31st July, 1800, he *m.* Mary Allyne OTIS, dau. of Hon. Joseph OTIS, of West Barnstable, a niece of James OTIS the patriot.

ISSUE

I. Mary Otis, *b.* 9th July, 1801; *d.* 6th January, 1853; *m.* Dr. Robert T. P. FISKE, 9th May, 1825.
II. Martin, *b.* 11th February, 1803; *d.* 15th May, 1850; *m.* Margaret ALLEN.
III. Charles William, *b.* 17th July, 1804; *d.* 1871.
IV. Henry Pinckney, *b.* 24th October, 1806; *d.* April 1852.
V. Frances Maria, *b.* 4th April, 1809; *d.* 1893.
VI. Elizabeth Margaret, *b.* 28th April, 1811; *m.* Jacob CHAPIN, 27th June, 1832.
VII. Sidney Howard, *b.* 22d May, 1814; *d.* 25th June, 1888; *m.* Elizabeth Downs NEAL.
VIII. Abby Frothingham, *b.* 14th May, 1816; *d.* 11th January, 1908; *m.* Isaac WINSLOW, 2d March, 1848.
IX. EBENEZER, *b.* 27th March, 1818; of whom later.
X. Arthur Otis, *b.* 31st August, 1819; *d.* 9th November, 1856.
XI. Winckworth Allan, *b.* 18th August, 1821; *d.* 23d February, 1910.

EBENEZER GAY, of Boston, Massachusetts, *b.* at Hingham, 27th March, 1818; *d.* 20th April, 1899; graduated Harvard College, 1841; he practised law in Boston; was Member of the Massachusetts Senate, 1862; *m.* 27th August, 1852, Ellen Blake BLOOD, of Worcester, Massachusetts, *b.* 13th September, 1831, *d.* 31st October, 1917.

ISSUE

I. Arthur Otis, *b.* Hingham, 12th January, 1854; *d.* 9th November, 1856.
II. Walter, *b.* Hingham, 22d January, 1856; has lived in Paris for many years and is a well-known artist, especially noted for his "portraits of interiors;" *m.* Matilda TRAVERS of New York.
III. EBEN HOWARD, *b.* Hingham, 6th February, 1858; the subject of the memoir.
IV. Harry Howard, *b.* Hingham, 13th December, 1859; *m.* 13th June, 1885, Caroline Louisa DORR, dau. of Joseph DORR, of Boston.

ISSUE

1. Caroline Humphrey, *b.* Boston, 16th February, 1886; *m.* 3d June, 1911, Albert Gardner MASON.
2. Marian Otis, *b.* Boston, 11th April, 1888; *m.* (firstly) 16th September, 1911, Francis Hathaway BURRAGE, *d.* 13th December, 1911; *m.* (secondly) Graeme DONALD, 2d June, 1914; she died in New York, 7th January, 1918.

ISSUE

1[1]. Marian (twin), *b.* 27th May, 1915.
2[1]. Jane (twin), *b.* 27th May, 1915.

V. William Otis, *b.* Dorchester, 10th May, 1866; *m.* 25th April, 1905, Annie Margaretta DUMARESQ, dau. of Philip DUMARESQ of Boston.

ISSUE

1. Sophie Margaretta, *b.* Boston, 28th April, 1907.
2. William Otis, *b.* Boston, 24th June, 1909.
3. Dorothea Ellen, *b.* Boston, 1st January, 1911.
4. Philip Dumaresq, *b.* Boston, 18th February, 1913.
5. John, *b.* Boston, 10th April, 1915.
6. Anne, *b.* New York, 19th February, 1917.

Arms.—Gules, three lions rampant, two, one argent.
Crest.—A demi-grey hound rampant sable, collared or.
Residence.—Brimmer Chambers, Boston, Massachusetts.
Clubs.—Country of Brookline; Boston Author's Club.

Gordon

ARMISTEAD CHURCHILL GORDON, LL.D., Lawyer and Author, of Staunton, Virginia; *b.* in Albemarle County, Virginia, 20th December, 1855; *m.* 17th October, 1883, Maria Breckinridge CATLETT, *b.* 5th November, 1860, dau. of Nathaniel Pendleton CATLETT and Elizabeth Thomas BRECKINRIDGE.

ISSUE

I. Margaret Douglas, *b.* 25th September, 1891.
II. Mary Daniel, *b.* 19th October, 1893.
III. James Lindsay, *b.* 19th May, 1895.
IV. Armistead Churchill, *b.* 9th July, 1897.
V. George Loyall, *b.* 26th November, 1899; *d.* 10th September, 1918.

ARMISTEAD CHURCHILL GORDON was educated at classical schools in Warrenton, North Carolina, and Charlottesville, Virginia, and at the University of Virginia; was admitted to the Bar in 1879; Mayor of Staunton, Virginia, from 1884 to 1886; visitor of the University of Virginia, 1894-1898, 1906-1918; Rector of same 1897-1898, 1905-1918; Chairman of State Library Board of Virginia 1903-1918; President General Alumni Association, University of Virginia, 1918-1920; President Virginia State Bar Association 1902-21; Doctor of Laws, College of William and Mary, 1906.

Lineage

JAMES GORDON, of Sheepbridge in the Barony of Newry, County Down, Ireland, settled there, 1692; will dated 7th July, 1707; *m.* Jean Campbell, dau. of Robert and Jean (WALLACE) CAMPBELL, of Newry.

ISSUE

I. JAMES, of Sheepbridge, Ireland, of whom later.
II. Robert, of Newry, County Down, Ireland.
III. George, of Newry, County Down, Ireland.

JAMES GORDON, of Sheepbridge, Ireland; will dated 27th February, 1747; *m.* Sarah GREENWAY, dau. of Samuel and Elinor (MATTHEWS) GREENWAY, of Newry.

ISSUE

I. James, of Lancaster County, Virginia (see GORDON, Edward Clifford),
II. Samuel, of Sheepbridge; *m.* Margaret HUNTER; had issue.

III. JOHN, *b.* in Ireland, of whom later.
IV. George, of Rockhamilton, County Down; had issue.
V. Anne, *m.* ———— TEMPLETON.
VI. Eleanor, *m.* Joseph CARSON, of Downpatrick, County Down, Ireland.
VII. Sarah, *d.* unmarried, circa 1757–1758.

JOHN GORDON, *b.* at Sheepbridge, County Down; went to Virginia with his brother James, about 1738, and was living in Lancaster County, Virginia, January, 1759; later at Urbana, Middlesex County, and afterwards removed to Richmond County; *d.* 1780; was a Justice of Richmond County, Virginia, and carried on a large tobacco business; *m.* 15th December, 1756, Lucy CHURCHILL, dau. of Col. Armistead CHURCHILL, of Middlesex County, and his wife, Hannah HARRISON, dau. of Nathaniel HARRISON of Brandon, on James River.

ISSUE

I. Hannah, *b.* 1758; *m.* William BEALE; had issue.
II. JAMES, *b.* 1759, of whom later.
III. Churchill, *b.* 10th February, 1761; Midshipman, Virginia Navy during Revolutionary War; *m.* Ann SPARKE; had issue.
IV. John, *b.* 28th September, 1762; *d.s.p.*
V. Sarah, *b.* 21st June, 1764; *d.s.p.*; *m.* Kendall LEE, of Ditchley, Virginia.
VI. William, *b.* 4th August, 1766; *d.s.p.*
VII. Mary, *b.* 14th March, 1768; *d.* 29th June, 1808, Nathaniel GORDON, son of Col. James and Mary (HARRISON) GORDON; had issue.
VIII. Nathaniel, *b.* 21st February, 1770; *m.* Elizabeth ELLIS; had issue.
IX. Lucy, *b.* 21st November, 1771; *m.* James Gordon WADDELL; had issue.
X. Armistead, *b.* 5th January, 1773; *d.s.p.*; *m.* Elizabeth CLAYTON.
XI. Samuel, *b.* 20th October, 1775; *m.* Elizabeth Cole FITZHUGH; had issue.
XII. Priscilla, *m.* Edmund EDRINGTON; had issue.

JAMES GORDON, *b.* 1759; *d.* 1799, of Germanna, Orange County, Virginia; Member of Virginia Convention, 1788; *m.* 13th August, 1777, his cousin, Elizabeth GORDON, *b.* 24th August, 1758, dau. of Col. James and Mary (HARRISON) GORDON.

ISSUE

I. Lucy Harrison *d.* unmarried.
II. John Churchill, *m.* Lucy HERNDON, of Fredericksburg, Virginia.
III. William Fitzhugh, *b.* 13th January, 1787, of whom later.
IV. Elizabeth, *d.* unmarried.
V. Armistead Churchill; *d.s.p.*
VI. Thomas, *m.* ———— KEY; *d.s.p.*

GEN. WILLIAM FITZHUGH GORDON, of Albemarle County, Virginia; *b.* 13th January, 1787; *d.* 28th August, 1858; Member of Virginia Convention, 1829-1830; Member United States Congress, 1829-1835; sometime Major-General in Virginia Militia. Originator of the Independent Treasury of the United States; he was a rigid disciple of the state's rights school, and an inflexible champion of the rights of the South; he was a man of incorruptible integrity; *m.* (firstly) 12th December, 1809, Mary Read ROOTES, who *d.s.p.*; *m.* (secondly) 21st January, 1813, Elizabeth LINDSAY, who *d.* 31st August, 1885, dau. of Col. Reuben and Hannah (TIDWELL)LINDSAY of Albemarle County, Virginia.

ISSUE BY SECOND MARRIAGE

I. James Lindsay, *b.* 13th October, 1813; *d.s.p.*, 7th December, 1877; *m.* (firstly) his cousin Mary BEALE, of Fredericksburg, Virginia; *m.* (secondly) Martha WINSTON.

II. Maria Lindsay, *b.* 2d December, 1815; *d.* unmarried 29th June, 1848.

III. Hannah Elizabeth, *b.* 28th September, 1817; *d.* 7th December, 1861; *m.* August, 1843, Judge William Joseph ROBERTSON, of the Supreme Court of Appeals of Virginia; had issue.

IV. Reuben Lindsay, *b.* 15th January, 1820; *d.* 13th September, 1887; *m.* 4th March, 1845, Eliza S. BEALE; sister of Mary BEALE; had issue.

V. William, *b.* 6th March, 1822; *d.* 26th November, 1822.

VI. William Fitzhugh, *b.* 26th November, 1823; *d.* 26th July, 1904; graduated as B.L., University of Virginia, 1842-1843; served in Confederate States Army, 1861-1865; *m.* 1852, Nancy MORRIS; had issue.

VII. Elizabeth, *b.* 9th July, 1826; *d.* 21st June, 1827.

VIII. GEORGE LOYALL (twin), *b.* 17th January, 1829, of whom later.

IX. Charles Henry (twin), *b.* 17th January, 1829; *d.* 23d January, 1899; Captain, Confederate States Army, 1861, 1865; *m.* 1847, his cousin, Mary BEALE; had issue.

X. John Churchill, M.D., of the Confederate States Army; *b.* 2d March, 1831; Graduated as M.D. of the University of Virginia, 1853; Assistant Surgeon, Confederate States Army, 1861-1865; *m.* 4th June, 1861, Mary B. PEGRAM; had issue.

XI. Alexander Tazewell, M.D. of the Confederate States Army; *b.* 12th May, 1833; *d.* 14th January, 1903; Private and Surgeon, Confederate States Army, 1861-1865; *m.* 1868, Lucy GORDON; had issue.

XII. Mason, *b.* 17th September, 1840; *d.* 9th July, 1914; Private and Lieutenant of Cavalry, Confederate States Army, 1861-1865; educated at the University of Virginia, 1859-1865; *m.* 4th January, 1867, Harriet HART, of Wilmington, North Carolina, *d.* 9th July, 1914; had issue.

GEORGE LOYALL GORDON, of Staunton, Virginia; *b.* 17th January, 1829; killed t the battle of Malvern Hill, 1st July, 1862; educated at the University of Virginia;

served in Confederate States Army, private and adjutant, 15th North Carolina Infantry; *m.* 20th December, 1854, Mary DANIEL, *b.* 20th August, 1829, *d.* 28th February, 1876, dau. of Judge Joseph J. DANIEL, of the Supreme Court of North Carolina, and Maria Bassett (SMITH) DANIEL.

ISSUE

I. ARMISTEAD CHURCHILL, *b.* 20th December, 1855, the subject of this memoir.
II. Frances Daniel, *b.* 3d May, 1857; *d.* young.
III. Lavinia Battle, *b.* 25th October, 1858; *d.* in infancy.
IV. James Lindsay, *b.* 9th January, 1860; *d.* 30th November, 1904; Member of Virginia Senate; removed to New York; Assistant District Attorney, and Assistant Corporation Counsel, of the City and State of New York; *m.* Emily Adele SLICHTER of Philadelphia, Pennsylvania.

ISSUE

1. Edith Churchill, *b.* 8th February, 1900.

V. Mary Long, *b.* 15th June, 1861; *d.* 13th August, 1895; *m.* 16th April, 1890, Dr. Richard Henry LEWIS, of Raleigh, North Carolina, *b.* 18th February, 1850, son of Richard Henry LEWIS and Martha Elizabeth (HOSKINS) LEWIS.

ISSUE

1. Nell Battle LEWIS, *b.* 28th May, 1893.

Arms.—Azure, a fess chequy argent and of the first, between three boars' heads erased or.
Crest.—A hart's head couped proper.
Motto.—Bydand.
Residences.—Newry House, 405 E. Beverly Street, Staunton, Virginia.
Clubs.—Westmoreland, Richmond, Virginia; National Arts (New York).
Societies.—Phi Beta Kappa (William and Mary College, Virginia); Virginia Historical Society (Executive Committee); American Historical Association; New Spalding Club of Aberdeen, Scotland; National Institute of Social Sciences; Authors' League of America; Virginia State Bar Association; American Bar Association.

Graham

KELLEY GRAHAM, of New York City, b. 3d January, 1889, at Austin, Texas; m. 15th October, 1914, Mary Valeria ATHERTON, b. 1890, a member of the Society of Colonial Dames of America, dau. of Peter Lee Atherton of Louisville, Kentucky, and Mary Goodenow (Kelsey) Atherton of New York City, New York.

ISSUE

I, John Macdougall Atherton, b. 29th November, 1915.

KELLEY GRAHAM attended public schools and then attended and graduated from Ogden College in Bowling Green, Kentucky; from there he went to the University of Virginia at Charlottesville for a year, leaving college at the age of nineteen to enter the banking business, in which he was engaged in Louisville, Kentucky, until 1917, in which year he removed to New York City, where he now resides and now (1918) holds the position of Vice-President of the Irving National Bank, which has its offices in the Woolworth Building.

Lineage

According to Scottish historians, this illustrious family is as ancient as the restoration of the Monarchy of Scotland by Fergus II and derive their origin from the renowned GREENE, who governing Scotland during the minority of his grandchild, Eugene II, whose reign began A.D. 419, had divers engagements with the Britons and by forcing the mighty rampart they had reared up between the rivers of Firth and Clyde, immortalized his name so much, as to this day that trench is called GRAHAMS-Dyke. It is certain the family is as ancient as any in Scotland now on record, for William DE GREENE is one of the witnesses to the foundation of Holy-Rood-House Abbey by David I in 1125, and after and at the special instance of said King, he gave to the Monks of Hadington, the lands of Clerkington, when Adda, Countess of Northumberland founded the Convent. It was from this distinguished family that the GRAHAMS herein recorded, who came from Scotland and settled in Virginia prior to the American Revolution are descended. About the year 1800 one branch of the family moved from Virginia to North Carolina, another branch, that from which the subject of the memoir is descended, went to Kentucky, settling in that portion of the state, now known as Warren County, and were the pioneers of the town of Bowling Green, where many of the name and family still reside and are prominent in the social and civic affairs of the county. The paternal gr. gd. father of the subject of this memorial was Judge Asher Waterman GRAHAM, for many years a distinguished lawyer, serving in the District bench and also was one of the Judges of the Court of Appeals of Kentucky. On the maternal side Mr. GRAHAM is a descendant of Gen. Henry CRIST who was also a pioneer settler in Kentucky and who fought in the many Indian battles in that state. He later served in the Congress of the United States and his remains are interred in the State Cemetery at Frankfort, Kentucky.

LUCIEN GRAHAM, of Austin, Texas; b. there 9th June, 1859; m. 10th November, 1886, Katherine E. FIELD, b. 25th July, 1863, dau. of Richard H. FIELD, b. 5th August, 1823, d. 4th April, 1880, who m. 7th August, 1851, Catherine S. SWEARINGEN.

ISSUE

I. KELLEY, b. 3d January, 1889, the subject of this memoir.
II. Hamilton Field, b. 27th April, 1898.
III. Lucien Dunavan, b. 6th July, 1900.

Arms.—Or, on a chief sable, three escallops of the first.
Crest.—A falcon proper, beaked and armed or, killing a heron or, armed gules.
Motto.—Ne oublie.
Residence.—244 Riverside Drive, New York City, Rye, N. Y.
Clubs.—Pendennis Club, Filson Club of Louisville, Kentucky; Union League Club, Church Club, Member Metropolitan Museum of Art, New York City, Ardsley Club, Ardsley-on-Hudson, New York.
Societies.—Colonial Wars.

Van Swearingen

The American ancestor of the family was Geret VAN SWEARINGEN, b. in Bemsterdam, Holland, in 1636; was a younger son of a family belonging to the nobility; came to America, 8th March, 1655, his ship being stranded off Fire Island, near Long Island, New York; d. at Marie's County, Maryland, 1698; was appointed Councillor under Governor STUYVESANT at Amstel on the Delaware, 26th November, 1659; Schout, 1660; called "Honorable President," in a letter from William BEEKMAN to STUYVESANT in 1663; commissioner to Holland from New Amstel, 1661–1662; removed to Maryland in 1664, and the meetings of the upper House of Maryland, were held in his house in St. Marie's City, from 1680 to 1692; Sheriff of St. Marie's County, 1686–1687; appointed for the Maryland Council, 12th March, 1687, one of three Commissioners of "A Special Court of Tryall;" Member of the Council, 1694; was, with his family, naturalized April, 1669, at St. Marie's, Maryland; m. (firstly) 1659, Barbara DEBARRETTE, b. at Valenciennes, France, circa 1670; m. (secondly) Mary SMITH, of St. Marie's County, Maryland; the antenuptial agreement being dated 5th October, 1676.

ISSUE BY FIRST MARRIAGE

I. THOMAS, *b.* circa 1665, of whom later.
II. Elizabeth.
III. Zacharias, *b.* circa 1663, at New Castle, Delaware; *m.* Martha (surname not given).

ISSUE BY SECOND MARRIAGE

I. Joseph, *b.* circa 1677, at St. Marie's, Maryland.
II. Charles, probably *d.* before his mother, not being mentioned in her will.
III. Eleanor, *m.* ———— CARROLL.
IV. Theresa.
V. Dorothy.
VI. A dau., who *m.* William BLADEN.

THOMAS SWEARINGEN, of Prince George County, Maryland; *b.* at St. Marie's County, circa 1665; *d.* 1710, probably lived at Somerset County, where he died; will probated there 19th March, 1710; *m.* Jane (surname not given).

ISSUE

I. Thomas, *b.* 1688; *m.* 1712, Lydia RILEY; *b.* 1691; *d.* 1764.
II. Van, known as "Maryland Van," *b.* 1692; *d.* 1811; aged one hundred and nine years; *m.* Elizabeth WALKER, *b.* 22d December, 1695.
III. Samuel, *b.* circa 1700; emigrated to North Carolina, 1735.
IV. JOHN, *b.* circa 1792, of whom later.

JOHN SWEARINGEN of Montgomery County, Maryland; *b.* circa 1702; probably in Somerset County; emigrated to Montgomery County, and settled on Rock Creek, not far from where Washington City now stands.

ISSUE

I. THOMAS, *b* circa 1730, of whom later.
II. Samuel, *b.* circa 1732; *m.* Catherine CORDELL.
III. Van, no record.
IV. John, *b.* 1751; *d.* circa 1830; *m.* (firstly) 17th January, 1771, Eleanor DAWSON; *m.* (secondly) 6th March, 1806, Fannie BAKER. (Also several daughters.)

THOMAS SWEARINGEN, of Montgomery County, Maryland; *b.* there circa 1730; *d.* there 15th October, 1794; *m.* (firstly) name not given; *m.* (secondly) Mary (surname not given); it is said his children numbered upward of twenty of whom are known.

ISSUE

I. John, *b.* 9th November, 1751; *d.* 1830; *m.* (firstly) 17th January, 1771, Elizabeth DAWSON.
II. Thomas, *b.* circa 1753; *d.* 1806; *m.* (firstly) Elizabeth POPER; *m.* (secondly) 6th March, 1806, Fannie BAKER.
III. Daniel, *b.* circa 1755; *m.* Eleanor DAWSON.
IV. Obed, *b.* 1757; emigrated to North Carolina.
V. ELIMELECH, *b.* circa 1760; of whom later.
VI. Samuel, *b.* 1762; *m.* Martha BELL; removed to Kentucky.
VII. William, *b.* 1770; *m.* (firstly) Sallie RAY; lived in Kentucky and Cole County, Missouri; *m.* (secondly) Rebecca Vaughn MUSAM.
VIII. Van, no record.
IX. Josiah, no record.
X. Hezekiah, no record.

ELIMELECH SWEARINGEN, of Bullett County, Kentucky; *b.* in Montgomery County, Maryland, circa 1760; *d.* in Bullett County, Kentucky, circa 1805; *m.* circa 1780, Elizabeth HIGGINS.

ISSUE

I. Samuel, *m.* Margaret PAYTON; went to Texas and with several sons fought in the Texan War.
II. George Washington, *m.* Elizabeth Crow BRASHIAR; removed to Grand Gulf, Mississippi, where he died.
III. WILLIAM WALLACE, *b.* November, 1803, of whom later.
IV. Elimelech, *d.* 1868; *m.* Mabalo CULVER.
V. Henry Hodger, *b.* 1825; *m.* Martha G. LLOYD.
VI. (and daughters.)

WILLIAM WALLACE SWEARINGEN, of Bullitt County, Kentucky; farmer and slave holder; *b.* 1st November, 1803, in Montgomery County, Maryland; *d.* in Bullitt County, Kentucky, 27th July, 1869; *m.* (firstly) December, 1822, Julia Franklin CRIST, *b.* 1806, *d.* 19th October, 1838, younger dau. of Henry CRIST, Representative in Congress and prominent farmer; *m.* (secondly) 1841, Mabel KING.

ISSUE BY FIRST MARRIAGE

I. Mary E.; *m.* Dr. James E. BEMISS.
II. Maria L. B., *m.* (firstly) Christopher WEATHERS; *m.* (secondly) Dr. J. H. DUPIN.
III. Sarah, *d.* in early girlhood.
IV. CATHERINE, *b.* 15th January, 1833, of whom later.
V. Julia F., *m.* A. H. FIELD.

vi. George Washington, *b.* 1838; *m.* 4th May, 1858, Mary EMBRY.
vii. Josephine, *m.* R. J. MEYLER.
viii. William E. C., of Memphis Kentucky.

CATHERINE S. SWEARINGEN, of Shepherdsville, Kentucky; *b.* in Bullitt County Kentucky, 15th January, 1833; *d.* in Shepherdsville, September, 1880; *m.* 7th August, 1851, in Bullitt County, Kentucky, Richard H. FIELD, of Shepherdsville, Kentucky; *b.* 5th August, 1823, in Bullitt County; *d.* in Shepherdsville, 4th April, 1880.

ISSUE

1. Katherine E. FIELD, *b.* 25th or 26th July, 1863, in Bullitt County, Kentucky; *m.* 10th November, 1886, Lucien GRAHAM, Sr., *b.* 9th June, 1859, in Bowling Green, Kentucky.

ISSUE

1. KELLEY GRAHAM, *b.* 3d January, 1889, the subject of this memoir.
2. Hamilton Field GRAHAM, *b.* 27th April, 1898.
3. Lucien Dunavan, *b.* 6th July, 1900.

Groser

SAMUEL HASKINS GROSER, B.A., M.A., of Brooklyn, New York; *b.* there 21st December, 1857; *m.* there 21st September, 1882, Bertha BROWN, *b.* there 6th November, 1863, dau. of Erasmus Dervan and Sarah Matilda (BEDELL) BROWN, of Brooklyn, New York.

ISSUE

I. Faith, *b.* 26th June, 1883; *m.* 20th November, 1907, Warren C. SWEETSER, son of William and Almira E. SWEETSER.

ISSUE

1. Converse Wentworth SWEETSER, *b.* 26th August, 1911.
2. Barbara SWEETSER, *b.* 5th April, 1914.

II. Kenneth Bedell, *b.* 26th January, 1886; *m.* (firstly) 14th September, 1906, Lola M. WAITE, dau. of Emmet E. and Georgia WAITE; *m.* (secondly) 1st June, 1916, Antoinette A. BORNARD, dau. of William and Emma BORNARD.

ISSUE BY FIRST MARRIAGE

1. Dorothy Lola, *b.* 8th June, 1908.

III. Marion, *b.* 16th October, 1896.
IV. Courtney Brown, *b.* 29th November, 1890.

SAMUEL HASKINS GROSER was educated at Trinity School, New York City and graduated 1879 with degree of B.A. in course from St. Stephens College, Annandale, New York; was awarded degree of M.A. in 1905 for thesis on the Race Problem in this country; now engaged in promoting trade relations between the manufacturers of hardware, iron and steel in the United States and the jobbers of these materials on the North American continent.

On the maternal side, Mr. GROSER comes of a long line of distinguished ancestors all of whom were prominently connected with the Colonial history of the United States.

Lineage

JOHN HOWLAND, *b.* 1592; *d.* 22d February, 1672, the thirteenth Signer of the *Mayflower* compact made at Cape Cod, 11th November (Old Style), 1620; he came from Essex, England; Queen Elizabeth granted the HOWLANDS their Coat

Armor in 1584, the family beginning with Bishop HOWLAND, who performed the obsequies for Mary, Queen of Scots; on the voyage to America, during a mighty storm, John HOWLAND, was thrown into the sea, but grasping the topsail halliards that were thrown out to him by his friends he was safely drawn on board the vessel; he was the last surviving passenger who *d.* in Plymouth; took part in the "First Encounter," Great Meadow Creek, December, 1620; Governor's Assistant, 1633-1635, in command of the Kennebec Trading Post, 1634; Deputy to General Court, 1641; *m.* 1623, Elizabeth TILLEY, *b* circa 1609, in Holland, *d.* 12th December, 1687, in Swanzey, age eighty, dau. of John TILLEY, one of the *Mayflower* Pilgrims. His house, built soon after the settlement of the colony at Plymouth, still survives the property of the Society of John HOWLAND Descendants and enjoys the distinction of being the sole remaining habitation which echoed to the tread of the Pilgrim Fathers.

ISSUE

    I. Desire, *b.* before 1627; *d.* 13th October, 1683; *m.* Capt. John GOTHAM.
   II. John, *b.* 1627, Ensign Barnstable Company, 1675, King Phillip's War.
 III. Jabez, *b.* 1628; served in King Philip's War as Lieutenant.
 IV. HOPE, *b.* 30th August, 1629, of whom later.
    V. Joseph, became a Military Officer during the Indian Wars; *m.* Elizabeth SOUTHWORTH.
 VI. Isaac, *d.* 1724; was an officer in the Indian Wars; kept an "Ordinary" (an Inn) 1684.
VII. Elizabeth, *m.* (firstly) no record; *m.* (secondly) John DILGAVSON.
VIII. Lydia, *m.* James BROWN, of Sivansea.

HOPE HOWLAND, *b.* 30th August, 1629; *m.* Elder John CHIPMAN, of Barnstable.

ISSUE

    I. LYDIA CHIPMAN, of whom below.

LYDIA CHIPMAN, *m.* John SARGENT.

ISSUE

    I. LYDIA SARGENT, of whom below.

LYDIA SARGENT, *m.* Joseph WAITE.

ISSUE

    I. HANNAH WAITE, of whom below.

HANNAH WAITE, *m.* Phineas UPHAM.

ISSUE

I. HANNAH UPHAM, of whom below.

HANNAH UPHAM, of Malden, Massachusetts, *b.* 6th May, 1734; *d.* 18th September, 1819; *m.* 12th March, 1752, John HASKINS, *b.* 12th March, 1729, *d.* 27th October, 1814; survived by his wife, thirteen children and forty-six grandchildren.

ISSUE AMONG OTHERS

I. Ruth, *b.* in Boston, 9th November, 1768; she was *m.* at her father's house by the Reverend Doctor PARKER, rector of Trinity Church, 25th October, 1796, to the Rev. William EMERSON; she *d.* in Concord at the house of her son, Ralph Waldo EMERSON, 16th November, 1853.
II. ROBERT HASKINS, *b.* 2d July, 1773, of whom below.

ROBERT HASKINS, *b.* 2d July, 1773; *d.* 6th January, 1855; *m.* 17th May, 1797, Rebecca EMERSON of Concord, Massachusetts.

Haskins

ROBERT HASKINS is the first of the name of whom there is any trace. He came to Boston from Virginia where his ancestors settled in the first years of that colony. He *m.* in 1728, Sarah COOK, dau. of Phillip COOK of Cambridge, whose name is on a tombstone of the old burying ground adjacent to the meeting house of the First Parish of that town. He lived, after his marriage, in Boston, on the northwest corner of Kingston and Essex Streets. His son John HASKINS was *b.* in Boston, in the house above referred to, 12th March, 1729. Mr. HASKINS business was that of a cooper. The coopers in those days, were an incorporated body, and had a large shipping trade, particularly with the West Indies. Before the Revolution, Mr. HASKINS was much interested in military affairs, and held the commission, first of Lieutenant and afterward of Captain in the old Boston Regiment. The latter commission is in the possession of Mr. David Greene HASKINS of Boston. It is issued to John HASKINS, Gentleman, by Thomas HUTCHINSON, Esquire, Governor in Chief of the Province of Massachusetts Bay, in the name of his Majesty King George III, and bears date, Boston, 20th February, 1772. Mr. HASKINS was over seventy years of age when he retired from active business. He had accumulated a handsome property, which was invested largely in real estate. His home was on the corner of Essex Street and Rainsfords Lane (now Harrison Avenue), a considerable tract of land extending to the Common on Boylston Street. His reputation for truth and rectitude gained for him the popular designation of "Honest John HASKINS." Mr. HASKINS' daughter Ruth was the mother of Ralph Waldo EMERSON.

Thomas Waldo HASKINS, the maternal gd. father of Samuel Haskins GROSER was a hardware merchant in Boston, Massachusetts, in 1823; his place of business being on Dock Square. The premises are still standing and until a few years ago displayed a prominent sign, "*A Hardware Store for a Hundred Years.*" An interesting incident is that his sister Hannah HASKINS, afterwards Mrs. PARSONS, was the first subscriber to the *Youths Companion*, her subscription having been taken by Nathaniel Parker WILLIS, first editor, in her brother's store.

On the paternal side, Mr. GROSERs father, Thomas Wentworth GROSER was *b.* in Spanishtown, West Indies on 9th May, 1818, and came to New York with his mother, about 1835. His father, Col. Thomas GROSER was Colonel St. Catherines Regiment and in command of His Imperial Majesty's forces in Jamaica, West Indies, under his brother-in-law Gen. Sir John Frederick Sigismund SMITH, who was commander-in-chief of all the West Indian forces. From 1800 to 1828 he was Colonial Secretary of the Island of Jamaica. Col. Thomas GROSER *m.* Charlotte Sophia Philopena SMITH the daughter of the Baroness Von KALKREUTH. Her father was Capt. Geo. SMITH in command of the flag ship under Admiral Lord HOWE and her brother, Lieut. William Murray SMITH was with his father on His Majesty's Ship *Gibraltar*, the sword he wore was sent to the nephew of the subject of this sketch, Lieut. Arthur GROSER of Beverly, West Australia, who lost his life in the Boer War. Gen. Sir John Frederick Sigismund SMITH'S daughter Eliza, first cousin to Thomas Wentworth GROSER *m.* Sir George ARTHUR, Governor General of Canada, Bombay and the West Indies. Their gd. son, the present Sir George ARTHUR, was aide-de-camp to General Lord KITCHENER. Sir George ARTHUR'S (the first) daughter Catherine ARTHUR *m.* Sir Bartle FRERE, Governor of South Africa. Thomas Wentworth GROSER, *m.* Mary Elizabeth HASKINS of Roxbury, thus reuniting two ancient English lineages. Thomas GROSER and Charlotte Sophia Philopena SMITH were *m.* in the Parish Church of St. Mary-le-bone, Middlesex, 21st June, 1804; sailed from Gravesend 13th October, 1805; arrived at Port Royal, Jamaica, West Indies, 30th November, 1805.

ISSUE AMONG OTHERS

I. THOMAS WALDO HASKINS, *b.* 1798. See HASKINS.

THOMAS WALDO HASKINS, of Waterford, Maine, *b.* there 1798; *d.* 1876; *m.* 11th April, 1826, Mary Ann SOREN, *b.* in Boston, *d.* 2d April, 1849, in Dorchester, Massachusetts, dau. of George and Mary SOREN.

ISSUE

I. Waldo Emerson.
II. MARY ELIZABETH HASKINS, *b.* 4th December, 1828, of whom later.
III. Edward Soren.
IV. George Shepherd.
V. Sarah Emerson.
VI. Thomas Wilson.

MARY ELIZABETH HASKINS, of Roxbury, Massachusetts; *b.* 4th December, 1828; *d.* 15th November, 1904; *m.* 18th October, 1854, Thomas W. GROSER, *b.* 9th May, 1818; *d.* 18th February, 1863, son of Col. Thomas GROSER, of Port Royal, Jamaica, British West Indies, *b.* 17th September, 1781, *d.* 1828, was colonel of St. Catherine Regiment, Colonial Secretary of Jamaica, *m.* 21st June, 1804, at the Parish Church of St. Mary-le-bone, Middlesex, England; Charlotte Sophia Phillipena SMITH, sailed from Gravesend, 13th October, 1805, arrived in Port Royal, Jamaica, 30th November, 1805.

ISSUE

I. Mary Soren, *b.* 24th July, 1855; *d.* 31st January, 1863.
II. Samuel Haskins Groser, *b.* 21st December, 1857, the subject of this memoir.
III. Charlotte Lilian, *b.* 14th February, 1860.
IV. Herbert Wilson, *b.* 1st October, 1862.
V. Wentworth, *b.* 20th May, 1820; *d.* 31st July, 1870.

Arms ((HASKINS).—Per chevron gules and azure a chevron engrailed or, between three lions rampant argent.
Crest.—A lion's head erased ppr.
Residences.—370 Park Place, Brooklyn, New York, and Shelter Island, Suffolk County, New York.
Clubs.—Shelter Island Yacht, Marine and Field, National Arts, Graduate, Hardware of New York.
Societies.—Empire State Society; Sons of the American Revolution; Mayflower Descendants; John HOWLAND Descendants.

Hall

THOMAS WILLIAM HALL, *b.* 17th February, 1840, at White Hall, in Anne Arundel County, Maryland. He was educated in the Public Schools, and at Anne Arundel Academy, and St. John's College. He *m.* 13th May, 1873, Violetta DUVALL, dau. of John Mortimer DUVALL, a son of Cornelius DUVALL, of Anne Arundel County, a direct descendant of Mareen DUVALL, the Hugenot, the first settler of that name in Maryland. At his marriage his father gave him a part of "White Hall," where he built his dwelling overlooking a wide valley, one of the head waters of South River from which fact the place was called "Valley View." Upon this part of "White Hall" stood the old HOOD residence, where Zacharia HOOD, the Tory and British Stamp Collector lived, and from which he was chased by patriots prior to the Revolution of 1776, and burnt in effigy. Up to a few years ago the graves of his two sisters could still be traced near the site of their old home in a grove of immense black walnut trees.

THOMAS WILLIAM HALL followed his father as an active worker in St. Stephen's Parish of which he was Vestryman, and Treasurer for many years, and as successor to his mother was the Organist of the Church. He was a Justice of the Peace of Anne Arundel County for a number of years.

In 1884 he removed to Baltimore City and shortly after to Talbot County, Maryland, to a farm between Cordova and Easton, where he was elected County Surveyor. He was also Organist of All Saints' Church in that County. In the autumn of 1891 he returned to Baltimore City where he engaged in business and still resides. After returning to Baltimore City he became a Vestryman of St. George's Church, and took an active part in the merger of the consolidated churches of St. George and St. Barnabas into the Pro Cathedral of the Incarnation, University Parkway, Baltimore, Maryland.

THOMAS WILLIAM HALL has been a wide reader and student of ecclesiastical history and literature, and has made many contributions to Church papers and periodicals and has written a short history of the origin and growth of St. Stephen's Parish, a copy of which may be found at the Maryland Historical Society Library.

ISSUE

1. Basil Duckett, III, *b.* in Anne Arundel County, 1st June, 1874, and now resides in Baltimore City, where he is engaged in business as a junior

---

This memoir was prepared and written by Mr. Richard M. DUVALL, of Baltimore, Md.

officer in a large manufacturing corporation. Like his father and brother, he is devoted to music and has been a member of the choirs of several of the Protestant Episcopal Churches of Baltimore. He *m.* 9th June, 1904, Alice Virginia HOMBURG, dau. of George William Albert HOMBURG, *b.* in 1827, in the Province of Mechlenburg-Schwerin, Germany, where his father, a man of means, was chief steward in charge of the estates of the Duke of that Province. He served two terms (six years), in the German army, during which time the abortive revolution of 1848 took pace. It is not known what part he bore in those stirring events, but it is evident that he had become dissatisfied with conditions there, as immediately upon his discharge about 1852 or 1853 he came to America and was naturalized, declaring that having served his time "he had paid Germany all he owed her, and was through with her for all time."

ISSUE

1. Henry Stevenson, *b.* 29th May, 1905.
2. Robert Gibson, *b.* 17th January, 1912.

II. Tyler, *b.* 6th December, 1879, in Anne Arundel County, now resides in Baltimore City, where he has been in business with his father for a number of years.

III. Mary Carolina, *b.* 28th November, 1888, in Talbot County, Maryland; *m.* 26th November, 1913, Robert Lawrence Cox, now of Belmar, New Jersey; he is a son of George Collins Cox, of Princeton, New Jersey, and Amelia Georganna Cox, his wife.

Lineage

HENRY HALL, Clergyman of the Church of England, and Planter, was a son of Robert and Ann (CRAG) HALL, his wife, was *b.* in the town of Horsham, County Sussex, England, 17th June, 1676, where he was *bapt.* in St. Mary's Church, on 29th June of that year. He entered St. Peter's College, Cambridge, 20th February, 1693, and was ordained Priest of the Established Church, 11th November, 1697, by the Lord Bishop of London, by whom he was sent, in the year 1698, with letters, to Hon. Francis NICHOLSON, Governor of the Province of Maryland.

On 7th May, 1698, he was, on the mandate of Governor NICHOLSON, formally inducted as the first Rector of St. James' Parish, Anne Arundel County. He continued as Minister of St. James, until his death in April, 1722. During his incumbency there was erected near Herring Creek in the center of the Parish, a new brick church, which stands today, a venerable monument to the fidelity and zeal of the minister and congregation. A part of the Communion Service still used in this Church was purchased and given to Saint James' Church during the lifetime of Rev. Mr. HALL. He is buried in the church yard and a marble slab with an appropriate inscription on it covers his grave. A memorial window has been erected in the church to the memory of its first Rector.

He was appointed by the Bishop of London, to whose jurisdiction the Churches of the Province were allotted, to the High Office of Commissary, whose functions it was to represent the bishop in the Province, but he declined the office preferring to confine his labors to the work of the Parish. He *m.* 5th February, 1701, Mary DUVALL, *b.* 1683, dau. of Mareen DUVALL, the French Hugenot, emigre, a merchant and planter, the owner of large tracts of land, and his second wife, Susanna. Mareen DUVALL was a man of prominence in the life of the Province, having been one of those, who in 1678 joined in the expedition against the Nanticoke Indians, and who in 1683 was appointed by the Governor and General Assembly, a Commissioner to purchase sites and lay out towns. He *d.* in 1694, and by his will gave to his dau. Mary, a large tract of land on South River, in Anne Arundel County. Mary HALL survived her husband and left a large landed estate to her children. St. James' Parish Register shows Henry HALL and Mary, his wife, had

ISSUE

I. HENRY, *b.* 12th March, 1702. (See further.)
II. Mary, *b.* 9th November, 1704; *m.* ———— ARNOLD.
III. Benjamin, *b.* 13th January, 1706; buried 6th December, 1708.
IV. Martha, *b.* 27th October, 1708; *d.* 8th April, 1752; *m.* 28th April, 1726, Stephen WEST, of Londontown, South River, and the "Woodyard", Prince George's County; he was a son of Sir John WEST, of Houghton, Buckinghamshire, England; they left numerous descendants.
V. Benjamin, *b.* 29th November, 1710 (see further).
VI. Magdelen, *b.* 26th December, 1712; further unknown.
VII. Edward, *b.* 4th May, 1714; *m.* 10th October, 1738, Mary BELT of All Hallows Parish, of Anne Arundel County.
VIII. John, *b.* 26th April, 1716 (see further).
IX. William, *b.* 23d October, 1719, *bapt.* 26th June, 1720; he resided at Elk Ridge, and Baltimore, where he became a wealthy shipping merchant, with London, England.

MAJ. HENRY HALL, son of Rev. Henry HALL and his wife Mary DUVALL, *b.* 12th March, 1702, *d.* in June, 1756; he was commissioned Major of Militia in Anne Arundel County; was a Planter and a man of prominence in the affairs of the Province; *m.* (firstly) 25th September, 1723, Martha BATEMAN, *d.* 25th August, 1734; *m.* (secondly) 12th November, 1734, Elizabeth LANSDALE, of Prince George's County, the ceremony being performed by Rev. Jacob HENDERSON of Queen Anne's Parish.

ISSUE BY FIRST MARRIAGE

I. Henry, *b.* 27th May, 1727; *d.* March, 1770 (see further).
II. John, *b.* 23d November, 1729; *d.* 23d November, 1797; was known as John HALL, Barrister, and as John HALL of Annapolis, and John HALL of "The

Vineyard," and was buried at his country place called "The Vineyard," about seven miles from Annapolis; he was a distinguished member of the Provincial and State Bar; refused a Commission as Judge of the Admiralty Court, but was a Member of the Council and of the Continental Congress; *m.* Eleanor DORSEY of "Hockley," but left no issue. A portrait of him is now in the possession of Miss Nellie RIDEOUT, of Annapolis, whose gd. mother was a sister of Barrister HALL's wife.

ISSUE BY SECOND MARRIAGE

I. EDWARD, *b.* 19th December, 1735 (see further),
II. ISAAC, *b.* 17th March, 1737 (see further).
III. Elizabeth, *b.* 10th February, 1739.
IV. Martha, *b.* 18th March, 1741; *d.* 28th May, 1747.
V. Thomas Henry, *b.* 13th September, 1743; *m.* Miss BOWIE, sister of Capt. Daniel BOWIE, of the Revolutionary Army, by whom he had issue.
VI. Margaret, *b.* 19th December, 1746; *m.* 3d February, 1767, Col. Richard HARWOOD.
VII. WILLIAM, III, *b.* 13th January, 1748 (see further).
VIII. Mary, *b.* 7th February, 1752.
IX. Martha, *b.* 27th March, 1755.

MAJ. HENRY HALL, *b.* 27th May, 1727; *d.* March, 1770 (son of Maj. Henry and Martha (BATEMAN) HALL, *m.* 27th December, 1748, Elizabeth WATKINS, dau. of ――― WATKINS, by Rev. William BROGDEN, Rector of All Hallows Parish. "He caught the smallpox in the natural way and *d.* when he was only about forty-three years of age, leaving his wife and nine children surviving him." He was commissioned in the Militia of Anne Arundel County, where he resided all his life, near Governor's Bridge.

ISSUE

I. Henry (Major), *b.* 21st July, 1751 (see further).
II. Nicholas, *b.* circa 1753; *d.* 29th December, 1821; *m.* (firstly) Ann GRIFFITH, *b.* 24th February, 1762, *d.* 27th April, 1791, dau. of Hon. Henry and Ruth (HAMMOND) GRIFFITH. They had issue, seven children— among their descendants were the late Charles F. PITTS, a prominent lawyer of Baltimore, and the late Sullivan PITTS of Baltimore; *m.* (secondly) ――― HOWARD, of Elk Ridge; he moved to Frederick County, and *d.* there.
III. WILLIAM, *b.* in 1755 (see further).
IV. John Stephen, *m.* ――― BOYD, dau. of Thomas BOYD, of Prince George's County, Maryland; he moved to New Market, Frederick County, where he *d.*
V. Martha, *m.* Joseph HOWARD, son of Joseph (see further).

VI. Margaret, *d.* unmarried.
VII. Anne, *m.* (firstly) Thomas RUTLAND; *m.* (secondly) John WATKINS (see further).
VIII. Mary, *m.* David STEWART, and had issue, sons and daughters.
IX. Elizabeth, *m.* John WATKINS, commonly called "Chunk" John.

MAJ. HENRY HALL (also known as Maj. Harry HALL), son of Maj. Henry and Elizabeth (WATKINS) HALL, his wife, *b.* 21st July, 1751; *d.* in 1798; *m.* (firstly) Sarah JACOB, dau. of Mordacci JACOB, of Prince George's County, and Jemina ISAAC, his wife; *m.* (secondly) 27th December, 1774, Margaret, sister of Joseph HOWARD; *m.* (thirdly) Rachel, dau. of Capt. Thomas HARWOOD, of South River; Maj. Henry HALL resided near the Governor's Bridge in Anne Arundel County; he had no issue by his first marriage.

ISSUE BY SECOND MARRIAGE

I. Henry, *b.* 7th December, 1776.
II. Joseph (M.D.), *m.* Harriet SELLMAN, dau. of William.

ISSUE

1. Sophia, *m.* R. Stockett MATHEWS, a distinguished lawyer of Baltimore, lately deceased; had issue.

III. Margery, *b.* 11th April, 1781; *m.* 28th April, 1799, the late S. Richard Galen STOCKETT, of Howard County.
IV. John Washington, *b.* 7th April, 1783.

ISSUE BY THIRD MARRIAGE

V. Elizabeth, *m.* Basil WARING, of Prince George's County, Maryland, and Washington, D. C.
VI. Mary Ann, *m.* 3d January, 1791, Thomas William HALL, her cousin, a son of Edward HALL.

ISSUE

1. Dr. Julius HALL, *m.* Jane CONTEE KENT, dau. of Joseph KENT, Governor of Maryland.

ISSUE

1[1]. Mary Ella, *b.* October, 1844; *d.* in 1916; *m.* Robert GRIFFITH; issue, four children; survived and live in Baltimore.
2[1]. Jullia, *b.* March, 1848; *d.* 1904; *m.* J. Alfred OSBOURNE, no issue.

3¹. Harriet, *d.* unmarried.
4¹. Joseph Thomas, *b.* November, 1849; *d.* in November, 1912; *m.* ——— GARRISON; had issue, two sons.
5¹. Wallace Kent, *b.* August, 1851.
6¹. Julius, Jr., *b.* 12th October, 1853; *m.* 27th April, 1887, Elizabeth Claude, daughter of Francis Henry STOCKETT, a distinguished lawyer of Annapolis, and Mary Priscilla HALL, his wife.

ISSUE

1². Julius, III, *b.* 21st August, 1888; *m.* 26th October, 1915 Florence Wode BECKER, of Buefield, West Virginia.

ISSUE

1³. Martha Elizabeth Becker, *b.* October, 1917.

2². Margaret Harwood, *b.* 17th September, 1890; *m.* 8th October, 1913, Ensign Harry W. HILL, United States Navy.

ISSUE

1³. Elizabeth Stockett HILL, *b.* 3d November, 1914.

3². Frances Stockett, *b.* 27th February, 1894.
4². Mary Priscilla.

7¹. William, *b.* August, 1857; *d.* January, 1916; *m.* Mary Etta WATERS, no issue.

VII. Thomas Harwood, probably *d.* young.
VIII. Richard Henry, *m.* Harriet KENT, a sister of Gov. Joseph KENT, of Maryland; he was a Commission Merchant in Baltimore City for many years.

ISSUE

1. Rachel Anne, *m.* Maj. William B. SLACK.

ISSUE

1¹. William Hall SLACK.
2¹. Addie SLACK, *m.* Lewis PERINE of New Jersey.

ISSUE

1². Rachel Hall Slack PERINE, *m.* in January, 1918, Eno CAMPBELL, of Artillery Corps.

IX. Osborne Sprigg, *d.* unmarried; held office in Washington.

EDWARD HALL, son of Maj. Henry HALL (and his wife Elizabeth LANSDALE), *b.* 19th December, 1735; *m.* 14th June, 1764, Martha ODELL, widow of Rignal ODELL, and dau. of Richard DUCKETT, Sr.

ISSUE

1. Richard, *m.* ——— COWMAN, of South River, Maryland.

ISSUE

1. A son, a Lieutenant of Marines of United States Navy; *m.* ——— COWMAN; had issue.
2. Edward Hall, *d.s.p.;* was a Member of the Executive Council of Maryland, and for several years of the General Assembly.
3. Thomas, *m.* dau. of Henry HALL, near Governor's Bridge; left issue; was a Member of the Council.
4. John, *d.* unmarried.
5. A dau., *m.* Joseph COWMAN, of South River, Anne Arundel County; left issue.
6. A dau., *d.s.p.*

Isaac, of West River, Anne Arundel County, Maryland; son of Maj. Henry HALL (and his wife, Elizabeth LANSDALE), *b.* 17th March, 1737, *m.* Ruth JACOB, only daughter of Mordacai and Ruth (TYLER) JACOB; his wife.

ISSUE

1. Edward, *m.* ——— STEVENSON.

ISSUE

1¹. A son, *m.* ——— ESTEP, dau. of Rezen ESTEP, of West River, Anne Arundel County, Maryland.

ISSSUE (AMONG OTHERS)

1². Estep.
2². Edward.
3². Alexander.

4^2. Augustus.
5^2. Frederick.

2. Mordacai, *d.* unmarried.
3. Henry, *m.* ——— STEVENSON, sister of his brother Edward's wife; had issue.

III. Margaret, third dau. of Maj. Henry HALL (and his wife Elizabeth LANSDALE), *b.* 19th December, 1746; *m.* 3d February, 1767, Col. Richard HARWOOD, son of Richard.

ISSUE

1. Anne Elizabeth, *m.* Maj. Jonathan SELLMAN.
2. Elizabeth Anne *m.* Osbourn Sprigg HARWOOD.
3. Richard Hall, Judge of Circuit Court of Anne Arundel County; *m.* Anne GREEN.
4. Henry Hall, *m.* 1805 Elizabeth LLOYD, dau. of Col. Edward LLOYD of Wye.
5. Joseph, *m.* (firstly) Ann CHAPMAN; *m.* (secondly) Matilda SPARROW.
6. Thomas, a lawyer of Baltimore; *d.* unmarried.
7. Mary, *m.* Thomas Noble HARWOOD, her cousin.
8. Henrietta, *m.* (firstly) Thomas COWMAN; *m.* (secondly) Thomas HALL; for issue see below.
9. Benjamin, *m.* (firstly) in 1783, Henrietta Maria BATTEE; *m.* (secondly) Margaret HALL dau. of Wm. HALL, III.

IV. William, III, son of Maj. Henry HALL (and his wife Elizabeth LANSDALE), *b.* 13th January, 1748; *d.* in 1815; *m.* 3d February, 1774, Margaret, dau. of Capt. Thomas HARWOOD, of St. James Parish. He was a gd. father of the wife of the late Francis H. STOCKETT, of Annapolis, and member of the Bar.

ISSUE

1. Thomas, *m.* (firstly) Henrietta, widow of Thomas COWMAN; *m.* (secondly) Mary WATKINS, 19th July, 1822.

ISSUE

1^1. John Thomas, *b.* 3d. June, 1826.
2^1. Watkins, *b.* 27th February, 1828.

2. Richard, *m.* (wife's name not given).

1¹. Richard, *m.*, and left descendants in Prince George's and Calvert Counties.

3. Margaret, *m.* Benjamin, son of Col. Richard HARWOOD and Margaret HALL, his wife.
4. Rachel, *m.* Soloman SPARROW; no issue.
5. Harry, *m.* Anne GASTON, of Delaware.

ISSUE

1¹. Anne, *d.* unmarried.
2¹. Susan, *d.* unmarried, 26th November, 1893.
3¹. William Henry, *m.* Henrietta HALL.

6. Mary Dryden, *d.* 25th December, 1883; *m.* Alfred SELLMAN; no issue.
7. Elizabeth, *m.* ——— WATKINS.

ISSUE

1¹. Eleanor WATKINS, *m.* Richard SELLMAN.
2¹. Rachel Sprigg WATKINS, *m.* Blake HALL.

8. William John, *b.* 1st January, 1791; *d.* 6th September, 1832; *m.* 18th November, 1819, Margaret Hall HARWOOD, dau. of Osbourn HARWOOD.

ISSUE

1¹. William Osbourn, *d.* young.
2¹. Maria, *d.* young.
3¹. Elizabeth Ann, *b.* 29th September, 1824; *d.* Easter Sunday, 1834.
4¹. Mary Priscilla, *b.* 14th January, 1827; *d.* 5th February, 1900; *m.* 19th November, 1846, Francis Henry STOCKETT, of Annapolis, a distinguished lawyer, and one time candidate for Attorney-General of Maryland, and for many years a Vestryman of St. Ann's Church.

ISSUE

1². Fannie STOCKETT, *b.* 19th April, 1848; *d.* 30th August, 1912.
2². Ann Sellman STOCKETT, *b.* 13th October, 1849.
3². Margaret Harwood STOCKETT, *b.* 1st October, 1851; *d.* 1871.
4². Elizabeth Claude STOCKETT; *b.* 11th December, 1853; *m.* 27th April, 1887, Julius HALL, Jr., (for issue see Julius HALL, Jr., ante).
5². Mary Priscilla STOCKETT, *b.* 5th September, 1856.
6². Francis Henry STOCKETT, *b.* 4th November, 1858.

7^2. Eleanor STOCKETT, *b.* 21st July, 1861; *d.* 23d July, 1861.
8^2. Ellen STOCKETT, *b.* 17th March, 1864; *d.* 1867.
9^2. Harriet Key STOCKETT, *b.* 29th January, 1866.

5^1. Harriet Kent, *b.* 14th August, 1829; *d.* 20th June, 1902; *m.* Phillip SCHWEAR.

ISSUE

1^2. William Hall SCHWEAR.
2^2. Florence SCHWEAR.
3^2. Cleland Nelson SCHWEAR.
4^2. Mary Walton SCHWEAR.

6^1. William Sprigg, *b.* 9th July, 1832; *d.* 25th February, 1875; *m.* Elizabeth Sellman WELSH.

ISSUE

1^2. Alfred Sellman.

2^2. William Sprigg.
3^2. Elizabeth Sellman.
4^2. Anna.
5^2. Margaret Harwood.

v. Martha, the fifth child of Maj. Henry HALL (and Elizabeth WATKINS, his wife) *m.* Joseph HOWARD, son of Joseph.

ISSUE

1. Joseph and five daughters, one of whom
2. Margaret, *m.* (firstly) 17th October, 1795, Allen Bowie DUCKETT, a distinguished lawyer, Member of the Legislature of Maryland, Member of the Governor's Council, 1803, and was appointed by President JEFFERSON, one of the first Judges of the District of Columbia, he was a son of Richard DUCKETT and Elizabeth WILLIAMS, his wife; *m.* (secondly) Daniel CLARK, also an eminent lawyer and afterward a Judge of the Circuit Court of Prince George's County, Maryland.

ISSUE BY FIRST MARRIAGE

1^1. Thomas DUCKETT, *b.* 1797; a member of the Bar; *m.* (firstly) Catherine E. W., dau. of William GOLDSBOROUGH, of Frederick County, Maryland (son of Hon. Robert GOLDSBOROUGH, of Cambridge, Maryland), and his wife Sarah WORTHINGTON, dau. of Col. Nicholas WORTHINGTON, of Sumner Hill, Anne Arundel County. Thomas DUCKETT, m. (secondly) Kitty, the widow of Daniel CLARK, Jr., and dau. of William BOWIE, and his wife, Kitty DUCKETT, dau. of Baruch DUCKETT and Mary BEANS, his wife.

ISSUE BY FIRST MARRIAGE

1². Richard DUCKETT, b. 1831; m. 1855 Elizabeth M. WARING (dau. of Col. John H. WARING, and his wife, Julia Maria WORTHINGTON), and had a dau., Kitty C., who m. the late Wm. B. CLAGGETT, a Member of the Senate of Maryland, from Prince George's County.

ISSUE BY SECOND MARRIAGE

1². Thomas A. DUCKETT, m. Lucy SELLMAN.

ISSUE

1³. Thomas Allan DUCKETT, killed by accident in his ninth year.
2³. Lucy DUCKETT, m. Ramsay HODGES.
3³. Oden Bowie DUCKETT, m. Estelle Bird ISRAEL.
4³. Richard Battee DUCKETT, m. Minnie HILL.
5³. Katherine Bowie DUCKETT, m. Thomson KING.

2². Elizabeth Howard DUCKETT, m. 20th December, 1804, Dr. Richard DUCKETT, brother of John DUCKETT, one time Treasurer of Maryland.
3². Eleanor Howard DUCKETT.
4². Margery Howard DUCKETT.
5². Martha Howard DUCKETT.
6². Kitty Howard DUCKETT, m. Rev. Mr. RAFFERTY, President of St. John's College; no issue.

VII. Anne, the seventh child of Maj. Henry HALL (and Elizabeth WATKINS, his wife) m. (firstly) Thomas RUTLAND; m. (secondly) John WATKINS.

ISSUE BY FIRST MARRIAGE

1. A dau., m. ——— BEARD, had issue.
2. A dau., m. ——— WATSON, had issue.

ISSUE BY SECOND MARRIAGE

1. A dau., m. ——— HOPKINS.
2. A dau., m. Leonard IGLEHART.

JOHN HALL, *b.* 26th April, 1716; *d.* 14th April, 1790; son of Rev. Henry HALL and Mary, his wife; *m.* about 1746, Ann WELLS, dau. of Thomas WELLS, of Anne Arundel and Calvert Counties, Maryland.

ISSUE

I. Martha, *b.* 23d December, 1747; *m.* 23d January, 1776, William TILLARD.
II. Elizabeth, *b.* 10th July, 1751; *d.* unmarried.
III. Anne, *b.* 10th May, 1754; *m.* ——— PINDELL.
IV. Mary Magdalen, *b.* 10th March, 1759; *m.* William URQUHART; no issue.
V. William Henry, *b.* 19th November, 1762; *d.* 1813; *m.* 27th January, 1788, Margaret Gassaway WATKINS, dau. of Col. Gassaway WATKINS, of the Revolutionary War, and Dinah, his wife; had twelve children, all *d.* in childhood, unmarried, but two.

ISSUE (AMONG OTHERS)

1. William Henry, *b.* 10th February, 1796; *m.* 10th February, 1825, Eleanor Deborrah SELLMAN, dau. of ——— SELLMAN.

ISSUE

1¹. Thomas Sellman.
2¹. Mary Sophia.
3¹. William Henry, *m.* Eleanor Maria ESTEP.

ISSUE

1². Eleanor Deborah.
2². William Henry.
3². Rachel Estep.
4². Thomas Sellman.

2. Thomas John, *b.* 24th June, 1800; *d.* October, 1880; for many years a prominent and useful citizen of the City of Baltimore, where he conducted the tobacco and grain commission business and as such accumulated a large fortune, and was the virtual banker and financial agent of a large part of the planters and farmers of Southern Maryland; *m.* (firstly) in November, 1821, Mary Ann HODGES, of Anne Arundel County, who *d.* in 1825; *m*, (secondly) 7th November, 1826, Rachel Sophia WATERS, dau. of Jacob WATERS, of Prince George's County, and Martha MULLIKEN, his wife.

ISSUE BY FIRST MARRIAGE

1¹. Charles William, *b.* 20th September, 1822; *m.* Alice STEWART, dau. of Dr. Hammond STEWART, of Calvert County.
2¹. John, *d.* unmarried.

ISSUE BY SECOND MARRIAGE

1¹. Harriet Ann, b. 18th August, 1829; m. 1862 Richard T. ESTEP.

ISSUE

1². Eleanor ESTEP, m. 1890, William HALL, nephew of William John HALL
2². Rachel Hall ESTEP, m. 1891, William Thomas SHACKELFORD.

ISSUE

1³. William Thomas Shackelford, Jr., m. 3d April, 1917, Mildred MARTIN.
2³. Richard Tillard Shackelford.

3². Richard ESTEP, m. 1894, Elizabeth Gordon SUDLER, of Virginia.
4². Mary L. ESTEP.
5². Sarah ESTEP (twin), m. Floyd LANKFORD, of Staunton, Virginia, now of Montreal, Canada.
6². Harriet ESTEP (twin).

2¹. Mary, b. 6th September, 1831; m. 1860, Otto BOEHME.
3¹. Martha, b. 22d April, 1834; d. young.
4¹. Thomas John, Jr., b. 18th June, 1836; m. 1874, Mary Esther LONEY, dau. of Francis Barton LONEY, of Baltimore, and Elizabeth K. his wife.

ISSUE

1². Anne Elizabeth, d. in infancy.
2². Rachel Sophia.
3². Mary, d. in infancy.
4². Margaret Gassaway.
5². Thomas John, III, of West River, Anne Arundel County, Maryland; m. 4th October, 1910, Issabelle Frances ALLEN, dau. of Benjamin W. ALLEN and Harriett WATERS his wife, of Tipperary, Ireland.

ISSUE

1³. Thomas Allen Waters, b. 6th September, 1911.
2³. Frances Barton Loney, b. 22d January, 1913.
3³. Catherine Sandes, b. 12th September, 1915.

5¹. Franklin Waters, b. 18th June, 1838; he succeeded his father in business from which he retired about 1890; m. in 1867 Katherine Gertrude ROBINSON, dau. of Alexander ROBINSON of Baltimore who m. a dau. of George APPOLD of Baltimore; she predeceased him; left no issue.

6¹. Laura, *b.* 1st December, 1840; *m.* 1870 Walter Scott KENNEDY, of Washington County, Maryland.

7¹. Virginia, *b.* 27th December, 1844; *m.* 1874, James CRANE of Baltimore.

8¹. Margaret, *d.* young.

BENJAMIN HALL, *b.* 29th November, 1710; *d.* 1760; a planter of Queen Anne's Parish, in Prince George's County; was the fifth child of Rev. Henry HALL and Mary DUVALL, his wife; *m.* 9th December 1731, Sophia WELSH, dau. of Maj. John WELSH, of All Hallows Parish, Anne Arundel County, and Thomasin HOPKINS, his wife. Major WELSH was Justice of the Quorum, High Sheriff, Commissioner for Building the Court House at Annapolis, and the owner of several thousand acres of land. Benjamin HALL *d.* on his plantation "Parrotts Mannor," in Queen Anne's Parish, leaving a will, which was probated in Prince George's County, 29th January, 1760, wherein he devises to his wife and seven surviving children many acres of land consisting of "Parrott's Manor," part of "Pleasant Grove," and also many slaves and much personalty of large value.

ISSUE

I. John, *b.* 30th November, 1732; *d.* young.

II. Benjamin, planter of Prince George's County; *b.* about 1734; *d.* leaving a will dated 3d July, 1780, and probated 8th November, 1783, whereby he devised all his lands, including his dwelling place near Governor's Bridge, to his wife Rebecca, and gave legacies to his brothers, William and Edward HALL, and to his sisters Sarah DUVALL, Sophia MULLIKEN, and Martha HALL. Benjamin HALL *m.* (firstly) Eleanor MURDOCK; (secondly) Rebecca MAGRUDER, but left no issue by either wife. He was a conspicuous citizen and took a prominent part in the stirring times in which he lived. He was one of the four Delegates elected from Prince George's County to the First Constitutional Convention of Maryland in 1776; was one of the Signers of the Declaration of Freemen, and a member of the State Convention of 1778.

III. William, planter of "Pleasant Grove," Prince George's County; *b.* about 1735–1736; *d.* in said County, leaving a will dated 6th January, 1791, and probated 6th January, 1792, whereby he devised his dwelling plantation, part of "Pleasant Grove" to his three sons, Isaac HALL, Rignal John Duckett HALL, and Grafton HALL; and makes bequests and devises to his gd. daughters, Elizabeth, Anne and Rebecca GODMAN, and to ten other children. He *m.* 15th March, 1764, Anne DUCKETT, dau. of Richard DUCKETT, and Elizabeth WILLIAMS, his wife. Her will dated 15th May, 1815, and probated 8th December, the same year disposes of a number of slaves and other personalty. William HALL, of Benjamin, was the owner of large tracts of land, and many slaves. He was a Member of the Committee of Safety for Prince George's County during the Revolutionary War, and was otherwise actively engaged during that period in public affairs. As shown by said wills and entries in the family Bible in the possession of the family of the late William Williams HALL, of Washington, D. C., the issue of William HALL, of Benjamin and Anne, his wife, were:

ISSUE

1. Elizabeth (twin), b, 4th May, 1765; m. ——— HOWARD.
2. Rachel (twin) b. 4th May, 1765; m. ——— GODMAN.

ISSUE

1^1. Elizabeth GODMAN.
2^1. Anne GODMAN.
3^1. Rebecca GODMAN.

3. Benjamin, b. 30th November, 1766; d. young.
4. Richard Duckett, planter; b. 6th May, 1768; d. 1819; m. 8th January, 1799, Elizabeth PERKINS, b. 7th June, 1778, dau. of William PERKINS, b. in England in 1750, d. 14th April, 1816, settled in Prince George's County in 1772, m. 18th June, 1777, Susannah CLARKE. He was a Tory. After the death of Richard Duckett HALL, his widow, Elizabeth (PERKINS), HALL m. Rev. Nathan HOSKINS. Richard Duckett HALL d. in 1819, as shown by an inventory of his estate filed by his brother Edward HALL, 8th June, 1819. He was a useful and trusted citizen of the community in which he lived and acted as executor of many estates, and was guardian for numerous infants.

ISSUE

1^1. Susannah, b. 14th September, 1800; d. prior to 1846; m. (firstly) 12tl December, 1822, Leonard BECK; m. (secondly) William ANDERSON, b. 30th August, 1797, d. 22d July, 1877. He m. (secondly) 3d November, 1846, his wife's sister Sarah HALL, b. 27th February, 1811, d. 1st May, 1875 (for whom see further).

ISSUE BY FIRST MARRIAGE

1^2. Richard S. BECK, b. 6th August, 1823; d. 8th March, 1824.

ISSUE BY SECOND MARRIAGE

1^2. William Henry Harrison ANDERSON, b. September, 1840; d. October, 1910; m. 1868, Cornelia M. BROCKET, dau. of Robert BROCKET and Anne MCCORMICK, his wife; he was a member of the Baltimore Bar; no issue.

2[1]. Mary Anne, *b.* 11th August, 1803; *m.* ———— BALDWIN; no issue.
3[1]. Eliza, *b.* 29th July, 1805; *m.* Samuel DUVALL, of Prince George's County, son of Tobias DUVALL, and ———— WILLETT, his wife (see DUVALL, MACKENZIE's "Colonial Families of America," 1907).

ISSUE

1[2]. Sue DUVALL, *d.* 1918; *m.* 19th October, 1859, Rev. George Williamson SMITH, *b.* 21st November, 1836, at Catskill, New York, removed to Rochester, New York, in 1843, where he prepared for College and entered the University in June, 1853, but changed to Hobart College, Geneva, New York, in the fall of that year. He graduated A.B. in 1857. He attended Bladensburg Academy from the fall of 1857 until March, 1860. He was clerk in the Navy Department until 2d July, 1864, and was Chaplain in the United States Navy from that date until 1st October, 1876, when he resigned. He was rector of Grace Protestant Episcopal Church, Jamaica, Long Island, New York, until September, 1881; Rector of The Church of the Redeemer, Brooklyn, New York, until September, 1883. He was President of Trinity College, Hartford, Connecticut until 1st July, 1904, when he resigned, and has since been the retired or Emeritus Professor of Metaphysics in the Institution; no issue.

2[2]. Anna DUVALL, *m.* ———— ROBINSON; no issue.
3[2]. Jackson DUVALL, *d.* unmarried.

4[1]. William Perkins HALL, *b.* 8th March, 1807; *m.* Elizabeth MEEKS, *b.* 26th March, 1810, dau. of Wesley MEEKS, and Susannah, his wife.
5[1]. Rev. John HALL, *b.* 5th March, 1809; *d.* 11th April, 1873; member of the Virginia Conference Methodist Episcopal Church; *m.* Angaline FRETWELL of Virginia; *d.* 20th August, 1886.

ISSUE

1[2]. John Edward HALL, *b.* 22nd February, 1845; deceased; *m.* Isabel HOPKINS, *b.* November, 1843. Issue: Seven children.
2[2]. Bettie HALL, *b.* 1846; *m.* Thomas BEALL.
3[2]. Richard Watson HALL, *b.* 17th November, 1847, *d.* 20th December 1913; *m.* Maria Overton Turner of Charlottesville, Virginia. Had issue: John T., Sammie, H. E., Mary, Nettie and Richard Overton Hall.
4[2]. Addie T. Hall, *d.* unmarried.

6[1]. Sarah HALL, b. 27th February, 1811; d. 1st May, 1875, became, 3d November, 1846, the second wife of William ANDERSON, the surviving husband of her deceased sister, Susannah HALL. They lived near Annapolis Junction in Anne Arundel County.

ISSUE

1[2]. Susannah ANDERSON, b. 27th April, 1850; m. Thomas John BOWIE, b. 22d February, 1837, d. 3d September, 1898.

ISSUE

1[3]. John BOWIE, b. 21st January, 1871; m. 17th October, 1900, Ethel Frances COOK, of Georgetown, D. C.

ISSUE

1[4]. One daughter and three sons.

2[3]. William BOWIE, b. 6th May, 1872; m. 28th June, 1899, Elizabeth Taylor WATTLES, of Alexandria, Virginia.

ISSUE

1[4]. Clagett Bowie, b. 6th February, 1907.

3[3]. Edward Hall BOWIE, b. 29th March, 1874; m. 12th December 1895, Florence HATCH.

4[3]. Henry Anderson BOWIE, b. 27th June, 1875; d. 11th February, 1888.

5[3]. Mary Tasker BOWIE, b. 18th October, 1878; d. 8th January, 1913; m. 27th September, 1905, Noah Ernest DORSEY, b. 15th March, 1873, A.B., Ph.D. of Johns Hopkins University; no issue.

5. William, Jr., b. 30th October, 1769; mentioned in the wills of his parents; further unknown.
6. Baruch, b. 16th January, 1773, d. about 1830, in Frederick County, where he lived; m. (wife's name not given) but left no issue.
7. Anne, b. 1st April, 1774; mentioned in her mother's will in 1815 as Anne MULLIKEN, but was single at the death of her father in 1792; further unknown.
8. Jacob Duckett, b. 6th April, 1775; d. between 30th September and 31st October, 1799, leaving a will by which he mentions his mother, brothers and sisters and nieces.

9. Martha, *b.* 8th June, 1777; *m.* Joshua DORSEY; was unmarried at death of her father, but is mentioned in her mother's will as Martha DORSEY; further unknown.
10. Edward, planter, *b.* 3d November, 1778; *d.* 21st April, 1834; he lived and died on his farm of 450 acres, near Beltsville, Prince George's County, which was devised to him and his brothers by their father by the name of part of "Pleasant Grove;" his uncle, Lieut. Edward HALL, by his will gave to him all his plate, wearing apparel, and certain negroes. Edward HALL, *m.* three times, but the name of the first wife is not known; he *m.* (secondly) August, 1824, Rebecca (WILLIAMS) HALL, *b.* 22d April, 1795, *d.* 27th July, 1829, the widow of his brother Grafton HALL; *m.* (thirdly) Sarah Beck (WILLIAMS) PARKER (widow), and sister of his second wife, Rebecca. By her first husband Sarah Beck WILLIAMS had two children, viz.: Ruth Anne Williams PARKER, *b.* 11th December 1820, and Samuel R. PARKER, *b.* 2d March, 1822.

ISSUE BY FIRST MARRIAGE

1^1. Andrew Jackson, *b.* 13th February, 1815; *d.* 24th August, 1826.
2^1. Rignal Duckett, *b.* 27th December, 1816; *d.* 29th August, 1826.
3^1. Elizabeth Anne, *b.* 10th October, 1818; *d.* 14th April, 1825.

ISSUE BY SECOND MARRIAGE

1^1. Edward Grafton Washington, *b.* 22d February, 1825; *m.* Isabella SCOTT; after the death of his sister Ruth Anne Rebecca, he became the owner of 450 acres of land of his father's known as "Pleasant Grove."
2^1. Ruth Anne Rebecca, *b.* 11th September, 1826; *d.* 6th August, 1851, unmarried.

ISSUE BY THIRD MARRIAGE

1^1. Mary, *b.* 14th February, 1834; *m.* (firstly) ——— FREEMAN; *m.* (secondly) Daniel MCCANN, further unknown.

11. Thomas, planter of Prince George's County; *b.* 17th July, 1781; *d.* intestate in spring of 1849; *m.* 1807–1808 Sue ANDERSON, dau. of ——— ANDERSON.

1^1. Absolam Anderson, *b.* November, 1810; *d.* 14th December, 1878; *m.* Julia BEARD of Anne Arundel County; *b.* 2d February, 1812, *d.* 22d May, 1881.

ISSUE

1^2. Anna May, *b.* 23d December, 1842; *d.* 14th February, 1857.
2^2. Margaret Jane, *b.* 28th September, 1850; *m.* 25th October, 1870, Rev. Isaac W. CANTER, of the Baltimore Conference of the Methodist Episcopal Church South.

ISSUE

1^3. Dr. Hall CANTER, *b.* 5th April, 1873; A.B., and A.M. from Randolph Macon College; Ph.D., Johns Hopkins University, 1890; Professor of Chemistry of Randolph Macon; *m.* (firstly) 8th August, 1900, Frances Cooksie BROWN, *d.* 3d August, 1911, dau. of Rev. Alexander BROWN, of Ashland, Virginia, a member of the Virginia Conference of the Methodist Episcopal Church South; *m.* (secondly) December, 1912, Caroline MIDYETTE, of Ashland, Virginia.
2^3. Rev. Harry M. CANTER, A.B., B.D., D.D.; *b.* 3d February, 1875; Presiding Elder of the Washington District of the Methodist Episcopal Church, South; *m.* 1st June, 1899, Margaret JONES.
3^3. Julia White CANTER, *b.* 21st September, 1880; *m.* Frank MAHOOD, *b.* 16th April, 1881, of Roanoke, Virginia, and is cashier of a bank.
4^3. Dr. Noland Mackenzie CANTER, *b.* 22d July, 1890; A.M. of Randolph Macon College, and M.D. of Johns Hopkins University.

3^2. Julia, *b.* 13th October, 1854; *m.* 7th February, 1882, Benjamin COLLISON, *b.* 11th June, 1855, of Anne Arundel County.

ISSUE

1^3. Jennie COLLISON, *b.* 21st July, 1884.
2^3. Benjamin COLLISON, *b.* 24th December, 1891; of Company B, 312th Machine Gun Battalion, and sailed for France 18th July, 1918.

2^1. Jacob, *b.* about 1812; *d.* unmarried.
3^1. Ann, *b.* about 1814; *m.* Isaac HOWARD, of Frederick, Maryland.

ISSUE

1^2. Clara Hall HOWARD.
2^2. Linden Hall HOWARD.

4[1]. Elizabeth, *b.* about 1816; *m.* Samuel ANDERSON, a merchant of Upper Marlborough, and Chase, Montgomery County, Maryland; he was a brother of William ANDERSON, of Annapolis Junction, Anne Arundel County.

ISSUE

1[2]. Thomas Hall ANDERSON, *m.* Virginia TURNER, of Frederick County.
2[2]. Martha ANDERSON, *m.* Abraham WOODWARD.
3[2]. Virginia ANDERSON, *m.* Daniel Dodge WOODWARD.
4[2]. Johns Hopkins ANDERSON, *m.* Mollie GRIFFITH.
5[2]. Dr. Samuel ANDERSON, *d.* unmarried; he resided at Woodwardville, Maryland.

5[1]. Mary Jane, *b.* about 1818; *d.* 188—; became the second wife of Rignal Duckett WOODWARD, planter, one time a Justice of the Peace for Anne Arundel County, and Chief Judge of the Orphan's Court.

ISSUE

1[2]. Ida WOODWARD, *m.* William F. WHITINGTON, of Anne Arundel County

ISSUE

A son and a daughter.

2[2]. Nannie WOODWARD, *m.* Albert HOLLAND, of Washington, D. C., left issue.

3[2]. William Isaac WOODWARD, *b.* 1859; *d.* January, 1915; *m.* (firstly) Miss Laura CHANDLER, by whom he had one child, a dau. Margaret WOODWARD, *m.* Edwin S. KELLOGG; *m.* (secondly) Aminee C. MATHIS, by whom he had three daughters, viz.:

1[3]. Neeta Hattie WOODWARD, *b.* 1896.
2[3]. Laura Adina WOODWARD, *b.* 1898.
3[3]. Jimmie Nellie WOODWARD, *b.* 1902.

4[2]. Mattie, *d.* about 1885; *m.* Thomas BEARD of Anne Arundel County, now deceased, by whom she had several children.

6[1]. Baruch, *b,* about September, 1817; *d.* May, 1886, of Washingron, D. C., where he was a successful merchant; *m.* 1841, Virginia Blagden GUNNELL, dau. of William Hunter GUNNELL, of Virginia; issue, ten children, of whom four only survived their minority, viz.:

COLONIAL FAMILIES OF THE UNITED STATES

ISSUE

1^2. Harry Walton, *m*. Anna MOHUN.
2^2. Rosa E., *m*. 1869, Rignal W. BALDWIN, *b*. 1835, *d*. on January 4th, 1891; he was a graduate of Dickinson College, and a prominent member of the Baltimore Bar, and among other large corporations, he was attorney for the Louisville and Nashville Railroad Company.

ISSUE

1^3. Rignal W. BALDWIN, a member of the Baltimore Bar; Graduate of the Baltimore City College; an alumnus of Johns Hopkins University, and is a Graduate of the Law Department of the University of Maryland; *m*. 1901, Augusta HOPKINS, dau. of J. Seth HOPKINS, now deceased, a prominent merchant of Baltimore City.

ISSUE

1^4. Rignal W. BALDWIN, III.
2^4. Ludlow BALDWIN.

2^3. Morgan H. BALDWIN, formerly of Baltimore and Anne Arundel County, but now of Denver, Colorado; *m*. 1901, Olive HILL, of South Carolina.

ISSUE

1^4. Mary Hamilton BALDWIN.
2^4. Morgan Hall BALDWIN, Jr.

3^3. Springfield BALDWIN, a Civil Engineer for the Illinois Central Railroad Company; a Graduate of the Baltimore City College and of Lehigh University; *m*. 1910, Mabel RANEY, of Chicago.

ISSUE

1^4. Rosa Hall BALDWIN.
2^4. Springfield BALDWIN, III.

4^3. Rosa BALDWIN, unmarried; Graduate of the Western High School of Baltimore City and of Goucher College, Baltimore.
5^3. Henry Wilson BALDWIN, *m*. Maude QUIRK.
6^3. Charles Severn Baldwin, unmarried; a Graduate of Baltimore City College and of Lehigh University, in Civil Engineering.

3². Baruch Crittenden, *b.* March, 1862; *m.* Emma Daingerfield TEN-
NANT, dau. of Rev. ———— TENNANT, of the Protestant Episcopal Church.

ISSUE

1³. A son.

4². Lola Anna, *b.* 1864; *m.* October, 1894, Austin C. STONEBURNER, of
Baltimore, Maryland, a financier; no issue.

7¹. Isaac, *b.* about 1823, *d.* unmarried.
8¹. Martha Thomas, *b.* about 1826; *d.* unmarried.

12. Rignal Duckett, *b.* 31st March, 1783; *d.* young.
13. Grafton, planter, of Prince George's County, Maryland; *b.* 1st September, 1784; *d.* 1st December, 1822; he served in the War of 1812 in
Captain ISAAC's Company; his home estate was known as "Catalpa,"
near what is now Springfield, Maryland; *m.* 11th January, 1811,
Rebecca WILLIAMS, *b.* 22d April, 1795, *d.* 27th July, 1829, dau. of
William WILLIAMS, of said County.

ISSUE

1¹. Ruth Anne, *b.* 28th March, 1812; *d.* 17th July, 1814.
2¹. William Williams, *b.* 12th December, 1814, at his father's homestead
near Springfield, in Prince George's County, where he lived until
after the Civil War, during which he was known as a Union man.
In his early life he was engaged in farming and took an active and
keen interest in politics. Later in life he entered the real estate
business both in his native county and in the City of Washington,
where he had lived for many years at the time of his death in his
hundredth year. He was a well known citizen, blessed with a
strong constitution and beloved by all. He was educated at a
private school conducted in the vicinity of his home. But few
could recall public events and family histories with more accuracy
or more interestingly than he could, or took more delight in doing
so even to his last years. He was familiarly and affectionately
known among his family connections as "Uncle Billy." He *m.*
February 18, 1857, Elizabeth Hinkle RITTENHOUSE, dau. of Smith
Baker RITTENHOUSE, of Bucks County, Pennsylvania, and Henrietta HATTON, his wife. Mr. RITTENHOUSE was *b.* in 1795, and
removed later to Baltimore, Maryland, where he taught in Gales
School, and *d.* 17th April, 1871.

ISSUE

1[2]. William Williams, *b.* 8th February, 1858; *d.* 11th December, 1897; *m.* 25th August, 1881, Rebecca Anne PEACH, dau. of John Gibson PEACH, of Virginia, a prominent lawyer.

ISSUE

1[3]. Mary Rebecca.
2[3]. John Grafton.
3[3]. William Thornton.
4[3]. Richard.

3[1]. Richard Duckett, Planter of Prince George's County, Maryland; *b.* 22d September, 1816; *d.* 24th April, 1864. He lived and *d.* at his homestead "Walnut Range," about ten miles from Washington, D. C. on the Baltimore and Ohio Railroad. He was an ardent Democrat, and his sympathies with the Southern cause during the Civil War induced him to become surety on a bond to furnish uniforms for the Confederate States to the amount of $80,000 of which $40,000 was paid by his widow to Johns HOPKINS, by way of compromise effected by his brother William Williams HALL as will appear from the Court Records at Upper Marlborough. Richard Duckett HALL, *m.* 10th February, 1842, Susannah PERKINS, *b.* 12th November, 1818, *d*, 14th January, 1901, dau. of John PERKINS, of Prince George's County, and Baltimore, Maryland, *b.* 13th November, 1781, *d.* 8th November, 1840, who served in Capt. David WARFIELD'S Company (Independent Command) "Baltimore United Volunteers," at the Battle of North Point, and at Fort McHenry, 12th September, 1814. John PERKINS, *m.* 12th May, 1809, Harriet GORSUCH, dau. of Robert GORSUCH, of Homestead, Baltimore County, Maryland.

ISSUE

1[2]. John Grafton, of Prince George's County, *b.* 6th February, 1843; *d.* 5th February, 1888. He was educated at private schools, and at Cumberland Valley Institute, at Mechanicsburg, Pennsylvania. He was prominent in the affairs of the State, and County for a number of years. He was Treasurer of Prince George's County, was appointed by President CLEVELAND, Internal Revenue Collector for the District of Maryland. He *m.* 6th February, 1878, Ruth Adella BEALL, *b.* November, 1845, *d.* in 1899, dau. of Thomas Birch BEALL, *b.* 1818, *d.* 1879, and Jane Beall MAGRUDER, his wife.

ISSUE

1[3]. Elsie, *d.* young.
2[3]. John Grafton.

2[2]. Rebecca Frances, *b.* 30th August, 1844; *m.* 20th January, 1877, George W. BEALL, *b.* 16th January, 1849, residing at Beltsville, Prince George's County, Maryland, son of John and Caroline (WALKER) BEALL, his wife. He is prominent in church and public life, and is now Superintendent of the District of Columbia, Department for opening and paving streets.

ISSUE

1[3]. George Hall BEALL, *b.* 30th March, 1879; *m.* 10th July, 1905, Agnes STEWART, dau. of William, McClure STEWART, of Washington, D. C., and Josephine A. (PLANT) STEWART, his wife.

ISSUE

1[4]. George Stewart BEALL, *b.* about 1st October, 1906; *d.* 2d May, 1907.
2[4]. Winifred BEALL, *b.* 13th March, 1908.
3[4]. John Rogers BEALL, *b.* 11th November, 1909.
4[4]. Stewart Hall BEALL, *b.* 2d November, 1912.

2[3]. Samuel Rogers BEALL, *b.* 14th October, 1880, unmarried.
3[3]. John Woolf BEALL, *b.* 12th March, 1882; *m.* October, 1914, Jane MARTIN, of New York.
4[3]. Susannah Catherine BEALL.

3[2]. Harriett Perkins, *b.* 16th September, 1845; *m.* 9th November, 1871, William Matthew MARINE, *b.* 25th August, 1843, *d.* 2d March, 1904. He was a prominent lawyer of the Baltimore Bar, and took an active interest in the politics of the State and City, where he died. He was appointed by President HARRISON, Collector of Customs, Port of Baltimore. He was a man of distinct literary and poetic talent, having written and published at times both history and poetry.

ISSUE

See MARINE family, this volume

4[2]. Richard Henry, farmer of Prince George's County, *b.* 5th June, 1847. He was educated at a Cumberland Valley Institute, Mechanicsburg, Pennsylvania. He *m.* 30th March, 1875, Henrietta Kerr SPALDING, *b.* 2nd November, 1851, *d.* 30th May, 1915, dau. of Charles Clement and Sophia Kerr (LEIGH) SPALDING, his wife.

ISSUE

1³. Mary Spalding.
2³. Henrietta Kerr.
3³. Ruth Leeds.
4³. Annie Leigh.
5³. Evelyn.

5². Robert Vinton, of Prince George's County, *b.* 28th September, 1848; *d.* 16th May, 1900; a member of the Legislature of Maryland from his native County; at the time of his death he was General Manager of the Union Mutual Life Insurance Company; *m.* 8th November, 1883, Virginia B. YOUNGER, dau. of Richard B. and Cecilia (WONN) YOUNGER.

ISSUE

1³. Robert Vinton.

6². Sarah Ryland, *b.* 18th February, 1850; educated at Patapsco Institute; *m.* 18th June, 1872, Rev. William Alexander McDONALD, *b.* in Virginia, 16th August, 1838, *d.* 14th May, 1902; he was a member of the Virginia Conference of the Methodist Episcopal Church South, which he joined in 1866, and in which he served in the Conference of Maryland from 1866 until his death; he was chaplain of the State Senate for several terms.

ISSUE

1³. William Bartholow McDONALD, M.D., *b.* 15th August, 1873; *m.* 3d April, 1907, Maude ARNOLD, dau. of John W. and Emma Cornelia (STANSBURY) ARNOLD, his wife.

7². Ruth Williams, *b.* 12th December, 1851; *d.* 13th October, 1852.
8². James Williams, *b.* 16th July, 1853; *d.* 24th March, 1854.
9². William Turner, *b.* 2d May, 1855; *d.* 8th August, 1902; educated at the Maryland Agricultural College; *m.* Louise HOPKINS, *b.* 1st February, 1856; *d.* 25th October, 1911.
10². Reuben Beauregard, *b.* 10th January, 1858; *d.* 26th September, 1869.
11². Mary Susannah, *b.* 15th January, 1860; resides at Beltsville, Maryland; she was educated at Lambs School, Baltimore, Maryland, and the Maryland Institute.

12². Summerfield Davis, *b.* 12th June, 1862; educated at Public Schools and Anne Arundel Academy, at Millersville, Md., is now Clerk of the Circuit Court for Prince George's County, and a member of the Local Draft Board.

4 . Jacob Thornton, son of Grafton HALL and Rebecca, his wife, *b.* 14th October, 1818; *d.* 16th November, 1891; *m.* 18th August, 1842, Altizera DUVAL, *b.* 3d July, 1824, *d.* 26th February, 1907, one of the five beautiful daughters of Thomas C. DUVAL, of Leesburg, Virginia, and Vansville Hill, Prince George's County, and Emma BARRON, his wife, dau. of Commodore James BARRON, *b.* in Virginia in 1769, commissioned Lieutenant in the United States Navy in 1798; Captain, in 1799, Commodore in 1806, assigned as Commander of the ill fated ship *Chesapeake* in 1820, out of which the controversy between him and Stephen DECATUR arose, and which lead to the duel between them, both being wounded, DECATUR mortally.

ISSUE.

1². Mary Eugenia, *b.* 25th August, 1843; *m.* 26th December, 1860, Dr. William WOODWARD, of Leonardtown, St. Mary's County, but later of Hyattsville, Prince George's County, where his widow now resides, *b.* 2d February, 1841, *d.* 2d January, 1890.

ISSUE

1³. Frank Thornton WOODWARD, *b.* 24th May, 1862, now of Dallas, Texas; *m.* Lucile WILLIAMS, of New Orleans.
2³. Alice Marie WOODWARD, *b.* 1st November, 1864, resides in Baltimore, Maryland.
3³. Mary Gertrude WOODWARD, *b.* 17th August, 1868; *m.* Dr. John WALTERMEYER, of Denver, Colorado.
4³. William WOODWARD, *b.* 3d February, 1871.
5³. Charles WOODWARD, *b.* 12th June, 1873; *d.* 28th June, 1874.
6³. Agnes Clare WOODWARD, *b.* 31st March, 1876; *m.* 22d June, 1898, Clarence Summerfield KESSLER, son of Lloyd Alexander and Mary Elizabeth (HOWARD) KESSLER.

2². Francis Asbury, *b.* 9th April, 1845; *d.* 2d February, 1906, unmarried; he was a soldier in the Federal Army during the Civil War.
3². Thomas Thornton, *b.* 8th November, 1849; *d.* 11th April, 1903; was in United States Revenue Marine Service; was accidentally drowned in the Potomac River, and buried in Glenwood Cem-

etery, Washington, D. C.; *m*. Mary Eleanor COOPER, dau. of Thomas Alexander and Anna (BROWN) COOPER, of Carroll County, Maryland; no issue.

14. Isaac, *b*. 28th June, 1788; *d*. young and unmarried; was living 7th August, 1809, when he gave a release to his mother as his guardian.
15. John, *b*. 3d May, 1791; further unknown.

IV. Lieutenant Edward, son of Benjamin and Anne HALL, *b*. in 1743; *d*. unmarried in 1785, in Frederick County, Maryland, where his will was probated 2d April, 1785. He was at one time a West India Merchant and amassed a considerable fortune. According to "Heitsman's Historical Register" and records at the United States War Department, he was a Lieutenant of GRAYSON's Additional Continental Regiment; was taken prisoner and on 5th November, 1780, was exchanged. His name appears, on a list dated at Amboy, New Jersey, 18th March, 1780, of American officers, who as prisoners of war are declared to be "unexceptionable;" also on one account dated at New Burgh, New York, 5th August, 1782, showing debts due by sundry American officers during their captivity to the inhabitants of Long Island. The Paymaster General's records show that he received an officer's pay from 1777 to 1780. After the War he settled in Frederick County, Maryland, where he died leaving a will whereby he devised a large landed estate to his two nieces, Elizabeth HALL, dau. of his brother William, and to his niece Sophia DUVALL, dau. of his sister Sarah, and her husband, Marsh Mareen DUVALL, and to his nephew, namesake and godson, Edward, son of his brother William, he left his watch, sword and all his plate, wearing apparel, and certain of his negroes.

V. John Henry, *b*. about 1745; he was a minor in 1759, when his father's will was executed, and was not mentioned in his brother Benjamin's will of 3d July, 1780, it would therefore seem probable as his name does not appear in any of the records, that he *d*. between those dates, a minor.

VI. Sarah, *b*. about 1746; *m*. Capt. Marsh Mareen DUVALL, of Prince George's County, *b*. 17th April, 1741, son of John and Anne (FOWLER) DUVALL, his wife; Marsh Mareen DUVALL was a Captain in the Revolutionary Army.

ISSUE

1. Sophia DUVALL, to whom her uncle, Lieut. Edward HALL, devised a part of the plantation whereon he lived, and the land he bought of Jerome PLUMMER, and all other lands, and one-half of his personal estate; further unknown.

VII. Sophia, *b.* about 1748; *m.* Belt MULLIKIN, son of James and Charity (BELT) MULLIKEN, his wife.

ISSUE

1. Benjamin Hall MULLIKEN.
2. Martha MULLIKEN, *m.* Jacob, son of Arnold WATERS.
3. Sophia MULLIKEN, *m.* (firstly) 13th February, 1798, Basil DUCKETT, son of Richard and Martha (WARING) DUCKETT, and had issue, sons and daughters; she *m.* (secondly) Col. Joseph CROSS, an officer of the Revolutionary Army; had issue.

VIII. Martha, *b.* about 1750; *m.* William HALL, son of Francis HALL,

ISSUE

1. Williams A. HALL, and others.

WILLIAM HALL, the third child of Maj. Henry HALL and Elizabeth WATKINS, his wife, was *b.* 1755, in Anne Arundel County, on the Hall Homestead, near Governors Bridge, and *d.* there in 18—. He *m.* 6th April, 1782, Martha DUCKETT, *b.* 1759, a dau. of Richard DUCKETT, Jr., of Prince George's County and Martha WARING, a dau. of Thomas WARING, of Prince George's County, Maryland, and Jane OXFORD, his wife. William HALL inherited a large number of acres of lands in Frederick County, Maryland, whither he removed and where his children were born. In 1816 he returned to Anne Arundel County, where he had bought a part of "White Hall," formerly owned by the father or uncle of the late Johns HOPKINS. This property was sold at a forced sale a few years later, and William HALL removed with his family to the old HALL place near Governor's Bridge, where he *d.*

ISSUE

I. Richard Henry, moved to Ohio.
II. Elizabeth, *m.* ——— JURNEY; had issue.
III. Margaret, *m.* ——— SMITH.
IV. Mary, *m.* about 1810 ——— ENOCH, of Frederick County, Maryland, and moved to Ohio; about 1816, they moved to Illinois, near where Rockford is now located. His farm was noted for having on it the only grove of trees and spring of water for many miles. He *d.* in 1858 while on a visit at the old DUCKETT homestead in Prince George's County. A gd. son, Harry ENOCH, now lives in Washington, D. C., where he *m.* a daughter of the late Phillip Dorsey CARR, of Anne Arundel County.
V. Nancy, *m.* Samuel HOPKINS, of Anne Arundel County, a cousin of the late Johns HOPKINS, the founder of the University and Hospital of that name in Baltimore.

ISSUE

1. Alexander Marshall HOPKINS, *d.* unmarried.
2. Montgomery HOPKINS, *d.* in Baltimore. He and his brother, Marshall HOPKINS, lived at "Lug Ox," adjoining "White Hall," the birthplace of the late Johns HOPKINS, to which place they later moved. Montgomery HOPKINS *m.* ———— GORDON, of Baltimore, Maryland, where he *d.*

ISSUE

1. Anna HOPKINS.
2. Gordon HOPKINS.

VI. Sophia, *m.* Benjamin DUCKETT, her cousin, of Prince George's County, gd. son of Richard DUCKETT, Jr.
VII. Lucy, *m.* Thomas HODGES of South River, Anne Arundel County.

ISSUE

1. Ramsay Hodges, *m.* ———— SELLMAN, dau. of John Stephen SELLMAN; had issue.

VIII. Basil Duckett, *b.* 21st August, 1797; see further.
IX. Caroline, *m.* Richard Francis HIGGINS, of Anne Arundel County, a brother of Dr. James HIGGINS, the eminent State Chemist.

ISSUE

1. Harriet HIGGINS, *m.* William Lafayette DORSEY of "Belvoir," Anne Arundel County; had issue.
2. Lucretia HIGGINS, *m.* Dr. Theodore LINTHICUM, and has issue: among others a dau., who *m.* the late Dr. William G. WILLIAMS. (See MACKENZIE's "Colonial Families.")
3. Sallie HIGGINS, *m.* Phillips Dorsey CARR, one time Sheriff of Anne Arundel County; had issue.
4. Richard Francis HIGGINS, *m.* Maria Eleanor DUVALL (sister of the wife of his cousin Thomas William HALL, of Basil), dau. of John Mortimer DUVALL, of Anne Arundel County. About 1880 he moved with his family to Wilmington, Delaware, where he *d.*; leaving three children surviving (others having died in infancy).

ISSUE

1[1]. Eleanor Ann HIGGINS, *d.* in 1914.
2[1]. George William HIGGINS, *m.* 26th December, 1917, his cousin, Dallas Hammond HIGGINS.
3[1]. Richard Mortimer HIGGINS, unmarried.

5. George William HIGGINS, *m.* Susan MEWBURN, dau. of Phillip MEWBURN, of Anne Arundel County and ———— HAMMOND, his wife.
6. Lackland HIGGINS, *m.* Augusta HAMMOND, dau. of Washington HAMMOND, of Anne Arundel County; had issue.

x. Catherine, *m.* ———— LYLES.
xi. Harriet, *d.* young.

BASIL DUCKETT HALL, Planter, *b.* 21st August, 1797, in Frederick County, Maryland; *d.* 5th May, 1875, at "White Hall," Anne Arundel County, Maryland. In 1830 he sold the HALL Homestead near Governor's Bridge, Anne Arundel County, and purchased and removed to that part of "White Hall" formerly owned by his father on the opposite side of the public road from the birthplace of Johns HOPKINS, and where the latter lived until he moved to Baltimore and accumulated his large fortune. Basil Duckett HALL was one of the founders of Severn Parish, Anne Arundel County, and was one of the original vestrymen of that Parish, and an active worker and supporter of St. Stephen's Church until his death. He, with members of his immediate family, are buried in the cemetery adjoining the Church. In 1855, with the late Richard I. DUVALL, Phil M. LEAKIN, William JONES, Benjamin E. GANTT, William H. BALDWIN, and others he was one of the Founders and an original Trustee of the Anne Arundel Academy. Basil Duckett HALL *m.* (firstly) 8th September, 1836, Margaret DAVIDSON, *b.* 29th September, 1810, *d.* 4th August, 1856, dau. of Samuel and Mary (BIRD) DAVIDSON, of Annapolis, Md. Samuel DAVIDSON was a son of John DAVIDSON, of Annapolis, and Eleanor, his wife. John DAVIDSON was an ardent patriot during the Revolutionary War. His ancestors were among the earliest settlers in Anne Arundel County. Samuel Davidson received wounds at the Battle of Bladensburg, in the War of 1812 from which he *d.* At his death his two children Margaret and Empson lived with their Aunt Margaret DAVIDSON on Georgetown Heights in the District of Columbia, in the old homestead, which is still in the possession of one of the DAVIDSON descendants. The DAVIDSONS are direct descendants of the famous Scotch Clan of that name, as is also the present Archbishop of Canterbury. A characteristic of the descendants of this Clan is their ruddy complexion and slightly reddish hair. Basil Duckett HALL *m.* (secondly) 30th June, 1863, Anne D. MULLIKEN, *d.* 20th April, 1896, in Baltimore, dau. of Basil Duckett MULLIKEN, of Prince George's County. By this marriage there was no issue.

ISSUE BY FIRST MARRIAGE

I. Martha Sophia, *b.* 3d April, 1838; *d.* 3d June, 1846.
II. THOMAS WILLIAM, *b.* 17th February, 1840; subjuct of this Memoir.
III. Rev. Samuel Davidson HALL, *b.* 22d April, 1842; *d.* 21st February, 1891; *m.* 27th December, 1866, Permelia Victoria IGLEHART, dau. of John Wilson IGLEHART, of South River, Anne Arundel County. Samuel DAVIDSON HALL was educated at Anne Arundel Academy and Mary-

land Agricultural College. He studied divinity under Bishop WHITTINGHAM by whom he was ordained a priest of the Protestant Episcopal Church about 1866. He was at various times Assistant Principal at Hannah Moore Academy. He was successively Rector of St. Stephen's Parish, Anne Arundel County, Shrewsbury Parish, Kent County, Maryland, Chapel of the Advent, Baltimore, Maryland, the Churches at Seaford, Delaware, and Denton, Maryland. He *d.* at the Church Home and Infirmary, Baltimore, while Rector of the Protestant Episcopal Church at Sykesville, Maryland.

ISSUE

1. Wilson Iglehart, *b.* 23d April, 1868.
2. Margaret Davidson, *b.* 23d September, 1870; *m.* 12th November, 1896, Frank Asbury MONROE, a merchant and prominent citizen of Annapolis, and a vestryman St. Ann's Church, and member of the School Board of Anne Arundel County.

ISSUE

1^1. Davidson Hall MONROE, *b.* 29th October, 1900; *d.* 19th January, 1903.
2^1. Frank Asbury MONROE, Jr., *b.* 21st March, 1904.
3^1. Permelia Victoria, *b.* 4th December, 1874; *m.* 14th May, 1904, Rev. Frederick Charles Frazier SHEARS, a minister of the Protestant Episcopal Church, *b.* in Newfoundland, and after coming to Maryland held the Rectorship of St. Thomas', Baltimore County, All Hallows and St. Stephens, Anne Arundel County, and is now Rector in Baltimore County, Maryland.

IV. Edward, *b.* 11th April, 1844; *d.* 8th May, 1913; *m.* 15th November, 1876, Eva Spence WALLACE, dau. of Arthur WALLACE, of Shrewsbury Parish, Kent County, Maryland, *d.* 15th November, 1908. Edward HALL was educated at Anne Arundel Academy, and Maryland Agricultural College, and for several years after graduating he taught school. For many years, until his death, he was one of the most useful and devoted trustees of Anne Arundel Academy. He was a Vestryman of St. Stephen's Church and a prominent citizen of the community in which he lived. He inherited and resided at "White Hall."

ISSUE

1. Anna, *b.* 9th September, 1877; *d.* 5th March, 1913.
2. Mary Davidson, *b.* 14th March, 1879, *d.* 11th April, 1880.
3. Edward, *b.* 31st December, 1880; *m.* 1st June, 1915, Margaret Augusta STUBBS, dau. of the late Francis and Mary Elizabeth (BURNETT) STUBBS, D.D., Ph.D., He inherited from his father "White Hall," where he now lives engaged in farming.

ISSUE

1[1]. Edward, *b.* 26th April, 1916.
2[1]. Elizabeth Burnett, *b.* 29th May, 1917.

4. Arthur Wallace, *b.* 28th May, 1883; *d.* 5th August, 1883.
5. Samuel Davidson, *b.* 27th February, 1885. Shortly after leaving school he became a newspaper reporter; later he went to West Virginia where he engaged in coal mining, and at the same time took a course in chemistry, specializing in explosives, and when the United States entered the Great War he volunteered among the first, and is now a first Lieutenant of Engineers in the United States Army; he is married.
6. Eva Spence, *b.* 24th January, 1889.

v. Basil Duckett, Jr., *b.* 3d May, 1846; *d.* 19th October, 1857.
vi. Francis Chapman, *b.* in Anne Arundel County, 8th June, 1848; *d.* in Baltimore, Maryland, 20th March, 1912; *m.* 22d January, 1879, Lucy CARR, dau. of the late Phillip Dorsey CARR, one time Sheriff of Anne Arundel County. He was educated in the Public Schools and at Anne Arundel Academy. He was a member of St. Stephen's Church, and of its Choir. Like his brother Thomas William, he was a student of church history. He was also interested in sociological problems and was the author of numerous, but unpublished manuscripts on that and kindred subjects, among them a novel dealing with the sweatshop evil.

ISSUE

1. Phillip Dorsey, *b.* 12th November, 1879; he is now an accountant and is connected with a Fiduciary Corporation in New York.
2. Frank, *b.* 10th September, 1882; *d.* 10th November, 1882.
3. Margaret Davidson, *b.* 22d September, 1883.
4. Thomas Irving, *b.* 21st August, 1886; *m.* 16th June, 1917, Lucy Orrick NICOLS, dau. of George Baynard NICOLS, of Baltimore.
5. Williams Edward Lucius Chapman, *b.* 24th March, 1889, was educated at the Baltimore Public Schools, and at the School of the Holy Cross Fathers in Connecticut, by whom he was sent to France to complete his education in the French language for the ministry of the Protestant Episcopal Church. Early in the Great War he was appointed on the Staff of the Belgian Relief Commission, and was active in that work there, until it was stopped by the Germans, he being among the last to leave, and in recognition of his work, has been awarded a gold medal.
6. Francis Chapman, *b.* 27th September, 1891.

VII. Mary, *b.* 1st January, 1852; *d.* 20th July, 1852.

Arms.—Argent, three talbot heads erased sable langued gules, between nine crosses crosslets gules.
Crest.—A talbot's head erased sable, langued gules.
Motto.—Esto quod esse videris.

Hancock

HARRIS HANCOCK of Cincinnati, Ohio; *b.* 14th May, 1867, at "Ellerslie," Albemarle County, Virginia; *m.* 30th September, 1907, at Cincinnati, Ohio, Belle Lyman CLAY, *b.* 4th November, 1872; her father, Hon Brutus Junius CLAY, *b.* 20th February, 1847, United States Commissioner to the Paris Exposition, 1900, American Minister to Switzerland, appointed by President Roosevelt 1905-1909, *m.* 20th February, 1872, Pattie Amelia FIELD of Richmond, Kentucky, *b.* 22d November, 1848, *d.* 23d December, 1891, dau. of Christopher and Charlotte (MARTIN) FIELD. Brutus Junius CLAY was son of Gen. Cassius Marcellus CLAY, United States Minister to Russia, who *m.* Mary Jane WARFIELD.

ISSUE

I. Thomasia Harris, *b.* 25th September, 1908.
II. Belle Clay, *b.* 15th January, 1912.

HARRIS HANCOCK, University Professor, educated under private tutors, graduated in School of Mathematics at the University of Virginia 1886 with first distinctions in Latin and Greek; A.B., Johns Hopkins University, 1888; post graduate in Mathematics, Physics and Astronomy at same, 1888-1891; honorary scholar at same, 1887-1891; studied at Cambridge, England, 1891; University of Berlin 1891-1892; 1893-1894; University of Paris (The Sorbonne), 1899-1900; University of Berlin, 1893; A.M., Ph.D. (Berlin), 1894; Dr. Sc. (Paris), 1901; Instructor University of Chicago, 1892-1893; and 1894-1899; Professor of Mathematics, University of Cincinnati since, 1900. Author of many works on advanced mathematical subjects; writer of numerous articles in the leading mathematical journals of America and Europe; interested in the improvement of the present system of education in the public schools and in the promotion of American education; member of many scientific societies in the United States and abroad. (See biographical sketches in the "National Cyclopedia of American Biography;" "American Men of Science;" "Who's Who in America.)"

Lineage

The first of this family in America was William HANCOCK who with his wife Eliza came to this country from England about 1707 as attorney for Lord POLLOCK. He held a grant from the King of Great Britain dated 1707 for a large tract of land situated on what is now known as Hancock's Creek, on the Neuse River below New-Bern, North Carolina. William HANCOCK with others (see North Carolina

Records, Vol. I, p. 820) makes a petition in 1711; Vol. II, p. 71, appraises an estate in 1713; Vol. II, p. 125, fights the Indians; Vol. XXIII, p. 98, Capt. William HANCOCK makes a road, 1722; Vol. XXIII, p. 8, one of the twelve Vestry of Craven Parish; in 1723 he is made by the General Assembly a commissioner with Cullen POLLOCK to sell the town lots of New-Bern.

ISSUE

1. William, was returned as member of the General Assembly July, 1733, see North Carolina Records, Vol. III, p. 562, and again in 1734. See Vol. IV, p. 115. From the Will Book, Secretary of State (North Carolina) Office, 1749–1753, page 69, it is seen that he was possessed of much land and many negroes.

ISSUE OF WILLIAM AND HIS FIRST WIFE DOROTHY

1. Durham.
2. James.
3. William.
4. Sarah.

II. HECTOR, of whom below.

HECTOR HANCOCK of Cartaret County, North Carolina in will probated December, 1751 (see HATHAWAY North Carolina Historical and Genealogical Records p. 224), mentions his wife Ann.

ISSUE

I. NATHANIEL, of whom below.
II. Benjamin.
III. Henry.
IV. Joseph, was one of the Representatives in the Provincial Congress held at Halifax, North Carolina, 4th April, 1776, and was again elected 15th October, 1776, to meet 12th November, 1776, and frame a constitution. Colonial Records of North Carolina, Vol. X, pp. 165, 167, 172, 500, 501.
V. Mary.
VI. John.
VII. William.

NATHANIEL HANCOCK of Onslow County, North Carolina; *m.* Sarah WARD, dau. of Enoch WARD, of Cartaret County, North Carolina; Enoch Ward was a member of the Provincial Congress, held at Hillsborough, North Carolina, 20th August, 1775. (See Colonial Records of North Carolina, Vol. X, p. 165.)

ISSUE

1. Gabriel.
II. ENOCH, of whom later.
III. Zebedee.
IV. Magdalen.
V. Dorothy.

ENOCH HANCOCK, of Onslow County, North Carolina, *m.* and had among other children

ISSUE

I. WILLIAM, *b.* 15th October, 1773, of whom later.

WILLIAM HANCOCK, of Onslow County, North Carolina; *b.* 15th October, 1773; *d.* 27th September, 1849; *m.* (firstly) Dorothy (surname not given); *m.* (secondly) the widow DUDLEY; *m.* (thirdly) Ruth HUGGINS, sister of Luke HUGGINS.

ISSUE BY FIRST MARRIAGE

I. NATHANIEL, *b.* 29th December, 1802, of whom later.

ISSUE BY SECOND MARRIAGE

I. Anna.

ISSUE BY THIRD MARRIAGE

I. Enoch.
II. Hull.
III. Noah.
IV. Joanna.
V. Roxanna.

NATHANIEL HANCOCK, *b.* 29th December, 1802, in Onslow County, North Carolina; *d.* 19th June, 1854, in Bossier Parrish, Louisiana; *m.* 28th January, 1824, Elizabeth HIGHTOWER, *b.* 16th November, 1801, *d.* 29th March, 1850, dau. of Jordan and Elizabeth (HAZELWOOD) HIGHTOWER, of Lunenberg County, Virginia.

ISSUE

I. William Jordan, *b.* 20th March, 1826.
II. John C., *b.* 5th May, 1829; *d.* 28th April, 1855.
III. James E., *b.* 15th February, 1853.
IV. Thomas Benton, *b.* 20th February, 1834; *d.* 29th March, 1870.
V. Elizabeth Ann, *b.* 26th March, 1836; *d.* 28th April, 1860.
VI. RICHARD JOHNSON, *b.* 22d March, 1838, of whom later.
VII. Emma V., *b.* 25th March, 1840; *d.* 9th February, 1901.

RICHARD JOHNSON HANCOCK, *b.* 22d March, 1838; *d.* 19th April, 1912; Captain of Company D, 9th Louisiana Regiment, C. S. A.; fought four years in the Civil War, severely wounded three times. See "Men of Mark of Virginia," Vol. IV, p. 164. *The Southern Planter and Farmer*, January, 1878; "Southern Historical Papers," Vol. VI, p. 218; *m.* 22d November, 1864, Thomasia Overton HARRIS, *b.* 27th. August, 1845. (See HARRIS family below.)

ISSUE

I. HARRIS, *b.* 14th May, 1867, the subject of this memoir.
II. Thomae Hightower, M.D., of whom in succeeding memoir.
III. Elizabeth Hazelwood, *b.* 10th September, 1871; *d.* unmarried April, 1915.
IV. Richard Jordan, *b.* 21st March, 1873.
V. Arthur Boyd, *b.* 26th June, 1875.
VI. Thomasia Overton, *b.* 1st July, 1877.
VII. Charles Russell, *b.* 27th September, 1879.
VIII. Emma Lewis, *b.* 12th December, 1881; *d.* unmarried 18th June, 1907.
IX. Jane Crawford, *b.* 16th July, 1887.

Arms.—(HANCOCK).—Gules, on a chief argent, three cocks of the field.
Crest.—A demi-griffin argent, armed or.
Motto.—Redeem time.
Residences.—2365 Auburn Avenue, Cincinnati, Ohio and "Ellerslie," Albemarle County, Virginia.

Harris

The first record we have of this family is that Capt. Thomas HARRIS and Thomas OSBORNE settled in Virginia in 1611 on lands that are now located in Henrico County. Captain HARRIS in the long Indian Wars of 1622 was second in command to Thomas OSBORNE. He was a member of the House of Burgesses in 1623, 1637, 1647. He *m.* Adria OSBORNE, and from this marriage descended Maj. Robert HARRIS of "The Forks" who *m.* a widow, Mrs. Mary (CLAIBORNE) RICE, youngest dau. of Col. William CLAIBORNE, the first Secretary of the Virginia Colony. Their son

WILLIAM HARRIS *m.* Temperance OVERTON, dau. of William OVERTON, the immigrant, and his wife, Mary WATERS; this William OVERTON was the son of Colonel OVERTON, Governor of Hull, England, under Oliver CROMWELL and later commanded a brigade at Dunbar and Inver Keithing. (See "HARRIS Family of Virginia," by Thomas Henry HARRIS of Fredericksburg, Virginia.)

ISSUE

I. Major Robert, *m.* Mourning GLEN; one of their daughters *m.* Joel CRAWFORD and they were the parents of the Hon. William Harris CRAWFORD of Georgia.
II. Overton, of "Cedar Hill," Virginia.
III. Frederick, of "Frederick's Hall," Virginia.
IV. Temperance.
V. Jemima.
VI. Keziah.
VII. Mary.
VIII. Anne Emillia, *m.* William DAY, son of John DAY, who *m.* ———— ESOM, their dau. Lucy DAY, *m.* her cousin, John HARRIS, of whom below.

JOHN HARRIS, *m.* his cousin Lucy DAY, dau. of William and Anne Emillia (HARRIS) DAY above.

ISSUE

I. Thomas.
II. William.
III. Sallie.
IV. JOHN OVERTON, *b.* 4th April, 1794, of whom below.
V. Mary (called Polly).
VI. Eusebia, *d.* young.

JOHN OVERTON HARRIS, *b.* at Oxford, in Caroline County, Virginia, 4th April, 1794; *d.* 18th May, 1878; *m.* 7th September, 1820, Barbara Wingfield TERRELL, *b.* 7th September, 1804, in Hanover County, Virginia; *d.* 11th February, 1883, at "Ellerslie." He was noted for his high sense of honor and his veracity.

ISSUE

I. Ann Lewis, *b.* February, 1835; *m.* John O. PENDLETON.
II. Thomasia Overton, *b.* 27th August, 1845; *m.* 22d November, 1864, Richard HANCOCK. (Vide HANCOCK supra.)

Arm.—(HARRIS).—Argent, a lion rampant sable, over all a chevron ermine.
Crest.—A falcon with outstretched wings.

Terrell=Lewis

Arms.—Argent two chevronels azure a bodure engrailed gule.

Crest.—A boars head couped and erect argent issuant out of the mouth a peacock, tail ppr.

Motto.—Sans crainte.

Joseph Terrell, *b.* 28th January, 1745; *d.* 9th April, 1787; *m.* 29th September, 1767, Elizabeth (nee Mills), *b.* 26th January, 1747, *d.* 22d November, 1833; their son, Charles Terrell, *b.* 3d July, 1768, *d.* August, 1839, *m.* Ann (Lewis) Phillips, *b.* 1745, in Spottsylvania County, Virginia, *d.* November, 1843, at Ellerslie, dau. of John Zachary Lewis and widow of William Phillips, by whom she had issue.

ISSUE

I. Lewis Phillips.
II. Launcelot Phillips.
III. William Phillips.

ISSUE OF CHARLES AND ANN (LEWIS) PHILLIPS TERRELL

I. Nicholas Terrell.
II. Zachary Terrell.
III. Barbara Terrell (see above).

John Zachary Lewis *m.* (firstly) ——— Woodfolk; *m.* (secondly) ——— Brock.

ISSUE BY FIRST MARRIAGE

I. Ann, who *m.* Charles Terrell.

ISSUE BY SECOND MARRIAGE

I. John Zachary, of whom below.
II. Augustin.
III. Betty.

John Zachary Lewis was a son of John Lewis, *b.* 18th October, 1729, in King and Queen's County, Virginia, and his second wife Mildred Lewis, dau. of Col. Robert and Jane (Merriwether) Lewis, dau. of Nicholas Merriwether of Albemarle County, Virginia. Col. Robert Lewis was a brother of Fielding Lewis who *m.* George WASHINGTON'S sister, Betty WASHINGTON. Col. Robert LEWIS was also the gd. father of the explorer Merriwether LEWIS. (See Spottsylvania County, Virginia Records, p. 41, and p. 490.)

Arms.—(LEWIS).—Argent, a dragon's head and neck erased vert, holding in the mouth a bloody hand, ppr.

Crest.—A dragon's head and neck, erased vert.

Motto.—Omne solum forti patria est.

Hancock

THOMAS HIGHTOWER HANCOCK, M.D., *b.* 9th January, 1869, at Ellerslie, near Charlotteville, Virginia; *m.* 24th September, 1894, at Mobile, Alabama, Marie Louise PRICE, *b.* 16th May, 1873, dau. of Thomas Henry PRICE, of Mobile, Alabama, *b.* in Prince Edward County, Virginia, *d.* near Bandera, Texas, March, 1883, Lawyer and Major in Confederate States Army during Civil War, *m.* Martha Elizabeth BYRD, *b.* 4th May, 1841, at Natchez, Mississippi, dau. of William BYRD, Judge of the Supreme Court of Alabama and his wife, Marie MASSIE, *b.* 1818, at Pulaski, Tennessee; dau. of William and Sarah (UPSHAW) MASSIE. Marie Louise PRICE is a first cousin to Gen. Sterling PRICE, U. S. A.

ISSUE

I. Elizabeth Erskine, *b.* 23d July, 1895; B.A., Smith College.
II. Richard Harris, *b.* 13th July, 1899; student in Students' Army Training Corps (Navy) United States Army; Emory University, Oxford, Georgia.
III. Emma Louise, *b.* 12th August, 1908; pupil Washington Seminary, Atlanta, Georgia.
IV. John Overton, *b.* 9th August, 1914.

THOMAS HIGHTOWER HANCOCK, M.D., was graduated from the College of Physicians and Surgeons (Columbia University), New York, in 1891; House Physician and Surgeon, New York Polyclinic Hospital, 1891–1892; commenced the practice of Medicine and Surgery at Atlanta, Georgia, 1st September, 1893; practice limited to General Surgery; Member of Fulton County Medical Society, Georgia State Medical Society, American Medical Association, Association of Surgeons of the Seaboard Air Line Railway and Central of Georgia Railway, Ex-President of the Association of Surgeons of the Southern Railway and also of the Southern States Association of Railway Surgeons.

(For related lineages see preceding memoir.)

Hart

CHARLES BYERLY HART, of Philadelphia, Pennsylvania; *b.* there 25 September 1846; *m.* there 12th October, 1876, Ida Virginia HILL, *b.* 9th February, 1856; dau. of George Washington HILL, *b.* 27th December, 1831, *d.* 13th December, 1913, *m.* 21st September, 1852, Sarah JANE WHITE, *b.* 14th April, 1835, *d.* 12th January, 1916.

ISSUE

I. Charles Byerly, *b.* 13th May, 1877; *d.* 13th July, 1877.
II. Ethel Hill, *b.* 21st January, 1879; *m.* 18th December, 1899, Ledyard HECKSCHER, *b.* 25th February, 1872, son of Richard HECKSCHER and Lucretia STEVENS of Philadelphia.

ISSUE

1. Ledyard Hart, *b.* 14th February, 1901.
2. Ida Virginia, *b.* 24th January, 1902.
3. Johanna Barbara, *b.* 20th June, 1904.
4. Ethel Hart, *b.* 2d July, 1906.
5. Charles Hart, *b.* 9th December, 1909.
6. Gustave Adolph, *b.* 4th November, 1914.

III. William Bryan, *b.* 29th May, 1884; member of the Philadelphia, St. Anthony, Merion Cricket Clubs; First Troop Philadelphia City Cavalry; *m.* 25th April, 1906, Nina Lewis JUSTICE, *b.* 9th February, 1884, dau. of George Randolph JUSTICE and Sallie Fisher LEWIS of Philadelphia.

ISSUE

1. William Bryan, *b.* 29th April, 1907.
2. Virginia Justice, *b.* 6th July, 1911.
3. Lewis Justice, *b.* 17th August, 1914.

IV. Thomas, *b.* 24th November, 1894; enlisted in the Aviation Service, United States Army; member of the Philadelphia, St. Anthony, Merion Cricket, and the Mask and Wig Club, all of Philadelphia and the St. Anthony Club of New York, Society of Colonial Wars, Historical Society of Pennsylvania and the Genealogical Society of Pennsylvania; *m.* 15th May, 1918, Margaret Newbold SMITH of Philadelphia, *b.* at Cape May, New Jersey, 31st August, 1899, dau. of the late Harry Hudson SMITH and Margaret M. NEWBOLD of Philadelphia.

ISSUE

1. Margaret Newbold, *b.* 17th March, 1919.

CHARLES BYERLY HART was educated at Friends Central School, and is engaged with his brother, William H. HART, Jr. in the manufacture of neckware supplies. He was one of the charter members of the Philadelphia Barge Club, of which he is the oldest active member (1918).

Lineage

SAMUEL HART, the emigrant ancestor of the HART family, *b.* about 1690; he came to America with his wife and family, from Belfast, in the province of Ulster, Ireland, about the year 1735. He came to Bucks County, Pennsylvania the settling ground of a large number of the Scotch-Irish and on 9th March, 1737, obtained a warrant of survey for 100 acres of land in Plumstead Township and settled thereon; he *d.* 1st April, 1750, leaving his plantation to his two eldest sons, James and William. He is buried in Deep Run Cemetery, Bedminster Township, where his grave may be seen to this day. His wife's name was Elizabeth. She *d.* shortly after her husband, in April, 1750. The respective wills of Samuel and Elizabeth HART are on file in the courthouse at Doylestown, Pennsylvania.

ISSUE

I. JAMES, *b.* April, 1717, of whom later.
II. William, *b.* about 1721; *m.* Margaret MEANS (the sister of Jean), served as Ensign in Capt. Charles STEWART's Company, Associated Regiment of Bucks County, during "King George's War."
III. Joseph.
IV. John.
V. Samuel.
VI. Mary, *m.* James McGLAUGHLIN.
VII. Jane, *m.* Samuel MATHERS.
VIII. Elinor.
IX. Elizabeth.

LIEUT. JAMES HART, *b.* April, 1717; *d.* 4th May, 1766; he *m.* Jean MEANS, *b.* 30th August, 1726, the dau. of William and Mary MEANS of Plumstead Township; she was the sister of John MEANS, whose dau. Elizabeth, later became the wife of Col. William HART; thus she became the mother-in-law of her niece in a day when family intermarriage was of common occurrence. After his marriage, James HART purchased a tract of about 400 acres of land, in 1751, adjoining the plantation of his father. Before becoming a landholder of Plumstead, he had served his country as an officer in the War of the Austrian Succession, "King George's War," holding the rank of Lieutenant in the Associated Regiment of Bucks County. His brother,

William, was Ensign of the same Company, captained by Charles STEWART. James HART *d.* 4th May, 1766, and was buried beside his father at Deep Run. On the brown headstone of his grave there is carved simply "J. H." His wife *d.* 31st January, 1799, and was buried at Abington, Montgomery County, Pennsylvania.

ISSUE

I. Samuel, *b.* 19th August, 1746; *d.* 21st January, 1831, unmarried; served as Private in Capt. Robert GIBSON's Company, of Plumstead, during the War of the Revolution.

II. Colonel William, *b.* 13th March, 1748; *d.* 2d January, 1831; *m.* his cousin, Elizabeth MEANS, in 1778; he served as Major of the Second Battalion of Bucks County Militia, during the War of the Revolution, eventually reaching the rank of Lieutenant-Colonel; he was one of the Captors of the Doans, and it is after him that Hartsville, Pennsylvania, is named; his wife *d.* 10th January, 1841.

III. John, *b.* 13th March, 1748 (his brother's twin); *d.* 24th February, 1803; *m.* Mary MCCALLA, *b.* 1762, *d.* 11th September, 1789; he served during the War of the Revolution as Lieutenant in Captain GIBSON's Company.

IV. Elizabeth, *b.* 2d February, 1750; *d.* in infancy.

V. Mary, *b.* 15th January, 1752; *d.* 3d April, 1817; *m.* 4th July, 1771, James RUCKMAN, *b.* 11th November, 1748, *d.* 26th August, 1834.

VI. James, *b.* 29th December, 1753; *d.* young.

VII. Joseph, *b.* 16th February, 1755; *d.* 3d May, 1826; *m.* Elinor WILSON.

VIII. Elizabeth, *b.* 28th February, 1757; *m.* John JOHNSTON.

IX. JAMES (again), *b.* 1759, of whom later.

X. Solomon, *b.* 31st August, 1762; *d.* 27th April, 1810; *m.* 10th April, 1789, Isabella LONG, *b.* 1754, *d.* 1st December, 1819.

XI. Jane, *b.* 4th August, 1765; *m.* Samuel OPDYKE.

JAMES HART, *b.* 17th March, 1759; *d.* 22d April, 1826; *m.* 14th January, 1785, Ann HANKINSON, *b.* 18th October, 1765, *d.* 20th November, 1820, the dau. of Thomas and Jemima HANKINSON, of Amwell, New Jersey. Until his marriage, he spent most of his time in Bucks County, upon the estate of his father, who *d.* some seven years after he was born, thus, James was one of the five children mentioned by his mother in her petition to the Court in 1768, when she states that she has "to bring up and support five children under the age of fourteen years." He served as a Private in Capt. Robert GIBSON's Company during the War of the Revolution. After his marriage he became a prosperous shipping merchant in Philadelphia, where he died. His remains now rest in the HART lot in South Laurel Hill Cemetery.

ISSUE

I. THOMAS, *b.* 30th November, 1786, of whom later.
II. Capt. William H., *b.* 16th November, 1789; *d.* 28th March, 1877; *m.* (firstly) 19th February, 1818, Matilda MAYBIN, *b.* 9th December, 1796; *d.* 14th April, 1832, she was the dau. of John MAYBIN of Philadelphia; from this marriage there were seven children; *m.* (secondly) 5th September, 1840, Mary Elizabeth SPERRY, *b.* 23d August, 1801, *d.* 14th May, 1874, dau. of Jacob SPERRY of Philadelphia; from this marriage there was no issue. William H. HART was Captain of the First Troop Philadelphia City Cavalry from 1827–1842, and Governor of the State in Schuylkill from 1838–1849.

THOMAS HART, *b.* 30th November, 1786; *d.* 29th August, 1852; *m.* 4th May, 1810; Mary McCALLA, *b.* 24th November, 1789; *d.* 1st September, 1823, the dau. of John and Rebecca Darrah (BRYAN) McCALLA. Mary McCALLA was the gd. dau. of Capt. William McCALLA of Plumstead, who served during the War of the Revolution as Captain of the 7th Company, 2d Battalion, Bucks County Associators and as Chief of the Forage Department, Commission of Purchase of that county. She was also the gd. dau. of William DARRAH, 1725–1808, who served in Benjamin FRANKLIN's Regiment on the Lehigh Frontier in 1756–1757. Her mother was the widow of William BRYAN. Thomas HART was a member of the State in Schuylkill, holding the office of First Counsellor therein at the time of his death. He and his brother who were associated with their father in business in Philadelphia, jointly purchased the family lot at South Laurel Hill Cemetery.

ISSUE

I. James Hankinson, *b.* 4th February, 1811; *d.* 4th October, 1862; *m.* 8th February, 1837, Catherine Louise BADGER, *b.* 28th November, 1814, *d.* 3d January, 1886, dau. of Bela and Catherine Penelope (WORRELL) BADGER.
II. WILLIAM BRYAN, *b.* 3d January, 1813, of whom later.
III. Francis, *b.* 5th January, 1815; *d.* 21st November, 1873; *m.* 10th October, 1837, Mary A. GILPIN, *b.* 11th October, 1817, *d.* 4th August, 1876, dau. of John GILPIN of Philadelphia.
IV. Nancy, *b.* 30th June, 1817; *d.* 23d April, 1843; *m.* James S. PRINGLE; *d.* November, 1860.
V. Thomas *b.* 28th July, 1819; *d.* 10th August, 1893; *m.* 21st June, 1856, Rebecca A. REEVES, *b.* 31st July, 1825, *d.* 29th October, 1869, dau. of David REEVES of Philadelphia.
VI. Mary Jane, *b.* 6th August, 1821; *d.* 30th May, 1916; *m.* 19th October, 1843, Edward Hough TROTTER, *b.* 27th November, 1814, *d.* 3d May 1872, son of Nathan and Susan (HOUGH) TROTTER.
VII. John Kirk, *b.* 25th August, 1823; *d.* 22d January, 1860, unmarried.

WILLIAM BRYAN HART, *b.* 3d January, 1813; *d.* 1st March, 1864; graduated from Princeton in 1831, A.M., Princeton, 1834; *m.* 10th July, 1838, Sara BYERLY, *b.* 5th February, 1817, *d.* 10th March, 1886, the dau. of John BYERLY, 1785-1837, and Anna LONG, *b.* 1796, *d.* 1865. During the War of 1812, John BYERLY served as Corporal under Capt. William RAWLE in the 2d Troop, Philadelphia City Cavalry. Sara BYERLY was the gd. dau. of Christopher BYERLY, *b.* 1737, *d.* 1823, and Elizabeth CLYMER, *b.* 1749, *d.* 1827.

ISSUE

I. Thomas, *b.* 14th April, 1839; *d.* 29th July, 1904, unmarried.
II. William Henry, *b.* 12th November, 1841.
III. Byerly, *b.* 15th February, 1844; *d.* 7th October, 1904; *m.* 26th June, 1873, Mary West HORSTMANN, *b.* 29th June, 1848, *d.* 11th November, 1899, dau. of Sigmund H. HORSTMANN of Philadelphia.
IV. CHARLES BYERLY, *b.* 25th September, 1846, the subject of this memoir.

Arms.—Argent, three hearts flammant gules.
Crest.—A dexter hand erect, grasping a couteau sword.
Motto.—Fide et amore.
Residence.—335 South 21st Street, Philadelphia, Pennsylvania, and "Antrim," Devon, Pennsylvania.
Clubs.—Art, Merion Cricket, Philadelphia Barge.

Helm

JAMES PENDLETON HELM, deceased, of Louisville, Kentucky; *b.* 7th January, 1850, at "Helm's Place," near Elizabethtown, Kentucky; *d.* 29th March, 1910, in Louisville, Kentucky; *m.* 14th January, 1874, at Louisville, Pattie Anderson KENNEDY, *b.* 18th March, 1854, dau. of Thomas Smith and Catharine M. (ANDERSON) KENNEDY, of Louisville, Kentucky..

ISSUE

I. Thomas Kennedy, LL.B., *b.* 18th November, 1874; attended Washington and Lee University, Lexington, Virginia; studied law at Charlottesville, Virginia, and University of Louisville; President of the Kentucky State Bar Association, August, 1906; *m.* 14th November, 1900, in Winchester, Kentucky, Elizabeth Tebbs NELSON, dau. of Judge George B. NELSON, and Kate (TEBBS) NELSON.

ISSUE

1. Pattie Anderson, *b.* 8th September, 1901.
2. George Nelson, *b.* 30th January, 1903.
3. Kate Tebbs, *b.* 5th October, 1907.
4. Thomas Kennedy, Jr., *b.* 16th September, 1918.

II. Katharine Anderson, *b.* 7th September, 1876, in Louisville, Kentucky; *m.* there 16th November, 1898, Samuel Hampton HALLEY, A.B., M.D., of Lexington, Kentucky, *b.* 21st September, 1871, son of Henry Simpson HALLEY, Orderly Sergeant of Company A of the 9th Kentucky Cavalry, BRECKINRIGDE'S Regiment of Morgan's Command, who *m.* 9th June, 1870, Alice Hunter BELL, dau. of James Franklin and Mary Jane (WILSON) BELL. (See HALLEY and WILSON, Vol. II, "Colonial Families of the United States.")

ISSUE

1. James Helm HALLEY, *b.* 26th August, 1899; *d.* 10th June, 1900.
2. Katharine Anderson Helm HALLEY, *b.* 20th April, 1901; *d.* 31st December, 1901.
3. Alice Bell HALLEY, *b.* 2d January, 1903.
4. Pattie Helm HALLEY, *b.* 1st March, 1905; *d.* 23d April, 1910.
5. Anne Hampton HALLEY, *b.* 24th October, 1907.
6. Samuel Hampton HALLEY, *b.* 24th July, 1914.

III. Lucinda Hardin, *b.* 17th January, 1880, in Louisville, Kentucky; *m.* 14th October, 1903, James CLARK, Jr., *b.* 29th August, 1869 of Louisville, son of James CLARK and Jessie (LA NAUZE) CLARK, *b.* in Scotland.

ISSUE

1. Helm CLARK, *b.* 7th May, 1906; *d.* 7th May, 1906.
2. James CLARK, *b.* 29th August, 1908.
3. Kennedy Helm CLARK, *b.* 19th September, 1910.

IV. James Pendleton, LL.B., *b.* 4th December, 1885; took his degree of B.A. at Yale, 1908, and M.A. at Yale, 1911, June; studied law at University of Louisville and Charlottesville, Virginia; *m.* 14th June, 1911, in New York, Dorothy Crosby WALKER, dau. of George and Jane (SMITH) WALKER, of Brooklyn, New York.

ISSUE

1. James Pendleton, III, *b.* 6th April, 1913.
2. George Crosby, *b.* 6th July, 1917.

JAMES PENDLETON HELM received his early education in the schools at Elizabethtown, Kentucky; after completing his various academic studies he graduated as LL.B. at the University of Louisville in 1870. After a few months practice in Elizabethtown he came to Louisville and began the practice of his profession there. For a time he was associated with Samuel RUSSELL, the firm being RUSSELL and HELM. He appeared before the Court of Appeals before twenty-one years old and won his case, and so continued until Mr. RUSSELL was elected President of the Bank of Louisville. In 1884 he formed a partnership with his nephew, Helm BRUCE. This partnership continued until 1907 and at the time of friendly dissolution was known as HELM, BRUCE, and HELM, later the firm continued as HELM and HELM, with Thomas Kennedy HELM constituting with his father the firm. Mr. HELM won success early and was in almost every important piece of litigation in the Kentucky courts during the last thirty years of his life. He was chief special counsel of the Louisville and Nashville Railroad Company; counsel for several of the largest banks of Louisville; General Counsel for the Kentucky Bankers Association, and for the Louisville, Henderson and St. Louis Railway Company, and legal representative of many other corporations. Was senior counsel for the *Evening Post* in the famous "Sharkey" case and shortly thereafter interested himself in the formation of the City Club in 1905. After the contested election of 1905 Mr. Helm volunteered his services, free of charge, to the citizens of Louisville in a fight to secure self government. He was the Senior Counsel for the contestants in that memorable contested election and also chairman of the Committee of One Hundred which raised the money and conducted that successful fight through the Court of Appeals.

As a lawyer his sterling integrity was never questioned. "He was regarded as one of the two Kentucky lawyers ranking among the few great lawyers of the United States."

Lineage

CAPT. THOMAS HELM, *b.* in Prince William County, Virginia, 14th September, 1731, *d.* in Hardin County, Kentucky, 21st April 1816, one of the pioneer settlers of Kentucky; removed in 1779, from Virginia where the family had first settled, to the Falls of the Ohio, in Kentucky. In 1780 with two others located one mile from where Elizabethtown, Kentucky, now stands, and each built a fort and block house forming a triangle of defense, one mile apart. His place was called "Helm Station" and later "Helm Place." He was a Lieutenant in Capt. Philip Richard Francis LEE's Company, 3d Virginia Regiment, commanded by Col. Thomas MARSHALL, his commission being dated 8th March, 1776; resigned 27th November, 1777; *m.* in Westmoreland County, Virginia, circa 1760, Jean POPE, *b.* circa 1744, *d.* in Hardin County, Kentucky, 1821, dau. of Worden and Hester POPE of Westmoreland County, Virginia, where his will was probated 29th August, 1749. He, son of Nathaniel, III, and Jane (BROWN) POPE. Nathaniel POPE was King's Attorney for Westmoreland County and guardian of Nathaniel WASHINGTON, and was the son of Nathaniel, II, *b.* in Maryland, 1640, *d.* in Virginia, 1675, and Mary (SISSON) POPE, who was the son of Nathaniel and Lucy POPE. Nathaniel POPE, I, was *b.* circa 1615, in probably London or Bristol, England, and emigrated to Maryland, 1635, and settled in what was known as St. Mary's Hundred; was a member of the Maryland Assembly, 1641–1642; was sent as agent to Kent Island, 1647; removed to Virginia, 1640, and settled in Westmoreland County; obtained a patent for 1050 acres and named it "The Cliffs;" was commissioned Lieutenant-Colonel of the Westmoreland County Troops, 4th April, 1655; his will was probated 28th April, 1660.

ISSUE

I. Thomas, killed by Indians while returning from the mill, fell from his horse at his mother's feet, just as she opened the gate to admit him, the Indians being in pursuit of him.
II. GEORGE, *b.* 2d April, 1773, of whom below.

GEORGE HELM of "Helm Place," Hardin County, Kentucky; *b.* 2d April, 1773, in Prince William County, Virginia; *d.* September, 1822, in Texas; was active in the affairs of Kentucky and represented his district in the Legislature for many years; *m.* 4th May, 1801, Rebecca LARUE, *b.* 2d May, 1784, in Frederick County, Virginia; *d.* 9th February, 1860, dau. of John and Mary (BROOKS) LARUE.

ISSUE

I. JOHN LARUE, *b.* 4th July, 1802, of whom later.
II. William.

iii. Squire.
iv. Lucretia.
v. Mary.
vi. Jane.
vii. Louisa.
viii. Melvina.
ix. Thomas.

HON. JOHN LARUE HELM, of "Helm Place,", Hardin County, Kentucky, *b.* there 4th July, 1802; *d.* there 8th September, 1867; was educated in the county schools of Hardin County; studied law in the office of Benjamin TOBIN; elected to the State Legislature eleven terms. In 1848 was elected Lieutenant-Governor on the Whig ticket with John C. CRITTENDEN and on the governor's resignation in 1850 filled out the remainder of his term to 1851. Served as Presidential Elector in 1853; chairman of the State Convention which met 8th January, 1861, to advocate the neutrality of Kentucky in the Civil War. In 1867 was elected Governor of Kentucky by an overwhelming majority of 60,000. On the day set for his inauguration 3d September, 1867, he was too ill to go to Frankfort and the oath of office was administered at his home. He did not live to assume the active duties of his office as he *d.* 8th September, 1867; was President of the Louisville and Nashville Railroad for some years; *m.* 10th August, 1830, Lucinda Barbour HARDIN, *b.* 2d February, 1809, Bardstown, Kentucky, *d.* 25th December, 1885, Elizabethtown, Kentucky, dau. of Benjamin HARDIN, *b.* 29th February, 1785, *d.* 17th September, 1852, who was one of Kentucky's greatest lawyers; *m.* 1808, Elizabeth Pendleton BARBOUR, *b.* 1788, Culpepper County, Virginia, *d.* 2d August, 1852, dau. of Ambrois BARBOUR, son of James BARBOUR, and Elizabeth (THOMAS) BARBOUR.

ISSUE

i. Gen. Benjamin Hardin, *b.* 2d June, 1831; *d.* 20th September, 1863, Graduate of West Point; *m.* 26th March, 1856, Emily P. TODD.
ii. George, studied law, *b.* 31st October, 1833; *d.* August, 1858, in Memphis, Tennessee; graduated at Harvard, 1858.
iii. Elizabeth Barbour, *b.* 11th April, 1836; *d.* 14th January, 1913; *m.* 12th June, 1856, Hon. H. W. BRUCE, formerly a member of the Confederate Congress, later Judge of Judicial Circuit of Kentucky.
iv. Rebecca Jane, *b.* 17th February, 1838; *d.* 23d August, 1859.
v. Lucinda Barbour, *b.* 23d December, 1839; *d.* unmarried, 15th November, 1897.
vi. Sara Hardin, *b.* 15th July, 1841; *d.* 2d June, 1868; *m.* 17th July, 1861, Maj. Thomas HAYS, C. S. A.
vii. Emily Palmer, *b.* 15th January, 1844; *d.* November, 1916; *m.* 24th December, 1868, Martin Hardin MARRIOTT.
viii. Mary, *b.* 18th May, 1845; *d.* 12th November, 1913.

ix. John Larue, *b.* 4th July, 1847; *d.* 6th June, 1917; *m.* 8th June, 1881; Lucy A. WASHINGTON, of Nashville, Tennessee.
x. William, *d.* in infancy.
xi. JAMES PENDLETON, *b.* 7th January, 1850, the subject of this memoir.
xii. Thomas Preston Pope, *b.* 17th August, 1851; *d.* 18th March, 1884.

Arms.—Or, on a field azure, between two griffin's segreant, respecting each other gules, an esquire's helmet ppr. garnished or.

Crest.—On a mount vert a demi-dragon azure, holding in the dexter paw a cross crosslet fitchée or, and supporting with the sinister paw an escutcheon gold, charged with a squire's helmet ppr.

Motto.—Cassis tutissima virtus.

Kennedy

The American ancestor of the family was MATTHEW KENNEDY, *b.* in Scotland, 1738; *d.* 1784; the third son of Walter KENNEDY, *b.* 1690 and his wife ———— MCDONALD. He was an officer in the English Navy, but resigned his commission and came to America before the Revolutionary War; when war was declared, he joined the Revolutionary Army, serving three years, as an Adjutant and Field Officer in Pennsylvania; *m.* 1770, Jane BUCHANAN, dau. of William BUCHANAN of Carlisle, Pennsylvania; in 1780 he settled in Augusta County, Virginia.

ISSUE

i. John.
ii. Walter.
iii. MATTHEW, Jr., *b.* 12th August, 1780, of whom below.

MATTHEW KENNEDY, JR., *b.* 12th August, 1780, near Staunton, in Augusta County, Virginia; *d.* 20th April, 1853, in Louisville, Kentucky; *m.* 15th September, 1811, at Versailles, Kentucky, Jane SMITH, *b.* in Richmond, Virginia, 6th March, 1796, *d.* 28th July, 1864; dau. of Capt. Samuel SMITH, an officer in the Revolutionary Army, *b.* 1752; *d.* 12th December, 1832; *m.* Tabitha MCLAUGHLIN, *b.* 1768; *d.* 12th December, 1834; dau. of Robert and Rebecca (CLARK) MCLAUGHLIN, the son of Laughlin MCLAUGHLIN of Scotland.

ISSUE

i. William Buchanan, *b.* 6th December, 1812; *d.* 19th August, 1814.
ii. Mary, *b.* 25th September, 1814; *d.* 18th July, 1815.

III. Alfred Worsley, *b.* 2d July, 1816; *d.* in Mexico, 1852. Assistant Surgeon United States Army; served in Florida and Mexican Wars under Gen. Zachary TAYLOR; *m.* July, 1844, in St. Louis, Missouri, Mimie BERTHOLD, who *d.* August, 1852.

ISSUE

1. Clarra, *m.* Robert LUCAS, of St. Louis.

IV. Samuel Smith, *b.* 26th February, 1818; *d.* 21st September, 1855; *m.* 1846 Mary BARRET.

ISSUE

1. Nannie, *m.* Carlisle PETERSILEA.
2. Laura, *m.* Frank P. TENNEY, of New York.

V. THOMAS SMITH, *b.* 18th June, 1820; of whom later.
VI. Rebecca, *b.* 4th February, 1822; *d.* 6th July, 1839.
VII. Henry Clay, *b.* 1st January, 1829; *d.* 21st February, 1832.
VIII. Ben Dudley, *b.* 6th July, 1832; *d.s.p.* April, 1884; *m.* 1856, Lucy CHAPMAN.
IX. Matthew Woodford, *b.* 16th October, 1834; *d.* 2d September, 1876.

THOMAS SMITH KENNEDY, M.D., of Louisville, Kentucky, *b.* there 18th June, 1820; *d.* there 12th March, 1902; Graduate of Transylvania University, Lexington, was associated in Louisville for many years with the Mutual Life Insurance Com; pany; *m.* 1st October, 1844, in Louisville, Kentucky, Catherine Martin ANDERSON, *b.* there 1st August, 1826, *d.* there 3d November, 1911, she dau. of John Foster ANDERSON, Lawyer, son of George ANDERSON *b.* in Ireland, 1749, *d.* in Lexington, Kentucky, 18th January, 1814, *m.* Rhoda OLIVER, *b.* in Culpeper County, Virginia, in 1776, *d.* in Louisville Kentucky, 5th December, 1849.

Catharine Martin ANDERSON was descended from the fine old stock of the WHITAKERS of Lancashire, England, 1400; the BAKERS; Sir Edward LEWIS, Wales, 1557; the BLANTONS, the MARTINS, and many distinguished allied families of the Old South. See MARTIN lineage later.

ISSUE

1. Sidney Anderson KENNEDY, *b.* 7th August, 1848; *m.* 1st December, 1869, David Murray RODMAN.

ISSUE

1. Kate RODMAN, *b.* 21st September, 1870; *m.* William FIELD.
2. Pattie RODMAN.
3. Lee RODMAN, *m.* Margharita WELLING.
4. Kennedy RODMAN.

II. Pattie Anderson KENNEDY, b. 18th March, 1854; m. James Pendleton HELM. See HELM memoir in preceding pages.

ISSUE

1. Thomas Kennedy HELM, b. 18th November, 1874.
2. Katharine Anderson HELM, b. 7th September, 1876.
3. Lucinda Harden HELM, b. 17th January, 1880.
4. James Pendleton HELM, b. 4th December, 1885.

III. Nancy Martin KENNEDY, b. 16th January, 1859; m. 9th February, 1881, James E. GAITHER, b. 10th June, 1852; d. 2d June, 1902.

ISSUE

1. Thomas Richard GAITHER, b. 8th November, 1884; m. 24th December, 1910, Marcia FRANCIS.

ISSUE

1[1]. Nancy Rose GAITHER, b. 12th July, 1912.

IV. Emily, b. 11th May, 1860; m. 17th October, 1881, Maxwell BARKER.

ISSUE

1. Carrie BARKER, b. 10th September, 1882.
2. Maxwell BARKER, b. 16th July, 1884.

V. Thomas Worsley, b. 20th December, 1861; m. 17th November, 1891; Madge WILLARD, dau. of James E. and Margaret (BRAYTON) WILLARD.

ISSUE

1. Thomas Willard.
2. Margaret.
3. Orville.
4. James.

VI. Orville Anderson, b. 3d November, 1864; d. 21st June, 1907; m. 27th December, 1889, Eugenia FERRELL, of Montgomery, Alabama.

ISSUE

1. Katharine, b. 17th December, 1891; d. 11th November, 1918.

Arms.—Sable on a fesse argent, between three helmets close, a fox courant ppr.
Crest.—A demi-arm embowed in armour ppr. holding a branch of oak.
Motto.—Ad haero vir tuti.

Martin

I. THOMAS MARTIN was *b.* circa 1720, and settled in Albermarle County, Virginia, prior to 1764, where he *d.* in 1792 and where many of his descendants reside. He *m.* Anne MOORMAN, by whom he had eleven children, of whom,

II. CAPT. JOHN MARTIN, *b.* 20th March, 1742; *d.* 3d December, 1837, *m.*, circa 1774, Elizabeth LEWIS, *b.* 1754, in Albermarle County, Virginia; *d.* November, 1838, Lexington, Kentucky. He was a Captain in the Revolutionary War; encharged with guarding of British prisoners to 1780; made a Major at the siege of Yorktown; removed to Fayette County, Kentucky, 1786, and was the first Sheriff of Clark County and later a Judge of the Quarter Sessions of that county. Their son,

III. JOHN LEWIS MARTIN, *b.* 14th August, 1779; *d.* 17th October, 1854; *m.* 1802, Catharine BLANTON, in Frankfort, Kentucky; *b.* 21st January, 1785, Augusta, Georgia; *d.* 20th August, 1830. Their daughter,

IV. NANCY OLIVER MARTIN, *b.* 5th February, 1804; *d.* 15th April, 1836; *m.* 29th September, 1825, at Lexington, Kentucky, John Foster ANDERSON, *b.* 10th September, 1802; *d.* 13th July, 1834. Their daughter,

V. CATHARINE MARTIN ANDERSON, *b.* 1st August, 1826; *d.* 3d November, 1911; *m.* 1st October, 1844, Thomas Smith KENNEDY, *b.* 18th June, 1820; *d.* 11th March, 1902, at Louisville, Kentucky. See KENNEDY Lineage in previous pages.

Hewins

HARRY WILLIAM HEWINS of Dedham, Massachusetts; *b.* 23d May, 1884, in Dedham, Massachusetts; son of George and Harriet Whiting (CARROLL) HEWINS. Harry William HEWINS was educated in the schools of Dedham; spent two years as a student in a mill in Lawrence, Massachusetts, learning to sort and judge wool; later was connected with the wool trade in Boston; attended the Plattsburg Training Camp in August, 1916, and studied for a reserve commission during the winter of 1916–1917; in May, 1917, enrolled in the 1st Provisional Training Regiment in Plattsburg Barracks, New York, serving as a Reserve Lieutenant during the camp; commissioned a Second Lieutenant in the Quartermasters' Corps; ordered to Camp Devens, and later to the Quartermasters' Depot in Boston; commissioned First Lieutenant April, 1918, commissioned Captain 24th October, 1918, and sailed to join American Expeditionary Forces in France shortly afterward; stationed (1919) in Tours; discharged 2nd September, 1919, at Camp Devens.

Lineage

The HEWINS family in America is connected with the family of that name of Warwickshire and Worcestershire, England. The name is found among the graves in the churchyard surrounding Holy Trinity Church, Stratford on Avon. Agnes ARDEN, the aunt of the great dramatist, *m.* John HEWINS of Bearley, and had two children, Thomas and Margaret. William Alfred Samuel HEWINS of London, a member of Parliament, and a writer and authority on Political Economy, has made extensive researches into the family in England.

Jacob HEWINS was a householder in Boston in 1656 and shortly afterwards bought a homestead of three acres of land in Dorchester. Through grants by the Dorchester Proprietors and by purchase he increased his holdings, until at his death, he owned about one hundred and seventy-five acres, most of which were within the present town of Sharon, formerly Stoughtonham. Jacob HEWINS *d.* 9th November, 1711, and Mary, his wife *d.* 12th March, 1715–1716.

ISSUE

I. Jacob, *m.* 24th February, 1681, Martha TRESCOTT.
II. Elizabeth, *m.* Nicholas IDE of Attleborough.
III. Samuel, *b.* 9th August, 1658; probably *d.* young.
IV. Mary, *b.* 9th August, 1660; probably *d.* before 1713.
V. Hannah, *b.* 29th April, 1665; *m.* ———FISHER.
VI. JOSEPH, *b.* 4th May, 1668; of whom later.
VII. Benjamin, *b.* 4th September, 1670; *d.* unm. circa 1690, at Castle William.

This biographical history of the HEWINS family and allied families was prepared for "Colonial Families of the United States of America" by Miss Clara Carroll HEWINS.

For other branches of this family, see, HEWINS genealogy, contained in "A Genealogical Register of Several Ancient Puritans," Vol. II, Boston, 1859.

JOSEPH HEWINS, *b.* 20th May, 1668, in Dorchester, Massachusetts; settled in that part of Dorchester, which became Sharon. On the establishment of the church in Dorchester precinct, which is now the First Congregational Parish Church of Canton, he was chosen Deacon and Ruling Elder; he often served the town as Assessor and Moderator; was repeatedly elected Selectman, and Town Clerk in 1730 and 1731; Joseph HEWINS *m.* 29th January, 1690, Mehetabel LYON, dau. of Peter LYON, a weaver of Dorchester, and *d.* 24th February, 1755.

ISSUE

I. Jacob, *b.* 4th January, 1691–1692; *d.* 22d October, 1711, at sea.
II. Mehetabel, *b.* 17th December, 1693; *m.* 3d March, 1717–1718, John HIXON.
III. Joseph, *b.* 26th March, 1696; *d.* young.
IV. Benjamin, *b.* 27th January, 1697–1698; *m.* Sarah—; *d.* 7th July, 1734.
V. Joseph, *b.* 26th February, 1696; *d.* 22d January, 1786; *m.* Catherine BIRD.
VI. Hannah, *b.* 10th April, 1703.
VII. Ebenezer, *b.* 24th March, 1707; of whom later.

EBENEZER HEWINS, *b.* 24th March, 1707; lived in Sharon, and held public offices, as had his father. He was a Lieutenant of Militia. His sons inherited love of country, four of them having been Lieutenants in the Continental Army, and a fifth as Corporal having served for the duration of the war. Lieutenant Enoch was the first volunteer from Sharon. Lieut. Ebenezer HEWINS *m.* 24th October, 1730, Judith PORTER, gr. gd. dau. of Maj. William HATHORNE, *b.* 1607, *d.* 1681, of Salem, Massachusetts, who was Deputy to the General Court sixteen years; Speaker of House of Deputies five years and for seventeen years Assistant; he was also a member of the Committee on Articles of Confederation 1648, and for Preservation of the Charter 1661; appointed Major before 1657, and at the age of nearly seventy years, Captain of the Salem Company in King Philip's War. Ebenezer HEWINS *d.* 22d July, 1751, and Judith (PORTER), HEWINS *d.* 30th June, 1753.

ISSUE

I. Ebenezer, *b.* 9th November, 1731; *d.* 8th May, 1806; *m.* 7th May, 1761 Mercy Guild; Lieutenant, Revolutionary Army.
II. Mehetabel, *b.* 10th October, 1733; *m.* Nathaniel BRADSHAW.
III. WILLIAM, *b.* 16th December, 1635; of whom later.
IV. Phebe, *b.* 30th March, 1737–1738; *d.* young.
V. Increase, *b.* 16th April, 1739; removed to Stockbridge; Captain, Revolutionary Army.
VI. Enoch, *b.* 16th May, 1641; *d.* 10th August, 1821; *m.* 18th December, 1766, Sarah HEWINS; Lieutenant, Revolutionary Army.
VII. Hannah, *b.* 12th July, 1743; *m.* John HEWINS of Dedham.

VIII. Joseph, *b.* 24th October, 1745; *d.* 15th December, 1813; *m.* 10th December, 1772, Anna GOULD; Private, Revolutionary Army.
IX. Elijah, *b.* 23d May, 1747; *d.* 21st May, 1827; *m.* (firstly) Lois WHITING, who *d.* 24th June, 1795, aged 50 years; (secondly) Irene BALCH of Dedham; Surgeon, Revolutionary Army.
X. Ruth, *b.* 4th March, 1748–1749; *m.* Asa HARDING of Franklin, Massachusetts.

WILLIAM HEWINS, *b.* 16th December, 1735, in Sharon; when twenty years of age, he volunteered for the Expedition against Crown Point, and as sentinel and corporal served in the French and Indian War throughout the Expedition for the Reduction, of Canada in 1758. He was a soldier under Washington from 1776 to 1783. He *m.* 27th November, 1759.
Ruth CUMMINGS, dau. of Samuel and Susanna (HOOD) CUMMINGS of Ipswich.

ISSUE

I. Ruth, *b.* 12th March, 1760; *m.* 8th January, 1783, John HEWINS resident of Sharon.
II. William, *b.* 12th March, 1762; *m.* ————INGRAHAM resident of Hallowell, Maine.
III. Ebenezer, *b.* 13th April, 1764; *m.* Elizabeth CUMMINGS resident of Hallowell, Maine.
IV. Amasa, *b.* 10th May, 1766, of whom later.
V. Rebecca, *b.* 28th June, 1768; *d.* unmarried 31st May, 1790.
VI. Elkanah, *b.* 9th September, 1773; *m.* 16th February, 1803, Hannah Capen FOSTER of Dorchester.

LIEUT. AMASA HEWINS, *b.* 10th May, 1766; *d.* 12th January, 1812, in Sharon, Massachusetts; *m.* 25th July, 1790, Esther KOLLOCK, whose gd. father, Cornelius KOLLOCK, was a member of the KOLLOCK family of Lewes, Delaware, and Philadelphia, of which Jacob KOLLOCK, as Judge, President of the Assembly, Treasurer of Sussex County and Register of Wills, was the distinguished founder. Cornelius KOLLOCK, traveling from Philadelphia to Boston sojourned at the famous Billings Tavern in Sharon, and *m.* 25th September, 1723, Jerusha BILLINGS, dau. of Ebenezer, the inn-keeper. This Capt. Ebenezer BILLINGS was the son of Roger, the emigrant ancestor, and owned several hundred acres in Sharon, including Moose Hill, and a large tract on Billings or Wollomolopoag Pond, adjoining land bought by Cornelius KOLLOCK, his son-in-law. The KOLLOCK homestead was owned successively by Cornelius KOLLOCK, his son Royall and his gd. dau. Esther who *m.* Amasa HEWINS, and Lemuel D. HEWINS, their son, all during a period of about one hundred and twenty-five years. Royall KOLLOCK derived his Christian name from the family of his mother, who were descendants of Capt. Isaac ROYALL, the owner of Blue Hill in 1720.

ISSUE

I. Simon K., *b.* 1st September, 1791; *d.* 26th March, 1859; *m.* Caroline T. BROWN of Boston.
II. Lemuel D., *b.* 19th August, 1793; *m.* (firstly) 26th February, 1818, Patty HEWINS; (secondly) 27th November, 1860, Sarah (SEAVEY) MARDEN.
III. AMASA, *b.* 11th July, 1795; of whom later.
IV. Royall, *b.* 24th December, 1796; *m.* Margaret————.
V. Esther, *b.* 19th June, 1799; *m.* Alpheus COWEN; resident of North Falmouth, Massachusetts.
VI. William, *b.* 7th June, 1801; *m.* Love HANDY; resident of Falmouth, Massachusetts.
VII. Nathaniel Adams, *b.* 3d June, 1803; *d.* 11th December, 1848; *m.* 23d September, 1827 Hannah HERSEY; resident of Dedham, Massachusetts.
VIII. Zebiah, *b.* 19th April, 1806; *m.* Charles SWIFT; resident of Pocasset, Massachusetts.

AMASA HEWINS, *b.* 11th July, 1795, in Sharon, where he attended the common schools. His education was extended by wide reading and travel. In middle age he acquired French and Italian, speaking and writing both languages fluently. He *m.* 22d August, 1820, Elizabeth ALDEN, a woman of strong character, dau. of Paul and Rebecca (NEWELL) ALDEN, by family tradition a descendant of John and Priscilla ALDEN of Plymouth, 1620. After ten years of commercial life Mr. HEWINS made portrait painting his profession, and had studios in Washington, Baltimore, and Boston. Between 1832 and 1855 he spent eight years in Europe, studying at the Academy in Florence, and traveling extensively. In 1852 he was appointed American Consular Agent at Florence, and he exported antiques, curios and works of art to America. Mr. HEWINS *d.* 18th August, 1855, in Florence, and his widow *d.* 4th October, 1862, in Dedham.

ISSUE

I. Charles Amasa, *b.* 4th January, 1822; *m.* 8th May 1845, Caroline L. CHAPIN, *d.* 11th November, 1898. Founded firm of HEWINS AND HOLLIS, Men's Outfitters, Boston.

ISSUE

1. Caroline Maria.
2. Frank Alden.
3. Elizabeth Fiske.
4. Lucy Chapin.
5. Edith.
6. Anna Fiske.
7. Bertha.

8. Florence Emmons.
9. Margaret.

II. Elizabeth Allin, *b.* 11th January, 1824; *m.* 24th December, 1846, John W. SEYMOUR. She *d.* 9th December, 1906.

ISSUE

1. Clara Alden SEYMOUR.
2. Gertrude Elizabeth SEYMOUR.
3. Evelyn Hewins SEYMOUR.

III. Richard, *b.* 7th February, 1827; *m.* (firstly) 25th December, 1851, Jerusha DAY; (secondly) 2d February, 1888, May PHILLIPS, resident of Philadelphia; *d.* 7th January, 1919.

ISSUE

1. Mary A.
2. Hattie E.
3. Edward.
4. George F.

IV. Esther, *b.* 18th April, 1829; *m.* 23d September, 1857, Nathaniel C. POOR, and *d.* 13th August, 1910.

ISSUE

1. James Ridgway POOR.
2. Alice Florence POOR.

V. Florence, *b.* 5th February, 1831; *d.* 21st March, 1882.
VI. Eben Newell, *b.* 5th September, 1834; Company F, 44th Regiment, in Union Army, War of Rebellion; later Treasurer of Boston Book Company; resident of Brookline, Massachusetts; *d.* 2nd May, 1919.
VII. GEORGE, of whom below.
VIII. Josephine, *b.* 12th March, 1839; conducted a private school in Dedham; *d.* 5th January, 1881.
IX. Louise, *b.* 17th August, 1841; resident of Jamaica Plain, Boston.

GEORGE HEWINS, *b.* 5th August, 1836, in Cornhill Court, Boston; *d.* 5th September, 1900, Dedham, Massachusetts, where he had made his home for nearly fifty years. The house in Dedham overlooking the Charles River now occupied by his family, was built by him in 1876. In his youth he went to work for a firm of chain makers in Boston, and in early manhood became a partner in the firm of John A.

EMMONS AND COMPANY, sugar brokers. He was a man of noted business integrity, a faithful citizen and always a doer of many kindnesses. Quiet in his tastes, he found his pleasure in his home and garden. He *m.* 14th November, 1861, Harriet Whiting CARROLL, in the First Parish Church, Dedham (Unitarian).

Carroll

HARRIET WHITING CARROLL, was a descendant in the fifth generation from Joseph CARYL of Walpole, Massachusetts; Jonathan, son of Joseph *m.* Lydia BOYDEN, a member of a family famous for its educators, founded by Thomas BOYDEN, who came from Ipswich, England, in the ship *Frances*, 1634. In 1665, he gave bonds that his stepsons should be taught to read and write, and later he contributed to the "new brick college," now Harvard University. Capt. Jonathan BOYDEN, his son, was one of the first settlers of Medfield, and his gr. gd. dau. the wife of Jonathan CARYL was a descendant of Joseph CLARK, Capt. Joshua FISHER, Lieut. Henry ADAMS, John FRAIRY and Hopestill LELAND, all early settlers of Medfield, Massachusetts. Jonathan CARYL, Jr. *m.* Esther POND, whose emigrant ancestors, Lieut. Daniel POND, Thomas FISHER, and Nathaniel FARRINGTON served in King Philip's War, and in the local militia.

JOSEPH CARREL, son of Jonathan CARYL, Jr., *m.* 27th October, 1803, Asenath CARPENTER, who traced her ancestry to William CARPENTER of Providence, son and heir of Richard CARPENTER of Amesbury, Wiltshire, England, and his wife Elizabeth ARNOLD of Cheselbourne, Dorsetshire. Both the ARNOLDS and CARPENTERS were eminent in the annals of Rhode Island. Thomas WIGHT, an emigrant ancestor of Asenath CARPENTER, was one of the seven original settlers of Medfield, and one of its most prominent townsmen, being Selectman for sixteen years, and the largest taxpayer. His dau. Mary *m.* Thomas ELLIS of Medfield, and through the marriage of their daughter Joanna to Nathaniel ROCKWOOD, Asenath CARPENTER was descended from Richard ROCKWOOD of Weymouth, England, who settled at Dorchester, Massachusetts and from Michael METCALF, a prosperous weaver of Norwich, England, son of Leonard METCALF, rector of the church in Tatterford, Norfolk. Michael METCALF had a grant of land on Dedham Island, bordering on Motley's Pond, later so named because the historian of the Dutch Republic was born on the estate. Ensign Francis CHICKERING, Deputy to the General Court, 1644, 1653, was also an ancestor of Asenath CARPENTER.

SANFORD CARROLL, son of Joseph and Asenath (CARPENTER) CARROLL, *b.* 22d October, 1810, in Walpole, Massachusetts; when eighteen years of age went to Dedham; here he engaged in business and took an active part in town affairs. He was a supporter of the great temperance movement of the 40's, and a faithful worker in the anti-slavery controversy, and for the protection of the slave. Mr. CARROLL *m.* (firstly) 22d October, 1834, Harriet WHITING, by whom he had three children, Charles Whiting, William Sanford, Harriet Whiting; (secondly) Clarissa ALDEN. By this union there were nine children. He *d.* 17th April, 1891, at Dedham.

Whiting

The emigrant ancestor of Harriet WHITING was Nathaniel WHITING, of Lynn, 1638, and Dedham, 1641, where he established the first corn mill, on the oldest canal in America, which connects the Charles with the lower levels of the Neponset River. His wife, Hannah, daughter of John and Hannah DWIGHT of Dedham, survived him thirty years, managed his business affairs and brought up a large family with rare discretion. The corn mill was in the possession of the WHITING family for more than two centuries. The last owner was William WHITING, son of Lemuel and Mary (GAY) WHITING, and of the sixth generation from the first miller, Nathaniel WHITING. Harriet, sister of William WHITING, was *b*. 9th February, 1814. Harriet WHITING was descended from three children of the emigrant Nathaniel, Timothy, Sarah and Judith, and in both paternal and maternal branches, with one exception, wholly from the first settlers of Dedham, William BULLARD, Nathaniel COLBURN, Ralph DAY, John DEAN, John DWIGHT, Joseph and Thomas ELLIS, Jonathan FAIRBANKS, John FARRINGTON, Thomas FULLER, John GAY and Thomas WIGHT. Harriet WHITING *m*. Sanford CARROLL, son of Joseph and Asenath (CARPENTER) CARROLL, and their only dau. Harriet Whiting CARROLL was *b*. 25th February, 1840, in Dedham. A woman of great warmth of temperament, she was ardently devoted to the affairs nearest her heart, her home, her church and her country. Her only surviving brother, Capt. Charles Whiting CARROLL, a young lawyer of great promise, was killed in the second Battle of Bull Run. It is significant that a silk American flag hangs in the First Parish Church, Dedham (Unitarian) in memory of Mrs. HEWINS. She *d*. 4th December, 1911.

George Hewins and Harriet Whiting CARROLL *m*. 14th November, 1861, in Dedham.

ISSUE

I. Elizabeth Alden, *m*. 19th September, 1889, Charles Elmer RUSSELL.

ISSUE

1. Philip Alden RUSSELL, Ensign, Naval Aviation, United States Naval Reserve Force.
2. Gertrude RUSSELL.

II. Charles Carroll, *b*. 3d August, 1864; *d*. 3d August, 1867.
III. Alice Emmons.
IV. Clara Carroll.
V. Josephine.
VI. George Sanford, *b*. 6th October, 1874; studied at Massachusetts Institute of Technology, Civil Engineer; built dam across the Connecticut River near Brattleboro, Vermont, Imperial Munition Plant at Toronto, Canada, etc.; general manager of plant for building wooden ships (Emergency

Fleet Corporation of the United States Shipping Board), Portsmouth, New Hampshire; *m.* 14th June, 1905, in Fairfax, Vermont, Mary Drake PHELPS.

ISSUE

1. Mary Phelps.
2. Harriet Caryl.

VII. Harriet, *d.* young.
VIII. Gertrude Newell, *b.* 22d September, 1880; *d.* 16th August, 1888.
IX. HARRY WILLIAM, the subject of this memoir.

Residence.—715 High Street, Dedham, Massachusetts.

Hollingsworth

JAMES EDWIN HOLLINGSWORTH of Memphis, Tennessee; *b.* 1st December, 1872, in DeKalb County, Georgia; *m.* 3d July, 1893, Atlanta, Georgia, Katharine McKEWEN, of Atlanta, Georgia, *b.* 8th January, 1874, dau. of William McKEWEN, *b.* in Baltimore, Maryland, 10th July, 1842, *d.* 5th October, 1910, and Martha Virginia (STODDARD) McKEWEN, of Washington, D. C., *m.* 4th September, 1866; *d.* 17th October, 1890.

ISSUE

I. Joseph Edwin, *b.* 17th October, 1896, at Shreveport, Louisiana; with United States Army in France, in 166th Ambulance Company, 42d Division, Sanitary Train No. 117.
II. Thelma Elizabeth, *b.* 26th August, 1900, at Ensley, Alabama.
III. Edna Earl, *b.* 9th December, 1904, at Birmingham, Alabama.

JAMES EDWIN HOLLINGSWORTH was educated in the Public Schools of Atlanta, Georgia; in General Contracting business in Memphis, Tenneseee; Member of General Contractors Association, Elks Lodge, and Kawannis, Memphis, Tennessee, and National Geographic Society, Washington, D. C.

Lineage

The HOLLINGSWORTH'S have held their own all along the ages. They were an old Saxon family said to have settled in the northeastern part of Cheshire, as early as 1022, in which year the ancestral estate, Hollingsworth Manor, in Cheshire was purchased. The name is a locality one, from the estate of that name, near Mottram, in the county in question. The name comes from the two words, "holly" and "worth," a farm; meaning a farm of holly trees. Annals dating from the Norman conquest, speak of the Domesday survey and the many manors, among them the Holinsworth Manor, situated on the edge of the great woods of Macclesfield. The visitation of Cheshire by the official herald in the year 1580 includes among the gentry residing in the hundred of Macclesfield "John HOLLINGSWORTH, gent," and "Robert HOLLINSWORTH" of Hollinsworth." A further record speaks of Robert HOLLINGSWORTH of Hollingsworth Hall; from whom the family is descended, and who was Magistrate for the counties of Chester and Lancaster. The church of the family and the hall, both several centuries old, are still standing, and upon both are emblazoned the family Coat of Arms. The buildings are much out of repair, and their later owner, Capt. Robert HOLLINGSWORTH, the last representative of the English branch of the family, *d.* in 1865. The picturesque red-berried holly trees abound upon the estate and when one realizes its nearness to the edge of the Macclesfield woods, the arms and crest handed down for the generations acquires picturesque significance. The tinctures of the shield are azure, suggestive of the blue sky; argent, the silvery streams that flow through the woodlands, and vert the green leafage of the forest trees. The virtues these colors express, are equally beautiful—loyalty, innocence and love. The crest is a stag, recalling the Saxon earls of Cheshire and merry hunting scenes, and three glistening holly leaves suggest Christmas in merry England. Motto: "Learn to suffer what must be borne." The usurpation of that Saxon shire by the Norman Earl Hugh LUPUS no doubt suggested the motto. At any rate the records state that these freemen of HOLLINGSWORTH and the seven other manors that make up Macclesfield, paid their yearly tax to the usurping Earls and held their manors in undisturbed possession.

The name HOLLINGSWORTH, so widely known and honored in the United States, is spelled severally: HOLLINGWORTH, HOLLINSWORTH, and HOLLINGSWORTH, the last has been clung to by a large majority of the descendants of the founder of the family in America, who was Valentine HOLLINGSWORTH, who came direct to the New World, from Ireland, in 1682, the year in which William PENN arrived in the Delaware, in front of what is now the city of Philadelphia, Pennsylvania.

VALENTINE HOLLINGSWORTH, the original emigrant ancestor was a son of Henry HOLLINGSWORTH of Belleniskcrannel, Parish of Legoe, County Armagh, Ireland, and Catharine, his wife and was born at Belleniskcrannel, about the sixth month in the year 1632. He was *m.* 7th April, 1655, to Ann REE, daughter of Nicholas REE, of Tanderagee, County Armagh. Ann REE was *b.* circa 1628, at Tanderagee, and *d.* 1st February, 1671. He then *m.* a second time, 12th April, 1672, Ann CALVERT, daughter of Thomas CALVERT, of Dromgora, Parish of Segoe, County Armagh, and Jane his wife. Valentine HOLLINGSWORTH was a Quaker and belonged to the Society of Friends; this in a way explains his departure for the New World when in 1682, Valentine HOLLINGSWORTH and his family, accompanied by his son-in-law, Thomas CONNAWAY, and by John MUSGRAVE an indented servant, sailed from Belfast, for the Delaware River, arriving a few months after William PENN's arrival in the good ship *Welcome*. He settled on a large plantation of nearly a thousand acres on Shelpot Creek in Brandywine Hundred, New Castle County, Delaware, about five miles northeast of the present city of Wilmington, and not far from the Fort Christina, or Christiana of the Swedes. That Valentine HOLLINGSWORTH was a man of extraordinary ability and influence is demonstrated from the fact that almost immediately after his arrival in the New World, he was called upon to hold office and participate in public affairs. He was a Member of the First Assembly of the Province of Pennsylvania, shortly after William PENN's advent, that of 1682-1683; also of the Grand Inquest empaneled 25th October, 1683, to consider the famous case of Charles PICKERING and others charged with counterfeiting. He served in several subsequent sessions of the Assembly, those of 1687, 1688, 1689, 1695, and 1700, from New Castle County, and was a Justice of the Peace from the same County. He was also a Signer of PENN's Great Charter and a Member of the Pro-Provincial Council. He *d.* circa 1711; his wife Ann, *d.* 17th August, 1697; both were buried in the old burial ground at Newark, Delaware, which he had presented to the Friends in 1687.

ISSUE BY FIRST MARRIAGE

1. Mary, *b.* 25th January, 1656, at Belleniskcrannel, Ireland; *m.* (firstly) Thomas CONOWAY, who *d.* 17th July, 1689; *m.* (secondly) Randal MALIN, in 1693.

ISSUE BY FIRST MARRIAGE

1. Elizabeth CONOWAY, *b.* 7th September, 1687; *m.* (firstly) 1705, Charles BOOTH; *m.* (secondly), 1720, Thomas CRABB.
2. Ann CONOWAY, *m.* 10th June, 1705, Philip TAYLOR.
3. Sarah CONOWAY, *m.* 1709–1710, John YEARSLEY.

ISSUE BY SECOND MARRIAGE

1. Hannah MALIN, *d.* young.
2. Rachel MALIN, *b.* 25th April, 1702.

II. Henry, *b.* 7th September, 1658, at Belleniskcrannel, Ireland; came to America in 1683; *d.* at Elkton, Cecil County, Maryland, 1721; will dated 23d February, 1721; probated 12th March, 1721; was a Surveyor and large land owner in Chester County, Pennsylvania, also in New Castle County, Delaware; was Coroner of Chester County, and Clerk of the Court, from 1700 to 1708; he represented New Castle County in the Assembly of Pennsylvania, in 1695, the same year with his father; in 1711–1712, he removed to the head of Elk River, now Elkton, Cecil County, Maryland, and was appointed Surveyor of the County by Lord Baltimore, 9th March, 1712; *m.* 22d August, 1688, in the Parish of Sligo, County Armagh, Ireland, Lydia ATKINSON.

ISSUE

1. Ruth, *m.* 24th December, 1706, George SIMPSON.
2. Stephen, was a Magistrate in Cecil County, Maryland in 1730; removed to Virginia and in 1734, obtained a grant of land of 472 acres on the west side of the Shenandoah River, Orange County.
3. Zebulon, *b.* 1696; *d.* 8th August, 1763, in Cecil County, Maryland; was a large land owner, also a Magistrate and President of the County Court; Vestryman of St. Mary Ann's Church in 1743; was engaged in the manufacture of flour with his son Levi, who afterward removed to Philadelphia; *m.* (firstly), 18th April, 1727, Ann MAULDEN, who *d.* November, 1740.

4. Catharine.
5. Abigail, *m.* 1720, Richard DOBSON.
6. Mary.

III. THOMAS, *b.* in March, 1661, of whom later.
IV. Catharine, *b.* in May, 1663; *d.* 29th June, 1746; *m.* 2d November, 1688, George ROBINSON, *b.* 1666-1667 in the North of Ireland, *d.* 8th September, 1738.

ISSUE

1. Mary ROBINSON, *m.* 13th August, 1710, Thomas JACOBS.
2. Ann ROBINSON, *m.* 1720, Jonathan OGDEN.
3. Valentine ROBINSON, *m.* 1740, Elizabeth BOOTH.

ISSUE BY SECOND MARRIAGE

V. Samuel, *b.* 27th January, 1673, in Ireland; *d.* 1748; will dated 30th August, 1748; proved 1st October, 1748; came from Belfast, Ireland, with his father in 1682; *m.* 1701, Hannah HARLAN; he represented New Castle County in the Assembly from 1725-1728.

ISSUE

1. Enoch, *m.* (firstly), 23d October, 1725; Joanna CROWLEY; *m.* (secondly) Betty (surname not given).
2. John, *m.* 1732, Mary REED.
3. Samuel, *m.* 1738, Barbary SHEWIN.
4. George, living in 1731 to 1737; *d.* before his father.
5. Betty, *m.* 1734, Henry GREEN.

VI. Enoch, *b.* 7th June, 1675; *d.* young, 1687.
VII. Valentine, of Kennett, Pennsylvania; *b.* 12th November, 1677, at Belleniskcrannel, Ireland; *d.* 1757; will dated 30th November, 1749; proved 25th March, 1757; *m.* in 1713, Elizabeth HEALD.

ISSUE

1. James, *m.* Mary (surname not given).
2. Rachel, *m.* (firstly) ——— HOPE; *m.* (secondly) in 1737, ——— BARNES.
3. Valentine, *m.* in 1743, Elizabeth HARLAN.
4. Elizabeth, *m.* in 1746, Samuel HARLAN; moved to North Carolina in 1753.
5. Sarah, *m.* in 1746, Aaron HARLAN; moved to Cane Creek, North Carolina, 1753.

VIII. Ann, *b.* 28th October, 1680; *m.* in 1700, James THOMPSON.
IX. John, *b.* 19th February, 1684, New Castle County, Delaware; *d.* 1722; *m.* in 1706, Catharine TYLER.
X. Joseph, *b.* 10th May, 1686, in New Castle County, Delaware.
XI. Enoch again, *d.* 26th September, 1690.

THOMAS HOLLINGSWORTH, of Rockland Manor, New Castle County, Delaware; *b.* in Belleniskcrannel, Ireland; he removed to Winchester, Virginia, where he died in 1733; will dated 30th October, 1723; he came to America with his father and settled in New Castle County, west side of the Brandywine in 1682; *m.* (firstly) Margaret (surname not given), who *d.* 1st August, 1687; *m.* (secondly) 31st January, 1692, Grace COOK, of Concord, Pennsylvania.

ISSUE BY FIRST MARRIAGE

I. ABRAHAM, *b.* 19th January, 1686, of whom later.

ISSUE BY SECOND MARRIAGE

I. Isaac, *b.* 16th April, 1693; *d.* in 1699.
II. Elizabeth, *b.* 8th November, 1694; *m.* 1718, ——— STROUD.
III. Hannah, *b.* 17th January, 1697; *m.* 1718, ——— DIXON.
IV. Thomas, *b.* 23d December, 1698; *d.* 1st September, 1753; *m.* 28th December, 1732, Judith LAMPLEY.
V. Ann, *b.* 6th May, 1701; *d.* in 1708.
VI. Jacob, *b.* 4th January, 1704; *m.* 23d September, 1729, Elizabeth CHANDLER, *b.* 4th January, 1704; purchased, 23d June, 1726, of James AUBREY, Attorney for Letitia AUBREY, dau. of William PENN, 225 acres of land in Mill Creek Hundred, New Castle County, Delaware; he *d.* intestate, leaving seven children.
VII. Sarah, *b.* 7th August, 1706; *m.* 1724, John DIXON.
VIII. Joseph, *b.* 11th March, 1709; *m.* in 1730, Martha HAUGHTON; removed to Virginia.
IX. Grace, *b.* 9th March, 1712.

ABRAHAM HOLLINGSWORTH, of near Winchester, Frederick County, Virginia; *b.* 19th January, 1686; *d.* October, 1748; he bought of Alexander Ross 582 acres of land in 1732 near Winchester, which his son, Isaac, inherited and a part of the Homestead is still owned by descendants; Isaac's title to this land was disputed by Lord FAIRFAX; to prevent legal proceedings he again purchased it in 1754; *m.* 13th March, 1710, Ann ROBINSON, dau. of George ROBINSON, *d.* in 1748; Abraham by will dated 23d September, 1748, recorded in Frederick County, Virginia, 1st November, 1748, disposed of 1232 acres of land.

ISSUE

I. GEORGE, *b.* 12th April, 1712, of whom later.
II. Margaret, *b.* 1715; *m.* Benjamin CARTER, of Virginia.
III. Lydia, *b.* 1718; *m.* Lewis NEILL of Virginia.
IV. Isaac, *b.* 1722; *m.* Rachel PARKINS, of Virginia.

GEORGE HOLLINGSWORTH, of Winchester, Virginia; *b.* 7th April, 1712; *m.* (firstly) Hannah McCoy, Sr., of Augusta County, Virginia; in 1762 he sold all his property near Winchester, Virginia, and he and all his family except his son Robert and his family, went to South Carolina, and then to the West; *m.* (secondly) Jane ELWELL.

ISSUE BY FIRST MARRIAGE

I. Joseph, *b.* 1735; *m.* (firstly) ———— FROST; *m.* (secondly) Margaret HAMMER, 1763; went to Bush River in South Carolina in 1768.
II. Isaac, *b.* 1737; *m.* Susanna WRIGHT, dau. of John WRIGHT; removed from Frederick County, Virginia, to Bush River Meeting, Newberry County, South Carolina and in 1805 to Miami County, Ohio.
III. ABRAHAM, *b.* 1739, of whom later.
IV. Ann, *b.* 1742.
V. Robert, *b.* 1744; *d.* 1799, in Virginia; family removed to Simpsonville, Shelby County; *m.* 1769, Susanna RICE, who *d.* of cholera in 1833.

ISSUE BY SECOND MARRIAGE

I. James, *b.* 1758-1759; *m.* (firstly) Sarah WRIGHT; *m.* (secondly), (wife's name not given).
II. Henry, *b.* 1760; *m.* Sarah COOK.
III. George, *b.* 1762; *m.* Jane HENRY.
IV. John, *b.* 1764; *d.* in Ohio, 1807; *m.* Rachel WRIGHT.
V. Nathan, *b.* 1766; unmarried.
VI. Susanna *b.* 1768; *m.* ———— MOTE.

ABRAHAM HOLLINGSWORTH, of Laurens, South Carolina; *b.* in Virginia, 1739; *m.* 1762, Margaret WRIGHT; moved to South Carolina with his father shortly after 1762.

ISSUE

I. George, *b.* 3d October, 1763.
II. JOSEPH, *b.* 22d September, 1765, of whom later.
III. Robert, *b.* 22d November, 1767, in Laurens County, South Carolina; *m.* 1791; Jennie HAMILTON, of Laurens County, South Carolina.
IV. Levi, *b.* 11th July, 1771.
V. Jemima, *b.* 25th September, 1773.

vi. Hannah, *b.* 10th March, 1776.
vii. Richard, *b.* 12th July, 1778.

Joseph Hollingsworth, son of Abraham, of Laurens District, South Carolina; *b.* 22d September, 1765; *d.* 8th April, 1844; moved to Georgia about 1834; *m.* Rosannah Nichols, *b.* 15th January, 1767; *d.* 10th March, 1839; he and his wife are buried at Smyrna, Rockdale County, Georgia.

ISSUE

i. Jennie, *b.* 27th September, 1720; *m.* William Bailey.
ii. James of Laurens, South Carolina; *b.* 13th September, 1792.
iii. John, *b.* 4th November, 1794; moved to Newton County, Georgia, 1833; *m.* October, 1817, Rebecca Bailey.
iv. Joseph, *b.* 10th April, 1797, of whom later.
v. William, *b.* 3d March, 1799; *d.* 28th March, 1883; *m.* 11th January, 1826, Pamelia McDowell; about 1828, moved from Laurens, South Carolina, to Smyrna, Georgia.
vi. Moses, *b.* 1st February, 1801; went to Georgia about 1824 from South Carolina; *m.* 26th September, 1821, Elizabeth or Betsie Rogers.
vii. Aaron, of Laurens, South Carolina; *b.* 23d February, 1803; *m.* Ruth Rogers.
viii. Mary, *b.* 11th October, 1805; *d.* 13th June, 1847–1848; *m.* 15th June, 1825, Nathaniel Rogers.
ix. Martha, *b.* 11th September, 1808, *d.* 30th March, 1888; *m.* 24th December, 1829, George Rogers.
x. George, *b.* 9th October, 1810; *m.* (firstly), 1835; Elizabeth Jackson; *m.* (secondly) 1842, Nancy Johnson Rogers.

Joseph Hollingsworth, of Smyrna, Georgia; *b.* 10th April, 1797, at Laurens, South Carolina; *d.* 13th June, 1859; moved to DeKalb County, Georgia, 1825, thence to Smyrna, Georgia; *m.* in 1815, Elizabeth Ann Jane Carr Rogers, *b.* 14th February, 1795, *d.* 4th February, 1881, dau. of Andrew and Lettie (Franks) Rogers. Joseph and his wife are buried at Hollingsworth Ferry, Heard County, Georgia.

ISSUE

i. James, *b.* 1st August, 1817; *d.* 23d September, 1864, at Mobile, Alabama; *m.* Joyce Eppison, of Ebenezer, Georgia; family moved to eastern Mississippi.
ii. Julia Ann, *b.* 9th February, 1819, at Laurens, South Carolina; *d.* 24th April, 1911, at Conyers, Georgia; *m.* 7th September, 1837, at home near Ebenezer, Georgia, John Lewis Stewart, of Ebenezer, Georgia, *b.* 19th September, 1810, in York District, South Carolina, *d.* 30th

April, 1886, at Conyers, Georgia, he was a son of Alexander and Sarah (STRIPLIN) STEWART and gd. son of Alexander and Juliatha (OLIVER) STEWART.

ISSUE

1. Sarah Elizabeth STEWART, *b.* 14th October, 1838, at Ebenezer, Georgia (living, 1918); *m.* (firstly) 22d October, 1857, Robert JONES, of Conyers, Georgia; *m.* (secondly) 16th October, 1864, Hiram HENSLEE, of Conyers, Georgia.
2. John Archibald Bellah STEWART, *b.* 2d December, 1840; *d.* 2d June, 1891, at Covington, Georgia; *m.* 4th April, 1867, at Atlanta, Georgia, Kitty Tennessee KING, dau. of Joseph KING.

ISSUE

1^1. J. King STEWART, *m.* Corinne BICKEL.
2^1. Eudox STEWART, *d.* young.
3^1. Julian Ann Hollingsworth STEWART, *m.* Rev. Jasper Keith SMITH, of Shreveport, Louisiana.
4^1. Mary STEWART, *m.* Beverly WALL.

3. Julia Crawford STEWART, *b.* 17th February, 1843; *d.* 12th November, 1887, at Birmingham, Alabama; *m.* 29th August, 1867, at Conyers, Georgia, Robert ETHERIDGE; issue, three sons and two daughters.
4. Joseph Alexander STEWART, of Covington, Georgia; *b.* 17th October, 1845, at Ebenezer, Georgia; *d.* 31st July, 1890, at Covington, Georgia; *m.* 30th January, 1873, in Newborn, Georgia, Carrie Julia ROBINSON, *b.* 19th February, 1852, living in 1918, dau. of James Hardwick and Martha (WEBB) ROBINSON.

ISSUE

1^1. James Hardwick Robinson STEWART, not married.
2^1. Joseph Adger STEWART, *m.* Anna Briggs CARTER.
3^1. Estelle STEWART, *m.* George Kearsley SELDEN.
4^1. Mary Daisy STEWART, *m.* Walter F. ROBERTS.
5^1. Emma Lucille STEWART, *d.* young.
6^1. Ann Eloise STEWART, *m.* James P. CHAMPION.
7^1. Francis Josephine STEWART, *m.* Dr. Hugh I. BATTEY.
8^1. Anita STEWART, *m.* R. Blair ARMSTRONG.

5. Frances Malinda STEWART, *b.* 23d December, 1847; living, 1918, Conyers, Georgia; *m.* 30th June, 1875, George W. GLEATON.

ISSUE

1¹. John S. GLEATON.
2¹. Stephen GLEATON.
3¹. Lucy GLEATON.
4¹. Sallie Fanny GLEATON.

6. Mary Matilda Stansell STEWART, *b.* 27th April, 1856, at Conyers, Georgia; *d.* 30th April, 1895, at Decatur, Georgia; *m.* 23d July, 1868, Walter Eudox McCALLA; no issue.
7. Martha Antoinette STEWART, *b.* 10th January, 1853; *d.* 12th June, 1863.
8. Thomas Dilworth STEWART, *b.* 7th April, 1856; living, 1918, at Atlanta, Georgia; *m.* there 15th October, 1879, Ida J. KISER.

ISSUE

1¹. Nellie Kiser STEWART, *m.* H. E. DEAN.
2¹. Mary Cliff STEWART, *d.* young.

9. Jackson Benjamin Levi STEWART, *b.* 27th August, 1858; *d.* 28th April, 1881; unmarried.
10. Jefferson Davis STEWART, of Louisville, Kentucky, *b.* 14th June, 1868, at Conyers, Georgia; President, Union National Bank, Louisville, Kentucky; *m.* 1st June, 1899, at Louisville, Kentucky, Abby Churchill BALLARD, dau. of Charles Thruston and Mina Breaux BALLARD, of Louisville, Kentucky.

ISSUE

1¹. Abby Ballard STEWART.
2¹. Jefferson Davis STEWART.

III. Letitia, *b.* Laurens County, South Carolina, 1820; moved to Georgia in 1825; *d.* in Coosa County, Alabama; *m.* Benjamin STEWART.
IV. Levi, *b.* Laurens, South Carolina, 1820; *d.* 23d May, 1899, on Chattahoochee River, in Heard County, Georgia; *m.* 19th December, 1844, Betsey ECHOLS.
V. Roseannah, *b.* 7th June, 1825, in Laurens County, South Carolina, 1st December, 1907, at Powder Springs, Georgia; *m.* William SCOTT.
VI. Sarah, "a beauty," *b.* 10th March, 1828, in DeKalb County, Georgia; *d.* 10th April, 1852, at Macon, Georgia; *m.* (firstly), 24th July, 1845, in Griffin, Georgia, John McDONALD; *m.* (secondly) Dr. Joshua CHERRY, of Macon, Georgia.

VII. Lizzie, *b.* 15th August, 1833, in Georgia; *m.* 20th September, 1853, WILLIAM W. WALCOTT.
VIII. Jane, *b.* 11th August, 1837, in Newton County, Georgia; *d.* 23d December, 1909, in Heard County, Georgia; *m.* Edward MOSELEY, of Heard County, Georgia.
IX. JOSEPH A., *b.* 2d July, 1835, of whom below.

JOSEPH A. HOLLINGSWORTH, of Atlanta, Georgia; *b.* 2d July, 1835, in Newton County, Georgia; *d.* 5th July, 1903 in Ensley, Alabama; *m.* 10th January, 1861, Lucy H. MOSELEY of Heard County, Georgia.

ISSUE

I. Mary Elizabeth, *b.* 4th May, 1864; *m.* 1884, W. B. BRADBURY, 66 Arkwright Place, Atlanta, Georgia.
II. William Henry, Birmingham, Alabama; *b.* 5th December, 1867; *m.* Darthalow GRIGGS.
III. Joseph, *b.* 31st August, 1870; *d.* 5th April, 1888; unmarried.
IV. JAMES EDWIN, *b.* 1st December, 1872, the subject of this memoir.
V. Julian, *b.* 29th August, 1883.
VI. Robert Emmett, *b.* 1st September, 1877; *d.* at six months of age.
VII. Charles Armstrong, *b.* 29th February, 1881; *d.* 8th July, 1883.

Arms.—Azure, on a bend argent, three holly leaves, slipped vert.
Crest.—A Stag lodged, ppr.
Motto.—Disce Ferenda Pati.
Residence.—328 North McNeill Street, Memphis, Tennessee.
Societies.—Memphis Chamber of Commerce, Masons, Elks.
Clubs.—Kawannas of Memphis.

Holloway

LIEUTENANT CHARLES THOMAS HOLLOWAY, II, of Baltimore, Maryland; United States Marine Flying Corps; *b.* 22d March, 1897; *m.* 20th June, 1918, Frances Allon FULLER, *b.* 11th February, 1897, dau. of James Edward FULLER, Jr., *b.* 28th October, 1865, in Athol, Massachusetts, *m.* 18th April, 1895, Maude Louise KNOWLTON, *b.* 3d March, 1872, in Worcester, Massachusetts, dau. of Frank Allan KNOWLTON, *b.* 7th June, 1849, in Shrewsbury, Massachusetts, *m.* Lucy Jane STRATTON. *b.* 25th September, 1853, in Worcester, Massachusetts; James Edward Fuller, Jr., was the son of James Edward FULLER, Sr., *b.* 8th October, 1836, in Warwick, Massachusetts, *d.* August, 1901, *m.* Clara Delia GOULD, *b.* 7th June, 1835, in Warwick. The immigrant ancestors of James Edward FULLER were Samuel and Edward FULLER who came in the *Mayflower*, 1620.

LIEUTENANT CHARLES THOMAS HOLLOWAY, II, received his education at Gilman School and Marstons, is a member of the United States Marine Flying Corps, First Squadron, First Marine Aviation Force, A. E. F., and was for a time instructor in acrobatic flying at Marine Flying Field, Miami, Florida; formerly United States Army Aviator instructor at Gerstner Field, Lake Charles, Louisiana.

ISSUE

1. Charles Thomas, III, *b.* 26th January, 1920.

Lineage

The first of the family we have knowledge of in America is Abraham HOLLOWAY, of Virginia. He was probably a member of the Society of Friends; *m.* Rachel (surname unknown), in Virginia.

ISSUE

1. ROBERT, of whom below.

ROBERT HOLLOWAY, of Fredericksburg, Virginia; *b.* 1786; *d.* 20th July, 1863; *m.* May, 1820, Eleanor Humphrey BOWEN, *b.* 6th January, 1793; *d.* 3d November, 1875; she dau. of Capt. Sabrite BOWEN, *b.* 10th December, 1758; *d.* 1811, who served from 1776 to 1783 in Flying Camp, Maryland, *m.* 4th January, 1792, Elizabeth HUMPHREY, *b.* in Gwynedd, Pennsylvania, 13th March, 1761, *d.* in Baltimore, Maryland, 29th April, 1847.

ISSUE

1. Catherine, *d.* 3d May, 1821.
2. William Henry, *b.* 18th February, 1823; *d.* 6th July, 1824.
3. John Merriman, *b.* 25th July, 1824; *m.* Fanny BAYLEY, dau. of William and Mary Ann BAYLEY.
4. Edward, *b.* 28th February, 1826; *d.* 20th July, 1866.
5. CHARLES THOMAS, *b.* 25th December, 1827, of whom later.
6. Mary Jane, *b.* 29th December, 1829.
7. Alexander, *b.* 25th December, 1831; *d.* 17th May, 1916.
8. Ellen Maria, *b.* 25th August, 1835; *m.* 22d June, 1875, Hugh W. BOLTON.
9. Eleanor, *m.* 3d August, 1843, James A. HOOPER.

CHARLES THOMAS HOLLOWAY, of Baltimore, Maryland; *b.* 25th December, 1827; *d.* 17th March, 1898; member of Maryland Society, Sons of the American Revolution at and one time its Vice-President; member of the Veteran Firemen Association and War of 1812; *m.* 12th October, 1854, Anne Harden Ross, *b.* 31st January, 1830, *d.* 31st January, 1909, dau. of Reuben and Sarah (name not given) Ross.

ISSUE

1. REUBEN ROSS, *b.* 13th June, 1855, of whom later.
2. Grace, *b.* 5th October, 1859; *d.* 10th January, 1911; *m.* 7th June, 1900, William J. SHURE, of Harford County, Maryland.

ISSUE

1. Daniel Ferree SHURE, *b.* 20th May, 1902.

REUBEN ROSS HOLLOWAY, of Baltimore, Maryland; *b.* 13th June, 1855; *d.* 13th December; 1908; member of Society 1812; Treasurer of Maryland Society, Sons of American Revolution; Knights Templar; *m.* 28th January, 1892, Ella Virginia HOUCK, *b.* 3d September, 1862, dau. of Jacob Wever HOUCK, *b.* 2d July, 1822, *d.* 22d May, 1888, *m.* 15th November, 1852, Susannah Frances PORTER. *b.* 27th September, 1832, *d.* 24th May, 1911. Ella Virginia (HOUCK) HOLLOWAY is Maryland State President, Daughters of 1812; Member Board of Managers, Francis Scott Key Chapter, Daughters of the American Revolution; Member Board of Managers, Children of the American Revolution; State Chairman Committee on Desecration of the American Flag, 1916–1920.

ISSUE

1. Virginia Leslie, *b.* 18th November, 1892; *m.* 26th April, 1913, Ernest Smith JEFFERIES, of Hamilton, Ontario, *b.* 18th July, 1887, son of Ebenezer Arthur William JEFFERIES, *b.* 23d February, 1862, at Malmsbury,

Wiltshire, England, *m.* in New York City, 14th September, 1883, Amelia M. SMITH, *b.* 13th September, 1863, at Gloucester, England, the son of John JEFFERIES, *b.* circa 1830, *m.* Sarah GREY; birth at Malmesbury, Wiltshire, England; removed to Gloucester, England, about 1864.

ISSUE

1. Ernest Smith JEFFERIES, Jr., *b.* 22d April, 1914.
2. Virginia Lovelace JEFFERIES, *b.* 16th July, 1916, in Canada.

II. CHARLES THOMAS, II, *b.* 22d March, 1897, the subject of this memoir.

Arms.—Gules, a fesse between three crescents argent.
Crest.—Out of a mural coronet argent, a lion's head or charged with a torteau.
Motto.—Toujours pret.
Residence.—Normandie Heights, Baltimore, Maryland.
Clubs.—Aero Club of America, Baltimore Country Club.
Societies.—Colonial Wars, Sons of the American Revolution, War of 1812, Maryland Historical, Thirty-second degree Scottish Rite Mason.

Foulke

See Foulke genealogical table for line back to Glonyio Glad Lydan: "King and Founder of the City of Caer Loreyon or Gloucester, England, A.D. 325." Published by Loughhead and Company, 919–921 Walnut Street, Philadelphia, 1898.

"I, Edward Foulke, was the son of Foulke ap Thomas, ap Evan, ap Thomas, ap Robert, ap David Lloyd, ap Evan Vaughan, ap Griffith, ap Madoc, ap Jerwerth, ap Madog, ap Ririd Flaidd, Lord of Penllyn, who dwelt at Rhiwaedog." My mother's name was Lowry, the daughter of Edward ap David, ap Ellis, ap Robert, of the parish of Llavor in Merionethshire, "I was born on the 13th of the 5th month, 1651, and when arrived at mature age, married Eleanor, daughter of Hugh ap Cadwalader, ap Rhys, of the Parish of Spytu, in Denbighshire; her mother's name was Gwen, the daughter of Ellis ap William, ap Hugh, ap Thomas, ap David, ap Madoc, ap Evan, ap Cott, ap Evan, ap Griffith, ap Madoc, ap Einion, ap Meredith, of Cai-Fa-dog; and was born in the same parish and shire with her husband.

"I had, by my said wife, nine children, whose names are as follows: Thomas, Hugh, Cadwalader and Evan; Grace, Gwen, Jane, Catherine and Margaret. We lived at a place called Coed-y-foel, a beautiful farm belonging to Roger Price, Esq. of Rhiwlas, Merionethshire, aforesaid. But in process of time, I had an inclination to remove with my family to the Province of Pensilvania; and in order thereto, we set out on the 3d day of the 2d month, A.D. 1698, and came in two days to Liverpool, where, with divers others who intended to go on the voyage, we took shipping the 17th of the same month on board the *Robert and Elizabeth*, and the next day set sail for Ireland, where we arrived and stayed until the first of the third month, May, and then sailed again for Pennsylvania, and were about eleven weeks at sea.

And the sore distemper of the bloody flux broke out in the vessel, of which died in our passage, five and forty persons. The distemper was so mortal that two or three corpses were cast overboard every day while it lasted. "But through the favor and Mercy of Divine Providence, I with my wife and nine children escaped that sore mortality, and arrived safe in Philadelphia, the 17th of the 5th month, July, where we were kindly received and hospitably entertained by our friends and old acquaintance.

"I soon purchased a fine tract of land of about seven hundred acres, sixteen miles from Philadelphia, on a part of which I settled, and divers others of our company who came over the sea with us, settled near me at the same time. This was the beginning of November, 1698, aforesaid, and the township was called Gwynedd, or North Wales. This account was written the 14th of the 11th month, January, A.D. 1702, by Edward Foulke." "Translated from the British into English by Samuel Foulke."

EDWARD FOULKE the emigrant, *b.* in Wales, 13th May, 1664; *d.* in Pennsylvania, 8th November, 1741; resided at Coldy foel, Rhiwlas, Merionshire; he left there for Liverpool, 3d February, 1698, and sailed thence with his wife and nine children, on the 17th of the same month, in the ship *Robert and Elizabeth*, Ralph WILLIAMS, Master. They arrived at Philadelphia 17th May, 1698, at Gwynedd, Pennsylvania, where he purchased 712 acres; *m.* Eleanor of the parish of Spytn, Denbigshire, she *d.* in Gwynedd, Pennsylvania, 16th January, 1733, was dau. of Hugh AP CADWALLADER AP RHYS.

ISSUE

I. Thomas, *b.* 7th August, 1685, in Merionshire, Wales; *d.* 1762; *m.* 27th June, 1706, at Gwynedd Meeting House, Gwen EVANS, eldest dau. of David EVANS of Radnor, Pennsylvania.
II. Hugh, *b.* 1685.
III. Cadwalader, *b.* 1691.
IV. Evan.
V. Gwen.
VI. Grace.
VII. Jane, *b.* in Wales, 10th January, 1683–1684.
VIII. Catherine.
IX. MARGARET, of whom below.

MARGARET FOULKE, *b.* in Wales, *d.* 23d March, 1717; *m.* Nicholas ROBERTS, son of Robert CADWALADER, of Gwynedd.

ISSUE

I. Jane ROBERTS.
II. Eleanor ROBERTS.
III. ELIZABETH ROBERTS, *b.* 11th June, 1723, of whom below.

ELIZABETH ROBERTS of Gwynedd, Pennsylvania; *b.* 11th June, 1723; *d.* 29th May, 1790; *m.* 12th February, 1743, David HUMPHREY of Gwynedd, Pennsylvania, son of Robert and Margeret (EVANS) HUMPHREY.

ISSUE

ELIZABETH HUMPHREY, *b.* 13th March, 1761, in Gwynedd, Pennsylvania; *d.* in Baltimore, Maryland, 29th April, 1847; *m.* January, 1792, Capt. Sabrett BOWEN, of the Continental Line.

ISSUE

ELEANOR HUMPHREY BOWEN, *b.* January, 1792; *d.* 2d November, 1874; *m.* 1820, Robert HOLLOWAY of Virginia, *b.* 1786, *d.* 7th July, 1863, son of Abraham and Rachel HOLLOWAY of Virginia.

ISSUE

I. CHARLES THOMAS, *b.* 25th December, 1827, of whom later.

CHARLES THOMAS HOLLOWAY, of Baltimore, Maryland; *b.* 25th December, 1827; *d.* 17th March, 1898; *m.* 12th October, 1854, Anna Harden Ross, *b.* 31st January, 1830, *d.* 31st January, 1909, dau. of Reuben and Sarah Ross (probably Alexander Ross who went to Virginia with a colony of Friends and purchased 100,000 acres of land for their settlement).

ISSUE

I. REUBEN ROSS, *b.* 13th June, 1855, of whom later.

REUBEN ROSS HOLLOWAY, of Baltimore, Maryland; *b.* 13th June, 1855; *d.* 13th December, 1908; member of Sons of the American Revolution, Society of War of 1812; *m.* 28th January, 1892, Ella Virginia HOUCK, *b.* 3d September, 1862, dau. of Dr. Jacob Wever HOUCK, Health Commissioner of Baltimore City, and Susannah Frances PORTER, both of Baltimore. Dr. HOUCK was the son of Dr. Jacob HOUCK of New Market, Maryland, who gave the half acre of ground on which the North Point Monument is erected, commemorating and marking the spot where the Battle of North Point was fought 12th September, 1812.

ISSUE

I. Virginia Leslie, *b.* 18th November, 1892; *m.* 26th April, 1913, Ernest Smith JEFFERIES, *b.* 18th July, 1887, of Hamilton, Ontario, Canada.

ISSUE

1. Ernest Smith JEFFERIES, Jr., *b.* 2d April, 1914.
2. Virginia Lovelace JEFFRIES, *b.* 16th July, 1916.
3. Eleanor Gorsuch JEFFRIES, *b.* 19th, 1920.

II. CHARLES THOMAS, II; *b.* 22d March, 1897, the subject of this memoir.

Arms (Foulke).—Vert, between a chevron argent, three dragon's heads erased argent, langued gules.
Crest.—A dragon's head erased argent, langued gules.
Motto.—Blaidd rhudd ar y blaen.

Lovelace

RICHARD LOVELACE, of Queenhite, London, England, purchased Bayfuce; his son
LAUNCELOT LOVELACE, of Bayluce in Sittingburne, possessed the Manor of Hever in Kingsdown; *m.* the only dau. and heiress of Eyneham; his son
WILLIAM LOVELACE, I, of Bayfuce, *m.* Lova, dau. of Peckham; his son,
WILLIAM LOVELACE, II; had a son
WILLIAM LOVELACE, III, Sergeant at Law; *m.* a dau. of Lewis, alderman of Canterbury; his son
SIR WILLIAM LOVELACE, IV, of Berchenden, Kent, afterwards of Grey Friars; Knighted, 30th June, 1599, by Robert, Earl of Sussex, Lord Lieutenant of Ireland; *m.* Elizabeth AUCHER, thirty-five generations in lineal descent from CHARLEMAGNE and HILDEGARDE, the dau. of CHILDEBRAND; Saubia, his son
SIR WILLIAM LOVELACE, of Kent; *b.* 1583; *d.* 1628; *m.* Anne BARNES, dau. of Sir William BARNES of Woolwick, Kent; his dau.
ANNE LOVELACE, *m.* Rev. John GORSUCH, son of Danyell GORSUCH, Alderman's Deputy, Bishop's Gate Ward, 1633, who *m.* Alice HALL, dau. of John HALL, of Lind. Danyell GORSUCH was a son of WILLIAM GORSUCH descended out of Lancashire from Gorsuch of Ormschurch, who *m.* Alice HILLSON; their dau.
ANN GORSUCH, of Baltimore County, Maryland, *m.* (firstly) Thomas TODD, I, of Toddesburg, Ware Parish, Gloucester County, Virginia, who came to Baltimore County, Maryland, and settled there in 1664. He came originally from England in 1637; was a member of the Maryland Assembly 1674–1675; he died while on a voyage to England and was buried at sea; his will was dated 26th February, 1675, and probated 30th May, 1677. Ann Gorsuch TODD *m.* (secondly) 16th January, 1678, David JONES.

ISSUE BY FIRST MARRIAGE

I. THOMAS, II, *b.* 1660, of whom later.
II. Christopher.
III. James.
IV. William.
V. Philip.
VI. Joanna.
VII. Anna.
VIII. Frances.
IX. Averilla.

CAPTAIN TODD, II of Baltimore County, Maryland; *b.* at Toddsburg, Wake Parish, Gloucester County, Virginia; came to Maryland, with his parents in 1664; *d.* 16th January, 1725, in Baltimore County; epitaph at Toddsburg reads: "Here lyes the body of Captain Thomas TODD who was born in the year of Our Lord 1660 and departed this life on the 16th day of January 1725." He *m.* Elizabeth (surname not given).

ISSUE

I. THOMAS, III, *d.* 1715, of whom later.
II. Annie, *b.* in the Parish of Ware, 9th November, 1682; *d.* 18th July, 1720; *m.* John COOKE of Wareham, Gloucester County, Virginia.
III. Christopher, of Toddsburg, *b.* 2d April, 1690; *d.* 26th March, 1743; *m.* Elizabeth (surname not given), *b.* 25th April, 1701, *d.* November, 1764.
IV. Frances, *b.* 1692; *d.* 1703.
V. Richard, *m.* (wife's name not given).
VI. William of King and Queen County, Virginia; will dated 1731; *m.* Martha VICUNES.
VII. Philip, *d.s.p.*; Sheriff of Gloucester County, Virginia, 1730.
VIII. Frances (again), *b.* 1710; *d.* 25th July, 1745; *m.* 2d July, 1729, Robert NORTH, of Baltimore County, Maryland.

THOMAS TODD, III, of Baltimore County, Maryland; *d.* 1715; will dated 11th January, 1715; proven in Baltimore, 11th June, 1715; he styles himself as "Thomas TODD the younger;" *m.* Elizabeth (surname not given).

ISSUE

I. THOMAS IV, *d.* 1739, of whom later.
II. Robert of "Showan," Baltimore County, Maryland.

THOMAS TODD, IV, of "Todd's Neck," Baltimore County, Maryland; will dated 9th December, 1736; probated 2d April, 1739; was appointed a Commissioner for laying out a town of ten acres with twenty lots valued at 150 pounds of tobacco each; the town was first called Jones, then Jones Town later Baltimore, which today is the present metropolis of the South; *m.* Eleanor Dorsey; she *m.* (secondly) William Lynch; her will was probated 1760; dau. of Caleb Dorsey, son of Hon. John and Ellen or Elinor (Warfield) Dorsey, she dau. of Richard Warfield, the immigrant.

ISSUE

    I. Thomas, V, *d.* 1798, of whom later.
   II. Elizabeth, *m.* John Cromwell.
  III. Eleanor, *m.* John Ensor.
  IV. Frances, *m.* 1757, George Risteau.
   V. Mary, *m.* John Worthington.

Thomas Todd, V, of Baltimore County, Maryland, *d.* 1798.

ISSUE

    I. William, *d.* 1813.
   II. Christopher, *d.* 1849; *m.* (wife's name not given).
  III. Bernard, *d.* 1816, of whom later.
  IV. George W., *d.* 1808; *m.* (wife's name not given).
   V. Thomas.

Bernard Todd of Baltimore County, Maryland; *m.* Mary Greene.

ISSUE

    I. Thomas J., *m.* Mary Trotten.
   II. George W.
  III. Nathan.
  IV. Richard.
   V. Elizabeth Frances, *b.* 29th January, 1809, of whom later.
  VI. Sarah Ann, *m.* (firstly) John Diffenderfer; *m.* (secondly) Thomas Trotten.

Elizabeth Frances Todd, of Todd's Inheritance; *b.* 29th January, 1809; *d.* July, 1860; *m.* James Porter, *d.* 30th September, 1843, son of Robert Porter *b.* 1757, *d.* 16th March, 1810, was First Lieutenant 3d Maryland Regiment, commissioned 20th February 1777, resigned April, 1777, *m.* Susannah Buck, they lived at Back River Neck at Porter's Bar.

ISSUE

    I. Mary George Porter.
   II. Susannah Frances Porter, *b.* 25th September, 1832, of whom later.
  III. John Mercer Porter.
  IV. Robert Porter.
   V. ―――― Porter.

SUSANNAH FRANCES PORTER, *b.* 26th September, 1832; *d.* 24th May, 1911; *m.* 15th November, 1852, Jacob Wever HOUCK, M.D., *b.* 2d July, 1822, *d.* 22d May, 1888.

ISSUE

I. Renthrope HOUCK.
II. Mary George HOUCK.
III. Bettie Trisler HOUCK, *m.* William Fletcher PENTZ.

ISSUE

1. Trisler Simmons PENTZ.
2. William Fletcher PENTZ.

IV. Jacob Adae HOUCK, *b.* 25th April, 1860.
V. Ella Virginia HOUCK, *b.* 30th September, 1862, of whom later.
VI. John Mercer Porter HOUCK.
VII. Caroline Somerville HOUCK.
VIII. Sudie Frances HOUCK, *b.* 27th March, 1870; *m.* Alfred Cookman THOMPSON of Maryland.

ISSUE

1. Raymond Webb THOMPSON.

IX. Hazeltine Howard HOUCK, *b.* 4th April, 1872; *d.* 29th November, 1917; *m.* Rose Burmingham, *b.* 4th July, 1873.

ISSUE

1. Howard Hawkens, *b.* 16th November, 1916.

ELLA VIRGINIA HOUCK, *b.* 3d September, 1862, *m.* 28th January, 1892, Reuben Ross HOLLOWAY of Baltimore, Maryland, *b.* 13th June, 1855, *d.* 13th December, 1908.

ISSUE

I. Virginia Leslie, *b.* 18th November, 1892, *m.* 26th April, 1913, Ernest Smith JEFFERIES.
II. CHARLES THOMAS, *b.* 22d March, 1897, the subject of this memoir.

Huger

WILLIAM ELLIOTT HUGER, of Charleston, South Carolina; *b.* 28th November, 1874.

Lineage

DANIEL HUGER, *b.* at Loundun, Tureene, France, 1st April, 1651; *d.* 24th December, 1711; son of John HUGER, a Huguenot, who was a Royal Notary at Loundun, emigrated to America, 1685; settled at Santee, Craven County, South Carolina; *m.* May, 1677, Margaret PERDRIAU, *d.* 1717, dau. of Orei PERDRIAU, silk merchant, of La Rochelle, France.

ISSUE

I. Margaret, *b.* at La Rochelle, 21st February, 1678; *m.* 17th August, 1704, Elias HORRY, of South Carolina, and had issue.
II. Magdalen, *d.* young.
III. DANIEL, *b.* 16th March, 1688, of whom below.

DANIEL HUGER, of Santee, Craven County, South Carolina; *b.* at Santee, 16th March, 1688; *d.* 8th December, 1754; *m.* (firstly) 25th January, 1710, Elizabeth GENDRON, who *d.s.p.* 23d May, 1740, dau. of Philip GENDRON; *m.* (secondly) 14th May, 1741, Mary CORDES, *d.* 30th December, 1746, dau. of Isaac CORDES; *m.* (thirdly) 4th December, 1747, Lydia JOHNSON, who *d.* 4th September, 1748, dau. of Robert JOHNSON; *m.* (fourthly) 19th October, 1749, Ann LE JAN, who *d.* 6th December, 1754, dau. of Col. Francis LE JAN.

ISSUE BY SECOND MARRIAGE

I. DANIEL, *b.* 20th February, 1742, of whom later.
II. Isaac, *b.* 19th March, 1743; *d.* 17th October, 1797; Brigadier-General in the Revolutionary Army; *m.* 23d March, 1762, Elizabeth CHALMERS; left issue.
III. John, *b.* 5th June, 1744; *d.* 22d January, 1804, Secretary of South Carolina; *m.* (firstly) Charlotte MOTTE; *m.* (secondly) Ann (BROWN) CUSAK, dau. of ——— BROWN, and widow of ——— CUSAK.
IV. Benjamin, *b.* 30th December, 1746; *d.* 11th May, 1779; Major in the Revolutionary Army; Member of the House of Assembly and Provincial Congress; *m.* (firstly) ——— GOLIGHTLY; *m.* (secondly) Mary KINLOCH; had issue.

ISSUE BY FOURTH MARRIAGE

I. Francis, *b.* 19th June, 1751; *d.* 18th August, 1811; Colonel in the Revolutionary Army; left issue.
II. Paul, *b.* 27th August, 1752; *d.s.p.*
III. Margaret, *b.* 23d August, 1754; *d.* in infancy.

DANIEL HUGER, of South Carolina; *b.* at the Limerick Plantation, Cooper River, South Carolina, 20th February, 1742; *d.* 6th July, 1799; Member of United States Congress, 1786-1793; *m.* Sabina ELLIOTT.

ISSUE

I. DANIEL ELLIOTT, *b.* 28th June, 1779, of whom later.
II. Sarah Elliott, *d.* unmarried at New York.
III. Ann Elliott, *m.* Edward LAIGHT, of New York; had issue.
IV. Sabina Elliott, *m.* John WELLS, of New York; had issue.

DANIEL ELLIOTT HUGER, of South Carolina, *b.* 28th June, 1779; *d.* 21st August, 1854; graduated at Princeton, 1798; Member of United States Congress, 1815-1819; Judge, South Carolina 1819; United States Senator, 1842-1845; *m.* 26th November, 1800, Isabella Johannes MIDDLETON, who *d.* 25th August, 1865, dau. of Arthur MIDDLETON, one of the signatories of the Declaration of Independence.

ISSUE

I. Mary Middleton, *b.* 1802; *d.* 1831; *m.* Joseph MANIGAULT; left issue.
II. William Elliott, *d.* unmarried.
III. DANIEL ELLIOTT, of whom later.
IV. John Middleton, *m.* Allen DEAS; had issue.
V. Joseph Alston, M.D., *m.* Mary ESTHER, dau. of Francis Kinloch HUGER; had issue.
VI. Arthur Middleton, *m.* Margaret Campbell KING, dau. of Hon. Mitchell KING; had issue.
VII. Emma Middleton, *m.* Allen Smith IZARD, *d.s.p.*
VIII. Sabina Elliott, *b.* 1811; *d.* 15th June, 1874; *m.* Charles Tidyman LOWNDES; had issue.
IX. Sarah Elliott, *m.* James W. WILKINSON; had issue.
X. Eliza Caroline Middleton, *m.* William Mason SMITH; had issue.

DANIEL ELLIOTT HUGER, of Charleston, South Carolina; *m.* Caroline PROCTOR.

ISSUE

I. Daniel Elliott, Captain in the Confederate States Army; killed in action 20th September, 1863.

II. Stephen Proctor, of the Confederate States Army; *d.s.p.* 25th January, 1862.
III. WILLIAM ELLIOTT, of whom later.
IV. Joseph Proctor, b. 1846, of the Confederate States Army; killed in action at Fort Sumpter, 13th April, 1864,
V. Richard Proctor.
VI. Mary, *m.* Gen. Arthur Middleton MANIGAULT, of the Confederate States Army; had issue.
VII. Caroline Proctor.
VIII. Isabella Middleton.

WILLIAM ELLIOTT HUGER, *m.* Elizabeth SMITH, dau. of John Julius Pringle SMITH.

ISSUE

I. Daniel Elliott.
II. WILLIAM ELLIOTT, the subject of this memoir.
III. Elizabeth.
IV. Caroline Proctor, b. 26th April, 1876; d. in infancy.

Residence.—34 Meeting Street, Charleston, South Carolina.
Arms.—Argent, a human heart emitting flame, between two laurel branches fructed saltirewise in chief, and an anchor erect in base, all proper, accompanied by as many flaunches azure, each charged with a fleur-de-lis or.
Crest.—On a wreath of the colours, a Virginia nightingale perched on a sprig proper.

Huntington

HENRY EDWARDS HUNTINGTON, of New York City, and San Marino, California; *b.* 27th February, 1850, in Oneonta, New York; *m.* (firstly) 1873, at Newark, New Jersey, Mary Alice PRENTICE; *m.* (secondly) in Paris, France, 16th July, 1913, Mrs. Arabella (DUVAL) HUNTINGTON.

ISSUE BY FIRST MARRIAGE

I. Howard Edward, *b.* 11th February, 1876, *m.* Leslie GREEN.
II. CLARA LEONORA, *b.* 2d February, 1878; *m.* Gilbert B. PERKINS, of New York.
III. Elizabeth Vincent, *b.* 8th February, 1880; *m.* John B. METCALF, of Berkeley, California.
IV. Marian PRENTICE, *b.* 3d October, 1883; unmarried.

HENRY EDWARDS HUNTINGTON began business life in the hardware business in Oneonta and later in New York City; was in the lumber business at St. Albans, West Virginia, 1874–1880; Superintendent of Construction Chesapeake Ohio and South western Railway, 1880–1884; Superintendent 1884, Receiver 1885; Vice President and General Manager 1886–1890, of the Kentucky Central Railway; Vice President and General Manager Elizabethtown, Lexington and Big Sandy and Ohio Valley Railways, 1890–1892; First Assistant to President Southern Pacific Company, 1892–1900, appointed Second Vice President March 1900, later First Vice President; President Southern Pacific Company Railways of Arizona and New Mexico, Carson and Colorado Railway, Market Street Cable Railway, San Francisco. At one time Mr. HUNTINGTON was in the directorate of fifty corporations from many of which he has resigned. He is now Chairman of Board the Chesapeake and Ohio Railway; the Columbus, Hocking Valley and Toledo Railway Company; Newport News (Virginia) Shipbuilding and Dry Dock Company; Safety Insulated Wire and Cable Company (New York); Director and Member Executive Committee Iowa Central Railway Company; Director and President Huntington Land and Improvement Company (California); Los Angeles Land Company; Los Angeles Railway Corporation; Los Angeles Railway Company; Oak Knoll Company; Director Chesapeake and Ohio Railway Company; Covina City Water Company; City Railway Company of Los Angeles; Des Moines and Fort Dodge Railway Company; Dodgeville (California) Land Company; Donner Boom and Lumber Company; Equitable Trust Company (New York); Hammond Lumber Company (California); Hocking Valley Railway Company; Kanawha (Virginia) Bridge and Terminal Company; Minneapolis and St. Louis Railroad Company; Newport News Light and Water Company; Old Dominion Land Company (Virginia); Pacific Light and Power Corporation (California); Redondo (California) Improvement Company; Southern Pacific Company; San Marino (California) Land Company; Wells, Fargo and Company; White Sulphur Springs Company.

In 1910 he retired from active business life and thenceforth devoted himself to the collection of a great library. His method, unlike that of most collectors, was to absorb entire collections. Thus he became possessed of many duplicates, which he later disposed of, retaining single copies. Today his library is famous and known as the greatest private collection of English literature and Americana in the world, containing some priceless tomes exceeding in rareness and value those in the British Museum and the Bodleian. Nearly all are first editions, of some of which there are only one or two in existence. Among the exceedingly rare Americana are included the "Hystorie of Virginia, New England and the Summer Isles, with the names of Planters and Governours from their first beginning" (1626), "The Book of Colonial Laws," the Diary and Autobiography of Benjamin Franklin, considered in value next to the Declaration of Independence. He has the first book ever printed in the English language: "The Recuyell of the Historyes of Troye" (1474); the first book in which color printing on wooden blocks was used, viz: "The Boke of St. Albans" (1486); the first book printed in the English Colonies of North America, "The Bay Psalm Book" (1640); the most famous manuscript of English literature, Chaucer's "Canterbury Tales" (1420) and perhaps the most valuable volume in the world, Shakespeare's Plays including the priceless Hamlet (1603). The collection of Shakespeare quartos and folios is the finest in the world. Included in the 400 Incunabula, or books printed before 1501, there are twenty-five Caxtons. There are the original editions of the letters of Columbus announcing the discovery of the New World (1493); the world-famous Guttenberg Bible, the first book, printed from movable type, for which the largest price ever paid for a single book was given. The collection has been made by the acquisition in toto of many celebrated libraries like the Church, Benedict, Beverly Chew, Stow, Halsey, etc., and the most important portions of the Duke of Devonshire, Britwell, Bridgewater, Hoe, Huth, Poor, and other libraries.

Lineage

This distinguished American family dates its origin from the Puritan, Simon HUNTINGTON, *b.* in England, who with his wife Margaret and children, *b.* in England, emigrated to New England in 1633. Simon *d.* of smallpox in 1633, and was buried at sea, though some accounts state he was brought ashore and buried at the mouth of the Connecticut River. He *m.* in England, Margaret BARRETT, dau. of Peter BARRETT, mayor of Norwich, England. The widow and her children settled first at Roxbury, Massachusetts, where she *m.* (secondly) Thomas STOUGHTON, a man of prominence and several times a Deputy to the General Court of Dorchester, Massachusetts, who *d.* 25th March, 1661. We have no record of any children, if any, by her second marriage.

ISSUE

 I. Thomas, *b.* in England, settled in Connecticut; *m.* (firstly) William SWAIN; *m.* (secondly) Hannah CRANE, dau. of Joseph CRANE.
 II. Christopher, *b.* in England; *m.* 7th October, 1652, Ruth ROCKWELL.
 III. SIMON, *b.* in England, 1629, of whom later.
 IV. Ann.

DEACON SIMON HUNTINGTON, of Norwich, Connecticut; *b.* 1629, in England, *d.* 28th June, 1721; settled in Norwich and was a member of Mr. FETCH's Church there; was Deacon until 1696, when his son succeeded him; was a member of the General Assembly in 1674, and had a grant of land in 1686; was townsman in 1690 and 1696; in 1694, he was on a committee to search out and reform the deficiencies in the public records; in 1700 he was on a committee to give deeds and fix titles in dispute or with defective title; *m.* October, 1653, in Saybrook, Connecticut, Sarah CLARK, dau. of Joseph CLARK, of Windsor, Connecticut, who *d.* 1721.

ISSUE

I. Sarah, *b.* August, 1654; *m.* 23d November, 1696, Dr. Solomon TRACY, son of Lieut. Thomas TRACY.
II. Mary, *b.* August, 1657; *m.* ——— FORBES of Preston.
III. Simon, *b.* 6th February, 1659; *m.* 8th October, 1663, Lydia GAGER, dau. of John GAGER; succeeded his father as deacon.
IV. Joseph, *b.* September, 1661; *d.* 29th December, 1747; *m.* 28th October, 1687, Rebecca ADGATE, *d.* 28th November, 1748, dau. of Thomas ADGATE.
V. SAMUEL, *b.* 1st March, 1665, of whom later.
VI. Elizabeth, *b.* 6th October, 1666; *m.* Joseph BACHUS.
VII. Nathaniel, *b.* 10th July, 1672; *d.* young.
VIII. Daniel, *b.* 13th March, 1675–1676; *d.* 13th September, 1741; *m.* (firstly) 31st January, 1705–1706, Abigail BINGHAM; *m.* (secondly) Rachel WOLCOTT.

LIEUTENANT SAMUEL HUNTINGTON, of Lebanon, Connecticut; *b.* 1st March, 1665, in Norwich, Connecticut; *d.* 10th May, 1717, in Lebanon. Removed to Lebanon in 1700. Before his removal, he held many local offices and was constable in 1692. Ten years after his removal to Norwich, the citizens of Lebanon appointed him on a commission to locate a new meeting house about which a dispute had arisen. He was a large land owner in Norwich and Lebanon and for services as a military officer, was entered in the records as Lieutenant. On 3d February, 1687, the town of Norwich granted him a parcel of land at Trading Cove Brook, "by the father's to be laid out by measure, 30 or 40 rods wide, the length of his father's land." He *m.* 29th October, 1686, Mary CLARK, *d.* October, 1743, probably dau. of William CLARK, of Wethersfield. Her name was entered on a list of Lebanon Churches, 1701.

ISSUE

I. Elizabeth, *b.* 24th April, 1688–1689; *d.* 27th December, 1761; *m.* 23d February, 1710, Moses CLARK.
II. Samuel, *b.* 28th August, 1691; *d.* circa 1785; *m.* 4th December, **1722**, Hannah METCALF.

III. Caleb, *b.* 8th February, 1693–1694; *m.* 28th January, 1720, Lydia GRISWOLD.
IV. Mary, *b.* 19th October, 1696; *d.* 30th July, 1717.
V. Rebecca, *b.* February, 1698–1699; *m.* 20th June, 1717, Joseph CLARK.
VI. Sarah, *b.* 22d October, 1701.
VII. JOHN, *b.* 17th May, 1706, of whom later.
VIII. Simon, *b.* 15th August, 1708; *d.* 22d August, 1753; *m.* 15th May, 1735, Sarah (surname not given).

JOHN HUNTINGTON, of Lebanon, Connecticut; *b.* 17th May, 1706; *m.* there circa 1728, Mehitable METCALF, *b.* 26th July, 1706, sister of his brother Samuel's wife.

ISSUE

I. Anna, *b.* 30th June, 1729; *m.* 1752, Charles COLLENS.
II. Elizabeth, *b.* 25th March, 1731; *d.* 1st December, 1736.
III. Eunice, *b.* 25th April, 1733.
IV. John, *b.* 4th May, 1735; *d.* 14th December, 1736.
V. John (again), *b.* 12th March, 1737; *d.* 5th March, 1830; *m.* 22d June, 1769, Lucy METCALF.
VI. JOSEPH, *b.* 6th May, 1739, of whom later.
VII. Israel, *b.* 6th April, 1741.
VIII. Daniel, *b.* 16th March, 1743.
IX. David, *b.* 24th November, 1745; graduated Dartmouth, 1763; A.M., Yale, same year; *m.* 5th November, 1778, Elizabeth FOOTE.
X. Nathaniel, *d.* soon after birth.

JOSEPH HUNTINGTON, of Harwinton, Connecticut; *b.* 6th May, 1739, in Lebanon, Connecticut; *d.* at Harwington, circa, 1820; *m.* Rachel PRESTON, *b.* 1st August, 1740; *d.* 1833; both are buried in the old graveyard of Harwinton.

ISSUE

I. Joseph, *b.* 1780, was a farmer at River Raisin, C. W.
II. WILLIAM, *b.* 1784, of whom later.
III. Lucy, lived and died in Vermont, *m.* Paul BLUZO.
IV. Rachel, *m.* Andrew FRANK of Starkboro, Vermont.
V. Rhoda, *m.* William TYRON, of New Hartford, Connecticut.

WILLIAM HUNTINGTON, of Wolcottville, Connecticut; *b.* 1784; *m.* Elizabeth VINCENT.

ISSUE

I. Mary, *b.* 13th January, 1812; *m.* 2d June, 1840, Daniel SAMMIS of Warsaw, New York.
II. SOLON, *b.* 13th January, 1812, of whom later.

III. Rhoda, *b.* 13th October, 1814; *m.* 10th May, 1834, Riley DUNBAR, of Wolcottville.
IV. Phebe, *b.* 17th September, 1817; *m.* 4th October, 1840, Henry PARDEE, of Oneonta, New York.
V. Elizabeth, *b.* 19th December, 1819; *m.* 5th April, 1842, Hiram YAGER, of Kortwright, New York.
VI. Collis Potter, of Oneonta, New York, and later of San Francisco, *b.* 22d October, 1821, *d.* 13th August, 1900; *m.* 16th September, 1844, Elizabeth STODDARD.
VII. Joseph, *b.* 23d March, 1823; *d.* unmarried 23d February, 1849.
VIII. Susan, *b.* August, 1826; *m.* 16th November, 1849, William PORTER, M.D., of New Haven, Connecticut.
IX. Ellen M., *b.* 12th August, 1835; *m.* Isaac E. GATES, of Orange, New Jersey.

SOLON HUNTINGTON, of Oneonta, New York; *b.* 12th January, 1812; *m.* 2d June, 1840, Harriet SAUNDERS.

ISSUE

I. Leonora, *b.* 7th August, 1841.
II. Howard, *b.* 13th December, 1843.
III. George, *b.* 26th September, 1847; *d.* 6th January, 1852.
IV. HENRY EDWARDS, *b.* 27th February, 1850, the subject of this memoir.
V. Harriet, *b.* 20th October, 1852; *d.* 1st August, 1855.
VI. Willard, *b.* 21st July, 1856.
VII. Caroline Densmore, *b.* 22d January, 1861; *m.* E. Burke HOLLADAY, of San Francisco, California.

Residence.—New York and San Marino, California.
Clubs.—Union League, Metropolitan, City Midday, Grolier, Hobby, Oneonta, Economic of New York; Los Angeles, California, Jonathan, Los Angeles Country, Gamut (Los Angeles), Pasadena Polo, Midwick Country, San Gabriel Valley Country, and Annandale Country of California, Bibliophile of Boston.
Societies.—Colonial Wars.

James

HOWARD KELLOGG JAMES, Attorney at Law, of Alameda, California; *b.* 20th July, 1867, at East Windsor, Connecticut; *m.* 23d March, 1897, Martha MESEROLE, dau. of George Frost MESEROLE.

ISSUE

I. Richard Leavitt JAMES, *b.* 21st April, 1898; enlisted, at the age of seventeen, in the Transport Service of the United States Army, making two trips to the Philippines and Japan; receiving an honorable discharge; he re-enlisted the following year; on his subsequent discharge from that service, he was one of the first to answer the volunteer call, 1917, being then just past nineteen years of age; serving in the Coast Artillery for some months, when he received an honorable discharge for disability and was refused re-enlistment upon that account; member Society of Mayflower Descendants, and Colonial Wars; through the maternal line he descends from the MESEROLE family of Huguenot days.

II. Donald Robertson JAMES, *b.* 6th July, 1905.

HOWARD KELLOGG JAMES, for some years a journalist whose experience brought him in intimate contact with local and city journalism of the United States and the Latin-American countries; night editor of New York dailies; Law writer and extensive traveler throughout the Continent; was admitted to the California bar in 1897, to the United States Courts the following year and is now practicing law in Oakland, California. He has been one of the very active men in the fostering of civic and commercial interests of the San Francisco Bay region; editor of a San Francisco trade journal, published in the interests of commercial associations which he organized; director of a number of California corporations; president of the Snipsic Company, which derives its name from the lake at Rockville, Connecticut, his parental home; and of the Dick and Don Mines which he, for some years, operated in northern Nevada; a Commissioner of the Superior Court of Alameda County; an active member of the Republican party; author; genealogist.

Arms.—Azure, a lion rampant argent, between two castles triple-towered in chief; a scaling-ladder in base, argent. A border or, charged with four roses, proper, and as many spear-heads, alternate, sable.

Crest.—A lion rampant argent, collared, holding between the forepaws a rose gules; the dexter hind-paw resting on an escutcheon argent, charged with a spear-head sable, as in the arms.

COLONIAL FAMILIES OF THE UNITED STATES 319

Motto.—"D'Huw a Digon"—God and Enough.
Residence.—Alameda, California.
Societies.—Mayflower Descendants, Colonial Wars, Sons of the American Revolution.

Lineage

This descent is traced as far back as the seventh century, to Pepin d'Heristal, a ruler of the Franks, before Charlemagne. Passing down to Gundreda, the fourth dau. of William the Conqueror, who *m.* William DE WARREN, who took so important a part in the battle of Hastings that the Conqueror gave him lands in almost every county in England; this WARREN became the first Earl of WARREN.

English Ancestry

I. William De WARREN, first Earl of Warren; *m.* Gundreda, fourth dau. of William the Conqueror; *d.* 1088, their son
II. William De WARREN, second Earl, who *m.* Isabel, dau. of Hugh the Great, Count de VERMANDOIS, and had
III. Reginald De WARREN, who *m.* Adelia, dau. of Roger De MOWBRAY, and had
IV. William De WARREN, who *m.* Isabel, dau. of William De HAYDON, Knight, and had
V. Sir John De WARREN, Knight, who *m.* Alice, dau. of Roger De TOWNSHEND, and had
VI. Sir John De WARREN, Knight, who *m.* Joan, dau. of Sir Hugh De PORT, of Etwall, and had
VII. Sir Edward De WARREN, Knight, who *m.* Maud, dau. of Richard De SKEGETON, and had
VIII. Sir Edward De WARREN, Knight, who *m.* Ciceley, dau. of Sir J. Nicholas De ETON, Knight, and had
IX. Sir John De WARREN, Knight, who *m.* Margaret, dau. of Sir John STAFFORD, and had
X. Sir Lawrence De WARREN, Knight, *b.* circa 1394; *m.* Margery BULKELEY, dau. of Hugh BULKELEY (see Governor Morgan G. BULKELEY of Connecticut), and had
XI. John De WARREN, Esquire, *b.* 1414; *m.* Isabel STANLEY, dau. of Sir John STANLEY, Knight of the Garter and Steward of the Household of King Henry IV; their son, who subsequently succeeded to the title,
XII. Sir Lawrence De WARREN, Knight, *m.* 1458, Isabel LEIGH, dau. of Sir Robert LEIGH, and had
XIII. William De WARREN, of Taunton, who, by his wife, Ann, had
XIV. John De WARREN, of Nottingham, *b.* 1525; who, by his wife Elizabeth, had
XV. John WARREN, of Devon, who had

xvi. Christopher WARREN, who had
xvii. William WARREN; *m.* Anne MABLE, dau. of Thomas MABLE, of Cornwall, and had
xviii. Christopher WARREN; *m.* Alice WEBB, dau. of Thomas WEBB, of Devon, and had

American Ancestry

xix. Richard WARREN, of Greenwich, England, who came to New England in the *Mayflower*, in 1620, and participated in the fight with the Indians at the field of the first encounter; he *m.* Elizabeth MARSH, in England, and had
xx. Ann WARREN, *b.* in England; *m.* Thomas LITTLE, and had
xxi. Patience LITTLE, *b.* in Hingham, Massachusetts; *m.* Joseph JONES, of Hingham, and had
xxii. Sarah JONES, *b.* in Hingham; *m.* Elijah BEAL, of Hingham, and had
xxiii. Sarah BEAL, of Hingham; *m.* Caleb LEAVITT, I, of Hingham, who had
xxiv. Caleb LEAVITT, II, of Hingham, who removed to Bath, Maine; *m.* Nancy SEWALL, of Bath, and had
xxv. Caleb LEAVITT, III, of East Windsor, Connecticut; *b.* in Bath; *m.* Delina ROBERTSON, of Stafford, gd. dau. of Patrick ROBERTSON, of Glasgow, Scotland; who settled in North Britain, near New London, Connecticut, and had Ann Francis LEAVITT, who *m.* Herbert Llewllyn JAMES, of Rockville, Connecticut, thence
xxvi. Herbert Llewllyn JAMES, *b.* 13th January, 1842, at Willington, Connecticut; *d.* 20th February, 1920; *m.* (firstly) 10th October, 1865, at Windsorville, Connecticut, Ann Francis LEAVITT, *b.* 18th February, 1844, in Bath, Maine; *d.* 12th February, 1890; dau. of Caleb and Delina (ROBERTSON) LEAVITT, of whom later; *m.* (secondly) 24th March, 1896, at Brooklyn, New York, Mrs. Ella Reed CRUTTENDEN. He was one of the leading citizens of his state; for many years general manager, secretary and treasurer of the Rock Manufacturing Company, of Rockville, until his retirement from business, in 1901; president of the Rockville Railroad Company and a director of the First National and Savings Banks, of that city, and an officer of many other companies; a Republican in politics, he took an active part in all civic affairs.

ISSUE (ALL BY FIRST MARRIAGE)

1. Howard Kellogg JAMES, of whom later.
2. Clara Leavitt JAMES, *d.* in infancy.
3. Mary Francis JAMES, *d.* in infancy,

xxvii. Howard Kellogg JAMES, *b.* 20th July, 1867, of Alameda, California, the subject of this memoir.

Collateral Families

James

The JAMES family in America, from which the subject of this memoir descends, originated through:

I. Benjamin JAMES, who came from England in the *William and Mary*, in 1665, settling in Narragansett Bay, on Prudence Island. From him descended a line of "Benjamins," the fifth of whom,

V. Benjamin JAMES, had

VI. Elisha Benjamin Reynolds JAMES, b. 28th January, 1814, at Union, Tolland County, Connecticut; m. 28th November, 1841, Mary Ann THOMAS (Rowland G.—Benjamin—Benjamin), of Willington, Connecticut, b. April, 1814; d. 29th January, 1878; he d. 24th March, 1876. He was an abolitionist of pronounced type, his home being a station of the "Underground Railroad" and a refuge for escaping slaves. He was a man of high attainment and deep sympathies, a very devoted citizen, participating in all movements for the support of the institutional life of his state and country.

ISSUE

1. HERBERT LLEWLLYN JAMES, of whom previously.
2. Sarah M. JAMES, b. 13th October, 1843; m. 17th December, 1878, Lebbeus Ensworth SMITH, of Putnam.
3. Albert E. JAMES, b. 4th December, 1851; d. 4th August, 1854.

Leavitt

I. JOHN LEAVITT, the immigrant ancestor, came from England to Dorchester, in 1634; removed to Hingham; a freeman, 1636; Representative to the General Court, 1656 to 1664; Selectman, 1661 to 1675; m. (firstly) wife's name unknown, she d. 4th July, 1646; m. (secondly) Sarah, surname unknown, 16th December, 1646; she d. 26th May, 1700; he d. 30th May, 1757, aged seventy-seven.

ISSUE

1. John LEAVITT.
2. ISRAEL LEAVITT, of whom later.

II. Israel LEAVITT, b. in 1648; m. Lydia JACKSON, and two later wives. By Lydia JACKSON, he had

III. Israel LEAVITT, II, b. in Hingham, 1st August, 1680; m. Mary BATE, 1716. Mary BATE was descended from Clement BATE, of Hingham, 1635, who was descended from Thomas BATE, in England, 1495. Their son

IV. Capt. Caleb LEAVITT, I, b. 1730, served in the campaign of Crown Point, 1756, and in Governor POWNALL'S expedition to the Maine Coast, 1759; he was also a Captain in the Revolutionary War; m. Sarah BEAL, who was descended through Elijah, Joseph and Caleb to John BEAL, of Hingham; also from Edmund HOBART, Hingham, 1633, and Margaret DEWEY. The Beal line also runs through Thomas NICHOLS, of Hingham, 1637, and Thomas JOSELYN, Hingham, 1637. Through Caleb LEAVITT, I, the line runs to William HILLIARD, of Boston, and through George LANE, Hingham, 1656, to William LANE, of England.

ISSUE

1. Elijah LEAVITT.
2. David LEAVITT.
3. CALEB LEAVITT, II, of whom later.

V. Caleb LEAVITT, II, b. 15th October, 1780, was one of the defenders of the Maine Coast in the War of 1812; m. Nancy SEWALL, of Bath, Maine. She is descended through Henry, Samuel, of York, Maine, John, Henry, of Newbury, Massachusetts, Representative to General Court, 1661, to Henry, Mayor of Coventry, England, and to Stephen DUMMER.

ISSUE

1. CALEB LEAVITT, III, of whom later.
2. Nancy LEAVITT, m. Freeman H. Morse, Congressman from Maine and our Consul to London during Civil War. (Friend of Lincoln.)

ISSUE

1[1]. Clara Francis MORSE was the authoress of "Blush Roses," published by Harpers as a résumé of her life at school in Dresden as companion of William HOHENZOLLERN'S sister.
2[1]. Howard Leavitt MORSE was at school at Bonn with William HOHENZOLLERN, erstwhile Emperor of Germany.

VI. CALEB LEAVITT, III, b. in Bath, Maine, 21st May, 1808; d. in Rockville, 1st May, 1897; m. Delina ROBERTSON, and had

ISSUE

1. Alice F. LEAVITT.
2. ANN FRANCIS LEAVITT, who m. Herbert Llewllyn JAMES, father of the subject of this memoir.
3. Martha S. LEAVITT.

Arms.—Argent, a series of crosses crosslet-fitchee, sable, a lion rampant sable.

Crest.—A demi-lion argent rampant, crowned or, holding a crosslet fitchee of the first.

Thomas

The THOMAS family is descended from an ancestry traced to 1680 in America.

I. The immigrant ancestor, BENJAMIN THOMAS, I, came to America from Wales between 1680 and 1685; *m.* and had

II. Benjamin THOMAS, II, who *m.* (firstly) ———— KIBBE, whose first name is unknown, and (secondly) Johannah RHODES, by whom he had

III. Rowland G. THOMAS, who *m.* Dorcas MAINE, and had

IV. Mary Ann THOMAS, who *m.* Elisha Benjamin Reynolds JAMES, as shown in JAMES lineage.

Jeffries

JOHN JEFFRIES (unmarried), of Boston, Massachusetts; *b.* Sunday, 27th July, 1890, at Milton, Massachusetts; was educated at Oxford University, England, 1911-1912; received the degree of A.B. from Harvard University in 1915; was prominent in Preparedness campaigns; in 1915, studied at two Federal Training Camps, Plattsburg, New York; and was recommended for a Captain of Volunteers; studied during 1916 at the Harvard Law School; in 1917, volunteered as a private in the Aviation Service in France, cadet pilot; was then commissioned Second Lieutenant of Field Artillery, and ordered to Saumur Academy, France; graduated with honor, April, 1918, from Saumur, and proceeded to the front with the 120th Field Artillery; was then attached to an Artillery Staff of the Seventh French Army; invalided to America, July, 1918; 1919-20 student of the Inner Temple, London, and the Honor School of Jurisprudence, Oxford University.

Lineage

The name of JEFFRIES means "at peace with God." The family of today are descendants in the thirty-fifth generation of the Earls of Chester. These earls of Chester were heirs to the Heptarch Kingdom of Mercia, whose monarchs sprang from fusion of the royal lines of the conquering Anglo-Saxons, the Bretwalds or overlords of Britain; the Lords of the Roman folk; and the line of TEA TEPHI, daughter of Zedekiah, last King of Judah, who fled to Ireland where she married HEREMON EOCHAID, King of Ireland and grandson of the Egyptian Pharoah, as shown in the Biblical and Jewish records, which descent is as follows:

ADAM, 4000-3070 B.C.
SETH, 3870-2978 B.C.
ENOS, 3765-2860 B.C.
CAINAN, 3675-2765 B.C.
MAHALALEEL, 3605-2710 B.C.
JARED, 3540-2578 B.C.
ENOCH, 3378-3013 B.C.
METHUSALEH, 3313-2344 B.C.
LAMECH, 3126-2344 B.C.
NOAH, 2944-2006 B.C.; *m.* NAAMA.
SHEM, 2442-2158 B.C.
ARPHAXAD, 2392-1904 B.C.
SALAH, 2307-2126 B.C.
HEBER, 2277-2187 B.C.

PELEG, 2243–2204 B.C.
REU, 2213–2026 B.C.
SERUG, 2181–2049 B.C.
NAHOR, 2052–2003 B.C.
TERAH, 2122–2083 B.C.; *m.* AMTHETA.
ABRAHAM, 1992–1817 B.C.; *m.* SARAH; *m.* (secondly) KETURAH.
ISAAC, 1896–1716 B.C.; *m.* REBEKAH.
JACOB, 1837–1690 B.C.; *m.* (firstly) RACHEL; *m.* (secondly) LEAH, whose son JUDAH, *b.* 1753 B.C.; *m.* TAMAR.
PHARES.
HEZRON.
ARAM.
AMINADAB.
NAASHON.
SALMON, 1451 B.C.; *m.* RAHAB (The Scarlet Woman).
BOAZ, 1312 B.C.; *m.* RUTH, daughter-in-law of NAOMI.
OBED.
JESSE.
DAVID, King of Judah and Israel, 1085–1015 B.C.; *m.* (fourthly) BATHSHEBA, widow of URIAH, the Hittite, dau. of ELIAM.
SOLOMON, *b.* 1033; *d.* 975 B.C.; King of Judah and Israel; *m.* NAAMAH, an Ammonitess.
REHOBOAM, *b.* 1016; *d.* 978 B.C.; King of Judah; *m.* MACAH, dau. of ABSALOM, for his third and favorite wife.
ABIJAM, King of Judah, 937–955 B.C.; *m.* MAACAH, dau. of ABISHOLAN.
ASA, King of Judah, 955–914, B.C.; *m.* AZUBAH, dau. of SHILKI.
JEHOSHOPHAT, King of Judah, 914–889, B.C.
JEHORAM, King of Judah, 889–885 B.C.; *m.* ATHALIAH, dau. of AHAB by JEZEBEL, dau. of ITHABAAL, King of Tyre.
AHAZIAH, *b.* 906; *d.* 885 B.C.; King of Judah; *m.* ZIBIAH, of Beersheba.
JOASH, King of Judah, 885–839 B.C.; *m.* JEHOADDAN of Jerusalem.
AMAZIAH, *b.* 864; *d.* 810 B.C.; King of Judah, 839–810; *m.* JECHOLIAH of Jerusalem.
UZZIAH, *b.* 826; *d.* 758 B.C.; King of Judah; *m.* JERUSHA, dau. of ZADOCK.
JOTHAM, *b.* 783; *d.* 742 B.C.; King of Judah.
AHAZ, *b.* 762; *d.* 726 B.C.; King of Judah; *m.* ABIJAH, dau. of ZECHERIAH.
HEZEKIAH, *b.* 751; *d.* 698 B.C. King of Judah; *m.* HEPHZIBAH.
MANASSEH, *b.* 730; *d.* 643 B.C.; King of Judah; *m.* MESHULLEMETH, dau. of HERUZ of Jotbah.
AMON, *b.* 691; *d.* 641 B.C.; King of Judah; *m.* Jedidah, dau. of ADAIAH of Boseath.
JOSIAH, *b.* 649; *d.* 610 B.C.; King of Judah; *m.* HAMUTAL.
ZEDEKIAH (whose name was changed from MATHANICAH by the King of Babylon); King of Judah, 619–587 B.C.; being the last of the Kings; his dau. TEA TEPHI who flourished 580 B.C.; *m.* Heremon EOCHAID, King of Ireland (gd. son to the Egyptian Pharoah mentioned in the Exodus, whose dau. SCOTA, *m.* MILESIUS, father of Here-

mon EOCHAID, supra), who reigned fifteen years; she took with her the Stone of Scone (the Pillow of Rock used by JACOB when he had his historical dream), which today remains with her descendants, the Kings of Great Britain and Ireland and is used at their coronations.

The JEFFRIES family is also descended from the more modern and less interesting Christian mediaeval royal houses of Castile, Aragon, Scotland, Hungary, Norway Denmark, Spain, England, and France.

DAVID JEFFRIES, the son of DAVID JEFFRIES and Dorothy Kinge, of Segell, was *b.* 18th November, 1658, at Rode, in Wiltshire, England; *d.* 10th November, 1742, at Boston, Massachusetts, at which place he landed 9th May, 1677; he *m.* 15th September, 1686, at Boston, Elizabeth USHER, *b.* there 18th June, 1669; *d.* there 17th June, 1698, dau. of John USHER, Royal Lieutenant and Acting Governor of New Hampshire, 1692-1697 and 1704-1715, Treasurer and Receiver-General of New England, who paid from his own fortune the cost of many Indian wars; Elizabeth USHER's mother was Elizabeth LIDGETT, dau. of Colonel LIDGETT.

ISSUE

I. Jane, *b.* 4th July, 1687; *d.* 13th March, 1703.
II. John, *b.* 5th February, 1689; *d.* 15th December, 1777; *m.* 24th September, 1713, Anne CLARKE, *b.* 24th September, 1696; *d.* 26th September, 1775.

ISSUE

1. Anne, *b.* 25th June, 1720; *d.* 23d August, 1720.

III. Elizabeth, *b.* 12th February, 1691; *d.* 25th July, 1737; *m.* (firstly) 13th January, 1708, Charles SHEPREVE, Esq., *d.* 28th May, 1717, and had issue; *m.* (secondly) Benjamin ELLIOTT.
IV. Rebecca, *b.* 9th December, 1693; *d.* 2d July, 1721; *m.* 9th August, 1711, Ebenezer WENTWORTH, and had issue.
V. DAVID, *b.* 15th June, 1690, of whom later.
VI. Sarah, *b.* 4th May, 1695; *d.* 12th January, 1734; *m.* 10th January, 1710, the Hon. George JAFFREY, Chief Justice of New Hampshire.
VII. Frances, *b.* 12th July, 1696; *d.* 7th October, 1714.
VIII. Peter, *b.* 18th November, 1697; *d.* 14th September, 1698.

DAVID JEFFRIES, of Boston, Massachusetts; *b.* there 15th June, 1690; *d.* in shipwreck, 13th September, 1716; graduated from Harvard in 1708 and upon graduation was listed as first in his class; in 1716 he travelled to England as Agent of Massachusetts; he set about the return voyage on the ship *Amity* in September of 1716; the ship was wrecked off Dungeness on 13th September, 1716, and save for one person, all souls on board were lost; *m.* 5th November, 1713, in Boston, Katherine EYRE, *b.* there 20th July, 1694, *d.* there 6th May, 1760, dau. of Capt. John EYRE, the famous Indian fighter, and his wife Katherine BRATTLE, dau. of Thomas BRATTLE, who led many expeditions against the Indians, was envoy to King Philip and a founder of the Old South Church; Katherine EYRE was a gr. gd. dau. of Capt. William TYNG, Treasurer of Massachusetts Bay.

ISSUE

1. DAVID, *b.* 23d October, 1714, of whom later.

DAVID JEFFRIES, A.B., of Boston, Massachusetts; *b.* 23d October, 1714; *d.* there 26th December, 1785; graduated from Harvard; A.B. in 1732; A.M. in 1735; *m.* (firstly) 21st October, 1741, his cousin, Sarah JAFFREY, *b.* 25th March, 1722, *d.* 11th July, 1753, dau. of George JAFFREY, Chief Justice of New Hampshire, and his wife Sarah JEFFRIES, who was gd. dau. of George JAFFREY, Councillor, Representative, and Speaker of the Assembly of New Hampshire and holder of broad grants of land; *m.* (secondly) in 1755, Deborah LYDE, *d.* May, 1767, gd. dau. of Governor BELCHER; *m.* (thirdly) 17th August, 1768, Hannah WINSLOW, *d.* 10th December, 1783; *m.* (fourthly) 2d November, 1784, Sarah widow of Henry RHOADS.

ISSUE BY FIRST MARRIAGE

I. John, *b.* 10th July 1742; *d.* 6th November, 1743.
II. David, *b.* 6th September, 1743; *d.* February, 1762.
III. JOHN, *b.* 5th February, 1745, of whom later.
IV. George, *b.* 13th July, 1746; *d.* 15th July, 1746.
V. Katherine, *b.* 5th April, 1748; *d.* before 1823.
VI. Ann, *b.* 8th November, 1749; *d.* 22d March, 1793; *m.* John EDDY and had issue.
VII. Sarah, *b.* 3d June, 1751; *d.* 24th October, 1753.
VIII. Elizabeth, *b.* 27th May, 1752; *d.* 31st May, 1752.

ISSUE BY SECOND MARRIAGE

I. Deborah, *b.* 10th January, 1756; *d.* about 1810.
II. Andrew Belcher, *b.* 31st July, 1757; *d.* August, 1757.
III. Sarah, *b.* 13th November, 1761; *d.* 6th July, 1825; *m.* Rev. Joseph ECKLEY, pastor of the Old South Church, and had issue.

DR. JOHN JEFFRIES, of Boston, Massachusetts; *b.* there 5th February, 1745; *d.* there 16th September, 1819; graduated from Harvard, A.B., 1763; A.M., 1766; and further studied abroad, receiving the degree of M.D. from Aberdeen, and honorary M.D. from Harvard; he began practice at Boston in 1769, and there his house became the Royalist headquarters; upon the outbreak of the Revolution he sent his family to England; he himself went with the troops to Halifax, and was made Surgeon-General of His Majesty's forces in America. After distinguished service in the fleet off South Carolina, he went, after peace was declared, to England; here he was offered the Surgeon-Generalship of India, and declined it. On March 1st, 1785, Doctor JEFFRIES made a Baron of the Cinq Ports. While in England he made two notable balloon ascensions, one in 1785 from England into France, he being the first man to cross the English Channel by air. He returned to Boston in 1789, where he had an extensive practice; he was a man of many scientific interests, and a great surgeon. Doctor JEFFRIES *d.* at Boston, 16th September, 1819, aged seventy-four years; *m.* (firstly) about 1770, Sarah RHOADES, *d.* 19th January, 1780, at London, England; *m.* (secondly) 8th September, 1787, at London, England, Hannah HUNT, *b.* there 4th November, 1764, *d.* 27th September, 1835, at Boston, Massachusetts; dau. of William HUNT, of London.

ISSUE BY FIRST MARRIAGE

I. John, *b.* 15th December, 1772; *d.* December, 1772.
II. John, again, *b.* 17th January, 1774; *d.* 5th September, 1796, at Paris, on his way to Russia.
III. Ann, *b.* 27th August, 1775; *d.* 29th April, 1807; *m.* 1800, Samuel BROWN, and had issue.

ISSUE BY SECOND MARRIAGE

I. Harriet Maria, *b.* 3d December, 1788, at London, England; smothered 6th May, 1789.
II. George Jaffrey, *b.* 21st December, 1789, at Boston; *d.* there 4th May, 1856; *m.* 18th January, 1814, Clementina Matilda WETHERED, of Baltimore, Maryland, had issue, who are extinct.
III. Robinson Ardesoif, *b.* 7th January, 1791, at Boston; burnt to death 24th February, 1796.
IV. Edward, *b.* 13th February, 1792; *d.* 9th June, 1813.
V. Harriet Maria, *b.* 26th February, 1793; *d.* 20th February, 1796.
VI. Eyre Massey, *b.* 11th September, 1794; *d.* 6th July, 1826; in Santa Martha, South America.
VII. JOHN, of whom later.
VIII. Catherine Matilda, *b.* 23d May, 1797; *d.* 15th March, 1859; *m.* Charles Chauncey HAVEN, of Portsmouth, and had issue.
IX. Julia Ann, *b.* 15th November, 1800; *d.* 8th February, 1874; *m.* 12th June, 1820, Thomas Jeffries ECKLEY, and had issue.
X. Sarah Augusta, *b.* 21st June, 1804; *d.* 14th August, 1830.

DR. JOHN JEFFRIES, of Boston, Massachusetts; *b.* there 23d March, 1796; *d.* there 16th July, 1876; graduated from Harvard; A.B., 1815; A.M., 1818; M.D., from Brown 1825; practiced his profession in Boston for fifty years; *m.* 8th November, 1820, at Boston, Anne Geyer AMORY (see AMORY family, Volume 2) *b.* there 14th May, 1802, *d.* 24th June, 1882, at Mattapoisett, Massachusetts; dau. of Rufus Greene AMORY, descended from Jonathan AMORY, Treasurer, Advocate-General, and Speaker of the

House of South Carolina; from John GREENE, Assistant of Roger WILLIAMS, the founder of Rhode Island; Thomas GREENE, Assistant of Rhode Island, and Arthur MACKWORTH, one of the original patentees of Maine; Anne Geyer AMORY's mother was Anne von GEYER, dau. of Frederich William von GEYER, of Boston.

ISSUE

I. Catherine Amory, *b.* 10th October, 1821; *d.* 9th July, 1910.
II. JOHN, *b.* 20th December, 1823, of whom later.
III. Ann McLean, *b.* 15th March, 1826; *d.* 6th October, 1874.
IV. Sarah Augusta, *b.* 17th July, 1828; *d.* 20th August, 1912; *m.* 28th April, 1851, Charles Lowell ANDREWS, and had issue.
V. George Jaffrey, *b.* 23d December, 1830; *d.* 20th September, 1853.
VI. Benjamin Joy, *b.* 26th March, 1833, at Boston; graduated from Harvard, 1854; *m.* 4th January, 1872, Marian SHIMMIN, dau. of Charles Franklin, and Marion Harriot (PARKMAN) SHIMMIN.

ISSUE

1. Charles Shimmin, *b.* 15th October, 1877, at Boston; *d.* 18th December, 1895.
2. Marian, *b.* 25th March, 1881; *m.* 11th July, 1915, Jas. Howard MEANS, M.D.

VII. Edward Payson, *b.* 1st August, 1835; graduated from Harvard, 1826; *d.s.p.*, 13th March, 1906; *m.* 1861, Almira McBURNEY.
VIII. Henry Upham, *b.* 7th December, 1840; graduated from Harvard, 1862.

COL. JOHN JEFFRIES, of Boston, Massachusetts; *b.* there 30th December, 1823; *d.* there 12th December, 1897; not eligible for active service; he was mustered into the United States service with the 1st Corps of Cadets of Boston as Major and did garrison duty in Boston Harbor; a successful yachtsman; *m.* 8th May, 1851, in Norwich, Connecticut, Anna Lloyd GREENE, *b.* there 5th January, 1829, *d.* 19th January, 1900, at Boston. Her father, William Parkinson GREENE, was twice descended from John Greene, Assistant of Roger WILLIAMS, who founded Rhode Island; twice from Thomas GREENE, Assistant of Rhode Island; twice from William HUBBARD, Representative of Massachusetts; twice from Lion GARDINER, holder of Gardiner's Island manorial grant; twice from Nathaniel SYLVESTER, holder of Shelter Island manorial grant; and was descended from William DOUGLASS, Representative of Connecticut; from Mary Neville; from Mabel HARLAKENDEN; Israel STOUGHTON, Assistant of Massachusetts; HUBBARD, the historian of the Indian Wars; Gen. Rufus BARTON; John HAYNES, Royal Governor of Massachusetts, and first Governor of Connecticut; George WYLLIS, Governor of Connecticut; Richard RUSSELL, Assistant of Massachusetts; Sir John LEVERETT, Major-General, Speaker, and Governor of Massachusetts.

Mrs. JEFFRIES' mother, Augusta Elizabeth BORLAND, was descended from Sir John TEMPLE, Kt. of Stanton Bury, who fled to America when CROMWELL was Protector and later returned to England; from William VASSAL, an original patentee of New England, who with his brother Samuel financed and sent to Massachusetts Bay, the expedition commanded by WINTHROP; Samuel PENHALLOW, of Penhallow County, Cornwall, Councillor, Secretary, Treasurer and Chief Justice of New Hampshire; Robert NELSON, of St. Bernard's Inn; Thomas BOURNE, of Kent, founder of Bourne; James LLOYD, of Somersetshire, holder of "Queen's village" manorial grant; Col. John POLE, famous Indian fighter; Capt. William POLE, Representative and Councillor of War of Massachusetts, son of Sir William POLE, gd. son of Sir William PERIAM, and gr. nephew of George POPHAM, the son of the Attorney-General, who founded the first Kennebec Colony; Francis BORLAND; John BORLAND; T. LINDELL. Judge, Representative, Councillor, and Speaker of the House of Massachusetts; William BRENTON Royal Governor of Rhode Island; and John CUTT, appointed by the Crown, first President of New Hampshire.

ISSUE

I. James Lloyd, *b.* 27th January, 1853 at Boston; *d.* 26th February, 1854.
II. Walter Lloyd, *b.* 26th November, 1854; graduated from Harvard, 1875; *d. s. p.* 30th August, 1898.
III. William Augustus, of 236 Marlborough Street, Boston; *b.* there 13th February, 1856; graduated from Harvard; A.B., 1875; *m.* 3d April, 1893, at La Grange, Illinois, Clemence EUSTIS, *b.* 8th March, 1859, at Baltimore, Maryland, dau. of Alexander Brooks EUSTIS, and gd. dau. of Brevet Brigadier-General EUSTIS; her father was descended from Lieut. Ralph SPRAGUE, Representative of Massachusetts; John JARVIS; James PEMBERTON; John SUNDERLAND; Nathaniel HANCOCK; Lieut. George INGERSOLL, Deputy of the Province of Maine; and Lieut. John REMINGTON. Her mother was Aurora GRELAUD, a gd. dau. of Jean Baptiste GRELAUD and Marie Claudine D'ESPAIGNE, who sought refuge in Philadelphia from a servile insurrection in Santo Domingo.

ISSUE

1. John Amory, *b.* 27th December, 1893, at Boston; graduated from Harvard, 1916; now First Lieutenant, American Expeditionary Force in France.
2. Clemence Despaigne, *b.* 20th November, 1898.

IV. John AMORY, *b.* 2d September, 1859, of whom below.

DR. JOHN AMORY JEFFRIES, of Boston, Massachusetts; *b.* at Milton, Massachusetts 2d December, 1859; *d.* 26th March, 1892, at Boston; graduated from Harvard; A.B., 1881; M.D., 1884; continued his medical studies at Vienna; was an ardent sportsman and naturalist; *m.* 26th September, 1889, at Milton, Massachusetts, Emily Augusta EUSTIS, *b.* 21st June, 1858, dau. of Rev. Frederick Augustus and Mary Ruth (CHANNING) EUSTIS; Emily Augusta EUSTIS is the gd. dau. of Brevet Brigadier-General EUSTIS and of the Rev. William Ellery CHANNING, founder of the American Peace Society; she is twice descended from Thomas DUDLEY, Royal Governor of Massachusetts, first Major-General of Massachusetts, one of the founders of Harvard, and President of the Confederated Colonies; twice from Mary ANTRIM; and is descended from Simon BRADSTREET, Royal Governor of Massachusetts, and New Hampshire, President of the United Colonies; Anne (DUDLEY) BRADSTREET, first American poetess; Benjamin ELLERY, Representative, Speaker of the Assembly, and Assistant of Rhode Island; William ELLERY, Judge, Deputy Governor, and Assistant of Rhode Island; William ELLERY, Signer of the Declaration of Independence, and Chief Justice of Rhode Island; Christopher ALMY, Representative and Assistant of Massachusetts; Nathaniel HANCOCK; Lieut. Ralph SPRAGUE, Representative of Massachusetts; Lieut. Edward HOWE; Jonathan REMINGTON, Representative, Judge, and Councillor of Massachusetts; Nicholas DANFORTH, Representative of Massachusetts; Rev. John WOODBRIDGE, Representative and Assistant of Massachusetts; Thomas CORNELL, Commissioner to Rhode Island Court of Commissioners; Lieut. George INGERSOLL, Deputy of the Province of Maine; and William CHANNING, Attorney General of Rhode Island.

ISSUE

1. John, *b.* 27th July, 1890.

Arms.—Sable, a lion rampant or, between three scaling ladders of the last.
Crest.—On a mountain vert, a castle with two towers or.
Motto.—Fac recte et nil time.
Residence.—105 Marlborough Street, Boston, Massachusetts.

Johnson

FRANCIS JEWETT JOHNSON, United States Army, of Chicago, Illinois; *b.* 2d May, 1880, at Saugatuck, Michigan; *m.* 2d December, 1911, at Minneapolis, Minnesota, Louisa Macalester NEVINS, *b.* 16th January, 1887, dau. of Richard NEVINS, *b.* 11th February, 1858, *d.* 5th April, 1902, *m.* Josephine MACCLOSKEY, *b.* 1st January, 1867, *d.* 24th March, 1906,

CAPTAIN FRANCIS JEWETT JOHNSON, United States Army, was educated at Griswold College, Racine; is of the banking house of Francis Jewett JOHNSON and Company of Chicago, Illinois.

Lineage

The members of this family were natives of Stamford and Rutlandshire, England, and are said to be descended from the same line as Isaac JOHNSON who came with WINTHROP in 1630 and was one of the signers of the compact and agreement at Cambridge, England in 1629. JOHN JOHNSON of England, *b.* 1609; *d.* 1640; *m.* (wife's name not given).

ISSUE

I. JOHN, *b.* 1630, of whom later.

CAPTAIN JOHN JOHNSON, of Rowley, Massachusetts; *b.* in England, 1630; *d.* there 29th January, 1685; at the commencement of King Philips' War he was Ensign in the Essex Regiment, commanded by Maj. Daniel DENNISON; was probably with Captain BROCKELBANK of Rowley, who was killed in the defense of Sudbury, Massachusetts, 21st April, 1676; was commissioned Captain 22d October, 1677; *m.* Hannah CROSBY, *b.* circa 1634, *d.* 5th December, 1717.

ISSUE

I. Hannah, *b.* 20th September, 1656; *m.* 9th January, 1677, Thomas PALMER.
II. Elizabeth, *b.* 16th January, 1659; *m.* 12th May, 1680, James BAILEY.
III. John, *b.* 3d February, 1665; buried 12th April, 1666.
IV. John, *b.* 31st January, 1667–1668; buried 7th October, 1670.
V. SAMUEL, *b.* 9th July, 1671, of whom below.

SAMUEL JOHNSON, of Rowley, Massachusetts; *b.* 9th July, 1671; *d.* before 6th August, 1753; *m.* Frances WICOM, *b.* 29th March, 1675, *d.* 13th September, 1750, dau. of Daniel WICOM. Daniel WICOM, *b.* 1635, in England, *d.* 15th April, 1700, *m.* (firstly) 14th October, 1658, in Rowley, Massachusetts, Mary SMITH, *d.* 29th January, 1690, dau. of Hugh SMITH, *m.* (secondly) 11th November, 1691, Lydia

(BAILEY) PLATTS, b. 1642, d. 24th November, 1722, dau. of James BAILEY and widow of Lieut. Abel PLATTS; was Captain of the Military Company; member of the General Court, 1689–1699; was a member of Capt. Nicholas PAIGE's troop, which accompanied Maj. Thomas SAVAGE in the expedition to Mount Hope, 23d August, 1675, and went with the Army to Narragansett; he was Quarter Master 24th June, 1676.

ISSUE AMONG OTHERS

1. SAMUEL, b. 11th June, 1699, of whom later.

SAMUEL JOHNSON of Rowley, Massachusetts; b. 11th June, 1699; d. 27th December, 1773; m. Rachel BOYNTON, d. 3d February, 1799, dau. of Ichabod BOYNTON, b. 19th April, 1677, m. Elizabeth HAZELTINE, b. 29th October, 1683; he son of John BOYNTON, b. 17th September, 1647, d. 22d December, 1719. John BOYNTON, II, b. in Rowley, Massachusetts, 17th September, 1647, d. 22d December, 1719; son of John BOYNTON, I, b. circa 1614, buried 18th February, 1670–1671, m. Ellen PELL. Removed to Bradford, Massachusetts, about 1678 and d. there 22d December, 1719. Was one of the ninety-five men who served under Capt. Joseph GARDINER of Ipswich, Massachusetts, in the expedition against the Narragansetts. Mustered in with the Army commanded by Maj. Samuel APPLETON at Dedham Plain, 9th December, 1675; marched to Wickford and Platts and took part in the Narragansett Fort Fight, 19th December, 1675; m. Hannah KEYS, b. 12th September, 1654, d. before 1719.

ISSUE AMONG OTHERS

1. SAMUEL, b. 22d April, 1748, of whom below.

SAMUEL JOHNSON, b. 22d April, 1748; d. 10th March, 1814; m. Susanna SEARLE, b. 28th January, 1750.

ISSUE AMONG OTHERS

1. MOSES, b. 1st September, 1787, of whom below.

MOSES JOHNSON, b. 1st September, 1787; d. December, 1822; m. Philomela JEWETT, d. 8th June, 1839.

ISSUE AMONG OTHERS

1. OTIS RUSSELL, b. 2d April, 1815, of whom below.

OTIS RUSSELL JOHNSON, b. 2d April, 1815; d. 6th March, 1895; m. Emily WELLES, b. 6th April, 1833; d. 1901.

ISSUE AMONG OTHERS

1. FRANCIS JEWETT, b. 2d May, 1880, the subject of this memoir.

Arms.—Argent, a chevron sable, between three lions' heads gules, crowned or.
Crest.—An eagle rising proper.
Motto.—Per aspera ad astra.
Residence.—Chicago, Illinois.
Clubs.—Chicago, Onwesntsia, Casino, Saddle and Cycle, all of Chicago; Minneapolis of Minneapolis, Minnesota; Metropolitan, Washington, D. C.
Societies.—Colonial Wars, Sons of the American Revolution.

Wells (Maternal)

The progenitor of this line and other lines of the WELLS family in America was Thomas WELLES, *b.* at Rothwell, Northamptonshire, England, about 1598 and is said to have been a descendant of the Essex an older branch of the family and much distinguished in England and having an estate and Manor House, Welles Hall first called Rayne Hall, in Essex, England. The founder of this family was Simon DE WELLES, who was at the siege of Jean D'Acre in Palestine, with Richard Coeur de Lion in 1191 and had this special grant of Arms by the King: Paly of five, gules and or, on a canton argent, a mullett sable.

GOVERNOR THOMAS WELLS, *b.* circa 1598 in Rothwell, England; *d.* 14th January, 1660, in Weathersfield, Connecticut, came to New England and settled at Hartford, Connecticut, in the summer of 1636. The next year was chosen Magistrate by the Planters and was in active participation of the duties of the office during the Pequot Wars in 1637. This office he held every successive year from this date until his decease in 1659–1660, a period of twenty-two years. In 1639 he was chosen the first Treasurer of the Colony, under the new Constitution and successively continued in this office until 1651, at which time on account of other duties asked to be eased of the Treasurer's place and the request was granted. In 1641 he was chosen Secretary of the Colony and held the office in subsequent years. In 1649 he was one of the Commissioners of the United Colonies. In 1654 Governor HOPKINS, being in England and Deputy Governor HAINES having died, he was elected by the whole body of the Freemen, convened at Hartford, Moderator of the General Court and this year was again appointed one of the Commissioners of the United Colonies, but other duties prevented him from serving and this year he was also chosen Deputy Governor in 1655 and in 1656 and 1657 Deputy Governor and in 1658 again Governor in 1659 again Deputy Governor; *m.* Elizabeth HUNT.

ISSUE AMONG OTHERS

1. John, *b.* 1621; *d.* 1660; *m.* Elizabeth BOURNE.

ISSUE AMONG OTHERS

1. JOHN, *b.* 1648 of whom below.

JOHN WELLES, *b.* 1648; *d.* 24th March, 1713; *m.* Mary HOLLISTER.

ISSUE AMONG OTHERS

1. JOHN, *b.* 1675–1676, of whom below.

JOHN WELLS, *b.* 16th October, 1699; *d.* 25th April, 1742; *m.* Mary THOMPSON, *b.* 9th September, 1706.

ISSUE AMONG OTHERS

1. DAVID, *b.* 28th March, 1738, of whom below.

DAVID WELLS, *b.* 28th March, 1738; *d.* 29th May, 1790; *m.* Johannah WILCOXSON, *b.* 11th February, 1741, *d.* 2d March, 1800.

ISSUE AMONG OTHERS

1. DAVID, *b.* 31st October, 1774, of whom below.

DAVID WELLS, *d.* 2d March, 1800; *m.* Abigail SHELTON, *b.* 13th August, 1775, *d.* 2d January, 1852.

ISSUE AMONG OTHERS

1. ANDREW SHELTON, *b.* 16th December, 1800, of whom below.

ANDREW SHELTON WELLS, *b.* 16th December, 1800; *m.* Mary WARNER, *b.* 22d December, 1805.

ISSUE AMONG OTHERS

1. EMILY, *b.* 6th April, 1833, of whom below.

EMILY WELLS, *b.* 6th April, 1833; *m.* Otis Russell JOHNSON of Saugatuck, Wisconsin; *b.* 2d April, 1815, *d.* 6th March, 1895.

ISSUE AMONG OTHERS

1. FRANCIS JEWETT JOHNSON, *b.* 2d May, 1880, the subject of this memoir.

Arms (WELLES).—Or, a lion rampant sable, langued gules, double queued.
Crest.—A demi-lion rampant sable, langued and queued as of the arms.

Lee

HONORABLE COLONEL JAMES FENNER LEE, deceased, of "Myrtle Point," St. Mary's County, Maryland; b. 9th July, 1843, at Providence, Rhode Island; d. 26th January, 1898, at "Myrtle Point," St. Mary's County, Maryland; m. 28th June, 1866, Mary Cornelia (READ) CARROLL, b. 25th December, 1839, at Baltimore, Maryland, d. 5th January, 1918, at "Myrtle Point," dau. of William George and Sophia Catherine (HOWARD) READ, she dau. of Col. John Eager and Margaret (CHEW) HOWARD. Mary Cornelia READ, m. (firstly) Albert Henry CARROLL, son of Charles and Mary Digges (LEE) CARROLL, d. 7th September, 1862, he was killed within a few weeks subsequent to his enlistment in a skirmish near Martinsburg, Virginia, while serving in the Confederate States Army; by this marriage there was

I. Mary Sophia CARROLL, b. 6th February, 1859; d. 21st April, 1883.
II. Mary Ellinor CARROLL, b. 7th December, 1860.
III. Agnes Carroll, b. 15th January, 1863; m. 13th April, 1887, Anton Otto Gräf VON HUISSENSTAMM zu Husinstein Gräfenhausen Freiherr zu Sterenberg, b. 13th April, 1856, K. u. K. Kämmerer u. Rittmiester; son of Alexander Gräf VON HUISSENSTAMM zu Husinstein Gräfhausen Freiherr zu Sterenberg, b. 18th November, 1812; m. 2d May, 1854, Caroline Gräfin VON HARRACH zu Rohran, b. 2d February, 1822, Stevus Kreutz Dammen St. Ks. D.

ISSUE OF JAMES FENNER AND MARY CORNELIA (READ) (CARROLL) LEE

I. Mary Cornelia, b. 8th July, 1867; d. November, 1875.
II. Arthur Fenner, b. 28th June, 1869; d. unmarried, 3d February, 1893, in Rio de Janeiro, Brazil.
III. Sarah Fenner, b. 17th December, 1870; d. 22d February, 1918, at "The Meadows," Owings Mills, Baltimore County, Maryland; m. 2d October, 1900, John Moseley WALKER (see WALKER, "Colonial Families," Vol. V, p. 537).

ISSUE

1. Sarah Fenner WALKER, b. 6th April, 1904.
2. John Moseley WALKER, b. 9th March, 1906.
3. Sophia Howard WALKER, b. 20th June, 1909.

iv. JAMES FENNER, of "Myrtle Point," St. Mary's County, Maryland; *b.* 9th June, 1872; *m.* 19th February, 1906, Lillian WATHEN, dau. of George Frank and Rose Victoria (GRAVES) WATHEN of St. Mary's County, Maryland.

ISSUE

1. Mary Sophia, *b.* 13th April, 1908.
2. Augusta Rose, *b.* 28th March, 1910.
3. James Fenner, *b.* 9th March, 1913.
4. John Eager Howard, *b.* 28th November, 1914.

v. Sophia Howard, *b.* 21st January, 1876; *m.* 22d November, 1897, JAMES BRISCOE, Jr., *b.* 3d March, 1873, son of Rev. James and Ann Sedgewick (HUPPMAN) BRISCOE of "Sotterley," St. Mary's County, Maryland.

ISSUE

1. James Howard BRISCOE, *b.* 22d August, 1898; *d.* July, 1899.
2. Cornelia Lee BRISCOE, *b.* 24th June, 1899.
3. Arthur Fenner Lee BRISCOE, *b.* 3d October, 1900.
4. Theodore Forbes BRISCOE, *b.* 18th November, 1902; *d.* 22d January, 1903.
5. John Douglas BRISCOE, *b.* 27th December, 1903; *d.* same day.
6. Elizabeth Sedgewick BRISCOE, *b.* 14th March, 1912; *d.* same day.
7. Ellinor Carroll BRISCOE, *b.* 15th November, 1914; *d.* same day.

JAMES FENNER LEE, diplomatist, was educated abroad. He attended prominent Swiss institutions of learning and was a graduate of the College of Louis le Grande at Paris; returned to America at the age of eighteen and studied law at Harvard. He completed his course with honors and entered the office of Messrs. BROWN and BROWN of Baltimore. While yet a youthful practitioner Colonel LEE in collaboration with Jacob I. COHEN, Esq., of this City compiled the third volume of a digest of the Court of Appeals of Maryland, which attracted general attention in legal circles because of the ability manifested by the compilers. Shortly after his marriage he purchased an estate in Carroll County to which he removed. He became prominent in politics and represented his county as Senator in the Maryland Assemblies of 1876 and 1878 and was an influential element in Democratic circles. Was appointed by President CLEVELAND, in 1865 Charge d'Affairs to the Court of Austria. His abilities won high appreciation in diplomatic circles. When the Republic of Brazil was organized after the deposition of Don Pedro, he was commissioned by President HARRISON as the Charge d'Affairs at Rio. Owing to climatic conditions he was forced to resign his post on account of failing health and returned to the United States.

Lineage

SIR ROBERT LEE, *b.* at Bridge North, Shropshire, England; *d.* 28th January, 1605, Lord Mayor of London, 1602.

ISSUE

HENRY LEE, one of the Captains of the city of London.

ISSUE

FRANCIS LEE, of Bridgetown, Barbadoes, who *m.* Mary, is said to have been the son of Henry LEE, one of the Captains of the Guard of London, who is said to have been the son of Sir Robert LEE, *b.* in Bridge North, Shropshire, England.

ISSUE

THOMAS LEE, *b.* at Bridgetown, Barbadoes; 6th February, 1710; *d.* 8th August, 1769; *m.* at Charleston, South Carolina, 26th May, 1732, Mary GILES, who *d.* 1st April, 1751.

ISSUE

I. Francis, *b.* 16th January, 1734; *d.* 29th November, 1767.
II. Mary, *b.* 7th January, 1738; *m.* Joshua LOCKWOOD.
III. Susannah, *b.* 2d October, 1740; *d.* 20th December, 1760; *m.* 19th April, 1759, ———— PINKNEY.
IV. Joseph, *b.* 11th November, 1742; *d.* 15th November, 1814; *m.* (firstly) Agnes HARPER; *m.* (secondly) 29th June, 1764, Mary Hay THORME, *b.* April, 1740, *d.* 1784.
V. Rebecca, *b.* 10th March, 1743; *d.* in infancy.
VI. Hannah, *b.* 17th July, 1745; *d.* in infancy.
VII. Col. William, of Charleston, South Carolina; *b.* 24th June, 1747; *d.* 29th November, 1803; *m.* Ann THEUS, *b.* 4th August, 1750, *d.* 5th August, 1797.
VIII. Rachel.
IX. STEPHEN, *b.* 21st January, 1750, at Charleston, South Carolina.

STEPHEN LEE, *b.* 21st January, 1750, at Charleston, South Carolina; *d.* 7th November, 1807; held as a hostage by the British during the Revolutionary War on board the schooner, *Pack Horse*, in Charleston Harbor, South Carolina; *m.* 1784, Dorothea ALISON, née SMISER, widow of Rev. Hugh ALISON.

ISSUE

I. PAUL S. H., *b.* 22d September, 1784.
II. Francis Joseph, *m.* 1st May, 1813, Ann BEEKMAN.

III. Marie.
IV. Caroline, *m.* Joshua LOCKWOOD.
V. Joseph.
VI. William States, D.D., of Edesto Island, South Carolina; *b.* 22d July, 1793; *m.* (firstly) M. C. Villepont EAUX; *m.* (secondly) Henrietta GAILLARD.

PAUL S. H. LEE, *b.* 22d September, 1784; *d.* 20th April, 1852; *m.* 10th January, 1809, Charleston, South Carolina, Jane Elizabeth MARTIN, dau. of Jacob and Rebecca (MURRAY) MARTIN; *m.* (secondly) Lynch VAN RYBURNE.

ISSUE BY FIRST MARRIAGE

I. Eliza.
II. J. Martin, *m.* Rebecca FISHBURNE.
III. STEPHEN STATES, *b.* 8th November, 1812, of whom later.
IV. Theodore B., *m.* Julia REYNOLDS.
V. Francis A.

ISSUE BY SECOND MARRIAGE

I. Hutson.
II. I. Allison.
III. P. Van Rhyne.

STEPHEN STATES LEE, of Baltimore, Maryland; *b.* 8th November, 1812; *d.* 22d August, 1892; *m.* 30th April, 1840, at Providence, Rhode Island, Sarah Fenner MALLETT, *b.* 14th August, 1821, *d.* 24th December, 1903, dau. of Gen. Edward Jones MALLETT, *b.* 1st May, 1797, in Fayetteville, North Carolina, *d.* 20th August, 1883, *m.* 11th September, 1820, Sarah FENNER, *b.* 13th May, 1797, *d.* 17th May, 1841. General MALLETT was the son of the Hon. Peter MALLETT, of Fayetteville, North Carolina; member of North Carolina Legislature, 1778; Commissary 6th Regiment Continental Line, October, 1776; he son of Peter MALLETT, the son of John MALLETT, who was the son of David MALLETT (Huguenot) of La Rochelle, France. Sarah FENNER, *b.* 12th July, 1773; *d.* 24th May, 1844; was the dau. of Arthur FENNER, *b.* 17th October, 1699, *d.* 2d February 1788, the son of Thomas FENNER, *b.* September, 1652, *d.* 27th February, 1718, who was the son of Capt. Arthur FENNER, *b.* September, 1622, *d.* 16th October, 1703, of Providence, Rhode Island, Assistant 1657–1690, Commander Providence Forces in King Philip's War; he son of Thomas FENNER of Branford, Connecticut.

ISSUE

I. JAMES FENNER, *b.* 9th July, 1843, the subject of this memoir.
II. Julian Henry, *b.* 2d November, 1845.

ISSUE

I. Elizabeth Tyson, *b.* 18th April, 1874; *m.* 28th September, 1898, Henry Arthur GUFFEY, son of Col. James GUFFEY, of Pittsburgh, Pennsylvania.

ISSUE

1[1]. Elizabeth GUFFEY.
2[1]. Nancy GUFFEY.
3[1]. ——— GUFFEY.

2. Stephen States, b. 8th March, 1876; unmarried.
3. Gulielma Poultney, b. 18th August, 1877; m. 2d November, 1898, Edward McCulloh FISHER, son of J. Harmanus and Josephine McCulloh FISHER, of Baltimore, Maryland.

ISSUE

1[1]. Josephine McCulloh FISHER.
2[1]. Julian Henry Lee FISHER.
3[1]. ——— FISHER.

4. Amabel, b. 15th April, 1879; m. 17th September, 1902, Colbert Anderson McCLURE.

ISSUE

1[1]. Amabel Lee McCLURE.

III. Hilyard Cameron, b. 8th December, 1854; now (1918) in the service of the American Red Cross in France.
IV. Amabel, b. 14th June, 1858; d. 1st March, 1895; m. 18th December, 1879, John Cowman GEORGE, son of Archibald and Henrietta (COWMAN) (Bowie) GEORGE, she dau. of ——— COWMAN and widow of Wm D. BOWIE.

ISSUE

1. Stephen Lee GEORGE, b. 26th August, 1882; m. Lillian Independence KELLEY, dau. of Independence and ——— KELLEY.

ISSUE

1[1]. Ann Lee GEORGE.

2. Amabel Lee GEORGE, b. 27th July, 1885; m. 28th June, ———, Heyward Easter BOYCE of Baltimore, Vice-President Drovers and Mechanics National Bank, son of Frederick A. and ——— BOYCE.

ISSUE

1[1]. Heyward Easter BOYCE, Jr.
2[1]. Rebecca Latimer BOYCE.

3¹. Amabel George BOYCE.
4¹. John George BOYCE (twin).
5¹. Elizabeth Lee BOYCE (twin).

3. Henrietta Cowman GEORGE, *b.* 5th December, 1888; *m.* 14th June, 1907, Marshall Langton PRICE, son of Maj. Curtis Ethelbert and Frances (SHAW) PRICE.

ISSUE

1¹. John Marshall PRICE, *b.* 24th December, 1908.
2¹. Amabel Lee PRICE, *b.* 4th May, 1910.

Arms.—Argent, a fesse sable, in chief three pellets, in base a martlet of the second.
Crest.—A talbot's head, erased.
Motto.—Fide et Constantia.

Lewis

EDWARD SIMMONS LEWIS, II, of St. Louis, Missouri; *b.* 22d August, 1848, in Richmond, Missouri; *m.* 4th April, 1876, in Nashville, Tennessee, Pattie COOKE, *b.* 29th September, 1851, at Gainesboro, Tennessee, dau. of Watson M. COOKE, *b.* 1817, *d.* 1877, *m.* 1841, Maria SHORES, *b.* 1815, *d.* 1903.

ISSUE

I. Watson Cooke, *b.* 22d November, 1879; *m.* 18th March, 1911, Helen CARRICK.
II. Augusta Bransford. *b.* 25th December, 1881; *m.* 6th May, 1905, Charles Van Dyke HILL, son of Ewing HILL.

ISSUE

1. Edward Lewis HILL, *b.* 1908.
2. Joyce Mallory, *b.* 1913.

III. Edward McElhiney, *b.* 26th January, 1884; unmarried; First Lieutenant 43d Company, 164th Depot Brigade, United States Army.
IV. Pattie Marian, *b.* 9th June, 1886; *m.* 20th May, 1916, Frederick Lewis ENGLISH, Judge Circuit Court, 1918, St. Louis, Missouri; son of Lewis W. ENGLISH and his wife Laura DULA.

EDWARD SIMMONS LEWIS was educated at St. Charles College, St. Charles, Missouri; formerly President of the Central National Bank; Star-Chronical Publishing Company (*St. Louis Star*), Board of Trustees, St. John's Methodist Episcopal Church, all of St. Louis, Missouri; now (1918) Excise Commissioner of St. Louis; Curator St. Charles College (Alma Mater); Second Lieutenant, 1st Regiment Missouri Home Guard.

Lineage

The American ancestor of this family was Edmund LEWIS, *b.* circa 1600; *d.* 1650; embarked at Ipswich, England with wife and two children 10th April, 1634; settled at Watertown, Massachusetts; *m.* Mary (surname not given), *d.* 7th September, 1658.

ISSUE

I. John, *b.* 1631, at Ipswich, England.
II. THOMAS, *b.* 1633, at Ipswich, England, of whom later.
III. James, *b.* 15th January, 1636.

COLONIAL FAMILIES OF THE UNITED STATES

    IV. Nathanial, *b.* 25th August, 1639.
    V. A child, buried 6th November, 1642.
    VI. A child (not named).
    VII. A child (not named).

THOMAS LEWIS, *b.* in England, 1633; *d.* 1709; *m.* 11th November, 1659, Hannah BAKER, dau. of Edward BAKER.

ISSUE

    I. Edward, *b.* 28th July, 1660.
    II. Thomas, *b.* 29th April, 1668.
    III. SAMUEL. *b.* 1673, of whom later.

SAMUEL LEWIS, of Woodbridge, New Jersey; *b.* 1673; *m.* 1698, Susannah JONES.

ISSUE AMONG OTHERS

    I. SAMUEL, *b.* 1st January, 1702, of whom below.

SAMUEL LEWIS, *b.* 1st January, 1702; *m.* Effe DAVENPORT.

ISSUE AMONG OTHERS

    I. JOHN, of whom below.

JOHN LEWIS, *d.* 1773; *m.* Mary GIFFORD.

ISSUE AMONG OTHERS

    I. SAMUEL, *b.* 1754, of whom below.

SAMUEL LEWIS, of Philadelphia, Pennsylvania; *b.* 1754; *d.* 1822; *m.* Elizabeth GODFREY.

ISSUE AMONG OTHERS

    I. EDWARD SIMMONS, *b.* 1794, of whom below.

EDWARD SIMMONS LEWIS, of Washington, D. C.; *b.* 1794; *d.* 1829; *m.* 1815, Susan Jean WASHINGTON, *b.* 1795, *d.* 1829, she dau. of Lund WASHINGTON, *b.* 1767, *d.* 1853, who *m.* Susannah GRAYSON. (See Excursus Washington.)

ISSUE AMONG OTHERS

    I. EDWARD AUGUSTUS, *b.* 1820, of whom below.

EDWARD AUGUSTUS LEWIS, of St. Louis, Missouri; Judge Supreme Court of Missouri, 1875; *b.* 1820; *d.* 1889; *m.* 1845, Parthenia BRANSFORD, *b.* 1826, *d.* 1893, dau. of Walter Lee BRANSFORD.

ISSUE

1. Walter Felix, *b.* 1846; *d.* 1903; *m.* 1872, Monimia CHASE, dau. of William H. CHASE.

ISSUE

1. George Chase, Lieutenant Colonel 38th Infantry, United States Army now in England (1918); *b.* 1876; *m.* 1914, Louise MANNING.

ISSUE

1[1]. Flora Louisa, *b.* 1917.

2. Florence Parthenia, *b.* 1877.
3. Walter Felix, *b.* 1889; First Lieutenant, United States Army, now (1918) in England.
4. Eugene Grayson, *b.* 1890, Private in 241st Highlanders, now (1918) in England.

II. EDWARD SIMMONS, *b.* 22d August, 1848, the subject of this memoir.
III. Florence Elizabeth, *b.* 1850; *m.* Robert ATKINSON, son of John ATKINSON.

ISSUE

1. Robert Lewis ATKINSON, *b.* 1879; *d.* 1903.

IV. Eugene Washington, *b.* 1855; *m.* 1913, Eva HUGHART.
V. Grayson, *b.* 1857; *m.* Mamie CARROLL.

ISSUE

1. Olive, *b.* 1884; *m.* Bernard POTTER.
2. Carroll Grayson, *b.* 1885, unmarried.

VI. Bransford, M. D., *b.* 1862; *m.* 1896, Jennie JAYNES, *b.* 1872.

Residence.—5855 Delmar Avenue, St. Louis, Missouri.
Societies.—Colonial Wars, Sons of the American Revolution, New England Colonial Society.

EXCURSUS WASHINGTON

LAURENCE WASHINGTON, *d.* 1677; *m.* Jane FLEMING, dau. Capt. Alexander FLEMING; their son
JOHN WASHINGTON, *m.* Mary TOWNSEND, dau. Robert TOWNSEND; their son
TOWNSEND WASHINGTON, *m.* Elizabeth LUND, dau. Christopher LUND; their son

ROBERT WASHINGTON, *d*. 1798; *m*. Alice STROTHER, dau. Benjamin STROTHER (see Strother, "Colonial Families," Volume V); their son

LUND WASHINGTON, *d*. 1853; *m*. Susannah GRAYSON, dau. of Capt. Spence GRAYSON of the Continental Army and his wife Mary Elizabeth WAGONER, she dau. of Peter WAGONER, who *m*. 1739, Catherine ROBINSON, she dau. of John ROBINSON, Speaker of Virginia House of Burgesses, who *d*. 1749, and his wife Catherine BEVERLEY who was the dau. of Robert BEVERLEY, who was *m*. in 1679, to Catherine HONE, who *d*. 1687, she the dau. of Theophilus HONE of Virginia.

SUSAN JEAN WASHINGTON, *b*. 1795; *d*. 1829; *m*. 1815, Edward Simmons LEWIS, of Washington, D. C.

Lewis Ancestral Charts

CHART I. *Colonial and Revolutionary Ancestry.* While directly recording the ancestry of the subject of this memoir, this chart includes many of the families of early Colonial history and has an important relation to numerous lineages heretofore published in Colonial Families.

CHART II. *A Certified Photographic Copy from the original Heraldic Records of Randle Holme, now in the British Museum, Including the Ancestry of* MARGARET BUTLER, *who m.* Lawrence WASHINGTON ancestor of the first President of the United States.

This most valuable original record sets aside the many controversies of the past involving that lineage. Since the chart is here reproduced in the old English of the original recorder, which might be difficult of interpretation by the reader, the following translation to modern print is given of that part covering the direct ancestry of Margaret BUTLER.

Aleanor, Lady Powys, was one of the dau. and co-heiress of Thomas Holand, Earl of Kent, son of Joan Countess of Kent, dau. and heiress of Edmond of Woodstock, son of Edward I and Margaret his wife, dau. of John Lord Wake, son of Hugh Lord Wake, son of Baldwyn Lord Wake, son of Hugh Lord Wake, and Jane his wife, dau. and heiress of Lord Somerville, Baron of Cottingham

Tho. Lord Somery, Baron of Dudley, was son of John Somery, Baron Dudley, and Beatrix his wife, dau. of David, Baron of Malpas John Somery was son to Rafe Somery, Baron Dudley, son of John Lord Dudley, who was son of Gervase Paganell, in right of his wife Felicia, dau. of Alfreton Dudley, Lord of Somery and Dudley, who was a son of Geoffrey Dudley, Earl of Conventry, *m.* to Alfreda dau. to Edmond Ironsides.
(King of England.)

Richard Sutton Kt. *m.* Margaret dau. Thos. Lord Somery, Baron of Dudley

Sir John Sutton, Lord Dudley *m.* dau. of Thos. Beauchamp Earl Warwick

John Sutton, Lord Dudley *m.* Alice dau. of Lord Spencer

John Sutton, created Baron Dudley, *m.* Constance dau. Sir Walter Blount Kt.

John Sutton, Baron Dudley *m.* Elizabeth dau. Sir John Berkeley

Payne Lord Tiptoft
|
Payne Lord Tiptoft
|
John Tiptoft *m.* Margaret dau. Lord Badlesmere
|
John Tiptoft *m.* Elizabeth dau. of Robt. Aspall Kt.
|
John Lord Tiptoft

Hawyse dau. and co-heiress of Lord Powys, *m.* John Cherlton Kt.
|
John Lord Powys *m.* Joan dau. of Earl of Stafford
|
Edward Cherleton Lord Powys, *m.*
|
Aleanor, co-heiress Earl of Kent
|
= Joyce dau. Edw. Lord Powys

Joyce Tiptoft = Sir Edmond Dudley
|
John Dudley of Aston le Walls 2nd son *m.* dau. of Darell
|
John Butler of Aston le Walls = Margaret dau. of John Dudley of Aston
|
William Butler 2nd son *m.* and had issue
|
Margaret Washington

She *m.* Lawrence Washington of Brington, *d.* 1614
|
Lawrence Washington, *d.* 1652
|
John Washington, *d.* 1675.   Lawrence *d.* 1677
|
Lawrence Washington, *d.* 1697
|
Augustine Washington, *d.* 1743
|
George Washington, *d.* 1799

ROYAL ANCESTRY OF ANDREW MONROE OF VIRGINIA

Charlemagne
Louis I, 840
Charles II, 877

Alfred the Great, 901　　　　　　　　　　　Baldwin I, 879 = Judith
Edward I, 925　　　　　　　　Aelfreth = Baldwin II, 918
Edmund I, 946　　　　　　　　　　　　　　Arnold I, 965
Edgar, 975　　　　　　　　　　　　　　　　Baldwin III, 962
Ethelred II, 1016　　　　　　　　　　　　　Arnold II, 989　　　　　　　Robert II,
　　　　　　　　　　　　　　　　　　　　　　　　　　　　　　　　　　King of
Edmund Ironsides, 1017　　　　　　　　　 Baldwin IV, 1036　　　　　　France
Edward Outlaw, 1057　　　　　　　　　　　Baldwin V, Earl of Flanders, 1067 = Adela
Margaret = Malcolm III, King of Scotland, 1093　Matilda = William the Conqueror, 1087
David I, 1153　　　　　　　　　　　　　　　Gundred = William of Warren, 1083
　　　　　　　　　　　　　　　　　　　　　William Earl Warren, 1138
　　　　　　　　　　　　　　　　　　　　　William Earl Warren, 1148

Henry Earl of Huntingdon, 1152 = Ada Warren 1178

Isabel = Robert Bruce, 1245

Robert Bruce, 1303

Robert I Bruce, King of Scotland, 1329

Margery = Walter Stewart, 1329

Robert II, King of Scotland, 1390

Robert Duke of Albany, 1420,

Margaret = Robert of Lorn　　　　Margery = Duncan Campbell, 1435

James Stewart of Lorn　　　　　　Archibald Campbell, v p

Isabel Stewart of Lorn　　=　　　Colin Campbell, Earl of Argyll, 1493

Agnes Campbell = Alex Mackenzie, 1488

Kenneth Mackenzie, 1507

Catherine Mackenzie = Hector Munro, 1541

Robert Munro, 1547 = Margaret Dunbar

Robert Munro, 1588 = Catherine Ross

Andrew Munro, 3rd son

Andrew Monroe of Virginia, 1668

Andrew Monroe, 2nd, 1714 = Elinor dau Patrick Spence

Susannah Monroe = Benjamin Grayson, 1757　　　Andrew Monroe, Sheriff, 1733

Spence Grayson, 1798　　　　　　　　　　　　　Spence Monroe, 1774 = Ely Jones

Susannah Monroe Grayson, 1822 = Lund Washington, 1853　James Monroe, 1831, President U. S.

Susan Jean Washington, 1829 = Edward S. Lewis I, 1829

Edward A. Lewis, 1889 = Parthenia Bransford

347

COLONIAL FAMILIES OF THE UNITED STATES

ROYAL LINEAGES OF SEVEN GENTLEMEN WHO SETTLED IN VIRGINIA ABOUT 1650 A.D.

Lawrence Washington	Alexander Fleming	William Strother	William Thornton	Gerard Fowke	Robert Beverley	Theophilus Hone

William the Conqueror
 |
Henry I — Adela
 | |
Matilda Stephen — Theobald
 | | |
Henry II Mary   Alice
 | | |
John   Matilda   Marie
 | | |
Henry III Godfrey Joan
 | | |
Edward I Matthew — Edward I = Eleanor
 | | Louvaine |
Joan of Acre — Edward II — Joan of Acre — Hawyse — Edward II — Joan of Acre
 | | | | Louvaine | |
Margaret Clare — Edward III — Margaret Clare — Louvaine — Edward III — Margaret Clare
 | | | | Aliva Basset | Lionel | Margaret Audley
Margaret Audley — John of Gaunt — Margaret Audley — Alenor Despencer — Phillippa — Hugh Stafford
 | | | | | |
Joan Stafford — John of Somerset — Joan Beaufort — Hugh Stafford — Aveline — Elizabeth Mortimer — Catherine Stafford
 | | | | | |
Edward Cherlton — Joan = James I King of Scots — George Nevill — Margaret Stafford — Courtney — Isabel Pole
 | | Janet | | | |
Joyce Cherlton — Elizabeth Gordon — Henry Nevill — Matilda Nevill — John Gifford — Elizabeth Percy — Anne Morley
 | | | | | |
Joyce Tiploft — Elizabeth Keith — Richard Latimer — Agnes Godard — Edmund Gifford — Thomas Clifford — Isabel Hastings
 | | | | | |
John Sutton — Robert Graham — Dorothy Latimer — Elizabeth Stapleton — John Gifford — John Clifford — Muriel Bosvile
 | | | | | |
Margaret Sutton — John Graham — Ann Dawnay — Agnes Plumpton — Elizabeth Kynnersly — Elizabeth Clifford — Muriel Burton
 | | | | | |
William Butler — Lillias Graham — John Conyers — Agnes Aldborough — John Kynnersly — Dorothy — Dorothy Everingham
 | | | | | |
Margaret Butler — Alexander Fleming — Elinor Conyers — Robert Thornton — Isabel Bradshaw — John Aske — Margaret Eyre
 | | | | | |
Lawrence Washington — Alexander Fleming — William Strother — Francis Thornton — Ann Fowke — Robert Aske — Mary Fanshaw
 | | | | | |
Lawrence = Jane Fleming — William Strother — William Thornton — Francis Fowke — Dorothy Aske — Mary Newce
 | Washington | | | | |
John Washington — William Strother — William Thornton — John Fowke — Francis Fairfax — Judith Alymer
 | | | | |
Townsend Washington — William Strother — William Thornton — Roger Fowke — Robert = Catherine Beverley Hone
 | | | | |
Robert Washington = Alice Strother — William = Margaret Thornton — Gerard Fowke — Catherine Beverley
                    | | |
              Benjamin Strother — Mary Fowke — Catherine Robinson
                    | |
              Alice Strother — Mary Mason — Mary Elizabeth Wagoner

Lund Washington = Susanna M. Grayson
 |
Susan Jean Washington = Edward S. Lewis I
 |
Edward A. Lewis = Parthenia Bransford

Walter F. Lewis Edward S. Lewis Florence E. Lewis Eugene W. Lewis P. Grayson Lewis Bransford Lewis

Marine

HONORABLE WILLIAM MATTHEW MARINE, deceased; *b.* in Sharpstown, Somerset County, Maryland, 25 August, 1843; *d.* 2d March, 1904, in Baltimore, Maryland; *m.* 9th November, 1871, at "Walnut Range," the Hall Estate in Prince George County, Maryland, Harriet Perkins HALL, *b.* 16th September, 1846, dau. of Richard Duckett HALL, *b.* 22d September, 1815, *d.* 24th April, 1864, *m.* 10th February, 1842, Susannah PERKINS, *b.* 12th November, 1818, *d.* 14th January, 1901 (see HALL Family, pp. 229–261).

HONORABLE WILLIAM MATTHEW MARINE, lawyer, orator, author and poet educated in private schools of Baltimore, Irving College, Cumberland Valley Institute; was appointed by President Benjamin HARRISON, Collector of the Port of Baltimore; studied law in the office of Thomas Yates WALSH, of Baltimore; admitted to the Baltimore Bar, 1864; was an accomplished orator and a gifted historian; was very active in political life and an ardent Republican in politics; author of the "British Invasion of Maryland, 1812–1814," "The Relation of Maryland to the Union during the Civil War." In 1901 a volume of his poems of unexceptional merit was published. Both he and his wife were descended from many of the most prominent families of the State. Distinguished for their services, in the Colonial and Revolutionary affairs of Maryland, among whom are the following of Mrs. MARINE's ancestors: Rev. Henry HALL, Benjamin HALL, Lieut. Richard DONOVAN, or DONAMHAM, Maj. John WELSH, Col. John WELSH, Richard DUCKETT, Sr., Richard DUCKETT, JR., Mareen DUVALL, Richard WELLS, Capt. Thomas STOCKETT, John NUTHALL, Lieut. Thomas SPRIGG, Thomas HILLEARY, Capt. Charles MERRYMAN.

ISSUE

1. Madison, LL.B., a successful practicing lawyer, of Los Angeles, California; *b.* at "Walnut Range," near Beltsville, Prince George County, Maryland, 7th September, 1873; educated in private schools in Maryland, 1881–1893; LL.B., University of Maryland, 1897; was associated with his father in the practice of his profession in Baltimore until 1904; member of the Bar of the Supreme Court of the United States, Court of Appeals of Maryland and all of the Courts of California; also of the Sons of the American Revolution in California; Society of War of 1812 in Maryland, of the Masonic Fraternity; Los Angeles County Bar Association, President Maryland Society of Southern California; one of the Counsellors of the War Board; *m.* December, 1912, Ida Irene

LAWRENCE, dau. of Thomas Henry LAWRENCE, who served for three years during the Civil War in the 96th Illinois Regiment, *m.* Mary EUSTICE.

II. Richard Elliott, A.B., LL.B., M.P.L., of Washington, D. C.; *b.* 6th February, 1875, at Ellicott City, Maryland; A.B., Johns Hopkins University, 1896; pursued a post graduate course in physics, mathematics and chemistry at the same institution, 1896-1897; attended National University Law School at Washington, D. C., and admitted in 1903 to the Bar of the District of Columbia; Master of Patent Law, Columbian (now George Washington) University, 1904; Charter Member of the University Club of Washington, D. C.; Assistant Principal and Instructor in Physics and Chemistry, Michigan City High School, Indiana, 1897-1900; Examiner United States Patent Office, 1900-1913; Principal Examiner in charge of the Division of Electricity, Generation and Motive Power, 1913-1917; appointed by President WILSON to the Board of Appeals of the United States Patent Office, 1917; otherwise known as the Board of Examiners in Chief; author of treatises on Principles of Patent Law and Patent Claims; *m.* 26th June, 1907, Marie St. Claire HOWELL, dau. of Charles E. HOWELL; of Washington, D. C., who *m.* Martha JEFFRIES; descended from THOMAS HUMPHREY, aide on Washington's staff; Col. John TAYLOE of Virginia, Richard CORBIN of Virginia, Col. George BRAXTON of Virginia; George BRAXTON, Jr. of Virginia; Robert CARTER of Virginia, Carter BRAXTON, of Virginia, Signer of the Declaration of Independence.

ISSUE

1. Martha Jeffries, *b.* 12th March, 1914, in Washington, D. C.

III. Harriet Perkins, Lecturer, Dramatist, Authoress and Orator; prominent in the social and civic activities of her city and state; *b.* at "The Devil's Elbow," near Hell Gate, Ellicott City, Maryland; member, Maryland Society Colonial Dames of America, Maryland Chapter Daughters of the American Revolution, being both Chapter 1905-1914 and State Historian since 1914; National Society of the United States Daughters of 1812; occupying the position of both Chapter and State Historian; Maryland Historical Society, First Vice-President and Recording Secretary; Children of the American Revolution; Woman's Literary Club, and a member of the Executive Committee of the Edgar Allen Poe Memorial Associates.

IV. Amelia Eleanor, *b.* at the family country seat, "Indian Springs," Harford County, Maryland; President of the Col. Nicholas Ruxton Moore Chapter Children of the American Revolution; Corresponding Secretary, Daughters of 1812 from 1905 to 1912, Registrar since 1913—; Member of the Board Francis Scott Key Chapter Daughters of the American

Revolution; National Society United States Daughters of 1812; Daughters of the Confederacy; Huguenot Society; Maryland Historical Society; Red Cross, etc.; *m.* 23d November, 1904, Nicholas Leeke DASHIELL, Jr., M.D., son of Nicholas Leeke DASHIELL, *b.* Somerset County, Maryland, 1st July, 1814, *d.* 28th February, 1895, *m.* Louisa Turpin WRIGHT. Dr. DASHIELL is a member of the Society of Colonial Wars, Huguenot Society of America, Sons of the American Revolution, Society War of 1812, Maryland Historical Society and numerous Medical Associations.

ISSUE

1. Eleanor Marine DASHIELL, *b.* 1st March, 1906.
2. Mary Leeke DASHIELL, *b.* 8th June, 1910.

v. Mary Susannah, *b.* at "Indian Springs," near Havre de Grace, Maryland; *d.* at "Walnut Range," the HALL Estate, 19th October, 1892.
vi. Frances Elizabeth, *b.* at "Indian Springs;" member Daughters of the American Revolution, Daughters of 1812, Daughters of the Confederacy; *m.* 21st June, 1911, Perry Belmont ROWE of New York, son of Dr. Walter Bosley and Caroline (BURROUGHS) ROWE of Maryland.

ISSUE

1. William Marine ROWE, *b.* 22d January, 1913, at Long Island, New York.
2. Walter Bosley ROWE, *b.* 14th June, 1914, at Malvern, Long Island, New York.
3. Perry Belmont ROWE, *b.* 5th June, 1916, at Malvern, Long Island, New York.

vii. Matthew Harrison, *b.* at "Indian Springs," Harford County, Maryland, 20th October, 1887; *d.* 20th January, 1891.

Lineage

The name is Norman-French and is variously given as MARINE, MERENÈ, MARIN, MAREEN, MAREAN and other abbreviations in America. The family of MARNE MARIN or MARIEN, were from their earliest record in France, warriors and were called the "sea-kings" and later the "sea-soldiers" of France. The name is an illustrious one in France and is traced back to the earliest antiquity, and has been borne by some of the most prominent of the Norman-French nobility for centuries. The first of the name in Maryland was Milleson MAREEN, planter, son of Alexander MARIN who *m.* ——— MILLESON, was *b.* in the Isle of France, 1634; *d.* 1679, in Sussex County, Delaware; he came to Maryland in 1655, with the Huguenots and settled in the northwest fork of the Nanticoke River; *m.* circa 1612–1664 Lavina MAJOR, dau. of

Thomas MAJOR of Accomac County, Virginia, also of French origin; they were among the first "Fox Quakers" of the Peninsula.

ISSUE

I. JONATHAN, b. circa 1665, of whom later.
II. William, b. circa 1667, d. 28th February, 1716; unmarried.
III. Charles, b. 1669; d. after 1717.
IV. James, b. 1671; will proved 28th February, 1748.
V. Alexander, b. 1673; d. young.
VI. Thomas, b. 1675; d. 1749; m. Mary (surname unknown).
VII. John, b. 1677; d. after 1716.
VIII. Major, b. circa 1679–1680.

JONATHAN MAREN or MARIEN, of Sewell Creek, Maryland; b. circa 1665; d. May, 1736; m. 1689, Kezia (surname not given); she d. circa 1738.

ISSUE

I. Millison, b. circa 1693–1694; d. in infancy
II. WILLIAM, b. 1696, of whom later.
III. Esther, b. circa 1698; no record.
IV. Jonathan, b. circa 1700; d. 4th January, 1756; m. December, 1726, Rachel VICTOR.
V. John, b. 1702; d. May, 1706.
VI. Thomas, b. 1704; d. August, 1775; m. Angel (ANEY) STEVENS or STEPHENS.
VII. Lovey, b. 5th January, 1708; no record.

WILLIAM MERINE, of "Buck's Lodge," Somerset-Worcester County, Maryland; b. 1696; d. November, 1767; m. Mary (surname unknown) who d. previous to 1762.

ISSUE

I. John, b. 1733; d. 1808.
II. Matthew, Gentleman, b. circa 1735; removed to Philadelphia and is given the title of "Gentleman" in some of the records there.
III. ZOROBABEL, b. 2nd June, 1736, of whom later.
IV. Charles, Gentleman, b. 11th September, 1738; d. 3d March, 1823; m. 1759, Anna ROBINSON, b. 20th October, 1733, d. 19th October, 1810.
V. James, b. 1740; d. young.
VI. David, b. 1742; d. young.
VII. William, b. June, 1744; m. in Somerset County, Maryland, wife's name unknown; d. in North Carolina.
VIII. Janet, b. circa 1748; no record.
IX. Esther, b. circa 1750; no record.

ZOROBABEL MARINE, of Lower Somerset and Dorchester Counties, Maryland, and Sussex County, Delaware; b. 2d June, 1736; d. 1st March, 1821; was one of the largest land owners and influential citizens and "Quakers" of that section; m. 1757-1758, Mary HAYWARD, dau. of Capt. Francis HAYWARD, d. 1757, of Dorchester County, Maryland; the son of Francis HAYWARD, son of Francis HAYWARD of Virginia, who m. Mary WARREN, dau. of Admiral WARREN, of London, England.

ISSUE

I. WILLIAM, b. circa 1759, of whom later.
II. Anna, b. circa 1761; no record.
III. Matthew, b. circa 1763; no record.
IV. Mary, b. circa 1765; m. Hatfield WRIGHT.
V. Esther, b. circa 1767; no record.
VI. Hayward, b. circa 1769; d. young.
VII. Sarah, b. 1771; m. Thomas GREY.
VIII. Rhoda, b. circa 1775; no record.
IX. John, b. May, 1778.
X. Charles, b. 11th January, 1781; d. young.

WILLIAM MARINE, planter, of "Fisher Farm;" b. circa 1759; d. in the winter of 1811; m. license 4th December, 1787, Mary FLETCHER, dau. of John FLETCHER, of New England, cousin of Grace FLETCHER, wife of Daniel WEBSTER.

ISSUE

I. Fletcher, b. 11th December, 1788; d. 1821; served in War of 1812; m. Polly ELLIOTT.
II. Levisa, b. circa 1792; d. 1821; m. William SMITH, of Quantico, Maryland.
III. Mary, b. 1795; m. John MOORE.
IV. MATTHEW, b. 19th August, 1797, of whom later.
V. William, Lieutenant; b. 1st May, 1799; d. 1833; m. Molly (surname not given).
VI. Sarah, b. 11th July, 1801; m. William SARD.
VII. Charles, b. 21st May, 1803; d. 22d November, 1869; m. 4th September, 1827, Rachel VAUGHAN, dau. of Joseph VAUGHAN.
VIII. Zorobabel, b. 11th July, 1805; d. June, 1857; m. (firstly) Vashti CHARLESCRAFT; m. (secondly) his sister-in-law Elizabeth CHARLESCRAFT.
IX. James, b. 1808; served in Delaware Militia; m. Eliza ROBINSON, dau. of Mrs. Rhoda ROBINSON of Somerset County.

MATTHEW MARINE, philanthropist, financier and man of public affairs, of Sharpstown, Wicomico County, Maryland; b. 19th August, 1797; d. 27th November, 1854; farmer and ship builder; served in the war of 1812; m. 9th April, 1818,

Nancy RAWLINGS, *b.* 9th January, 1803, *d.* 16th April, 1870, dau. of John RAWLINGS and Mary MEZWICK, dau. of Luke and Leah MEZWICK of Somerset County, Maryland.

ISSUE

    I. Polly Mezwick, *b.* 24th May, 1819; *d.* 24th September, 1823.
   II. FLETCHER ELLIOTT, *b.* 1st March, 1821, of whom later.
  III. Nancy Mezwick, *b.* 11th October, 1823; *d.* 18th May, 1824.
  IV. Vashtie, *b.* 15th September, 1825; *m.* (firstly) Capt. James Osmond ADAMS, lineally descended from President John ADAMS; *m.* (secondly) John B. TWIFORD, who *d.s.p.*

ISSUE BY FIRST MARRIAGE

1. Nancy Ellen ADAMS.
2. Matthew Washington ADAMS.
3. John Quincy ADAMS.
4. James Fletcher ADAMS.
5. Alice ADAMS.

    V. Matthew Washington, *b.* 7th May, 1828; *d.* 28th June, 1845.
   VI. Nancy Elizabeth, *b.* 20th May, 1830; *d.* 5th May, 1876; *m.* Maj. Allen ROBINSON, *b.* 27th November, 1819; *d.* 15th July, 1893, son of John and Sallie (ALLEN) ROBINSON.
  VII. Margaret Ann Levisa, *b.* 23d August, 1833; *d.* 27th April, 1836.
 VIII. William John, Lieutenant, lawyer; *b.* 4th April, 1836; *d.* 26th August, 1883; was appointed during the Civil War, a Lieutenant in the 12th Missouri, United States Volunteers, and participated in the Western battles under Gen. George H. THOMAS; was wounded at the battles of Chickamauga, Lookout Mountain, Missionary Ridge, and before Nashville.
   IX. Martha Ann, *b.* 20th August, 1839; *d.* 19th June, 1913; *m.* 1855, Henry Flower RAWLINGS, *b.* 2d June, 1832, *d.* 28th February, 1910, son of Jesse son of John and Molly (MEZWICK) RAWLINGS.

ISSUE

1. Cordelia Jane RAWLINGS, *d.* 17th August, 1909.
2. Nannie Leonard RAWLINGS, *m.* 1855, Marmaduke Goodhand WHITE, of Kent Island.
3. Hester RAWLINGS.
4. Emma Purner RAWLINGS, *m.* 22d April, 1889, Samuel Maith NORTH, B.S., M.A., Columbia University; 1894–1914, Head of Department of English, Baltimore Polytechnic School; 1918, Journalist.

    1^1. Marie Rawlings NORTH.

COLONIAL FAMILIES OF THE UNITED STATES

ISSUE

x. Sarah Jane, *b.* 19th June, 1841; *m.* Thomas James TWILLEY, *b.* 24th April, 1835, *d.* 24th February, 1898, son of Robert and Nancy (WALKER) TWILLEY, of Somerset County, Maryland.

REV. FLETCHER ELLIOTT MARINE, *b.* 1st March, 1821, in Sussex County, Delaware; *d.* 19th September, 1889; educated at Dickinson College; was an ordained preacher of the Baltimore Conference of the Methodist Episcopal Church; publisher of *The Pioneer*, a monthly religious magazine; Chaplain of his lodge Independent Order of Odd Fellows; *m.* 7th September, 1842, Hester Eleaner KNOWLES, *b.* 7th July, 1820, in Sussex County, Delaware, *d.* 17th December, 1896, in Baltimore, dau. of Judge William KNOWLES, who served in Capt. Thomas RIDER'S Company, 9th Regiment Delaware Militia which saw active service in the War of 1812.

ISSUE

I. WILLIAM MATTHEW, the subject of the sketch.
II. Louisa Emmalla, *b.* 18th July, 1848; *m.* 22d June, 1868, J. W. CATHCART, son of Robert and Martha Ann (COOPER) CATHCART.

ISSUE

1. Maxwell CATHCART.
2. Martha Cooper CATHCART, *m.* 14th November, 1900, Lewis Stewart ELMER.
3. Blanche CATHCART.
4. Frances Josephine CATHCART.

III. Thomas Price, *b.* 17th September, 1850; *d.* 29th June, 1851.
IV. John Fletcher, *b.* 28th May, 1852; *d.* 30th June, 1854.
V. James Hargis, *b.* 22d March, 1854; *d.* 16th January, 1912; *m.* Anna Barbara RUPP, *b.* 5th September, 1854; *d.* 12th June, 1918.

ISSUE

1. Elizabeth Hester, *b.* 23d April, 1873; *m.* 1st March, 1894, Rev. Robert M. MOORE, of the Methodist Episcopal Church.
2. Minnie Elizabeth, *b.* 10th May, 1875; *d.* young.
3. Emma Hargis, *b.* 18th February, 1877; *d.* in early womanhood.
4. Annie Eugenia, *b.* 24th August, 1881; *m.* David SALMON, of Washington, Chief of the War Department.

ISSUE

1^1. Barbara SALMON.

VI. Hester Ann, *b.* 16th March, 1856; *m.* 17th August, 1875, W. J. DAVIS.

ISSUE

i. Marie DAVIS, *d.* aged twenty-three years.

VII. Mary Jane, *b.* 12th May, 1858; *d.* 28th February, 1920; *m.* 6th December, 1882, Frank Thomas LERCH, son of Augustus LERCH, of West River, Anne Arundel County, Maryland, and Martha WATKINS, dau. of Richard WATKINS, of South River, whose grandfather (according to family tradition) founded the historic old South River Club of Anne Arundel County, Maryland, the oldest social organization in the country.

ISSUE

1. Harry Miltenberger LERCH, *m.* Florence Louise CARTER.

ISSUE

1. Martha Watkins LERCH.
2. Florence Louise LERCH.

VIII. Fletcher Columbus, *b.* 23d November, 1860; *d.* 6th March, 1864.

Arms.—Azure, between a chevron or, three martlets argent.

Morris

MAJOR EFFINGHAM BUCKLEY MORRIS, JR., A.B., LL.B., of Philadelphia, Pennsylvania; *b.* 26th August, 1890, at his father's country residence "Ty'n-Coed," Lower Merion Township, Montgomery County, Pennsylvania; *m.* 19th February, 1917, at Chestnut Hill, Philadelphia, Julia Peabody Lewis, dau. of Francis D. and Mary (Chandler) Lewis.

ISSUE

1. Effingham Buckley, III, *b.* 21st November, 1917.

Effingham Buckley Morris, Jr., a lawyer; was educated at Haverford School and was graduated from Yale where he received degree of A.B. in 1911, and LL.B. from the Law School of the University of Pennsylvania, 1915; played center in Yale Freshman football team, 1907; same position on Yale University football team, 1908–1911; member First Troop, Philadelphia City Cavalry, 1912 et seq.; served on Mexican Border with the troops in 1916; seven months, from 6th July, 1916 to 22d January, 1917; enlisted as Second Lieutenant 10th May, 1917, Officer's Reserve Corps, Fort Niagara, New York; promoted 15th August, 1917, to Captain of Cavalry, Officer's Reserve Corps, served as Captain, 313th Regiment Co. "K," Infantry National Army, Camp Meade, Maryland; went to France with his regiment in July, 1918. He participated in the Argonne offensive and led his men at Monfaucon Hill; his Company being one of the two Assault Companies in that action on 26th September, 1918. He was shot in the leg on 27th September, but declined to leave the field and took command of the Battalion on the death of the Major, remaining in command for four days until the regiment was relieved, and he was sent to the hospital. For this action he was cited in the dispatches, was promoted to Major, and was awarded the Distinguished Service Cross by General Pershing. He was subsequently given the Croix de Guerre, with Palm, by Marshall Petain of the French Army, and made a Chevalier of the Legion d' Honneur of France with the cross of that Order. He returned to the United States in command of the Second Battalion, 313th Regiment, in July, 1919; was mustered out of service, and resumed the practice of law in Philadelphia. He resides in the old Morris house, No. 225 South Eighth Street. His son, Effingham B. Morris, III, representing the sixth generation of the family, in continuous residence there.

Lineage

Anthony Morris, "Mariner," of Old Gravel Lane, in the Parish of Stepney, London, England; *b.* 1630; *d.* at sea; according to tradition he was of Welsh extraction.

The progenitor of this family was another Anthony Morris, *b.* circa 1600, of whom little is known except that he was at one time a resident of Reading in Great Britain but subsequently he became a resident of Barbadoes in the West Indies; one of the records referring to him states "The family removed from Leicestershire, to London;" he had a son

ANTHONY MORRIS, I, "Mariner," of Old Gravel Lane, in the Parish of Stepney, London, England, who was b. circa 1630, and was the father of Anthony MORRIS, II, the emigrant (below); made voyages between London and the Island of Barbadoes; m. probably 1653, Elizabeth SENIOR, in Barbadoes, she d. in Barbadoes in 1660, having gone there to settle her husband's estate. According to one account he was lost at sea in 1655-1656, on a return voyage from Barbadoes to Britain, or according to an entry in an old family Bible "he died in Barbadoes."

ISSUE

I. ANTHONY, II, only child, b. 23d August, 1654, of whom below.

ANTHONY MORRIS, II, Merchant, of Philadelphia, Pennsylvania, b. 23d August, 1654, in Old Gravel Lane, Stepney, London, in the Kingdom of Great Britain; bapt. 25th August, 1654, at At Dunstan Chapel, Stepney; d. 23d August, 1721, in Philadelphia, where he settled before the close of 1685. He was in London at the time of the Plague and also the Great Fire, during his minority, at which period of his life through conviction, he became a member of the Society of Friends or Quakers. In the Charter granted to the City of Philadelphia 20th March, 1691, he is named one of the Six Aldermen; 6th September, 1692, was commissioned a Justice of the Peace of the County Courts, Philadelphia, reappointed 6th May, 1693, and is mentioned as a Justice of the Peace, 12th February, 1697. On 6th September, 1692, he was commissioned a Justice of the Court of Common Pleas, Quarter Sessions of the Peace and the Orphans Court of the City and County of Philadelphia. Was reappointed by Governor FLETCHER 5th May, 1693, being commissioned the Presiding Justice of the Court of Common Pleas and also Presiding Justice of the County Court of Quarter Sessions on 29th May, 1693; in August, 1694, commissioned a Justice of the Supreme Court of Pennsylvania. Elected to the Provincial Council 1675-1676; Member of the Assembly, 1701-1702; Mayor of Philadelphia, 1703-1704; m. (firstly) 30th January, 1676, at the Meeting of the Savoy on the Strand, London, England, Mary JONES, d. 3d August, 1688; m. (secondly) 26th August, 1689, Agnes BARR, who d.s.p. 26th May, 1692, widow of Cornelius BARR. Anthony MORRIS was probably her fourth husband as her first husband's name was Herman VAN SNYDER and she was betrothed to Cornelius BARR as Agnes MAKEMAN; he m. (thirdly) 18th January 1683-1684, at Newport, Rhode Island, Mary CODDINGTON, who d. 25th September, 1699, widow of Thomas CODDINGTON, of Rhode Island; he m. (fourthly) 30th August, 1700, Elizabeth WATSON, b. circa 1661, d. 2d February, 1767, dau. of Luke and Sarah WATSON.

ISSUE BY FIRST MARRIAGE

I. Susanna, b. in London, 7th March, 1676-1677; "dyed about 6 years old."
II. Mary, b. in London, 18th July, 1678, and "departed this life one year old."
III. Anthony, b. in London, 24th February, 1683, "dyed about one yeare old."

IV. ANTHONY, *b.* in London, 15th March, 1681–1682, of whom later.
V. John, *b.* 17th February, 1685, at Burlington, New Jersey; *d.* in Philadelphia, 12th April, 1690.
VI. Samuel, *b.* in Philadelphia, 28th December, 1686–1687; *d.* 2d November, 1689.
VII. James, *b.* Philadelphia, 8th May, 1688; *d.* October, 1747, at Duck Creek, Delaware; *m.* 8th January, 1709, Margaret COOK.

ISSUE BY THIRD MARRIAGE

I. William, *b.* in Philadelphia, 2d May, 1695; *d.* 6th November, 1776; *m.* (firstly) 14th November, 1718, Sarah DURY; *m.* (secondly) 2d November, Rebecca CADWALADER.
II. Elizabeth, *b.* in Philadelphia, 28th April, 1697; *m.* (firstly) 13th October, 1716, Samuel LEWIS; *m.* (secondly) William DURY.
III. Joseph, *b.* in Philadelphia, 12th March, 1699; *d.* in Philadelphia, 25th May, 1699.

ISSUE BY FOURTH MARRIAGE

I. Isaac, *b.* in Philadelphia, 24th October, 1701; *d.* there after 24th October, 1755 (date of the will of his mother Elizabeth MORRIS).
II. Sarah, *b.* in Philadelphia, 16th November, 1703–1704; *d.* unmarried in Philadelphia, 24th October, 1774.
III. Israel, *b.* in Philadelphia, 25th October, 1705; *d.* there 1729.
IV. Luke, *b.* in Philadelphia, 25th August, 1707; *d.* there 17th November, 1793; *m.* February, 1749, Mary RICHARDS.
V. Hannah, *b.* in Philadelphia, 4th May, 1717; *d.* there unmarried 25th June, 1741.

ANTHONY MORRIS, III, Brewer, of Philadelphia, Pennsylvania, *b.* 15th March, 1681–1682, in London, England; *d.* 23d September, 1763, in Philadelphia; received his scholastic education at the Public School in Philadelphia, which his father, with other "Friends" of the Monthly Meeting, had been instrumental in founding in 1689. At the age of fourteen apprenticed himself to learn the art and mysteries of brewing, to serve for seven years from 29th December, called February in the year 1695–1696. In 1721 was chosen a Representative in the Assembly of the Province of Pennsylvania; re-elected 1722–1723–1724 and 1725, and sat until the close of the session 6th June, 1726; was appointed one of the Signers of paper money; elected Alderman 29th September, 1726; again, 2d October, 1733, and same day commissioned an Associate Justice of the City Court; his will dated 29th September, 1760, is sealed with his crest; *m.* in Philadelphia 10th March, 1704, Phoebe GUEST, *b.* 28th July, 1685, dau. of George and Alice (BAILYES) GUEST, *d.* 18th March, 1768, she dau. of William and Alice (CHANDERS) BAILYES; he son of William and Alice (SOMMERLAND) BAILYES of Birmingham, England.

ISSUE

I. ANTHONY, IV, *b.* 14th November, 1705, of whom later.
II. James, *b.* 8th July, 1707, *d.* 29th January (as November), 1750; *m.* 18th January, 1734, Elizabeth KEARNEY.

ISSUE

1. Anthony.
2. Mary.

III. John, *b.* 23d April, 1709; *d.* 3d February, 1782; *m.* 18th February, 1734, Mary SUTTON.

ISSUE

1. William.
2. Mary.

IV. Samuel, *b.* 20th July, 1710; *d.* 7th August, 1710.
V. Samuel, *b.* 21st September, 1711; *d.* 31st March, 1782; *m.* 26th March, 1737, Hannah CADWALADER.

ISSUE

1. John, and others

VI. Mary, *b.* 13th October, 1713; *d.* 31st October, 1759; *m.* 9th September, 1732, Samuel POWELL.
VII. Joseph, *b.* 10th January, 1714-1715; *d.* July, 1785; *m.* (firstly) 18th December, 1741, Martha FITZWATER; *m.* (secondly) 7th November, 1765, Hannah MICKLE.

ISSUE

1. George, and others.

VIII. Elizabeth, *b.* 21st October, 1716; *m.* 6th September, 1739, Benjamin SHOEMAKER.
IX. Benjamin, *b.* 30th October, 1717-1718; *d.* 7th July, 1719.
X. Phoebe, *b.* 24th May, 1721; *d.* 5th March, 1722.
XI. Susanna, *b.* 27th July, 1722; *d.* 13th June, 1724.
XII. Deborah, *b.* 13th November, 1723-1724; *d.* unmarried 31st March, 1793.
XIII. Benjamin (M.D.), *b.* 7th March, 1725; *d.* unmarried 14th May, 1755.
XIV. A dau., unnamed, *b.* and *d.* 19th May, 1726.

ANTHONY MORRIS, IV, of Philadelphia, Pennsylvania, *b.* there 14th November 1705; *d.* there 2d October, 1780, at his country seat "Peckham," in Southwark; was connected with his father in the brewing business; he was one of the Signers of the Non-importation Agreement, 7th November, 1765; *m.* (firstly) December, 1730, Sarah POWELL, *b.* 29th April, 1713, *d.* 10th February, 1751, dau. of Samuel and Abigail (WILCOX) POWELL. Samuel POWELL, *b.* 2d November, 1673, in Great Britain, came of a Somersetshire family, many of the name and apparently his kinsmen being residents in the Parish of North Curry and its neighborhood, but they came originally from Wales. Their Coat of Arms bore: Party per fesse, argent and or, a lion rampant gules; Crest: a star of eight points above a cloud—all proper. From this Coat of Arms it is evident that the family claimed descent from the princes of Powis through Einion Efell, Lord of Cynleath, who flourished in the twelfth century. ANTHONY MORRIS, IV, *m.* (secondly) 30th April, 1752, Eizabeth HUDSON *b.* 20th February, 1720–1721, *d.* 22d May, 1783, dau. of William and Jane (EVANS) HUDSON, a gd. dau. of William HUDSON, a member of the Provincial Council, and Mayor of Philadelphia, 1725-1726, and his wife Mary RICHARDSON, dau. of Samuel RICHARDSON also a Provincial Councillor.

ISSUE BY FIRST MARRIAGE

I. Anthony, V, *b.* 25th September, 1731; *d.* 29th November, 1732.
II. SAMUEL, *b.* 24th April, 1734, of whom later.
III. Deborah, *b.* 15th September, 1736; *d.* 23d September, 1787; *m.* 8th September, 1756, John FRANKLIN of New York.
IV. Anthony, VI, Major, *b.* 8th August, 1738; killed at the Battle of Princeton, New Jersey, 3d January, 1777.
V. Israel, *b.* 6th February, 1741; *d.* 30th October, 1806; *m.* Mary HARRISON.
VI. Sarah, *b.* 2d May, 1743; *d.* 20th January, 1830; *m.* 11th April, 1771, William BUCKLEY.
VII. Thomas, *b.* 25th November (January), 1745–1746; *d.* 2d October, 1809; *m.* 6th October, 1768, Mary SAUNDERS.

ISSUE BY SECOND MARRIAGE

I. William Hudson, *b.* 10th March, 1753; *d.* 14th September, 1807; *m.* 5th September, 1776, Sarah WARDER.
II. Luke, *b.* 10th April, 1760; *d.* 20th March, 1802; *m.* 9th May, 1786, Ann WILLING.
III. Isaac, *b.* 28th November, 1761; *d.* in "the following week."

CAPT. SAMUEL MORRIS, V, of Philadelphia, *b.* 14th April, 1734, at Reading, Pennsylvania during his parents temporary sojourn there; *d.* July, 1812 (styled as Junior) in Philadelphia, at his Philadelphia residence; Captain 1st Troop Philadelphia Light Horse, which was organized 17th November, 1774. In 1763 was a member of the Society of St. David's; President for forty years of Gloucester Fox Hunting Club out of which two organizations the 1st Troop of Philadelphia Light Horse

Cavalry was formed; Governor for forty years of the State in Schuykill (the noted Fish House Club); one of the subscribers to the Non-Importation Resolutions, 25th October, 1765, the first "Pledge of Honor" before the Declaration of Independence; member of the Committee of Safety from 30th June, 1775, until 10th October, 1775, and from 20th October, 1775, to 22d July, 1776. In 1776 was elected to the Provincial Assembly of Pennsylvania and again in 1781-1782 and 1783. In 1776-1777 the Philadelphia Troop of Light Horse, commanded by Capt. Samuel MORRIS, served as WASHINGTON's Body Guard. At the Battle of Trenton the members of the Troop distinguished themselves by their bravery; Captain MORRIS took part at the battle of Brandywine and Germantown, camped at Valley Forge, and on other active duties during the Revolutionary War. He resigned his Captaincy 11th April, 1786; *m.* at Christ Church, Philadelphia, 11th December, 1755, Rebecca WISTAR, *b.* 25th January, 1735-1736, *d.* 22d January 1791, dau. of Caspar and Katherine JOHNSON (JANSEN) WISTAR. Caspar WISTAR the founder of the family in America was *b.* in Hilsbach in the Electorate of Heidelberg in Germany 3d February, 1696, *d.* 21st March, 1752, being the eldest son of Johannes Caspar WISTER, *b.* 1670, *d.* 15th January, 1726, and Anna Catharina his wife. His father held the hereditary office of Electoral Huntsman (Fürst Jäger) to Carl Theodore of Bavaria, the Elector of Baden. The appellation "Herr" appears on the Church Record, prefixed to his name and distinguished him from the Bourgeois.

ISSUE

I. Samuel, *d.* young.
II. Sarah, *b.* 19th January, 1758; *d.* 31st January, 1831; *m.* 14th March, 1782, Richard WISTAR.
III. Benjamin WISTAR, *b.* 14th August, 1762; *d.* 24th April, 1825; *m.* 24th November, 1758, Mary WELLS.
IV. Caspar Wistar, *b.* 12th September, 1764; *d.* 27th February, 1828; *m.* 24th November, 1795, Elizabeth GILES.
V. Anthony, *b.* 10th February, 1766; *d.* 3d November, 1860; *m.* 13th May, 1790, Mary Smith PEMBERTON.
VI. Luke Wistar, *b.* 25th June, 1768; *d.* 4th June, 1830; *m.* (firstly) 24th March, 1791, Elizabeth Morris BUCKLEY; *m.* (secondly) 4th April, 1800, Ann PANCOAST.
VII. Isaac Wistar, *b.* 19th July, 1770; *d.* 8th May, 1831; *m.* 17th December, 1795, Sarah PASCHALL.
VIII. Catharine Wistar, *b.* 22d April, 1772; *d.* unmarried 10th December, 1859.
IX. Samuel, *b.* 14th March, 1775; *d.* 17th September, 1793, of yellow fever.
X. ISRAEL WISTAR, *b.* 27th February, 1778, at Reading, Pennsylvania, of whom below. (All of the above children were born in Philadelphia except the last named.)

ISRAEL WISTAR MORRIS, Broker and Commission Merchant of Philadelphia, *b.* 27th February, 1778, at Reading, Berks County, Pennsylvania, during the occupation of Philadelphia by the British; *d.* 17th August, 1870; was elected a member of the Philadelphia Troop of Light Horse 31st May, 1798; *m.* 12th June, 1799, Mary HOLLINGSWORTH, *b.* 19th April, 1776, *d.* 23d June, 1820, dau. of Levi and Hannah (PASCHALL) HOLLINGSWORTH. He son of Zebulon and Ann (MAULDEN) HOLLINGSWORTH), who was the son of Henry and Elizabeth (ATKINSON) HOLLINGSWORTH. He the son of Valentine and Catherine (CORNISH) HOLLINGSWORTH, she dau. of Henry CORNISH, High Sheriff of London, who was unjustly executed during the reign of James II, 23d October, 1685, for alleged complicity in the Monmouth Plot. His innocence was later clearly established and his confiscated estate restored to his family. Valentine HOLLINGSWORTH, the progenitor of the Delaware, Maryland and Pennsylvania families, was probably born in Cheshire, England about 1630–1640.

ISSUE

I. Stephen P., *b.* 3d June, 1800; *d.* 13th August, 1865; *m.* (firstly) 21st February, 1827, Rachel JOHNSON, who *d.* 30th August, 1837; *m.* (secondly) 9th December, 1854, Mary Ann C. COPE, *b.* 11th January, 1803, dau. of Israel COPE, of Philadelphia and Margaret COOPER.

II. Henry, *b.* 27th January, 1802; *d.* 20th December, 1881; *m.* about 1830, Caroline OLD.

III. Samuel, *b.* 25th November, 1803; *d.* 18th June, 1804.

IV. CASPAR, M.D., *b.* 2d May, 1805, of whom later.

V. Levi, *b.* 24th April, 1807; *d.* 26th February, 1868; *m.* 1830, Naomi MCCLENACHAN.

VI. Hannah, *b.* March, 1809; *d.* January, 1892.

VII. Israel, *b.* 22d October, 1811; *m.* 25th September, 1839, Elisabeth LONGSTRETH.

VIII. Jane, *b.* 13th August, 1813; *d.* 12th March, 1897.

IX. Wistar, *b.* 6th September, 1815; *d.* 23d March, 1891; *m.* 22d January, 1863, Mary HARRIS.

CASPAR MORRIS, M.D., of Philadelphia, Pennsylvania; *b.* 2d May, 1805; *d.* 17th March, 1884; M.D., University of Pennsylvania, 1826, and after serving as Resident Physician to the Pennsylvania Hospital and making a voyage to India as Ship's Surgeon, he began practice in Philadelphia. Was a founder and manager and from 1860–1880 Vice President of the Institute for the Blind; a founder and manager of the Protestant Episcopal Hospital; *m.* 12th November, 1829, in Baltimore, his cousin, Ann CHESTON, *b.* 9th May, 1810, *d.* 27th November, 1880, eldest dau. of James and Mary (HOLLINGSWORTH) CHESTON.

ISSUE

I. James Cheston, M.D., *b.* 28th May, 1831; *m.* (firstly) 8th March, 1854, Hannah Ann TYSON, *d.* 2d February, 1867, dau. of Isaac, Jr. and Hannah Ann (WOOD) TYSON of Baltimore, Maryland; *m.* (secondly) 11th January, 1870, Mrs. Mary Ella (JOHNSON) STUART, dau. of Lawrence JOHNSON of Philadelphia.

II. Israel Wistar, *b.* 1st June, 1833, of whom later.
III. Mary Hollingsworth, *b.* November, 1835; *m.* 1856, Henry M. Murray.
IV. Galloway Cheston, *b.* 26th June, 1837; *m.* 1861, Hannah Perot.
V. Cornelia, *b.* 26th June, 1840; *d.* 12th April, 1842.
VI. Daniel Corrie, *b.* 17th May, 1842.

Israel Wistar Morris of Philadelphia, *b.* 1st June, 1833; *d.* 18th December, 1909; a Mining Engineer of high standing; President of the Locust Mountain Coal and Iron Company and other mining corporations connected with the Lehigh Valley Railroad; *m.* 3d December, 1855, Annie Morris Buckley, *b.* 13th January, 1836, *d.* 4th March, 1915, dau. of Effingham L. and Hannah A. (Morris) Buckley and gd. dau. of Thomas Buckley, President of the Bank of America, New York.

ISSUE

1. Effingham Buckley, *b.* 23d August, 1856, only child, of whom below.

Effingham Buckley Morris, of Philadelphia, *b.* 23d August, 1856, at the old Morris mansion, 225 South Eighth Street, Philadelphia; graduate of University of Pennsylvania, 1875; A.B., Law School of University of Pennsylvania, 1878 LL.B. Practised law in association with P. Pemberton Morris, LL.D.; General Attorney for the Lehigh Valley Railroad for a number of years and solicitor for the Girard Trust Company, until election as President of that Corporation in 1887, since which time the company has greatly prospered. Represented the Eighth Ward on Councils for two years, 1880, 1881. Director of Union League Club for three years, the full term of service. Member of the Philadelphia, University and other clubs. Manager of the Pennsylvania Hospital, where he succeeded his uncle, the late Wistar Morris. Director of the Pennsylvania Railroad 1896 and allied roads to date. Manager of the Philadelphia Savings Fund Society and other corporations; *m.* 5th November, 1879, Ellen Douglas Burroughs, dau. of H. Nelson and Caroline (Mitchell) Burroughs, banker of Philadelphia and gd. dau. of Samuel Augustus Mitchell, publisher of *Mitchell's Atlas*.

ISSUE

I. Rhoda Fuller, *b.* 5th November, 1880; *m.* 12th February, 1901, George Clymer Brooke of Birdsboro, Pennsylvania, he *d.* 7th May, 1915; *m.* (secondly) 15th February, 1917, Trenchard Emlen Newbold of Philadelphia.
II. Eleanor Burroughs, *b.* 6th October, 1881; *m.* 25th October, 1902, Stacy Barcroft Lloyd of Philadelphia.
III. Caroline Mitchell, *b.* 24th June, 1886; *m.* 6th December, 1905, John Frederic Byers of Pittsburg, Pennsylvania.
IV. Effingham Buckley, *b.* 26th August, 1890, the subject of this memoir.

Arms.—Sable, a lion passant between three scaling ladders argent.
Crest.—A castle domed argent.
Motto.—Proprium decus et patria.
Residence.—No. 225 South Eighth Street (the Morris Homestead), Philadelphia, Pennsylvania.
Clubs.—Philadelphia, Racquet, Radnor Hunt, Pickering Hunt, White Marsh Valley Hunt, Yale Club of New York, Merion Cricket.

Payne

EDWARD WALDRON PAYNE, of Springfield, Illinois, *b.* 19th March, 1857, at Cincinnati, Ohio; *m.* 23d April, 1885, Ida KEYS, *b.* 21st October, 1863, dau. of James and Nannie (GARDNER) KEYS, Springfield, Illinois.

ISSUE

1. Nanette, *b.* 16th September, 1887, at Springfield, Illinois; *m.* 10th April, 1917, Charles Crankshaw THOMAS, son of Henry Wailes and Margaret (CRANKSHAW) THOMAS (see THOMAS family, p. 453).

    ### ISSUE

    Payne, *b.* 11th May, 1919.

II. Coirnne, *b.* 24th October, 1891, at Springfield; *m.* William Hughes DILLER, of Springfield, son of Isaac and Addie (HUGHES) DILLER, of Springfield, Illinois.

    ### ISSUE

    1. William DILLER, *b.* 15th July, 1916.
    2. Corinne DILLER, *b.* 16th December, 1917.
    3. Jane LOUISE, *b.* 8th June, 1919.

III. Alida, *b.* 10th December, 1898, at Springfield.

EDWARD WALDRON PAYNE was President of the State Bank of Springfield for many years and is interested in various civic, state and industrial developments. He has established the Payne Collection of prehistoric implements of the Stone Age.

Lineage

ROGER HASKELL, *b.* in England, 1613; *d.* 1667; was the first American Ancestor. In 1632 he came to America accompanied by his brothers, William and Mark, and settled in that part of Salem, Massachusetts, which was cut off and became known as Beverly. He was at first a shipmaster and had land grants made him in Salem. He *m.* (firstly) ——— STONE, dau. of John and Abigail STONE; *m.* (secondly) Elizabeth HARDY, dau. of John and Elizabeth HARDY, of Beverly.

ISSUE BY FIRST MARRIAGE

1. ROGER, II, *b.* in Beverly, of whom later.

ISSUE BY SECOND MARRIAGE

I. John.
II. William.
III. Mark.
IV. Elizabeth.

ROGER HASKELL, II, was *b.* in Beverly and moved from there to Norwich, Connecticut, in 1708; *m.* circa 1680, Hannah WOODBURY, dau. of John WOODBURY.

ISSUE

I. Abigail, *b.* 18th October, 1681.
II. Josiah, *b.* 16th August, 1685.
III. Hannah, *b.* 23d January, 1687.
IV. Mary, *b.* 23d April, 1689.
V. Judith, *b.* 1690; *d.* circa 1691.
VI. Daniel, *b.* 11th January, 1691.
VII. ROGER, III, *b.* 16th October, 1697, of whom later.
VIII. Elizabeth (twin).
IX. Judith (twin).
X. Sarah.

ROGER HASKELL, III, of Norwich, Connecticut, *b.* 16th October, 1697; *m.* (wife's name not given, the supposition being she predeceased him).

ISSUE

1. Elijah HASKELL, the eldest son of Roger, III, *b.* Norwich, Connecticut, 17th March, 1721; *d.* at Tolland, Vermont, 1774; *m.* 11th April, 1745, Sarah READ.

ISSUE

1. Charlotte, *b.* 18th August, 1754, in Norwich Connecticut; *d.* 1838, in Baltimore, Vermont; *m.* (firstly) Thomas DUMPHY; *m.* (secondly) Joshua MARTIN, of Weathersfield, Vermont, *b.* 1st December, 1764, at Tolland, Vermont, *d.* February, 1836.
2. Hannah, *b.* 1st December, 1764, in Tolland.
3. Diadama, *b.* 3d March, 1756, at Norwich, Connecticut; *d.* 28th May, 1847; *m.* Jonathan NYE.
4. Jacob, *b.* 21st October, 1759, in Norwich; *d.* 25th June, 1835; *m.* Diantha ROBINSON, dau. of Elijah ROBINSON; served three years in the Revolutionary Army.

5. John, *b.* 28th February, 1762; served three years in the Revolutionary Army; *m.* (firstly) Amy CHANDLER; *m.* (secondly) Grace BARNARD.
6. Gideon, *b.* 10th November, 1766, Tolland, Connecticut; *d.* 25th February, 1842; *m.* Mahitable BARNARD.
7. ROGER, IV, *b.* 6th May, 1763, of whom below.
8. Peres, *b.* 26th September, 1770, in Tolland, Connecticut; *d.* in Lyme, New Hampshire, *m.* Hannah BALDWIN.

ROGER HASKELL, IV, of Weathersfield, Vermont; *b.* 5th May, 1763, Tolland, Connecticut; *d.* 9th February, 1838, at Ascutneyville, Vermont; removed to Weathersfield, Vermont; *m.* 13th September, 1796, Hannah WHITE, who *d.* 25th November, 1856, at Weathersfield, dau. of John WHITE, a lineal descendant of Peregrine WHITE the first child born in the first Plymouth Colony.

ISSUE

I. Daniel, *b.* 17th October, 1797; *d.* 25th February. 1882; *m.* 24th November, 1822, Betsey RICHARDS, who *d.* 24th March, 1869.
II. Horace, *b.* 17th December, 1793; *d.* 15th February, 1851, at Glenn, New York; *m.* February, 1828, Elizabeth ELLIS, who *d.* 25th October, 1871.
III. ROXANA ATILDA, *b.* 28th October, 1800, of whom later.
IV. Content, *b.* 29th September, 1802; *d.* 3d May, 1877; *m.* 19th February, 1846, Elijah WILSON.
V. Luctus, *b.* 1st April, 1804; *d.* at Guild Hall, Vermont; *m.* (firstly), April, 1831, Marilla COWLES; *m.* (secondly) Adeline HATCH.
VI. Zenas, *b.* 22d August, 1805; *d.* 10th January, 1827.
VII. Roswell, *b.* 2d July, 1808; *d.* 2d April, 1883, at Windsor, Vermont; *m.* 15th October, 1849, Charlotte Jane DEFOREST of Staten Island, New York, who *d.* 30th June, 1891.
VIII. Elijah, *b.* 1st April, 1810; *d.* 16th May, 1833.
IX. Lorenzo Cogswell, *b.* 18th March, 1819; *d.* 28th August 1824.
X. Jacob Reed, *b.* 25th January, 1815; *d.* 10th October, 1875; *m.* 4th March, 1857, Mariett THRASHER, *d.* 1st May, 1885.
XI. Lucy Bates, *b.* 3d October, 1816; *d.* 11th October, 1875.
XII. Henry Louis Shafter, A.B., A.M.; *b.* 12th December, 1818, at Weathersfield, Vermont; *d.* 5th December, 1902, near Bloomington, Illinois; *m.* (firstly) Mary SPAULDING, of Bloomington, Illinois; *m.* (secondly) Sarah BANTS, of Matamora, Illinois, 25th December, 1862; A.B., A.M., Norwich University. Illinois bar, 1850; enlisted Company K, 11th Illinois Infantry, 26th May, 1861; prominent in Illinois educational and political affairs.
XIII. Susan Atlantic, *b.* 4th August, 1822; *m.* (firstly) Cullen BOWEN, who *d.* 4th September, 1843; *m.* (secondly) 23d January, 1850, Joseph WHITCOMB, who *d.* 6th February, 1877.

Roxana Atilda Haskell, of Springfield, Illinois, b. 29th October, 1800; d. there 2d December, 1875; m. 26th March, 1829, John G. Waldron of Albany, New York.

ISSUE

I. Charles Henry Waldron, b. 9th January, 1831, in Albany; d. 1st August, 1889, in Ludlow, Illinois; m. 23d July, 1860, Emma Neal of Matamora, Illinois.
II. William J. Waldron, b. 21st December, 1832; d. 4th September, 1858.
III. Maryette Waldron, b. 4th February, 1836, of whom later.

Maryette Waldron, of Springfield, Illinois; b. 4th February, 1836, at Buffalo, New York; d. 4th February, 1884, at Springfield; m. 13th May, 1855, Francis Edward Payne, of Utica, New York, who d. 30th December, 1897, at Springfield.

ISSUE

I. Elizabeth Waldron Payne, b. 26th March, 1856, Cincinnati, Ohio; d. 25th May, 1856.
II. Edward Waldron Payne, b. 19th March, 1857 the subject of the memoir.
III. William Morris Payne, b. 5th November, 1859, at Springfield; d. 9th November, 1910.
IV. Richard J. Payne, b. 2d February, 1864, at Springfield; d. 20th November, 1886.
V. Julia Etta Payne, b. 10th April, 1872, at Springfield; d. 22d August, 1878.
VI. Minnie Ada Payne, b. 6th January, 1876, at Springfield; m. 21st October, 1897, James A. Easley, of Springfield.

ISSUE

1. Frances Easley, b. 21st August, 1898.
2. Edward Easley, b. 23d April, 1901.

Arms.—(Haskell) Vaire, or and sable.
Crest.—On a mount azure, an apple tree fructed proper.
Motto.—Vincet Veritas.

ARTHUR EMMONS PEARSON, son of William Henry and Nancy Delia (BENJAMIN) PEARSON, b. in Boston, 9th January, 1869. He is connected with HOLLINGSWORTH AND WHITNEY COMPANY, one of the largest manufacturers of paper and paper bags, and has been with them for nearly thirty years. He has compiled and published biographical histories of the PEARSON* and BENJAMIN families and he also contributed to the publication of the NOYES genealogy. He presented the New Hampshire Bay in the Cloister of the Colonies of the Washington Memorial Chapel at Valley Forge, Pennsylvania. This is the Sanctuary Bay, and was given by Mr. PEARSON in honor of the troops of New Hampshire and in memory of his seven ancestors who gave military service in the War of American Independence.† The New Hampshire State Panel in the Ceiling of the Chapel was the gift of Mr. PEARSON and his sister, Miss Nella Jane PEARSON.

The following account of the dedication of the John BENJAMIN tablet, which occurred 19th June, 1908, appeared in the *Washington Chapel Chronicle* of 18th July, 1908:

". . . . As soon as the processional hymn was sung the choirs and congregation united in singing "America." On the wall adjoining the doorway into what will in the future be the "Porch of the Allies" an American flag had been hung, falling gracefully from a crown of oak leaves. During the singing of the first stanza, Mr. Arthur E. PEARSON, of Boston, Massachusetts, a son of the donor, unveiled the John BENJAMIN tablet.

The inscription was read by the Rev. W. Herbert BURK, as follows—
WITH . THANKSGIVING . UNTO . ALMIGHTY . GOD . AND . IN . LOVING MEMORY . OF . JOHN . BENJAMIN . OF . MASSACHUSETTS . BORN . FEBRUARY 5 . 1758 . DIED . DECEMBER . 2 . 1814 . ARTILLERIST . IN . THE . CONTINENTAL ARMY . GIVING . TO . HIS . BELOVED . COUNTRY . A . SERVICE . OF . SEVEN YEARS . AND . SHARING . THE . PRIVATIONS . OF . VALLEY . FORGE . THIS TABLET . IN . TRIBUTE . TO . HIS . HONOR . HIS . VALOR . AND . HIS . FAITHFUL LIFE . IS . ERECTED . BY . HIS . GRANDDAUGHTER . NANCY . DELIA BENJAMIN . PEARSON

---

* See memoir of William Henry PEARSON, "Colonial Families of the United States of America," Vol. II, 1911; "Benjamin Genealogy" (Winthrop, 1900); "American Families of Historic Lineage," which includes charts (New York); "Noyes Genealogy" (Boston, 1904); "The Cyclopedia of American Biography" (Appleton's Revised, New York, 1918); "Biographical History of Massachusetts" (Eliot, Vol. IX, 1918); "Colonial Wars," Vol. I, No. I, 1913; "Chart Book of the Society of Colonial Wars in the Commonwealth of Massachusetts" (in preparation).

† The print of the Dedication party at the Massachusetts Bay, in the Cloister of the Colonies, of the Washington Memorial Chapel at Valley Forge, 19th June, 1909, including the clergy, guests and the choir, together with the complete key was prepared by Mr. PEARSON, and presented by him to The Massachusetts Society of the Sons of the American Revolution, and was reproduced in their Year Book of 1910. This was the first society to present a Bay in the Cloister or to take part in the erection of the Memorial.

"The tablet was dedicated by the Rev. Roberts COLES, Rector of the Church of Our Saviour, Jenkinton, and Dean of the Convocation, acting for Bishop WHITAKER, this being his first official act as Dean. . . . .

"In designing the . . . . tablet . . . . the architect of the Chapel, has done a work full of artistic merit. The graceful Gothic border, the richly decorative lettering and the illustrative details of cannon, balls and rammers, combine to make a tablet worthy of a place upon the Chapel walls.

"The John BENJAMIN tablet is the gift of Mrs. William Henry PEARSON, of Boston.

"John BENJAMIN was a descendant, in the fifth generation, from John BENJAMIN, of Watertown, Massachusetts, and his wife Abigail EDDY. His father perished in the expedition to Fort William Henry in the year 1758. In the year 1773 he chose his kinsman, Richard HUNNEWELL, as his guardian. He enlisted into the Continental Army from Col. William McINTOSH's Regiment known as the 'First Suffolk County Regiment.' He participated in the principal engagements of the war. He was in the regiment commanded by Colonel CRANE. His youthful patriotism had undoubtedly been whetted by his being a witness of the "Boston Tea Party." He married, on 15th February, 1781, in Needham, Massachusetts, Jemima MILLS, a descendant, in the fourth generation, of Samuel MILLS, of Dedham, Massachusetts, and his wife Frances PEMBROKE. Jemima (MILLS) BENJAMIN died after a married life of about twenty years. There were children by a second marriage as well as by this union. About the year 1793 the family removed to Maine. After a life of honor and industry, a life blessed through a consecrated service to his country and to his home, he passed from this life, at the home of his son, Benaiah BENJAMIN, in Whitefield, Maine."

A reproduction of the tablet was printed in *The Churchman* of 4th July, 1908.

Mr. PEARSON was unanimously elected a Vice President of the Valley Forge Historical Society upon the organization of the Society (1918). The Washington Memorial Library and the Valley Forge Museum of American History are under the care of the Society.

Mr. PEARSON has enabled a number of public libraries to include many and costly volumes in their collections, that they otherwise would not have possessed.

Mr. PEARSON presented to the State of New Hampshire during the administration of Governor Keyes, a whip made and used by Daniel WEBSTER in driving his old white horse "Morgan," when hunting and fishing in the vicinity of Marshfield. The whip is in the keeping of the New Hampshire Historical Society at Concord.

Mr. PEARSON effected an agreement with the American Unitarian Association and donated a fund for the establishment of the perpetual series of addresses known as The Unification Addresses. The fund is to be continuously invested in securities of the United States of America as the President and Directors of the Association shall determine. As Rev. Samuel A. ELIOT, D.D., President of the American Unitarian Association so happily expresses the purpose of this agreement, it is intended to assist in "unifying all the forces of righteousness and good will in the World." Dr. Charles W. ELIOT has accepted the invitation to deliver the First

Unification Address in the Horace Mann Auditorium, Columbia University, New York City, on 20th October, 1918.‡ The selection of the persons to give the addresses must always be open to "such scholars of humane and cultured attributes" as by inclination and ability shall most perfectly assist in consummating "complete mutual understanding and helpfulness between the people of all denominations and creeds"—and the addresses shall never become an agency "to further the particular beliefs of any sect or association of persons in any manner such as a just interpretation could regard as an unwarranted affront to the followers of any faith."

The addresses are to be given once in every five years.

At the entrance of the United States of America into the World War, Mr. PEARSON was considerably over the enlistment age, yet he made two trips to Washington and offered his services for the period of the war without remuneration.

Lineage

I. JOHN PEARSON, (1615–1679), emigrated from England and settled in Lynn in the year 1637 and later in Reading, Massachusetts. He was one of the first seven members of The First Church in Christ of Reading and a Deacon (1652). His wife, Maudlin (Madeline) survived him. Their son,

II. LIEUT. JOHN PEARSON (1650–1728) was chosen as chairman of the committee appointed for the establishment of the town of Lynnfield and acted in a similar capacity for the construction of the Meeting House on Lynnfield Common. This was built in the same year as St. Michael's (Episcopalian), at Marblehead, and the church of the Unitarian Society at Hingham, known as the "Old Ship," is the only church edifice still standing in Massachusetts that was constructed at an earlier date. The Meeting House at Lynnfield was the gathering place for the transaction of all the civil affairs of the town until the year 1892, when the new town hall was built; it is still used for town purposes and is in an excellent state of preservation. Lieutenant PEARSON was Representative to the General Court of Massachusetts (1702–1703; 1710–1711). He *m.* Tabitha KENDALL, daughter of Deacon Thomas and Rebecca KENDALL. Their son,

III. CAPT. JAMES PEARSON (1680–1744) was active in the town and parish affairs of Lynnfield. About ten years before his death, he removed to Haverhill, Massachusetts, having purchased the Wainwright property from Nathaniel SALTONSTALL, JR. He *m.* Hepsibah SWAYNE, dau. of Maj. Jeremiah SWAYNE and Mary SMITH, his wife. Major SWAYNE was a distinguished officer of the Massachusetts Company in the Narragansett Campaign against King Philip, and he was severely wounded at the Great Swamp Fight. He later was appointed by the Governor

‡ Owing to the national epidemic a postponement of the first Unification Address was necessary. Dr. Eliot delivered the address at the Copley-Plaza Hotel, Boston, 22nd May, 1919.

as Commander-in-Chief of all forces of the Province of Massachusetts Bay, and led an expedition "against the Indian Enemy,—in the direction of the Kennebec." He was repeatedly chosen as Representative Deputy and Member of the Council. Hepsibah SWAYNE was a gr. gd. dau. of Isaac MORRILL, of Roxbury, and her mother inherited his farm of two hundred acres in Reading. Isaac MORRILL was a progenitor of Gen. Joseph WARREN, who fell at the Battle of Bunker Hill. He was a member of the Military Company of the Massachusetts, now the Ancient and Honorable Artillery Company, in the year of its formation (1638). The son of Capt. James PEARSON and Hepsibah SWAYNE, his wife,

IV. JONATHAN PEARSON (1704–circa 1798) was a resident of Andover, Massachusetts; at the close of the Revolutionary War, he removed to Lyndeborough, New Hampshire. He *m.* Abigail GATES, dau. of Amos and Hannah (OLDHAM) GATES. She was a descendant of Sir Geoffrey GATES, who *m.* Elizabeth, dau. of Sir William CLAPTON, Knight, of Kentwell, Sussex, England. The son of Jonathan and Abigail (GATES) PEARSON,

V. AMOS PEARSON (1734–ante 1783) was Sergeant of the Reading Military Company and answered the call at Lexington on 19th April, 1775. He *m.* Elizabeth NICHOLS, a gd. dau. of Capt. Thomas NICHOLS of the Reading Military Company, a soldier in King Philip's War and a Selectman of Reading for thirty-one consecutive years. The son of Amos and Elizabeth (NICHOLS) PEARSON,

VI. HIRAM PEARSON (1770–1856) lived in Bradford, Vermont, where his house is still standing. He removed to the nearby town of Orford, New Hampshire. He *m.* Alice BARRON, dau. of Ensign Joshua BARRON (a Revolutionary soldier, and later under arms as a Green Mountain Boy) and Lavina DERBY, his wife. The son of Hiram and Alice (BARRON) PEARSON,

VII. WILLIAM PEARSON (1807–1887) was born at Orford, New Hampshire. He *m.* Lucinda Maria GREENLEAF, and resided in Lancaster, New Hampshire, until the year 1845, when he made his home in Boston, Massachusetts. Their son,

VIII. WILLIAM HENRY PEARSON, of Boston and Newton, Massachusetts (q.v., Vol. II, of this work), *m.* Nancy Delia BENJAMIN, dau. of Benaiah and Elizabeth (NOYES) BENJAMIN. Their children,

IX. Seth Greenleaf PEARSON, *d.* 1864.

IX. Nella Jane PEARSON.

IX. ARTHUR EMMONS PEARSON, the subject of this memoir.

Arms.—Az. between two pallets wavy ermine, three suns, or.
Crest.—A sun ppr. issuing out of a cloud.
Residence.—West Newton, Massachusetts.

Clubs.—Brae-Burn Country Club, Neighborhood Club, West Newton.

Societies.—Member of the Unitarian Laymen's League, Patron of the Valley Forge Historical Society, Life member of Society of Colonial Wars in the Commonwealth of Massachusetts, the Bostonian Society, New England Society for the Preservation of New England Antiquities, Member of the Massachusetts Society of the Sons of the American Revolution, Society of the War of 1812 in the Commonwealth of Massachusetts, and the New Hampshire Historical Society.

Pearson

MAXWELL JOHN PEARSON, *b.* 24th February, 1885, Orange, New Jersey; *m.* 19th October, 1910, Ethel Bennett CONANT, *b.* 3d December, 1884, Campello, Massachusetts.

ISSUE

 i. Maxwell John PEARSON, Jr., *b.* 4th October, 1911.
 ii. Margaret Conant PEARSON, *b.* 27th January, 1913.
 iii. Leonard PEARSON, *b.* 22d September, 1917.
 iv. Edward PEARSON, *b.* 10th April, 1920.

Mr. PEARSON for many years has been identified with one of the largest shoe manufacturing concerns of Brockton, Massachusetts. He is a communicant of St. Paul's Episcopal Church of that city, and a member of Paul Revere Lodge, Free and Accepted Masons, of Brockton, Massachusetts.

Through the descent from JOHN PEARSON, of Lynn and Reading and the marriage alliances, Maxwell John PEARSON, is lineally descended from more than a score of progenitors who gave Colonial services civil and military and from six participants in the Revolutionary War.

Mrs. PEARSON is the dau. of Alton Leonard and Hattie (JENKS) CONANT and gd. dau. of Galen and Sarah COLLINS (REDLINGTON) CONANT. Roger CONANT was the founder of the family in America. The maternal gd. father of Mrs. PEARSON was George Albert JENKS; he served in the Union Army in the Civil War. Her maternal gd. mother was Martha BENNETT, whose ancestry was allied with the DALES family.

Lineage

JOHN PEARSON (1615–1679), emigrated from England and settled in Lynn, Massachusetts (1637) and later in Reading. He was one of the first seven members of The First Church of Reading and sometime Deacon. His wife, Maudlin (Madeline), survived him. Their son,

LIEUT. JOHN PEARSON (1650–1728), was chairman of the Committee that effected the establishment of Lynnfield and of the committee to build the meeting-house on Lynnfield Common, which edifice is still used for town purposes (1918). He was Representative to the General Court (1702–1703, 1710–1711). His wife was Tabitha KENDALL, dau. of Deacon Thomas and Rebecca KENDALL. Their son,

CAPT. JAMES PEARSON (1680–1744), a resident of Lynnfield for many years, purchased a property in Haverhill (circa 1732), from Nathaniel SALTONSTALL and lived there until his death twelve years later. He *m.* Hepsibah SWAYNE, dau. of Maj.

Jeremiah and Mary (SMITH) SWAYNE. The services of Major SWAYNE, both civil and military were many and distinguished. The son of Capt. James and Hepsibah PEARSON,

JONATHAN PEARSON (1704-5-circa 1798), *m.* Abigail GATES in Cambridge (1729-30). Their son,

AMOS PEARSON (1734-ante 1785), as Sergeant of the Reading Military Company responded to the call at Lexington, 19th April, 1775. He *m.* Elizabeth NICHOLS. Their son,

HIRAM PEARSON (1770-1856), was one of the petitioners for the incorporation of the first public library in Vermont. He *m.* Alice BARRON. Their son,

WILLIAM PEARSON (1807-1887), *m.* Lucinda Maria GREENLEAF. Their son,

EDWARD ASHER PEARSON (1840-), *m.* (firstly) Adeline Chamberlain CROCKER; (secondly) Sophia Downing OWENS; (thirdly) Annie Anderson LOWRY.

ISSUE BY THIRD MARRIAGE

I. Edward Lowry PEARSON, *b.* 16th November, 1880.
II. Annie May PEARSON, *b.* 13th May, 1882; *m.* 15th June, 1908, Lester Earle PACKARD.

ISSUE

1. Lester Earle PACKARD, Jr., *b.* 15th February, 1911.
2. David Charles PACKARD, *b.* 2d October, 1917.

III. MAXWELL JOHN PEARSON, the subject of this memoir.
IV. Alice LeBarron, *b.* 14th November, 1888; *m.* 8th December, 1914, Lewis Henry CONNOR.

Arms.—Az. between two pallets wavy ermine, three suns, or.
Crest.—A sun ppr. issuing out of a cloud.
Residence.—Campello, Massachusetts.

Penniman

JAMES LANMAN PENNIMAN, deceased, of Philadelphia, Pennsylvania; *b.* 9th July, 1832, in Cincinnati, Ohio, *d.* 2d August, 1890, in Philadelphia; Graduated from Yale, A.B., 1853; A.M., 1855; *m.* 17th August, 1859, Maria Davis HOSMER, *b.* 1st February, 1830, in Concord, Massachusetts, *d.* 15th January, 1914, in Philadelphia, Pennsylvania, dau. of Abel and Olive Parlin (DAVIS) HOSMER of Concord, Massachusetts.

ISSUE

I. James Hosmer, *b.* 8th November, 1860, at Alexandria, Virginia; unmarried; A.B., Yale, 1884; Litt.D. (Honorary) Franklin and Marshall College, 1914; taught in the De Lancey School, Philadelphia, 1886–1912; author of "Common Words Difficult to Spell," "The School Poetry Book," "Prose Dictation Exercises," "Practical Suggestions in School Government," "New Practical Speller," "Books and How to make the Most of Them," "George Washington as Commander in Chief," "George Washington as Man of Letters," also various papers in *The Forum, The School Journal, The Journal of Education,* etc. A notable contribution of Dr. PENNIMAN to the cause of education is the "Maria Hosmer Penniman Memorial Library of Education" established by him in 1915 at the University of Pennsylvania, as a tribute to his mother. This library now numbers over ten thousand volumes, many of which are of the greatest rarity. To it the founder is making considerable additions from time to time, the gathering of volumes from all parts of the world, constituting an important part of his labor of filial love. He is a member of the following Societies: Societe de Sport de l'Ile de Puteaux, Paris; National Geographical Society; Philadelphia Geographical Society; Fellow of the American Geographical Society; life-member of the Historical Society of Pennsylvania; life member of the Society of the Sons of the Revolution; The Yale Club of New York.

II. Josiah Harmar, *b.* 20th July, 1868, Concord, Massachusetts; unmarried; A.B., 1890; Ph.D., 1895, University of Pennsylvania; LL.D., University of Alabama, 1906; Washington College, Maryland, 1907; taught in the De Lancey School, Philadelphia, 1890–1892; Instructor, Assistant Professor, English, University of Pennsylvania, 1892–1905; Professor of English Literature University of Pennsylvania, 1905; Dean of the College, 1897–1909; Vice Provost, 1911–to date. Author of "The War of the Theatres," "A Book about the Bible" and many articles on literary and educational topics. Editor of Jonson's "Poetaster" and

Dekker's "Satiromastix" Belles Lettres Series. Member of The American Philosophical Society; The Modern Language Association of America (life); The American Dialect Society; The English Association (Great Britain); Sons of the Revolution (life); Society of Colonial Wars (life); American Association for the Advancement of Science (life); National Institute of Social Sciences; Clubs: Contemporary Club, Franklin Inn, University.

Dr. James Hosmer PENNIMAN and his brother come of a long line of distinguished ancestors among whom on the maternal side are to be found the names of the Rev. Peter BULKELEY, the learned first minister of the Concord settlement, whose book "The Gospel Covenant" printed in London in 1649 and again in 1651 (second edition) was one of the earliest written in America; Dr. Jonathan PRESCOTT, who m. Peter BULKELEY's gd. dau., and their son, Col. Charles PRESCOTT, who distinguished themselves in the service of the Colonies, and Col. Charles PRESCOTT in the Revolution as well.

The HOSMERS, who came to America in 1635 in the ship *Elizabeth*, and settled in Concord, were among the first defenders of American Liberty and were numerously represented in the Revolution, as they had been in the Colonial Wars. Capt. Isaac DAVIS, Abner HOSMER and James HAYWARD who fell, and Joseph HOSMER who was Adjutant, at the Concord fight, 19th April, 1775, were all near kinsmen of Dr. PENNIMAN's mother. (See Memorial of Rev. G. W. HOSMER and PRESCOTT Memorial, also Concord and Acton Town Records.)

On the PENNIMAN side are found the names of Col. Benjamin CHURCH, Col. Charles CHURCH, Col. John CHANDLER, Capt. Samuel CHANDLER of Colonial Wars and Revolution; of Judge Charles Church CHANDLER, who at his death 8th August, 1787, was a member of the Continental Congress. A contemporary notice of him says:

"He was an eminent practitioner of the Law. He sustained several important public characters with great reputation and ability; as Judge of Probates, Representative of the Town in the General Assembly, and has been elected a Member of Congress. As a man of genius he was universally known and respected, as a man of philanthropy and goodness, he was universally beloved. He needs not the soft hand of flattery to portray his virtues. His best and most honourable epitaph is engraven in the memory of all who had the pleasure of his acquaintance."

Judge CHANDLER's wife was Marian GRISWOLD, dau. of Matthew GRISWOLD, and gd. dau. of Roger WOLCOTT, both Colonial Governors of Connecticut. Judge James LANMAN was Dr. PENNIMAN's gr. gd. father, who m. Judge CHANDLER's dau. Marian. Judge LANMAN was Senator from Connecticut, 1819–1825, and was also a member of the Convention that formed the first Constitution of the State. He was a member of the Legislature and a Judge of the Superior Court, greatly beloved and respected for his character and for his distinguished public services to State and Nation (see CHANDLER Family, BACKUS Family, Records of Connecticut, and of Rhode Island).

Lineage

JAMES PENNIMAN, the emigrant ancestor of the PENNIMAN family in America, was one of the settlers of the town of Braintree, Massachusetts, having gone there from Boston where he at first lived. He came over in the ship *Lion* in 1631 with his wife Lydia ELIOT (sister of John ELIOT, the Apostle to the Indians), and having as fellow passengers, John WINTHROP, Jr. (son of the Governor of Massachusetts Bay, and himself first Governor of Connecticut), John ELIOT and his brother Jacob ELIOT. The ELIOTS came from Naseing, Essex, while the seat of the PENNIMAN family was probably in Yorkshire, where the English PENNYMAN family still live at Marske, in Ormesby Hall (see PENNYMAN Records). The connection between the English and the American families has never been satisfactorily established. The statement sometimes made that James, the emigrant was a brother of Sir William PENNYMAN, the distinguished Royalist is not substantiated by any known record, though it is not impossible that it may be true. As James was a Puritan it has been suggested that his Royalist relations kept no record of him or that the records were destroyed. (For James, the Emigrant, see Town Records of Braintree, Massachusetts. For Lydia, his wife, see Town Records of Medfield, Massachusetts where her second marriage as widow of James, is mentioned and she is stated to have been the sister of John ELIOT, the Apostle. For Penniman see the PENNYMAN Records, York 1904, Appendix N, American Pennimans.)

THE PENNIMAN FAMILY OF BRAINTREE

JAMES PENNIMAN, *b.* in England, came in the *Lion*, 1631, with John WINTHROP, Jr.; admitted as Freeman 6th March, 1631–1632; of Boston at first; of Braintree, 1639; wife, Lydia ELIOT; he *d.* 26th December, 1664. Lydia *m.* (secondly) 7th December, 1665, Thomas WRIGHT, of Medfield (Medfield Records). James PENNIMAN'S will is dated 18th December, 1664; proved 31st January, 1664–1665; recorded Suff. Prob., 1: 443. Mentions his oldest son James, son Joseph, youngest son Samuel. He says, "God hath blessed me with many children." His son James "had been educated into such a way of living, as he is having already had a portion." Most of the children, he says, were young. Inventory, 31st January, 1664–1665, including dwelling house, £45; barn and stable, old house and orchard, £70; thirty acres of land near the Mill-Pond, £70; fifteen acres near Knight's Neck, (Quincy), £30; eighteen acres "nigh Weymouth ffery," £55, etc. Total, £505, 3s. Sworn to in court by Lydia PENNIMAN, widow of James. (Suff. Prob., 4: 207.)

ISSUE

 I. James, *bapt.* 26th March, 1633; *m.* 10th May, 1659, Mary CROSS.
 II. Lydia, *bapt.* 22d February, 1634–1635.
 III. John, *bapt.* 15th January, 1636–1637; *m.* 24th February, 1664–1665, Hannah BILLINGS.
 IV. Joseph, *b.* 1st August, 1639; *m.* (firstly) Waiting ROBINSON; *m.* (secondly) widow Sarah (BASS) STONE.

v. Sarai (Sarah), *b.* 6th May, 1641.
vi. SAMUEL, *b.* 14th November, 1645; of whom later.
vii. Hannah, *b.* 26th May, 1648.
viii. Abigail, *b.* 27th December, 1651; *m.* 18th April, 1678, Samuel NEALE, son of Henry NEALE.
ix. Mary, *b.* 29th September, 1653; *m.* 4th April, 1678, Samuel PAINE.

LIEUTENANT SAMUEL PENNIMAN, son of James and Lydia, *b.* 14th November, 1645; he was admitted as Freeman, 1678; by occupation "cordwinder;" Lieutenant; appraiser of Thomas Faxon's estate, 26th April, 1694; of estate of John Mills, 7th November, 1695; he *d.* intestate, 16th January, 1704–1705. Joseph PENNIMAN and Joseph PARMENTER, administrators, 2d February, 1704–1705. (Suff. Prob., 15: 478); *m.* 6th January, 1673–1674, Elizabeth PARMENTER, dau. of Robert and Leah PARMENTER, and gd. dau. of Martin SANDERS, who (Martin) *d.* July, 1658; Robert PARMENTER was a deacon of the First Church in Braintree.

ISSUE

i. Elizabeth, *b.* January, 1674–1675; *m.* 8th November, 1699, Joshua MORSE of Medfield.
ii. Samuel, *b.* 15th March, 1675–1676; *d.* in infancy.
iii. Samuel, *b.* 5th November, 1677; *m.* 14th May, 1707, Ellen PAINE.
iv. Josiah, *b.* 21st November, 1678; *d.* 29th November, 1678.
v. Hannah, *b.* 12th February, 1682–1683.
vi. Jonathan, *b.* 12th February, 1682–1683.
vii. James, *b.* 29th March, 1695.
viii. NATHAN, *b.* March, 1689, of whom below.

NATHAN PENNIMAN, of Mendon, Massachusetts, *b.* March, 1689; *m.* 5th December, 1716, Mary FARNUM.

ISSUE

i. SAMUEL (Lieutenant), *b.* 11th October, 1717, of whom later.
ii. Jonathan, *b.* 30th July, 1719.
iii. Nathan, *b.* 8th May, 1721.
iv. Ann, *b.* 23d October, 1723.
v. Peter, *b.* 11th September, 1728.

LIEUT. SAMUEL PENNIMAN, of Mendon, Massachusetts, *b.* 11th October, 1717; *d.* 7th October, 1807; *m.* (firstly) Huldah WHITE, 3d December, 1741, *d.* July, 1769; *m.* (secondly) Mrs. Deborah TAFT, 25th October, 1770; *b.* 4th November, 1734, *d.* 2d April, 1797; *m.* (thirdly) Mrs. Sarah ALBEE, previously widow BUGBEE, maiden name Sarah GORE, 1799. (Milford and Mendon Records.)

ISSUE BY FIRST MARRIAGE

I. William.
II. Huldah.
III. Silence.
IV. ELIAS, b. 1st December, 1748, of whom later.
V. Nathan.
VI. Phineas.
VII. Mary.

ISSUE BY SECOND MARRIAGE

I. Samuel, b. 24th June, 1773.
II. James, b. 28th January, 1777.

DOCTOR ELIAS PENNIMAN of Mendon and Hardwick, Massachusetts, b. Mendon, Massachusetts, 1st December, 1748; d. 9th February, 1830, in Hardwick; graduated at Brown University, 1774; m. 8th December, 1773, Ann JENKS, dau. of Capt. Ebenezer JENKS of Providence, Rhode Island.

ISSUE

I. CHIRON, b. Milford, Massachusetts, 8th January, 1775, of whom later.
II. Obadiah, b. Milford, 1st November, 1776; d. Troy, New York, 14th September, 1820; a publisher and bookseller.
III. William.
IV. Sylvanus Jenks (see "Annals of Albany," vol. 4, p. 439).
V. John Ritto, b. Milford, 30th January, 1783; d. New York; he was a portrait painter.
VII. Polly (see Mendon and Hardwick Records).

CHIRON PENNIMAN, b. Milford, Massachusetts, 8th January, 1775; m. 30th November, 1796, Olive WHIPPLE, dau. of Samuel WHIPPLE; Chiron d. in St. Johnsbury, Vermont, before 22d October, 1815, at which time his widow Olive presented for baptism in Hardwick, Massachusetts.

ISSUE

I. John Ritto.
II. Elias.
III. Anson Whipper.
IV. OBADIAH, was an older son, b. 1797, of whom below.

OBADIAH PENNIMAN, b. 1797, Milford, Massachusetts; d. 13th September, 1836, Cincinnati, Ohio; m. 29th January, 1829, Marian Chandler LANMAN, b. 7th September, 1797, d. 31st October, 1851. She was the dau. of Judge James LANMAN of Norwich, Connecticut, b. 14th June, 1769; graduated at Yale, 1788, d. 7th August, 1841, and Marian CHANDLER, *b.* 29th July, 1774, *d.* 7th September, 1817, *m.* 18th May, 1794. Marian CHANDLER was the dau. of Judge Charles Church CHANDLER of Woodstock, Connecticut, *b.* 1746, *d.* 8th August, 1787, and Marian GRISWOLD, *b.* 1750, *d.* 1829. Marian GRISWOLD was the dau. of Gov. Matthew GRISWOLD and his wife Ursula WOLCOTT, the dau. of Gov. Roger WOLCOTT of Connecticut (see CHANDLER Family).

ISSUE

1. JAMES LANMAN, *b.* 9th July, 1832; *d.* 2d August, 1890, of whom below.

JAMES LANMAN PENNIMAN, only child of Obadiah and Marian Chandler, *b.* 9th July, 1832, Cincinnati, Ohio; *d.* 2d August, 1890, Philadelphia; *m.* 17th August, 1859, Maria Davis HOSMER, *b.* 1st February, 1830, Concord, Massachusetts; *d.* 15th January, 1914, Philadelphia, dau. of Abel Hosmer and Olive Parlin DAVIS, of Concord, Massachusetts. James Lanman PENNIMAN graduated from Yale, A.B., 1853; A.M., 1855.

    I. James Hosmer PENNIMAN, *b.* 8th November, 1860.
    II. Josiah Harmar PENNIMAN, *b.* 20th July, 1868.

Arms.—Gules, a chevron, ermine between three half spears broken, the staff, or, and iron, argent.

Crest.—In a mural crown, gules, a lion's head erased or, pierced through the neck with a broken spear, as in arms.

Motto.—Fortiter et Fideliter.

Pepper

CHARLES HOVEY PEPPER, A.B., A.M., L.H.D., of Concord Massachusetts, *b.* 27th August,1864, at Waterville, Maine; *m.* 16th July, 1889, at Skowhegan, Maine, Frances E. Coburn, dau. of Stephen Coburn, *b.* 11th November, 1817, at Bloomfield, now Skowhegan, Maine, *d.* there 4th July, 1882, *m.* 29th June, 1853, Helen Miller, *b.* 25th March, 1832, at Turner, Maine, *d.* 27th June, 1910, at Skowhegan.

ISSUE

1. Stephen Coburn, *b.* 29th April, 1891; *m.* 12th February, 1914, Ellen Hoar, dau. of Sherman Hoar, of Concord, Massachusetts.

ISSUE

1. Sherman Hoar, *b.* 29th August, 1915.
2. Elizabeth Hoar, *b.* 31st July, 1917.

II. Eunice Gordon, *b.* 28th January, 1906.

Charles Hovey Pepper received the degrees of A.B., Colby College, 1889; A.M., 1891, and L.H.D., 1912.

Lineage

Robert Pepper, the ancestor of the American family of this name, came to New England about 1640 and settled at Roxbury, Massachusetts; *b.* in England; was Freeman 10th May, 1643; *d.* 7th July, 1684; *m.* 14th March, 1643, Elizabeth Johnson, *d.* 5th January, 1684.

ISSUE

I. Elizabeth, *bapt.* 3d March, 1644; *d.* in a few days.
II. Elizabeth, *b.* 25th May; *bapt.* 1st June, 1645.
III. John, *b.* 8th April; *bapt.* 11th April, 1647.
IV. Joseph, *b.* 18th March, 1649.
V. Mary, *b.* 27th April, 1651.
VI. Benjamin, *b.* 15th May, 1653; *d.* young.
VII. Robert, *b.* 21st, *bapt.* 29th April, 1655; captured in Squakheog fight, 4th September, 1675; probably *d.* in captivity.
VIII. Sarah, *b.* 28th April, 1657.

IX. Isaac, *b.* 26th April, 1659.

X. JACOB, *b.* 28th July; *bapt.* 4th August, 1661, of whom later.

JACOB PEPPER, of Roxbury, Massachusetts; *b.* 28th July; *bapt.* 4th August, 1661; *d.* there; *m.* 10th February, 1684, Elizabeth PAYNE.

ISSUE AMONG OTHERS

1. JOSEPH, *b.* 1696, of whom below.

JOSEPH PEPPER, of Roxbury, Massachusetts; *b.* there 1696; *m.* 15th December, 1720; Anna YOUNGMAN.

ISSUE AMONG OTHERS

1. JACOB, *b.* 7th April, 1733, of whom below.

JACOB PEPPER, of Dudley, Massachusetts; *b.* there 7th August, 1733; *d.* 7th April, 1812; *m.* Abigail (surname not known).

ISSUE AMONG OTHERS

1. STEPHEN, *b.* 1762, of whom below.

STEPHEN PEPPER, of Braintree, Massachusetts; *b.* there 1762; *d.* 11th November, 1809; *m.* 14th April, 1788, Sarah SIMONDS.

ISSUE AMONG OTHERS

1. JOHN, *b.* 19th January, 1791, of whom below.

JOHN PEPPER, of New Braintree, Massachusetts; *b.* there 19th January, 1791; *d.* there 24th October, 1860; *m.* there 7th February, 1822, Eunice HUTCHINSON.

ISSUE AMONG OTHERS

1. GEORGE DANA BOARDMAN, *b.* 5th February, 1833, of whom below.

GEORGE DANA BOARDMAN PEPPER, of Ware, Massachusetts; *b.* there 5th February, 1833; *d.* 30th January, 1913; *m.* 29th November, 1860, Annie GRASSIE.

ISSUE AMONG OTHERS

1. CHARLES HOVEY, *b.* 27th August, 1864, the subject of this memoir.

Arms (PEPPER).—Quarterly, first and fourth gules a griffin segreant or, over all a bend argent; second and third vair argent and sable (for WARD).
Crest.—A stag trippant, argent.
Motto.—Semper erectus.
Residence.—Concord, Massachusetts.
Clubs.—Concord Social Circle (founded 1782), St. Botolph of Boston, Twentieth Century, Boston Art, Delta Kappa Epsilon Club of New York, New York Watercolor Club, Metropolitan Automobile Club.
Societies.—Phi Beta Kappa, Delta Kappa Epsilon, Japan Society of New York, Copley Society, Boston, National Geographic, American Asiatic Association, Forestry Association.

Prentis

HONORABLE ROBERT RIDDICK PRENTIS, LL.B., of Richmond and Suffolk, Virginia, *b.* 24th May, 1855, at University, Albemarle County, Virginia; *m.* 6th January, 1887, at Suffolk, Virginia, Mary Allen DARDEN of Suffolk, Virginia, *b.* 8th September, 1861, *d.* 27th June, 1904, dau. of Algernon Sidney DARDEN of Suffolk, Virginia, *b.* 28th January, 1829, *d.* 3d April, 1893, *m.* 27th November, 1855, Mary Swepson ALLEN, *b.* 4th October, 1837, *d.* 16th October, 1913. She was dau. of Archibald ALLEN and Mary SWEPSON, his wife and he the son of Capt. Edward ALLEN of "Rose Hill," Nansemond County, Virginia.

ISSUE

1. Janet Whitehead, *b.* 28th October, 1887; *d.* 20th August, 1888.

HON. ROBERT RIDDICK PRENTIS, graduate, Eastman Business College, Poughkeepsie, New York, 1874; graduate LL.B., University of Virginia, 1876; practiced at Charlottesville, Virginia, 1876–1879; Norfolk, January–November, 1879; Suffolk, 1879–1895; Mayor of Suffolk, 1883–1885; Judge of Virginia Circuit Court, Norfolk Circuit, 1895–1907, resigned; Chairman State Corporation Commission 1st June, 1907–1916, resigned; President National Association Railway Commissioners, 1915–1916; Member Democratic State Committee, 1887–1892; Presidential Elector, 1892; Director Lee Camp Soldiers Home, State Institution for Disabled Confederate Veterans, 1907–1916, Justice Supreme Court of Appeals of Virginia, since 1916.

Lineage

The American ancestor of this family was William PRENTIS, of Williamsburg, Virginia, from County Norfolk, England; merchant, partner of John BLAIR, of BLAIR and PRENTIS, Williamsburg, Virginia; *b.* 1701; *d.* 4th August, 1765; *m.* Mary BROOKE, *b.* 1710; *d.* 9th April, 1768, dau. of John BROOKE, and his wife Ann (surname not given) of York County, Virginia.

ISSUE

1. William Prentis, will probated 19th August, 1765.

ISSUE

1. John, *b.* 24th January, 1754.
2. JOSEPH, *b.* 24th January, 1754, of whom later.
3. Daniel.

COLONIAL FAMILIES OF THE UNITED STATES 387

 4. William.
 5. Sarah, *m.* William WATERS.
 6. Elizabeth.

None of whom have any descendants so far as is known, except JOSEPH.

HON. JOSEPH PRENTIS, of Williamsburg, Virginia; *b.* 24th January, 1754; *d.* 18th June, 1809; Member Virginia Convention, December, 1775; House of Delegates, 1777-1788; Speaker, 1788; Privy Council, 1779-1781; Code Revisor, 1792; Judge of the General Court of Virginia, 1788-1809; *m.* 16th December, 1778, Margaret BOWDOIN, *b.* 27th November, 1758; *d.* 27th August, 1801; dau. of John BOWDOIN, *d.* 1775, of Northampton County, Virginia, and his wife, Grace STRINGER, *m.* 10th January, 1754, dau. of Hilary STRINGER, III, and Alicia HARMANSON, his wife; she dau. of Col. George HARMANSON, and Elizabeth YEARDLEY, his wife, who was dau. of Capt. Argall YEARDLEY, and Sarah MICHAEL, his wife. He son of Col. Argall YEARDLEY and Ann CUSTIS, his wife. He son of Sir George YEARDLEY, Governor of Virginia, who *m.* Temperance WEST.

ISSUE

None of his children have descendants except,

JOSEPH, *b.* 24th January, 1783, of whom below.

HON. JOSEPH PRENTIS, JR., of Suffolk, Virginia, *b.* Williamsburg, 24th January, 1783; *d.* Suffolk, Virginia, 29th April, 1851; *m.* 10th January, 1810, Susan Caroline RIDDICK, *b.* Nansemond County, Virginia, *d.* 19th October, 1862, dau. of Col. Robert Moor RIDDICK and Elizabeth RIDDICK his wife. She the dau. of Col. Willis RIDDICK and Mary FOULKE, his wife.

ISSUE

 1. Margaret Susan, *b.* 29th December, 1810; *m.* Dr. Robert Henning WEBB, of Suffolk, Virginia, 22d January, 1834; *d.* 24th March, 1882.

ISSUE

 1. Joseph Prentis WEBB, *b.* 30th October, 1843; *d.* 27th December, 1892; Company I, 13th Virginia Cavalry, C. S. A.; *m.* 27th January, 1881, Annie Jordan DARDEN, *b.* 17th August, 1858, dau. of Algernon Sidney DARDEN (Aide to General ARMSTEAD and General CHAMBLISS, C.S.A.) and Mary Swepson ALLEN, his wife; she dau. of Archibald ALLEN, and he son of Capt. Edward ALLEN, of "Rose Hill," Nansemond County, Virginia.

ISSUE

1[1]. Robert Henning WEBB, Ph.D. (Harvard); b. 21st February, 1882; Professor of Greek University of Virginia; m. Blanche F. MILLER, Lisbon, Ohio, and has issue.

II. ROBERT RIDDICK, of Suffolk, Virginia, b. 11th April, 1818, of whom later.
III. Peter Bowdoin, b. 5th April, 1820; m. Eliza WRENN, of Isle of Wight County, Virginia, 23d December, 1841; d. 5th March, 1889.

ISSUE

1. Martha Josephine, b. 21st March, 1845; d. 17th February, 1909; m. 1864, Capt. Charles Henry CAUSEY, Company B, 3d Virginia Cavalry, C.S.A., State Senator, b. 14th July, 1837, d. 27th August, 1890; leaving issue.

ROBERT RIDDICK PRENTIS, of Charlottesville, Virginia, b. Suffolk, Virginia, 11th April, 1818, d. Charlottesville, Virginia, 23d November, 1871; m. Margaret Ann WHITEHEAD; b. 8th August, 1826; d. 16th February, 1910; dau. of Elliott and Catherine (FLYNN) WHITEHEAD.

ISSUE

I. Henning Webb, b. 22d October, 1851; m. Mary Morton MCNUTT, 1876; d. 1st January, 1918.

ISSUE

1. Margaret Whitehead, b. 11th November, 1877; m. 21st August, 1912, Robert Lee RAMSAY.
2. Henning Webb, b. 11th July, 1884; m. 6th September, 1909, Bernice COLE.
3. Hally Morrison, b. 22d September, 1885; m. 5th August, 1916, William Pierrepont NELSON, Jr.
4. Morton McNutt, b. 2d January, 1887.
5. Joseph Elliott, b. 10th July, 1888; m. 1st February, 1917, Eleanor GORDON.

II. ROBERT RIDDICK, b. 24th May, 1855, the subject of this memoir.
III. Peter Bowdoin, b. 4th April, 1857; m. Rose Hortense COSTER.

ISSUE

1. Peter Bowdoin, b. 26th March, 1894.
2. Mary Hortense, b. 12th March, 1896.
3. Rose Marie, b. 15th September, 1900.

IV. John Brooks, b. 26th February, 1859; m. Martha ALEXANDER.

ISSUE

1. John Brooks, *b.* October, 1895.

v. Susan Josephine, *b.* 10th March, 1864; unmarried.
vi. Katherine Lewis, *b.* 16th August, 1866; *m.* Hon. Nathaniel BEAMAN, Norfolk, Virginia.

ISSUE

1. Sallie Louise BEAMAN, *b.* 14th March, 1889.
2. Robert Prentis BEAMAN, *b.* 13th December, 1891.
3. Nathaniel BEAMAN, *b.* 16th July, 1898.

There were other children who died young, unmarried and without issue. The eldest being Joseph, *b.* 13th January, 1846; Confederate soldier, killed at the battle of Malvern Hill, Virginia, 1st July, 1862.

Arms.—Per chevron or and sable, three grey hounds, courant and counterchanged collared gules.
Crest.—A demi grey hound, rampant or, collared, ringed and lined sable, the line coiled in a knot at the end.
Residence.—Richmond; Domicile; Suffolk.
Clubs.—Westmoreland, Commonwealth (Richmond), Virginia (Norfolk), Country Club of Virginia.
Societies.—Colonial Wars, Sons of the Revolution, Phi Beta Kappa, Chi Phi, American Bar Association, Virginia State Bar Association, Virginia Historical Society.

Littleton

COLONEL NATHANIEL LITTLETON, of Accomack County, Virginia, 1640; *d.* 1654; was Counsellor, 1640; Chief Magistrate of Northampton County; Member of the Virginia House of Burgesses, 1652; Member of the Council, 1652; *m.* Ann SOUTHEY; he was the son of Sir Edward LITTLETON of Henley Shropshire, England. She was the dau. of Lewis and Elizabeth SOUTHEY. Their dau.

ESTHER LITTLETON, *m.* Col. John ROBINS, who *d.* 1709; their dau.
GRACE ROBBINS, *d.* 1722; *m.* Hilary STRINGER, II; their son
HILARY STRINGER, III, *d.* 1744; *m.* Elishe (Alicia) HARMANSON; their dau.
GRACE STRINGER, *m.* 10th January, 1754, in Northampton County, Virginia, John BOWDOIN, *d.* 1775; their dau.
MARGARET BOWDOIN, *b.* 27th November, 1758; *d.* 27th August, 1801, at Williamsburg, Virginia; *m.* 16th December, 1778, Joseph PRENTIS (Judge), *b.* 24th January, 1754, *d.* 18th June, 1809; their son
HONORABLE JOSEPH PRENTIS, JR., *b.* 24th January, 1783, at Williamsburg, Virginia; *d.* 29th April, 1851, at Suffolk, Virginia; *m.* 18th January, 1810, Susan Caro-

line RIDDICK, b. 6th October, 1791, in Nansemond County, Virginia, d. 19th October, 1862, at Suffolk, Virginia, gd. dau. of Col. Willis RIDDICK, their son
ROBERT RIDDICK PRENTIS, b. 11th April, 1818, in Suffolk, Virginia, d. 23d November, 1871, in Charlottesville, Virginia; m. 21st March, 1845, Margaret Ann WHITEHEAD, b. 8th August, 1826, in Suffolk, Virginia, d. 16th February, 1910.

ISSUE

1. ROBERT RIDDICK PRENTIS, b. 24th May, 1855; m. 6th January, 1887. Mary Allen DARDEN, who d. 27th June, 1904.

Bowdoin

PIERRE BAUDOUIN (BOWDOIN) a French Huguenot refugee, with his wife Elizabeth, settled in Massachusetts.

ISSUE

I. James; his descendant James was Governor of Massachusetts in 1785-1787.
II. JOHN.

JOHN BOWDOIN, I, of Northampton County, Virginia; d. 1717; settled in Northampton County, Virginia, 1700; m. Susannah STOCKLEY; their son
PETER BOWDOIN, of Northampton County, Virginia; m. (firstly) ———— HARMANSON; m. (secondly) 13th May, 1733, Susanna PREESON; their son
JOHN BOWDOIN, II, of Northampton County, Virginia; d. 1775; in 1759 he bought from Severn EYRE, the farm "Hungars;" m. 10th January, 1754, Grace STRINGER, and left descendants; their dau.
MARGARET BOWDOIN, b. 27th November, 1758; m. 16th December, 1778, Judge Joseph PRENTIS of Williamsburg, Virginia; their son
HON. JOSEPH PRENTIS, JR., of Suffolk, Virginia, b. 24th January, 1783; d. 29th April, 1851; m. 18th January, 1810, Susan Caroline RIDDICK, b. October, 1791, d. 19th October, 1862; he was a member of the Virginia Constitutional Convention, 1829-1830; Attorney at law, and for many years Clerk of the Court. Descendants leaving issue
Margaret Susan, m. Dr. Robert Henning WEBB.
Robert Riddick, b. 11th April, 1818; m. Margaret Ann WHITEHEAD.
Peter Bowdoin, m. Eliza WRENN.

Yeardley

SIR GEORGE YEARDLEY, Knight, b. 1577; d. 13th November, 1627; Governor and Captain General of Virginia, 1619; m. 1618, Temperance WEST; their son
COL. ARGALL YEARDLEY, b. 1621; d. 1655; Member of the Council of Virginia, 1643; m. 1649, Ann CUSTIS, dau. of John and Joane; their son

CAPT. ARGALL YEARDLEY, *d.* 1683; Member of the Council of Virginia; *m.* 23d January, 1682, Sarah MICHAEL, dau. of Capt. John and Elizabeth (THOROUGHGOOD) MICHAEL. She dau. of Capt. Adam THOROUGHGOOD, *b.* 1603, *d.* 1640; their dau.

ELIZABETH YEARDLEY, *m.* Col. George HARMANSON, who *d.* 1734; he was a member of the Virginia House of Burgesses; their dau.

ELISHE (ALICIA) HARMANSON, *d.* 1744; *m.* Hilary STRINGER, who *d.* 1760; their dau.

GRACE STRINGER, *m.* John BOWDOIN, who *d.* 1775; he was a member of the Virginia house of Burgesses; their dau.

MARGARET BOWDOIN, *b.* 27th November, 1758; *d.* 27th August, 1801; *m.* 16th December, 1778, Judge Joseph PRENTIS, *b.* 24th January, 1754, *d.* 18th June, 1809; their son

HON. JOSEPH PRENTIS, JR., *b.* 24th January, 1783; *d.* 29th April, 1851; *m.* 18th January, 1810, Susan Caroline RIDDICK, gd. dau. of Col. Willis RIDDICK; their son

ROBERT RIDDICK PRENTIS, *b.* 11th April, 1818; *d.* 23d November, 1871; *m.* 21st March, 1845, Margaret Ann WHITEHEAD, *b.* 8th August, 1826; *d.* 16th February, 1910; their son

HON. ROBERT RIDDICK PRENTIS, *b.* 24th May, 1855; *m.* 6th January, 1887, Mary Allen DARDEN, who *d.* 27th June, 1904.

Fielding-Reid

CAPT. FRANCIS FIELDING-REID, B.A., United States Army, of Baltimore, Maryland; *b.* there 15th April, 1892; *m.* 3d February, 1917, at Fort Leavenworth, Kansas, Marie Magdalene SVENDSEN, *b.* 4th October, 1895, at Drammen, Norway, dau. of Olaf SVENDSEN, *b.* 1857, in Dramen, Norway, and his wife, Lena Marie JENSEN, *b.* 1855, at Haugesund, Norway.

ISSUE

I. Francis Dorian Fielding, *b.* 13th November, 1917.
II. Ernest Brooke Fielding, *b.* 10th February, 1920.
III. Elizabeth Washington Fielding, *b.* 10th February, 1920.

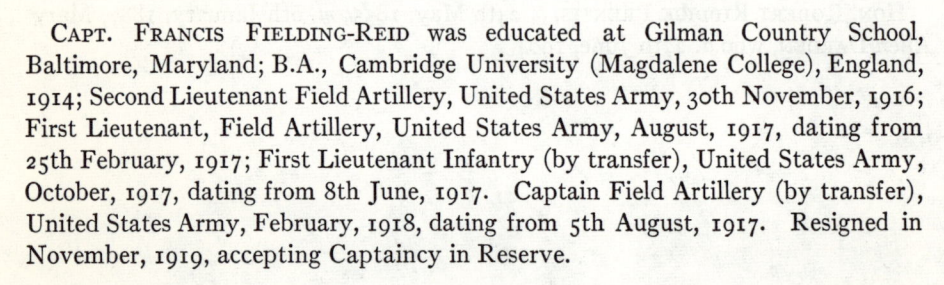

CAPT. FRANCIS FIELDING-REID was educated at Gilman Country School, Baltimore, Maryland; B.A., Cambridge University (Magdalene College), England, 1914; Second Lieutenant Field Artillery, United States Army, 30th November, 1916; First Lieutenant, Field Artillery, United States Army, August, 1917, dating from 25th February, 1917; First Lieutenant Infantry (by transfer), United States Army, October, 1917, dating from 8th June, 1917. Captain Field Artillery (by transfer), United States Army, February, 1918, dating from 5th August, 1917. Resigned in November, 1919, accepting Captaincy in Reserve.

Lineage

GEORGE REID, a native of Scotland, came to Virginia and settled in Norfolk, Virginia, 1801; *d.* there 1849; he was the son of William REID of Farfar, Scotland; the old manor of the REID family is one of the residences of the Earl of GREY; *m.* Elizabeth TAYLOR, *b.* 12th April, 1777, *d.* 1862, in Baltimore, dau. of John and Elizabeth (CAN) TAYLOR of Scotland, who was of Aberdeen.

ISSUE

1. Andrew, *b.* 22d September, 1818, of whom below.

ANDREW REID, of Baltimore, Maryland, *b.* 22d September, 1818, in Norfolk, Virginia; *d.* in Baltimore, Maryland, 4th January, 1896; *m.* 8th December, 1853, in Richmond, Virginia, Fanny Brooke GWATHMEY, *b.* 8th September, 1835, dau. of Humphrey Brooke GWATHMEY, *b.* 29th March, 1794, in Canterbury, Virginia. *d.* in Richmond, Virginia, 22d October, 1852, *m.* 27th June, 1822, Frances Fielding LEWIS, *b.* 11th February, 1805, in Culpepper County, Virginia, *d.* 28th May, 1888, in Wilmington, North Carolina, she dau. of Howell LEWIS, b. 11th or 12th of December, 1771, m. 26th December, 1795, Ellen Hackley POLLARD, b. 7th December, 1776, d. 15th January, 1859, in Marietta, Ohio. Howell LEWIS, was the son of Col. Fielding LEWIS, b. 7th July, 1725, in Virginia, d. there December, 1781, or January, 1782, m. (secondly) 7th May, 1750, Betty WASHINGTON, b. 20th June, 1733, in Wakefield, Virginia, d. 31st March, 1797, dau. of Augustine and Mary (BALL) WASHINGTON. Fielding LEWIS was commissioned County Lieutenant, 1758; Commander-in-Chief Spottsylvania County Militia, 1761; Member of the Virginia Assembly from 1761 to 1768.

ISSUE

1. Harry FIELDING, b. 18th May, 1859, of whom below.

HARRY FIELDING REID of Baltimore, Maryland, b. there 18th May, 1859; m. there 22d November, 1883, Edith GITTINGS, dau. of James GITTINGS and Elizabeth (MACGILL) GITTINGS, of Baltimore, Maryland.

ISSUE

1. FRANCIS FIELDING, b. 15th April, 1892, the subject of this memoir.
II. Doris Fielding, b. 4th September, 1895.

Arms.—Argent an eagle displayed sable, on the breast an escutcheon of the first.
Crest.—A cubit arm issuing out of the clouds, holding the Holy Bible open, at Job IX, all ppr., leaves or.
Motto.—Pro Virtute.
Residence.—No. 608 Cathedral Street, Baltimore, Maryland.
Clubs.—Beef Steak, and University Pitt Club, of Cambridge, England, Maryland, and Elkridge Hunt Clubs of Baltimore, Maryland.
Societies.—Colonial Wars.

Rhoades

NELSON OSGOOD RHOADES, of Los Angeles, California, b. 2d June, 1869, in Franklin, Wisconsin; m. 18th September, 1887, in Van Wert, Iowa, Lotta M. FARNSWORTH; m. (secondly), 27th January, 1911, Frances James BROWN, b. 28th December, 1872, in Kenoza Lake, New York; dau. of Renwick BROWN, b. 2d June, 1837, in New York City, who m. 7th November, 1860, Mary Agnes MOULTHROP, whose lineage is recorded later in this memoir.

NELSON OSGOOD RHOADES was educated by tutelage; teacher at seventeen, in Iowa; thereafter, successively, teacher of Spanish schools, in New Mexico; San Luis, Fort Garland, County Superintendent of Schools, Principal of High School, Normal School, Superintendent of City Schools, all in State of Colorado. His early engineering experience was gained in the construction of the Great Western Railway, State of Iowa; had responsible charge railway construction on Red River of the North; extensive Government survey work in Colorado; professional experience covered survey and abstracting of titles of the Spanish grants of Colorado and New Mexico, involving abstract work in Mexico and Spain; designed and constructed many millions of dollars of irrigation plants, water-supply and sewage plants, nitrofaction plants for sewage disposal; designing and building of storage, slow-sand-filtration and chemical plants, conduit systems of water-supply; also railway survey work and scientific work in India, Africa and Europe; construction of Chihuahua and Pacific Railway, Mexico; geographical survey and revalidation of title work, original designing and direction of construction of public works, all in Mexico. Designing and construction of irrigation system in Sinaloa, amongst largest in the Republic of Mexico; establishing and operating of sugar plantation and refineries in Sinaloa; consulting and contracting engineer through above periods. Now a member of the association of GARFIELD and RHOADES, Latin-American Counsellors and Fiscal Agents, with offices in Cleveland, Ohio, Los Angeles, California, and Mexico City, Mexico; the senior associate is Hon. James R. GARFIELD of Ohio.

Arms. (RHOADES)—Argent on a cross engrailed, between four lions rampant, gules, as many bezants.
Crest.—A leopard sejeant, or spotted sable, collared and ringed argent.
Residences.—Los Angeles, California and University Club, Mexico City, Mexico.
Offices.—Los Angeles, California, Cleveland, Ohio and Mexico City, Mexico.
Clubs.—California, Jonathan and Los Angeles Country Club, Los Angeles, California; University, Reforma, American and Country Clubs, Mexico City, Mexico.
Societies.—Society Mayflower Descendants, Order Founders and Patriots, Society Colonial Wars, Order of Washington, Society Sons of Revolution, New York

Genealogical and Biographical Society, New England Historic Genealogical Society, National Historical Society, Valley Forge Historical Society, Utah Genealogical Society, National Genealogical Society, California Genealogical Society, American Academy Sciences, Pacific Astronomical Society, York and Scottish Rite Masonry, etc.

Lineage

I. 1. HENRY RHODES, *b.* in Lancashire, England, 1608, came to the Massachusetts Bay Colony, settling at Lynn before 1640, where he *d.* in 1675. He *m.* Elizabeth WHITE (or PAUL) who *d.* in Lynn 25th November, 1700. He was an ironmonger in Lynn, 1640; a witness 1647; representative to the General Court 1657. Served in King Philip's War and fought against the Indians in the Nipmugg Country, and at Narragansett in 1675. He signed his name with various spellings, but commonly "RODES." BODGE, in his "History of King Philip's War," records him as "Henry RHOADES," as he is frequently quoted in other historical references. There are many branches of the RHODES family existing in the United States, practically none are found spelling their names "RHOADES," except the descendants of Henry, of Lynn. In England, where the family originated, but one family is found which so spells its name and that is the one from which Amphillis RHOADES, great-grandmother of George WASHINGTON, descended.

This branch of the RHODES family descended from a long line of English ancestors, tracing back to Willemus, of Rode, on many of whom heraldic honors had been conferred. Henry RHODES brought to America a coat-of-arms and copy of the original charter inscribed, "These are the ancient names of the family of RHODES of Adrod, Cheshire, whereof James RHODES, of Lancashire, is descended of the second house, Henry RHODES, son of George."

All descendants of Henry RHODES are qualified for membership in the Society of Colonial Wars and Order of Founders and Patriots of America.

ISSUE, ALL BORN IN LYNN, MASSACHUSETTS

2. I. Eleazer RHODES, *b.* 6th February, 1640; *d.* 15th May, 1716.
*3. II. Samuel RHODES, of whom later.
4. III. Joseph RHODES, *b.* January, 1645; *m.* Jane COATES (COOTES).
5. IV. Joshua RHODES, *b.* April 1648; *m.* Ann GRAVES; *d.* 29th December, 1725.
6. V. Josiah RHODES, *b.* April, 1651; *m.* Elizabeth COATES.
7. VI. Jonathan RHODES, *b.* August, 1654; *d.* 7th April, 1677.
8. VII. Elizabeth (Eliza) RHODES, *b.* March, 1657; *m.* 5th November, 1695, Nathaniel WHITTEMORE of Boston.
9. VIII. Henry RHODES, Jr., *b.* circa 1659.

(*Authorities;* Family bibles and records, vital statistics of Massachusetts and Colonial War Registers, BODGE'S "History King Philip's War.")

II. 3. SAMUEL RHODES, b. Lynn, Massachusetts, February, 1642; d. 1718; m. 16th January, 1681-1682, Lynn, Abigail COATES, dau. of Robert COATES, b. 1627, England, d. Lynn; great-granddaughter of Thomas COATES who came in 1635, from Sarum, Wilts, England. Abigail, b. Lynn, 10th April, 1663; d. 20th August, 1743. They lived at Lynn, Massachusetts. Samuel served in King Philip's War under Captain GARDNER. Robert COATES served under Captain TURNER in garrison at Hadley, Massachusetts, 1676, et seq.

ISSUE, ALL BORN IN LYNN, MASSACHUSETTS

- 10. I. Jonathan RHODES, b. 28th November, 1683; d. 3d February, 1745; m. Sarah BAXTER.
- 11. II. Samuel RHODES, b. 2d August, 1685.
- 12. III. Abigail RHODES, b. 19th January, 1686-1687.
- 13. IV. Eleazer RHODES, b. 3d November, 1688; d. 1727, m. Sarah NEWMAN.
-     V. Sarah RHODES, b. 31st July, 1690; d. 8th October, 1690.
- *14. VI. OBADIAH RHODES, of whom later.
-     VII. Sarah RHODES. b. 16th August, 1696; d. July, 1698.
- 15. VIII. Joane RHODES, b. 19th August, 1699; m. Ralph MERRY, 12th January, 1720.
- 16. IX. Joseph RHODES, b. 25th August, 1701; d. 8th April, 1765; m. Mary FULLER, 14th November, 1723.
- 17. X. Benjamin RHODES, b. 12th June, 1704; m. Rachel SILSBY, 1727.

(*Authorities:* Family records, Colonial War Registers, BODGE's "History of King Philip's War," vital statistics of Massachusetts.)

III. 14. OBADIAH RHODES, b. in Lynn, Massachusetts, 13th May, 1693; removed to Voluntown, Connecticut, admitted to First Church, 15th September, 1728; m. 1717, Abigail, whose family name is unknown, but who was admitted to First Church, Voluntown, 1729. Obadiah was one of the earliest settlers of Voluntown where he was a respected citizen, serving as selectman and in other official capacities.

ISSUE

- 49. I. Abigail RHODES, b. 3d December, 1719, at Voluntown, Connecticut.
- *50. II. OBADIAH RHODES, of whom later.
- 51. III. Martha RHODES, b. 29th May, 1725, at Voluntown; d. 7th October 1725, at Voluntown.
- 52. IV. John RHODES, b. 15th April, 1727; m. Joanna CADY, 16th March, 1748
    (*Authorities:* Family records, LARNED's "History of Windham County Connecticut," vital statistics of Lynn, Massachusetts, Stonington and Voluntown, Connecticut.)

IV. 50. OBADIAH RHODES, *b.* in Voluntown, Connecticut, 20th July, 1722; will proven in Voluntown, 12th August, 1760; *m.* at Voluntown, 4th June, 1747, Mary STANDBERRY (STANBURY), whose antecedents are unknown. She *m.* (secondly), a Mr. WILLIAMS, whose first name is not recorded. Obadiah and his father were extensive land owners in Connecticut.

ISSUE

82. I. Obadiah RHODES, *b.* 5th June, 1748, at Voluntown, Connecticut; *m.* Lydia JONES, at Voluntown, 30th December, 1773.
83. II. John RHODES, *b.* 15th December, 1749, at Voluntown; *m.* Rebecca STEWART, at Voluntown, 14th November, 1771.
84. III. Jane RHODES, *b.* 15th February, 1752, at Voluntown; *m.* Oliver STEWART, 17th February, 1772, at Voluntown.
*85. IV. BENJAMIN RHODES, of whom later.
86. V. Sarah RHODES, *b.* circa 1756.
(*Authorities:* Vital and family records of Voluntown and Stonington, Connecticut.)

V. 85. BENJAMIN RHOADES, *b.* in Voluntown, Connecticut, 3d January, 1754; *d.* Wallingford, Vermont, 24th August, 1791; *m.* circa, 1780, Judith RICHMOND (Eliakim-Christopher-Joseph-John-John); *bapt.* 1772, Cheshire, Massachusetts; *d.* Ashford, New York, 1849, aged ninety-six. Benjamin removed to Vermont at an early age and became an extensive owner of land in that state as his father had been in Connecticut. He died as a result of accident. He served in the Revolutionary War from Vermont; Vermont Military Rolls, page 446. Judith, his widow, remained in Vermont until after 1800, when she, with other members of the RHOADES and RICHMOND families, removed to New York, where she *m.* (secondly), a Mr. PARIGO whose first name is unknown.

The descendants of Benjamin and Judith are qualified for membership in the Society of Mayflower Descendants through Thomas ROGERS. See RICHMOND-ROGERS lineage later.

ISSUE

87. I. Sarah RHOADES, *b.* 26th December, 1781, Wallingford, Vermont.
88. II. Eliakim RHOADES, *b.* 9th February, 1784, Wallingford; *m.* Aurilly GROVER, 3d July, 1808, at Wallingford.
89. III. Betsey RHOADES, *b.* 1st May, 1786; Wallingford; *m.* Almon FULLER.
*90. IV. BENJAMIN RHOADES, of whom later.
91. V. Deliverance RHOADES, *b.* 1791, Wallingford.
(*Authorities:* Family and vital records of Voluntown, Connecticut, Wallingford, Vermont, Springville and Ashford, New York and the genealogy of the RICHMOND family by Joshua Bailey RICHMOND.)

VI. 90. BENJAMIN RHOADES, *b.* in Wallingford, Vermont, 19th March, 1789; *d.* Viroqua, Wisconsin, 1865; *m.* Nellie BISHOP, *b.* in Vermont, 1799; *d.* Cambridge, Pennsylvania, 9th January, 1866. Benjamin and family removed to New York, where most of their children were born; removed in 1849 to Wisconsin. Benjamin was a pioneer and farmer; served in the War of 1812, from New York. Nellie BISHOP's parents came from Cumberland, Rhode Island, where her brother, Reuben BISHOP of Meadville, Pennsylvania, was born.

ISSUE

92. I. Hannah RHOADES, *m.* Nelson Carrier; lived Missouri.
*93. II. BELA RHOADES, of whom later.
94. III. Lavisa RHOADES, *b.* 1831, in New York.
95. IV. Serafina RHOADES, *m.* Jerome GILLETTE, circa 1850.
*96. V. NELSON CARRIER RHOADES, of whom later.
97. VI. Axa RHOADES.
98. VII. Ann RHOADES.

(*Authorities;* Family, probate and vital records of Wallingford, Vermont; Viroqua, Wisconsin, Cambridge, Pennsylvania and Springville, New York.)

VII. 93. BELA RHOADES, *b.* in New York in 1825; *d.* in Wisconsin; *m.* in Wisconsin, 1852, Jane JOHNSON. They resided at Wilton. He was a farmer.

ISSUE

106. I. Emily RHOADES, *b.* 1854, at Wilton; *d.* aged twenty-two; unmarried.
107. II. Benjamin D. RHOADES, *b.* 5th December, 1856, at Wilton; *m.* and had one son, *b.* 1882; living New Lisbon, 1920.
108. III. Simeon B. RHOADES, *b.* 1860, at Wilton; *m.* Rena McKNIGHT; had four sons and two daughters; living 1920, Lillie, Louisiana.
109. IV. Henry RHOADES, *b.* 1863, at Wilton; *d.* aged twenty-four, accident; unmarried.
110. VI. Ernest B. RHOADES, *m.* Louisa GOFF, at Wilton; living 1920, Oklahoma; no issue.
111. VI. Ralph H. RHOADES, living 1920, Prentice, Wisconsin.

VII. 96. NELSON CARRIER RHOADES, *b.* in Cattaraugus County, New York, 16th May, 1836; *d.* at Leon, Iowa, 9th January, 1905; *m.* at Viroqua, Wisconsin, Temperance HART, a niece of General Jeremiah RUSK, Governor of Wisconsin. He *m.* (secondly), 13th September, 1866, Lucy Eunice OSGOOD (Joshua-Joshua-William-Joshua-Hooker-Stephen-John). See OSGOOD lineage later. They lived in the state of Wisconsin until about 1878, where he was engaged in farming and lumbering. They later removed to Nebraska and from there, in 1881, to the state of Iowa. His widow, Lucy RHOADES, is living, 1920, in Los Angeles, California.

COLONIAL FAMILIES OF THE UNITED STATES

ISSUE

(By first marriage)

*112. I. Francis Marion Rhoades, of whom later.

(By second marriage)

113. II. Nellie Rhoades, *b.* 7th June, 1867, at Viroqua, Wisconsin; *d.* 14th August, 1882, at Garden Grove, Iowa; unmarried.

*114. III. Nelson Osgood Rhoades, of whom later.

115. IV. Mary Alice Rhoades, of whom later.

116. V. Lucy Maud Rhoades, *b.* 17th May, 1873, at Franklin, Wisconsin; *d.* 19th May, 1874, at Franklin.

117. VI. Ida May Rhoades, *b.* 18th March, 1875, at Wilton, Wisconsin; *d.* 19th August, 1876, at Wilton.

*118. VII. Edward James Rhoades, of whom later.

119. VIII. Minnie E. Rhoades, *b.* 22d July, 1880, at Lincoln, Nebraska; *d.* 6th May, 1888, at Garden Grove, Iowa.

*120. IX. Eva May Rhoades, of whom later.

(*Authorities;* Family bible.)

VIII. 112. Francis Marion Rhoades, *b.* 7th June, 1862, at Viroqua, Wisconsin; living, 1920, at Redfield, South Dakota; *m.* 9th August, 1882, at Garden Grove, Iowa, Manetta Holland, descended from John Holland, of Dorchester, Massachusetts, 1636, *b.* 5th September, 1864, at Garden Grove. He is a merchant.

ISSUE

121. I. Winifred May Rhoades, *b.* 16th December, 1883, at Garden Grove, Iowa; *m.* William Nuhn, in Montana.

122. II. Archie Lumnin Rhoades, *b.* 8th January, 1887, at Garden Grove; living, 1920, in South Dakota; *m.* Nora Juanita Baker.

123. III. Bertha Alice Rhoades, *b.* 14th October, 1888, at Garden Grove; living, 1920, at Redfield, South Dakota; *m.* Henry G. Wilson, 8th June, 1910, at Des Moines, Iowa.

124. IV. A child, *b.* 23d September, 1890, at Garden Grove; *d.* soon.

125. V. William Francis Rhoades, *b.* 24th April, 1892, at Garden Grove; living, 1920, at Redfield, South Dakota; *m.* Bernice Clayton Hazen, 26th November, 1915, of Huron, South Dakota.

126. VI. Nellie Rhoades, *b.* 22d August, 1894, at Garden Grove; living, 1920, at Redfield, South Dakota; *m.* Chester B. Thomas, at Redfield.

127. VII. Ralph Benjamin Rhoades, *b.* 23d October, 1897, at Garden Grove; living, 1920; *m.* 18th June, 1918, Huron, South Dakota, Cora L. McCoy.

128. VIII. Cecil Peter RHOADES, *b.* 20th June, 1900, at Leon, Iowa; living, 1920, at Redfield; *m.* 5th March, 1918, at Huron, Cecilia Varonica LAWLER.
129. IX. Enid Frances RHOADES, *b.* 23d April, 1902, at Blocton, Iowa; living 1920.
130. X. Inez B. RHOADES, *b.* 9th February, 1905, at Lamoni, Iowa; living 1920.
131. XI. Invert D. RHOADES, *b.* 9th February, 1905, at Lamoni; living 1920.

VIII. 114. NELSON OSGOOD RHOADES, subject of this memoir and whose vital record is shown in the introduction, had

ISSUE

(By first marriage)

132. I. Ewell Nelson RHOADES, *b.* 1893, at Rouse, Colorado; living, 1920, in Washington.
133. II. Roger Farnsworth RHOADES, *b.* 1903, at Denver, Colorado; living, 1920, California.

(By second marriage)

134. III. Alan RHOADES, *b.* 11th November, 1911, at Detroit, Michigan; *d.* 14th November, 1911, at Detroit.
135. IV. Mary Agnes RHOADES, *b.* 1911. Ad.

VIII. 115. MARY ALICE RHOADES, *b.* 3d July, 1871, at Franklin, Wisconsin; living, 1920, at Hecla, Nebraska; *m.* 10th August, 1889, at Garden Grove, Iowa, Charles KELLEY, descended from Edward KELLEY, of Boston, 1635.

ISSUE

136. I. Alta Maud KELLEY, *b.* 31st October, 1891, at Garden Grove; living, 1920, Hecla, Nebraska; *m.* 14th February, 1912, at Seneca, Kansas, Lawrence Henry LACKEY.
137. II. Ida Fern KELLEY, *b.* 4th April, 1894; *d.* 11th September, 1896.
138. III. Charles William KELLEY, *b* 12th July, 1897; living 1920.
139. IV. Robert Nelson KELLEY, *b.* 22d August, 1901, at Leon, Iowa; living 1920.
140. V. Ruth Inez KELLEY, *b.* 9th May, 1905, at Chicosa, Colorado; living 1920.
141. VI. Evelyn Rosette KELLEY, *b.* 4th June, 1907, at Eagle, Colorado.

VIII. 118. EDWARD JAMES RHOADES, *b.* 9th July, 1877, at Wilton, Wisconsin; living, 1920, at Los Angeles, California; *m.* 25th December, 1906, at Eldorado, Oklahoma, Launa Viola LONG.

ISSUE

142.   I. Ethel Grace RHOADES, *b.* 2d April, 1908, at Eldorado, Oklahoma; living, 1920, Los Angeles.
143.   II. Frances Nell RHOADES, *b.* 16th November, 1910, at Stephenville, Texas; living, 1920, Los Angeles.
144.   II. Edward James RHOADES, *b.* 15th October, 1913, at Los Angeles; living, 1920.

VIII.   120.   EVA MAY RHOADES, *b.* 10th January, 1886, at Garden Grove, Iowa; living, 1920, at Tulsa, Oklahoma; *m.* 10th May, 1904, Clarence MATTHEWS, at Des Moines, Iowa, who *d.* in 1904; *m.* (secondly), in 1912, in Oklahoma, George W. OLDHAM, living, 1920, Tulsa, Oklahoma. He is a merchant.

ISSUE

145.   I. Ollie D. OLDHAM, *b.* 7th October, 1913, Tulsa, Oklahoma.
146.   II. Palmer D. OLDHAM, *b.* 21st August, 1917, Tulsa, Oklahoma.

Richmond

The family is definitely traced from A. D. 1040, as follows, see the "RICHMOND Family," by Joshua Bailey RICHMOND.

1. ROALDUS MUSARD DE RICHMOND, one of the most powerful leaders who accompanied William the Conqueror into England.
2. HASCULFUS MUSARD DE RICHMOND.
3. ROALDUS DE RICHMOND, "Le Ennase," second Constable of Richmond Castle under Alan III, Earl of Richmond.
4. SIR ALAN, FIL ROALD DE RICHMOND, third Constable of Richmond Castle.
5. SIR ROALD, FIL ALAN DE RICHMOND, Knight, fourth Constable of Richmond Castle, to whom King John, in 1208, gave the lands of William de Rollos, including the manors of Caldewell, Croft, Kipling.
6. ALAN, FIL ROALD RICHMOND DE CROFT, to whom his brother gave the manor of Burton.
7. SIR ROALD, FIL ALAN RICHMOND DE CROFT, to whom his uncle Roald fil Roald gave the manors of Caldwell and Croft.
8. EUDO DE RICHMOND, had possessions in Staynwriggis, County of York.
9. ELYAS DE RICHMOND, was living during the time of Edward III, 1327–1377.
10. ELYAS DE RICHMOND, was living during the time of Edward III and Richard II, 1327–1399. Arms of Elyas de RICHMOND: Or; on a bend engrailed gules, 3 crosslets or.
11. THOMAS DE RICHMOND, was living in the time of Richard II, Henry IV and Henry V.

12. WILLIAM DE RICHMOND, assumed the name of WEBB upon his marriage, about 1430, and quartered the WEBB arms.
13. WILLIAM RICHMOND, alias WEBB, of Draycott Foliott, Wilts.
14. WILLIAM RICHMOND, alias WEBB, of Stewkley Grange, Bucks County, and Over-Wroughton, Wilts.
15. EDMUND RICHMOND, alias WEBB, Esq., of Denvord (Durnford), Wilts, was living in 1575.
16. HENRY RICHMOND, alias WEBB.
17. JOHN RICHMOND, eldest son; was an officer of distinction during the civil war.

American Lines

I. JOHN RICHMOND, the emigrant, was *b.* in 1594; he came to America from Ashton, Wiltshire, England. He probably left England about 1635, and was one of the purchasers of Taunton, in 1637. He was married before he came to this country, but neither the name of his wife, the date of their marriage, nor the date of her death, has been found.

He was away from Taunton much of his life—through the records he is known to have been at Newport and other places—but he returned to Taunton and *d.* there 20th March, 1664, aged seventy.

ISSUE

*2.   I. JOHN RICHMOND, of whom later.
3.   II. Edward RICHMOND, *b.* circa 1632.
4.   III. Sarah RICHMOND, *b.* circa 1638.
5.   IV. Mary RICHMOND, *b.* circa 1639.

II. 2. JOHN RICHMOND, was *b.* circa 1627, before his father came to this country; *d.* 7th October, 1715, aged eighty-eight; *m.* Abigail ROGERS, *b.* 1641; *d.* 1st August, 1727, aged eighty-six; dau. of John ROGERS of Duxbury, who came to America on the *Mayflower*. Both John and Abigail are buried in Taunton, Massachusetts. Their descendants are all qualified for membership in the Society of Mayflower Descendants.

ISSUE

6.   I. Mary RICHMOND, *b.* 2d June, 1654, in Bridgewater.
7.   II. John RICHMOND, *b.* 6th June, 1656, in Bridgewater; killed 20th September, 1672, by the upsetting of a cart.
8.   III. Thomas RICHMOND, *b.* 2d February, 1659, in Newport, Rhode Island; *d.* in Middleboro, 14th December, 1705; unmarried.
9.   IV. Susanna RICHMOND, *b.* 14th November, 1661, in Bridgewater.
*10. V. JOSEPH RICHMOND, of whom later.
11.   VI. Edward RICHMOND, *b.* 8th February, 1665, in Taunton.
12.   VII. Samuel RICHMOND, *b.* 23d September, 1668, in Taunton.

COLONIAL FAMILIES OF THE UNITED STATES 403

13. VIII. Sarah RICHMOND, *b.* 26th February, 1671, in Taunton.
14. IX. John RICHMOND, *b.* 5th December, 1673, in Taunton.
15. X. Ebenezer RICHMOND, *b.* 12th May, 1676, in Newport, Rhode Island.
16. XI. Abigail RICHMOND, *b.* 26th February, 1679, in Newport.

III. 10. (LIEUTENANT) JOSEPH RICHMOND, *b.* in Taunton, 8th December, 1663; date of death unknown; *m.* 26th June, 1685, Mary ANDREWS, dau. of Henry and Mary ANDREWS of Taunton.

ISSUE, BORN IN MIDDLEBORO

52. I. Joseph RICHMOND, *m.* Hannah DEANE; *m.* (secondly), Abigail (PHILLIPS) FRENCH.
53. II. Margaret RICHMOND, *d.* in 1737; unmarried.
54. III. Mary RICHMOND, *m.* William REED; *m.* (secondly), Stephen ANDREWS.
55. IV. Abigail RICHMOND, *m.* Mathew GOODING.
56. V. John RICHMOND, *m.* Sarah THRASHER.
*57. VI. CHRISTOPHER RICHMOND, of whom later.
58. VII. Henry RICHMOND, *m.* Mehitable CASWELL.
59. VIII. Josiah RICHMOND, *m.* Elizabeth POOL; *m.* (secondly), Joanna BRIGGS.
60. IX. William RICHMOND, *m.* ———— MACOMBER

IV. 57. CHRISTOPHER RICHMOND, was *b.* in Middleboro, in 1688; *m.* Phebe WILLIAMS, dau. of Joseph and Elizabeth (WATSON) WILLIAMS, *b.* 25th September, 1687; she *d.* and he *m.* (secondly), 15th November, 1750, Susanna BARDEN of Middleboro, widow.

ISSUE, BORN IN MIDDLEBORO

(By first marriage)

190. I. Judith RICHMOND, *b.* 29th May, 1717; *m.* William CLAGGETT, of Newport, Rhode Island.
191. II. Elizabeth RICHMOND, *b,* 1st October, 1719.
192. III. Mary RICHMOND, *b.* 18th October, 1721; *m.* STEPHENS.
*193. IV. ELIAKIM RICHMOND, of whom later.
194. V. Phebe RICHMOND, *b.* 2d January, 1727–;8 *m.* Gershom RICHMOND.
195. VI. Joseph RICHMOND, *b.* 4th February, 1730–1731; *d.* young and unmarried.

V. 193. ELIAKIM RICHMOND, *b.* in Middleboro, 28th January, 1724–1725; *m.* 19th November, 1747, Sarah HACKETT, dau. of George and Lydia (THOMAS) HACKETT, *b.* in Middleboro, 19th May, 1725; and had amongst others, Judith RICHMOND, who *m.* Benjamin RHOADES, of Wallingford, Vermont, ancestor of the subject of this memoir.

Rogers

ANCESTORS OF ABIGAIL ROGERS, WHO M. JOHN RICHMOND (JOHN)

I. 1. THOMAS ROGERS came over in the *Mayflower* with his son Joseph; *d.* early in the winter of 1621, of hardships in the new Colony.

ISSUE

2.   I. Joseph ROGERS.
3.   II. Eleazer ROGERS.
*4. III. JOHN ROGERS, of whom later.

II. 4. JOHN ROGERS, *m.* Ann Churchman. He lived in Plymouth in 1631; and in Duxbury in 1634; he was Representative to the General Court in 1657.

ISSUE

5.   I. John ROGERS, *m.* Elizabeth (ALDEN) PABODIE.
6.   II. Joseph ROGERS.
7.   III. Timothy ROGERS.
8.   IV. Ann ROGERS, *m.* John HEMSDON.
9.   V. Mary ROGERS.
10. VI. Abigail Rogers, *m.* John RICHMOND, whose descendant, Judith RICHMOND, *m.* Benjamin RHOADES of Wallingford, Vermont; ancestor of the subject of this memoir.

Osgood (Maternal)

I. JOHN OSGOOD, of Andover, Essex County, Massachusetts, was *b.* in the parish of Wherwell, Hampshire, England, 23d July, 1595; *d.* in Andover, 24th October, 1651; *m.* in England, circa 1627, Sarah BOOTH, who *d.* 8th April, 1667. (See "OSGOOD Genealogy" by Eben PUTNAM, 1894.)

Before the Norman Conquest, Clapa OSGOOD was living at Lambeth, and it was at the marriage feast of his daughter, Cytha, in 1042, that Harthacnut, or "Hardicanute," died, as he drained his goblet. Osgood was second only to the King in power. After the battle of Hastings, the Saxon monks, Osgod and Alrik, removed Harold's remains to their monastery at Waltham. In "Domesday Book," mention is made of several OSGOODS holding lands in a number of counties. Osgot was a great landed proprietor, probably one of the Saxons who made his peace with the Conqueror and was confirmed in his possessions. Robertus OSGOOD was a burgess of Willshire, living in the thirteenth century. In 1316, Adam de OSGODBY of Yorkshire was keeper of the Great Seal.

For nearly three centuries the Osgood family has been prominent in Massachusetts and New York. The Pilgrim ancestor, John, came from Wherwell, near Andover, England, and is said to have named Andover, Massachusetts, which town he helped to found. His was the second house there, and religious services were held in it until the church was built. The property has been in possession of the family until within the last few years. According to tradition, John "feared neither the theological devil or the red ones" who prowled in the neighborhood. He went to church with his musket, and he and his sons went armed when trouble with the Indians threatened. John Osgood was a religious enthusiast who "devoted all his leisure to the glory of God," as it has been expressed. No better type of the God-fearing, stout-hearted pioneer can be found. He was the first representative from Andover to the General Court, 1651.

Massachusetts Revolutionary Rolls of those who flew to arms upon the "Lexington Alarm" give the names of six Osgoods from Andover, eight from Salisbury and twelve from other towns. Under "Miscellaneous Service," Benjamin Osgood "marched twenty-six miles from home." Thomas "enlisted 10th October, 1777, discharged 18th October, twenty miles from home."

Samuel Osgood of Andover, the fifth in descent from John, commanded a company of minute men at Lexington and Concord, and served on many important committees in the Provincial Congress. He helped to frame the Constitution of the United States, and was a member of the Cabinet. This position, however, he resigned when the capital was removed from New York to Philadelphia. He was conspicuous in all public movements. The first two names on the list of incorporators of the present public school system of New York are those of De Witt Clinton and Samuel Osgood. Another Samuel Osgood, b. 1812, is regarded as one of the literary lights of the family. Samuel is a name of honor; the representative in art is Samuel, b. 1808. Many of his canvases are treasured in the great public collections of the country. His wife was Frances Sargent Locke, better known by her pen name, "Fanny Forester."

The Arms were granted by King James Stuart I, as a reward for military achievement; they were the Arms of John the Immigrant.

On the esquire's helmet, mantled gules, doubled argent, a torce argent and gules, thereon, a demi-lion, rampant, proper, supporting a garb gules. In heraldry, the garb denotes plenty, and that the first bearer of the Arms did deserve well for his hospitality. Another symbolic meaning is that "the harvest of first hopes had been secured." The tressure flory is an emblem signifying preservation or protection. It is borne in the arms of Scotland, and the legend is that it was given to Achaius, King of Scotland, by Charlemagne in order to signify that the French lilies should defend the Scottish lion. The double tressure was first assumed by Robert Stuart to testify his approval of the alliance which he had renewed with Charles V of France.

The lion has always held a high place in heraldry as an emblem of deathless courage. The helmet denotes wisdom and surety in defense. As to the colors, gules stands for fortitude, and argent, peace and security.

John OSGOOD, upon his arrival in New England, sojourned at Ipswich, but shortly after chose Newbury as the place of his residence. There he remained until his removal and settlement at Andover which occurred in or just previous to 1645. That he had early determined to remove from Newbury, which, in the view of the inhabitants, was already overcrowded, is shown by the fact that he was one of the petitioners for, and chairman of, the committee to obtain a settlement at Winnacunnet, now Hampton, New Hampshire. This was in 1638.

In September, 1644, an attempt was made to form a church at Andover, the meeting being held at Rowley, as there were not sufficient accommodations at Andover, but on account of a technicality the organization was not effected until October, 1645. The names of the first ten members, freeholders (as required by law to constitute a church), were John WOODBRIDGE, teacher, John OSGOOD, Robert BARNARD, John FRYE, Nicholas HOLT, Richard BARKER, Joseph PARKER, Nathan PARKER, Richard BLAKE, Edmund FAULKNER; given in order of their signing.

ISSUE

2. I. Sarah OSGOOD, b. England, 1629; m. 1st June, 1648, John CLEMENTS of Haverhill, 1645, perhaps at Marblehead 1651, representative 1654; d. by shipwreck on a voyage to England soon after.
3. II. John OSGOOD, b. England, probably 1630.
4. III. Mary OSGOOD, b. England, 1633; m. Henry INGALLS.
5. IV. Elizabeth OSGOOD, b. England, 1635–1636; bapt. Wherwell, 14th October, 1636; m. 12th or 18th October, 1653, John BROWN of Reading.
*6. V. STEPHEN, of whom later.
7. VI. Hannah OSGOOD, b. Andover, 1644; m. 21st May, 1660, Samuel ARCHER, son of Samuel and Susanna, who went from Salem to Andover. He was freeman 1668.

Arms (OSGOOD).—Three garbs in a double tressure, flory, counter-flory, gules.
Crest.—A demi-lion rampant proper, supporting a garb, gules.

II. 6. STEPHEN OSGOOD, of Andover, Massachusetts, b. circa 1638, in Ipswich or Newbury; d. 15th January, 1690–1691; m, 24th October, 1663, Mary HOOKER.

ISSUE

20. I. Stephen OSGOOD, b. 11th March, 1665; d. 1st October, 1667.
*21. II. HOOKER OSGOOD, of whom later.
22. III. Stephen OSGOOD, b. 16th August, 1670; d. 1749.
23. IV. Joseph OSGOOD, b. 1st June, 1673.
24. V. Mary OSGOOD, b. 23d December, 1677; d. 4th March, 1677 or 1678.

III. 21. HOOKER OSGOOD, of Lancaster, Massachusetts, b. in Andover, 24th August, 1668; d. Lancaster, 29th January, 1748; m. 26th April, 1692, Dorothy WOODMAN, b. 23d November, 1669. See WOODMAN lineage later.

ISSUE, BORN IN LANCASTER

57.   I. Hooker Osgood, *b.* 26th March, 1693; *d.* 1765.
*58. II. Joshua Osgood, of whom later.
59. III. Jonathan Osgood, *b.* 16th September, 1696; *d.* 10th February, 1766.
60.   IV. David Osgood, *b.* 8th October, 1698; *d.* 1771.
61.   V. Benjamin Osgood, *b.* 21st May, 1700; *d.* 29th October, 1798.
62.   VI. Moses Osgood, *b.* 1702; *d.* March, 1776.
63. VII. Aaron Osgood, *b.* 1706.
64. VIII. Dorothy Osgood; *b.* 1707; *m.* Josiah Whitcomb of Lancaster. Many of their descendants are to be found in Swanzey, New Hampshire.
65.   IX. Elizabeth Osgood, *b.* 1709; *m.* Thomas Sawyer, at Lancaster, 21st October, 1736.
66.   X. Sarah Osgood, *b.* 1710; *m.* 16th November, 1726, John Divoll of Lancaster.

IV. 58. Joshua Osgood, of Leominster, and Barre, Massachusetts, *b.* 2d September, 1694; *d.* 31st January, 1783; *m.* 20th December, 1722, Ruth Divoll, *d.* 28th May, 1782. He was a farmer. Ruth Divoll was descended from William-John, of Braintree.

ISSUE

152.   I. Joshua Osgood, *b.* 13th April, 1724; *d.* young
153.   II. Ephraim Osgood, *b.* 22d January, 1726; *d.* 1787.
154. III. Ruth Osgood, *b.* 22d November, 1727; *d.* 10th January, 1805; *m.* 6th June, 1753, Phineas Houghton, probably son of John and Mehitable Houghton, of Lancaster, *b.* 10th April, 1725.
155.   IV. Sarah Osgood, *b.* 7th December, 1729; *d.* young.
*156.   V. William Osgood, of whom later.
157.   VI. Asahel Osgood, *b.* 23d March, 1735; *d.* 21st July, 1812.
158. VII. Abel Osgood, *b.* 25th April, 1738; *m.* 9th March, 1814.
159. VIII. Sarah Osgood, *b.* 7th December, 1740.
160.   IX. Manasseh Osgood, *b.* 30th April, 1745; *d.* 26th November, 1830.
161.   X. Lemuel Osgood, *b.* 6th November, 1747; *d.* 23d October, 1821.
162.   XI. Joshua Osgood, *b.* 10th August, 1749; *d.* 28th July, 1826.

V. 156. William Osgood, of Barre, Massachusetts; Claremont, New Hampshire and Cabot, Vermont, *b.* 20th August, 1732; *d.* in Cabot, 5th February, 1801; *m.* 3d June, 1756, Hepsibeth Dunton of Reading, who *d.* 31st October, 1809.

William Osgood removed from Barre to Claremont, New Hampshire, in 1775; thence, 1794, to Cabot, Vermont. He was a farmer. His family was the largest of the Lancaster branch of the Osgood family. He had a long and distinguished service in the American Revolution and his descendants are qualified for admission to the Societies, Sons of the Revolution and Colonial Wars, Daughters of the Revolution and Colonial Dames.

ISSUE

426. I. William Osgood, *b.* Barre, 17th January, 1760; *d.* 4th October, 1823.
427. II. Thomas Osgood, *b.* 1st August, 1761, Barre; *d.* 10th November, 1843.
428. III. Levi Osgood, *b.* Barre, 25th April, 1763; *d.* circa 1812.
429. IV. Abijah Osgood, *b.* Barre, 23d February, 1765; *d.* 17th April, 1826.
430. V. Mary Osgood, *b.* Barre, 5th February, 1767; *d. s. p.* 1793; *m.* Joshua Chase, farmer of Cornish, Vermont.
431. VI. Sarah Osgood, *b.* Barre, 17th February, 1769; *d.* 2d July, 1839; *m.* Joseph Fisher, farmer of Cabot, Vermont.
432. VII. Amasa Osgood, *b.* Barre, 18th September, 1771; *d.* 1811.
*433. VIII. Joshua Osgood, of whom later.
434. IX. David Osgood, *b.* 5th November, 1774; *d.* 29th May, 1848.
435. X. Solomon W. Osgood, *b.* Claremont, New Hampshire, 18th October, 1776.
436. XI. John Osgood, *b.* Claremont, 1779.
437. XII. Samson Osgood, *b.* Claremont, 28th July, 1738; *d.* 5th May, 1851.
438. XIII. Hepsebeth Osgood, *b.* Claremont, 1787; *d.* March, 1855; *m.* Edward Gilman, farmer and clothier, of Ogden and Byron, New York, who *d.* 31st December, 1867.
439. XIV. Anne Osgood, *d.* 26th June, 1866; *m.* David Haines, farmer, of Cabot, Vermont.

VI. 433. Joshua Osgood, of Cabot, Vermont; *b.* in Barre, Massachusetts, 18th January, 1773; *d.* in Cabot, Vermont, 23d April, 1820; *m.* Lucy Russell, of Lee, Massachusetts, who *m.* (secondly), Robert Lance.

ISSUE

1089. I. Hannah Osgood, *b.* 20th August, 1801; *d.* young.
1090. II. Zenas Osgood, *b.* 16th August, 1804; *d.* circa 1862.
1091. III. Eunice Osgood, *b.* 7th November, 1807; *m.* Porter Cushman of Tunbridge, Vermont.
*1092. IV. Joshua W. Osgood, of whom later.
1093. V. Elijah Osgood, *b.* 3d July, 1816.

VII. 1092. Joshua W. Osgood, *b.* Montpelier, Vermont, 5th January, 1812; *d.* Gery City, Kansas, 20th July, 1876; *m.* Mary (Elizabeth) Russell, of Lee, Massachusetts, in Albany, New York, 15th October, 1831. They resided till about 1840 in Montpelier; removed to Wisconsin; removed to Kansas about 1865.

ISSUE

2161. I. Francis Wright Osgood, *b.* in Vermont, 21st December, 1835; *d.* in Arkansas, 1912; *m.* Mary J. Pannel, 7th March, 1858.

2162. II. Henry Elijah Osgood, *b.* in Vermont, 28th February, 1838; *d.* in Columbus, Nebraska, August, 1886. Served in Civil War.
2163. III. Charles Joshua Osgood (first), *b.* 23d May, 1841; *d.* 29th September, 1841.
2164. IV. Charles Joshua Osgood (second), *b.* in Waukesha, Wisconsin, 6th February, 1843; *d.* in Arkansas in 1912; *m.* in 1869; *m.* (secondly and thirdly), no data. Served in Civil War.
2165. V. Lucy Eunice Osgood, *b.* in Waukesha, Wisconsin, 8th February, 1846; *m.* Nelson Carrier Rhoades at Viroqua, Wisconsin, 13th September, 1866. Parents of the subject of this memoir.
2166. VI. Clarinda J. Osgood, *b.* in Sullivan, Wisconsin, 25th November, 1848; *d.* at Palmyra, Wisconsin, 30th November, 1848.
2167. VII. Mary Elizabeth Osgood, *b.* in Sullivan, 31st July, 1851; *d.* in Mt. Ayr, Iowa, August, 1886; *m.* Johnny ―――, who lived but one month; *m.* (secondly), Levy Newman, in 1873.
2168. VIII. Alphonso George Osgood, *b.* in Orian, Wisconsin, 2d October, 1854; *m.* at Mt. Ayr, Iowa.

Woodman

The long English ancestry, introducing the American line, closes with Edward Woodman, who *m.* Olive Mallot, and had:

ISSUE

I. Lieutenant Edward Woodman, *b.* 27th December, 1606, in England; *d.* 1694, Newbury, Massachusetts; *m.* Joanna Salway, *b.* 1614; *d.* 1687. In Newbury, 1635; called "Mr." in the early records; Deputy to the General Court 1636-1637, 1639, 1643; who had,

II. Joshua Woodman, *b.* 1636; *d.* 30th May, 1703; *m.* Elizabeth Stevens, *b.* 1645; *d.* 1714; who had,

III. Dorothy Woodman, *b.* 13th November, 1669; *m.* Hooker Osgood. See Osgood Lineage.

Moulthrop

Frances James Brown, who *m.* Nelson Osgood Rhoades, is a direct descendant from the Moulthrop family of Connecticut. Amongst her immigrant ancestors are,

Thomas Stewart;
John Thompson of New Haven;
Thomas Wheeler of Concord, Massachusetts, 1636;
William Tuttle, who came to Boston in the *Planter*, 1635;
Edward Howe, who came to Lynn, Massachusetts, in the *Truelove*, in 1635, and was Representative to the General Court in 1638;
Isaac Bradley of Branford, Connecticut.

I. MATTHEW MOULTHROP, the founder of the MOULTHROP family in America, was *b.* in England; was at New Haven in 1639; *d.* 22d December, 1668. Admitted to First Church, New Haven, before 1644; *m.* in England, Jane, surname unknown, who *d.* in May, 1672, in New Haven. Wills of both are found in Volume I of the New Haven Probate Records. Matthew was prominent in the affairs of the New Haven and East Haven Colonies, in both of which he held office; he fought in the Indian Wars.

ISSUE

*2. I. MATTHEW MOULTHROP, of whom later.
3. II. Elizabeth MOULTHROP, *b.* in England, in 1638; *bapt.* 1642; *m.* 1663, John GREGORY.
4. III. Mary MOULTHROP, *b.* 1641; *bapt.* 1642.

II. 2. MATTHEW MOULTHROP, *b.* in England; *d.* 1st February, 1690–1691, in East Haven, aged fifty-three. He was at East Haven in 1638; *m.* 26th June, 1662, Hannah THOMPSON, dau. of John and Eleanor THOMPSON. His death record, shown above, places his birth in 1638, but history refers to his birth in England as stated. He lived in East Haven from which he served in the Indian Wars.

ISSUE

5. I. Hannah MOULTHROP, *b.* 2d November, 1663; *d.* 2d January, 1663–1664.
6. II. Hannah MOULTHROP, *b.* 20th April, 1665; *m.* 17th August, 1687, Capt. John RUSSELL, *b.* 14th December, 1664; *d.* 3d February, 1724; son of Ralph and Mary RUSSELL.
7. III. JOHN MOULTHROP, of whom later.
8. IV. Matthew MOULTHROP, *b.* 18th July, 1670; *d.* 12th May, 1740.
9. V. Abigail MOULTHROP, *d.* soon (twin of Matthew).
10. VI. Lydia MOULTHROP, *b.* 8th August, 1674.
11. VII. Samuel MOULTHROP, *b.* 24th June, 1677; *d.* 14th October, 1677.
12. VIII. Samuel MOULTHROP, *b.* 13th April, 1679; *d.* 30th January, 1713; *m.* Sarah BARNES, *b.* 1689, dau. of Thomas BARNES and Keziah MOULTHROP.
13. IX. Keziah MOULTHROP, *b.* 13th April, 1682; *d.* aged fifty-three.

III. 7. (SERGEANT) JOHN MOULTHROP, *b.* 5th February, 1667–1668; *d.* 14th February, 1713; *m.* 29th June, 1692, Abigail BRADLEY, *b.* 9th September, 1671; *d.* 3d September, 1743; dau. of Joseph, *b.* 4th January, 1646, who *m.* Silence (BROCKETT), 25th October, 1667, dau. of John BROCKETT, of New Haven. He served in Colonial Wars.

John BROCKETT, son of Sir John, of England, was the young engineer chosen to lay out the village or colony of New Haven. The "Green" or "Public Square," and its surroundings for two blocks deep, remain practically unchanged in form from that established by the first survey. John, *d.* 12th March, 1689, aged eighty.

ISSUE

26.   I. Abigail MOULTHROP, *b.* 12th August, 1693; *d.* young.
27.   II. John MOULTHROP, *b.* 17th March, 1696; *d.* 1727; *m.* Sarah TUTTLE, *b.* 1698; *d.* 3d November, 1734.
28.   III. Mary MOULTHROP, *b.* 5th April, 1700; *d.* 1st July, 1708.
29.   IV. Sarah MOULTHROP, *b.* 10th October, 1701; *m.* Adonijah MORRIS, son of Eleazer and Anna MORRIS.
30.   V. Daniel MOULTHROP, *b.* 1st December, 1703; *d.* 29th January, 1759; *m.* Hannah BELCHER.
31.   VI. Israel MOULTHROP, *b.* 7th June, 1706; *d.* 15th October, 1787; *m.* Lydia PAGE.
*32. VII. SERGEANT JOSEPH MOULTHROP, of whom later.
33.   VIII. Timothy MOULTHROP, *b.* 1708–1709, twin of Joseph.

IV. 32. (SERGEANT) JOSEPH MOULTHROP, *b.* 1708; *d.* 1771; *m.* Mary WHEDON; *d.* before 13th May, 1783. Will, January 23, 1771, probated May, 1771; lived in East Haven. See Volume ii of New Haven Probate Records. Joseph served as a sergeant in the French and Indian Wars.

ISSUE; BORN IN EAST HAVEN

69.   I. Adonijah MOULTHROP, *d.* in French Wars, 11th November, 1760, in hospital at Albany, New York; unmarried.
70.   II. Joseph MOULTHROP, *m.* 1766, Lucretia BRADLEY, dau. of Caleb and Sarah (RUSSELL) BRADLEY; Sergeant, Revolution.
71.   III. Elihu MOULTHROP, *b.* 1747; *d.* 27th October, 1782; Revolution.
*72. IV. JUDE MOULTHROP, of whom later.
73.   V. Rhoda MOULTHROP.
74.   VI. Hannah MOULTHROP.
75.   VII. Mary MOULTHROP, *m.* 30th December, 1771, in East Haven, Ebenezer BURRINGTON.
76.   VIII. Abigail MOULTHROP, of New Haven, *m.* 18th June, 1776, ——— CARTER, of Farmington, at North Haven.
77.   IX. Lucretia MOULTHROP, *m.* before 1st November, 1781, John TALMADGE.

V. 72. JUDE MOULTHROP, *d.* 10th December, 1800; *m.* 30th July, 1777, Betsey WHEELER of Southbury, *b.* 1st January, 1755; *d.* 16th August, 1842; dau. of Obadiah and Agnes (TUTTLE) WHEELER. Both Jude and Betsey MOULTHROP are buried in the North Main Street Cemetery, Rutland, Vermont. He was one of the pioneer settlers of Rutland, Vermont. He and his descendants were amongst the prominent and progressive men of that region until the death of his last male descendant there, in 1885. The greater part of his original homestead is now occupied by the city of Rutland, on the edge of which the old MOULTHROP house still stands in perfect condition, typical of the times when it was built. Jude MOULTHROP was the progenitor of a large branch of the family which moved to New York and has since become very numerous.

ISSUE

*132.   I. NATHAN MOULTHROP, of whom later.
133.   II. Trueman MOULTHROP, b. 1788; m. Delia, surname unknown.
133a.   III. Esther MOULTHROP. d. young.
134.   IV. Laura MOULTHROP, b. 1800; m. 9th November, 1820, Daniel GLEASON, at Rutland, Vermont.

VI. 132. NATHAN MOULTHROP, b. 20th December, 1778, at Southbury, Connecticut; d. 27th September, 1851, at Kenoza Lake, New York; m. 7th July, 1803, Agnes NEWBY of Poughkeepsie, New York, b. 7th September, 1783, in England; d. 3d September, 1847, at Kenoza Lake; dau. of Robert, of England, and Isabella ATKINSON. They were m. in First Presbyterian Church in New York City. He was made a Mason in New York City in 1802.

Nathan MOULTHROP left Vermont as a young man and became a sea captain, plying between American and European coasts. He was a captive of the English during the War of 1812. In 1827, he and the STEWART family appeared in the vicinity of Pike's Pond, now Kenoza Lake, New York. He acquired a considerable amount of landed property, raised a large family and was a prominent citizen. His family has multiplied numerously, remaining in that district, and still constitute a large part of the representative population of that place. A later branch of the family moved into Michigan.

ISSUE

197.   I. Agnes MOULTHROP, b. 7th April, 1804, at Rutland, Vermont; d. at Bethel, New York; m. Samuel BROWN.
*198.   II. ROBERT MOULTHROP, of whom later.
199.   III. Elizabeth (Betsey) MOULTHROP, b. 29th May, 1808, at New York City; d. at Poughkeepsie; m. probably at Poughkeepsie.
200.   IV. Nathan MOULTHROP, Jr., b. 9th May, 1813, at Poughkeepsie; d. 3d March, 1867, at Pike's Pond; m. 27th November, 1834, at Pike's Pond, Phoebe WOOD.
201.   V. Jane MOULTHROP, b. 30th May, 1815, at Poughkeepsie; d. 24th November, 1888 (G. S. I.) at Newburg, New York, m. 9th March, 1842, Christopher SLEE, at Poughkeepsie. She d. at Newburg, New York.

202. VI. JOHN MOULTHROP, b. 23d July, 1817, at Poughkeepsie; d. 9th August, 1874, at Kenoza Lake; unmarried.
203. VII. Isabella MOULTHROP, b. 4th June, 1820, Poughkeepsie; d. 23d January, 1892, at Newburg; buried Kenoza Lake, New York; m. Capt. John D. KIDD, at Newburg.
204. VIII. Truman MOULTHROP, b. 29th October, 1822; d. 1891 at Kenoza Lake; m. 7th November, 1849, Hannah Catherine WOOD, at Kenoza Lake.
205. IX. Sarah Jane MOULTHROP, b. 28th January, 1825; at Poughkeepsie; d. 8th May, 1911 at North Branch; m. 2d September, 1846, William B. HUNT, at Kenoza Lake.
206. X. Gideon MOULTHROP, b. 17th December, 1827, at Cochecton, New York; d. 4th January, 1907; m. 8th October, 1856, at Kenoza Lake, Isabella Eliza NEWBY. He d. at Kenoza Lake.

VII. 198. ROBERT MOULTHROP, b. 12th October, 1805, at Poughkeepsie, New York; d. 9th March, 1891, at Kenoza Lake, New York, aged eighty-five; m. Margaret Ellen STEWART, at Hurds Settlement; dau. of Thomas and Nancy STEWART, b. in 1811; d. 9th March, 1879, aged sixty-eight, at Hurds Settlement; buried Kenoza Lake.

Robert MOULTHROP resided at Kenoza Lake, and following the habits of his father, became a prominent landholder. The descendants of Robert and Margaret STEWART are qualified for membership in the Society of Americans of Royal Descent.

ISSUE

246. I. Sarah Jane MOULTHROP, b. 14th February, 1832, at Kenoza Lake; d. at Delhi, New York; m. Cornelius FLINT at Kenoza Lake.
247. II. Thomas Taylor MOULTHROP, b. 31st May, 1834, at Hurds Settlement; d. 7th May, 1911, at Kenoza Lake; m. in 1867, at Kenoza Lake, Hannah J. BARLOW.
*248. III. MARY AGNES MOULTHROP, of whom later.
249. IV. Alexander MOULTHROP, b. 28th May, 1839, at Kenoza Lake; d. 17th September, 1907, at Kenoza Lake; unmarried.
250. V. William H. MOULTHROP, b. 14th June, 1844, at Kenoza Lake; d. 14th December, 1906, at Kenoza Lake; unmarried.
251. VI. Elizabeth MOULTHROP, b. 26th March, 1847, at Kenoza Lake; living, 1920, at Kenoza Lake; m. James FULTON at Kenoza Lake.
252. VII. Grace MOULTHROP, b. 10th August, 1850, at Kenoza Lake; living, 1920; m. 18th November, 1890, William MAGAR, b. 23d February, 1847; d. 28th October, 1918.
253. VIII. Ellen MOULTHROP, b. 15th July, 1853, at Kenoza Lake; d. 17th October, 1881, at Kenoza Lake; m. Samuel THOMPSON.

VIII. 248. MARY AGNES MOULTHROP, *b.* 3d December, 1836, at Kenoza Lake; *d.* 6th September, 1913, at Alpena, Michigan; *m.* 7th November, 1860, at Kenoza Lake, Renwick BROWN, *b.* 2d June, 1837, in New York City; living, 1920, Orting, Washington.

ISSUE

304.	I.	Elizabeth BROWN, *b.* Bethel, New York; *d.* young, at Bethel.
305.	II.	Victoria BROWN, living, 1920, Tacoma, Washington.
306.	III.	FRANCES JAMES BROWN, *m.* 26th January, 1911, Nelson Osgood RHOADES; living, 1920, Los Angeles, California.
307.	IV.	Mary Agnes BROWN, living, 1920, Detroit, Michigan.
308.	V.	Charles Edgar BROWN, *d.* young.
309.	VI.	Walter Scott BROWN, living, 1920, Detroit, Michigan; *m.* 1909, at Detroit, Frances Elizabeth BARTLETT, who has *Mayflower* ancestry.

ISSUE

Walter Edgar BROWN

Rickard

ORLIN LUMAN RICKARD of Chicago, Illinois, *b.* 6th August, 1855, at Massena, New York; *m.* 25th July, 1876, at Augusta, Wisconsin, Barbara SHONG, *b.* 20th September, 1854, at Lowville, New York, dau. of John Michael SHONG, *b.* 1810, *d.* 1894, soldier of France, *m.* 1831, in Metz, France, Margaret PELOW, *b.* 1810, *d.* 12th June, 1887.

ISSUE

1. Fay Ebben, *b.* 11th August, 1878; *m.* 22d August, 1900, Martha SCHWAB, *b.* 27th June, 1880, dau. of Julius and Louise (TROY) SCHWAB.

ISSUE

I. Lester Earle, *b.* 20th December, 1908.
II. Anna Mary (adopted dau.), *b.* 7th December, 1884; *m.* 23rd July, 1906, Walter Munford.

ISSUE

Clarence, *b.* 19th July, 1907.
Evelyn, *b.* 19th November, 1909.

ORLIN LUMAN RICKARD, received a public school education. For fifteen years was engaged in railroad office work and in 1883 became one of the founders of the Railway Station Agents Association. Was Adjutant General and afterwards Commander in Chief of United Boys Brigade of America. Holds interest in Rickard Circular Folding Company; President and General Manager Lakewood Lot Owners Association; Lakewood Utilities Company and Lakewood Street Railway; Registrar Illinois Society Founders and Patriots.

Lineage

The family of RICKARD or RICKANDIS an ancient family of County Radnor, England were frequently High Sheriffs of the County. One of the family, whose monument remains on Old Radnor Church, was Auditor of Wales to Charles I. A junior branch of the family settled at Llantrissant, County Glamorgan in the seventeenth century and still exists there; other branches were also seated in Counties Hereford and Somerset. The American ancestor of this family was Giles RICKARD, of Plymouth, Massachusetts, *b.* circa 1597 in England; *d.* at Plymouth, 1684; *m.* (firstly) March, 1622, Judith whose surname is not given and who *d.* 6th February, 1661; *m.* (secondly) 2d March, 1662, Joan TILSON at Plymouth, Massachusetts, *d.s.p.; m.* (thirdly) 24th January, 1669, Mrs. Hannah POTTS, at Plymouth, Massachusetts, *d.s.p.*

ISSUE

I. GILES, *b.* 1623, of whom later.
II. John, *b.* 1627, *m.* 1651, Esther BARNES.
III. Sarah, *m.* George PADDOCK.

GILES RICKARD, of Plymouth, Massachusetts, *b.* there 1623; *m.* 3d October, 1651, Hannah DUNHAM, dau. of Deacon John and Abigail (WOOD) DUNHAM, who were married in Holland.

ISSUE

I. John, *b.* 1652; *m,* Mary COOK.
II. SAMUEL, *b.* 14th January, 1662, of whom later.
III. Henry, *b.* 1667, *m.* (firstly) Mary COOK, dau. of John COOK *d.* 17th September, 1726-1727; *m.* (secondly) Mercy MORTON, *b.* 1662, *d.* 10th January, 1729-1730.
IV. Eleazer, *m.* Sarah (surname not given).
V. Abigail, *m.* ———— WHITNEY.
VI. Giles, *b.* 1654; *m.* 1688 Hannah SNOW; no issue.
VII. Judith, *m.* 1678, Joseph FAUNCE.
VIII. Mercy, *b.* 12th February, 1683.
IX. Hannah, *b.* 1701, *m.* Ebenezer EATON.

SAMUEL RICKARD, of Plympton, Massachusetts, *b.* there 14th January, 1662; *d.* there 7th September, 1727; *m.* 31st December, 1689, at Plympton, Rebecca SNOW, *b.* 23d July, 1676, near Eastham, Massachusetts, *d.* 4th April, 1740, dau. of William and Rebecca (BROWN) SNOW, she dau. of Peter BROWN of the *Mayflower.*

ISSUE

I. Rebecca, *b.* 9th February, 1691; *m.* 1735 Deacon Seth ALLEN.
II. Hannah, *b.* 25th September, 1693; *m.* (firstly) 1720, Țhaniel WHITMAN; *m.* (secondly) Joseph BRYAN.
III. Samuel, *b.* 21st May, 1696; *d.* 18th August, 1796; *m.* 1721 Rachel WHITON, who *d.* 30th January, 1792.
IV. Bethiah, *b.* 10th October, 1698.
V. HENRY, *b.* 4th February, 1700, of whom later.
VI. Mary, *b.* 8th April, 1702.
VII. Elkanah, *b.* 7th June, 1704; *m.* (firstly) Keturah BISHOP; *m.* (secondly) Bertha CONANT.
VIII. Mehitable, *b.* 1st April, 1707; *m.* 1730, Arthur HARRIS.
IX. Eleazer, *b.* 8th March, 1709.

HENRY RICKARD, of Pembroke, Massachusetts, b. 4th February, 1700; m. 13th February, 1723–1724, Alice OLDHAM, b. 22d June, 1703, dau. of Isaac OLDHAM, of Oldham, Massachusetts.

ISSUE

I. Judith, b. 1725–1726.
II. SAMUEL, b. 12th October, 1726–1727, of whom below.
III. Isaac, b. 1728–1729.

SAMUEL RICKARD, of Bridgewater, Massachusetts, b. 12th October, 1727, at Plympton, Massachusetts; m. (firstly) 30th March, Sarah JOSLYN, d. 11th April, 1747, m. (secondly) 3d November, 1749, Zeraviah BUMPUS, b. 5th April, 1729, d. 30th January, 1792.

ISSUE BY FIRST MARRIAGE

I. Sarah, b. 29th March, 1747.

ISSUE BY SECOND MARRIAGE

I. Allis, b. 27th September, 1750; m. William REED.
II. Jacob, b. 23d December, 1751; unmarried; d. near Utica, New York.
III. Samuel, b. 3d April, 1753; m. 12th November, 1778, Marion BARNES.
IV. Cleo, b. 16th September, 1754; m. 21st November, 1777, James TINKHAM.
V. Mary, b. 21st April, 1756; m. 1775, Nathaniel HOLMES.
VI. ISRAEL, b. 27th January, 1757, of whom later.
VII. Deborah, b. 12th September, 1759.
VIII. Hannah, b. 8th September, 1761.

ISRAEL RICKARD, of Middleboro, Massachusetts, b. 27th January, 1757; m. 22d November, 1781, Voadica WESTON, b. 16th January, 1760, d. 14th May, 1834, dau. of Lieut. John WESTON, a descendant of John SOULE of the *Mayflower*.

ISSUE

I. Weston, b. 11th May, 1785, d.s.p. in Vermont.
II. ISRAEL, b. 21st October, 1786, of whom below.

ISRAEL RICKARD, of Massena, New York, b. 21st October, 1786, in Middleboro, Massachusetts; d, 15th March, 1850, in Massena; m. 5th December, 1811, at Bethel, Vermont, Lucy KINNEY, b. 10th January, 1786, at Bethel, Vermont, d. 26th March 1849, at Massena, dau. of Daniel and Polly (SPRAGUE) KINNEY of Bethel, Vermont.

ISSUE

I. LEONARD, b. 10th September, 1812, of whom later.
II. Weston, b. 25th April, 1814; d. 6th July, 1889; m. (firstly) 6th March, 1836, Betsey Keyser; m. (secondly) 27th July, 1860, Mary KIRKHAM.

III. Voadica, *b.* 5th December, 1815; *d.* young.
IV. Polly, *b.* 13th December, 1818; *m.* 20th September, 1849, John D. BEEBE.
V. Daniel, *b.* 8th July, 1820; *m.* 24th October, 1839, Louisa JONES,
VI. Joseph, *b.* 7th May, 1823; *d.* 1st October, 1873; *m.* 25th November, 1840, Emily MORRISON.
VII. Lorenzo, *b.* 8th August, 1824; *d.* 19th June, 1886; *m.* 2d August, 1845, Lucy PARKER.
VIII. Frederick, *b.* 2d March, 1828; *d.* 15th September, 1886; *m.* Martha M. FANSHAW.
IX. Lucy, *b.* 20th June, 1829, *d.* 13th October, 1860; *m.* Asive VARNUM.

LEONARD RICKARD, of Massena, New York, *b.* 10th September, 1812, at Bethel, Vermont; *d.* 18th March, 1886, at Massena; *m.* 1st March, 1834, Rhoda RUSSELL, *b.* 11th May, 1811, at Mount Holly, Vermont, *d.* 25th October, 1883, at Massena, New York, dau. of Benjamin and Merribah (DOOLITTLE) RUSSELL.

ISSUE

I. MARCELLUS BENJAMIN, *b.* 22d December, 1834, of whom later.
II. Charles, *b.* 1st June, 1836; *d.* March, 1899; *m.* 4th July, 1861, at Louisville, New York, Marie H. KNIPE, *b.* 1st April, 1837.
III. Voadecia, *b.* 18th December, 1838; *d.* 6th December, 1898; *m.* 9th February, 1858, Hiram VANTYNE.
IV. Alphus, *b.* 27th September, 1841; *d.* March, 1908; *m.* (firstly) 18th October, 1866, Helen M. COATES, *b.* 16th September, 1844; *m.* (secondly) Margaret CLINE, *b.* 10th May, 1861, dau. of William CLINE and May CARPENTER.
V. Albert, *b.* 29th September, 1844; *d.* 21st May, 1913; *m.* 22d January, 1863, Philena DAY, *d.* 25th February, 1907, dau. of Joseph and Elisa PROCTOR DAY.
VI. Myron, *b.* 29th September, 1851, *d.* 1916; *m.* (firstly) Martha C. CARTER; *m.* (secondly) Mrs. Lucy C. LAMB.
VII. Marabah Charlotte, *b.* 25th December, 1852; *d.* 2d September, 1880; *m.* 3d January, 1880, George B. SCOTT.

MARCELLUS BENJAMIN RICKARD, Blacksmith, of Augusta, Wisconsin, *b.* 22d December, 1834, at Massena, New York; *d.* 22d January, 1879, at Augusta, Wisconsin; *m.* 11th February 1854, at Massena, Sarah Ann DEXTER, *b.* 11th August, 1832, *d.* 6th December, 1883, at Augusta, dau. of Joseph and Sally (THOMPSON) DEXTER.

ISSUE

I. ORLIN LUMAN, *b.* 6th August, 1855, the subject of this memoir.
II. Harlow Ebben, *b.* 26th May, 1858; *d.* 18th May, 1916, *m.* Myra HOUGHTON, *b.* 22d March, 1860, at Humbird, Wisconsin; *d.* 18th November, 1906.

ISSUE

1. Oscar Marcellus, *b.* 27th May, 1885; *m.* 1st September, 1909, Emma Monson, *b.* 4th May, 1886.

III. Myra Adaline, *b.* 21st December, 1867; *d.* in infancy.
IV. Harvey Joseph, *b.* 3d October, 1869; *m.* (firstly) 25th November, 1891, Mattie Enright (divorced); *m.* (secondly) 20th November, 1915, Cora Ester Greenburg, *b.* 2d March, 1892.

ISSUE BY FIRST MARRIAGE

1. Blanch Sarah Anne, *b.* 3d June, 1893; *m.* Harry Saunders (divorced).
2. Grace Jesse, *b.* 30th June, 1894; *m.* Hugh Shelton.
3. Harvey Joseph, *b.* 5th April, 1897.
4. Francis, *b.* 12th March, 1901.
5. Maxin, *b.* 5th April, 1908; *d.* May, 1908.

Arms (Rickards–Rickard).—Argent on a bend gules three garbs or.
Crest.—Out of the battlements of a tower ppr. a demi-talbot argent, collared gules.
Motto.—Este quod esse videris.
Residence.—No. 3330 W. 62nd Street, Chicago, Illinois.
Societies.—Founders and Patriots of America, Odd Fellows, Knights of Pythias.

Rockwood

LUBIM BURTON ROCKWOOD, *b.* 8th August, 1816, in Wilton, New Hampshire; *d.* 7th May, 1872, in Roxbury, Massachusetts; *m.* 1st May, 1845, at Wilton, Abby Ann ABBOT, dau. of Ezra and Rebekah (HALE) ABBOT.

ISSUE

I. Arthur Burton, *b.* 20th November, 1846, in New York City; *d.* 4th October, 1847.
II. Edward Nelson, *b.* 9th October, 1848, in New York City; *d.* 14th February, 1849.
III. Sarah Hale, *b.* 9th December, 1849, in New York City; *m.* 7th September, 1871, at Roxbury, Massachusetts, Charles Avery PLUMER of Boston, Massachusetts.
IV. Fanny Larcom, *b.* 23d August, 1851, in Rocky Hill, Connecticut; *d.* 10th January, 1902, in Philadelphia, Pennsylvania; *m.* 2d December, 1874, at Roxbury, James Cook MILLER, of Boston and Philadelphia; he *d.* 1st February, 1908.

ISSUE

1. Burton Rockwood MILLER, *b.* 6th October, 1875, in Boston, Massachusetts; Princeton University, 1897; member of Sons of the Revolution and Massachusetts Society of the Order of Founders and Patriots of America; enlisted and appointed Lieutenant (junior grade) United States Naval Reserves, March, 1917, stationed at Boston; Section Commander, Provincetown, Massachusetts, August, 1918, to January, 1919; then appointed Member of Board detailed to write history of 1st Naval District.
2. Florence Hale MILLER, *b.* 31st August, 1877, in Boston.

V. William Emerson, *b.* 5th November, 1854, in Rocky Hill, Connecticut; *d.* 24th June, 1899; *m.* 19th September, 1883, at Brooklyn, New York, Persis Abbot LOVEJOY, dau. of Henry and Melinda (WHEELER) LOVEJOY; educated at Andover, Meriden, and Dartmouth College; built home at Englewood, New Jersey; drowned in Oyster Bay, through attempting to rescue the life of another man, who was also swept from the deck of the yacht in which he was cruising.

ISSUE

1. Melinda Wheeler, *b.* 12th July, 1884, in Brooklyn, New York; *m.* 7th May, 1918, at Brown's Mills, New Jersey, Edmund Quincy ABBOT; 311th Infantry, United States National Army; Second Lieutenant, 316th Machine Gun Battalion, United States Army, in France.

This historical and biographical account of the ROCKWOOD and ABBOT families was edited and furnished by Miss Henrietta ROCKWOOD.

2. Persis, *b*. 3d May, 1889, in Englewood, New Jersey; *d*. 26th June, 1889.
3. Richard Burton, *b*. 30th June, 1894, in Wurtsboro, New York; educated at Geneva, Switzerland, and Williams College, 1916; Second Lieutenant, Headquarters Company 310th Infantry, United States Army, in France; upon returning to the headquarters of the 155th Infantry Brigade at Thiaucourt during a heavy bombardment, after the successful execution of a most important commission, he was hit by a piece of shrapnel, 26th September, 1918; he *d*. 28th September, 1918, and the very day he had been recommended by his commanding general for the award of the Distinguished Service Cross for gallantry and "exceptionally meritorius service." The award was later made and the Order of the Crown was also conferred by the King of Belgium.

VI. Annie Abbot, *b*. 6th September, 1856, in Rocky Hill, Connecticut, *m*. 17th October, 1878, in Roxbury, Massachusetts, Clarence HAZLEWOOD, who *d*. 10th January, 1888, in the Bradford, Massachusetts, railroad accident.

ISSUE

1. Grace Burton HAZLEWOOD, *b*. 5th August, 1879, in Roxbury, Massachusetts; *m*. 24th September, 1903, at Roxbury, Horton Gregory IDE of Boston.

ISSUE

1^1. Ann Daggett IDE, *b*. 15th September, 1904.
2^1. Melinda Rockwood IDE, *b*. 31st January, 1906.
3^1. Horton Francis IDE, *b*. 23d March, 1910.
4^1. Edith Burton IDE, *b*. 10th April, 1912.
5^1. Grace Shirley IDE, *b*. 23d August, 1916.

2. William Plumer HAZLEWOOD, *b*. 10th May, 1881, in West Roxbury, Massachusetts; *m*. 15th April, 1905, Leora B. HALEY, of Providence, Rhode Island.

ISSUE

1^1. Gordon Clarence HAZLEWOOD, *b*. 24th January, 1906.
2^1. Lillian HAZLEWOOD, *b*. 8th November, 1908.
3^1. Ruth HAZLEWOOD, *b*. 20th September, 1911.

VII. Elizabeth Davis, *b*. 28th September, 1858; *d*. 24th March, 1885.
VIII. Grace Burton, *b*. 8th May, 1861; *d*. 20th November, 1861.
IX. Henrietta, *b*. 25th April, 1863.

Rev. LUBIM BURTON ROCKWOOD was the son of Lubim and Lydia (BURTON) ROCKWOOD, of Wilton, New Hampshire, and gd. son of Ebenezer ROCKWOOD, M.D. He received his education at New Ipswich Academy, Dartmouth College and Andover Theological Seminary. In 1844 he was ordained a Presbyterian minister and became financial agent of Union Theological Seminary in New York City, where he remained seven years. In July, 1850, he was installed over the Congregational Church in Rocky Hill, Connecticut, as colleague with Dr. CHAPIN. He resigned his pastorate in 1859 and for one year, he was agent of the American Tract Society for Connecticut, being appointed in April, 1860, Secretary of the New England Branch of the American Tract Society, with an office in Boston. He then made his resi-residence in Roxbury, Massachusetts. He travelled extensively throughout New England, making public addresses. During the Civil War, his duties took him to the South, where he gave generously of his time and abilities in work among the soldiers. The Walnut Avenue Congregational Church was organized at his home in Roxbury and the Immanuel-Walnut Avenue Church now worships in the original church edifice. Mr. ROCKWOOD was a man in whom wisdom and sincerity of purpose were happily united and his genial personality and friendly optimism brought many appeals for his counsel and generosity which were always met with cheerfulness and bounty.

He *m.* 1st May, 1845, at Wilton, New Hampshire, Abby Ann ABBOT, whose emigrant ancestor was George ABBOT of Yorkshire, England and Andover, Massachusetts. She was *b.* 13th December, 1818, in Wilton, New Hampshire; educated at New Ipswich Academy; teacher in Wilton, Peterborough and Franklin, New Hampshire. Her father was Ezra ABBOT, a farmer on the homestead in Wilton, New Hampshire. He was Captain of the South Company of Militia; Selectman; Deacon for twenty-five years; a man greatly respected for his benevolence, love of justice, liberality in support of schools and libraries. Her mother Rebekah (HALE) ABBOT, was the dau. of Lieut. Joseph HALE of Coventry, Connecticut, and niece of Capt. Nathan HALE, patriot soldiers in the Continental Army. The dying words of the latter, "I only regret that I have but one life to lose for my country," were reverently remembered in that New England household. The early years of her married life were spent in New York City, but after 1860 and until her death, which occurred 12th May, 1912, at the age of ninety-three years, she resided in Roxbury, Massachusetts. Mrs. ROCKWOOD was greatly interested in the temperance movement; founder of the Maternal Association, member of the King's Daughters and Honorary President of the Woman's Association of Immanuel-Walnut Avenue Church; Vice President of the Florence Crittenden League of Compassion; member of the corporation of the Willard Settlement in Boston; member of the Connecticut Society of the Sons of the American Revolution.

Abbot

1. George ABBOT, *b.* 1615; *d.* 24th December, 1681; came from Yorkshire, England, about 1640; one of the first settlers of Andover, Massachusetts in 1643–1644; *m.* 12th December, 1646, Hannah CHANDLER, *b.* 1629, *d.* 2d June, 1711, dau. of William and Annis CHANDLER.

II. John ABBOT, son of George ABBOT, the emigrant and Hannah CHANDLER, his wife; *b.* 2d March, 1648; *d.* 19th March, 1721; Deacon; Selectman; Representative; *m.* 17th November, 1673, Sarah BARKER, *b.* 1647, *d.* 8th February, 1729, dau. of Richard and Johanna BARKER; residence Andover.

III. John ABBOT, son of John and Sarah (BARKER) ABBOT, *b.* 2d November, 1674; *d.* 1st January, 1754; Deacon for thirty-four years; Selectman; *m.* 6th January, 1703, Elizabeth HARNDEN; she *d.* 9th August, 1756.

IV. John ABBOT, son of John and Elizabeth (HARNDEN) ABBOT, *b.* 3d August, 1704; *d.* 10th November, 1793; Captain of 2d Andover Foot Company, 4th Regiment of Essex County Militia, Col. Richard SALTONSTALL, 1754, French and Indian War; *m.* 28th September, 1732, Phebe FISKE, *b.* 4th August, 1712, dau. of John FISKE of Boxford (1711) and Abigail POOR, his wife. Abigail POOR was the dau. of Henry POOR, *b.* 13th December, 1650, of Newburyport and Rowley, a soldier in King Philip's War, and Abigail HALE, his wife, *b.* 8th April, 1662, the dau. of Thomas HALE, Jr. and Mary HUTCHINSON, his wife. His father Thomas HALE, *bapt.* 1606, Watton, England; Sergeant Newbury Militia Company; *m.* 1632, St. Helens, Bishopsgate, London, Thomasine DOWSETT. His father was Thomas HALE, who *m.* Joan KIRBY. Mary HUTCHINSON was the dau. of Richard HUTCHINSON and Alice BOSWORTH, his wife, and gd. dau. of Thomas HUTCHINSON, who was descended in the eighth generation from Bernard HUTCHINSON of Cowlan, York, and his wife Alice. The parents of Henry POOR, were John and Sarah POOR. He was *b.* 1615, a native of Wiltshire, England. The gd. father of Phebe FISKE was Samuel FISKE, who *m.* Phebe BRAGG. He *d.* 31st October, 1716. His father was William FISKE, *b.* 1614; first Town Clerk of Wenham; Representative to General Court. Phebe Fiske *d.* 7th December, 1802.

V. Abiel ABBOT, son of Capt. John ABBOT and Phebe (FISKE) ABBOT, *b.* 19th April, 1741, in Andover, Massachusetts; *d.* 19th August, 1809; settled in Wilton, New Hampshire, 1764; Deacon for sixteen years; Justice for fifteen years; Selectman for eleven years; Representative to General Court; Captain, 1769, also 1776; second Major, 5th Regiment of New Hampshire Militia, raised to reinforce the Continental Army at Ticonderoga, 29th June, 1777; first Major, 5th Regiment of New Hampshire Militia, 30th March, 1781; member of New Hampshire Provincial Congress (Registry New York Society Sons of the Revolution); *m.* 20th November, 1764, Dorcas ABBOT, *b.* 1st August, 1744; *d.* 23d February, 1829, a gr. gd. dau. of George ABBOT, of Andover. Their dau. Rhoda, *b.* 17th March, 1784, *m.* 14th November, 1805, Ephraim PEABODY. Their son Ephraim PEABODY was Minister of King's Chapel, Boston, 1846–1856.

VI. Ezra ABBOT, son of Maj. Abiel and Dorcas (ABBOT) ABBOT, *b.* 8th February, 1772, in Wilton, New Hampshire; *m.* 6th October, 1799, at Coventry, Connecticut, by Rev. Abiel ABBOT, D.D., Rebekah HALE, *b.* 9th January, 1781, dau. of Joseph HALE, Lieutenant in KNOWLTON's and WEBB's Regiments of the Revolutionary War. He is also recorded as a Corporal in the company that marched from Coventry, Connecticut, in the Lexington alarm. In 1776 he was an Ensign in Colonel WARD's Regiment, which joined WASHINGTON's army at New York in August, and was stationed at first near Fort Lee. Marching with the troops to White Plains, and subsequently into New Jersey, the command participated in the battles of Trenton and Princeton, and encamped with WASHINGTON at Morristown. In 1777 he was Lieutenant in a Connecticut Militia Regiment, commanded by Col. John ELY; and in 1781, he was Lieutenant in a provisional regiment, "ordered by the General Assembly to be raised and put in readiness to march at the shortest notice, in case his excellency, General WASHINGTON shall call for them." He was a brother of Nathan HALE, the martyr spy. The wife of Lieut. Joseph HALE was Rebekah HARRIS, gr. gr. gd. dau. of Walter and Mary HARRIS. Rebekah (HALE) ABBOT was gd. dau. of Richard HALE, *b.* 28th February, 1717, who *m.* Elizabeth STRONG, *b.* 2d February, 1728, dau. of Capt. Joseph STRONG and Elizabeth STRONG his wife, and gr. gd. dau. of Thomas STRONG, who emigrated from England. Richard HALE was the gd. son of Rev. John HALE, son of Robert HALE, emigrant from England, and Johanna his wife; *b.* 3d June, 1636; Harvard College, 1657; settled church at Beverly, 1667; Chaplain of Canadian Expedition under Sir William PHIPPS, 1690. His wife was Sarah NOYES, dau. of Rev. James NOYES. Rebekah Hale ABBOT, *d.* 5th May, 1860. Ezra ABBOT, *d.* 3d April, 1847.

ISSUE

1. Rebecca ABBOT, *b.* 16th July, 1800; *d.* 5th April, 1882; *m.* Rev. Isaac KNIGHT, pastor of Congregational Church, Franklin, New Hampshire, *b.* 29th December, 1797, *d.* 24th July, 1850, graduate of Bowdoin College.
2. Son, *b.* and *d.* 13th September, 1801.
3. Joseph Hale ABBOT, *b.* 25th September, 1802; *d.* 7th April, 1873; *m.* 13th May, 1830, at Beverly, Massachusetts, Fanny Ellingwood LARCOM, dau. of Henry and Fanny (ELLINGWOOD) LARCOM and gd. niece of Hon. Nathan DANE, LL.D., member of Continental Congress 1785–1788; educated at Bowdoin College and Harvard College; Professor at Phillips Exeter Academy; elected Resident Fellow of American Academy of Arts and Sciences; author. Henry Larcom ABBOT, *b.* Beverly,

Massachusetts, 13th August, 1831; graduated at West Point, 1854; brevet Second Lieutenant, Topographical Engineers; brevet Brigadier-General, United States Army, 13th March, 1865; wounded at Bull Run, 1861, the father of Frederic Vaughan ABBOT; graduated at West Point, 1879; Colonel, United States Army; Brigadier-General, United States National Army, was the son of Joseph Hale and Fanny Ellingwood (LARCOM) ABBOT (see "Cyclopedia of American Biography"). Another son, Edward Stanley ABBOT, *b.* 22d October, 1841, entered Harvard College, 1860; enlisted, 1862, 17th Regiment Infantry, United States Army; was at Chancellorsville and at Gettysburg, where he was shot 2d July, Little Round Top, and *d.* 8th July, 1863; First Lieutenant and brevet Captain.

4. Dorcas ABBOT, *b.* 24th January, 1804; *d.* 2d November, 1833; *m.* 21st September, 1825, Ebenezer BISHOP of Lisbon, Connecticut, *b.* 1798, *d.* 6th January, 1827.
5. Ezra ABBOT, *b.* 27th November, 1805; *d.* 16th August, 1876; educated at Phillips Exeter Academy, and Bowdoin College; *m.* 29th April, 1846, at Leeds, Virginia, Sarah HOOKER, *b.* 7th August, 1824, *d.* 13th February, 1905.
6. Abiel ABBOT, *b.* 11th May, 1808; *d.* 23d August, 1896; educated at Phillips Exeter Academy, and Bowdoin College; Justice; Representative; surveyor.
7. Emily ABBOT, *b.* 16th August, 1810; *d.* 10th June, 1835.
8. Harris ABBOT, *b.* 19th September, 1812; *d.* 20th March, 1884; *m.* 20th November, 1860, at Pelham, New Hampshire, Caroline Ann GREELEY, *b.* 20th October, 1836, *d.* 8th November, 1911; educated Pinkerton and Phillips Exeter Academy; settled on the homestead, now in the possession of his son Stanley Harris ABBOT. Charles Greeley ABBOT, another son, is Director of the Astrophysical Department of the Smithsonian Institution, Washington, D. C.; Draper and Mumford medals, American Academy of Arts and Sciences.
9. Harriet ABBOT, *b.* 19th June, 1814; *d.* 16th July, 1886; *m.* 5th January, 1837, Hermon ABBOT of Wilton, *b.* 20th February, 1814, *d.* 17th November, 1878; he was a Deacon and Selectman.
10. Nelson ABBOT, *b.* 17th November, 1816; *d.* January, 1890; *m.* 17th October, 1848, at Greenfield, New Hampshire, Hannah Holt PEVEY, *b.* 31st October, 1821, *d.* 21st March, 1891; settled on part of the homestead.
11. Abby Ann ABBOT, *b.* 13th December, 1818; *d.* 12th May, 1912; *m.* 1st May, 1845, Rev. Lubim Burton ROCKWOOD.
12. Sarah Jane ABBOT, *b.* 15th May, 1821; *d.* 18th January, 1857.
13. John Hale ABBOT, *b.* 2d September, 1825; *d.* 20th January, 1905; surveyor.

Lineage

RICHARD ROCKWOOD emigrated from Weymouth or Dorchester, Dorsetshire, England, and settled in Dorchester, Massachusetts, in 1636; *m.* (firstly) Agnes BICKNELL, who *d.* at Braintree, Massachusetts, 9th October, 1643; *m.* (secondly) Ann (surname not given); he *d.* at Braintree, 1660.

ISSUE

I. NICHOLAS, *b.* 1628, of whom below.

NICHOLAS ROCKWOOD, *b.* 1628; *d.* 26th January, 1680, at Medfield, Massachusetts; *m.* (firstly) Jane (ADAMS?), who *d.* 15th December, 1654; *m.* (secondly) Margaret HOLBROOK, 2d July, 1656, who *d.* 23d April, 1670; *m.* (thirdly) Silence (surname not given), who *d.* November, 1677; he was one of the first settlers of Medfield.

ISSUE

I. Josiah.
II. Samuel.
III. Joseph.
IV. Benjamin.
V. dau.
VI. John.
VII. NATHANIEL, *b.* 23d February, 1665, of whom below.

NATHANIEL ROCKWOOD, *b.* 23d February, 1665; *d.* 24th September, 1721, in Wrentham, Massachusetts; *m.* 7th December, 1698, Joanna ELLIS.

ISSUE

I. Margaret, *b.* 4th September, 1699.
II. Nathaniel, *b.* 7th September, 1700,
III. Benjamin, *b.* 8th March, 1702.
IV. Abigail, *b.* 2d January, 1703–1704.
V. Ebenezer, *b.* 2d November, 1705.
VI. Hannah, *b.* 9th October, 1707.
VII. Mary, *b.* 17th October, 1709
VIII. Thomas, *b.* 25th February, 1711.
IX. Abigail.
X. ELISHA, *b.* 11th June, 1716, of whom below.

ELISHA ROCKWOOD, *b.* 11th June, 1716, in Wrentham, Massachusetts; *d.* 5th December, 1788, in Groton, Massachusetts; *m.* 17th August, 1738, Elizabeth ADAMS, *b.* 3d September, 1719, in Sherburne, Massachusetts, *d.* 16th May, 1799; she was a relative of Robert Treat PAINE, the signer of the Declaration of Independence.

ISSUE

 I. Elizabeth, *b.* 6th May, 1739; *d.* 17th September, 1753.
 II. Elisha, *b.* November, 1740; *d.* 1831.
 III. Samuel, *b.* 11th August, 1742; *d.* 2d September, 1753.
 IV. Joseph, *b.* 13th June, 1744; *d.* 9th June, 1816.
 V. EBENEZER, *b.* 13th August, 1746, of whom below.
 VI. Lydia, *b.* 27th May, 1748; *d.* 17th September, 1753.
 VII. Abigail, *b.* 13th August, 1751; *d.* 28th February, 1825.
 VIII. Moses, *b.* 11th July, 1753; *d.* 7th September, 1753.
 IX. Samuel, *b.* 6th December, 1754; *d.* 29th May, 1804.
 X. Elizabeth, *b.* 17th April, 1757; *d.* 11th December, 1847.
 XI. Lydia, *b.* 23d August, 1759.
 XII. Sibbel, *b.* 11th August, 1761; *d.* 21st March 1818.
 XIII. Sarah, *b.* 3d July, 1763.

EBENEZER ROCKWOOD, M.D., *b.* 13th August, 1746, in Groton, Massachusetts; *d.* 10th February, 1830, in Wilton, New Hampshire; graduated at Harvard College, 1773; Surgeon in United States Army; accepted Wilton invitation to settle as physician; eminent in profession, extensive practice; farmer, house he built in Wilton, now standing (1920); through his influence, largely, the Second Congregational Church was organized; *m.* 10th June, 1779, Mary, dau. of Rev. Daniel EMERSON, of Hollis, New Hampshire. He was *b.* 20th May, 1716, in Reading, Massachusetts; *d.* 30th September, 1801; educated at Harvard College; minister at Hollis; Chaplain in French and Indian War, 1755–1758; *m.* Hannah EMERSON, dau. of REV. Joseph EMERSON, of Malden, Massachusetts, *b.* 1700, and Mary MOODY, his wife; she was the dau. of Samuel Moody, *b.* 1676, educated at Harvard College, minister at York, Maine, 1700, *d.* 1745. Mary EMERSON'S gr. gd. father, Joseph EMERSON, of Mendon, later of Concord, New Hampshire, emigrated from England. His wife was Elizabeth BULKLEY, dau. of Rev. Peter BULKLEY, D.D., *b.* in England, 1583. Mary EMERSON'S brother, Rev. William EMERSON, was gd. father of Ralph Waldo EMERSON.

ISSUE

 I. William EMERSON, *b.* 23d. March, 1780; *d.* 16th April, 1873; *m.* 22d October, 1812, Abigail CONANT of Hollis, New Hampshire.
 II. Ebenezer, *b.* 2d June, 1781; *d.* 8th May, 1815; graduate of Harvard College; studied law and settled in Boston; formed a partnership with Hon. Samuel HOAR, whose son Ebenezer Rockwood HOAR, was named for him; *m.* 9th September, 1807, Elizabeth Breeze HAZARD, dau. of Hon. E. HAZARD of Philadelphia, Pennsylvania.
 III. Betsey, *b.* 9th December, 1782; *d.* 6th October, 1846; *m.* 4th November, 1812, Timothy ABBOT of Wilton, New Hampshire, *b.* 2d September, 1777, *d.* 27th October, 1863; he was Representative and Senator in the New Hampshire Legislature.

IV. Polly, *b.* 6th August, 1784; *d.* 16th May, 1874.
V. Lubim, *b.* 6th April, 1786.
VI. Daniel, *b.* 15th October, 1787; *d.* 31st January, 1821, Cuba; graduate of Dartmouth College; studied law and settled in Boston; was an early partner of Chief Justice Lemuel SHAW of Massachusetts.
VII. Hannah, *b.* 19th February, 1790; *d.* 7th November, 1808.
VIII. Sally, *b.* 18th January, 1792; *d.* 12th August, 1884, in Hollis, New Hampshire; *m.* 1st October, 1833, Rev. Leonard JEWETT, of Temple, New Hampshire; they later removed to Hollis.
IX. Matilda, *b.* 30th November, 1793; *d.* 21st April, 1823.

LUBIM ROCKWOOD, *b.* 6th April, 1786; *d.* 15th May, 1826; a farmer and settled on the homestead in Wilton, New Hampshire; *m.* Lydia BURTON, *b.* 7th May, 1793, *d.* 8th October, 1869; she *m.* (secondly) Elijah CHANDLER. Lydia BURTON was the dau. of Abraham BURTON and Betty DALE, his wife. He settled in Wilton, New Hampshire; was at Winter Hill, in Captain TAYLOR's Company and at Ticonderoga, 1776, in Captain BARRON's Company; Selectman. She was descended from John BURTON, Freeman, Salem, Massachusetts, 1638, whose farm joined that of Governor ENDICOTT, and from Boniface BURTON, Freeman, Lynn, Massachusetts, 1635; he *d.* 13th June, 1669, at the age of 113 years; farmer; ancestor of nearly all the BURTONS in this country.

ISSUE

I. Hannah, *b.* 8th July, 1814; *d.* 13th April, 1832.
II. LUBIM BURTON, the subject of this memoir.
III. Lydia Henrietta, *b.* 24th May, 1819; *d.* 22d June, 1840.
IV. Mary Emerson, *b.* 14th May, 1821; *d.* 18th July, 1904; *m.* 5th December, 1839, Col. John P. CLARK of New Ipswich, New Hampshire; he *d.* 3d March, 1889.
V. Betsey Dale, *b.* 19th April, 1825; *d.* 1857; *m.* 1845, Charles S. DAVIS of Hancock and Newton Centre, Massachusetts; he *d.* 1907.

Ruggles

JOHN RUGGLES, deceased, Major, *b.* 3d February, 1776, at Pomfret, Connecticut; *d.* 19th February, 1831, at Rutland, Vermont; *m.* (firstly) 17th January, 1800, Mary GOULD, dau. of Henry GOULD, of Concord, Massachusetts; *m.* (secondly) 15th December, 1807, Eunice KINGSLEY, dau. of Phineas KINGSLEY, of Rutland, Vermont; *m.* (thirdly) 30th December, 1821, Sarah BEAMAN, dau. of Nathaniel BEAMAN, of Rutland, Vermont.

ISSUE BY FIRST MARRIAGE

I. Mary Gould, *b.* 18th December, 1800; *m.* Benjamin SMITH.
II. Jane Augusta, *b.* 2d May, 1804; *m.* Adams HARRINGTON.
III. John Gould, *b.* 19th April, 1806.

ISSUE BY SECOND MARRIAGE

IV. Julia Sparrow, *b.* 9th December, 1808; *m.* William H. ELMORE.
V. Gershom Cheney, *b.* 3d February, 1810.
VI. Henry Bond, *b.* 9th July, 1813.
VII. George Fitch, *b.* 12th December, 1818.

ISSUE BY THIRD MARRIAGE

VIII. Edmund Ingalls, *b.* 31st October, 1822.
IX. Sarah Beaman, *b.* 6th January, 1830, *m.* Francis BRADLEY.

Lineage

All the family legends point to the Staffordshire house of RUGGELEY, as the source of the RUGGLES family of Essex and of Suffolk, but in two migrations separated by a period of two hundred years. The first is claimed to trace from William DE RUGGELE of Stafford, thirteenth century, who having incurred the royal displeasure, and suffered banishment from the kingdom, was known to have established a new home in Flanders. Although, for service in the Wars, he had subsequently received the pardon of his sovereign, King Edward I, he never returned to the land of his birth. Three of his sons, however, are said to have crossed the Straits of Dover, and to have settled in the County of Essex and from them, it is alleged, the early generations in that and the adjoining counties, descended. Children of a fourth son went to Switzerland and the name (RUGGLE) is still perpetuated there. The later migration, according to John Sydney HAWKINS, the biographer in 1787 of George RUGGLES, a founder of Virginia and an eminent scholar of the reign of King James I, was from

Warwick to Lincoln, and thence to Suffolk, being a branch from Nicholas RUGGELEY, Lord of the Manors of Hawkesbeard in Stafford and Downton-Ruggeley, in Warwick. It was this second migration which supplied later the Puritan emigrants to New England as well as the English RUGGLES family of Spains Hall, Essex. In support of the first claim, it has been pointed out that RIETSTAP discovered the family in Flanders and in his "Armorial Général" has recorded for that family the same arms as those given by English authorities as the bearings of the Staffordshire house. Though RIETSTAP'S work registers some English arms, he mentions no other RUGGELEY, than the branch in Flanders. The identity of coat-armor has always, been held to be confirmatory of a common origin, and Dr. BARBER in his work on British family names, edition 1903, cites such identity for RUGGELEY, of Stafford and RUGGLES of Essex. The name RUGGELEY, in England is now extinct, and only in those having the name of RUGGLES is the stock represented there.

THOMAS RUGGLES, of Sudbury, Suffolk, England; will dated 21st June, 1547.

ISSUE

I. NICHOLAS, of whom later.
II. John, will proved 19th May, 1566.
III. Ann.
IV. Elizabeth.

NICHOLAS RUGGLES, of Sudbury, Suffolk, England.

ISSUE

I. Roger.
II. George, will proved 16th May, 1616.
III. THOMAS, of whom later.
IV. Edward.
V. William.
VI. Robert.
VII. Margery, *m.* John Drury.

THOMAS RUGGLES, of Sudbury, Suffolk, England, and of Nasing, Essex, England.

ISSUE

I. THOMAS, *b.* in England, 1584, of whom later.
II. Florence, buried 3d May, 1603.
III. John.
IV. Mary, *bapt.* 13th February, 1597.
V. Samuel, *bapt.* 8th July, 1599.
VI. Nathaniel, *bapt.* October, 1602.

THOMAS RUGGLES, of Nasing, Essex, England, and Roxbury, Massachusetts, *b.* at Sudbury, Suffolk, England, 1584; *d.* at Roxbury 16th November, 1644; will dated 9th November, 1644; his holdings are scheduled on page 1, "Roxbury Book of Possessions," 1639; *m.* 1st November, 1620, at Nasing, Mary CURTIS, dau. of Thomas CURTIS, of Nasing, and sister of the first William CURTIS of Roxbury.

ISSUE

 I. Thomas.
 II. JOHN, *bapt.* 6th January, 1625, of whom later.
 III. Sarah, *bapt.* 17th February, 1628; *m.* William LYON.
 IV. Samuel, *bapt.* 14th March, 1629.

JOHN RUGGLES, of Roxbury, Massachusetts; *bapt.* at Nasing, England, 6th January, 1625; *d.* at Roxbury, 15th September, 1658; will dated 9th September, 1658; his holdings are scheduled "Roxbury Book of Possessions," 1654; *m.* Abigail CRAFT, dau. of Griffin CRAFT, the founder of Roxbury.

ISSUE

 I. JOHN, *b.* 22d January, 1654, of whom later.
 II. Thomas, *b.* 28th January, 1655.
 III. Samuel, *b.* 16th August, 1657.

JOHN RUGGLES, of Roxbury, Massachusetts, *b.* at Roxbury, 22d January, 1654; *d.* 16th December, 1694; *m.* 2d September, 1674, Martha DEVOTION, dau. of Edward DEVOTION (DE VAUTION) a Huguenot, of noble family from Rochelle, France.

ISSUE

 I. Abigail, *b.* 5th June, 1675; *m.* Thomas RICHARDSON.
 II. John, *b.* 16th March, 1680.
 III. Martha, *b.* 21st December, 1686.
 IV. EDWARD, *b.* 2d October, 1691, of whom later.

EDWARD RUGGLES, of Roxbury, and Cambridge, Massachusetts, *b.* at Roxbury, 2d October, 1691; *d.* at Cambridge, 16th September, 1765; will dated 4th December, 1764; he left for the times a large property, including estates in Cambridge, Roxbury, Newton, and Warwick, Massachusetts, Pomfret, Connecticut, and vast woodlands in Canada; he was in 1739 the largest slaveholder in Roxbury; *m.* (firstly) 24th June, 1716, Hannah CRAFT, dau. of Samuel CRAFT, of Roxbury; *m.* (secondly) 11th January, 1733, Mrs. Abigail (DAVIS) WILLIAMS, widow of Joseph WILLIAMS of Roxbury, and dau. of John and Mary (TORREY) DAVIS, of Roxbury.

ISSUE BY FIRST MARRIAGE

 I. Samuel, *b.* 29th March, 1717.
 II. Hannah, *b.* 22d December, 1718.

III. Elizabeth, *b.* 20th October, 1722; *m.* James NOBLE.
IV. EDWARD, *b.* 22d June, 1724, of whom later.
V. Abigail, *b.* 12th May, 1726.
VI. Thomas, *b.* 15th November, 1729.
VII. Benjamin, *b.* 19th February, 1731.

EDWARD RUGGLES, of Pomfret, Connecticut, a soldier of the Revolution; *b.* at Roxbury, Massachusetts, 22d June, 1724; *d.* at Montague, Massachuetts, 25th December, 1797; *m.* Ann SUMNER, dau. of Samuel SUMNER, of Pomfret.

ISSUE

I. Benjamin, *b.* 10th August, 1747; a soldier of the Revolution (his son Benjamin was United States Senator from Ohio, 1815–1833).
II. Abigail, *b.* 23d June, 1749; *m.* Samuel SESSIONS.
III. SAMUEL, *b.* 25th February, 1751; a soldier of the Revolution, of whom later.
IV. Elizabeth, *b.* 20th April, 1754.
V. Ann, *b.* 1st October, 1756.
VI. Hannah, *b.* 15th August, 1758; *m.* Alexander WATKINS.
VII. Edward, *b.* 3d April, 1763.
VIII. Thomas, *b.* 11th August, 1765.

SAMUEL RUGGLES, of Pomfret and Willington, Connecticut, a soldier of the Revolution; *b.* at Pomfret, 25th February, 1751; *d.* at Willington, 23d October, 1778; *m.* 17th September, 1772, Lucy ROBINSON, dau. of John ROBINSON, of Lebanon, Connecticut (she *m.* as her second husband 1781 Col. Christopher WEBBER, of Walpole, New Hampshire).

ISSUE

I. Ebenezer, *b.* at Pomfret, 17th December, 1773.
II. JOHN, *b.* 3d February, 1776, the subject of this memoir.
III. Edward, *bapt.* at Willington, May, 1778.

Arms.—Argent a chevron between three roses gules.
Crest.—A tower or, inflamed ppr. and pierced with four arrows in saltire, argent.
Motto.—Struggle.

Sloan

FRANCIS BURNS SLOAN, of Baltimore, Maryland (Frank B. SLOAN), *b.* there 16th March, 1846; *m.* there 3d December, 1872, by Rev. A. M. RANDOLPH, D.D., later Protestant Episcopal Bishop, of Virginia, Susan Lucket BASH, dau. of Henry M. BASH, Banker, of Baltimore, who was *b.* in 1801, *d.* 14th November, 1885, *m.* Susan Anne ROWLES, *b.* 1809, *d.* 24th January, 1898.

ISSUE

I. Francis Eugene, *b.* 20th September, 1873; *m.* 11th February, 1902, Josephine RICHARDS.

II. George Frederick, *b.* 3d June, 1877; *m.* 14th November, 1905, Helena Buelah PARKER.

ISSUE

1. George Frederick, *b.* 10th July, 1915.

III. Elizabeth Bash, *b.* 15th February, 1882; *m.* 11th November, 1902, in Emmanuel Protestant Episcopal Church, by Rev. J. Houston ECCLESTON, D.D., George David Francis ROBINSON, of Washington, D. C.

ISSUE

1. Virginia Cushing ROBINSON, *b.* 17th October, 1903.
2. Elizabeth Conrad ROBINSON, *b.* 9th September, 1906.
3. George David Francis ROBINSON, *b.* 9th February, 1909.

IV. Mildred Cushing, *b.* 11th November, 1886.

FRANCIS BURNS SLOAN was engaged for a quarter of a century as an active partner in the hardware firm of C. Sidney NORRIS and Company, one of the leading firms of the country. Mr. SLOAN is a member of the Maryland Club, and Society of Colonial Wars, Red Cross and Navy League, and a former member of the Athenaeum, Baltimore Country Club, the Kennels, Merchant, Yacht Club, all of Baltimore and the Southern Maryland Society, of New York. Mr. SLOAN's father was a member of the well known lumber firm of BURNS and SLOAN of Baltimore and Mrs. SLOAN's father was the well known banker and capitalist, also of the same city.

Cushing (maternal line)

WILLIAM CUSHING (CUSSYN or CUSSEYN) was b. sometime during the fourteenth century. He was either the son or gd. son of Galfridus CUSYN of Hardingham, County Norfolk, England, who is mentioned in the Subsidy Rolls for Norfolk, in 1327. He added to the original estate in Hardingham the estates in Hingham which were inherited by his son Thomas.

THOMAS CUSHING (CUSSEHYN or CUSSHYN) was b. in Hardingham, County Norfolk, England, in the latter part of the reign of Richard II, 1377-1399. A deed dated 1466 contains not only his name but the name of his son William. He is also named in other deeds and charters dated 1474, 1480, and 1484. He possessed large estates in Hardingham, Hingham and other parts of his natural country.

WILLIAM CUSHING (CUSSHYN) of Hingham, England, eldest son and heir of Thomas CUSHING, was b. in the early part of the fifteenth century, and m. Emma (surname not given). His long and explicit will was dated 26th September, 1492 and proved in the Bishop's Court of Norwich 11th March 1493. In ancient deeds he is styled "Gentleman." His wife Emma was executrix of his will; her own dated 16th July, 1507, was proved 26th July, 1507.

ISSUE

I. JOHN, the elder, of whom later.
II. Robert of Hingham, styled "Gentleman;" m. Joan (surname not given); his will was proved 10th July, 1547; they had a son Robert under eighteen in 1547.
III. Thomas, of Hardingham, and afterwards of East Dereham, Norfolk; will dated 20th December, 1503; proved 15th January, 1504; his children were John, William, Parnell, Rose and Alice.
IV. John, junior, inherited by his father's will his house in East Row, Hingham; his will is dated 29th July, 1515; proved 1st August, 1515; he left a wife Isabel, but no children.
V. Evelyn.
VI. Annabel.
VII. Margaret, m. Thomas CROWE.
VIII. Agnes.

JOHN CUSHING (CUSHYN or CUSHYNG), the elder, was b. in Hingham, but lived in Hardingham, where he possessed estates; also owned large properties in Lombard Street, London; called "Gentleman" in a survey of the manor of Floskthorp in Hardingham, dated 1512; his will is dated 21st February, 1522, and proved 5th March, 1523; it mentions his wife and six children; he is mentioned in the Subsidy Rolls of Henry VIII, for 1523.

ISSUE

I. John, Lord of the manors of Flockthorpe, in his native place, Markhams in Tothington, and Statworthy, in Wymondham; *m.* (firstly) Alice CLINE, dau. of Richard CLINE, of Hingham; *m.* (secondly) Rose (surname not given); his will is dated 1st March, 1532, and proved in the Prerogative Court, London, 11th May, 1532.

ISSUE BY FIRST MARRIAGE

1. Etheldreda.
2. Edward, *m.* Elizabeth CANZ, dau. and heiress of Robert CANZ, of Hingham.
3. Edmund, of Swannington in Norfolk, *d.* 14th August, 1555; *m.* Frances RICHARDS, dau. of Henry RICHARDS, of Swannington.

II. THOMAS, of Hardingham, of whom later.
III. William, of Hardingham, to whom his father gave a house called "Gilberts;" *m.* Joan (surname not given).
IV. Margaret.
V. Isabel.
VI. Margery.
VII. Elyne.
VIII. Agnes.

THOMAS CUSHING (CUSHYN), *d.* April, 1558, in Hardingham, inherited the homestead of his father with all the lands pertaining thereto; his wife's name not given.

ISSUE

I. John of Knapton, in Norfolk; his will is dated 21st October, 1585, and proved 26th November, 1586; he inherited his father's estate.
II. Ursula.
III. Nicholas.
IV. Edward.
V. Stephen.
VI. PETER of whom below.

PETER CUSHING, of Hingham; was born at Hardingham but removed to Hingham about 1600 in which year the parish register of Hingham begins; *m.* 2d June, 1583, at Hardingham, Susan HAWES, buried 26th April, 1641; he was buried 2d March, 1615, at Hingham, England; he was probably one of the first CUSHINGS to embrace the Protestant faith, for the wills of the father and the eldest brother are not in the Protestant form.

ISSUE

I. Theophilis, *bapt.* 4th November, 1584; *d.* 24th March, 1679; he came to New England, 1633, in the Ship *Griffin*, in company with Governor HAYNES, and the eminent Puritan divines, COTTON and HOOKER. For a time he resided on the farm with his friend (afterwards the celebrated Governor HAYNES) as his adviser and secretary. When his younger brother Matthew, following his example came to New England, Theophilus, who appears never to have married, settled with him in Hingham, Massachusetts. He was blind for twenty-five years previous to his death.

II. Bridget, *bapt.* 19th February, 1586; *m.* 15th July, 1627, George MORE.

III. MATTHEW, *bapt.* 2d March, 1589, of whom later.

IV. William, *bapt.* 1st April, 1593; *m.* Margery (surname not given).

ISSUE

1. William.
2. Robert.
3. Anne.
4. Elizabeth.

V. Barbara, *bapt.* 16th June, 1569; *d.* January, 1632.

VI. Peter, of London, *d.s.p.*, Godey PAYNE, widow of Simon PAYNE; his will is dated 2d February, 1644; probated 2d January, 1665; his wife made her will 11th April, 1675, and *d.* the same year.

VII. Katherine, *m.* ——— LONG, of Cotton Road, near Wymondham in Norfolk.

VIII. Thomas, of London, *bapt.* 15th May, 1603; his will is dated 10th August, 1669; he calls himself of London, "Gentleman," unmarried.

MATTHEW CUSHING, of Hingham, Massachusetts; *bapt.* 2d March, 1589, in Hingham, England; *d.* 30th September, 1660, in Hingham, Massachusetts; *m.* 5th August, 1613, Nazareth PITCHER, dau. of Henry PITCHER, of England; he lived for fifty years in Hardingham and Hingham, County Norfolk, England. In 1638, with his wife, five children and his wife's sister Frances RIECROFT, he embarked in the ship *Deligent* of Ipswich, 350 tons, John MARTIN, master, which sailed from Gravesend, 26th April, 1638, with 133 passengers, among whom was Robert PECK, M.A., Rector of the parish of Hingham, England. The party arrived at Boston, 10th August, 1638; immediately proceded to their destination, Hingham, Massachusetts, so named after the name of the former home of the CUSHING family in England; a house lot of five acres, first below Pear Tree Hill, on Bachelor (Main) Street, was given to Matthew CUSHING and it continued in the possession of the family until 1887. Became a deacon in Mr. HOBART's church. His will was verbal and written after his death, by direction of his children under date of 15th November, 1660.

All the persons bearing the surname of CUSHING in the United States and Canada are his direct descendants, with exception of a few families who have come to this country during the past century.

ISSUE; ALL BORN IN HINGHAM, ENGLAND

I. DANIEL, *bapt.* 20th April, 1619, in Hingham, England, of whom later.
II. Jeremiah, *b.* 21st July, 1621; was lost at sea; became a mariner and commanded a ship trading between Boston (where he resided) and Liverpool; *m.* 11th March, 1662, Elizabeth WILKIE, widow of John WILKIE. In her will she mentioned dau. Elizabeth CONDY and gd. son John CONDY, and sister Martha MUZER, in Redrif near London.
III. Matthew, *bapt.* 5th April, 1623; *d.s.p.* 9th January, 1701; was Selectman thirteen times between 1661 and 1695; Freeman, 1679; was known as Sergeant, Cornet and later as Lieutenant; *m.* 25th February, 1653, Sarah JACOB, who *d.* 8th August, 1701, dau. of Nicholas and Mary JACOB.
IV. Deborah, *bapt.* 17th February, 1625; *d.* 25th September, 1701; *m.* 9th May, 1648, Matthew BRIGGS, who *d.* 24th February, 1697.
V. John, *b.* 1627; *d.* 31st March, 1708; Deputy, 1674, and many years thereafter; Selectman, 1674 to 1686, inclusive; County Magistrate, 1685–1692; Assistant, 1689–1691; Representative to the General Court at Boston, 1692, and for several succeeding years; Member of the Council, 1706 and 1707; also Colonel of the Plymouth Regiment; *m.* 20th January, 1658, at Hingham, Massachusetts, Sarah HAWKE, *bapt.* 1st August 1641, *d.* 9th March, 1679, dau. of Matthew and Margaret HAWKE.

DANIEL CUSHING, of Hingham, Massachusetts, *bapt.* 20th April, 1619, in Hingham, England; *d.* 3d December, 1700, in Hingham, Massachusetts; Freeman, 1671; an active Magistrate and for many years thereafter; Delegate to the General Court, 1680–1682, and 1695; *m.* (firstly) 19th January, 1645, Lydia GILMAN, *b.* in England, *d.* 12th March, 1689, in Hingham, Massachusetts, dau. of Edward and Mary (CLARK) GILMAN; *m.* (secondly) 23d March, 1691, Elizabeth (JACOB) THAXTER, dau. of Nicholas and Mary THAXTER, and widow of Capt. John THAXTER.

ISSUE BY FIRST MARRIAGE

I. Peter, *b.* 29th March, 1646; *d.* 14th April, 1719; Constable, 1688; Selectman, 1689 and 1702; *m.* 4th June, 1685, Hannah HAWKE, *bapt.* 22d July, 1655, at Hingham, *d.* 4th April, 1737, dau. of Matthew and Margaret HAWKE; left issue.
II. Daniel, *b.* 23d July, 1648; *d.* 5th May, 1716; Constable, 1684; *m.* 8th December, 1680 Elizabeth THAXTER, *b.* 19th February, 1661, *d.* 6th April, 1727, dau. of Capt. John and Elizabeth (JACOB) THAXTER.

III. Deborah, *b.* 13th November, 1651; *d.* 15th January, 1710; *m.* (firstly) 25th September, 1679, Henry TARLETON; *m.* (secondly) 31st August 1686, Rev. Benjamin WOODBRIDGE.
IV. Jeremiah, *b.* 3d July, 1654; *d.* 22d March, 1706; Graduated Harvard College, 1676; ordained 27th May, 1691, Pastor at Scituate; *m.* 5th June, 1685, Hannah LORING, *b.* 9th August, 1664, *d.* 30th May, 1710, dau. of Thomas and Hannah (JACOB) LORING.
V. THEOPHILUS, *b.* 7th June, 1757, of whom later.
VI. Matthew, *b.* 15th July, 1660; *d.* 23d June, 1715; was known as Lieutenant and also Captain; Constable, 1693; Selectman, 1710; *m.* 31st December, 1684, Joel JACOB, *b.* 7th September, 1662, *d.* 23d December, 1708, dau. of Capt. John and Mary (RUSSELL) JACOB; left issue.

THEOPHILUS CUSHING, of Hingham, Massachusetts, *b.* there 7th June, 1657; will dated 3d January, 1718; Selectman, 1697, 1707, 1715; Representative, 1702-1704; 1707, and 1713; *m.* 28th November, 1688, Mary THAXTER, *b.* 19th August, 1657, *d.* 1737, dau. of John and Elizabeth (JACOB) THAXTER.

ISSUE

I. Nehemiah, *b.* 18th July, 1689; *d.* 11th December, 1774; settled in Pembroke, Massachusetts, 1711; March, 1719, was chosen Town Treasurer, and served until 1724; May, 1722, Representative to the General Court, at Boston; Coroner, 1739 and 1762; *m.* 20th March, 1711, Sarah NICHOLS, *b.* 30th January, 1688, dau. of Nathaniel and Sarah (LINCOLN) NICHOLS; left issue.
II. Mary, *b.* 9th February, 1691; *d.* 8th August, 1699.
III. Adam, *b.* 1st January, 1693; *d.* 21st January, 1752; Graduated Harvard College, 1714; in 1720 was a Selectman, styled Captain; *m.* 25th September, 1718; *m.* Hannah GREENWOOD, dau. of Rev. Thomas GREENWOOD; left issue.
IV. David, *b.* December, 1694; *d.* 3d September, 1723; Constable, 1721; *m.* 14th May, 1718, Rachel LEWIS, *b.* 19th June, 1694, dau. of John and Hannah (LINCOLN) LEWIS; left issue.
V. ABEL, *b.* 26th October, 1696, of whom later.
VI. Rachel, *b.* 17th August, 1689; *d.* 9th September, 1699.
VII. Mary, *b.* 26th September, 1701; *d.* 30th August, 1716.
VIII. Theophilus, *b.* 16th June, 1703; *d.* 15th June, 1779; for many years held offices of Constable and Selectman; *m.* 18th September, 1723, Hannah WATERMAN, *b.* 22d May, 1704, dau. of Robert and Sarah (LEWIS) WATERMAN; left issue.
IX. Seth, *b.* 13th December, 1705; *d.* 17th May, 1761; Inn-Keeper; *m.* 9th January, 1729, Lydia FEARING, *b.* 3d September, 1709, dau. of John and Margaret (HAWKE) FEARING; left issue.

x. Deborah, *b.* 26th September, 1707; *d.* 20th November, 1730.
xi. Lydia, *b.* 13th February, 1710; *d.* before her father.

ABEL CUSHING, of Hingham, Massachusetts, *b.* 24th October, 1696; *d.* 20th May, 1720; was a farmer and mill owner; was styled Captain; *m.* 24th November, 1720, Mary JACOB, *b.* 29th September, 1698, dau. of Peter and Hannah (ALLEN) JACOB.

ISSUE; ALL BORN AT HINGHAM

 i. Mary, *b.* 12th August, 1722; *d.* 12th October, 1726.
 ii. David, *b.* 12th July, 1724; *d.* 17th October, 1726.
 iii. DAVID, *b.* 7th September, 1727, of whom later.
 iv. Abel, *b.* 26th January, 1730; *d.* circa 1761; *m.* 29th January, 1758, Hannah CROCKER, dau. of Samuel and Ruth (HAMBLIN) CROCKER, of Barnstable; left issue.
 v. Mary, *b.* 28th January, 1732; *m.* 25th March, 1753, Rev. Daniel SHUTE.
 vi. Laban, *b.* 21st February, 1734; *d.* 18th May, 1747.
 vii. An infant
 viii. An infant } *b.* 21st January, 1737; *d.* same day.
 ix. Lydia, *b.* 23d April, 1738; *m.* 31st January, 1759, Gideon HAYWARD; left issue.
 x. Abigail, *b.* 14th June, 1741; *d.* 11th January, 1810; *m.* 2d October, 1761, Thomas HERSEY, *b.* 22d September, 1734, *d.* 12th January, 1810, son of Jonathan and Lydia (CUSHING) HERSEY, as his second wife. He was a soldier in the Crown Point Expedition and Captain of a Military Company in the Revolutionary War; left issue.

COL. DAVID CUSHING, of Hingham, Massachusetts, *b.* there 7th September, 1727; *d.* there 15th February, 1800; Selectman several years; was Lieutenant-Colonel of Col. Solomon LOVELL's 2d Suffolk County Regiment, in 1776, and Colonel of 2d Suffolk County Regiment, 1778, and 1779; *m.* (firstly) 9th April, 1752, Ruth LINCOLN, *b.* 25th February, 1733, *d.* 6th July, 1761, dau. of Samuel and Ruth (CUSHING) LINCOLN; *m.* (secondly) 23d January, 1763, Mabel GARDNER, *b.* 6th January, 1729, *d.* 14th August, 1798, dau. of Hosea and Mary (WHITNEY) GARDNER.

ISSUE BY FIRST MARRIAGE

 i. Ruth, *b.* 11th November, 1752; *m.* 30th August, 1770, Perez CUSHING.
 ii. DAVID, *b.* 2d July, 1754, of whom later.
 iii. Mary, *b.* 6th September, 1756; *m.* 30th January, 1783, Joshua MANN, of Hanover.
 iv. Jonathan, *b.* 13th April, 1759; *d.* 25th January, 1847; enlisted as seaman 1777, and was captured while serving on the *Hazard;* he was imprisoned at Halifax in 1778, and in the *Jersey* Prison Ship, 1780; Selectman,

1804; Representative, 1808 to 1813 inclusive; *m.* 15th January, 1788, Sarah SIMMONS, of Scituate, *b.* circa 1767, *d.* 25th April, 1845, or 1878, left issue.

ISSUE BY SECOND MARRIAGE

I. Abel, *b.* 22d October, 1763; *d.* 30th September, 1843; served as a private for three years from 22d July, 1780 to 1782; in the War of the Revolution under General LINCOLN; in the suppression of the "Shay Rebellion;" *m.* 1st January, 1784, Sarah WILDER, *b.* 1st March, 1768, *d.* 31st March, 1832, dau. of Jabez and Martha (COLLMAN) WILDER; left issue.

II. Hosea, *b.* 29th May, 1756; *d.* 22d November, 1736; *m.* 8th January, 1792, Cecelia WILDER, *b.* 15th July, 1766, *d.* 22d December, 1864, dau. of Edward and Hannah (LEWIS) WILDER; left issue.

III. Charles Whiting, *b.* 7th November, 1766; *d.* 21st June, 1828; Representative, 1816; styled Captain; *m.* 29th November, 1795, Deborah Richmond JACOBS, *b.* 22d June, 1776, *d.* 8th November, 1841, dau. of James and Deborah (RICHMOND) JACOBS.

IV. George Russell, *b.* 24th April, 1768; *d.* 2d February, 1751. In early life was a seafaring man in the European and West India trade. At the time of the French Revolution he was obliged to remain in France on account of the embargo laid on his vessel. He amassed quite a fortune. He had a miniature of himself made in London, England, with the CUSHING Coat of Arms upon its back, which is now in the possession of his descendants. Was a Justice of the Peace at Ashburton for a number of years, was also elected Captain of a Company in the 4th Regiment of Infantry, 2d Brigade, 7th Division of the Militia; *m.* (firstly) 13th August, 1801, Catherine WILLARD, who *d.* 28th April, 1825, dau. of Jacob WILLARD; *m.* (secondly) 22d March, 1826, Hannah Russell HILL, dau. of Issac HILL and sister of Isaac HILL, Jr., the noted Governor of New Hampshire; left issue, by first wife.

V. Nancy, *b.* 10th March, 1770; *d.* unmarried, 27th December, 1825.

VI. Jane, *b.* 3d April, 1772; *m.* 5th November, 1796, Lemuel DWELLY, of Hanover, Massachusetts.

VII. Lucy, *b.* 18th October, 1773; *d.* 21st November, 1840; *m.* 24th May, 1798, David LEWIS, *b.* 16th November, 1771, was a master mariner and lost at sea, son of Elijah and Elizabeth (WHITON) LEWIS; left issue, all born at Hingham.

VIII. Christiana, *b.* 14th March, 1775; *d.* 1st July, 1821.

IX. Elnathan, *b.* 30th April, 1777; *m.* Mary THOMAS; left issue.

X. Jerusha, *b.* 13th February, 1779.

XI. Josiah, *b.* 6th April, 1781.

XII. Mabel, *b.* 6th March, 1783; *m.* 1810, William ROUSE, of Bath, Maine.

DAVID CUSHING, of Hingham and Ashburnham, Massachusetts; *b.* 2d July, 1754, at Hingham; *d.* 3d May, 1728, Ashburnham, where he removed his family in 1798; served in the Revolutionary War as Fourth Lieutenant, in Capt. Jotham LORING's Hingham Company in 1775; also a Sergeant in Capt. Pyan CUSHING's Company, Col. Solomon LOVEL's Regiment in 1776; was Constable in Hingham, 1784 to 1787, inclusive, and from 1790 to 1794 inclusive; was an innholder, tanner and farmer; was known as Captain; *m.* 14th October, 1779, Hannah CUSHING, *b.* 26th April, 1760, *d.* 13th March, 1823, dau. of Joseph and Sarah (LEAVITT) CUSHING, of Hingham.

ISSUE, FIRST SEVEN BORN IN HINGHAM

I. JOSEPH, *b.* 23d January, 1781, of whom later.
II. Hannah, *b.* 9th June, 1783; *m.* Silas WHITNEY.
III. David, *b.* 7th November, 1785; *d.* November, 1851; *m.* 17th April, 1807, Polly ADAMS, *b.* 25th June, 1789, *d.* 15th August, 1854, dau. of John ADAMS; left issue.
IV. Susannah, *b.* 25th March, 1788; *m.* 8th October, 1851, Joseph JEWETT.
V. Laban, *b.* 29th April, 1791; *d.* 17th October, 1847; served in the War of 1812, as a drummer; *m.* 23d April, 1811, Nancy WHITNEY, *d.* 27th January, 1871; left issue.
VI. Deborah, *b.* 6th September, 1793; *m.* Josiah FLETCHER, Jr.
VII. Moses, *b.* 20th March, 1796; *d.* 29th November, 1883; *m.* 25th December, 1818, Gertrude POLLY; left issue.
VIII. Sarah Leavitt, *b.* 7th December, 1798, in Ashburton, Massachusetts; *d.* circa 1830; *m.* Ephram May CUNNINGHAM, a lawyer who removed to Reading.

JOSEPH CUSHING, of Hingham, Massachusetts, and Baltimore, Maryland; *b.* in Hingham, 23d January, 1781; *d.* in Baltimore, 2d August, 1852; he was a printer in Boston and succeeded William BIGLOW, M.A., in editing *The Village Messenger*, in Amherst, New Hampshire, 1796, 1800; this publication continued to 1801, and was succeded in 1803 by *The Farmers Cabinet* (Coll. Mass. Hist. Soc., Vol. II); he established this newspaper himself as a bookseller; he served in the Maryland Legislature and City Government, and aided in the establishment of the first Public School in Baltimore City, as also in 1816, the Savings Bank of Baltimore, of which he was President for twenty-five years until his death; *m.* 1st November, 1804, Rebecca EDMANDS, *b.* 3d April, 1782, *d.* in Baltimore, December 1836.

ISSUE

I. JOSEPH, *b.* in Amherst, New Hampshire, in 1806; *m.* 1834, Ann MACKENZIE, *d.* 6th July, 1879, dau. of Dr. Colin and Sarah (PINKERTON) MACKENZIE, of Baltimore (see MACKENZIE, Vol. I, p. 341).

ISSUE

1. Joseph Mackenzie, *b.* 15th December, 1835, in Baltimore; *d.* there 23d November, 1902; Graduated from Harvard College, A.B., 1855; was a member of the "Maryland Constitutional Convention," in 1864.
2. Wiley Edmands, *b.* 1841; *d.* 1st January, 1904; *m.* Emily Grace MARRIOTT, dau. of William, Haddon and Sophia Keyser (BOYD) MARRIOTT, of Baltimore.

ISSUE

1¹. Joseph Wiley.
2¹. Thomas Morris.

3. Ann, *b.* 1828.
4. Sarah Pinkerton, *b.* 1843; *m.* 11th June, 1868, Hon. Thomas John MORRIS, of the United States District Court of Maryland.

ISSUE

1¹. Josephine Cushing MORRIS, *b.* 1877.

II. John, *b.* 29th August, 1808; removed to Baltimore and became connected with his father and brother in the book and stationery business on Howard Street; was a member of the Eutaw Infantry, of the First Baltimore Hose Company, and for twenty-five years its Treasurer. President of the Fire Department of Baltimore under Mayor Thomas SWANN, Director of the Commercial and Farmers National Bank, Member of the Associate Reform Church, of which his father was one of the founders, also the last charter member of the Eutaw Savings Bank, with which he was connected, from 1847 for forty years. The last twenty years of his life was President of the Associated Firemen's Insurance Company of Baltimore; *m.* 14th October, 1830, Frances CROMWELL, *d.* 13th March, 1865.

ISSUE

1. Joseph, *b.* 5th August, 1831; *d.* 18th November, 1864; *m.* 24th June, 1857, Ella V. WHITMAN; left issue.
2. Rebecca Edmands, *b.* 16th February, 1834; *d.* 23d December, 1894.
3. Elizabeth Waters, *b.* 26th April, 1835; *d.* 15th August, 1880; *m.* 6th June, 1854, Henry Latimer NORRIS, *b.* 3d August, 1831, *d.* 21st February, 1903; left issue.
4. John, *b.* 18th March, 1837; *d.* 17th August, 1877, at Laurel, Maryland; *m.* Etta WHELAN, dau. of William WHELAN, of Baltimore.

1[1]. Edith, *b.* in Baltimore, 11th October, 1841.
2[1]. Francis Cromwell, *b.* 21st November, 1875, in St. Louis, Missouri; enlisted during Cuban campaign in Spanish American War, in the 5th Maryland Infantry, and re-enlisted in 41st United States Volunteers and served two years in the Philippine Islands; now deputy Collector of Malolos, Philippine Islands.
3[1]. Elizabeh Norris, *b.* 14th July, 1878, in St. Louis, Missouri; *m.* Charles W. KNAPP, lawyer, of Baltimore.
4[1]. William Whelan, *b.* 20th July, 1881, in Baltimore.

5. Francis, *b.* 5th June, 1838; *d.* 2d November, 1838.
6. Henry Miller, *b.* 8th January, 1841; *d.* 6th June, 1896; *m.* 13th February, 1868, Margaret E. FOLSON, dau. of Dr. George S. FOLSON, of Prince George County, Maryland.
7. Richard Cromwell, *b.* 27th April, 1842; served in the Civil War, 1861–1865, as Quarter Master Sergeant, 10th Maryland Infantry, and First Lieutenant and Regimental Quarter Master of the 11th Maryland Volunteer Infantry; *m.* 24th October, 1884, Kate E. EADIE.
8. Francis Cromwell, *b.* 10th August, 1844; *d.* 13th July, 1874.

III. David, *b.* 30th August, 1811; *d.* 26th August, 1875; *m.* 11th December, 1834, Catherine Jane MCCLELLAN, who *d.* 24th February, 1845; left issue.
IV. Rebecca Ann, *m.* 29th October, 1835, Hon. John Wiley EDMANDS of Boston; have issue.
V. Mary, *d.s.p.* 10th April, 1840; *m.* 1839, Erastus EDGARTON.
VI. Sarah, *d.* 14th September, 1886; *m.* 1st June, 1848, William Henry CALWELL, of Baltimore; have issue.
VII. Elizabeth, *b.* 14th September, 1818; *m.* 15th January, 1841, George F. SLOAN, of Baltimore, *b.* 24th March, 1819, *d.* 30th March, 1866. He *m.* (secondly) R. E. WATT, of Philadelphia.

ISSUE BY FIRST MARRIAGE

1. George F. SLOAN, *b.* 3d February, 1842; *d.* 24th December, 1914.
2. Joseph Cushing SLOAN, *b.* 4th January, 1844; *d.* 3d November, 1901.
3. FRANCIS BURNS SLOAN, *b.* 16th March, 1846, the subject of this memoir.

ISSUE BY SECOND MARRIAGE

1. Isabella Highland SLOAN, deceased.
2. Elizabeth Burns SLOAN.
3. Fisher SLOAN, *d.* 24th December, 1918; *m.* Anne BUZBY.

ISSUE

1[1]. Mary Buzby SLOAN, *m.* Capt. Charles H. REEVES, of Baltimore.

Arms (CUSHING).—Quarterly, first and fourth gules an eagle displayed argent for CUSHING; second and third gules, three dexter hands couped or, in bend sinister a canton compony of eight, azure and or for DENNIER.
Crest.—Two lions gambs erased sable supporting a ducal coronet or, from which hangs a human heart gules.
Motto.—Virtute et numine.

Southgate

HUGH MACLELLAN SOUTHGATE, of Chevy Chase, Maryland, *b.* 3d September, 1871, at St. Johnsbury, Vermont; *m.* 12th December, 1900, at Orange, New Jersey, Alice Austen MACLAREN, *b.* 24th April, 1872, dau. of Rev. Donald MACLAREN, D.D., Chaplain United States Navy, with rank of Rear Admiral, *m.* 14th July, 1858, Elizabeth Stockton GREEN, who *d.* 20th September, 1906, she dau. of Dr. Jacob and Ann Eliza (MCCULLOH) GREEN.

ISSUE (ALL BORN AT ALTRINCHAM, CHESHIRE, ENGLAND)

I. Elizabeth MacLaren, *b.* 30th June, 1903.
II. Isabel Frances, *b.* 10th February, 1906.
III. Hugh MacLellan, Jr., *b.* 14th January, 1907.

HUGH MACLELLAN SOUTHGATE, graduated at Worcester Polytechnic Institute 1892, B.S.; Postgraduate, 1893, B.S., Electrical. With the Westinghouse Electrical and Manufacturing Company in Pittsburg and Boston, 1893-1899; British Westinghouse Company, London and Manchester, England, 1899 to 1911, returning to represent the Westinghouse Electrical and Manufacturing Company as Manager of their Government Office, Washington, D. C., to date (1918).

Lineage

The emigrant ancestor of this family was Richard SOUTHGATE, the son of John and Elizabeth (BENNETT) SOUTHGATE of England; he was *bapt.* 7th March, 1670-1671, at Combs, Suffolk County, England; *d.* 1st April, 1758, at Leicester, Massachusetts; arrived in Boston, 12th September, 1715; was the first Treasurer of the town of Leicester; *m.* 16th October, 1700, at Badley, Suffolk, England, Elizabeth STEWARD, dau. of William STEWARD.

ISSUE (FROM HIS FAMILY BIBLE)

I. STEWARD, *b.* 8th September, 1703, of whom later.
II. Elizabeth, *b.* 23d March, 1705; *d.* 4th November, 1788.
III. Richard, *b.* 2d August, 1708; *d.* 24th August, 1708.
IV. Hannah, *b.* 10th December, 1709; *d.* 30th March, 1754.
V. Mary, *b.* 9th January, 1712; *d.* 7th February, 1766.
VI. Richard, *b.* 23d July, 1714; *d.* 2d November, 1798.

STEWARD SOUTHGATE, *b.* 8th September, 1703, at Combs, Suffolk County, England, *d.* 18th December, 1764, at Leicester, Massachusetts; he was Proprietor's Clerk and Town Clerk of Palmer, Massachusetts; Town Surveyor, etc.; *m.* (firstly) 28th March, 1735, Elizabeth SCOTT, dau. of William and Sarah (FOOTE) SCOTT; *m.* (secondly) Elizabeth POTTER, dau. of Nathaniel and Rebecca POTTER.

ISSUE BY FIRST MARRIAGE

I. Elizabeth, b. 26th January, 1735-1736, at Palmer; d. there 28th January, 1737-1738.
II. John, b. 15th January, 1737-1738, at Palmer; d. 7th August, 1806, at Penobscot, Maine.
III. William, b. 29th August, 1739, at Palmer; d. 25th September, 1747, at Leicester.
IV. ROBERT, b. 26th October, 1741, at Leicester, of whom later.
V. Margaret, b. 17th July, 1743, at Leicester; d. 17th July, 1743.
VI. Sarah, b. 18th June, 1744, at Leicester; m. Araziah DICKENSON, of Hadley.
VII. Mary, b. 16th October, 1746, at Leicester; d. 13th May, 1756, at Leicester.
VIII. Steward, b. 10th September, 1748, at Leicester; d. 29th September, 1820, at Bronson, Ohio.

ISSUE BY SECOND MARRIAGE

I. Son, b. 21st October, 1750, at Leicester; d. same day.
II. Amos, b. 3d December, 1751, at Leicester; d. 30th September, 1775, at Boston.
III. Rebecca, b. 23d August, 1754, at Leicester; d. there 14th October, 1756.
IV. Son, b. 11th March, 1757, at Leicester; d. there same day.
V. Ruth, b. 3d December, 1758, at Leicester; d. 16th October, 1777, at Boston.
VI. Moses, b. 19th July, 1761, at Leicester; d. September, 1777 at Boston.

DR. ROBERT SOUTHGATE, of Scarborough, Maine, b. 26th October, 1741, at Leicester, Massachusetts; d. 2d November, 1833, at Scarborough, Maine; was Judge of the Court of Pleas, 1800-1810; Trustee of Bowdoin College; m. 23d June, 1773, Mary KING, dau. of Richard and Isabella (BRAGDON) KING, the brother of Rufus KING, whose guardian Dr. SOUTHGATE was.

ISSUE (FROM HIS FAMILY BIBLE)

I. Mary King, b. 4th September, 1775; d. 22d June, 1795, at Scarborough.
II. Daughter, b. 4th January, 1777; d. same day.
III. Son, b. 4th November, 1777; d. same day.
IV. Isabella, b. 29th March, 1779; d. 28th January, 1821, at Portland.
V. HORATIO, b. 9th August, 1781, of whom later.
VI. Elizabeth, b. 24th September, 1783; d. 19th February, 1809, at Charleston, South Carolina.
VII. Octavia, b. 13th September, 1786; d. 9th January, 1815, at Portland.
VIII. Miranda, b. 15th February, 1789; d. 17th July, 1816.
IX. Frederick, b. 9th August, 1791; d. 28th May, 1813, at Scarborough.
X. Arixene, b. 17th September, 1793; d. 6th December, 1820, at Portland.

XI. Robert, b. 14th October, 1796; d. 6th July, 1799, at Scarborough.
XII. Mary King, b. 6th May, 1799; d. 13th May, 1829, at Scarborough.

(All children born in Scarborough, Maine.)

JUDGE HORATIO SOUTHGATE of Scarborough, Maine, and Portland, Maine, b. in Scarborough, 9th August, 1781; d. there 7th August, 1864, graduated at Exeter Academy in the class with Daniel WEBSTER, Augustine and Bushrod WASHINGTON and Henry WADSWORTH; was County Treasurer in 1814; Registrar Cumberland County Probate Court, 1815–1836; m. (firstly) 1st November, 1805, Abigail McLELLAN, dau. of Maj. Hugh and Abigail (BROWNE) McLELLAN; m. (secondly, 10th May, 1818, Mary WEBSTER, dau. of Noah WEBSTER; m. (thirdly), 14th October, 1821, Eliza NEAL, dau. of James NEAL.

ISSUE BY FIRST MARRIAGE (FROM FAMILY BIBLE)

I. Robert, b. 4th September, 1806, at Portland; d. 25th July, 1807.
II. ROBERT, b. 28th January, 1808, of whom later.
III. Abagail Browne, b. 28th October, 1809; d. 19th May, 1834, at Portland.
IV. Horatio, b. 5th July, 1812; d. 12th April, 1894 (Bishop SOUTHGATE of the Episcopal Church) at Astoria, Long Island.
V. Frederick, b. 23d October, 1814; d. 29th February, 1844, at Quincy, Illinois.

ISSUE BY SECOND MARRIAGE

I. Mary Webster, b. 5th February, 1819; d. 2d May, 1860, in Paris.

ISSUE BY THIRD MARRIAGE

I. Richard, b. 27th January, 1822; d. 15th November, 1852, at Scarborough.
II. Elizabeth, b. 20th July, 1823; d. 17th December, 1862, at Scarborough.
III. Emily, b. 13th November, 1824; d. 29th September, 1852, at Scarborough.
IV. Julia, b. 5th February, 1826; d. 8th October, 1837, at Scarborough.
V. Edward Payson, b. 17th September, 1827, d. 23d January, 1846, at Portland.
VI. Ellen, b. 7th May, 1829; d. 26th November, 1852, at Boston.
VII. William Scott, b. 10th April, 1831; d. 21st May, 1899, at Annapolis, Maryland.
VIII. John Barrett, b. 25th July, 1833; d. 7th February, 1862, at Scarborough.
IX. Henry Martin, b. 4th August, 1835; d. 30th December, 1852, at Portland.
X. Julia Abbey, b. 25th January, 1838; d. 23d January, 1883, at Brooklyn, New York.

All born at Portland, Maine, except Julia Abbey who was born at Scarborough.

REV. ROBERT SOUTHGATE, *b.* 28th January, 1808 at Portland, Maine; *d.* 6th February, 1873, at Woodstock, Vermont; he was graduated at Bowdoin College and Andover Theological Seminary, 1829; he occupied Congregational pulpits at Woodstock, Vermont; Wethersfield, Connecticut; Monroe, Michigan; Ipswich, Massachusetts, and Hartford, Vermont; *m.* 2d September, 1832, Mary Frances SWAN, dau. of Benjamin and Lucy (GAY) SWAN.

ISSUE

I. Robert Swan, *b.* 7th August, 1834, at Woodstock, Vermont; *d.* 10th December, 1898, at Detroit, Michigan.
II. Horatio, *b.* 24th August, 1836, at Woodstock, Vermont; *d.* 30th January, 1842, at Weathersfield, Connecticut.
III. Frances Swan. *b.* 14th May, 1843, at Weathersfield, Connecticut; *m.* Edward DANA.
IV. CHARLES MCLELLAN, *b.* 18th November, 1845, of whom later.
V. Frederick Chester, *b.* 25th January, 1853, Judge Probate Court, Windsor, Vermont.

REV. CHARLES MCLELLAN SOUTHGATE. *b.* 18th November, 1845, in Monore, Michigan; *d.* 5th June, 1912, at his summer home, Bass Rocks, Gloucester, Massachusetts; was graduated from Phillips Andover Academy, 1862; Yale University, 1866; Andover Theological Seminary, 1870; occupied Congregational pulpits at St. Johnsbury, Vermont; Dedham, Massachusetts; Worcester, Massachusetts; Auburndale, Massachusetts; at the time of his death he was Superintendent of the Massachusetts Bible Society, Boston, Massachusetts; he was Trustee of Harford Theological Seminary; Director Congregational Sunday School and Publishing Society; *m.* 30th November, 1870, Elizabeth Virginia ANDERSON, dau. of Dexter and Sophia (FOSTER) ANDERSON.

ISSUE

I. HUGH MACLELLAN, *b.* 3d September, 1871, the subject of this memoir.
II. Isabel Anderson, *b.* 22d August, 1881; *m.* 1st June, 1907, at Auburndale, Massachusetts, Guy Crosby RIDDELL, son of Robert Hugh and Annie (DAGGETT) RIDDELL.

ISSUE

I. Robert Southgate RIDDELL, *b.* 6th April, 1912, at Helena, Montana.

III. Stuart Leicester, *b.* 26th April, 1889; *m.* 31st July, 1915, Alice DARLEY, of Farmington, Connecticut, dau. of Henry Samuel and Florence (BRADLEY) DARLEY.

ISSUE

1. Barbara Gay, *b.* 4th June, 1917, at Boston, Massachusetts.

Residences.—Chevy Chase, Maryland; Bass Rocks, Gloucester, Massachusetts.
Clubs.—Metropolitan and University of Washington, Chevy Chase, and Engineers Club of New York.
Societies.—Baronial Order of Runnemede, Colonial Wars, Sons of the Revolution, American Institute of Electrical Engineers, New England Historical and Genealogical Society.

Talcott

REVEREND JAMES FREDERICK TALCOTT, A.B., A.M., of New York City, *b.* there 14th September, 1866; *m.* there (firstly) 28th October, 1890, Frank Vanderbilt CRAWFORD, *b.* 24th August, 1859, *d.* 19th August, 1915, dau. of Robert Singleton and Julia (LAKE) CRAWFORD; *m.* (secondly) 17th February, 1917, Louise SIMMONS, *b.* 1st February, 1872, dau. of Cheston H. and Louise (MAYNARD) SIMMONS.

ISSUE BY FIRST MARRIAGE

I. James, Jr., *b.* 21st November, 1893; *m.* 14th April, 1917, Mary Stoddard JOHNSON, dau. of Arthur S. JOHNSON, of Boston, Massachusetts.
II. Frederick Hooker, *b.* 13th April, 1895.
III. Julia Lake, *b.* 28th October, 1898.
IV. Martha Eveleth, *b.* 16th March, 1904.

JAMES FREDERICK TALCOTT, A.B., Princeton, 1888; A.M., Princeton, 1890; student at Oxford, England, 1890-1891; studied at Berlin, Germany, 1891; graduate Union Theological Seminary, 1892; Assistant Minister of St. Bartholomew's Church of New York City, 1893-1898; Minister in charge, St. George's Church, Rumson, New Jersey, 1898-1903; Chaplain, Water Street Mission, New York City; Director, Bowery Branch, Young Men's Christian Association; Director, St. Ambrose Italian Mission; President James Talcott Company.

Lineage

The family originated in Warwickshire, England, from which line descendants were living in Colchester, County Essex, prior to 1558. The Motto on the Coat Armor granted in that year is "Virtus sola nobilitas." Members of the family were clergymen of the Church of England, Aldermen, Justices of the Peace and Merchants. The line of the American branch is from

JOHN TALCOTT, I, of Colchester, England, *d.* 1606; *m.* (firstly) ——— WELLS, the mother of the American branch; *m.* (secondly) Marie PULLEN, the mother of Thomas TALCOTT, the head of the English branch.

ISSUE

I. JOHN, II, *bapt.* 4th October, 1562, of whom below.

JOHN TALCOTT, II, *bapt.* 4th October, 1562; *d.* 1604; of Braintree, County Essex, England; *m.* Anne SKINNER, dau. of William SKINNER of Braintree, Massachusetts.

ISSUE

I. JOHN, III, *b.* circa 1690, in Braintree, County Essex, England of whom later.
II. A dau.

III. A dau.
IV. A dau.
V. A dau.
VI. A dau.

HON. JOHN TALCOTT, III, of Cambridge and Hartford, Connecticut, b. in Braintree, County Essex, England; d. 1660; he came to Cambridge with his wife and two children in the Company of the Rev. Thomas HOOKER, leader of the Expedition which founded the Colony of Connecticut, in 1635, which sailed in the ship *Lion* from England, 22d June, 1632, and arrived at its destination 16th September of that year. He was Freeman 6th November, 1632; Representative to the First General Assembly in May, 1634, and five following courts including May, 1636. He soon after accompanied the Rev. Thomas HOOKER and his church to Connecticut and became one of the founders of the City of Hartford. In that Colony he was a member of the First General Court, 1637, and every year following to 1654, when he was raised to Assistant and one of the two "Commissioners" of the New England Colonies, was styled "The Worshipful" and served as Treasurer of the First Assembly from 1652 to 1659; m. in England, Dorothy MOTT, d. 1670, dau. of Mark MOTT, D.D., who came with his wife Dorothy and several children in the *Lion* (SAVAGE says Dorothy SMITH, dau. of Benjamin SMITH, was the name of his wife).

ISSUE

I. John, b. in England; d. 23d July, 1688; succeeded his father as Treasurer, holding the position from 17th May, 1660, to 1676; was Lieutenant-Colonel; m. 29th October, 1650, Helena or Helen WAKEMAN.
II. Mary, b. in England; m. 28th June, 1649, Rev. John RUSSELL, of Wethersfield.
III. SAMUEL, b. 1635, of whom later.

CAPTAIN TALCOTT of Newton Massachusetts, b. 1635, in Newton, Massachusetts; d. 10th November, 1691; leaving a large estate; was Captain; Freeman, 1662; Representative, 1669–1677; m. (firstly) 7th November, 1661, Hannah HOLYOKE, d. 2d February, 1679; (secondly) 6th August, 1679, Mary (surname unknown), who *d.s.p.*

ISSUE BY FIRST MARRIAGE

I. Samuel, b. 1663.
II. John, d. young, but probably after his father.
III. Hannah, b. 1665; m. 26th November, 1686, John CHESTER.
IV. Elezur, b. 31st July, 1669.
V. Joseph, b. 20th February, 1672.
VI. BENJAMIN, b. 1st March, 1674, of whom later.
VII. Rachel, b. 2d April, 1676; m. 1700, Peter BUCKLEY.
VIII. Nathaniel, b. 28th January, 1679.

Deacon Benjamin Talcott, of Wethersfield, Connecticut, *b.* 1674, in Wethersfield, Connecticut; *m.* (wife's name not given); his son
Capt. Samuel Talcott, had a son
Samuel Talcott, *b.* in 1733; who had a son
Samuel, *b.* 1765; who had a son
Samuel Talcott, *b.* 1765; who had a son
Seth Talcott, of West Hartford, Connecticut, *b.* 1801; who had a son
James Talcott, of West Hartford, Connecticut, *b.* there 1835; who had
James Frederick, *b.* 14th September, 1866, the subject of this memoir.

Arms.—Argent on a pale sable, three roses of the field.
Crest.—A demi-griffin erased argent, gorged with a collar sable, charged with three roses of the field.
Motto.—Virtus sola nobilitas.
Residences.—No. 16 East 66th Street, New York City; "Harbourage," Seabright, New Jersey.
Clubs.—Republican, Princeton.
Societies.—Geographical, Asiatic.

Thomas

CHARLES CRANKSHAW THOMAS, of Baltimore, Maryland, *b.* at Atlanta, Georgia, 20th December, 1882; *m.* 10th April, 1917, Nanette PAYNE, dau. of Edward Waldron and Ida (KEYS) PAYNE, of Springfield, Illinois (see HASKELL family).

CHARLES CRANKSHAW THOMAS is a graduate of Washington and Lee University, Virginia, 1904; attended Georgia School of Technology, Georgia; Johns Hopkins University, Maryland; Lawyer; special investigator for American manufacturers in South America, 1914-1915; interested in publishing scientific journals; editor.

ISSUE

1. Payne, *b.* 11th May, 1919.

Lineage

The founder of the family was Thomas THOMAS, of St. Mary's County, Maryland. The THOMAS family supposedly originated from Wales. Thomas THOMAS is understood to have come from County Sussex, England, the latter part of 1639. For transporting himself, wife Elizabeth, son James; his servants, Robert and Eleanor PATTERSON and Matthew SMITH, to the Province in 1651, he demanded and received a warrant with one William BATTEN, 22d November, 1652, for eleven hundred acres on the north side of the Patuxent River, over against or near Buzzard Island; 31st March, 1656, he was one of the High Commissioners of the Provincial Court held at Patuxent. He made his will 28th December, 1670, proved 2d February, 1671. His wife was Elizabeth, a dau. of William BARTON, Sr.

ISSUE

1. JAMES THOMAS, *b.* in England prior to 1651; he made his will as of Charles County, Maryland, 7th June, 1701, leaving his estate, "Ware," on the Patuxent, to his children; his will was proved 29th November, 1701; he *m.* Teratia (surname not given).

ISSUE

1. John, of whom later.
2. Thomas, *d.* before 20th February, 1723-1724; *m.* Susanna (surname not given).

ISSUE

1¹. Thomas, of Charles County; will dated 6th March, 1733-1734; probated 22d October, 1734; *m.* Elizabeth (surname not given).
2¹. George, *m.* (wife's name unknown); she *d.* before him.
3¹. William.
4¹. Elizabeth, *m.* ———— ADAMS.

3. Anna Mary.

JOHN THOMAS, of Charles County, Maryland, *b.* 1682, will dated 30th April, 1756; probated 7th July, 1757; his wife's name is unknown as she predeceased him.

ISSUE

I. JOHN of "Ware," Charles County, of whom later.
II. Leonard, *b.* circa 1711, of "Bowling Green;" moved to North Carolina, prior to 1773.
III. James, *d.* 1782; *m.* Catherine (surname not given).

ISSUE

1. Susanna, *m.* James MILLS.
2. Zachary, *m.* Mary EDEN, dau. of Hon. John EDEN.

ISSUE

1¹. Elizabeth EDEN, *m.* Thomas BUCKNER.

IV. Jane, *d.* before 1756; *m.* Edward SWANN.
V. Elizabeth, *b.* before 1756; *m.* Benjamin WOOD.
VI. Major William, *b.* 1714; *d.* 25th March, 1795; *m.* Elizabeth REEVES.

JOHN THOMAS, *b.* 1705, *m.* Mary WILSON, of Montgomery County, Maryland; she made her will in 1763, as of Dorchester County, and as the wife of John THOMAS, who predeceased her.

ISSUE

I. Jonathan, *b.* 1725; *d.* 1780.
II. Elizabeth, *b.* 1726; *m.* Peter WOOD.
III. John, *b.* 1728; *m.* Nancy TAYLOR.
IV. Nancy, *b.* 1729; *m.* Mevoral MORAN.
V. Hezekiah, *b.* 1731; *d.* 1778.
VI. Caleb, *m.* Mary CAVE, 29th December, 1784.
VII. William, *b.* 1737; *m.* Elizabeth COLLINS.

VIII. Martha, b. 1739; m. John Rouse ADAMS.
IX. Nathan, b. 1740; m. Mary BRUCE, of St. Mary's County, Maryland.
X. Rebecca, b. 1742; m. Hezekiah BILLINGSLEY.
XI. Mary, b. 1744; m. ——— LYON.
XII. Nathaniel, b. 1745; d. 1815, an officer in the Continental Army.
XIII. Catherine, b. 1747; m. ——— PARKER.
XIV. PHILIP, b. 1750; d. 1821; of whom later.

PHILIP THOMAS, of Charles County, Maryland, b. circa 1750; d. 1821; m. circa 1773, Elizabeth Covington WAILES, dau. of Capt. Benjamin and Sarah (HOWARD) WAILES of Prince George's County, Maryland (Maryland Archives, XXI, p. 414). Philip THOMAS was an officer in the Continental Army and was presented with a sword for meritorious conduct in battle. About the year 1797, in the company with the brothers of his wife, Edward LLOYD WAILES, m. Sarah Biggs ODEN, 22nd March, 1780 and Levin WAILES (Surveyor-General, Mississippi, 1807), he removed to Fauquier County, Virginia; then to Columbia County, Georgia; then to Franklin County, Georgia, where Philip THOMAS died.

ISSUE

I. John, b. 1773; m. Nancy (surname not given).
II. Philip, b. 1774; m. Nancy (surname not given).
III. Elizabeth, b. 1776; d. 1822.
IV. EDWARD LLOYD, b. 1778; d. 1850; of whom later.
V. William, b. 1784; m. Nellie (surname not given).
VI. Wesley, b. 1791.
VII. James, b. 1795; m. Rebecca AVERY.
VIII. Lovick, b. 1798; d. 1870; m. Captain 35th Georgia Regiment, Confederate States Volunteers.

EDWARD LLOYD THOMAS, of Georgia, b. 1778; d. 1850, at Thomas Place, Gwinnett County, Georgia, He removed from Franklin County, Georgia, to Oxford, Georgia, and then to Gwinnett County, Georgia. He controlled the Patterson grants, a large tract of land in Georgia. He was Surveyor-General of Georgia, a planter of extensive holdings, and a minister of the gospel. He m. circa 1808, Mary HOUGE, of Columbia County, Georgia.

ISSUE

I. HENRY PHILIP, of whom later.
II. Wesley, of Newman, Georgia, b. 1824; d. 1910; Major, 1861–1864, Cavalry, Philips Legion, Confederate States Volunteers; Representative, Georgia Legislature, for many years.
III. Edward Lloyd, b. 1826; Emory College, 1846; Captain, Mexican War; Brigadier-General, 1863–1864, Confederate States Volunteers; m. Jennie H. GRAY, of Cullodon, Georgia, d. 1907.

COL. HENRY PHILIP THOMAS, *b.* 25th May, 1810, at Thomas Place, Gwinnett County, Georgia; killed at Fort Saunders, Tennessee, 29th November, 1863; Graduate University of Georgia, 1832; Lawyer; Member of State Legislature; State Senator; Member Charleston Convention, 1860; Member Baltimore Convention, 1860; Lieutenant-Colonel, United States Volunteers, Creek War; Captain, Georgia Volunteers, and aide to Gen. Winfield SCOTT, Mexican War; organized and captained the first company from Gwinnett County, Georgia, 1861, for the Confederate Army; Lieutenant-Colonel and Colonel, 16th Georgia Regiment, Confederate States Volunteers; killed while in command WOFFORD's brigade, Fort Saunders, Knoxville, Tennessee, 29th November, 1863. He *m.* 5th December, 1837, Ellen BURROUGHS, *b.* 25th December, 1814; *d.* August, 1894, a dau. of James and Elizabeth (WOOD) BURROUGHS (a dau. of Capt. Jonathan WOOD, wife's name unknown; War of Revolution), of Columbia County, Georgia.

ISSUE

I. Winfield Scott, *b.* 9th May, 1839; *m.* Mary C. GERMANY; United States Military Academy, 1860; Captain, Company K, 13th Georgia Cavalry, Confederate States Volunteers.
II. Edward Burroughs, *b.* 29th July, 1841; Captain, Company F, 24th Georgia Infantry; Confederate States Volunteers; *d.* 8th April, 1915.
III. Charles, Company K, 18th Georgia Cavalry, Confederate States Army.
IV. HENRY WAILES, *b.* 9th August, 1844, of whom later.
V. James Lovick Albert, *b.* 12th September, 1853; *d.* 1914, Dallas, Texas.

HENRY WAILES THOMAS, *b.* 9th August, 1844, at Thomas Place, Gwinnett County, Georgia; *d.* Atlanta, Georgia, 11th October, 1913; Member Company F, 35th Georgia Confederate States Volunteers; Merchant; *m.* 9th November, 1881, Margaret CRANKSHAW, *b.* 10th September, 1859, dau. of Hamilton (of Darwin, England) and Mary Alice (FLINN) CRANKSHAW (of Newark, Delaware).

ISSUE

I. Charles, *b.* 20th December, 1882, at Atlanta, Georgia; *m.* 10th April, 1917, Nanette PAYNE, dau. of Edward Waldron and Ida (KEYS) PAYNE, of Springfield, Illinois.
II. Mary, *b.* 1st September, 1886, at Atlanta, Georgia; *m.* 16th October, 1909, A. Pratt ADAMS, a son of Judge and Mrs. Samuel Barnard ADAMS, of Savannah, Georgia.

ISSUE

1. Samuel ADAMS, *b.* 25th July 1910.
2. Margaret ADAMS, *b.* 3d January, 1913.
3. Pratt ADAMS, *b.* 24th May, 1914.
4. Thomas ADAMS, *b.* 3d April, 1917.

III. Margaret, b. 9th June, 1891, at Atlanta, Georgia; m. 15th November, 1911, Eli Shorter RANKIN, d. 20th December, 1918, son of Jesse and Frances (LAMAR) RANKIN, of Atlanta, Georgia.

ISSUE

1. Eli Shorter RANKIN, b. 23d May, 1915.
2. Margaret RANKIN, b. 16th May, 1918.

Arms.—Argent three lions rampant gules, a chief azure.
Crest.—A demi-lion rampant gules.
Motto.—Honesty is the best policy.
Residence.—Roland Park, Baltimore, Maryland.
Clubs.—University, Baltimore, Maryland; Capitol City, Atlanta, Georgia; Muscogee, Columbus, Georgia.
Societies.—American Chemical Society; American Electrochemical Society; American Society for Testing Materials; American Association for the Advancement of Science; Sigma Alpha Epsilon; Theta Nu Epsilon; Old Guard of the Gate City Guards, Atlanta, Georgia; Sons of the American Revolution.

Tiffany

HONORABLE GEORGE TIFFANY, LL.B., of Brooklyn, New York, *b.* 22d July, 1859, in the village of Quaker Street, Schenectady County, New York; *m.* 3d December, 1884, Eliza A. ESTES, *b.* 15th August, 1862, *d.* 4th February, 1915, dau. of Ira ESTES, *b.* 4th September, 1820, *d.* September, 1913, and Jane M. (LOOMIS) his wife, *b.* 16th February, 1827, *d.* 8th August, 1904, *m.* 25th February, 1857.

ISSUE

I. George B., *b.* 6th December, 1885; *m.* 27th June, 1917, Idella Gibson MINKS, of Camden, New Jersey, *b.* October 22d, 1896, at Woodbury, New Jersey, dau. of William L. and ELIZABETH H. MINKS, his wife.
II. Marguerite, *b.* 22d June, 1890.

GEORGE TIFFANY, Attorney and Counsellor at Law, was educated at Quaker Street Literary Institute, and Union University; Member of Assembly for New York State from the 18th District, King's County, 1898; has acted as Counsel to take Appeals for the Government under designation pursuant to Act of Congress to authorize the President to increase temporarily the military establishment of the United States, 18th May, 1917; Elder in "The Reformed Protestant Dutch Church of the Town of Flatbush in King's County," one of the oldest and most historic Churches in the United States, founded 1654; is a member of "The Board of Domestic Missions of the Reformed Church in America" and a member of its Executive Committee; the degree of LL.B. was conferred upon him 28th May, 1885, by Union University; is First Vice President and Treasurer of King's County Historical Society, Incorporated; President of the South Classis of Long Island Reformed Church in America, 1919-1920.

Lineage

It is the theory of some members of the family that this family originated about the time of the Early Crusades to "The Holy Sepulchre" and that some member of the family returning from the Crusades settled in Brittany, France. That following the Norman Conquest, the English left Brittany at different periods and that it is from some of these English TIFFANYS that the American TIFFANYS are descended. The name is Norman French. On the revocation of the Edict of Nantes by Louis XIV of France, many Huguenots emigrated to England and some to America, among them were certain families of the name of TIFFANY, among whom was a James TIFFANY, from the Province of Champagne, who was naturalized in the year 1682.

As no effort has been made to trace the line in England or France this memoir will begin with the first TIFFANY in America.

The earliest TIFFANY mentioned in colonial history is Squire Humphrey TIFFANY, who went to Massachusetts Bay Colony about 1660. In the records of the ancient town of Rehoboth, "Baylis History of New Plymouth" Volume I, page 209, under the date of 22d January, 1663, it states "Humphrey TIFFANY permitted to be a Sojourner and to buy or hire." At this date he became a citizen of the Town and was a Justice of the Peace. He was killed by a stroke of lightning on 15th July, 1685, while on the way to Boston with a party of friends. The following quaint lines have recorded the event: "Humphrey Tiffany and Mistress Lowe, by a stroke of lightning into eternity did go." His wife was Elizabeth (surname not given). The four great branches of the family whose descent is unquestioned, are his four sons.

ISSUE

I. James.
II. THOMAS, b. 1665–1670, of whom later.
III. Ebenezer.
IV. Consider.

THOMAS TIFFANY, b. 1665–1670, in Swansea, Massachusetts, about 1698 moved to Bristol, Rhode Island, then to Ashford, Connecticut; 15th March, 1718, Thomas TIFFANY was admitted a Freeman of Ashford, Connecticut, and on this date he and his son Thomas, James TIFFANY and others, drew each 200 acres by lot, of the undivided public lands, the citizens having, at a Town Meeting held on 11th January, 1718, voted to distribute among themselves the surplus land by drawing lots. Records show that he bought a great deal of land in Ashford, was a man of substance and for those times a large land owner. From 1735 to 1741 he was a Selectman and Town Clerk and with the exception of two years was Town Clerk from 1721 to 1748; *m.* Hannah (surname not given); the records of the birth of his three oldest children are in Swansea and five were baptized in Christ Church, Bristol.

ISSUE

I. Eliezer, b. at Swansea, Massachusetts, 30th April, 1690.
II. THOMAS, b. at Swansea, Massachusetts, 22d May, 1692, of whom later.
III. Recompence, b. Swansea, Massachusetts, 11th March, 1694.
IV. Isaiah, b. at Bristol, Rhode Island, 1698; d. at Lebanon, Connecticut, 1780; Lieutenant Isaiah TIFFANY, an officer in the American Revolution, was a gd. son of THOMAS TIFFANY of the second generation and *was also one of the Charter Members of the Order of the Cincinnati in the State of Connecticut.* "*He fought in eighteen battles of the Revolution, including Monmouth and Yorktown and was at Valley Forge. He was one of the forlorn hope in storming the redoubts at Yorktown.*" Lieut. Isaiah TIFFANY's grandson Henry Frederick PHINNEY, *m.* Caroline Martha COOPER,

a dau. of J. Fennimore COOPER, the novelist, at Cooperstown, New York, 8th February, 1849. Rev. Frederich Trench TIFFANY another in this line was Chaplain of Congress, in 1845.
v. Edward, b. at Bristol, Rhode Island, d. Ashford, Connecticut, 29th June, 1770.
vi. Nathaniel, bapt. at Bristol, Rhode Island.

THOMAS TIFFANY, b. Swansea, Massachusetts, 22d May, 1692; d. 29th January, 1768; 7th December, 1720, admitted an inhabitant of the Town of Ashford, Connecticut; in 1731 was a Deputy to the General Court; in 1740 was appointed Justice of the Peace, of Windham County, Connecticut, and reappointed until 1752; was a man of wealth and influence; m. 1719, Mercy REED of Weymouth, Massachusetts; in 1756 he signed Congregational Church Covenant at Ashford, Connecticut.

ISSUE; ALL BORN IN ASHFORD, CONNECTICUT

I. Abigail, b. 10th August, 1720.
II. Bethyah, b. 18th November, 1721.
III. Annie, b. 7th July, 1723.
IV. Ezekiel, b. 30th December, 1725, of whom later.
V. Mary, b. 24th November, 1726.
VI. Thomas, b. 30th December, 1728.
VII. Simeon, b. 24th August, 1732.
VIII. Hannah, b. 11th November, 1735.
IX. Sarah, b. 27th June, 1736.

EZEKIEL TIFFANY, b. 30th December, 1725; d. 30th July, 1795; 1st December, 1760, was elected Clerk and Constable of Ashford, Connecticut; 23d November, 1765, was elected Collector of the Westford Society of Ashford, Connecticut; his son Capt. Stephen TIFFANY was a soldier in the War of 1812, and was Captain of the Walpole Rifle Company; Ezekiel TIFFANY m. 19th March, 1749, Mary KNOWLTON. Mary KNOWLTON, *was a sister of Lieut.-Col. Thomas* KNOWLTON *of Ashford, Connecticut, Captain of* KNOWLTON'S *Rangers*, who took part in capture of Fort Ticonderoga in July, 1759; in battle of Breeds Hill, 16th June, 1775; commanded a Division at the Battle of Bunker Hill; in battle of Long Island, 27th August, 1776; in battle of Harlem Heights, 16th September, 1776, where he fell mortally wounded; he was buried with military honors on the field of battle, now 143d Street, New York City. Mary (KNOWLTON) TIFFANY was also a sister of Lieut. Daniel KNOWLTON, also of KNOWLTONS' Rangers, who was in the Crown Point Expedition and in many battles of the Revolution. Ezekiel TIFFANY in 1756 signed the Congregational Church Covenant at Ashford, Connecticut, said Church founded 26th November, 1718.

ISSUE; ALL BORN IN ASHFORD, CONNECTICUT

I. Sarah, *d.* 22d March, 1814; *m.* ———— STEBBINS.
II. Simeon, *b.* 29th May, 1751; at Lexington Alarm, served seven days.
III. WILLIAM, *b.* 30th July, 1753, of whom later.
IV. Mary, *b.* 1st December, 1755.
V. Ezekiel, *b.* 12th March, 1763; enlisted twice for service in the Revolutionary War.
VI. Ezra, *b.* 27th June, 1765.
VII. Amasa, *b.* 6th November, 1767; *d.* Bennington, Vermont, 17th April, 1850.
VIII. Calvin, *b.* 5th November, 1772.

WILLIAM TIFFANY, *b.* at Ashford, Connecticut, 30th July, 1753; *m.* there (firstly) 16th November, 1775, Molly CLARK, dau. of Lemuel CLARK, a soldier in the Revolution, and Mercy (BRIDGES) CLARK his wife, *b.* 14th August, 1755; *d.* 3d July, 1778; *m.* (secondly) 30th April, 1783, Anne PETTES, *b.* 12th November, 1754, *d.* 5th January, 1791, dau. of Joshua PETTES and Elizabeth CROCKER, his wife, of Norwich, Connecticut; *m.* (thirdly) 4th September, 1791, Marjory LA CORE, of Montgomery, Massachusetts.

ISSUE BY FIRST MARRIAGE

I. William, *b.* at Ashford, 1776.
II. CLARK, *b.* 20th June, 1778, of whom later.

ISSUE BY SECOND MARRIAGE

I. Almira, *b.* 27th February, 1784, at Mansfield, Connecticut.
II. Wealthy, *b.* 15th January, 1786, at Mansfield, Connecticut.
III. Anna, *b.* 9th August, 1788, at Montgomery, Massachusetts.
IV. Pettes, *b.* 17th December, 1790, at Montgomery, Massachusetts.

ISSUE BY THIRD MARRIAGE

I. Jared, *b.* at Montgomery, Massachusetts.

CLARK TIFFANY, *b.* at Ashford, Connecticut, 20th June, 1778; *m.* about 1798, Submit BROWN; he died near Albany, New York, after an operation, about 1818; he was a farmer and landowner, his wife *d.* 3d March, 1866, in Oneida County, New York, aged eighty-four years and was buried in the cemetery near McConnellsville, New York; before his death the family resided in the Town of Duanesburgh, Schenectady County (formerly Schoharie County), New York, and his widow and family continued to reside there for some years thereafter, when she moved to Oneida County, where one of her sons, Alanson TIFFANY, resided.

ISSUE

I. William, *b.* 22d October, 1801; *m.* Mary RECTOR, *b.* 14th February, 1802, *d.* July, 1865; he *d.* 1st January, 1885.
II. Jonathan R., *d.* 23d October, 1843; held many public offices in the town of Duanesburgh; *m.* Sally Ann (surname not given).
III. Calvin.
IV. Alanson, *b.* 10th March, 1808; *d.* 1890; *m.* Catherine RECTOR, who was *b.* February, 1810.
V. JOSEPH, *b.* 1809, of whom later.
VI. Jared, *b.* 1st January, 1811; *d.* 30th October, 1887; *m.* 1st January, 1834, Margaret MOTT.
VII. Almira, *m.* Gideon WELLS.
VIII. Wealthy.
IX. Elizabeth.
X. Sarah, *b.* 1816; *d.* 6th August, 1877; *m.* Walton CLARK.

JOSEPH TIFFANY, farmer, *b.* 1809, at Oak Hill, Town of Duanesburgh, Schenectady County, New York; *d.* 1849; *m.* early in 1827, Mary CORNELL, *b.* 28th April, 1809; he *d.* at Oak Hill and is buried in the TIFFANY burial plot in the cemetery at Esperance, Schoharie County, New York; his wife Mary, who survived him many years, lies beside him in the same plat.

ISSUE

I. WASHINGTON, *b.* 13th July, 1828; *d.* 9th November, 1886, of whom later.
II. Elizabeth Ann, *b.* 1829–1830; *m.* William EFFNER.
III. George, *b.* 1831; served through the Civil War; was Sergeant of Company A, in the 134th Regiment of New York Volunteers, Infantry; *d.* unmarried in 1887; buried in the TIFFANY plot in the cemetery at Esperance, Schoharie County, New York.
IV. Eleanor, *b.* 1833; *m.* Charles HAVENS about 1893; *d.* about 1903, buried in the cemetery at Esperance, with her mother and brother and father.
V. Sergeant Harvey J., served through the Civil War; was Sergeant of Company D, of the 134th Regiment of New York Volunteers, Infantry; wounded in the Battle of Dug Gap, Georgia; now (1918) living in Hoosick Falls, Rensselaer County, New York; *m.* Sarah GALLUP, *b.* 24th April, 1848. Sergeants George and Harvey J. TIFFANY were actually engaged in the following battles of the Civil War and went on SHERMAN'S march from Atlanta to the sea, viz.: Gettysburg, Chancellorsville, Missionary Ridge, Knoxville, Atlanta, Resaca, Dallas Pine Knob, Lost Mountain, Peach Tree Creek, Savannah, Goldsboro and Dug Gap.

WASHINGTON TIFFANY, *b.* at Oak Hill, in the town of Duanesburgh, Schenectady County, New York, 13th July, 1828; *d.* at the Village of Quaker Street, Schenectady County, New York, 9th November, 1886; was buried in the Friends Cemetery, in that village; he was greatly interested in the cause of education; for some years was School Trustee in his town and was a man of affairs, universally respected and liked and of wide influence; m. 3d November, 1850, Ruth UNDERHILL, b. 8th October, 1828, in the Town of Rensselaerville, Albany County, New York, who is still living, dau. of Daniel and Philena (TITUS) UNDERHILL.

ISSUE

I. Ruth A., b. 16th September, 1851; d. 25th November, 1860.
II. Mary, b. 11th January, 1853; unmarried.
III. Orlando J., b. 1st June, 1855; d. 14th November, 1860.
IV. GEORGE, b. 22d July, 1859, the subject of this memoir.
V. William H., b. 6th January, 1862; m. September, 1887, Edith LEWIS.
VI. Elizabeth, b. 1863; d. 9th September, 1863.
VII. Philena, b. 31st October, 1865; d. 14th February, 1866.
VIII. Alice E., b. 29th August, 1867; m. (firstly) Charles CARTWRIGHT, 18th October, 1884; m. (secondly) William LEVEY, 14th September, 1911.
IX. Florence A. L., b. 2d June, 1873; m. (firstly) Harry E. WICKHAM, he d.; m. (secondly) Sidney NEWMAN.

Arms.—Argent, a chevron between three lions heads erased gules.
Crest.—A grey hound's head erased, in the mouth a stag's foot erased, all ppr.
Motto.—Patria Fidelis.
Residences.—No. 178 Hawthorne Street, Brooklyn, New York; (summer) "Tarrymore," Tyringham, Berkshire County, Massachusetts.
Societies.—Colonial Wars, Kings County Historical Society, St. Nicholas, Society of Nassau Island, Brooklyn Bar Association.

Underhill

Lineage of George TIFFANY by right of descent through the line of his mother, Ruth (UNDERHILL) TIFFANY. From Reports of the UNDERHILL Society of America, D. Harris UNDERHILL, Historian, 248 Maple Street, Brooklyn, New York, and from English Public Records and Public Records of New York, New Hampshire, Massachusetts, Rhode Island and Connecticut.

This line begins with TIMOTHEUS UNDERHILL, b. in Yorkshire, England in 1248.

EDWARD UNDERHILL, "the Hot Gospeller," gd. father of Capt. John UNDERHILL, was b. 1512; d. 1576; was Gentleman-in-Waiting to Queen Mary and to Queen Elizabeth of England; Gentleman Pensioner; Man at Arms under Sir Richard CROMWELL, who was Captain of the Horsemen in the contingent sent to assist the Emperor in the siege of Londreci Hainault. One of 200 men who attended upon King Henry when he went to Boulougne. Went to France again on military service under the Earl of Huntington to check the French, who were aiming at recapture of Boulougne; *m.* March, 1545, at London Joan PERRINS; their son,

SIR JOHN EDWARD UNDERHILL was *b.* 10th February, 1556, *m.* Mary MOSELY; their son,

CAPT. JOHN UNDERHILL, was *b.* in Bagington, Warwickshire, England, on 7th October, 1597; *d.* in Matincock, New York, 21st July, 1672; came to Boston with WINTHROP's fleet as Captain of any military force that might be employed. Speedily joined the Church. Previously served under the great Dutch Prince in the war of the Netherlands. Sworn in as Freeman; Officer of Ancient and Honorable Artillery Company, Boston; Deputy to first General Court, Massachusetts (Legislature); appointed Selectman; appointed by General Court with Daniel PATRICK and Robert FEAKE to fix upon a site for a fort on Castle Island in the Bay; ordered by the Magistrates, with a shallop, to bring Roger WILLIAMS from Salem to Boston; on account of murder of Captain OLDHAM by Block Island Indians, Governor VANE and Council, ordered sent thither ninety men, distributed to four commanders, Capt. John UNDERHILL, with commission to put to death the men, but spare the women. Commander with Captain MASON in Pequot War; Colonial Governor of Dover and Exeter, New Hampshire; Representative from Stamford, Connecticut, in General Court. Led the Dutch against the Simaroy Indians; appointed member of Council of New Netherland; commanded by the Director to attack and subdue certain hostile Indians on Long Island, which was done; elected one of the eight men of New Amsterdam to adopt measures against the Indians. Governor KIEFT grants to Capt. John UNDERHILL, Meutalers (Bergens) Island. Sheriff of the North Riding of Long Island; Magistrate at Flushing; command by Rhode Island, Newport and Providence Plantations to Privateers to go against the Dutch, Capt. John UNDERHILL made Commander in Chief of the land forces. Appointed Deputy by Governor NICHOLLS, with sober and discreet powers, etc. Mrs. Schuyler VAN RENSSELAER in her history of the City of New York says: "The most conspicuous Englishmen in New Netherland in the time of Governor KIEFT were Isaac ALLERTON and John UNDERHILL." See above History, Volume 1, page 215. "That he had served with credit in the army in the low Countries, Ireland and Spain." Same History and Volume, p. 216. Sherman WILLIAMS in his book called "New York's Part in History" at page 124, referring to the Indian Wars of New Netherland and particularly to the Battle of Stricklands Plain where the Colonists were led by Capt. John UNDERHILL says: "The Colony was saved from utter destruction chiefly through the efforts of John UNDERHILL." He led several expeditions against the Indians and the last one compelled a peace. "At Stricklands Plain not far from Stamford a decisive battle was fought." "It was a stunning blow for the Indians and it ended the war and saved the Colony." "KIEFT proclaimed a Public Thanksgiving for the result of UNDERHILL's Expedition." Capt. John UNDERHILL *m.* (secondly) 1658–1659 probably at Flushing, Elizabeth FEAKE, *b.* in Watertown, Massachusetts, 1633, *d.* in Killingworth on Matincock, in 1674–1675, dau. of Lieut. Robert FEAKE and Elizabeth (FONES) WINTHROP, his wife; their son,

NATHANIEL UNDERHILL, *b.* in Killingworth, Oyster Bay, New York, 22d February, 1663; *d.* 10th September, 1710; *m.* October, 1685, Mary FERRIS, of Westchester County, New York, dau. of John FERRIS, one of the ten proprietors of Throckmortons neck, and Mary FERRIS his wife, their son

BENJAMIN UNDERHILL was *b.* August, 1694; was of Northcastle, Westchester County, New York; *m.* Hannah (surname not given); their son

JOHN UNDERHILL, was *b.* in Westchester County, New York, in 1719; *d.* in Town of Carlisle, Schoharie County, New York; *m.* 19th December, 1771, in Chappaqua, Westchester County, New York, Deborah DICKINSON, *b.* in Westchester County, New York, about 1740, dau. of Zebulon and Joyce (HANCE) DICKINSON and a direct descendant of John HOWLAND, the *Mayflower* Pilgrim; their son

HENRY UNDERHILL, was *b.* in Westchester County, New York, September, 1772; *d.* in Town of Westerlo, Albany County, New York, November, 1864; *m.* about 1800–1801, Ruth SPENCER, *b.* in East Greenwich, Rhode Island, 1st March, 1767, *d.* 2d May, 1813, in Watervliet, New York, dau. of William and Margaret (JOHNSON) SPENCER; their son

DANIEL UNDERHILL, *b.* in town of Rensselaerville, Albany County, New York, 8th August, 1802; *d.* in Quaker Street, New York, 5th January, 1874; *m.* in Rensselaerville, New York, 3d January, 1828, Philena TITUS, *b.* in Rensselaerville, New York, 13th May, 1809, *d.* in Quaker Street, New York, 30th August, 1884, dau. of Richard and Elizabeth (HAIGHT) TITUS; their dau.

RUTH UNDERHILL, was *b.* in the town of Rensselaerville, Albany County, New York, 8th October, 1828; still living (1918); *m.* in Oak Hill, Schenectady County, New York, 3d November, 1850, Washington TIFFANY, *b.* in town of Duanesburgh, New York, 13th July, 1828, *d.* in Quaker Street, Schenectady County, New York, 9th November, 1886; their issue, among others, is

GEORGE TIFFANY, the subject of this memoir.

Arms.—Argent, a chevron sable between three trefoils slipped vert.
Crest.—On a mount vert, a hind legged or.

Van Santvoord

SEYMOUR VAN SANTVOORD, of Troy, New York, *b.* there 17th December, 1858; *m.* (firstly) 4th June, 1884, Virginia SHIELDS, *b.* 1862, *d.* 1886, dau. of Capt. Hamilton Le Roy SHIELDS, United States Army, of Virginia, and Caroline HART, dau. of Richard P. HART and Betsey A. HOWARD. Captain SHIELDS was a graduate of West Point, was breveted twice for gallantry in Mexican War, Member of Aztec. Richard P. HART was a wealthy merchant and prominent citizen of Troy; *m.* (secondly) 4th January, 1888, his sister-in-law, Caroline Hart SHIELDS, *b.* 1860.

ISSUE BY FIRST MARRIAGE

1. Edith, *b.* 26th January, 1886; *m.* Donald Argyll CAMPBELL, of Cornell, 1908, Private, U. S. A., son of Rev. Frederick A. CAMPBELL of Rochester, New York.

ISSUE BY SECOND MARRIAGE

I. Virginia, *b.* 29th May, 1889; *m.* Lieut. Raymond Brower BOWEN, United States Army, of Yale, 1911.

II. George, *b.* 5th August, 1891; A.B., Yale, 1912; Oxford, 1915; Litt.B., Oxford, 1917; Rhodes Scholar, 1914; served American Ambulance Field Service; Master Winchester College, England; Instructor, Yale College, 1919; Sergeant, 39th Regiment, United States Infantry, 4th Division in France. Received Croix de Guerre and Citation from French Government for gallantry in 2nd Battle of Marne; promoted 1st Lieut., 167th Regiment, Rainbow Division; severely wounded October, 1918.

III. Agnes, *b.* 8th August, 1892; *m.* 1912 Lieut. William T. RICE, United States Army.

IV. John Griswold, *b.* 24th February, 1895; Yale, 1916; Ensign, United States Naval Reserve.

V. Richard Staats, *b.* 31st January, 1898; Yale, 1920; Private 36th Balloon Company, U. S. A., in France.

VI. Alexander Seymour, *b.* 23d October, 1899; Yale, 1921; Private U. S. A. (Artillery).

SEYMOUR VAN SANTVOORD, A.B., Union College, 1878; LL.B., Albany Law School, 1881; Lawyer, Troy, N. Y.; Farmer, Manufacturer, Banker; President Walter A. Wood Mowing Machine Company, 1896–1906; President Security Trust Company, and Safe Deposit Company of Troy, 1906–1911; Counsel to Governor,

N. Y., 1912; Chairman N. Y. Public Service Commission, 1914–1918; Ex-President New York State Trust Company Association; Alternate Delegate at Large Democratic National Convention, 1904; President Holland Society, 1916–1919; Vice-President Albany Law School; Trustee Troy Public Library; Troy Orphan Asylum; Samaritan Hospital; Member New York State National Guard, 1882–1887; Presidential Elector, 1908; received votes for United States Senator from New York in Legislative Ballot, January, 1911.

Lineage

The progenitor of the VAN SANTVOORD family in America was Rev. Cornelius VAN SANTVOORD, b. in Holland, 1686; graduated from University of Leyden; settled in Staten Island, 1717, and preached there in French, Dutch and English until 1742, when he removed to Schenectady and became pastor of the Old Dutch Church there; he was a scholar and prolific writer (see "Appleton's Encyclopedia of American Biography," Tit. VAN SANTVOORD); he m. Anna STAATS of Staten Island.

ISSUE

I. Cornelius, m. Ariantje BRATT.
II. STAATS, m. Geertge BRATT.
III. ZEGER, b. 12th October, 1733, of whom later.
IV. Jacoba, m. Peter TRUAX.
V. Geertje, m. Ryk VANDERBILT.
VI. Anne.
VII. Maria, m. Johannes E. WENDELL.

ZEGER VAN SANTVOORD, b. 12th October, 1733; was a soldier in the Revolutionary Army; m. 9th April, 1756, Catlyna POST of Schenectady.

ISSUE

I. Sarah, m. Jacob VAN NOAST.
II. Nancy, m. William DE GRAFF.
III. CORNELIUS ZEGER, b. 22d May, 1757, of whom below.

CORNELIUS ZEGER VAN SANTVOORD, of Schenectady; enlisted as a private in 1776; was commissioned Ensign by Governor CLINTON in 1778 and became Captain in 1780; he fought throughout the War; m. 11th September, 1782, Eva SWITS, dau. of Maj. Abram SWITS, of Schenectady, a gallant officer in the Revolution; several of her ancestors were killed and others taken captive to Canada in the French and Indian War in 1690.

ISSUE

I. Zeger, b. 1783; was a Colonel in the War of 1812.
II. Abraham, 1784.

III. STAATS, *b.* 15th March, 1790, of whom later.
IV. Catlyna, *b.* 1794.

STAATS VAN SANTVOORD, D.D., *b.* in Schenectady, 15th March, 1790; was a Clergyman of the Dutch Reformed Church; graduated from Union College, 1811; New Brunswick Theological Seminary, 1814; *m.* 31st December, 1812, Margaret VAN HARLINGEN, of a French Huguenot family which had found refuge in Holland after the revocation of the Edict of Nantes.

ISSUE

I. Rev. Cornelius, A.B., Union College, 1839; author, "Life of Dr. Nott," Chaplain 18th Regiment Infantry, 1862–1865.
II. George, enlisted in the War of the Rebellion, but was killed in a railroad accident before he enrolled.
III. Eugene, *b.* 1842; Captain 169th Regiment New York Infantry, 1862–1865.

GEORGE VAN SANTVOORD was *b.* Belleville, New Jersey, 8th December, 1819; *d.* in 1862; graduated from Union College, A.B., class of 1841, as valedictorian of his class, and Φ B K; he was a brilliant classical scholar, lawyer and author. Besides various law books he wrote "Lives of the Chief Justices of the United States," "Life of Algernon Sydney," biographies of leaders of French Revolution including ROBESPIERRE, DANTON, VERGNIAUD, MARAT and CARNOT, and a brilliant eulogy of Andrew JACKSON, the latter when the author was only twenty-four years of age; *m.* at Kinderhook, New York, 7th November, 1844, Elizabeth VAN SCHAACK, *b.* Kinderhook, 10th October, 1824; she was highly gifted and educated, published many poems and translations from the French and Italian. On account of delicate health she lived in Italy the last twenty years of her life and died there in Turin, 1st January, 1913, in her eighty-eighth year. On the occasion of the twenty-fifth anniversary of the marriage of King Humbert and Queen Margherita, she addressed a congratulatory poem to the Queen, by whom it was translated into Italian and by royal decree published in all the papers in Italy. The father of Elizabeth VAN SCHAACK was Peter VAN SCHAACK, *b.* Kinderhook, 1796; A.B., Union College, 1819; a lawyer and editor of *Kinderhook Rough Notes*, a newspaper which he founded. His father was Peter VAN SCHAACK, B.A., LL.D., Kings College (now Columbia), 1768, a celebrated lawyer of Colonial times. He made the first revision of the Colonial Laws of New York State (Appletons "Encyclopedia of American Biography"). The mother of Elizabeth VAN SCHAACK was Dorcas MANTON, *b.* Providence, 22d September, 1798; *d.* Kinderhook, 21st May, 1894. Her ancestry included many men of attainments and prominence, among them Dr. Thomas MANTON, a celebrated non conformist clergyman of the time of CROMWELL, at whose installation he made the prayer. He was a graduate of Oxford and tutor of Lord BOLINGBROKE. The first MANTON in this country was Edward who prior to 1640 settled in Providence, Rhode Island, where five generations of his descendants lived and are buried.

In the fifth generation was Captain Daniel Manton, who commanded a Rhode Island Company in the Revolutionary war; his son was John MANTON (father of Dorcas above), *b.* 1776, *d.* in 1791, *m.* Mary BROWN of Providence, Rhode Island, *b.* there 10th May, 1778; she was a descendant of Rev. Chadd BROWN, the first Elder of the oldest Baptist Church in America. He came to Providence from Salem in 1637 and succeeded Roger WILLIAMS in the pastorate. Mary BROWN's gd. father James BROWN was one of the founders of the Commercial House of BROWNS and his brother John was the founder of Brown University, Providence, Rhode Island.

CHILDREN OF GEORGE AND ELIZABETH VAN SANTVOORD

I. Margaret, *b.* 1850.
II. Frank, *b.* 1851; *d.* 1874.
III. Harold, *b.* 1854; *d.* 1914.
IV. George Bancroft, *b.* 1856, *m.* 15th January, 1909, Alice Brewer GLAZIER.
V. SEYMOUR, *b.* 17th December, 1858, the subject of the memoir.

Arms.—Azure, three salmon conjoined at the fesse point, or.
Crest.—A salmon between a pair of wings erect or.
Residences.—Washington Park, Troy, New York, and Shadowbrook Farm, Bennington, Vermont.
Clubs.—Camp Fire of America, University of New York City.
Societies.—Holland, St. Nicholas, Huguenot, Colonial Wars, Sons of the Revolution, Kappa Alpha (Greek Letter), National Institute of Social Sciences, Archaeological of America, New York State Bar Association, American Bar Association, New York State Historical Society.
Author: "The House of Caesar;" "The Roman Forum," etc.

Walling

WILLIAM ENGLISH WALLING, *b.* 14th March, 1877, in Louisville, Kentucky; *m.* 28th June, 1906, in Paris, France, Anna Seraphine STRUNSKY, *b.* 21st March, 1879, the well known authoress and lecturer, dau. of Elias STRUNSKY, of New York City, *b.* October, 1847; *m.* 1866, Anna HOROWITZ, *b.* March, 1846.

ISSUE

I. Rosamond, *b.* 29th January, 1910.
II. Anna Strunsky, *b.* 31st December, 1912.
III. Georgia, *b.* 14th October, 1914.
IV. William Hayden English, *b.* 22d December, 1916.

WILLIAM ENGLISH WALLING, of Brookside Drive, Greenwich, Connecticut; Economist, Author, Lecturer, *b.* in Louisville, Kentucky, 14th March, 1877; B.S., University of Chicago, 1897; Post Graduate Work in Economics and Sociology, 1899–1900; Factory Inspector, Illinois, 1900–1901; Resident University Settlement, New York from 1902 until marriage, 1906; contributor to leading American and European journals; author of "Russia's Message;" "The Larger Aspects of Socialism;" "Socialism as It Is;" "Socialists and the War," etc.
Clubs.—New York City, Civic and Liberal Clubs.

Immigrant Colonial Ancestors

CORNELIS BARENTSE SLECHT, of Holland; in Esopus, Ulster County, New York, 1655.
MATHEW BLANSHAN, of Artois; Ulster County, New York; arrived 1660.
LOUIS DU BOIS, of Artois; in Ulster County, New York, 1661.
JAN JOOSTAN VAN METEREN, of Holland; Ulster County, New York, 1662.
JOOST JANS (JOHN) VAN METEREN, of Holland; Ulster County, New York, 1662.
JAN ROELOFFSEN ELTING, of Holland; in Long Island, New York, 1665; Ulster County, New York, 1667.
JOST HEYDT (HITE), of Alsace; in Ulster County, New York, 1710.
CASPER DILLER, of Alsace; Lancaster County, Pennsylvania, 1729.
PHILIP ADAM DILLER, of Pfalz, Germany; Lancaster County, Pennsylvania, 1729.
LEONARD ELLMAKER, of Germany; Lancaster County, Pennsylvania, 1726.
JOSEPH ABEL, of London; Maryland and later Kentucky.
RANDALL REVEL, of England; in Virginia, 1632.
ROBERT WHARTON, of England; in Pennsylvania, 1697.

THOMAS ELLIS, of Wales; in America previous to 1684–1685, when Thomas PENN wrote: "Dearly salute me to dear Thomas ELLIS of the Welsh Friends." Thomas ELLIS settled in Pennsylvania.

JOHN GRIGSBY, of England; came to Virginia about 1660, with brother James; both soldiers under Cromwell; *m.* Jane ROSSER, who came over on the same vessel.

JOHN CALDWELL, of Ireland; settled in Maryland.

CAPT. EDMOND SCARBOROUGH, of England; in Virginia, 1620.

JOSEPH MAHEW, of Hartwell, Northamptonshire, England; Maryland.

Immigrant Colonial Ancestresses

MADELINE (JORISSE) BLANSHAN, of Artois, France; New York, 1660.
TRYNTJE TYSSE (BOS) SLECHT, of Holland; New York, 1655.
FANTA LENA, of Spain; Maryland.
CATHERINE (BLANSHAN) DU BOIS, of Artois, France; New York, 1661.
JACOMYNTJE (SLECHT) ELTINGE, of Holland; New York, 1655.
MACYKEN (HENDRYGKEN) VAN METEREN, of Holland; New York, 1662.
ANNE MARIE (DU BOIS) HEYDT, of Artois, France; New York, 1710.
BARBARA DILLER, of England; Pennsylvania, 1729.
JANE ROSSER, of England; Virginia, 1660.
HANNAH SCARBOROUGH, of England; Virginia, 1635.

William English Walling Descent

LOUIS DU BOIS, of Artois, and Catherine BLANSHAN; had issue.

SARAH DU BOIS, *b.* 14th September, 1664; *m.* Joost Janse VAN METEREN (John VAN METER), son of Joosten VAN METEREN and Macyken HENDRICKSEN of Holland; had issue.

Rebecca VAN METEREN, *b.* 26th April, 1686; *m.* Cornelius ELTING, son of Jan, son of Roeloff and Aeltje ELTING, of Holland, and Jacomyntje, dau. of Cornelius Barentse SLECHT and Tryntje Bos, of Holland; Rebecca and Cornelius ELTING had issue.

SARA ELTING, *m.* Col. John HITE, son of Jost HITE, and had

Rebecca HITE, *m.* Col. Charles SMITH, son of John, and had

SARAH SMITH, *m.* Lieut. Philip EASTIN and had

MAHALA EASTIN, *m.* Maj. Elisha G. ENGLISH and had

WILLIAM HAYDEN ENGLISH, *m.* Mardulia E. S. JACKSON, dau. of Capt. John Farrow and Elizabeth Butler (GRIGSBY) JACKSON and had

CAPT. WILLIAM E., and Rosalind ENGLISH, who *m.* Dr. Willoughby WALLING and had

ISSUE

I. William English.
II. Willoughby George.
III. Mardy Jackson.

Blanshan

MATHEU BLANJEAN, *b.* in Nieuville, Artois, France; *m.* Madeline JORISSE, and had

CATHERINE BLANJEAN, *m.* Louis du Bois DE FIENNES, of Artois, in Manheim, 10th October, 1655.

ISSUE

I. Marie, *m.* Antoine CRÉPEL, of Artois, in Manheim.
II. Madalena.
III. Elizabet.
IV. Mattys.

Who embarked in the *Gilded Otter*, 27th April, 1660; he had one of the first cases in Ulster County before the Schepens in 1661; he was in the Colonial service with his son-in-law, Louis DU BOIS and Antoine CRÉPEL; signed 1684 petition to Governor-General; signed pledge to support their Representatives with Jan ELTINGE, Mattys SLEGHT, Anthony CRESPEL.

Du Bois

LOUIS DU BOIS was born at Wiores, Province of Artois, 27th October, 1626, son of Chretien Maxmillian DU BOIS, DE FIENNES, Seigneur de Beaufermez and de Bourse; *m.* 10th October, 1655, in Manheim, Catherine BLANSHAN, dau. of Matheu and Madeline (JORISSE) BLANSHAN. Two sons Abraham and Isaac, were *b.* before they sailed to America. The third child, Jacob, was *b.* in Ulster County, New York, in 1661. Catherine Blanshan DU BOIS and three children were captured by Indians in 1663; she was respited from burning by singing the 137th Psalm as a death chant, which gave her husband and New Amsterdam soldiers the time to save her. Sara, the only daughter to reach maturity, was *bapt.* 14th September, 1664; *m.* 12th September, 1682, Joost Janz VAN METEREN, he was probably one of the VAN METEREN children in captivity with her mother. Louis DU BOIS was the founder of New Paltz. He with his two young sons and nine other Huguenots, called the twelve Patentees, secured a land patent from Governor ANDROS, September, 1677. Four months previous and before PENN's famous purchase, they had purchased this land of the Indians. DU BOIS was in the first Court of Sessions in Kingston. He was a leader in demanding of the English Government under the Duke of York, an assembly and taxation by consent and was put out of commission for his daring.

Slecht

CORNELIS BARENTSE SLECHT of Woerden, Holland; *m.* Tryntje Tysse Bos. He was in Esopus, New York, in 1655; Now Ulster County. He was Sergeant of a Military Company and signed an agreement 31st May, 1658, with Governor STUYVESANT to build a stockade and to make peace with the Indians. His son was captured, 1659, and tortured to death, and his daughter, 1663, was captured and made to *m.* an Indian. Esopus was made Wiltwyck, 1661, and SLECHT was on the first board of three Schepens (Aldermen). He was one of the four leaders in an insurrection against the oppression of the English Commandant, 1667. Wiltwyck become Kingston, 1669, and SLECHT was a Member of the Court of Sessions, 1676. In 1683 he was arrested with his son, Mattys, son-in-law Jan ELTINGE and Matheu BLANCHAN for signing a petition to Governor DONGAN asking liberty to choose their own officers to town courts and to transport their own produce. Daughter Jacomyntje, *b.* in Woerden, Holland; *m.* 1677, Jan ELTINGE. Petronella, Annetje, Cornelis and Hendricus were other children.

Elting

JAN ELTING, son of Roeloff and Aaltje ELTING, was *b.* in Switchelaer, Holland, 29th July, 1632, O. S., Province of Drenthe, a dependency of Beyle; he was in Long Island, New York, in 1663; Jan and Jacomyntje (SLECHT) ELTINGE signed as witnesses to Indian signatures in purchase of New Paltz by Louis DU BOIS and partners, 1677; Jan with others held a Court of Sessions, commissioned 1675.

ISSUE

I. Geertje.
II. Aaltje.
III. Roeloff.
IV. Cornelis, *b.* 1681; *m.* Rebecca VAN METER.
V. William.

Van Meter

JAN JOOSTEN VAN METEREN with wife, Maycken HENDRICKSEN, and five children came to New York in 1662 in the *Fox* and settled in Ulster County in same year.

ISSUE

I. Lysbeth.
II. Catherine.
III. Geertje.
IV. JOOST JANSE of whom later.
V. Gysbert.

He took oath of allegiance 1664; was referee in a lawsuit, 1665, and Schepen, 1665 and 1668; in 1673 he was one of four Magistrates of Hurley and Marbletown and in 1676 petitioned for a minister to Governor ANDROS.

JOOST JANSE VAN METEREN, *b.* about 1656, in Guelderland, Holland; *m.* 12th December, 1682, Sara DU BOIS, dau. of Louis DU BOIS.

ISSUE

I. Jan.
II. REBECCA, *bapt.* 26th April, 1686, of whom later.
III. Lysbeth.
IV. Isaac.
V. Hendrix.

JOHN VAN METER (JOOST JANS), a "Dutchman from the Hudson," was an Indian trader and pioneer explorer of the Shenandoah Valley who "spied out the land" about the time of Governor SPOTSWOOD's expedition, 1716; he equipped a band of Delaware Indians at his own expense and traveled far southward over unknown lands; on his return he advised his sons to take up lands in "The Wappatomica Valley in the South Branch bottom, above the Trough," as it was the finest land he had discovered; John and Isaac took his advice and petitioned Governor GOOCH in 1731 for 40,000 acres which was granted; in 1731 they transferred their grant to Joost HITE, whose wife, Anne Marie DU BOIS, was a near relative of their grandfather, Louis DU BOIS.

See *"Colonial Families," Volume IV*

Heydt (Hite)

HANS JOOST HEYDT, colonizer of the Shenandoah Valley, is said to have been "a baron of Alsace;" he came to America with his wife, Anne Marie DU BOIS, dau. Mary and sixteen, or more, families in two vessels of his own, the *Swift* and the *Friendship*, his dau. Elizabeth was *bapt.* in Kingston, 1710; in 1716, he was in Pennsylvania with a colony; in 1730 he sold his Pennsylvania lands, and in 1731 started with sixteen families from York Pennsylvania, for their new Virginia home.

ISSUE

I. COLONEL JOHN, of whom later.
II. JACOB.
III. Mary.
IV. Elizabeth.
V. Magdalena.
VI. Isaac, *m.* Eleanor ELTINGE, dau. of Cornelis ELTINGE.
VII. Abraham.
VIII. Joseph.
IX. (Possibly) Maria Susannah.

COL. JOHN HEYDT (HITE) was in French and Indian and Revolutionary Wars; Captain of Precinct; President Courts Martial and County Courts, 1760; Colonel Frederick County Militia and succeeded Lord FAIRFAX as C nty Lieutenant; *m.* Sara ELTINGE, dau. of Cornelis and Rebecca (VAN METER) E INGE.

Smith

REBECCA HITE, *b.* 1740; *d.* 1785; *m.* Col. Charles SMITH (son of John SMITH), *b.* 1726, served in French and Indian War and lost left hand at Great Meadows. Charles SMITH, Gentleman, Sheriff of Frederick County, Virginia, 1772 and Vestryman of Frederick Parish; will 1774–1776.

ISSUE

I. John SMITH, in Revolutionary War.
II. Charles SMITH, in Revolutionary War.
III. Elizabeth Hite SMITH, *m.* William MORTON.
IV. SARAHANNA SMITH, of whom below.

Eastin

SARAHANNA SMITH, *b.* 1767; *d.* 1843; *m.* Lieut. Philip EASTIN, 4th Virginia Continentals, 1782, and settled in Kentucky.

ISSUE

I. George EASTIN, captured by Indians.
II. Fanny EASTIN.
III. Charles EASTIN.
IV. Rebecca EASTIN.
V. Martin EASTIN.
VI. David EASTIN.
VII. Philip EASTIN.
VIII. William EASTIN.
IX. Lucy EASTIN.
X. Rachel EASTIN.
XI. Sarah EASTIN.
XII. Mahala EASTIN.

English

MAHALA EASTIN, *b.* 2d March, 1799, in Fayette County, Kentucky; *d.* 3d June, 1882, in Indianapolis, Indiana; *m.* 9th November, 1819; Maj. Elisha Gale ENGLISH, *b.* in Kentucky, 23d March, 1798, *d.* 14th November, 1874, son of Elisha ENGLISH and Sarah (WHARTON) ENGLISH; he was United States Marshal for Indiana and in the State Senate for many years.

ISSUE

I. WILLIAM HAYDEN ENGLISH, only child, of whom below.

WILLIAM HAYDEN ENGLISH, *b.* 27th August, 1822; *d.* 7th February, 1896; was Speaker of the Indiana House of Representatives; Member of Congress 1852–1861;

author of Compromise Measure for admission of Kansas, known as the "English Bill;" President Indianapolis Street Railway; President First National Bank; Vice-Presidential candidate with General HANCOCK in 1880; author of "Conquest of the Northwest," etc.; *m.* Mardulia Emma Sybil JACKSON, dau. of Capt. John Farrow and Elizabeth Butler (GRIGSBY) JACKSON, of Fauquier County, Virginia.

ISSUE

I. WILLIAM EASTIN ENGLISH, of whom later.
II. Rosalind ENGLISH, *m.* Dr. Willoughby WALLING.

CAPT. WILLIAM EASTIN ENGLISH, was in the Indiana House of Representatives and Senate; Member of Congress; on General WHEELER's Staff in Spanish American War and was severely wounded at Santiago; Author of "History of Masonry in Indianapolis," etc.,

ELISHA ENGLISH, Kentucky pioneer, 1790; *b.* Sussex County, Delaware, 2d March, 1768; *d.* 7th March, 1857, in Kentucky; son of James ENGLISH, *b.* 1708, Maryland, *m.* Amy WALLER, 10th February, 1743, son of James and Mary ENGLISH in Somerset County, Maryland, 1689, son of Thomas and Margaret ENGLISH.

Wharton

SARAH WHARTON, *b.* 26th September, 1768; *d.* 27th November, 1849, dau. of Capt. Revel WHARTON and Mary SCROGIN, *m.* in 1763.

CAPT. REVEL WHARTON, *b.* in Northampton County, Virginia; killed in Revolutionary service by the British on his own vessel; was son of Thomas WHARTON and Sarah REVEL, dau. of John REVEL, son of Edward REVEL and Rachel HALL, son of Randall REVEL and Katherine SCARBOROUGH, dau. of Capt. Edmond SCARBOROUGH.

RANDALL REVEL, of England; in Virginia, 1632; burgess etc., in Northampton County, Virginia, and in Somerset County, Maryland; will 1685-1686.

THOMAS WHARTON, was a son of Robert WHARTON, County of Cumberland, England, and Delaware County, Pennsylvania; *m.* 1701, Rachel ELLIS, dau. of Thomas and Ellen ELLIS, of Redstone, Pembrokeshire, Wales and Haverford, Pennsylvania. (See "Register-General of Pembrokeshire.")

MARY SCROGIN, widow of Capt. Revel WHARTON, on the way to Kentucky about 1790; *m.* a brother of Daniel BOONE, who was killed shortly after; she *d.* in Kentucky, 1824.

CAPT. EDMOND SCARBOROUGH, of England, Burgess in Virginia, 1620-1635; *d.* 1635, *m.* Hannah (surname not given).

ISSUE

I. Sir Charles SCARBOROUGH of England, physician to Charles II, James II and William III.

II. Col. Edmond SCARBOROUGH, of Virginia; Burgess, Surveyor-General, etc.; *d.* 1671.

III. Katherine SCARBOROUGH, *d.* previous to 5th May, 1688; *m.* Randall REVELLE.

Scrogin

MARY SCROGIN, *b.* 1745; dau. of Joseph SCROGIN and Sarah CALDWELL, dau. of John and Mary CALDWELL.

JOSEPH SCROGIN, *d.* 1772; son of Jane and John SCROGIN, *d.* 1743, of Charles County, Maryland; son of Joseph SCROGIN and Fanta LENA of Spain.

FANTA LENA of Spain; a lady of rank, imprisoned by her father in a tower near the water, escaped by a rope ladder to her lover and sailed with him in his vessel anchored nearby to Maryland, where her husband *d.*; she is said to have *m.* a second husband, a widower with children, named ———— DAVIDSON, and to have become estranged from her own child, who *m.* in opposition to her wishes; her gd. son, Joseph SCROGIN, settled near Snow Hill, Maryland, where he *m.* Sarah CALDWELL, dau. of John CALDWELL, who *d.* in 1747, in Somerset County, Maryland.

William English Walling's Descent from John Grigsby and Jane Rosser of England

John, I, of Stafford County, Virginia, had James Redmond, who *m.* Susannah and had Nathaniel, who *m.* Elizabeth BUTLER, dau. of William BUTLER and Anne (?) MASON, and had William, who *m.* Jane KING, dau. of George Hales KING and Sarah GARRARD, dau. of William GARRARD and Mary, dau. of Charles and Ann SMITH, and had Elizabeth Butler GRIGSBY, who *m.* Capt. John Farrow JACKSON, son of Samuel and Mary (FARROW) JACKSON, dau. of Issac and Ann (SCOTT) FARROW, son of Abraham and Sybil FARROW, son of Abraham FARROW.

SAMUEL JACKSON was son of Francis JACKSON and Sally TYLER, dau. of Judge Charles TYLER. Francis JACKSON was the son of John JACKSON and Miss KENNY Johns JACKSON was a son of Samuel JACKSON, in Stafford County, Virginia, in 1694. Capt. John Farrow JACKSON and Elizabeth Butler GRIGSBY had Mardulia Emma Sybil JACKSON who *m.* William Hayden ENGLISH and had Rosalind ENGLISH who *m.* Dr. Willoughby WALLING and had

ISSUE

I. William English WALLING.
II. Willoughby George WALLING.
III. Mardy Jackson WALLING.

Grigsby

ELIZABETH BUTLER (GRIGSBY) JACKSON, *b.* 7th February, 1791; *m.* 1813; *d.* 2d December, 1878; was dau. of William and Jane (KING) GRIGSBY, of Fauquier County, Virginia, who *m.* in 1786; Jane KING was dau. of George Hales KING and Sarah GARRARD, dau. of William GARRARD, *d.* 1747, and Mary SMITH, dau. of Charles, *d.* 1714, and Ann SMITH of Westmoreland County, Virginia.

King

GEORGE HALES KING, of Prince William County, Virginia, Revolutionary soldier and supposed to have been in Colonial service; son of John KING and Mary HALES, dau. of John HALES, who *d.* 1728, Westmoreland County, Virginia, William GRIGSBY, *b.* 1760, son of Nathaniel GRIGSBY, Loudoun County, Virginia, *d.* 1801, Kentucky, and Elizabeth BUTLER, dau. of William BUTLER and Anne (?) MASON. Nathaniel GRIGSBY, son of James Redmond GRIGSBY, will 1752, and Susannah of Stafford County, son of John GRIGSBY, I, of Stafford, *d.* 1729, son of John GRIGSBY and Jane ROSSER of England and Virginia.

Jackson

CAPT. JOHN FARROW JACKSON, *b.* 15th March, 1788; was the son of Samuel JACKSON, of Prince William County, Virginia, *d.* 1815, and Mary FARROW, *b.* 1759, dau. of Isaac and Ann (SCOTT) FARROW. Isaac FARROW *d.* 1804, Prince William County, Virginia. Isaac FARROW was the son of Abraham and Sybil FARROW, *d.* 1741. Abraham FARROW was son of Abraham FARROW, in Stafford County, 1694.

SAMUEL JACKSON was son of Francis JACKSON, of Prince William County, *d.* 1782, and Sallie TYLER, dau. of Judge Charles TYLER.

FRANCIS JACKSON was son of John JACKSON of Stafford, 1738, and Miss KENNY.

JOHN JACKSON was son of Samuel JACKSON, in Stafford, 1694.

William English Walling Descent

CASPAR DILLER, of Alsace, and Barbara, of England, had Philip Adam DILLER of Pfalz, Germany, who *m.* Elizabeth ELLMAKER, dau. of Leonard ELLMAKER, of Germany, and had Leonard DILLER, of Lancaster County, Pennsylvania, who *m.* Mary Magdalena HINKLE and had Jeremiah DILLER of Louisville, Kentucky, who *m.* Elizabeth ABLE, dau. of Joseph ABLE of London and Catherine HARTLEY of Maryland, dau. of John HARTLEY and had Ellen M. DILLER, who *m.* Dr. George H. WALLING, son of Capt. Henry M. R. WALLING of Maryland, and Sarah CAKE, and had Dr. Willoughby WALLING, who *m.* Rosalind ENGLISH, and had

DR. WILLOUGHBY WALLING, *b.* 3d March, 1848; *d.* 28th November, 1916, in Chicago; only son of Dr. George Henry WALLING, a man of great courage, integrity and ability, a Mason, elected twenty times Master of his Lodge, and a prominent physician of Louisville, Kentucky, and Ellen Maria DILLER, *b.* 17th May, 1825, *d.* 20th July, 1886, dau. of Capt. Jeremiah DILLER; was educated in Louisville, London and Vienna and was Professor of Anatomy in the University of Louisville, President of the Louisville Medical Society; President of Pendennis Club, a leading social organization; delegate to National Democratic Convention in 1880; head of wholesale drug house of WALLING and Company; United States Consul to Edinboro, Scotland, under CLEVELAND; Professor of Laryngology and Rhinology, Post Graduate Medical School; and practiced specialty of Throat, Nose and Ear in Chicago, until retirement from ill health. Dr. George H. WALLING, *b.* 29th February, 1820, in Canton, Ohio, *d.* 23d August, 1893, in Louisville, Kentucky, and Dr. Willoughby WALLING (the first), *b.* 28th May, 1818, in Lexington, Kentucky, were sons of Capt. Henry Mesel Reid WALLING, in war of 1812, and Sarah CAKE of Washington County, Maryland, dau. of Henry CAKE, Revolutionary soldier and Catherine MILLER, only dau. of John MILLER, *d.* about 1787. Capt. Henry Mesel Reid WALLING, *b.* 23d March, 1788, was a son of John WALLING, Revolutionary soldier of Frederick County, Maryland, and Susannah REID, dau. of Dorothy Roher and John Reid of Pennsylvania, Commissary in Revolution. John WALLING was the son of John WALLING, descendant of George WALLING, Burgess, Isle of Wight, Virginia, 1663, and Ann MAYHEW, dau. of Elizabeth and Joseph MAYHEW, *d.* 1763, of Frederick County, Maryland. The WALLINGS were in Virginia as early as 1634 and came from the border between Scotland and England.

CAPTAIN JEREMIAH DILLER, *b.* Lancaster County, Pennsylvania, 1786; *d.* 16th April, 1869, aged eighty-three; son of Leonard DILLER, *b.* 1759, *d.* 1798, and Mary Magdalena HINKLE, of Hinkletown, Pennsylvania, went to Kentucky about 1805, was in the first Council, and was one of the first trustees of Louisville, and was a large steamboat owner. He *m.* Elizabeth ABEL, dau. of Joseph ABEL, born in London, 1752, son of Joseph and Deborah (BURTON) ABEL, who came to America as a boy, *m.* Catherine HARTLEY, *b.* 1772, of Frederick, Washington County, Maryland, and became a Kentucky pioneer. He *d.* at Middletown, Kentucky, 22d July, 1848, in his ninety-fourth year. Leonard DILLER was son of Philip Adam DILLER, *b.* in the Palatinate near Heidelberg, Germany, 8th March, 1723; *d.* 8th September, 1777, in Pennsylvania; *m.* Elizabeth ELLMAKER, *b.* 1727, *d.* 1807, dau. of Leonard ELLMAKER of Germany, who was in Earl Township, Lancaster County, Pennsylvania, in 1726. Philip Adam DILLER was a son of Caspar DILLER of Alsace, *b.* 1670–1675, whose Huguenot father, descendant of Michael DILLER, Court Preacher, 1543, fled from Alsace to Holland with his family. Caspar DILLER went to England when between ten and fifteen years of age, *m.* Barbara there, and went later to the Palatinate, where two sons, Philip Adam and Jean (Han) MARTIN were born. He came to America about 1729 and settled on a farm "Loch Platz" near New Holland, Pennsylvania; he *d.* aged about one hundred, between 1770 and 1775. Dr. Willoughby WALLING and Rosalind (ENGLISH) WALLING had

ISSUE

I. WILLIAM ENGLISH WALLING, *b.* 14th March, 1877, the subject of this memoir.
II. Willoughby George WALLING, of Chicago, Illinois; *b.* in Louisville, 23d May, 1878; graduate of Chicago University, 1899; Law Course, Harvard University 1899–1900; Ex-National President Delta Kappa Epsilon Society; Secretary Western Trust and Savings Bank, Chicago; Trust Officer Central Trust Company of Illinois; Director Fletcher Trust Company, Indianapolis; Morris Plan Bank of Chicago; Winnetka State Bank of Winnetka, Illinois; Director, General Civilian

Relief American Red Cross; *m.* at Columbia, South Carolina, 25th December, 1902, Frederika Christina HASKELL, dau. of Judge Alexander Chevis HASKELL, Ex-Judge Supreme Court of South Carolina, who served during the Civil War with rank of General, C. S. A., and Alice (VAN YEVEREN) ALEXANDER.

ISSUE

1. Willoughby Haskell, *b.* 23d April, 1904, in Chicago, Illinois.
2. William English, *b.* 19th April, 1907, in Chicago.
3. Frederika Christina, *b.* 25th November, 1909, in Chicago.
4. Cheves Thompson, *b.* 28th February, 1916, in Chicago.

III. Mardy Jackson WALLING, *b.* 1st July, 1884, at Indianapolis; *d.* 25th January, 1887, at Indianapolis.

Arms (WALLING).—Sable a fesse argent between three roses of the second two, one.
Residence.—Brookside Drive, Greenwich, Connecticut.
Clubs.—City, Civic and Liberal Club of New York.
Societies.—Delta Kappa Epsilon Society; Society of Colonial Wars; American Academy Political and Social Science; American Economic Association.

The Watson Family

Lineages of the Watson, Clark, La Nauze, Washington and Allied Families

THE records of these families include lineages reaching back to generations which participated in many of the most notable events of history. Some of them were present at the Battle of Crecy, others participated with the Barons at Runnymede in securing from the reluctant sovereign, John, that charter of rights and liberties which were perpetuated in the Magna Charta.

These ancestral lines, by intermarriage at a later day, brought to their lines the blood of the WASHINGTONS, revered in the history of this country. Springing from other directions they have touched the lines of the Honorable George READE, "Gentleman," descended from Alfred the Great; the stern old Puritan, Elder BREWSTER, of the Plymouth Colony; of that fine and brave line of classic soldiers, the LEES; of James TAYLOR, Knight of the Golden Horseshoe; of the ERSKINES, of the THORNTONS, the STEVENSONS, the LYNES; the LA NAUZES, representative of the noble-hearted Huguenots, and many others.

In the history here recorded will be found the foundation of a large number of other notable American Colonial families.

Watson

MAJOR ALEXANDER MACKENZIE WATSON, United States Marine Corps; *b.* 4th January, 1883, in Detroit, Michigan; *m.* 2d April, 1913, in Louisville, Kentucky, Jessie (CLARK) STRATER, dau. of James and Jessie (LA NAUZE) CLARK of Louisville, Kentucky and widow of William Edward STRATER, *b.* 28th January, 1866, in Chillicothe, Ohio, *d.* 24th May, 1908, in Jefferson County, Kentucky.

ALEXANDER MACKENZIE WATSON was educated in the public schools and at the Tamalpais Military Academy, San Rafael, California; appointed to the United States Marine Corps from the District of Columbia; commissioned Second Lieutenant 2d April, 1904; promoted to First Lieutenant 31st December 1907; Captain 14th June, 1914; Major 22d May 1917; served afloat and ashore in the United States Pacific Fleet; the United States Atlantic Fleet; the Philippine Islands; the American Legation at Peking, China; Santo Domingo and various posts in the United States. Served in the World War from 6th April, 1917, to 11th December, 1917, on board *U. S. S. Oklahoma*, and from 13th December, 1917, to 4th April, 1918, on board *U. S. S. Utah*, as Aide on the Staff of the D.vision Commander, Sixth Division, U. S. Atlantic Fleet, and from 8th April, 1918, to date of armistice (11th November, 1918) at Headquarters, U. S. Marine Corps, Washington, D. C., as an Assistant Adjutant and Inspector.

Lineage

The founder of this branch of the American family was originally Scotch but removed to Ireland where the immediate ancestor Christopher WATSON was *b.* in County Cavan, Ireland, as also his wife Margaret BOURLAND. Josiah WATSON, gd. son of Christopher and Margaret (BOURLAND) WATSON who was of Pennsylvania and Virginia, was *b.* 15th October, 1748, and *d.* June, 1828, in Washington, D. C. A memorandum in his handwriting states his paternal grandparents were Christopher and Margaret (BOURLAND) WATSON, and his maternal grandparents were Robert and Jane (ROBERTS) COUCH, but does not give the names of his father and mother. In 1771 he laid claim to 300 acres in Cumberland County, Pennsylvania, which had been evacuated to his sister Margaret WATSON, 24th June, 1763. She *d.* unmarried and intestate and her brother Josiah WATSON was granted letters of administration on her estate 25th September 1769; he was then living in Sussex County, New Jersey; *m.* Jane TAYLOR, *b.* 11th August, 1752, *d.* 10th August, 1830, in Washington, D. C., dau. of ———— and Sarah (FINNEY) TAYLOR. Her brothers were Andrew, James and Hugh TAYLOR, whose will was probated in Cumberland

County, Pennsylvania 1st February, 1782. Her sisters were Sarah TAYLOR and Mrs. VANCE. Her uncle, Alexander FINNEY, in his will, probated in Cumberland County, Pennsylvania, 24th January, 1767, left her land in Letterkenny Township in now Franklin County, and constituted Adam HOOPS of Carlisle, Philadelphia and Bucks County, Pennsylvania, Executor of that part of his estate. Adam HOOPS who *d.* in Philadelphia in June, 1771, was *m.* to her aunt, Elizabeth FINNEY, *b.* 1720, *d.* 1782, in Philadelphia, and he, too, left Jane TAYLOR land in Letterkenny Township adjoining the tract left her by her uncle, Alexander FINNEY. The daughters and sons of Adam and Elizabeth (FINNEY) HOOPS were Isabel HOOPS, who *m.* 10th January, 1763, James MEASE, who was *b.* in Strabane, County of Tyrone, Ireland, *d.* June, 1785, in Philadelphia. He was Paymaster and Treasurer of the Continental Army in 1775; appointed in 1777 by WASHINGTON, Clothier-General of the Army; in 1780 he subscribed £5000 to the stock of the bank organized to supply the Army with provisions; his widow, Isabel (HOOPS) MEASE, *m.* (secondly) 8th May, 1788, Jasper MOYLAN of Philadelphia, *b.* in Ireland, son of John MOYLAN and half brother of Stephen MOYLAN, *b.* 1734, Commandant of the American Light Dragoons. Col. Stephen MOYLAN'S mother was the Countess of Limerick, and his wife whom he *m.* 1778, in New Jersey, was Mary Ricketts VAN HORNE, dau. of Col. Philip VAN HORNE. Margaret HOOPS *m.* 16th September, 1772, Thomas WALKER of Virginia, *b.* 1748, son of Dr. Thomas and Mildred (THORNTON) (MERIWETHER) WALKER of Castle Hill. Mildred THORNTON was the dau. of Francis and Mary (TALLIAFERRO) THORNTON and widow of Nicholas MERIWETHER. Jane HOOPS *m.* before 1771 Daniel CLARKE and they moved to New Orleans. Sarah HOOPS, *m.* 1768, Col. John SYME of Virginia, half brother of Patrick HENRY. Mary HOOPS, *m.* 18th October, 1770, Thomas BARCLAY, Consular Agent of the United States in France at the end of the American Revolution. Robert HOOPS a member of the Legislative Council of Sussex County, New Jersey, 1778. David HOOPS of Virginia and Maryland. Maj. Adam HOOPS, United States Army, *b.* 9th January, 1760, at Carlisle, Pennsylvania, *d.* 9th June, 1846 at West Chester, Pennsylvania. ——— WATSON, *m.* ——— COUCH, dau. of Robert and Jane (ROBERTS) COUCH.

ISSUE

I. Margaret, *b.* prior to 1742; *d.* 1769, in Philadelphia.
II. JOSIAH, *b.* 15th October, 1748, of whom below.

JOSIAH WATSON, of Pennsylvania and Virginia, *b.* 12th October, 1748, in Philadelphia (?); *d.* 28th June, 1828, in Washington, D. C., came from Pennsylvania circa 1771; settled at "Turkey Ridge" and later at "Bush Hill" near Alexandria, Virginia; was Postmaster at Alexandria from June, 1814, to April, 1821; was member of the First Presbyterian Church in Alexandria, founded in 1772, and one of the Trustees authorized to raise the funds for completing the church building; a deed recorded 2d of October, 1800, in Alexandria shows he purchased and had issued a patent for 12,687 acres of land in Powell Valley, on Clinch River, Tennessee; besides this he had 35,000 acres of land claimed under Martin ARMSTRONG, in the state of Tennessee; 16,374 acres of military land in Tennessee; 5,063 acres military land, HENDERSON and Company grants, state of Tennessee; 14,519 acres of military land, HENDERSON & Company grants, state of Kentucky; 50,000 in Randolph County, Virginia; land in Shenandoah and Frederick Counties, Virginia, and elsewhere; in all a total of 133,643 acres of land; *m.* 28th June, 1771, in Cumberland County, Pennsylvania, by the Rev. James LANG, of the Falling Spring Presbyterian Church, Jane TAYLOR, dau. of ——— and Sarah (FINNEY) TAYLOR.

ISSUE

1. James, *b.* 7th April, 1772, in Alexandria, Virginia; *d.* 12th October, 1822, in Washington, D. C.; served in the War of 1812 in Col. George MAGRUDER'S 1st Regiment of Infantry, District of Columbia Militia; *m.* 1796, in Fairfax County, Virginia, Elizabeth Courts LOVE, *b.* there 5th October, 1777, *d.* 20th December, 1853, in Washington, D. C., dau. of Samuel LOVE of "Salisbury," Fairfax County, Virginia, *d.* 22d July, 1800, and Anne JONES of "Cleandrinking," Montgomery County, Maryland.

ISSUE

1. Samuel, *b.* 1797, in Alexandria; *d.* in infancy.
2. Jane Love, *b.* 25th December, 1799, in Alexandria; *d.* 20th December, 1869, in Washington, D. C.; *m.* 5th July, 1825, in Washington, D. C., George GRAHAM, who was Secretary of War, 1817, Commander of Fairfax Light Horse in War of 1812, and Commissioner of the General Land Office, he *d.* 9th August, 1830; son of Richard GRAHAM, who *m.* 10th February, 1758, Jennie BRENT, *b.* 10th April, 1738, dau. of George and Catherine (TRIMMINGHAM) BRENT.

ISSUE

1[1]. Jennie Brent GRAHAM, *b.* 9th March, 1826, in Washington, D. C.; *d.* there 1st July, 1899; *m.* there 9th December, 1847, Capt. Henry K. DAVENPORT, United States Navy, *b.* 10th December, 1820, at Savannah, Georgia, *d.* 18th August, 1872, at Franzensbad, Bohemia.

ISSUE

1[2]. Richard Graham DAVENPORT, Commodore, United States Navy; *b.* 11th January, 1849, in Washington, D. C.; *m.* 20th November, 1884, in New York City, Serena Hale GILMAN, *b.* there 10th March, 1856.

2². Thomas Corbin DAVENPORT, First Lieutenant, United States Army; *b.* 11th April, 1850, in Washington, D. C., *d.* there, 6th May, 1887.

3². Jennie Brent DAVENPORT, *d.* in infancy.

4². George Graham DAVENPORT, *b.* 17th March, 1859, in Washington, D. C.; *d.* there 7th December, 1883; unmarried.

2¹. James Watson GRAHAM, *b.* 3d September, 1827, in Washington, D. C.; *d.* there 5th July, 1832.

3¹. George Richard GRAHAM, *b.* 14th November, 1829, in Washington, D. C.; *d.* there 25th July, 1889.

3. Andrew Jackson, *b.* 1802, at the "Hermitage," the home of Gen. Andrew JACKSON, in Tennessee; was Purser in the United States Navy; lost on the *U. S. S. Levant,* 1860.

4. James Muir, *b.* 1803, in Alexandria, Virginia; *d.* 17th April, 1873, at Mare Island Navy Yard, California; Commodore United States Navy; *m.* at Pensacola Navy Yard, Flo CROSBY, dau. of Paymaster CROSBY, United States Navy, who *m.* Theresa ROBERGAT.

ISSUE

1¹. Zelie, *b.* in Pensacola; *m.* Otway Calvert BERRYMAN, Colonel, United States Marine Corps.

5. Harriet Love, *b.* 1805, at "Buckland," Prince William County, Virginia; *d.* 1883, in Ripon, Wisconsin; *m.* 1834, in Washington, D. C., John Scott HORNER, *b.* 5th December, 1802, in Warrenton, Virginia, *d.* 3d February, 1883, in Ripon, Wisconsin, appointed by President JACKSON in 1835 Secretary, and Acting Governor of Michigan, including the territories of Wisconsin and Iowa; had issue.

6. Mary Eleanor, *b.* 1806, in Alexandria; *d.* unmarried, 1865, in Washington, D. C.

7. Elizabeth Love, *b.* 1807, in Alexandria; *d.* unmarried, 1886, in Washington, D. C.

8. Fanny, *b.* in Alexandria, *d.* in infancy.

9. John, *b.* 1811, in Alexandria; was a Cadet at West Point from which place he disappeared when about nineteen years of age.

10. Olivia M., *b.* 1812, in Alexandria; *d.* unmarried, 1888, in Washington, D. C.

11. William Henry, *b.* 8th January, 1814, in Washington, D. C.; *d.* unmarried, 1st March, 1868.

12. Josiah, *b.* 1816, in Washington, D. C.; *d.* 5th February, 1864; Major United States Marine Corps; served in the Mexican and Civil Wars; *m.* 6th November, 1856, in Philadelphia, Abbie MURDOCH, *b.* in Plymouth County, Massachusetts.

ISSUE

1[1]. Warren Murdoch, *b.* 19th February, 1861, in Brooklyn, New York.

II. Elizabeth, *b.* 5th October, 1773, in Alexandria; *m.* John LOVE, of "Buckland," Prince William County, Virginia, son of Samuel LOVE of "Buckland," *d.* April, 1785, and half brother of Samuel LOVE of "Salisbury," Fairfax County, Virginia, *d.* 22d July, 1800.
III. JOHN, *b.* 31st March, 1775, of whom later.
IV. Robert, *b.* 17th February, 1777, in Alexandria, Virginia, *d.* in infancy.
V. Josiah, Jr., *b.* 9th August, 1778, in Alexandria, Virginia; *d.* unmarried, in Frankfort, Kentucky, after 1821; was a graduate of Princeton College, New Jersey.
VI. Robert, *b.* 19th September, 1779, in Alexandria, Virginia; *d.* after 1799.
VII. Andrew, *b.* July, 1781, in Alexandria; went South when grown and nothing further known of him.
VIII. Sarah, *b.* 1785, in Alexandria; *d.* unmarried, 1868, in Washington, D. C.
IX. William Henry, Lieutenant United States Navy; *b.* circa 1789, in Alexandria, Virginia; *d.* 13th September, 1823, at Key West, Florida, while in command of the corvette *John Adams*; in the summer of 1823 while in command of the barges *Gallinipper* and *Musquito* he captured the celebrated pirate Diableto; was Lieutenant on the *Argus* when she was compelled to surrender and was imprisoned for awhile at Yarmouth, England; he *d.* unmarried.
X. Jane, *b.* in Alexandria; *d.* 1805, at "Potomac Hill," Virginia; *m.* Capt. James V. (?) BALL; leaving a son.

ISSUE

1. John L. BALL, United States Navy.

DR. JOHN WATSON, of Frankfort, Kentucky; *b.* 31st March, 1775, in Alexandria Virginia; *d.* 12th April, 1821, in Frankfort, Kentucky; *m.* 28th July, 1804, at "Cove Spring," near Winchester, Frederick County, Virginia, Ann Bannister HOWE, *b.* 20th September, 1785, in Frederick County, Virginia, *d.* 1835, at Frankfort, Kentucky, dau. of Capt. Edward HOWE, an officer in the Revolutionary War, in Capt. Henry LEE's Light Horse Brigade, *b.* 1743 in Virginia, *d.* 1823, near Versailles, Kentucky, he *m.* Ann LYNE, *b.* in King and Queen County, Virginia, *d.* in Frankfort, Kentucky, dau of Col. William LYNE, *b.* 1737 in King and Queen County, Virginia, *d.* 27th September, 1808, near Dunkirk, Virginia, and his wife Lucy Foster LYNE, who was also his first cousin. Col. William LYNE was an officer in the Revolutionary War; Member of the Committee of Safety, King and Queen County, 1775; Burgess for same county, 1769, 1770 and 1771. Ann Bannister HOWE, *m.* (secondly) 4th January, 1824, Col. John BUFORD, by whom she also had issue.

ISSUE

I. Jane Love, *b.* 28th May, 1806, at Frankfort, Kentucky; *d.* there 10th July, 1890; *m.* Philip SWIGERT who *d.* 31st December, 1871.

ISSUE

1. Mary SWIGERT, *m.* Rev. Mr. HENDRICK, of Frankfort, Kentucky; had issue.
II. Anne, *b.* 1st July, 1808, in Frankfort, Kentucky; *d.* 18th September, 1829, at Versailles, Kentucky; *m.* there 1st February, 1825, William BARR, *b.* 4th April, 1796, in Fayette, Kentucky, *d.* 5th June, 1844, in Mississippi, son of Thomas BARR, Jr., *b.* in Pennsylvania, *d.* in Kentucky, *m.* 25th March, 1776, Mary Toland BARCLAY of Philadelphia, Pennsylvania.

ISSUE

1. John Watson BARR, United States District Judge for Kentucky; *b.* 17th December, 1826, at Versailles; *d.* 31st December, 1907, in Louisville, Kentucky; *m.* 23d November, 1859, Susan Preston ROGERS, dau. of Jason and Josephine (PRESTON) ROGERS.

ISSUE

1^1. Anna Watson BARR.
2^1. John Watson BARR, Jr., *m.* Margaret McFERRAN.
3^1. Caroline Hancock Preston BARR, *m.* Morton Venable JOYES.
4^1. Susan Rogers BARR, *m.* Edward J. McDERMOTT.
5^1. Jason Rogers BARR, *m.* Elizabeth Nelson WOOD.
6^1. Josephine Preston BARR, *m.* John B. McFERRAN.
7^1. Elise Rogers BARR, m. William Wallace McDowell.

III. Elizabeth, *b.* 17th December, 1809, at Frankfort, Kentucky; *d. s. p.*, 1827; *m.* ——— MOORE.
IV. Rebecca, *b.* 16th January, 1812, at Frankfort, Kentucky.
V. EDWARD HOWE, *b.* 27th February, 1814, of whom later.
VI. John, *b.* 21st April, 1817, at Frankfort; *d.* 24th September, 1882; *m.* 14th November, 1844, Sallie Ann RODES, *b.* 1st September, 1825, *d.* 20th October, 1890, dau. of William RODES, *b.* 24th February, 1794, *d.* 17th October, 1877, and his wife, Pauline Green CLAY, *b.* 7th September, 1802, *d.* 1886.

1. Pauline Clay, *b.* 22d January, 1846; *m.* 26th July, 1881, Rev. Robert CHRISTIE.

ISSUE

1¹. John Watson CHRISTIE.
2¹. Robert Dobbie CHRISTIE.
3¹. Mary Rodes CHRISTIE.

2. Philip Swigert, *b.* 12th October, 1847; *d.* young.
3. Adaline Crittenden, *b.* 8th October, 1849; *m.* 25th December, 1873, Knox BROWN.

ISSUE

1¹. Pauline BROWN, *m.* Rev. Hugh LEITH.
2¹. John BROWN.
3¹. Knox BROWN.
4¹. Rodes BROWN.
5¹. Joseph Bailey BROWN.

4. William Rodes, *b.* 8th October, 1851; *m.* 10th March, 1901, Nellie BONSALL.
5. Henry Howe, *b.* 30th December, 1853; *d.* 20th August, 1897; *m.* 7th December, 1882, Charlotte E. SMITH.

ISSUE

1¹. George C.
2¹. Jane, *m.* Frank CLAY.
3¹. Rebecca, *m.* Rev. William BYERS.
4¹. Charlotte.

6. John, Jr., *b.* 22nd October, 1857; *d.* unmarried, 23rd December, 1877.
7. Eliza, *b.* 21st May, 1859; *d.* 8th March, 1901; *m.* 25th March, 1886, William MCEWAN.

ISSUE

1¹. Sallie Rodes MCEWAN.
2¹. William MCEWAN.

8. Dudley, *b.* 10th July, 1861.

VII. William Henry, *b.* 23d April, 1820, at Frankfort, Kentucky; *d.* there; *m.* Elizabeth Ann TODD, dau. of John Harris TODD, who *m.* his first cousin, Maria Knox INNES, *d.* 1851, and gd. dau. of Judge Thomas TODD of the United States Supreme Court, who *m.* Elizabeth HARRIS, dau. of John and Hannah (STEWART) HARRIS, she dau. of Charles STEWART.

ISSUE

1. Kate C., *b.* 7th August, 1849; *m.* Henry Lyne STARLING, *b.* 23d August, 1848.
2. Maria Innes, *m.* Joseph W. LINDSEY.
3. Lina, *m.* Robin Alexander WALLER of Chicago.

DR. EDWARD HOWE WATSON, *b.* 27th February, 1814, in Frankfort, Kentucky; *d.* there 7th April, 1868; *m.* (firstly) Louisa F. HICKMAN, *b.* 23d July, 1815, *d. s. p.* 29th April, 1837; *m.* (secondly) 1st October, 1840, in Frankfort, Kentucky, Sarah Lee CRITTENDEN, *b.* 8th January, 1821, in Frankfort, Kentucky, *d.* 27th March, 1887, while on a visit in Danville, Kentucky, dau. of Gov. John Jordan CRITTENDEN, *b.* 10th September, 1787, in Woodford County, Kentucky, *d.* 26th July, 1863, in Frankfort, Kentucky, *m.* there in 1811, Sallie O. LEE, *b.* in Woodford County, Kentucky, *d.* 1824, in Frankfort, Kentucky. Governor CRITTENDEN was a graduate of William and Mary College, Virginia, class of 1806; was Attorney General of the territory of Illinois in 1809–1810; served in the campaigns of the War of 1812 as aide to General RAMSEY, in the expedition commanded by General HOPKINS, and as Aide on the Staff of Gov. Isaac SHELBY, whose report of the Battle of the Thames praises his conspicuous gallantry; he was often a Representative in the Kentucky Legislature and was four times elected Speaker of that body; was Secretary of State and Governor of Kentucky, 1850–1853; Representative in Congress, 1861–1863 and author of the Crittenden Compromise; was four times Senator of the United States and twice Attorney General; he *m.* (secondly) Mrs. Maria Knox (INNES) TODD, who *d.* 1851, dau. of Judge Harry INNES of Kentucky and his second wife, Mrs. Ann (HARRIS) SHIELDS. His third wife, whom he *m.* 3d February, 1853, was Mrs. Elizabeth (Moss) (WILCOX) ASHLEY, *b.* 1804, *d.* 1873, dau. of Dr. James W. Moss and widow, first of Dr. Daniel P. WILCOX, and next of Gen. William H. ASHLEY, who *d.* 1838. Maj. John CRITTENDEN, father of Governor CRITTENDEN, was *b.* circa 1750, in Virginia, *d.* 1805, in Kentucky; *m.* 21st August, 1783, in Powhatan County, Virginia, Judith HARRIS, *b.* in Cumberland County, Virginia, *d.* in Kentucky, dau. of Col. John HARRIS, of "Norwood," in now Powhatan County, *b.* 1732, in Virginia, *d.* 19th November, 1800, at "Norwood," *m.* 24th August, 1754, in Cumberland County, Obedience TURPIN, *b.* in Goochland County, Virginia, dau. of Thomas TURPIN *d.* 1790, and Mary JEFFERSON, who was the aunt of President Thomas JEFFERSON. John CRITTENDEN was Major of the Virginia State Line and Lieutenant in the Virginia Continental Army in the War of the Revolution; Member of the Committee of West Fincastle to the Convention of Virginia, 20th June, 1776; representative from Fayette County in the Virginia House of Burgesses, 1783–1784; Original Member of the Cincinnati; his son Robert CRITTENDEN was Governor of Arkansas; his son Thomas T. CRITTENDEN was Secretary of State for Kentucky and a distinguished Judge; his son Henry CRITTENDEN was the father of Thomas T. CRITTENDEN, Governor of Missouri and of William Logan CRITTENDEN, Captain United States Army, shot by Spaniards in Cuba in 1851. Maj. John LEE, father of Sallie (LEE) CRITTENDEN, was *b.* 20th September, 1742, in Fauquier County, Virginia; *d.* 1802, in Woodford County, Kentucky; *m.* 18th December, 1781, in Orange County, Virginia, Elizabeth BELL, *b.* there, *d.* in Kentucky, dau. of Capt. Thomas BELL of Orange County, where he *d.* 4th October, 1795; Captain BELL was a member of GRAYSON's Additional Continental Regiment and one of the Original Members of the Cincinnati; his wife was Elizabeth TAYLOR, *b.* circa 1740, dau. of Zachary TAYLOR of Orange County, and his wife Elizabeth LEE, *b.* 1709 (twin), sister of Hancock LEE, II. Maj. John LEE, son of Hancock and Mary (WILLIS) LEE, II, was Captain in the Continental and Major in the Virginia State Line and a Member of the Cincinnati in Virginia. Mary WILLIS *b.* 1716; *d.* 4th December, 1766, was the dau. of Col. John WILLIS, *d.* 1740, of Fredericksburg, Virginia and Anne ALEXANDER.

ISSUE

I. JOHN CRITTENDEN, *b.* 24th August, 1842, of whom later.
II. Jane Swigert, *b.* 1844, in Frankfort, Kentucky, *d.* there, unmarried, 1892.
III. George Crittenden, *b.* 28th August, 1846, in Frankfort, Kentucky; *m.* Corinne QUIGLEY.

ISSUE

1. Thomas Quigley.
2. Edward Howe.
3. Belle Quigley.
4. William P.
5. George Crittenden.
6. Eleanor Quigley.
7. Robert Waller.

IV. Anne Innes, *b.* in Frankfort, Kentucky; *m.* 1874, Edmund H. TAYLOR, *b.* 1845, son of Thomas Hart TAYLOR, *b.* 1825

ISSUE

1. Sarah Crittenden TAYLOR.
2. Thomas H. TAYLOR.
3. Edmund B. TAYLOR.
4. Adeline C. TAYLOR.

REAR ADMIRAL JOHN CRITTENDEN WATSON, *b.* 24th August, 1842, in Frankfort, Kentucky; appointed to United States Naval Academy from Kentucky, 1856; graduated 1860; promoted Midshipman, 15th June, 1860. Among his various duties he served in Western Gulf Blockading Squadron, 1862–1864; participated in bombardment and passage of Forts Jackson and St. Philips and Chalmette batteries June–July, 1862; served as Flag Lieutenant to Admiral David Glasgow FARRAGUT during operations in Mississippi River and the Battle of Mobile Bay, 5th August, 1864; passage of Port Hudson, 14th March, 1863; passage of Grand Gulf, 19th and 30th March, 1863; served in European Squadron 1865–1869; Commanded a Division of North Atlantic Fleet, May–September, 1898, during war with Spain; Commander-in-Chief, Eastern Squadron, July, 1898, to threaten coast of Spain and reinforce DEWEY's Fleet; Commander-in-Chief United States Asiatic Fleet, 1899–1900, as the relief of Admiral George DEWEY; Naval Representative to the Coronation of Edward VII of England, 1902; *m.* 29th May, 1873, in San Francisco, California, Elizabeth Anderson THORNTON, *b.* 27th May, 1850, at Eutaw, Alabama, dau. of James Dabney THORNTON, Judge of the Supreme Court of California, who was *b.* 18th January, 1823, at "Oak Hill," Cumberland County, Virginia, *d.* 25th September, 1902, in San Francisco, where he had moved in 1854; from Virginia he went first to Eutaw, Alabama, where he *m.* 17th February, 1848, Sarah Frances THORNTON. Judge James Dabney THORNTON was the son of William Mynn THORNTON, *b.* 1773 at "May Fair," Hanover County, Virginia, *d.* 1856, in Cumberland County, and Elizabeth ANDERSON, dau. of Samuel ANDERSON of Cumberland County, *b.* 25th June, 1757, at "Gold Mine," Hanover County, Virginia, *d.* 24th February, 1826, and his wife Ann DABNEY. He was the gd. son of Col. John THORNTON of Hanover County and Sarah THRUSTON, his wife, *b.* 1743, at "Landsdowne," Gloucester County, Virginia. Sarah Frances THORNTON, *b.* 31st July, 1825, at Huntsville, Alabama; *d.* May, 1904, in San Francisco, California, was the dau. of Judge Harry Innes THORNTON, *b.* 3d April, 1797, at "Fall Hill," Fredericksburg, Virginia, *d.* 1867, in San Francisco and his wife Lucy CRITTENDEN, *b.* 3d October, 1803, in Woodford County, Kentucky, *d.* 25th December, 1885, in San Francisco, *m.* 1824 in Kentucky, sister of Gov. John Jordan CRITTENDEN. Judge Harry Innes THORNTON was the son of Francis THORNTON of "Fall Hill," and Sally INNES, and after his mother's death in 1807 was brought up by his grandfather, Judge Harry INNES of Kentucky. In 1823 he moved to Huntsville, Alabama; he was appointed by John Quincy ADAMS, Federal District Attorney; elected to the Supreme Court Bench of Alabama; State Senator in Alabama for three years; appointed Commissioner of Lands, California, 1849 to 1862; Judge of the Court of Claims, San Francisco.

ISSUE

I. Edward Howe, Captain United States Navy; *b.* 28th February, 1874, in Frankfort, Kentucky; *m.* 20th October, 1909, in St. Louis, Missouri, Hermine GRATZ, *b.* 1884, dau. of Benjamin and Caroline Clifford (BRYAN) GRATZ.

ISSUE

1. Clifford Bryan, *b.* 13th July, 1914, at Newport, Rhode Island.

II. James Thornton, Lieutenant-Colonel, United States Army; *b.* 25th April, 1875, Mare Island Navy Yard, California, *m.* 22d February, 1917, in New York City, Marie SINCLAIR.

III. Ann Mary, *b.* 15th September, 1876, at Mare Island Navy Yard, San Francisco, California.

IV. John Jordan Crittenden, in the United States Consular Service; *b.* 18th February, 1878, at Frankfort, Kentucky; *m.* 3d October, 1917, in Yarmouth, Nova Scotia, Mary Gertrude SEELEY, *b.* 27th September, 1892, at Yarmouth, Nova Scotia, only child of Col. Thomas Melville SEELEY, of Nova Scotia, *b.* at Argyle, Nova Scotia, 20th July, 1864, and Joanna ARCHIBALD, *b.* 31st March, 1865, at Stewiacke, Colchester County, Nova Scotia.

ISSUE

1. John Crittenden, *b.* 28th July, 1918.

V. Lucy Crittenden, *b.* 20th May, 1879, in Frankfort, Kentucky, *d.* young.
VI. Sarah Thornton, *b.* 7th April, 1881, at Detroit, Michigan.
VII. ALEXANDER MACKENZIE, *b.* 4th January, 1883, the subject of this memoir.
VIII. David Loyall Farragut, *b.* 25th June, 1885, Brooklyn Navy Yard, New York; *m.* 30th April, 1919, in Little Rock, Arkansas, Florence LEIGH.

Arms (WATSON of Scotland).—Argent on a mount vert an oak tree inclining to the sinister ppr. acorned or, debruised by a fesse azure.

Crest.—Two arms issuing from clouds, holding the stump of a tree fructed at the top, with branches on each side, all ppr.

Residence.—Stoneleigh Court, Washington, D. C.

Clubs.—Chevy Chase, and Army and Navy of Washington, D. C., and Pendennis of Louisville, Kentucky.

Societies.—Colonial Wars and Sons of the American Revolution of Kentucky, and Sons of the Revolution of the District of Columbia; Society of the Cincinnati, and the Order of Runnemede.

Arms (Lee).—Gules a fesse chequy azure and or, between ten billets argent, four in chief, three, two and one in base.

Crest.—On a staff raguly, lying fessways, a squirrel sejant proper, cracking a nut; from the dexter end of the staff a hazel branch vert, fructed or.

Motto.—Non Incautus Futuri.

Arms (Erskine).—Argent, a pale sable.
Crest.—A cubit arm grasping a club all proper.

Arms (Thruston).—Sable three bugle horns argent stringed or, garnished azure.
Crest.—A heron argent.
Motto.—Esse Quam Videri.

Arms (Innes).—Argent three estoiles with a bordure, chigney of the first and second.
Crest.—A branch of palm slipped, proper.
Motto.—Ornatur Radix Fronde.

Arms (Willis).—Argent, three griffins passant sable, a bordure engrailed gules bezantee.
Crest.—A griffin rampant upholding palewise a spear.

Arms (Thornton).—Argent, a chevron sable between three hawthorn trees proper.
Crest.—Out of a ducal coronet or, a lion's head proper.

Arms (Anderson).—Or, on a chevron gules between three hawks' heads, erased sable, as many acorns slipped vert.
Crest.—An eagle's head erased argent, holding in the beak palewise an arrow gules, headed and feathered or.
Motto.—Nil desperandum auspice Deo.

Arms (Taylor).—Quarterly first and fourth argent, on a chief sable, two boars' heads of the field, couped, second, argent, a chevron, between three greyhounds, courant, proper, third, argent, a chevron ermine, between three mullets, gules.
Crest.—A naked arm couped at the shoulder embowed, holding an arrow proper.
Motto.—Consequitur quod cunque petit.

Arms (Lyne).—Gules, three bucks' heads, or, on a chief argent, two griffins' heads couped, sable.
Crest.—A demi-griffin, sable.

Clark—La Nauze

ROBERT CLARK of the "Shitterflat," Renfrewshire, Scotland; *m.* post 1682, Janet (MUIR) MONTGOMERY, dau. of William MUIR, of Bruntwood, and widow of Matthew MONTGOMERY of the Bogstone, whom she *m.* in 1682.

ISSUE (AMONG OTHERS)

1. WILLIAM CLARK, *b.* at the "Shitterflat," latter part of the seventeenth century; *m.* (firstly) Margaret SIMPSON, dau. of William SIMPSON of "Willowyard;" *m.* (thirdly) surname not given.

   ISSUE BY FIRST MARRIAGE

   1. Mary, *m.* 1740, John DUNLOP, Eighth Laird of Borland; had issue.

   ISSUE AMONG OTHERS BY THIRD MARRIAGE

   1. WILLIAM CLARK, eldest son, *b.* at the "Shitterflat," 1730; *m.* (firstly) (name not given); *m.* (secondly) (name not given); *m.* (thirdly) 1763 Marian GILMOUR, *b.* 24th November, 1731, dau. of John and Agnes (ANDERSON) GILMOUR, they *m.* 11th January, 1723; John GILMOUR was son of Thomas and Marian (STIRLING) GILMOUR, who were *m.* in 1702.

      ISSUE (AMONG OTHERS)

      1. William, only son, *b.* at the "Shitterflat," 1764; *d.* there 10th June, 1812; *m.* 1793, Janet KERR, *b.* 12th April, 1775, *d.* 8th March, 1796, dau. of Hugh and Jean (STERROT) KERR, *m.* in 1752. Hugh KERR was son of Hugh and Mary (WILSON) KERR, *m.* in 1728.

ISSUE

1². **William Clark**, of the "Shitterflat," Renfrewshire, Scotland; *b.* there 27th September, 1794; emigrated with his family to Ontario, Canada, in 1837, becoming one of the first settlers of Scarboro, at which place he was for many years identified with the inception and execution of all public enterprises. When but a young man he was ordained to the Eldership of the Relief Church of Scotland (Presbyterian) in which office his father served before him; his son and gd. son were associated with him in the Session of the Knox Church, Scarboro, at the time of his death, which occurred 20th July, 1881; *m.* 15th April, 1814, in Scotland, Isabella Stevenson, *b.* 28th October, 1794; *d.* at Scarboro, 20th May, 1848, she, dau. of Robert and Margaret (Cochrane) Stevenson, *b.* 1764, *m.* 20th June, 1787. Robert Stevenson was the son of Robert and Margaret (Burns) Stevenson. Margaret Cochrane was the dau. of Robert and Isabella (Burns) Cochrane, *b.* at "Ladyland."

ISSUE

1³. William, *b.* 4th December, 1814; *d.* 9th June, 1888; *m.* Helen Crawford.

ISSUE

1⁴. William.
2⁴. John.
3⁴. Robert.
4⁴. Margaret.
5⁴. Isabella.
6⁴. James.
7⁴. David.

2³. Robert, *b.* 1st April, 1816; drowned in the Ohio River, 1861.
3³. Margaret, *b.* 29th March, 1818; *d.* May 1st, 1888; *m.* Samuel Kennedy.

ISSUE

1⁴. Samuel Kennedy.
2⁴. Isabella Kennedy.
3⁴. Robert Kennedy.
4⁴. William Kennedy.
5⁴. Ellen Kennedy, *m.* John Green.
6⁴. John Kennedy, *m.*

ISSUE (AMONG OTHERS)

1⁵. William Thomson KENNEDY, Captain Canadian Army Medical Corps; *m.* 7th August, 1918, in Milwaukee, Wisconsin, Janet Gordon CAMP.

4³. Janet, *b.* 18th December, 1819; *d.* 10th March, 1887 *m.* William GEORGE.

ISSUE

1⁴. James GEORGE, D.D.
2⁴. Isabella GEORGE.
3⁴. Janet GEORGE, deceased; *m.* circa 1876, in Glasgow, Scotland, John DAVIDSON.

ISSUE

1⁵. Robert DAVIDSON, *b.* 1877, in Bearsden, Scotland.
2⁵. Janet Clark DAVIDSON, *b.* October, 1886, in Bearsden, Scotland; *m.* 24th July, 1918, William McDOUGALL.

4⁴. William GEORGE, D.D.
5⁴. Robert GEORGE, *b.* in Scotland, 2d February, 1853; *m.* 13th September, 1892, Julia LOVING, *b.* 6th November, 1870.

ISSUE

1⁵. Julia Courtenay GEORGE, *b.* 24th July, 1896.
2⁵. Robert Clark GEORGE, *b.* 17th November, 1907.

6⁴. Lizzie GEORGE, *m.* 1886, at Bowling, Scotland, Charles SCOTT.

ISSUE

1⁵. William SCOTT.
2⁵. James SCOTT.
3⁵. Janet Clark SCOTT, *m.* 20th September, 1917, Alexander MACGREGOR.
4⁵. Charlotte SCOTT.
5⁵. Charles SCOTT.

7⁴. Peter GEORGE, *m.* (firstly) Nannie PHELPS, deceased of Nitta Yuma; Mississippi; *m.* (secondly) May ANKENY, of Minneapolis, Minnesota; no issue.

ISSUE BY FIRST MARRIAGE

1⁵. Alonzo Phelps GEORGE, *b.* 1898.
2⁵. Nannie GEORGE, *d.* in infancy.

5³. Isabella, *b.* 20th December, 1821; *d.* 11th June, 1906; *m.* William YOUNG.

ISSUE

1⁴. William YOUNG, *m.* and has issue.
2⁴. Isabella YOUNG, *d.*
3⁴. James YOUNG, *d.*
4⁴. Marian YOUNG, *d.*; *m.* and left issue.
5⁴. Margaret YOUNG, *d.*
6⁴. John YOUNG, *m.* (firstly) Margaret McCOWAN.

ISSUE BY FIRST MARRIAGE

1⁵. William YOUNG.
2⁵. Clark YOUNG.

6³. John Stevenson, *b.* 23rd December, 1823; *d.* 25th October, 1848.
7³. David, *b.* 27th September, 1825; *d.* 27th February, 1900; *m.* 24th August, 1865, Georgina LA NAUZE, *b.* October, 1840, Ellichpur, India.

ISSUE

1⁴. Agnes Parry, *b.* in Henderson, Kentucky, September, 1866; *m.* there, 18th December, 1895, James Whittle CLARKE, *b.* in Virginia, 1852.
2⁴. Isabel Stevenson, *b.* in Henderson, Kentucky, April 1868.
3⁴. David, Jr., *b.* in Henderson, Kentucky, 10th June, 1869; *m.* there 11th November, 1896, Julia Ballard DIXON, *b.* 29th August, 1871, in Henderson, Kentucky, dau. of Archibald DIXON, M.D., who *m.* Margaret HERNDON.

ISSUE

1⁵. David Henderson, *b.* 25th February, 1899; Ensign, United States Navy, June, 1918.
2⁵. Archibald Dixon, *b.* 26th March, 1901.

4⁴. Christiana Parry, *b.* in Henderson, Kentucky, 23d April, 1872; *m.* there, 15th February, 1916, William Hopkins STITES, *b.* 3d June, 1862.

5⁴. William, *b.* 1st October, 1874; *d.* 17th September, 1895.
6⁴. Jessie La Nauze, *b.* in Henderson, Kentucky, 16th January, 1876; *m.* in Santa Barbara, California, 1st December, 1908, William Rankin MARRS, *b.* in Henderson, Kentucky, 4th July, 1873.

ISSUE

1⁵. Paul Rankin MARRS, *b.* 17th March, 1914.

7⁴. Margaret Annette (twin), *b.* in Henderson, Kentucky, 16th October, 1878; *m.* there, 1900, Campbell Housman JOHNSON, M.D., *b.* 1870.

ISSUE

1⁵. Georgina La Nauze ("Nina") JOHNSON, *b.* 1st January, 1902; *d.* in Paducah, Kentucky, 20th February, 1914.

8⁴. Georgina La Nauze (twin), *b.* in Henderson, Kentucky, 16th October, 1878; *m.* there, December, 1903, Robert BRODIE, M.D., *b.* in Owensboro, Kentucky, 1875.

ISSUE

1⁵. Robert BRODIE, *b.* 2d December, 1904.
2⁵. David Clark BRODIE, *b.* November, 1906, in Henderson, Kentucky.

9⁴. James, *b.* in Henderson, Kentucky, July, 1883; *d.* there, September, 1883.

8³. Hugh, *b.* 11th June, 1827; *d.* 21st September, 1891; *m.* Elizabeth CRAWFORD.

ISSUE

1⁴. William, *m.*
2⁴. Margaret, *d.*
3⁴. Isabella.
4⁴. Elizabeth.
5⁴. John.
6⁴. Hugh, *m.*
7⁴. Janet, *m.*

9[3]. Marion, *b.* 1828; *d.* in infancy.
10[3]. James, *b.* 28th June, 1830, of whom below.
11[3]. Andrew, *b.* 19th September, 1832; *d.* 20th July, 1862; *m.* Mary DIXON.

ISSUE

1[4]. Mary Dixon, *m.* Thomas Woodbridge BUCKNER.

ISSUE

1[5]. Mary Clark BUCKNER, *m.* and has issue.

12[3]. Walter Symington, *b.* 12th November, 1836; *d.* 30th April, 1857.

JAMES CLARK, of Louisville, Kentucky; *b.* 28th June, 1830, in Renfrewshire, Scotland, at the "Shitterflat," which estate has been in possession of his ancestors for more than three hundred years; *d.* 27th April, 1902, at his residence, 1114 Third Avenue, Louisville, Kentucky; at the age of seven came with his parents to Canada; in 1848, engaged in tobacco business in Pittsburgh, Pennsylvania, removing to Louisville, Kentucky, two years later, where, in 1850, he became one of its pioneer buyers, rehandlers and exporters of leaf tobacco; on 20th November, 1852, he became a naturalized citizen of the United States; was one of the organizers, also Director and Vice-President of the First National Bank (Louisville), the oldest National bank in the South; Treasurer and Vice-President of the Ohio Valley Telephone Company; Director in the Louisville Tobacco Warehouse Company and President of the Farmers' Tobacco Warehouse Company; member of the old Prentice Club, Union Club, Ananias Fishing Club, and, in 1887, President of the Pendennis Club, all of Louisville; Director and Vice-President of the Middle Bass Club on Lake Erie; *m.* in Beith, Scotland, 26th September, 1865, Jessie LA NAUZE, *b.* 18th January, 1837, in Ellichpur, India, *d.* 19th November, 1908, in Louisville, Kentucky, she dau. of Capt. George LA NAUZE, of the British Army, *b.* 15th August, 1805, at Kill, County Cavan, Ireland, *d.* 17th January, 1841, at Aurungabad, India, *m.* in Madras, India, Chirstiana PARRY, she *b.* there 15th April, 1815, *d.* 19th January, 1854, in Dublin, Ireland.

ISSUE

I. Christiana Parry, *b.* 24th July, 1866; *d.* in Maine, 11th August, 1872.
II. Isabel Stevenson (twin), *b.* 24th February, 1868, in Louisville, Kentucky; *m.* 27th April, 1893, William Howard COURTENAY, *b.* 30th July, 1858.

ISSUE

1. Erskine Howard COURTENAY, *b.* 25th April, 1895; Ensign, United States Naval Reserve Force, 1918.

2. James Clark COURTENAY, *b*. 14th January, 1897; Quartermaster Aviation, Second Class, United States Navy, 1918.

III. Jessie La Nauze (twin), *b*. 24th February, 1868, in Louisville, Kentucky; *m*. (firstly) in Louisville, 14th December, 1893, William Edward STRATER, *b*. 28th January, 1866, in Chillicothe, Ohio, *d*. 24th May, 1908, in Jefferson County, Kentucky; *m*. (secondly) 2d April, 1913, in Louisville, Kentucky, Maj. Alexander Mackenzie WATSON, United States Marine Corps.

ISSUE BY FIRST MARRIAGE

1. Edward La Nauze STRATER, *b*. in Louisville, Kentucky, 2d December, 1894; was graduated from Hill School, Pottstown, Pennsylvania, 1913, and from Princeton University, 1917; from May until November, 1917, Member of S. S. U. 1, American Ambulance Field Service on active duty at the Front in France; was graduated from Third Officers Training Camp, Camp Dix, New Jersey, 19th April, 1918; commissioned Second Lieutenant, Field Artillery, United States Army, 1st June, 1918; returned to France, June, 1918; graduated at the Artillery School, Saumur; assigned to the Air Service and took a course as balloon observer of artillery fires; assigned by the Army to University College, Oxford, England; returned to the United States 15th July, 1919, and released from the Army at Camp Dix, New Jersey, 17th July 1919; member the Country Club, and River Valley Club, both of Louisville, Kentucky.

IV. James, Jr., *b*. 29th August, 1869; *m*. in Louisville, Kentucky, 14th October, 1903, Lucinda Hardin HELM ("Inda"), *b*. 17th January, 1880, dau. of James Pendleton and Pattie Anderson (KENNEDY) HELM.

ISSUE

1. Helm, *b*. 7th May, 1906; *d*. the same day.
2. James, III, *b*. 29th August, 1908.
3. Kennedy Helm, *b*. 19th September, 1910.

V. William Kerr, *b*. 30th November, 1871; *m*. (firstly) in Clayville, New York, October, 1895, Rebecca Maillard SCHEUCH; *m*. (secondly) 24th November, 1909, Lenore DURBECK.

VI. George David, *b*. 16th January, 1874; *d*. 8th January, 1875.

VII. Walter Symington, *b*. 9th November, 1880; *m*. in Louisville, Kentucky, 12th June, 1906, Margaret COLEMAN, *b*. 29th January, 1882, dau. of John and Susan (NORTON) COLEMAN.

ISSUE

1. Susan Norton, *b.* 14th March, 1907; *d.* 20th March, 1907.
2. Jessie La Nauze, *b.* 18th November, 1908.
3. Constance, *b.* 15th July, 1914, at Easthampton, Long Island, New York.
4. Margaret, *b.* 14th December, 1916.

Arms (CLARK).—Or, a fesse chequey azure and argent in chief two crescents gules, in base, a boar's head couped sable.
Crest.—A demi huntsman, habited vert, winding a huntsman's horn ppr.
Motto.—Free for a blast.

Arms (COCHRANE of "Ladyland").—Argent, a chevron gules, between three boars' heads erased, azure.
Crest.—A horse sable, trotting.
Motto.—Vertute et labore.

Arms (KERR).—Vert, a chevron argent, charged with three mullets sable.
Crest.—A unicorn's head, erased argent, armed and maned or.
Motto.—Pro Christo, et patria dulce periculum.

La Nauze

DOCTOR ANDREW GEORGE LA NAUZE, known as the "Good Physician," member of the noble family of DE LA NAUZE, which lived near the Huguenot center, Castres, in the south of France, after the Revocation of the Edict of Nantes, 22d October, 1685, fled the country, crossed the Straights of Dover and finally settled in Ireland, where he *m.* 20th January 1689, Anne HIEROME (JEROME) only dau. of Count and Countess LA FAVRE, *b.* in France, *d.* 9th June, 1715, and is interred in the church at Killishandra, County Cavan, Ireland. In a French prayer book (Episcopal) published in 1683, Dr. LA NAUZE, entered the dates of his marriage, his wife's death and the names of their children.

ISSUE

1. James, *b.* 16th November, 1690; christened the next day by Mr. BREDIN, Minister of Carrick, brother-in-law of Dr. LA NAUZE; god-parents were Dr. FITZMAURICE, Mr. FENNARD, Mrs. STANDIS and Mrs. Rachel HYEROME.

COLONIAL FAMILIES OF THE UNITED STATES 503

 II. John Paul, *b.* 4th July, 1692, christened the 6th by Mr. ROSSEL; godparents were Mr. Gabriel BARBIER, Minister of the French Church, Mr. Paul AUGIER, Mrs. ROSSEL and Mrs. Magdelon MARIEL.

 III. Ysaac, *b.* 16th September, 1693; christened the 16th by Mr. ROSSEL, Minister of the Parish of Dromline; god-parents were Mr. Thomas HUME, Captain ROSSEL and Mrs. Henriette BREDIN.

 IV. Rachel, *b.* 2d April, 1696, christened the 7th by Dr. JUISON; god-parents were Dr. JUISON, Mr. Robert MAXWELL, Minister of Turbet and Mrs. WILSON.

 V. St. Cyre, *b.* 16th July, 1699; *d.* 27th July, 1699; christened the 21st by Dr. JUISON; god-parents were Captain ST. CYRE, Captain DEBOISE, Madam DE MILLIERE, and Mrs. Henriette BREDIN; he *d.* 27th July, 1699.

 VI. Peter Marc Antony, *b.* 18th June, 1701; christened 2d July, by Dr. JUISON; god-parents were Dr. JUISON, Mr. GUILARMINE, Mr. BONSON, Mrs. JUISON and Mrs. HUME.

 VII. Alexander, *b.* 12th April, 1705; *d.* 31st January, 1768; christened the 20th by Mr. HARRIS, Minister of Carrighan; god-parents were Captain MILLIERE, Mr. SIMPILL, Madam DEBOISE, and Mrs. Katherine HUME.

 VIII. GEORGE LA NAUZE, *b.* 21st September, 1706, of whom below.

GEORGE LA NAUZE, *b.* 21st September, 1706, *d.* 28th May, 1800; will probated in County Cavan; christened 26th September, 1706, by the Rev. Mr. SKELERNE, Minister of Killishandra; *m.* (firstly) 30th October, 1736, in parish of St. Brides, Dublin, Guillermine Martha DE LA PIERRE, *bapt.* by the Rev. Mr. VIRIDET, 12th June, 1717, *d.* May 1754, dau. of Sieur Estienne DE LA PIERRE, of Dublin, and his wife, Prudence HIEROME, *b.* 1677, *d.* 10th August, 1765, to whom he was *m.* 4th May, 1698, by the Rev. Mr. BARBIER. Estienne DE LA PIERRE was the son of Pierre DE LA PIERRE, Surgeon, of Lyons, and Marye VESIAN, of the Province of Languedoc. Prudence HIEROME was the dau. of Jacques HIEROME, D.D., and Marthe LE ROY. The Rev. Jacques HIEROME was before 1660, French Minister in Somerset House, the Chapel of which was originally granted by Charles I, to his Queen, Henrietta Maria, and was afterwards appropriated by Parliament in 1653, for the use of the French Protestants in London. He removed to Ireland where he was naturalized in 1665, and was for a while Chaplain in the household of the Duke of ORMOND, Lord Lieutenant of Ireland. On 29th April, 1666, he was installed as the first minister of the French Church in the Lady Chapel of St. Patrick's Cathedral, Dublin (Episcopal). George LA NAUZE, *m.* (secondly) ———— STOREY, *b.* 1738, *d.* at Kill, 22d February, 1788, dau. of Archdeacon STOREY.

ISSUE BY FIRST MARRIAGE

 I. Robert, *b.* 1740; *d.* 8th January, 1777.
 II. Martha, *b.* 1742; *d.* 9th May, 1778.
 III. ANDREW, *b.* August 1748, of whom later.

ISSUE BY SECOND MARRIAGE

I. Charles, *b.* June 1760; *d.* 26th September, 1761.
II. George John, *b.* 1761; *d.* 30th January, 1824.
III. Francois, *b.* 1764; *d.* December, 1788; interred on Christmas Day.

ANDREW LA NAUZE, *b.* August, 1748; *d.* 1st February, 1831; buried at Kill, County Cavan; *m.* 1800, Anne O'REILLY, *d.* before 1854, dau. of Myles O'REILLY, and gd. dau. of Col. John O'REILLY and his wife Margaret O'REILLY, she dau. of Owen O'REILLY. Col. John O'REILLY, *d.* 17th February, 1717, and is buried in the churchyard at Kill, parish of Crossarlough, County Cavan; he resided at Clonlyne, County Cavan, from which he was returned as Member of Parliment held in Dublin by James II.

ISSUE

I. Andrew, *b.* 4th August, 1802; *d.* in India, in 1857.
II. Robert, *b.* 2d January, 1804, *d.* in Dublin in 1884.
III. GEORGE, *b.* 15th August, 1805, of whom later.
IV. Charles, *b.* 28th May, 1807; *d.* 17th February, 1838.
V. Richard, *b.* 18th February, 1809; *d.* 10th May, 1871.
VI. William Henry, *b.* 2d July, 1815; *d.* 22d December, 1835.
VII. Martha, *b.* 25th January, 1818; *d.* 23d June, 1844.

CAPT. GEORGE LA NAUZE, of the British Army, *b.* 15th August, 1805, at Kill, in County Cavan, Ireland; *d.* 17th January, 1841, at Aurungabad, India; *m.* September, 1830, in Madras, India, Christiana PARRY, *b.* there, April, 1815; *d.* in Dublin, 19th January, 1854; she, dau. of Capt. George PARRY, Royal Navy, Commander of His Majesty's Ship "Quail"; he *b.* in Wales circa 1780; *d.* in Calcutta, India, 1820; *m.* in South Leith, Scotland, 11th April, 1810, Agnes NICOL, *b.* 1792; *d.* 27th April, 1877, in Edinburgh, Scotland; she, dau. of Robert NICOL, of Bo'ness, Scotland, and his wife, Christian ERSKINE.

ISSUE

I. Agnes Alicia, *b.* in Ellichpur, India, 14th June, 1831; *d.* in Glasgow, Scotland, 3d January, 1897; *m.* 1854, John Newton WHYTLAW, of Natchez, Mississippi; *d.* 30th November, 1904.

ISSUE

1. Harriette Sophia Newton WHYTLAW, *b.* and *d.* in Scotland; *m.* William B. PAXTON; no issue.
2. George La Nauze WHYTLAW, *b.* November, 1859; *d.* 11th October, 1884.

II. Andrew Henry, *b.* Ellichpur, 1833; *d.* in infancy.
III. Anne Martha, *b.* Ellichpur, India, 16th September, 1834; *m.* (firstly) in Scotland, the Rev. David WILLIAMSON, *b.* Beith, Scotland, 17th September, 1833, he *d.* at Ajaccio, Corsica, 23d April, 1875; *m.* (secondly) 1895, David BLACKBURN-ADAM; no issue by second marriage.

ISSUE BY FIRST MARRIAGE

1. Annette de La Nauze WILLIAMSON, *b.* Bombay, India, 15th November, 1863; *m.* St. George's Chaple, Edinburgh, Scotland, 19th April, 1892, George Stanser McNAIR, *b.* at Sandown, Isle of Wight, England, 14th January, 1867, *d.* in West New Brighton, Staten Island, New York, 26th June, 1917.

ISSUE

1. George Henderson Stanser McNAIR, *b.* Glasgow, Scotland, 22d August, 1893; naturalized citizen of the United States; was graduated with degree of C. E. from Cornell University, May, 1918.
2. James Edward Parry Aust McNAIR, *b.* Glasgow, Scotland, 4th April, 1895.
3. Dorothy Mildred Trelawney McNAIR, *b.* Kilmalcolm, Renfrewshire, Scotland, 8th April, 1897.
4. Hugh Noel de La Nauze McNAIR, *b.* Glasgow, Scotland, 6th June, 1901.

IV. Jessie, *b.* Ellichpur, India, 18th January, 1837; *d.* Louisville, Kentucky, 19th November, 1908; *m.* in Beith, Scotland, 26th September, 1865, James CLARK, *b.* 28th June, 1830, Renfrewshire, Scotland, *d.* 25th April, 1902, in Louisville, Kentucky. (See CLARK, pp. 495–502.)
V. Georgina, *b.* Ellichpur, India, October, 1840; *m.* in Beith, Scotland, 24th August, 1865. David CLARK, *b.* 27th September, 1825, in Renfrewshire, Scotland; *d.* 27th February, 1900, in Henderson, Kentucky; had issue. (See CLARK, pp. 495–502.)

Arms (LA NAUZE).—Argent, a lion rampant gules.
Crest.—Out of a mural crown or, a demi lion rampant gules.
Motto.—J'ai Travaille Dieu a beni.

Arms (ERSKINE).—Argent, a pale sable.
Crest.—In a dexter hand a club, raguly ppr.
Motto.—Judge Nought.

Washington

THE Virginia WASHINGTONS claim descent from John WASHINGTON of Whitfield, County Lancaster, England, who lived about 1450, and who had

ISSUE

I. John, of Whitfield.
II. ROBERT, of Warton, of whom below.

ROBERT WASHINGTON, Gentleman, of Warton, County Lancaster; *m.* (firstly) (wife's name unknown); *m.* (secondly) ―――― WHITTINGTON, a dau. of Miles WHITTINGTON of Berwick, County Lancaster, by whom he had issue; *m.* (thirdly) Agnes BATEMAN, dau. of ―――― BATEMAN of Haversham, Westmoreland, and had issue.

ISSUE BY FIRST MARRIAGE

I. JOHN, of Warton, of whom below.
II. Ellen, *m.* James MASON, of Warton.
III. Thomas.

JOHN WASHINGTON, of Warton, County Lancaster; *m.* Margaret KITSON, dau. of Robert KITSON, of Warton, son of Sir Thomas KITSON, Knight, Alderman of London; he had a son

LAWRENCE WASHINGTON, of Northampton and Gray's Inn; Mayor of Northampton, 1532-1545; Grantee of the Manor of Sulgrave, 1539; *d.* 19th February, 1594; *m.* for his second wife, Amy PARGITER, *d.* 7th October, 1564, dau. of Robert PARGITER of Gretworth, Gentleman; their son

ROBERT WASHINGTON, Esquire, of Sulgrave, who was forty years old in the twenty-sixth year of Queen Elizabeth, *m.* for his first wife, Elizabeth LIGHT, dau. and heiress of Robert LIGHT of Radway, County Warwick; their son

LAWRENCE WASHINGTON, of Sulgrave and Brington; *d.* 13th December, 1616; *m.* 3d August, 1588, Margaret BUTLER, *d.* after 1641, dau. of William BUTLER of Tighes, Sussex. Margaret BUTLER was descended from the ancient and noble family of the ORMONDES, tracing back through the DE BOHUNS to King Edward I of England; issue:

LAWRENCE WASHINGTON, *b.* 1602; buried near Maldon, 21st January, 1652; Rector of Purleigh, Essex, 1633-1643; entered Brasenose College, 2d November, 1621; M.A., Fellow of Brasenose College, Oxford, 1627-1632; *m.* Amphillis ROADES, *d.* 19th January, 1654, dau. of John ROADES of Middle Claydon; their son

COL. JOHN WASHINGTON, *b.* at Warton, County Lancaster, England, 1627, emigrated to America, 1659, and settled on Bridge's Creek, Virginia; *d.* January, 1677;

m. Ann POPE, dau. of Col. Nathaniel and ———— (LUCE) POPE, of Pope's Creek, Virginia; their son

LAURENCE WASHINGTON, *b.* about 1661, at Bridge's Creek; *d.* at same place, 1697; *m.* in Gloucester County, Virginia, 1690, Mildred WARNER, dau. of Col. Augustine and Mildred (READE) WARNER; their dau.

MILDRED WASHINGTON, *b.* circa 1696; *d.* 5th September, 1745; *m.* Roger GREGORY; issue:

FRANCES GREGORY, *m.* 3d November, 1736, Col. Francis THORNTON, *b.* 1711, *d.* 7th April, 1749; issue:

FRANCIS THORNTON, *d.* 8th April, 1795; *m.* 1759, Ann THOMPSON, *b.* 1744, *d.* 1815; issue:

FRANCIS THORNTON, *b.* 11th June, 1767; *d.* 15th July, 1836; *m.* 2d June, 1792, Sally INNES, *b.* 1776, *d.* 2d May, 1807; issue:

JUDGE HARRY INNES THORNTON, *b.* 3d April, 1787; *d.* 1867; *m.* 1824, Lucy CRITTENDEN, *b.* 3d October, 1804, *d.* 25th December, 1885; issue:

SARAH FRANCES THORNTON, *b.* 31st July, 1825; *d.* May, 1904; *m.* 17th February, 1848, Judge James Dabney THORNTON, *b.* 18th January, 1823, *d.* 25th September, 1902; issue.

ELIZABETH ANDERSON THORNTON, *b.* 27th May, 1850; *m.* 29th May, 1873, Rear Admiral John Crittenden WATSON, *b.* 24th August, 1843; issue:

MAJ. ALEXANDER MACKENZIE WATSON, United States Marine Corps, *b.* 4th January, 1883.

Arms (WASHINGTON).—Argent two bars gules, in chief three mullets of the second.
Crest.—Out of a ducal coronet or, an eagle, wings endorsed sable.
Motto.—Virtus Sola Nobilitas.

Wilbur

LAFAYETTE WILBUR, Lawyer, of Jericho, Vermont, *b.* 15th May, 1834, in Waterville, Vermont; *d.* 11th August, 1918, at Portland, Oregon; *m.* 9th January, 1861, at Underhill, Vermont, Mercy Jane MORSE, *b.* 12th May, 1840, Underhill, Vermont, dau. of Calvin MORSE, *b.* 7th January, 1804, at Dublin, New Hampshire, *d.* 11th September, 1880, at Jericho, Vermont, *m.* at Underhill, Vermont, 14th January, 1830, Mercy MEAD, *b.* 11th January, 1807, at Pittsford, Vermont, *d.* 26th December, 1881, at Jericho.

ISSUE

I. Gratia, *b.* 20th May, 1864; *d.* 4th June, 1864.
II. Earl Morse, *b.* 26th April, 1886; *m.* 30th June, 1898, Dorothea Dix ELIOT, dau. of Thomas Lamb ELIOT and Henrietta MACK, *b.* 14th February, 1871, at Portland, Oregon.

ISSUE

1. William Eliot, *b.* 30th September; *d.* 23d October, 1902, Meadville.
2. Elizabeth Fuller, *b.* 27th August, 1907, Portland, Oregon.
3. Thomas Lamb Eliot, *b.* 9th November, 1912, Berkeley, California.

III. Ralph William, *b.* 30th March, 1869; *m.* 26th June, 1894, Alice Dunbar HEUSTIS, dau. of James Farrington HEUSTIS, of Boston, Massachusetts, *b.* 11th February, 1871.

Lineage

The immigrant ancestor of this branch of the American WILBURS, was Samuel WILDBORE who came from Yorkshire, England to Boston, Massachusetts, 1633; *d.* 29th September, 1656; *m.* Ann BRADFORD.

ISSUE

I. Samuel, *d.* 1710; *m.* Hannah PORTER.
II. Joseph, *d.* 27th August, 1691; *m.* Elizabeth FARWELL who *d.* 9th November, 1670.
III. William, *b.* 1630?; *d.* 1710.
IV. SHADRACH, *b.* 1632, of whom below.

SHADRACH WILDBORE, of Taunton, Massachusetts, *b.* 1632; *d.* February, 1697–1698; *m.* MARY DEAN, *d.* 27th March, 1691.

ISSUE

I. Mary, *b.* 11th November, 1659; *d.* 19th June, 1674.
II. Sarah, *b.* 18th March, 1661; *m.* Nathaniel HOAR, *b.* 1656.
III. Samuel, *b.* 1st April, 1663; *d.* 16th December, 1695; *m.* Sarah PHILLIPS, *b.* 17th March, 1667.
IV. Rebekah, *b.* 13th January, 1664; *d.* 23rd August, 1725; *m.* Abraham HATHAWAY, *d.* 30th August, 1727.
V. Hannah, *b.* 24th February, 1667–1668; *d.* 30th December, 1675.
VI. Joseph, *b.* 27th July, 1670; *d.* 1720; *m.* Mehitable DEANE, *b.* 9th October, 1671, *d.* circa 1757.
VII. SHADRACH, *b.* 5th December, 1672, of whom later.
VIII. John, *b.* 2d March, 1674–1675; *d.* 1718; *m.* Alice PITTS, *b.* circa 1665.
IX. Eliezer, *b.* 1st July, 1677; *d.* September, 1700.
X. Benjamin, *b.* 23d July, 1683; *d.* circa 1750; *m.* Jane BIRD, *b.* 25th June, 1693, *d.* before 1758.

SHADRACH WILBORE, of Taunton, Massachusetts, *b.* 5th December, 1672; *d.* 8th November, 1749; *m.* Joanna NEAL, *b.* 27th May, 1680, dau. of Henry and Hannah (PRAY) NEAL of Braintree, Massachusetts.

ISSUE

I. Shadrach, *b.* circa 1700; *d.* 26th April, 1793; *m.* Anna (surname not given), *d.* 7th July, 1737.
II. Meshach, *b.* circa 1702; *d.* 25th December, 1793; *m.* Elizabeth LEONARD, *d.* 30th November, 1776.
III. Joseph, *m.* Susanna HARRIS.
IV. Jacob.
V. Abijah, *b.* 1716; *d.* 29th January, 1776; *m.* Phebe WHITE, *b.* 1726, *d.* 26th August, 1812.
VI. Ebenezer, *d.* 1761; *m.* Lydia DEANE, *b.* 11th December, 1704.
VII. PHILIP, of whom later.
VIII. Benjamin, *d.* 16th August, 1763; *m.* (firstly) Elizabeth LEONARD, *d.* 17th September, 1756.
IX. Joanna, *m.* Josiah LEACH.
X. Abiah, *b.* circa 1714; *d.* 15th May, 1792; *m.* Joan LEA, *d.* 1750.

PHILIP WILBORE, of Taunton, Massachusetts; *m.* 29th December, 1737, Mary LEONARD, *b.* circa 1705.

ISSUE

1. Philip, *m.* Bathsheba WITHERELL.
2. Zilpah, *d.* 13th August, 1756.
3. DAVID, *b.* 1743, of whom later.
4. Lydia, *m.* Jacob LEACH.

DAVID WILBORE, of Westmoreland, New Hampshire, and Waterville, Vermont, *b.* 1743, *d.* 2d August, 1819; *m.* Tabitha BRITTON, *b.* 11th April, 1748, *d.* 28th March, 1840, dau. of Ebenezer and Tabitha (LEONARD) BRITTON.

ISSUE

1. WILLIAM, *b.* 13th August, 1772, of whom later.
2. Solomon, *m.* Patty STAPLES.
3. Nathan, *m.* Lucinda LINCOLN.
4. Tabitha, *m.* Azariah LEACH.
5. Lois, *m.* Abiathar WITHERELL.
6. Theodora, *m.* Benjamin WINCHESTER.
7. Wealthy, *m.* Alpheus WINCHESTER.
8. Elisha, *m.* Jerusha LINCOLN.

WILLIAM WILBUR, of Westmoreland, New Hampshire, and Waterville, Vermont, *b.* 13th August, 1772; *d.* 19th April, 1835; *m.* 7th October, 1795, Asenath WILBORE, *b.* 13th April, 1770, *d.* 26th February, 1832, dau. of Abijah and Rachel (WITTAM) WILBORE.

ISSUE

1. Asenath, *b.* 22d January, 1797; *d.* 21st March, 1883; *m.* (firstly) Ziba ELLIS; *d.* 15th September, 1840; *m.* (secondly) TIMOTHY BROWN.
2. Armelia, *b.* 28th April, 1798; *d.* 6th June, 1879; *m.* Richard HAWLEY, *d.* 15th December, 1843.
3. Diana, *b.* 18th October, 1799; *d.* 28th January, 1882; *m.* Hiram FRENCH, *d.* 7th September, 1881.
4. WILLIAM, *b.* 8th March, 1801, of whom later.
5. Salina, *b.* 20th June, 1802; *d.* 3d April, 1864; *m.* Welcome BROWN.
6. Achsah, *b.* 12th October, 1803; *d.* January, 1887; *m.* (firstly) Stephen WILLEY; *m.* (secondly) ―――― AVERY.
7. George Washington, *b.* 18th December, 1805; *d.* 20th September, 1856; *m.* Betsey E. McFARLAND, *d.* 26th January, 1882.
8. Wealthy, *b.* 5th May, 1808; *d.* 10th January, 1892; *m.* Ephraim W. BROWN, *d.* 10th January, 1892.
9. Clarissa, *b.* 12th August, 1809; *d.* 16th November, 1825.
10. Delana, *b.* 13th June, 1811; *d.* 26th August, 1849; *m.* Seymour HESELTINE.

WILLIAM WILBUR, of Waterville, Vermont, *b.* 8th March, 1801; *d.* 7th March, 1882; *m.* 21st February, 1826, Westmoreland, New Hampshire, Betsey FULLER, *b.* 6th October, 1802, *d.* 12th November, 1888, dau. of Joshua, *b.* February, 1774, *d.* 22d April, 1849, and Mercy (FELT) FULLER, *b.* 14th December, 1776, *d.* 17th December, 1862.

ISSUE

I. Almina Jane, *b.* 8th December, 1826; *d.* 27th June, 1893; *m.* (firstly) Nelson FASSETTE, *d.* 12th March, 1894; *m.* (secondly) Charles E. FURNALD, *d.* 1887.

II. Seymour, *b.* 10th November, 1828; *d.* 25th December, 1904; *m.* Sarah E. PAINE., *d.* 29th July, 1856, and five others later.

III. Clarissa Maria, *b.* 19th May, 1830; *d.* 11th January, 1912; *m.* (firstly) W. Harrison DEAN, *b.* 24th August, 1811, *d.* 7th September, 1878; *m.* (secondly) Charles H. LYMAN, *b.* 8th May, 1820, *d.* 4th September, 1889.

IV. Sylvia Ann Fuller, *b.* 29th January, 1832; *d.* 5th October, 1905; *m.* Bartlett N. ADAMS, *d.* 20th December, 1905.

V. Emily Ware, *b.* 23d January, 1833, *d.* 3d March, 1881; *m.* I. Austin DENIO, *b.* 28th January, 1824, *d.* 3d June, 1901.

VI. LA FAYETTE, *b.* 15th May, 1834, *d.* Portland, Oregon, 11th August, 1918, the subject of this memoir.

VII. Elizabeth Stocker, *b.* 14th November, 1835; *d.* 6th September, 1851.

VIII. Gratia Bragg, *b.* 22d March, 1837; *d.* 20th June, 1862.

IX. David, *b.* 3d April, 1838; *d.* 18th July, 1838.

X. Elbridge, *b.* 30th July, 1839; *m.* (firstly) Viola BUNDY; *m.* (secondly) Ida M. TILLOTSON, *b.* 10th May, 1856.

XI. Ruth Ann, *b.* 14th August, 1841; *d.* 2d March, 1842.

XII. Meribah Esther Hyde, *b.* 16th December, 1843; *d.* 2nd April, 1908; *m.* Martin SHATTUCK, *b.* 5th February, 1842, *d.* 3d January, 1911.

Arms.—Sable, on a fesse between two boars passant, a javelin point of the field.
Crest.—The upper part of a spear ppr. through a boar's head erased, argent, dropping blood ppr.
Residence.—Jericho, Vermont.

Wood

HENRY WOOD, A.B., Ph.D., LL.D. of Baltimore, Maryland, *b.* 8th July, 1849, in New Bedford, Massachusetts; *m.* (firstly) June, 1878, at Gotha, Germany, Alida NICHOLSON, who *d.* 17th May, 1900; *m.* (secondly) 16th June, 1902, at Potsdam, Germany, Clotilde Jenny Marie Therese VON KRETSCHMAN, *b.* 23d August, 1872, dau. of Oscar Karl Paul Theodor VON KRETSCHMAN, *b.* 11th July, 1837, at Frankfurt, *d.* at Scherbitz, 3d March, 1885; *m.* 3d May, 1870, at Potsdam, Germany, Magdalene Therese Friedericke Freiin VON ESBECK, *b.* 24th January, 1842, in Koenigsberg, Prussia, *d.* 28th February, 1898, in Potsdam.

ISSUE

I. Carl-Anton Oscar Henry, *b.* 18th May, 1903, in Baltimore, Maryland.
II. Henry Russell Oscar Friedrich, *b.* 21st August, 1905, New Bedford, Massachusetts.
III. Ernst Friedrich Edmund Earle, *b.* 26th September, 1918, Baltimore, Maryland.

HENRY WOOD, University Professor, A.B., Haverford College, 1869; Ph.D., Leipzig, 1879; Instructor Modern Literature, Friends' School, Providence, Rhode Island, 1879–1881; Associate in English, 1881–1885, Associate Professor of Germanic languages, 1885–1892; Professor of German since 1892, Johns Hopkins University; President American Folk-Lore Society, 1898–1899; created Knight of the Order of the Red Eagle, 3d Class, by the Emperor of Germany, 1910; LL.D., Wake Forest College, North Carolina, 1914; Author of "Faust-Studien, Ein Beitrag zum Verstaendnis Goethes in seiner Dichtung," (Berlin), 1912; "Study of Bettina Von Arnim" (Volume VII, German Publication Society); also of various monographs on German and English literature in *American Journal of Philology, Vierteljahrschrift fur Litteraturgeschichte*, etc.

Lineage

JOHN WOOD, the immigrant ancestor of this family of Portsmouth on the Island of Newport, Rhode Island, *d.* before 17th March, 1655; he *m.* twice; his second wife, Sarah MASTERSON, dau. of Richard MASTERSON, survived him as is shown by the court records; having died intestate certain lands were awarded by the Court for her life; she *d.* after her husband, but also in the year, 1655.

ISSUE

 i. George.
 ii. JOHN, of whom later.
 iii. Thomas, *m.* Rebecca (surname not given).
 iv. Margaret, *d.* 1693; *m.* Thomas MANCHESTER.
 v. William, *d.* 1697; *m.* Martha EARLE.
 vi. Susanna.
 vii. Elizabeth, *m.* Samuel WHEATON.

JOHN WOOD, of Newport, Rhode Island; was a Freeman in 1655 and a Deputy to the General Court in 1673, 1674 and 1675; *m.* Mary (surname not given).

ISSUE

 i. THOMAS, *b.* 1666, of whom later.
 ii. Henry.
 iii. Walter.

THOMAS WOOD of Little Compton, Massachusetts, *b.* 1666; *d.* 10th May, 1729; his wife's name is not given.

ISSUE

 i. WILLIAM, *b.* 7th February, 1700, of whom later.
 ii. Thomas.
 iii. John.
 iv. Elizabeth, *m.* ——— FINNEE.
 v. Content, *m.* ——— SHAW.
 vi. Rebecca, *m.* ——— SHAW.
 vii. Mary, *m.* ——— SISSON.
 viii. Desire.
 ix. Deliverance.

WILLIAM WOOD, of Dartmouth, Massachusetts, *b.* 7th February, 1700; *d.* 1778; removed from Little Compton, Rhode Island, first to Fairhaven, then a part of Dartmouth, Massachusetts; *m.* (firstly) Hannah SHAW, *b.* 7th March, 1699; *m.* (secondly) Patience (ELLIS) WING, widow of Edward WING.

ISSUE BY FIRST MARRIAGE

 i. Zaruiah, *m.* 5th August, 1750, Rhoda ELDREDGE.
 ii. Hannah, *m.* Caleb MANDELL.

ISSUE BY SECOND MARRIAGE

 i. JOHN, *b.* 9th July, 1742, of whom later.
 ii. Rebecca, *m.* Amos ELDREDGE.

III. Zilpha, *m.* Onesipharus WEST.
IV. Anstis, *m.* Abraham WING.
V. Content, *m.* ——— WING.

JOHN WOOD, of Dartmouth, Massachusetts, *b.* 9th July, 1742; *d.* 1775; *m.* 26th August, 1760, Sarah RUSSELL, *b.* 3d January, 1742, *d.* 1816, dau. of Caleb Senior, and Rebecca (BORDEN) RUSSELL.

ISSUE

I. Thomas.
II. Joseph.
III. GIDEON, *b.* 28th August, 1765, of whom later.
IV. Walter.
V. Russell.
VI. Richard.
VII. John.
VIII. Caleb.

GIDEON WOOD, of Dartmouth, Massachusetts, *b.* 28th August, 1765; *d.* 19th February, 1838; *m.* 23d September, 1787, Thankful TABER, *b.* 2d May, 1768, dau. of Amaziah TABER.

ISSUE

I. THOMAS, *b.* 10th February, 1790, of whom later.
II. Sally.
III. Phebe.
IV. Thankful.
V. Taber.

THOMAS WOOD, of Fairhaven, Massachusetts, *b.* 10th February, 1790; *d.* 26th July, 1872; *m.* 5th October, 1814, Betsey Pope GORDON, *b.* 8th January, 1796, *d.* 18th August, 1886, dau. of William, and Nabby (POPE) GORDON, of Boston, Massachusetts.

ISSUE

I. Betsey Gordon.
II. Gideon.
III. HENRY TABER, *b.* 21st September, 1820, of whom later.
IV. Abby.
V. George.
VI. Walter.
VII. Albert.
VIII. Jabez.
IX. William Gordon.

HENRY TABER WOOD, *b.* 21st September, 1820; *d.* 23d November, 1883; *m.* 4th August, 1845, Anna Greene RUSSELL.

ISSUE

I. Walter.
II. HENRY, *b.* 8th July, 1849, the subject of this memoir.
III. George Russell.
IV. Edmund.
V. Augustus.

Arms.—Quarterly 1–4 (WOOD) Or, on a mount vert, an oak tree fructed ppr. 2–3, between three crescents sable a chevron.
Crest.—A demi-wild man, wreathed head and middle with laurel gules in the dexter hand an oak slip, in the sinister a spiked club resting over the shoulder, all ppr.
Motto.—Diruit Aedificat.
Residence.—No. 109 North Avenue, West, Baltimore, Maryland.
Clubs.—Johns Hopkins, Germania.
Society.—Colonial Wars.

Russell

JOHN RUSSELL of Dartmouth, Massachusetts, *b.* 1608, *d.* 13th February, 1695, was one of the first proprietors and settlers of the Township of Dartmouth, Massachusetts. He purchased the share of Captain Miles STANDISH' land 9th March, 1664. He took the oath of fidelity 1684. Was the first Representative Dartmouth had at the Old Colony Court, Plymouth, 1665. He represented the town from 1665 to 1683 with the exception of two years, viz., 1666 and 1673. Was Freeman 29th May, 1670, *m.* Dorothy, surname not given, who *d.* 18th December, 1687.

ISSUE

I. John, Jr., *d.* 25th March, 1695; *m.* 16th July, 1644, Mehitable SMITH.
II. JOSEPH, *b.* 6th May, 1650, of whom later.
III. Dorothy, *d.* 3d January, 1657.
IV. Mary, *b.* 1645, *m.* John CORNELL.
V. Jonathan, *d.* 1727; *m.* Hozodiah SMITH, *b.* 11th January, 1650.

JOSEPH RUSSELL, of Dartmouth, Massachusetts, *b.* 6th May, 1650; *d.* 11th December, 1739; *m.* Elizabeth RICKETSON, *b.* there 6th March, 1657, *d.* 25th September, 1737.

ISSUE

I. JOSEPH (twin), *b.* 22d November, 1679, of whom later.
II. John (twin), *b.* 22d November, 1679, *d.* 20th March, 1695; *m.* Rebecca RICKETSON.

  III. William, *b.* 20th May, 1681; *d.* 9th April, 1708.
  IV. Mary, *b.* 10th August, 1683; *m.* 3d April, 1700, John LAPHAM.
  V. Joshua, *b.* 26th January, 1686; *d.* 23d December, 1692.
  VI. Rebecca, *b.* 3d January, 1686; *m.* 6th April, 1710, Jabez BARKER.
  VII. Benjamin, *b.* 11th May, 1691; *d.* 31st October, 1732; *m.* 22d December, 1720, Abigail HOWLAND.
  VIII. Seth, *b.* 7th April, 1696; *d.* 23d August, 1728; *m.* 21st June, 1722, Hannah ALLEN.
  IX. Sarah.

JOSEPH RUSSELL, of Dartmouth, Massachusetts, *b.* 22d November, 1679; he and his brother John were born within the famous RUSSELL stockade or garrison on the RUSSELL land on the east shore of Apponegansett River in Dartmouth 22d November, 1679, where all settlers had taken refuge from the many attacks of the Indians during King Philip's War; *d.* 13th April, 1748; *m.* Mary TUCKER, *b.* there 1st July, 1682, *d.* there 5th December, 1769, dau. of Abraham TUCKER, Senior.

ISSUE

  I. Mary, *b.* 1st April, 1704.
  II. Abraham, *b.* 19th March, 1705; *d.* 4th September, 1770; *m.* Dinah ALLEN, who *d.* 1784.
  III. Mary, *b.* 18th February, 1708.
  IV. William, *b.* 10th December, 1708.
  V. Abigail, *b.* 19th March, 1711; *m.* 13th August, 1730, Joseph BORDEN.
  VI. CALEB, *b.* 9th August, 1713, of whom later.
  VII. Martha, *b.* 24th April, 1716; *m.* 13th February, 1734, Rufus GREENE.
  VIII. Joseph, III, *b.* 8th October, 1719; *d.* 1804; *m.* 29th August, 1744, Judith HOWLAND, *b.* 14th March, 1723; *d.* 26th July, 1803.
  IX. Mary, *b.* 20th December, 1723; *m.* 13th March, 1739, Peleg CORNELL.
  X. Patience, *b.* 8th October, 1727; *m.* 13th March, 1739, William GIFFORD.

CALEB RUSSELL, of Dartmouth, Massachusetts, *b.* there 9th August, 1713; *d.* there 30th August, 1804; *m.* there Rebecca BORDON, *b.* there 18th August, 1712, *d.* 30th April, 1752.

ISSUE

  I. Peace, *b.* 10th January, 1735; *m.* 24th March, 1764, John AIKEN.
  II. Mary, *b.* 7th January, 1740; *m.* 14th December, 1758, Philip SHERMAN.
  III. Sarah, *b.* 3d January, 1742; *d.* 1816; *m.* 26th August, 1760, John WOOD.
  IV. Anna, *b.* 6th September, 1743; *m.* 28th August, 1764, Enoch CUNDALL.
  V. CALEB, *b.* 11th March, 1747, of whom later.

CALEB RUSSELL, of Dartmouth, Massachusetts, *b.* there, 1747; *d.* there 15th October, 1827; *m.* 9th May, 1770, Content GIFFORD.

ISSUE

I. REUBEN, *b.* 29th August, 1771, of whom later.
II. Asa, *b.* 7th October, 1774; *d,* 15th November, 1808; *m.* (firstly) Vertue SMITH, *d.* 18th September, 1798; *m.* (secondly), Alice HATHAWAY, *d.* 12th February, 1808; *m.* (thirdly) Mehitable EARLE, *d.* 15th July, 1810.
III. Rebecca, *b.* 15th February, 1778; *m.* 31st December, 1795, Humphrey ALLEN.
IV. Caleb, *b.* 28th January, 1783.
V. Sarah, *b.* 2d March, 1795; *d.* 19th March, 1879; *m.* 5th May, 1825 (as his second wife) Timothy AKIN.

REUBEN RUSSELL, of Dartmouth, Massachusetts, *b.* there 29th August, 1771; *d.* in New Bedford, Massachusetts, 24th October, 1846; *m.* 29th December, 1809, Anna (TUCKER) SHEARMAN, *b.* there 27th August, 1772, *d.* 10th June, 1842, dau. of Joseph and Mary (WING) TUCKER, and widow of David SHEARMAN.

ISSUE

I. Mehitable Earle, *b.* 24th October, 1810; *d.* 26th August, 1892; *m.* 23d September, 1829, Abraham H. HOWLAND.
II. Mary Ann, *b.* 10th May, 1812; *d.* 20th December, 1863; *m.* 1st September, 1831, Benjamin Franklin HOWLAND.
III. Anna Greene, *b.* 14th September, 1822, in New Bedford, Massachusetts; *d.* 3d August, 1913; *m.* 4th September, 1845, Henry Taber WOOD, *b.* 21st September, 1820, in that part of Fairhaven now called Acushnet, near New Bedford, Massachusetts.

ISSUE

I. Henry Wood, *b.* 8th July, 1849 (see WOOD record, preceding pages).

Index

A

Abbot, Abby Ann, 420, 422, 425
  Abiel, 423, 424, 425
  Betsey (Rockwood), 427
  Caroline Ann (Greeley), 425
  Charles Greeley, 425
  Dorcas, 423, 424, 425
  Dorcas (Abbot), 423, 424
  Edmund Quincy, 420
  Edward Stanley, 425
  Elizabeth (Harnden), 423
  Emily, 425
  Ezra, 420, 422, 424, 425
  Fanny Ellingwood (Larcom), 424, 425
  Frederick Vaughan, 425
  George, 63, 422, 423
  Hannah (Chandler), 422, 423
  Hannah Holt (Pevey), 425
  Harriet (Abbot), 425
  Harris, 425
  Henry Larcom, 424
  Hermon, 425
  John, 423
  John Hale, 425
  Joseph Hale, 424, 425
  Melinda Wheeler (Rockwood), 420
  Nelson, 425
  Phebe (Fiske), 423
  Rebecca, 424
  Rebekah (Hale), 420, 422, 424
  Rhoda, 423
  Sarah (Barker), 423
  Sarah (Hooker), 425
  Sarah Jane, 425
  Stanley Harris, 425
  Timothy, 427
Abbott, Elizabeth (Ballard), 63
Abel, Deborah (Burton), 479
  Elizabeth, 479
  Joseph, 470, 479

Able, Catherine (Hartley), 478
  Elizabeth, 478
  Joseph, 478
Ackincloss, Mary (Fillis), 33
Adams, ———, 454
  A. Pratt, 456
  Alice, 354
  Andrew Robert, 37
  Anne, 119
  Bartlett N., 511
  C. H., 37
  Charles Henry, 37
  David Bain, 37
  Eliphalet, 126
  Elizabeth, 63, 426
  Elizabeth (Thomas), 454
  Francis Valleé, 37
  Henry, 288
  Jane, 426
  James Fletcher, 354
  James Osmond, 354
  John, 6, 354, 441
  John Quincy, 354
  John Rouse, 455
  Margaret, 456
  Marguerite Desloye (Bain), 37
  Marguerite Marie, 37
  Marie (Ziegler), 37
  Martha (Thomas), 455
  Mary, 126
  Mary (Thomas), 456
  Matthew Washington, 354
  Nancy Ellen, 354
  Polly, 441
  Pratt, 456
  Samuel, 456
  Samuel Barnard, 456
  Sylvia Ann Fuller (Wilbur), 511
  Thomas, 456
  Vashtie (Marine), 354
Addison, John, 176, 180
  Rebecca (Wilkinson) Dent, 176, 180
Adgate, ———, 50, 53
  Elizabeth (Dorsey), 50, 53

Adgate—*Continued*
  Rebecca, 315
  Thomas, 315
Ahles, Clara, 18
  Emma, 18
  Evaline, 18
  Fannie, 18
  George, 18
  Georgia, 18
  Gertrude F., 16, 18
  Helen Wilmer (Kemper), 3
  John William, 15, 18
  Lydia Ann (Bell), 15, 18
  Lydia Bell, 3
  Robert Lawrence, 3, 16, 18
  Virginia, 16, 18
  Zoe, 18
  Zoe Parine (Charruaud), 18
Aiken, John, 516
  Peace (Russell), 516
Akers, *Arms*, 19, 20
  Amelia (Garritson), 20
  Charles Lawson, 20
  Frank (Guthrie), 19
  Frank Guthrie, 19
  George, 19
  Hiram, 19, 20
  Louisa Abraham (Miller), 20, 21
  Matthew Love, 19, 20
  Millicent, 19
  Minnie Caroline, 20
  Nancy, 19
  Nancy (Akers), 19
  Owen Miller, 20
  Reason Lawson, 20, 21
  Sarah (Malone), 19
  Simon, 19
  Thomas, 19
Akin, Sarah (Russell), 517
  Timothy, 517
Albee, Sarah (Gore), 380
Aldborough, Agnes, 348
Alden, Clarissa, 288
Alden, Elizabeth, 286, 404
  John, 286
  Paul, 286

INDEX

Alden—*Continued*
  Priscilla (———), 286
  Rebecca (Newell), 286
Alexander, Alice (Van Yeveren), 480
  Anne, 490
  John, 194
  Ludwell Brooke, 100
  Martha, 388
  Mary Breckenridge (Maltby), 10
Alison, Dorothea (Smiser), 338
  Hugh, 338
Allison, Martha Bell (Bullitt), 137
  Richard, 137
Alston, Catherine (Hamilton), 148
  James, 148
  Jane C., 148
Allaway, Sarah, 188
Allen, Archibald, 386, 387
  Benjamin W., 241
  Dinah, 516
  Edward, 386, 387
  Harriett (Waters), 241
  Hannah, 439, 516
  Humphrey, 517
  Issabelle Frances, 241
  Jane, 125
  Lydia, 79, 81, 84
  Margaret, 213
  Mary Swepson, 386, 387
  Mary (Swepson), 386
  Matilda J., 17
  Rebecca (Rickard), 416
  Rebecca (Russell), 517
  Sallie, 354
  Seth, 416
  Thomas, 125
  William, 81
Almy, Christopher, 331
  Helen Martin (Gordon), 134
  John, 134
Alymer, Judith, 348
Ambler, Eliza Jacqueline, 113
Amory, Anne Geyer, 328, 329
  Anne (Von Geyer), 329
  Jonathan, 326
  Rufus Greene, 328
Anderson, *Arms*, 494
  ———, 246
  Absalom, 246

Anderson—*Continued*
  Agnes, 495
  Ann (Dabney), 491
  Catharine M., 275
  Catherine Martin, 280, 282
  Cornelia M. (Brocket), 243
  Dexter, 448
  Elizabeth, 491
  Elizabeth (Hall), 248
  Elizabeth Virginia, 448
  Elizabeth Virginia (Anderson), 448
  George, 280
  John, 87
  John Foster, 280, 282
  Johns Hopkins, 248
  Julia, 132
  Julia (Beard), 246
  Martha, 248
  Mollie (Griffith), 248
  Nancy Oliver (Martin), 282
  Rhoda (Oliver), 280
  Samuel, 248, 491
  Sarah (———), 87
  Sarah (Hall), 87, 243, 245
  Samuel, 248
  Sophia (Foster,) 448
  Sue, 246
  Susannah, 87, 91, 245
  Susannah (Hall) Beck, 243
  Thomas Hall, 248
  Virginia, 248
  Virginia (Turner), 248
  William, 87, 243, 245, 248
  William Henry Harrison, 87, 243
Andrews, Charles Lowell, 329
  Henry, 403
  Mary, 403
  Mary (———), 403
  Mary (Richmond) Reed, 403
  Sarah Augusta (Jeffries), 329
  Stephen, 403
Ankeny, May, 497
Anterbus, Jane (Arnolde), 6
  Joane, 6
  Walter, 6
Antrim, Mary, 339
Appold, George, 241
Archer, Hannah (Osgood), 406
  Samuel, 406
  Susanna (———), 406
Archibald, Joanna, 492

Arden, Agnes, 283
Ariss, Elizabeth, 188
  Sarah (Allaway), 188
  Spencer, 188
Armitage, Frances Elizabeth (Cooch), 161
  John, 161
Armstrong, Anita (Stewart), 298
  R. Blair, 298
Arnold, *Arms*, 22
  ———, 231
  Abbie (Stone), 28
  Abigail (Wilbur), 25
  Ada Caroline Margaret, 25
  Amy (Waterman), 27
  Ann Marten (Brown), 24
  Archer Seymour, 25
  Barbary, 27
  Benedict, 23, 24
  Caleb, 26
  Charles Lowther, 25
  Charlotte Georgiana (Cholmondeley), 25
  Christian (Peak), 22, 182
  Christine (———), 26
  Clara Louise (Wright), 29
  Damaris, 26
  Damaris (Westcott), 23
  Edith Genevieve, 29
  Edward Cholmondeley, 25
  Edward Gladwin, 25
  Edward Shippen, 24
  Elisha, 26, 27
  Elizabeth, 23, 26, 27, 28, 288
  Elizabeth (Arnold), 27
  Elizabeth Cecila (Ruddach), 24
  Elizabeth (Padelford), 27
  Elizabeth (Rhodes), 27
  Elizabeth (Smith), 26
  Elizabeth Sophia, 25
  Emma Charlotte Georgiana, 25
  Emma Cornelia (Stansbury), 253
  Esther, 26, 182
  Flora Etta (Richards), 22
  Freelove, 26
  George, 23, 24, 27
  George C., 28
  George Carpenter, 22, 23, 27, 28, 29

INDEX

Arnold—*Continued*
  George Hugh Bryant, 25
  George Jay, 29
  George R., 28
  Georgiana Phipps, 25
  Godsgift, 26
  Hannah (Ten Eyck), 24
  Hannah (Waterman) King, 23
  Henry, 24
  Henry Abel, 25
  Herbert Tollemache, 25
  Hettie F., 28
  Israel, 27, 182
  James, 26, 27
  James O., 28
  James Oliver, 28
  James Robertson, 24
  James Utter, 28
  Joanna, 26, 182
  John Holden, 28
  John Rice, 29
  John W., 253
  Joseph, 27
  Josiah, 26, 27
  Lincoln Richards, 22
  Louisa Russell, 25
  Lydia (Greene), 182
  Mabel Caroline Frances, 25
  Madeline W. (Webster), 22
  Marcia Elizabeth, 25
  Margaret (Mansfield), 24
  Margaret (Shippen), 24
  Margaret Steuart, 25
  Margaret (Weatherhead), 24
  Marian B. (Harris), 22
  Mary, 28
  Mary (Barker) Smith, 26
  Mary (Brinley), 25
  Mary E. W. (Brayton), 29
  Mary (Hall), 231
  Mary (Turner), 23
  Maude, 253
  Mehetable, 28
  Mehetabel (Carpenter), 28
  Mitchell Wright, 29
  Moses, 27
  Oliver, 26, 27
  Penelope, 26
  Phebe, 26
  Phebe Ann (Low), 28
  Phebe (Cook), 26
  Phebe (Rhodes), 28

Arnold—*Continued*
  Philip, 27
  Philip Rhodes, 22
  Richard, 24
  Ruth (Utter), 27
  Sally, 27
  Samuel Low, 28
  Sarah, 26, 28
  Sarah (———), 27
  Sarah (Green), 27
  Sarah Hill (Carpenter), 29
  Sarah (Mills), 25
  Sarah (Munford), 23
  Sarah Rhodes, 29
  Sarah (Smith), 26
  Simon, 182
  Sion, 27
  Sophia, 24
  Sophia Mary, 24
  Sophia Matilda, 25
  Stephen, 23, 26, 27, 182
  Susanna (Carpenter), 26
  Susanna (Potter), 27
  Virginia (Goodrich), 24
  Waterman, 27
  William, 22, 26, 27, 182
  William Fitch, 24
  William Henry, 25
  William James, 28
  William Penn Rhodes, 29
  William Rhodes, 29
  William Trail, 25
  William Utter, 28
Arnolde, Jane, 6
Arnoux, Agnes, 115
Arthur, Catherine, 227
  Eliza (Smith), 227
  George, 227
Arundel, Winifred, 103
Ashley, Elizabeth (Moss) Wilcox, 489
  William H., 489
Ashe, Dorothy, 348
  John, 348
  Robert, 348
Aspall, Elizabeth, 346
Atchison, Mary, 189
Atherton, Catherine, 38
  Humphrey, 38, 39
  Mary Goodenow (Kelsey), 219
  Mary Valeria, 219
  Peter Lee, 219

Atkins, Ruth, 213
Atkinson, Elizabeth, 363
  Florence Elizabeth (Lewis), 344
  Isabella, 412
  John, 344
  Lydia, 293
  Mary Brent, 193
  Mary Brent (Nuttall), 193
  Robert, 344
  Robert Lewis, 344
  William B., 193
Aucher, Elizabeth, 306
Audley, Margaret 348
Augier, Paul, 503
Austin, Jennie, 199
Avenell, Adelina (D'Abrincis), 165
  Matilda, 165
  Randolph, 165
Avery, *Arms*, 30, 35
  ———, 510
  Abigail, 32, 33
  Achsah (Wilbur) Willey, 510
  Ann, 33
  Bertha (Blanpied), 30
  Charles French, 30, 35
  Charles Henry, 30
  Deborah, 33
  Deborah (Lothrop), 33
  Deborah Putnam, 33
  Ebenezer, 32
  Elisha, 33
  Elisha Lothrop, 30, 33, 34
  Elizabeth, 32, 33
  Elizabeth Draper, 33
  Elizabeth (Lane), 32
  Emma (Putnam), 33
  Elizabeth (White), 31
  Ephraim, 32, 33
  Frances, 31
  Florence Adelaide (Topping), 30
  Florence Gladys, 30
  Florence May, 30
  Hannah, 32
  Hannah Ann (Park), 34
  Hannah (Platt), 33
  Hannah Platt, 33
  Harriet, 35
  Helen Ogden, 30
  Jane (Gunning), 34
  Jane Gunning, 34

INDEX

Avery—*Continued*
Job, 33
John, 32, 33
John William, 33, 34
Jonathan, 32
Joseph Platt, 33
Lydia (Healey), 32
Lester Hobart, 30
Margaret, 31
Mary, 31, 33
Mary (Deming), 32
Mary (Fillis)Ackincloss, 33
Mary (Lane), 31
Mary Rotch, 32
May Hepzebah (Urquhart), 30
Mary (Woodmansey) Tapping, 31
Mehitable (Hinckley) Worden, 31
Ogden, 35
Rachel, 32
Rebecca, 455
Richard, 31
Robert, 31, 32
Ruth, 32, 33
Ruth (Knowles), 32
Ruth (Little), 32
Ruth (Smith), 33
Samuel, 33
Samuel Putnam, 34
Sarah (Coit), 34
Sarah Coit, 34
Sarah Elizabeth, 34
Sarah (Fairchild), 33
Septimus, 33
Thomas, 31
William, 31
Aylett, Mary, 113
Aylmer, Judith, Lewis Chart No. 1
Mary (Newce), Lewis Chart No. 1
Theophilus, Lewis Chart No. 1

B

Babcock, James, 152
John, 152
Mary, 152
Mary (Champlin), 152
Mary (Lawton), 152
Sarah (———), 152

Bachus, Elizabeth (Huntington), 315
Joseph, 35
Bacon, Ann, 74
Nicholas, 74
Badger, Bela, 273
Catherine Louise, 273
Catherine Penelope (Worrell), 273
Badlesmere, Margaret, 346
Bailey, Elizabeth (Johnson), 332
Ellen (Lawson), 188
George, 106
Hellen, 106
Helen (Newsome), 106
James, 332, 333
Jennie (Hollingsworth), 297
Lydia, 333
Rebecca, 297
Sarah, 106
Stephen, 188
William, 297
Bailyes, Alice (Chanders), 359
Alice (Sommerland), 359
William, 359
Bain, Catherine Louise, 36
Charlotte Louise, 40
Clara Louise (Gregg), 37
Clara Lucie Vallé, 40
George, 40
George Grantham, 40
George Valleé, 37
Lucie Clara, 37
Margaret Louise, 37
Marguerite Desloge, 37
Marie Zoé, 36
Mary (Vallé), 36
Robert Edward Mather, 36, 37, 40
Walter Howard, 40
William Brown, 40
Baker, Catherine (Bulkeley), 125
Deborah (Avery), 33
Edward, 343
Fannie, 221, 222
Frances, 110
George, 125
Hannah, 343
Joseph, 33
Margaret (Emerson) McKim Vanderbilt, 202

Baker—*Continued*
Mary, 178
Nora Juanita, 399
Ray, 202
Thomas, 178
Balch, Irene, 285
Baldwicke, Joanna (———), 211
Baldwin ———, 244
Augusta (Hopkins), 249
Charles Severn, 249
Hannah, 368
Henry Wilson, 249
Ludlow, 249
Mabel (Raney), 249
Mary Anne (Hall), 244
Mary Hamilton, 249
Maude (Quirk), 249
Morgan H., 249
Morgan Hall, 249
Olive (Hill), 249
Rignal W., 249
Rosa, 249
Rosa E. (Hall), 249
Rosa Hall, 249
Springfield, 249
William H., 258
Ball, *Arms*, 41, 46
Achsah, 46
Albert Day, 41
Albert Ritchie, 43
Alexander, 44
Alexis Smith, 43
Alfred Harvey, 43
Alice Worthington, 46
Ann Liza (Schminke), 44
Anne Virginia, 44
Annie Boyd, 41
Annie Clay (De Vere), 41, 42
Arthur Dorsey, 46
Catherine, 43
Charles, 42
Charles Alexander, 44
Constance Mildred, 43
David Charles, 41, 42
Edwin Barclay, 43
Edwin Dorsey, 44
Eleanor, 45
Eleanor De Vere, 41
Eleanor Randall (Ford), 46
Elizabeth, 46
Elizabeth Bruce, 43

INDEX

Ball—*Continued*
Elizabeth Dorsey, 44
Elizabeth (Dorsey), 42, 53
Elizabeth Francis (Boyd), 42
Elizabeth Prudence, 42
Elizabeth Rogers, 41
Elizabeth Walker, 45
Ella, 44
Emily Ann (Cole), 46
Fannie (Walker), 46
George Fisher, 43
George Henry, 44
Helen Frances, 43
Henrietta, 46
Henrietta Handy, 44
James McCabe, 46
James V., 486
Jane (Watson), 486
Jeannetta Wilkins (Minter), 43
John, 44, 46
John Arthur, 43
John Edwin, 44
John L., 486
Joshua Dorsey, 46
Lloyd Dorsey, 46
Louisa, 46
Lula (Blair), 43
Mary, 44, 393
Mary (Ball), 44
Mary (Barbee), 43
Mary Henrietta, 43
Mary (Jurdan), 42
Mary Louisa, 45
Mary Virginia, 41
Mildred (San Souci), 43
Owen Davis, 43
Owen Dorsey, 42, 43
Owen Lester, 41
Prudence Gough, 42
Raymond, 44
Robert Owen, 44
Roberta (Fisher), 43
Rosalia Barrett, 41
Samuel Boyd, 43
Sara Jenetta, 41
Sarah Ann, 46
Sarah (Dorsey), 42, 50, 53
Sarah Virginia, 43
Summerfield, 44
Walter, 44, 46
Walter Summerfield, 44
William, 42, 50, 53

Ball—*Continued*
William Dorsey, 42, 53
William Edwin, 42
William Owen, 44
Ballantine, Eliza H., 17
Elizabeth (Bryant) Bonnell, 17
John, 17
Ballard, *Arms*, 62, 65
Abby Churchill, 299
Abigail, 63
Addison, 65
Adelaide (Fitch), 65
Alice Whiting (Barker), 62
Ann, 63
Charles, 65
Charles Thruston, 299
Dolly, 64
Dorothy, 63, 64, 65
Electa (Hawkes), 65
Eliza Whitney, 65
Elizabeth, 63
Elizabeth Bishop, 62
Elizabeth (Whitney), 64
Elizabeth Whitney, 65
Ellenor, 63
Emily (Palmer), 65
Eunice (Hibbard), 65
Grace (———), 62
Hannah, 63, 64
Harlan Hoge, 62, 65
Hezekiah, 63
Humphrey, 63
James, 64, 65
Jeremiah, 63, 64
John, 63, 64, 65
Jonas, 64
Jonathan, 64
Joseph, 63
Josiah, 63, 64
Julia Perkins (Pratt), 65
Julia Spaulding, 65
Laura Walker, 65
Lucy Bishop, 62
Lucy Bishop (Pike), 62
Lydia, 63, 64
Margaret, 62
Mary, 63, 64
Mary (Chandler), 63
Mary Swift, 65
Mina Breaux, 299
Olive Barker, 62
Otis, 64, 65

Ballard—*Continued*
Pamelia (Bennett), 65
Phebe, 64
Rebecca, 64
Rebecca (Rea) Stevens Horne, 63
Sarah, 63, 64
Sarah (Carter), 64
Tabitha, 63
Thomas, 64
Uriah, 63
William, 62, 63, 64, 65
William Whitney, 65
Winifred Pamelia, 65
Bants, Sarah, 368
Barbarie, John, 8
Barbee, Mary, 43
Barbier, Gabriel, 503
Barbour, Ambrois, 278
Elizabeth Pendleton, 278
Elizabeth (Thomas), 278
James, 278
Barcelo, Frances Augusta (Charruaud), 17
Juan, 17
Barclay, Mary (Hoops), 483
Mary Toland, 487
Thomas, 483
Barden, Susan (———), 403
Barker, Alice Whiting, 62
Carrie, 281
Emily (Kennedy), 281
Jabez, 516
James, 26
James Madison, 62
Johanna (———), 423
Maxwell, 281
Rebecca (Russell), 516
Richard, 406, 423
Sarah, 423
Barlow, Hannah J., 413
Barnard, Grace, 368
Mahitable, 368
Robert, 406
Barnes ———, 294
Adams, 56
Anne, 306
Emily, 160
Esther, 416
Hannah (Dorsey), 56
John, 56
Keziah (Moulthrop), 410
Marion, 417

INDEX

Barnes—*Continued*
  Rachel (Hollingsworth)
    Hope, 294
  Sarah, 410
  Sarah (Bullitt), 131
  Thomas, 410
  William, 131, 306
Barr, Agnes (———) Van Snyder Makeman, 358
  Anna Watson, 487
  Anne (Watson), 487
  Caroline Hancock Preston, 487
  Cornelius, 358
  Elise Rogers, 487
  Elizabeth Nelson (Wood), 487
  Jason Rogers, 487
  John Watson, 487
  Josephine Preston, 487
  Margaret (McFerran), 487
  Mary Toland (Barclay), 487
  Susan Preston (Rogers), 487
  Susan Rogers, 487
  Thomas, 487
  William, 487
Barret, Hugh L., 139
  Mary, 280
  Sue Bullitt (Chenoweth), 139
Barrett, Anna, 208
  Margaret, 314
  Peter, 314
Barritt, Hannah Platt (Avery), 33
  Stephen, 33
Barron, Alice, 373, 376
  Emma, 254
  James, 254
  Joshua, 373
  Lavina (Derby), 373
Bartlett, Frances Elizabeth, 414
  Margaret (Brent), 105
  Thomas, 105
Barton, Elizabeth, 453
  John, 17
  Phoebe (Bryant), 17
  Rufus, 329
  Sallie, 184
  William, 453
Bash, Henry M., 433
  Susan Anne (Rowles), 433
  Susan Luckett, 433

Bass, Sarah, 379
Basset, Aliva, 348
Bate, Clement, 321
  Helen Martin (Bullitt), 133
  Mary, 321
  Philip Barbour, 133
  Thomas, 321
Bateman, ———, 506
  Agnes, 506
  Martha, 231, 232
Battee, Henrietta Maria, 236
Batten, William, 453
Battey, Francis Josephine (Stewart), 298
  Hugh I., 298
Baugh, Anne, 106
Baxter, Sarah, 396
Bayley, Fanny, 302
  Mary Ann (———), 302
  William, 302
Beacham, Robert, 10
Beal, Caleb, 322
  Elijah, 320, 322
  John, 322
  Joseph, 322
  Sarah, 320, 322
  Sarah (Jones), 320
Beale, Eliza S., 217
  Hannah, 58
  Hannah (Gordon), 216
  Mary, 217
  William, 216
Beall, Agnes (Stewart), 252
  Bettie (Hall), 244
  Caroline (Walker), 252
  Elizabeth (Brooke), 180
  George, 90, 180
  George Hall, 252
  George Stewart, 252
  George W., 252
  Jane Beall (Magruder), 251
  Jane (Martin), 252
  John, 252
  John Rogers, 252
  John Woolf, 252
  Mary, 92
  Ninian, 90
  Rebecca Frances (Hall), 252
  Ruth Adella, 251
  Samuel Rogers, 252
  Stewart Hall, 252
  Susannah Catherine, 252
  Thomas, 244

Beall—*Continued*
  Thomas Birch, 251
  William, 92
  Winifred, 252
Beaman, Katherine Lewis (Prentis), 389
  Nathaniel, 389, 429
  Robert Prentis, 389
  Sallie Louise, 389
  Sarah, 429
Beans, Mary, 239
  Mary (Bowie), 92
  William, 92
Beard ——— (Rutland), 239
  Julia, 246
  Mattie (Woodward), 248
  Thomas, 248
Beauchamp, Thomas, 346
Beaufort, Joan, 348
Beaumont, Katerin, 5
Beaupre, Edward, 67
Beck, Leonard, 243
  Richard S., 243
  Susannah (Hall), 243
Becker, Florence Wode, 234
Becket, Mary, 13
  Eleanor (Percy), 13
Bedell, Sarah Matilda, 224
Bedford, Mary C., 162
Bedon, Mary, 123
Beebe, Jerusha, 207
  John D., 418
  Jonathan, 207
  Polly (Rickard), 418
Beekman, Ann, 338
Belcher ———, 327
  Hannah, 411
Bell, *Arms*, 66, 69
  Abigail (Roach), 67
  Alice (Colston), 67
  Alice Hunter, 275
  Anne (Osborne), 67
  Anne Virginia, 66
  Anne Virginia (Land), 66, 74
  Anthony, 67
  Barbara Robins (Wise), 67
  Catherine H. (Lawrence), 15
  Catherine (Lawrence), 18
  Charles Gibson, 66
  Edmund, 67
  Edward Land, 66
  Elizabeth, 67, 70, 490

INDEX

Bell—*Continued*
  Elizabeth Harmanson
    (Spiers), 68, 69
  Elizabeth Land, 66
  Elizabeth (Savage), 68, 71
  Elizabeth (Scott), 68
  Elizabeth (Taylor), 490
  Emily Newbold, 15
  Ernestine, 66
  Ezekiel, 70
  Ewell, 68
  George, 67, 68, 70
  Hannah (Brickhouse), 67
  Henry Lawrence, 15
  James Franklin, 275
  James Ernest, 66
  James Ewell, 66, 67, 68, 74
  Joab, 68
  Julia Newbold (Black), 15
  Kesiah (———), 68
  Leah (———) ,68
  Lelia, 66
  Lilian, 66
  Lisa (Ridgely), 15
  Lydia, 15
  Lydia Ann, 15, 18
  Maria Louisa, 66
  Martha, 222
  Mary, 66, 67, 68, 74
  Mary Jane (Wilson), 275
  Mary (Neale), 67, 71
  Mary (Watson), 67
  Richard Moore, 15
  Rosa, 66
  Robert, 67, 68, 71
  Robert Moore, 15, 18
  Sarah W. (Flagg), 204
  Savage, 68, 69
  Susanna, 68
  Susanna (Bell), 68
  Tabitha (Scarborough), 67, 71
  Thomas, 67, 70, 71, 490
  Walter Land, 66
  William, 67, 68, 71
  William Keeling, 66
Belt, Agnes, 54
  Charity, 256
  Humphrey, 94
  Joseph, 90
  Margaret, 94
  Mary, 59, 231
  Mary (Brooke), 94

Bemiss, James E., 222
  Mary E. (Swearingen), 222
Benjamin *Arms*, 79, 82, 83, 85
  Abel, 79, 81, 82, 84
  Abigail (———), 79, 81, 84
  Abigail (Eddy), 79, 81, 84
  Addison, 79, 80, 82, 84
  Benaiah, 79, 80, 81, 82, 83, 84, 371, 373
  Catherine Emma, 80, 82, 84
  Elizabeth (Noyes), 79, 80, 81, 82, 83, 84, 373
  Elizabeth (Nutting), 79, 82, 84
  Ephraim Mellen, 80, 82, 84
  Helen Augusta (Turner), 80, 82, 83
  Hester Ann, 80, 82, 84
  Jemima (Mills), 79, 82, 84, 371
  Jesse, 82
  John, 79, 80, 81, 82, 84, 370, 371
  Jonathan, 79, 81, 84
  Lois Noyes, 80, 82, 84
  Lydia (Allen), 79, 81, 84
  Martha, 82
  Mary Ann (Murphy), 80, 82, 84
  Mary Elizabeth, 80, 82, 84
  Mary Washburn, 83
  Meriam (Hunt), 80, 82, 84
  Milton, 80
  Milton Noyes, 82, 84
  Nancy Delia, 80, 82, 84, 370, 373
  Parson, 80, 82, 84
  Richard, 79
  Samuel, 82
  Susanna (Norcross), 79, 81, 84
  Tabitha (Livermore), 82
  Washburn, 80, 82, 83, 84, 85
Benner, Catherine Emma (Benjamin), 80, 82, 84
  Miles Leroy, 80, 82, 84
Bennett, Catherine Louise (Bain), 36
  E. C., 36
  Elizabeth, 445
  Elliott Chalmers, 36
  Elliott Walter Mather, 36
  Joseph, 65

Bennett—*Continued*
  Julia, 36
  Julia (Chittenden), 36
  Martha, 375
  Mary (Swift), 65
  Pamelia, 65
  Robert Chalmers, 36
  Theodora Valleé, 36
  Vallé Chittenden, 36
  Virginia Louise, 36
Benney, Ida Horsey, 193
Benson, Eliza, 169
Berkeley, Elizabeth, 346
  John, 346
Berkley, Mary Ann, 188
Berners, Margery, 115
Berry, Richard, 52
  Sarah (Dorsey), 52
Berryman, Otway Calvert, 485
  Zelie (Watson), 485
Berthold, Minnie, 280
Beverley, Catherine, 345
  Catherine, Lewis Chart No. 1
  Catherine (Hone), Lewis Chart No. 1
  Catherine (Hone), 345, 348
  Robert, 345, 348
  Robert, Lewis Chart No. 1
Bickel, Corinne, 298
Bicknell, Agnes, 426
Bigelow, Elizabeth (Bryant), 17
  Jackson, 17
Billings, Ebenezer, 285
  Hannah, 379
  Jerusha, 285
  Roger, 285
  Sarah Jane, 119
Billingsley, Hezekiah, 455
  Rebecca (Thomas), 455
Bingham, Abigail, 315
Bird, Catherine, 284
  Jane, 509
  Mary, 258
Birney, Hannah, 21
Bishop, Dorcas (Abbot), 425
  Ebenezer, 425
  Keturah, 416
  Lucy, 62
  Nellie, 398
  Reuben, 398

INDEX

Black, Jacob, 40
  Julia Newbold, 15
  Louise M. (Mather), 40
  Mary (Gay), 213
  William, 213
Blackburn-Adam, Anne Martha (La Nauze) Williamson, 505
  David, 505
Blackwell, Fitzalan, 67
  Sarah (Richardson) Dorsey, 58
  Thomas, 58
Bladen, ——— (Swearingen), 221
  Ann, 94
  John, 47
  William, 221
Blair, John, 68
  Lula, 43
Blake, Avery Hobart, 30
  Charles Avery, 30
  Dexter Barnes, 30
  Francis Clark, 65
  Frederick Henry, 30
  Helen Ogden (Avery), 30
  Richard, 406
  Winifred Pamelia (Ballard), 65
Blanpied, Bertha, 30
  Bertha (Sawyer), 30
  David, 30
Blanshan, Catherine, 471, 472
  Madeline (Jorisse), 471, 472
  Mathew, 470, 472, 473
Blanton, Catharine, 282
Bliss, Damaris (Arnold), 26
  Helen L. (Mather), 40
  John, 26
  P. Y., 40
Blood, Ellen Blake, 214
Blossom, Thankfull, 207
Blount, Constance, 346
  Walter, 346
Blunt, Elizabeth (Ballard), 63
  William, 63
Blush, Anna (Fuller), 207
  Tristram, 207
Bluzo, Lucy (Huntington), 316
  Paul, 316
Boehme, Mary (Hall), 241
  Otto, 241

Bolton ———, 127
  Ellen Maria (Holloway), 302
  Hugh W., 302
  Sarah Chauncey (Bulkeley), 127
Bolyne, Ann, 74
  Anne, 74
  Anne (Calthrope), 74
  Mary, 74
  Thomas, 74
  William, 74
Bonham, Hannah (Fuller), 206
  Nicholas, 206
Bonnell, Charlotte, 17
  Elizabeth (Bryant), 17
  Jonathan, 17
Bonsall, Nellie, 488
Bonson ———, 503
Bonville, Margaret, 166
Bonville, William, 166
Boone, Daniel, 476
  Mary (Scrogin) Wharton, 476
Booth, Charles, 293
  Elizabeth, 294
  Elizabeth (Conoway), 293
  Sarah, 404
Borden, Abigail (Russell), 516
  Joseph, 516
  Rebecca, 514
Bordon, Rebecca, 516
Borland, Augusta Elizabeth, 330
  Francis, 330
  John, 330
Bornard, Antoniette A., 224
  Emma (———), 224
  William, 224
Bos, Tryntje Tysse, 471, 472
Bostwick, Joel, 154
  Mary (Stone), 154
  Sylvia, 154
Bosvile, Muriel, 348
Bosworth, Alice, 423
Bourchier, Anne (Plantagenet), 115
  Jane, 115
  Margery (Berners), 115
  William, 115
Bourland, Margaret, 482
Bourn, Alice Mansfield Wentworth, 86
  Augustus Osborn, 86
  Charity (Chase), 86

Bourn—*Continued*
  Charity (Wheaton), 86
  Deborah, 86
  Deborah (Bourn), 86
  Elizabeth (Brayton), 86
  Elizabeth Roberts, 86
  Elizabeth Roberts (Morrill), 86
  Frances (———), 86
  Francis, 86
  George Osborn, 86
  Huldah Battey (Eddy), 86
  Jared, 86
  Stephen, 86
  Stephen Wentworth, 86
Bourne, Elizabeth, 334
  Thomas, 330
Bowdoin (Harmanson), 390
  Elizabeth (———), 390
  Grace (Stringer), 387, 389, 390, 391
  James, 390
  John, 387, 389, 390, 391
  Margaret, 387, 389, 390, 391
  Peter, 390
  Pierre, 390
  Susanna (Preeson), 390
  Susannah (Stockley), 390
Bowen, Cullen, 368
  Eleanor Humphrey, 301, 305
  Elizabeth (Humphrey), 301, 305
  Raymond Brower, 466
  Sabrett, 301, 305
  Susan Atlantic (Haskell), 368
  Virginia (Van Santvoord), 466
Bower, Mary, 122
Bowie, *Arms*, 87, 94
  ———, 332, 340
  Allen, 92, 93
  Amelia Gantt, 94
  Clagett, 89, 245
  Daniel, 232
  Edward Hall, 89, 245
  Eleanor, 91
  Elizabeth, 93
  Elizabeth (Pottinger), 92
  Elizabeth Taylor (Wattles), 88, 245
  Esther (Sprigg), 92
  Ethel Frances (Cook), 87, 245

INDEX

Bowie—*Continued*
  Florence Clara (Hatch), 89
  Florence (Hatch), 245
  George Washington, 94
  Hannah, 93
  Hannah (Lee), 92
  Henry Anderson, 87, 89, 245
  Helen McKinstry, 89
  Henrietta (Cowman), 340
  Humphrey Belt, 94
  James, 92
  John, 87, 91, 92, 93, 94, 245
  Kitty, 239
  Kitty (Duchett), 239
  Margaret(Belt), 94
  Margaret Crabb (Johns) Chew, 93
  Margaret (Dallas), 92
  Margaret Lowndes, 89
  Margaret Lowndes (Gantt), 94
  Margaret Ruth, 94
  Margaret (Sprigg), 92
  Martha (———), 92
  Martha Magdalene (Rapine), 94
  Mary, 92, 93
  Mary Ann, 94
  Mary (Beall), 92
  Mary (Mullikin), 91
  Mary (Rapine), 94
  Mary Tasker, 90, 245
  Priscilla (———) Finch, 92
  Rachel (Pottinger), 92
  Rezin P., 92
  Richard, 93
  Richard Cramphin, 94
  Robert Monroe, 87
  Ruth (Crampin), 93
  Susan (Fraser), 92
  Susannah (Anderson), 87, 91, 245
  Susannah Anderson, 89
  Susannah Frances, 87
  Thomas, 92, 93
  Thomas J., 94
  Thomas John, 87, 90, 94, 245
  Washington, 93
  William, 87, 92, 239, 245
  William Tasker, 89
Bowling, James, 179
  Mary (Brooke), 179

Bowman, Edmund, 70
  Elizabeth, 67, 70
  Gertrude, 69
  Southey Littleton, 69
Bowne, Elizabeth (Lawrence), 12, 13
  Hannah, 13
  John, 6, 12, 13
  Mary (Beckett), 13
  Samuel, 13
Boyce, ———, 340
  Amabel George, 341
  Arthur Cauchoir, 44
  Edna (Grandveaux), 44
  Elizabeth, 44
  Elizabeth Dorsey (Ball), 44
  Elizabeth Lee, 341
  Frederick A., 340
  Heyward Easter, 340
  James Raymond, 44
  John George, 341
  Natalie (Goffe), 44
  Raymond, 44
  Rebecca Latimer, 340
  Wallace Campbell, 44
  Walter Ball, 44
Boyd, ———, 232
  David, 42
  Elizabeth Francis, 42
  Mary, 42
  Sophia Keyser, 442
  Thomas, 232
Boyden, Jonathan, 288
  Lydia, 288
  Thomas, 288
Boyle, Celia (Gay), 213
  John, 213
Boynton, Elizabeth (Hazeltine), 333
  Ellen (Pell), 333
  Hannah (Keys), 333
  Ichabod, 333
  John, 333
  Rachel, 333
Bradbury, Mary Elizabeth (Hollingsworth), 300
  W. B., 300
Bradford, Ann, 508
  Hannah (Rogers), 212
  Jerusha, 212
  Samuel, 212
Bradley, ———, 198
  Abigail, 410

Bradley—*Continued*
  Caleb, 411
  Florence, 448
  Francis, 429
  Isaac, 409
  Joseph, 410
  Lucretia, 411
  Sarah Beaman (Ruggles), 429
  Sarah (English), 198
  Sarah (Russell), 411
  Silence (Brockett), 410
Bradshaw, Ann, 348
  Mehetabel (Hewins), 284
  Nathaniel, 284
Bradstreet, Anne (Dudley), 331
  Simon, 331
Bragdon, Isabella, 446
Bragg, Phebe, 423
Branch, Anne Harris, 146
  James Read, 146
  Martha Louise (Patteson), 146
Brandt, Elizabeth, 130
  Randolph, 129, 130
Bransford, John, Lewis Chart No. 1
  Nancy (Snoddy), Lewis Chart No. 1
  Parthenia, 343, 347, 348
  Parthenia, Lewis Chart No. 1
  Patsy, Lewis Chart No. 1
  Thomas, Lewis Chart No. 1
  Virginia (Settle), Lewis Chart No. 1
  Walter L., Lewis Chart No. 1
  Walter Lee, 343
Brashiar, Elizabeth Crow, 222
Bratt, Ariantje, 467
  Geertge, 467
Brattle, Katherine, 326
Brattle, Thomas, 326
Braxton, Carter, 350
  George, 350
Bray, Ann (Keeling), 75
  Edward, 75
  Robert, 75
Brayton, Elizabeth, 86
  Francis, 86
  Margaret, 81
  Mary E. W., 29
Breckinridge, *Arms*, 95, 100
  ——— (Murphy), 99
  Alexander, 95

INDEX

Breckinridge—*Continued*
  Anna Sophonisba (Preston), 97
  Ben Johnson, 99
  Caroline Laurence, 97
  Charles David, 98
  Clifton Rodes, 95, 99
  Elizabeth Lee, 100
  Elizabeth Thomas, 215
  Ethel Ludlow Dudley, 97
  Florence, 99
  Frances, 99
  Frances Anne, 97
  Frances (Prevost), 97
  Harriet (———), 99
  Helen (Steele), 99
  Henry Skillman, 97
  Isabell (Goodrich), 98
  James, 96
  James Carson, 95
  Jane (———), 95
  John, 96, 97, 99
  John Cabell, 98
  John Preston, 97
  John Witherspoon Owen, 99
  Joseph Cabell, 96, 97, 98
  Katherine (Breckinridge) Carson, 95
  Laura Johnson, 98
  Letitia Porter, 98
  Letitia Preston, 96
  Lloyd Trevis, 99
  Louise Ludlow (Dudley), 97
  Louise (Trevis), 99
  Lucien Scott, 97
  Lucy Hayes, 97
  Margaret Scott Skillman, 97
  Mary Ann, 96
  Mary Cabell, 98
  Mary Carson, 95
  Mary Cryene (Burch), 98
  Mary Desha, 100
  Mary Dudley, 97
  Mary (Hopkins) Cabell, 96
  Mary Marvin, 98
  Robert, 96, 98
  Robert Jefferson, 97
  Robert Johnson, 99
  Sally Frances (Johnson), 98
  Sarah (Tomkins) Garnett, 97
  Scott Dudley, 97
  Susanna Preston Lees, 95
  William Lewis, 97

Bredin, Henriette (———), 503
Brent, *Arms*, 101, 111
  Adelaide, 113
  Agnes, 102, 103, 104
  Ann (Carroll), 107
  Anna Maria, 109
  Anna Maria (Parnham), 108
  Anna Maria Parnham, 109
  Anne, 103, 104, 105, 106, 108, 113, 178
  Anne (Baugh), 106
  Anne (Brent), 108
  Anne (Calvert) Brooke, 106, 112
  Anne Fenton (Lee), 113
  Anne (Stourton), 103
  Arthur Lee, 113
  Barbara, 102, 103
  Barbara (———), 105
  Benjamin, 108
  Catherine, 104, 105, 108
  Catherine (———), 105
  Catherine (Trimmingham), 107, 484
  Catherine Walker (Johnson), 108
  Cecila (———), 104
  Clare, 107
  Daniel, 108
  Daniel Carroll, 113
  Dorothy, 106
  Dorothy (Leigh), 109
  Duncan Kenner, 101, 111
  Edward, 105, 106
  Edward Cole, 110
  Edward Watkins, 110
  Eleanor, 104, 105, 108, 113, 114
  Elinor, 109
  Elinor (Carroll), 113
  Eliza Jacqueline (Ambler), 113
  Eliza (Walsh), 108
  Elizabeth, 103, 104, 105, 106, 107, 108, 109
  Elizabeth (———), 104
  Elizabeth (Greene), 106
  Elizabeth Hager, 110
  Elizabeth (Neale), 108
  Elizabeth (Reed), 104, 112, 115
  Elizabeth (Worth), 104

Brent—*Continued*
  Emma Fenwick, 110
  Flora, 114
  Flora (Deshler), 114
  Frances, 105
  Frances (Baker), 110
  Frances Rosella (Kenner), 111
  Frances Wharton, 109
  Frances (Whitgreaves) Harrison, 112
  Francis, 108, 109
  Fulke, 104, 112
  George, 105, 106, 107, 108, 109, 112, 484
  George Lee, 113
  Giles, 103, 105, 106, 112, 193, 194
  Hally Brown (Richardson), 101
  Harriet Carrington, 101
  Helen, 104
  Henrietta, 110
  Henry, 106, 107, 108, 112
  Hugh, 102
  Ida (De Beauchamp), 102
  Ida Schreve, 110
  James, 109
  James Fenwick, 110
  Jane, 105, 106, 108
  Jane (Chandler), 112
  Jane (Mudd), 107
  Jane (Thompson), 107
  Jane (Wilkins), 113
  Jennie, 484
  Joan, 102
  Joan (Harewell), 102
  Joan (Latimer), 102
  Joan Le Eyre, 102
  Joan (Malet), Crewkern, 103
  John, 102, 103, 106, 108
  Joseph Lancaster, 101, 110, 117
  Katherine, 105, 112
  Katherine (Greville), 104
  Laura (Overton), 110
  Leila Lawrence, 110
  Margaret, 103, 104, 105, 106, 112, 178, 194
  Margaret (Malet), 103
  Margaret (Peshell), 104
  Margery (Colchester), 104

INDEX

Brent—*Continued*
  Maria, 110
  Maria (Fenwick), 109
  Marianne, 107
  Marianne (Peyton),106, 112
  Marie Louise, 114
  Martha, 107, 108
  Mary, 104, 105, 106, 107, 108, 109, 112, 114
  Mary Aylett, 113
  Mary (Brent), 106, 112
  Mary (Culpeper), 103
  Mary (Fitz-Hugh), 107
  Mary Hoke, 110
  Mary (Huggerford), 104
  Mary (Ludlow), 103
  Mary (Sewell) Chandler, 107
  Mary (Wharton), 108
  Mary (Young), 108
  Matilda (Lawrence), 109
  Matilda (Thomas), 109
  Maude (Pauncefoot), 103
  Millicent (———), 101
  Nanine, 111
  Nicholas, 104, 107, 108
  Princess (Kitomagund), 112
  Richard, 102, 103, 104, 106, 112, 113, 115
  Robert, 103, 104, 105, 106, 107, 108, 109
  Robert Fenwick, 110
  Robert J., 111
  Robert James, 109
  Rosella (Kenner), 117
  Sarah, 107
  Sarah Anne, 110
  Sarah (Gibbons), 113
  Stephen, 103
  Susannah, 107, 108
  Susannah (Seymour), 107
  Teresa, 109
  Thomas, 104, 108
  Thomas Lee, 113, 114
  Thomas Ludlow Lee, 114
  Thomas Ludwell Lee, 113
  Thomasine, 102
  Ursula, 106
  William, 102, 103, 104, 105, 106, 108, 109, 110, 112, 113
  William Leigh, 109, 110
  Winifred (Arundel), 103
  Winifred Beale (Lee), 113

Brent—*Continued*
  Winifred Eleanor, 114
  Winifred Lee, 114
Brenton, William, 330
Brewerton, Henry, 169
  Sarah (Courtenay), 169
Brice, Ann, 61
  John, 60, 61
  Rachel, 61
  Sarah (Frisby), 61
  Sarah (Howard) Worthington, 60
Brickhouse, Hannah, 67
Bridge, James Howard, 151
  Margery Howard, 151
  Mary Ellen (Taylor), 151
  Pauline W., 201
Bridges, Charles, 6
  Elizabeth (Peirce), 187
  Mercy, 461
  Rozier, 187
Briggs, Deborah (Cushing), 437
  Joanna, 403
  Matthew, 437
Bringier, Aglae, 117
  Aglae (Du Bourg), 117
  Agnes (Arnoux), 115
  Amedee, 116
  Anne Guilhelmine Nanine, 111
  Augustine (Tureaud), 116
  Browse, 116
  Du Bourg, 116
  Elizabeth Aglae (Du Bourg), 115
  Ignace, 115
  Jean, 115
  Louise, 117
  Marie (Douradou), 115
  Marie Frances (Durand), 115
  Marius Pons, 115
  Marius Ste. Colombe, 116, 117
  Michel Douradou, 115, 116, 117
  Myrthe, 117
  Nanine, 117
  Octavie, 117
  Pierre, 115
  Trist, 116
  Stella (Tureaud), 116

Brinley, Mary, 26
Briscoe, Ann Sedgewick (Huppman), 337
  Arthur Fenner Lee, 337
  Cornelia Lee, 337
  Elizabeth Sedgewick, 337
  Ellinor Carroll, 337
  James, 337
  James Howard, 337
  John Douglas, 337
  Sarah, 176
  Sophia Howard (Lee), 337
  Theodore Forbes, 337
Britton, Ebenezer, 510
  Tabitha, 510
  Tabitha (Leonard), 510
Brock, ———, 267
Brocket, Anne (McCormick), 243
  Cornelia M., 243
  Robert, 243
Brockett, John, 410
  Silence, 410
Brodie, David Clark, 499
  Georgina La Nauze (Clark), 499
  Robert, 499
Brogden, William, 232
Brooke, *Arms*, 178
  Ann (———), 386
  Anne (———), 179
  Anne (Calvert), 106, 178
  Baker, 106, 178, 180
  Barbara, 178
  Barbara (Dent), 176, 179
  Benjamin, 91, 179
  Clement, 179
  Eleanor, 179
  Eleanor (Bowie), 91
  Eleanor (Hatton), 178
  Elizabeth, 180
  George Clymer, 364
  Ignatius, 179
  Jane, 179
  Jane (Sewell), 179
  John, 179, 386
  Lucy, 180
  Mary, 94, 178, 179, 386
  Mary (Baker), 178
  Mary (Engham), 178
  Mary (Mainwaring), 178
  Matthew, 179
  Nathaniel, 179

INDEX

Brooke—*Continued*
Rebecca, 176, 179, 180
Rhoda Fuller (Morris), 364
Robert, 90, 173, 178, 179
Susan (Foster), 178
Thomas, 90, 173, 176, 178, 179, 180
Brooks, Mary, 277
Brown, ———, 310
Ann, 310
Ann (Jeffries), 328
Ann Marten, 24
Anna, 255
Abial, 181, 182
Abigail, 203
Adaline Crittenden (Watson), 488
Agnes (Moulthrop), 412
Alexander, 247
Asenath (Wilbur) Ellis, 510
Bertha, 224
Caroline T., 286
Charles Edgar, 414
Daniel, 198
Ebenezer, 197
Edith, 154
Eleanor (Fitz-Alan), 197
Elizabeth, 414
Elizabeth (Osgood), 406
Ellen (Bryant), 17
Ephraim W., 510
Erasmus Dervan, 224
Frances Cooksie, 247
Frances Elizabeth (Bartlett), 414
Frances James, 394, 409, 414
Francis, 197, 204
Gustavus, 129
Gustavus Richard, 131
Hally, 101
Hannah (English), 198
Hannah 'Vincent), 197
Hopestill (———), 181, 182
James, 17, 225, 469
Jane, 277
Joanna, 181
John, 406, 469, 488
Joseph Bailey, 488
Katherine (McKenna), 174
Knox, 488
Lydia (Howland), 225
Maria Stockton, 136
Mary, 469

Brown—*Continued*
Mary Agnes, 414
Mary Agnes (Moulthrop), 394, 414
Mary (Edwards), 197
Mary Elizabeth (Hynson), 101
Mary (English), 198
Mercy, 204
Nancy, 181, 182
Pauline, 488
Peter, 416
Rebecca, 197, 416
Renwick, 394, 414
Rodes, 488
Roswell, 198
Salina (Wilbur), 510
Samuel, 328, 412
Sarah, 131
Sarah B., 3
Sarah Matilda (Bedell), 224
Submit, 461
Thomas, 197
Thomas C., 101
Timothy, 510
Victoria, 414
Walter Edgar, 414
Walter Scott, 414
Wealthy (Wilbur), 510
Welcome, 510
Browne, Abigail, 447
Elinor, 59
Bruce, Elizabeth Barbour (Helm), 278
H. W., 278
Helm, 276
Isabel (Huntingdon), 347
Margaret, 347
Margery, 347
Mary, 455
Robert, 347
Bryan, Alexander Hamilton, 120
Amanda Stewart, 119
Anne Eliza (Tennant), 119
Caroline Clifford, 491
David Tennant, 119
Delia (Forman), 123
Elizabeth (Pendarvis), 123
Elizabeth Tucker (Coalter), 123
Emily Page (Kemp), 119
Evelyn, 140

Bryan—*Continued*
Grace (Hamilton), 119
H. Georgia, 123
Hannah, 122
Hannah (Rickard) Whitman, 416
Helen McGill, 120
Helen McGill (Hamilton), 120
Hugh, 122
Isobel Lamont (Stewart), 119
Isobel Stewart, 120
Janet (Cochran), 122
John Randolph, 123, 140
John Stewart, 119
Jonathan, 119, 122
Joseph, 119, 120, 122, 123, 416
Joseph St. George, 119
Josiah, 122, 123
Lamont Stewart, 120
Margaret Randolph (Minor), 140
Mary (Williamson), 122
Norma Stewart, 120
Rebecca (Darrah), 273
Robert Carter, 119
Robert Coalter, 119
Thomas Forman, 123
Thomas Pinckney, 120
Virginia, 123
William, 273
Winifred (Duffy), 119
Bryant, Benjamin, 17
Cornelius, 16
Elizabeth, 17
Ellen, 17
Ellen (Sparling), 16
Frances (Deleval), 16
George, 17
Hannah, 17
Hannah (Carteret), 16
Jane, 17
Johannes, 16
John, 16, 17
Mary, 17
Nancy, 17
Phoebe, 17
Sarah, 17
Simeon, 16
Buchanan, Jane, 279
William, 279

INDEX

Buck, Charles Neville, 133
  Charles William, 133
  Elizabeth (Bullitt), 133
  Mamie, 133
  Margaret Field De Motte, 133
  Susannah, 308
Buckbee, Henry H., 17
  Mary (Bryant), 17
Buckley, Annie Morris, 364
  Effingham L., 364
  Elizabeth Morris, 362
  Hannah A. (Morris), 364
  Peter, 451
  Rachel (Talcott), 451
  Sarah (Morris), 361
  Thomas, 364
  William, 361
Buckner, Elizabeth (Ariss), 188
  Elizabeth Eden (Thomas), 454
  Mary Clark, 500
  Mary Dixon (Clark), 500
  Richard, 188
  Thomas, 454
  Thomas Woodbridge, 500
Buffington, Willie Anne, 119
Buford, Ann Bannister (Howe) Watson, 486
  John, 486
Bugbee, Sarah (Gore), 380
Bulkeley, *Arms*, 124, 128
  Ann, 125, 127
  Ann (Bulkeley), 127
  Ann (Latimer), 126
  Catherine, 125, 126
  Charles, 126, 127
  Charles E., 127
  Charles Edwin, 127
  Clarissa, 127
  Clarissa (Bulkeley), 127
  Daniel, 125
  Dorothy, 125, 126
  Dorothy (Prescott), 126
  Edward, 124, 125, 126
  Elijah, 127
  Elinor Houghton, 124
  Eliphalet, 126, 127, 128
  Eliphalet Adams, 127
  Eliza, 125
  Elizabeth (Grosvenor), 124
  Fannie Briggs (Houghton), 124

Bulkeley—*Continued*
  Frances, 127
  George, 125
  Gershom, 125, 126
  Grace (Chetwode), 125
  Houghton, 124
  Hugh, 319
  Jabez, 125
  Jane (Allen), 125
  John, 125, 126
  John Charles, 127
  John Taintor, 127
  Jonathan, 127
  Joseph, 125
  Julia, 127
  Julia (Worthington), 127
  Lucy, 126
  Lydia, 126
  Lydia Ann, 127
  Lydia Smith (Morgan), 127
  Margaret, 125
  Margaret (Whittemore), 124
  Margery, 319
  Mary, 125, 126, 127
  Mary (Adams) Gardiner), 126
  Mary (Isham), 127
  Mary Morgan, 128
  Morgan G., 319
  Morgan Gardner, 124, 127
  Nathaniel, 125
  Olive (Irby), 125
  Oliver, 126
  Orlando, 127
  Patience, 126, 127
  Patience (Prentice), 126
  Paul, 125
  Peter, 125, 126, 378
  Rebecca (Talcott), 126
  Richard, 125
  Roland, 124
  Ruth (Collins), 124
  Sarah, 126
  Sarah (Chauncey), 126
  Sarah Chauncey, 127
  Sarah (Taintor), 127
  Thomas, 124, 125
  William, 125
  William Henry, 127
Bulkley. Elizabeth, 427
  Peter, 427
Bull, Godsgift (Arnold), 26
  Jireh, 26

Bullard, William, 289
Bullitt, *Arms*, 129, 140
  A. C., 134
  Agatha Marshall, 140
  Alexander Scott, 131, 134, 135, 140, 177
  Ann Eliza, 134
  Anne, 136
  Annie Christian, 132, 134, 177
  Annie Priscilla (Logan), 139
  Benjamin, 130
  Charles Smith, 135
  Clare Selby (Ralston), 135
  Cuthbert, 130, 132, 134, 173
  David Bell, 137
  Dorothy Frances (Stimson), 140
  Dorothy (Terry), 140
  Edith, 133
  Edna (———), 137
  Edward Crowe, 133
  Elizabeth, 130, 133, 135
  Elizabeth (Brandt), 130
  Elizabeth (Harrison), 130
  Elizabeth R. (Smith), 135
  Elizabeth (Selby), 135
  Emilie (Tathman), 136
  Ernesta (Drinker), 136
  Evelyn (Bryan), 140
  Frances, 131
  Frances (Weston), 135
  George Smith, 135
  Gordon, 134
  Harriet, 134
  Harriet (Willett), 132
  Helen, 134
  Helen Eleanor Grant, 131
  Helen Key, 137
  Helen Martin, 133, 137
  Helen (Scott), 131
  Helen Scott, 134
  Helen (Willard), 134
  Henrietta, 134
  Henrietta Massie, 135
  Henry Massie, 132, 139
  Irene Smith, 135
  James Bell, 135, 139, 140
  James Fry, 137
  Jean Christian, 137
  Jeanette Langhorne, 137
  John Christian, 135, 136, 137, 140

INDEX

Bullitt—*Continued*
Joseph, 130
Joshua Fry, 135
Julia, 133
Julia (Anderson), 132
Julia Dunlap), 136
Kate (Steele), 134
Keith Logan, 140
Logan M., 137
Logan McKnight, 136
Louisa Gross (Horwitz), 136
Margaret, 140
Margaret (Emmons), 137
Margaret Emmons, 137
Margaret (Talbott), 135
Maria Stockton, 137
Maria Stockton (Brown), 136
Maria (Strother), 127
Mary, 131
Mary A., 155
Mary Caile (Harrison), 131
Mary (Churchill) Prather, 131
Martha Bell, 135, 137
Martha Davis, 137
Mary L. (Frederick), 139
Maurice Langhorne, 136
Mildred Ann, 140
Mildred Ann (Fry), 135
Minar Dixon, 135
Mirah Logan, 140
Nora (Iasigi), 129
Nora Isaigi, 129
Pauline, 136
Polly, 131
Priscilla, 134
Priscilla (Christian), 131, 177
Priscilla Christian, 137
Orville, 136
Ralston, 135
Richard Stockton, 137
Samuel, 134
Sarah, 131
Sarah Crow (Paradise), 132
Seth, 130
Sophia, 131
Susan Dixon, 136
Susan (Ingersoll), 136
Susan Peachy, 137
Therese, 136
Therese Caldwell (Langhorne), 135

Bullitt—*Continued*
Thomas, 130, 131
Thomas James, 131
Thomas Walker, 129, 139, 140
Virginia Anderson, 133
Willett, 134
William, 134
William Christian, 135, 136
William Marshall, 129, 139
Bullock, Caroline Lawrence (Breckinridge), 97
J. J., 97
Bumpus, Zeraviah, 417
Bundy, Viola, 511
Burbank, David, 137
Burbank, Kate (Dixon), 137
Burch, Clifton Rodes, 98
Mary Cryene, 98
Burdick, Deborah, 152
Mary (———), 152
Samuel, 152
Tacy, 152
Burgess, Bryant, 25
Elizabeth (Dorsey), 52
Elizabeth Sophia (Arnold), 25
John, 52
Mary Ridgeley (Dorsey), 48
Philemon, 48
Rebecca (Dorsey), 48
Susannah, 179
Vachel, 48
Burks, Elizabeth, 144
Mary (Davis), 144
Samuel, 144
Burling, Ann, 14
Edward, 14
Elizabeth, 14
James, 14
Mary (Lawrence), 14
Sarah, 14
Burmingham, Rose, 309
Burnett, Mary Elizabeth, 259
Burns, Isabella, 496
Margaret, 496
Burrage, Francis Hathaway, 214
Burrage, Marian Otis (Gay), 214
Burrington, Ebenezer, 411
Mary (Moulthrop), 411

Burroughs, Caroline, 351
Caroline (Mitchell), 364
Ellen, 456
Elizabeth (Wood, 456
Ellen Douglas, 364
H. Nelson, 364
James, 456
Burton, Abraham, 428
Betty (Dale), 428
Boniface, 428
Deborah, 479
John, 428
Lydia, 422, 428
Media, 189
Muriel, 348
Butler, Anne (Mason), 477, 478
Elizabeth, 477, 478
Jane Short, 132, 174, 177
John, 346
Julia (Bulkeley), 127
Margaret, 346, 348, 506
Margaret (Dudley), 346
Stueben, 127
William, 346, 348, 477, 478, 506
Butt, Jane (———), 76
Joshua, 76
Olive, 76
Robert, 76
Thomas, 76
Butterfield, Ann (Bollard), 63
Joseph, 63
Lydia (Ballard), 63
Samuel, 63
Buzby, Anne, 443
Byerly, Ann (Long), 274
Christopher, 274
Elizabeth (Clymer), 274
John, 274
Sara, 274
Byers, Caroline Mitchell (Morris), 364
John Frederick, 364
Rebecca (Watson), 488
William, 488
Byrd, Marie (Massie), 269
Martha Elizabeth, 269
Mary, 77
Richard, 77
William, 269

INDEX

C

Cabell, *Arms*, 142, 150
  Abraham Joseph, 146
  Adah (Wymond), 147
  Agness Bell, 147
  Agnes Sarah Bell (Gamble), 146
  Agness C. (Coles), 148
  Alfred, 150
  Anna Maria (Wilcox), 147
  Anne, 143
  Anne Harris (Branch), 146
  Anthony, 143
  Arthur Grattan, 147
  Ashley, 147
  Bridget, 143
  Catherine Ann, 146
  Christopher, 143
  Clarence, 150
  Dorothy Temple, 142
  Edward Carrington, 146, 147
  Eliza Fitzhugh (May), 145
  Elizabeth, 143, 144, 145, 146
  Elizabeth Brierton (Jones), 145
  Elizabeth (Burks), 144
  Elizabeth (Cabell), 146
  Elizabeth Caskie, 146
  Elizabeth Crittanden, 147
  Elizabeth (Fowell), 143
  Elizabeth Hannah, 147
  Emily Corbett (Failing), 149
  Emma Catharine, 146
  Ethel Alston, 142
  Elthel Hoyt (Scott), 142
  Florence, 148
  Florida, 147
  George, 143, 145
  Hannah, 145
  Hannah (Carrington), 145
  Heningham, 145
  Henry Coalter, 148, 149
  Henry Failing, 149
  Henry Landon, 147
  Isa (Carrington), 146
  J. J. Crittenden, 147
  James Alston, 142, 148
  James Caskie, 146
  Jane C. (Alston), 148
  Joanna, 144
  John, 143, 145
  John Grattan, 148

Cabell—*Continued*
  Joseph, 144, 145
  Joseph Carrington, 145
  Julian Mayo, 150
  Katherine Hamilton, 142, 148
  Louisa Elizabeth, 146
  Margaret Constance, 147
  Margaret Hodges (Stretch), 147
  Margaret (Jordan), 144, 146
  Margaret (Meredith), 144
  Margaret Read (Venable), 145
  Margaret Sophia (Caskie), 146
  Margery Wade, 142
  Mary, 144
  Mary (———), 143
  Mary Anne, 145
  Mary Hope, 147
  Mary (Hopkins), 96, 145
  Mary (Prestwood), 143
  Mary Walker (Carter), 145
  Mayo Carrington, 145
  Nannie (Enders), 146
  Nicholas, 143, 144, 145
  Nicholas Carrington, 146
  Paul C., 145
  Paulina (Jordan), 145
  Rachel (Hooper), 144
  Richard, 142, 143
  Robert Gamble, 146, 147
  Samuel, 143
  Sarah, 144
  Sarah Marshall (Tankersley), 148
  Susan, 143
  Susanna (Wyatt), 145
  Susannah (Peter), 143
  Thomasin (———), 142
  Walter Coles, 148
  William, 143, 144, 146
  William H., 145, 146, 147
  William Wirt, 147
  William Wymond, 147
Cadwalader, Eleanor, 303, 304
  Hannah, 360
  Hugh, 303, 304
  Rebecca, 359
  Robert, 304
Cady, Joanna, 396

Cake, Catherine (Miller), 479
  Henry, 479
  Sarah, 478, 479
Caldwell, Gabriel, 189
  John, 471, 477
  Lucinda (Moss), 189
  Mary (———), 477
  Sarah, 477
Calthorpe, Anne (Bolyne), 74
  Anne, 74
  Elizabeth, 74
  Philip, 74
Calvert, Anne, 106, 112, 178, 292
  Anne (Brent), 105, 178
  Anne (Crupper), 105
  Anne (Nottley), 105
  Elizabeth, 106
  Elizabeth (Harrison), 105
  Elizabeth (Stone), 105
  George, 105
  Hellen (Bailey), 106
  John, 105, 106
  Jane (———), 292
  Leonard, 105, 112, 178
  Mary (Strother) Deatherage, 105
  Sarah (Bailey), 106
  Thomas, 292
  William, 105
Calwell, Sarah (Cushing), 443
  William Henry, 443
Camp, Janet Gordon, 497
Campbell, ———, 97
  Agnes, 347
  Archibald, 347
  Colin, 347
  Donald Argyll, 466
  Duncan, 347
  Edith (Van Santvoord), 466
  Elizabeth (Henry), 97
  Eno, 235
  Frederick A., 466
  Isabel (Stewart), 347
  Jean, 205, 215
  Jean (Wallace), 215
  Kate Bradshaw, 189
  Margaret, 37
  Margery (Bruce), 347
  Rachel Hall Stack (Perine), 235
  Robert, 215
Can, Elizabeth, 392

INDEX

Cannon, Elizabeth, 193
  Margaret, 193
  Nutter, 193
Canter, Caroline (Midyette), 247
  Frances Cooksie (Brown), 247
  Hall, 247
  Harry M., 247
  Margaret Jane (Hall), 247
  Margaret (Jones), 247
  Isaac W., 247
  Noland Mackenzie, 247
  Julia White, 247
Canz, Elizabeth, 435
  Robert, 435
Carlile, David, 171
  Jane, 171
  Jane (Medill), 171
Carpenter, ———, 26
  Asenath, 288, 289
  Elizabeth (Arnold), 23, 288
  Emma Eliza (Clarke), 29
  Joseph, 29
  May, 418
  Mehetabel, 28
  Richard, 288
  Sarah (Arnold), 26
  Sarah Hill, 29
  Susannah, 26
  William, 23, 26
Carr, Jane, 153
  Lucy, 260
  Phillip Dorsey, 256, 257, 260
  Sallie (Higgins), 257
Carrel, Asenath (Carpenter), 288
  Joseph, 288
Carrick, Helen, 342
  Helen, Lewis Chart No. 1
Carrier, Hannah (Rhoades), 398
  Nelson, 398
Carrington, Anne (Mayo), 145
  Benjamin, 145
  Emma Catherine (Cabell), 146
  George, 145
  Hannah, 145
  Henry, 146
  Isa, 146
  Louisa Elizabeth (Cabell), 146

Carrington—*Continued*
  Mary Anne (Cabell), 145
  Mary (Penniman), 101
  Paul S., 146
Carrol, Asenath (Carpenter), 289
Carroll, ———, 221
  Agnes, 336
  Albert Henry, 336
  Anne, 107
  Anne (Brent), 113
  Charles, 179, 336
  Charles of Carrollton, 179
  Charles Whiting, 288, 289
  Clarissa (Alden), 288
  Daniel, 113
  Eleanor, 113
  Eleanor (Darnall), 113
  Eleanor (Swearingen), 221
  Harriet (Whiting), 288, 289
  Harriet Whiting, 283, 288, 289
  Joseph, 289
  Mamie, 344
  Mary Cornelia (Read), 336
  Mary (Darnall), 179
  Mary Digges (Lee), 336
  Mary Ellinor, 336
  Mary Sophia, 336
  Sanford, 288, 289
  William Sanford, 288
Carson, Eleanor (Gordon), 216
  James Green, 95
  Joseph, 216
  Katherine Breckinridge, 95
Carter, ———, 411
  Abigail (Moulthrop), 411
  Anna Briggs, 298
  Benjamin, 296
  Breckinridge, 99
  Caroline Dupre (Steele), 99
  Christopher, 144
  Florence Louise, 356
  Frances, 113
  George, 145
  Joseph Coleman, 99
  Margaret (Hollingsworth), 296
  Martha C., 418
  Mary (Cabell), 144
  Mary Walker, 145
  Robert, 350
  Ruth (Phelps), 64

Carter—*Continued*
  Sarah, 64
  Sarah Fullerton, 99
  Thomas, 64
Carteret, Elizabeth, 11, 16
  Elizabeth (Smith) Lawrence, 11
  George, 16
  Hannah, 16
  James, 16
  Phillip, 11
Cartwright, Alice E. (Tiffany), 463
  Charles, 463
Cary, Katherine, 74
  Mary (Bolyne), 74
  William, 74
Caryl, Esther (Pond), 288
  Jonathan, 288
  Joseph, 288
  Lydia (Boyden), 288
Caskie, Elizabeth (Pincham), 146
  James, 146
  Margaret Sophia, 146
Cassel, Anna Bella, 174
Cassie, Jane (Brent), 105
  Thomas, 105
Castleman, David, 96
  Mary Ann (Breckinridge), 96
Caswell, Mehitable, 403
Catesby, Mary (Brent), 104
  Richard, 104
Cathcart, Blanche, 355
  Caroline, 170
  Frances Josephine, 355
  J. W., 355
  Louisa Emmalla (Marine), 355
Cathart, Martha Ann (Cooper), 355
Cathcart, Martha Cooper, 355
  Maxwell, 355
  Robert, 355
Cathell, Margaret J., 209
Catlett, Elizabeth Thomas (Breckinridge), 215
  Maria Breckinridge, 215
  Nathaniel Pendleton, 215
Causey, Charles Henry, 388
  Martha Josephine (Prentis), 388

INDEX

Cave, Mary, 454
Chalmers, Elizabeth, 310
Champernowne, Agnes, 166
  Alexander, 166
Champion, Ann Eloise (Stewart), 298
  James P., 298
Champlin, *Arms*, 151, 156
  Adam, 153
  Ann, 152, 153
  Anne, 153
  Anstis, 153
  Bridget (Thompson), 152
  Caroline Brown, 155
  Christopher, 151
  Christopher Grant, 151
  Deborah, 153
  Deborah (Burdick), 152
  Edward Elmore, 155
  Elizabeth, 153, 154
  Elizabeth (Wells), 154
  Esther (Smith), 155
  Eunice, 153
  Eunice Thruston (Melville), 153
  Franka E. (Colvocoresses), 156
  Geoffrey, 151
  George, 151
  Hannah (Gardner), 152
  Hannah (Stetson), 153
  Henrietta (Coggshall), 153
  Isaac, 154
  Isabella, 155
  James, 152
  James Tift, 151
  James Wells, 154
  Jane (Carr), 153
  Jeffrey, 151, 152, 153
  John, 153
  John Denison, 151, 154, 155
  John Drew, 154
  Joseph, 152, 153
  Joshua, 152
  Lois, 153
  Lucy, 153
  Margaret, 154
  Margaret (Drew), 154
  Margery Howard (Bridge), 151
  Mary, 152, 153, 154
  Mary A. (Bullitt), 155
  Mary (Babcock), 152

Champlin—*Continued*
  Mary (Clarke), 152
  Mary (Denison), 154
  Mary Elizabeth, 154
  Mary (Maxon), 152
  Nora (Crusman), 154
  Oliver, 153
  Pamelia, 153
  Phoebe, 153
  Prudence (Hallam), 152
  Prudence (Thompson), 152
  Rowland, 153
  Samuel, 152
  Sarah, 153, 154
  Sarah (Pendleton), 153
  Sarah (Thompson), 152
  Stephen, 151
  Susanna, 152
  Sylvia (Bostwick), 154
  William, 151, 152, 153, 154
  William Belden, 155
Chanders, Alice, 359
Chandler, Amy, 368
  Annis (———), 422
  Charles Church, 378, 382
  Elijah, 428
  Elizabeth, 295
  Hannah, 422, 423
  Hannah (Ballard), 64
  Isaac, 64
  Jane, 112
  John, 378
  Laura, 248
  Lydia (Burton) Rockwood, 428
  Marian, 378, 382
  Marian (Griswold), 378, 382
  Mary, 63, 357
  Mary (Ballard), 63
  Mary (Sewell), 107
  Mary (Stevens), 63
  Samuel, 378
  Thomas, 63
  William, 63, 112, 422
Chanler, Ann (Throughgood), 77
  Job, 77
Channing, William, 331
  William Ellery, 331
Chapell, Patience, 207
Chapin, Caroline L., 286
  Elizabeth Margaret (Gay), 213

Chapin—*Continued*
  Jacob, 213
Chapman, ———, 127
  Ann, 236
  Caroline Matilda (Fuller), 208
  Benjamin, 208
  Lucy, 280
  Patience (Bukleley), 127
Charlescraft, Elizabeth, 353
  Vashti, 353
Charleton, Ann (West), 71
  Elizabeth, 71
  Mary, 71
  Stephen, 71
Charruaud, Ada Geraldine, 17
  Eliza H. (Ballantine), 17
  Emma Serena, 17
  Frances Augusta, 17
  John Henry, 17
  John J., 17
  Matilda J. (Allen), 17
  Pierre Eugene, 17
  Zoe Parine, 17, 18
Chase, Charity, 86
  Elisha, 86
  Flora Louisa, 344
  Harriet, 28
  Joshua, 408
  Louise (Manning), 344
  Mary (Osgood), 408
  Monimia, 344
  William H., 344
Chauncy, Charles, 126
  Sarah, 126
Cheney, Cicely, 166
  Elizabeth (Hill), 166
  John, 166
Chenoweth, Fannie Bell, 139
  Helen Bullitt, 139
  Helen Martin (Bullitt), 137
  Henry, 137
  Henry Walker, 139
  James Shreve, 139
  Mary Thompson (Creel), 139
  Mildred Ann, 138
  Nancy Creel, 139
  Sue Bullitt, 139
Cherlton, Edward, 348
  Hawyse (Powys), 346
  John, 346
  Joyce, 348

INDEX

Cherry, Joshua, 299
  Sarah (Hollingsworth) McDonald, 299
Chester, Hannah (Talcott), 451
  John, 451
Cheston, Ann, 363
  James, 363
  Mary (Hollingsworth), 363
Chetwode, Grace, 125
  Richard, 125
Chew, Margaret, 336
  Margaret Crabb (Johns), 93
  Thomas J., 93
Chickering, Frances, 288
Chipman, Hope (Howland), 225
  John, 225
  Lydia, 225
Childs ———, 56
  Elizabeth (Frost), 56
Chittenden, Julia, 36
Cholmondeley, Charlotte Georgiana, 25
  Henry, 25
Christian, *Arms*, 141, 180
  Anne (Henry), 131
  Priscilla, 131, 177
  William, 129, 131, 173
Christie, John Watson, 488
  Mary Rodes, 488
  Pauline Clay (Watson), 487
  Robert, 487
  Robert Dobbie, 488
Church ———, 33
  Benjamin, 378
  Charles, 378
  Elizabeth Draper (Avery) 33
Chudleigh, Agnes (Champernowne), 166
  John, 166
Churchill, Armistead, 216
  Hannah (Harrison), 216
  Lucy, 216
  Mary, 131
Clagett, Caroline, 88
  Edward, 91
  Eleanor (Bowie) Brooke, 91
  Joseph White, 94
  Mary Ann (Bowie,) 94
  William D., 94
Claggett, Judith (Richmond), 403

Claggett—*Continued*
  Kitty C. (Duckett), 239
  William, 403
  William B., 239
Claiborne, Hamilton Cabell, 149
  Herbert Augustine, 148, 149
  Jeanie Alston, 149
  Katherine Hamilton (Cabell), 148
  Mary, 265
  William, 265
Clapton, Elizabeth, 373
  William, 373
Clare, Margaret, 348
Clark, *Arms*, 502
  Agnes Parry, 498
  Andrew, 500
  Archibald (Dixon), 498
  Christiana Parry, 498, 500
  Constance, 502
  David, 496, 498, 505
  David Henderson, 498
  Daniel, 238, 239
  Elizabeth, 499
  Elizabeth (Crawford), 499
  Elizabeth (Huntington), 315
  George David, 501
  Georgina (La Nauze), 498, 505
  Georgina La Nauze, 499
  Helen (Crawford), 496
  Helm, 276, 501
  Hugh, 499
  Isabel Stevenson, 132, 164, 498, 500
  Isabella, 496, 498, 499
  Isabella (Stevenson), 496
  James, 164, 276, 482, 496, 499, 500, 501, 505
  Janet (Kerr), 495
  Janet (Muir) Montgomery, 495
  Janet, 497, 499
  Jessie, 482
  Jessie (La Nauze), 164, 276, 482, 500, 505
  Jessie La Nauze, 499, 501, 502
  John, 496, 499
  John P., 428
  John Stevenson, 498
  Joseph, 36, 315, 288

Clark—*Continued*
  Julia Ballard (Dixon), 498
  Kennedy Helm, 276, 501
  Kitty (Bowie), 239
  Lemuel, 461
  Lenore (Durbeck), 501
  Lucinda Hardin (Helm), 276, 501
  Margeret, 496, 499, 502
  Margaret Annette, 499
  Margaret (Coleman), 501
  Margaret (Howard) Duckett, 238
  Margaret (Simpson), 495
  Marian (Gilmour), 495
  Marian Lawrence, 160
  Marion, 500
  Mary, 315, 437, 495
  Mary (Dixon), 500
  Mary Dixon, 500
  Mary Emerson (Rockwood), 428
  Mary (Haines), 160
  Mercy (Bridges), 461
  Molly, 461
  Moses, 315
  Rebecca, 279
  Rebecca (Ballard), 64
  Rebecca (Huntington), 316
  Rebecca Maillard (Scheuch), 501
  Robert, 495, 496
  Sarah, 315
  Sarah (Tiffany), 462
  Susan Norton, 502
  Walter Symington, 500, 501
  Walton, 462
  William, 315, 495, 496, 499
  William Henry, 160
  William Kerr, 501
Clarke, Agnes, 157
  Agnes Parry (Clark), 498
  Ann (Champlin), 152
  Anne, 326
  Arnold, 153
  Bethiah (Hubbard), 152
  Charity, 12
  Daniel, 483
  Emma Eliza, 29
  Hannah (Cottrell), 153
  James Whittle, 498
  Jane (Hoops), 483
  John, 152, 157

INDEX

Clarke—*Continued*
  Joseph, 152, 153
  Lucy (Champlin), 153
  Mary, 152
  Samuel, 152
  Susannah, 243
  Thomas, 12
Clay, Belle Lyman, 262
  Brutus Junius, 262
  Cassius Marcellus, 262
  Frank, 488
  Jane (Watson), 488
  Mary Jane (Warfield), 262
  Pattie Amelia (Field), 262
  Pauline Green, 487
Clayton, Elizabeth, 216
Clements, John, 406
  Sarah (Osgood), 406
Cleveland, Catherine Romano (Marsiglia), 18
  Ezra, 18
  Francis A., 18
  Grover, 18
Clifford, Elizabeth, 348
  John, 348
  Thomas, 348
Clifton, Anne (Brent), 106
  James, 106
Cline, Alice, 435
  May (Carpenter), 418
  Margaret, 418
  Richard, 435
  William, 418
Clinton, De Witt, 405
Clymer, Elizabeth, 274
Coalter, Elizabeth Tucker, 123
  John, 123
Coates, Abigail, 396
  Elizabeth, 395
  Helen M., 418
  Jane, 395
  Robert, 396
  Thomas, 396
Cobb, Jennie (Mary Virginia), 194
  Lois, 152
Coburn, Frances E., 383
  Helen (Miller), 383
  Stephen, 383
Cochran, Janet, 122
Cochrane, *Arms*, 502
  Isabella (Burns), 496
  Margaret, 496

Cochrane—*Continued*
  Robert, 496
Coddington, Mary (———), 358
  Thomas, 358
Coggshall, Henrietta, 153
Coit, David, 34
  Sarah, 34
  Sarah (Ogden), 34
Colburn, Nathaniel, 289
Cochester, George, 104
  Margery, 104
Cole, Bernice, 388
  Emily Ann, 46
Coleman, John, 501
  Margaret, 501
  Susan (Norton), 501
Coles, Agnes C., 148
  Anna Belle, 189
  John Woolston, 136
  Therese (Bullitt), 136
  Therese Pauline, 136
  Walter C., 148
Collens, Anna (Huntington), 316
  Charles, 316
Collins, Elizabeth, 454
  Ruth, 124
Collison, Benjamin, 247
  Jennie, 247
  Julia (Hall), 247
Collman, Martha, 440
Colston, Alice, 67
  Ralf, 67
Colvocoresses, Franka E., 156
  George M., 156
  George P., 156
Combs, Elizabeth (Bullitt), 130
  John, 130
Conant, *Arms*, 157, 159
  Abigail, 427
  Agnes (Clarke), 157
  Alton Leonard, 375
  Bertha, 416
  Bethia (Mansfield), 158
  Caleb, 157
  Debach (Lowell), 158
  Elizabeth, 158
  Elizabeth (Walton), 158
  Ethel Bennett, 375
  Exercise, 158
  Galen, 375

Conant—*Continued*
  Hannah (Mansfield), 158
  Hattie (Jenks), 375
  Ira, 159
  Isadora (Shepardson), 159
  Joana (Washburn), 159
  John, 157, 158
  Joshua, 158
  Lot, 157, 158
  Lucy (Leonard), 159
  Martha, 158
  Mary, 158
  Mary (Woodbury), 158
  Nathaniel, 158
  Phineas, 158, 159
  Phineas (Pratt), 158
  Rebecca, 158
  Richard, 157
  Roger, 157, 158, 375
  Sarah, 157, 158
  Sarah (———), 158
  Sarah Collins (Redlington), 375
  Sarah (Horton), 157
  W. H., 157
  William, 158
  William Albert, 157, 159
  William Henry, 159
Condy, Elizabeth, 437
  John, 437
Connaway, Thomas, 292
Connor, Alice Le Barron (Pearson), 376
  Lew Henry, 376
Conoway, Ann, 293
  Elizabeth, 293
  Mary (Hollingsworth), 293
  Sarah, 293
  Thomas, 293
Contee, Alexander, 179
  Jane (Brooke), 179
Conyers, Elinor, 348
  John, 348
Cooch, *Arms*, 160, 163
  Ann (Heide), 162
  Annie M. (Curtis), 162
  Caroline, 160
  Edward Allyn, 160
  Edward Webb, 160
  Eleanor B., 163
  Eleanor Bedford (Wilkins), 160
  Eliza B., 163

INDEX

Cooch—*Continued*
Elizabeth, 161
Elizabeth (Marvis), 161
Frances Elizabeth, 161
Francis Allyn, 160
Francis Lowen, 161
Frank, 163
Hannah (———), 161
Harriette, 162
Helen, 162
Isabella, 161
Isabella (———), 161
Joseph Wilkins, 160, 161, 162
Lester Wilkins, 163
Levi Griffith, 160, 162
Levi Hollingsworth, 160
Margaret (Hollingsworth), 162
Margaret Hollingsworth, 160
Marian Lawrence (Clark), 160
Mary Bedford, 163
Mary Evarts (Webb), 160
Mary Josephine (Logan), 160
Nettie E. (Dix), 163
Nina, 163
Phoebe Lawrence, 160
Richard Logan, 160
Sara, 163
Sarah Conant (Wilkins), 162
Sarah (Griffith), 161
Sarah (Lowen), 161
Sarah (Welsh), 161
Tamar (Miller), 162
Thomas, 160, 161, 162
Thomas P., 163
William, 161, 162
Zebulon Hollingsworth, 162, 163
Cood, Helen Bullitt, 133
John, 133
Virginia Anderson (Bullitt), 133
Cook, Ethel Frances, 87, 245
Grace, 295
John, 416
John George, 87
Margaret, 359
Mary, 416
Mary Eliza (Monroe), 87
Olivia Walter, 45
Phebe, 26

Cook—*Continued*
Philip, 226
Sarah, 226, 296
Cooke, Annie (Todd), 307
John, 307
Maria (Shores), 342
Maria A. (Shores), Lewis Chart No. 1
Pattie, 342
Pattie, Lewis Chart No. 1
Patsy (Bransford) Shores, Lewis Chart No. 1
Richard F., Lewis Chart No. 1
Robert, Lewis Chart No. 1
Watson M., 342
Watson M., Lewis Chart No. 1
Coons, Mary Angeline, 185
Cooper, Anna (Brown), 255
Caroline Martha, 459
J. Fenimore, 460
Margaret, 363
Martha Ann, 355
Mary Eleanor, 255
Thomas Alexander, 255
Cope, Israel, 363
Margaret (Cooper), 363
Mary Ann C., 363
Corbett, Emily, 149
Corbin, Richard, 350
Cordes, Isaac, 310
Mary, 310
Cornell, Elizabeth, 12
John, 515
Mary, 462
Mary (Russell), 515, 516
Peleg, 516
Richard, 12
Thomas, 331
Cornhill, Richard, 6
Cornish, Catherine, 363
Henry, 363
Coster, Rose Hortense, 388
Cotton, Anna (Lake), 38
Eleazer, 38
Esther (Warham), 38
John, 38
Marie, 38
Sarah (Handbridge) Story, 38
Cottrell, Hannah, 153

Couch ———, 483
Jane (Roberts), 482, 483
Robert, 482, 483
Coulburn, Mary, 192
William, 194
Coulter ———, 46
Florence (Ridgely), 46
Helen, 46
Courtenay, *Arms*, 164, 175
——— (Savage), 168
Agnes (Champernowne) Chudleigh, 166
Alexander Dallas Bache, 169
Alice, 167
Ann Boyd, 170
Anna Maria, 171
Anne, 172
Anne (Wake), 166
Annie Christian (Howard), 132, 173, 177
Aveline, 348
Carl Butler, 174
Carrie Lillian (Hitchcock), 169
Catherine, 167
Catherine Sarah (Murphy), 172
Catlyna Totten, 169
Charles, 167, 171, 172
Charlotte Jane (Irving), 171
Charlotte Mary, 172
Charles Henry, 171
Chichester, 171
Cicely (Cheney), 166
Conrad, 170
Conway, 170
David, 171
David Carlile, 171
David Stewart, 168, 170
Edward, 167, 170, 171, 172, 175
Edward Henry, 169, 170, 171
Edward Smith, 172
Elizabeth, 171, 172
Elizabeth Cathcart (Doon), 170
Elizabeth Dorsey (Hawkins), 168
Elizabeth (Hungerford), 166
Elizabeth Isabella (Purviance), 168
Elizabeth (Manners), 167
Elizabeth (Paulet), 167

INDEX

Courtenay—*Continued*
  Elizabeth (Seymour), 167
  Elizabeth Storer (Wade), 172
  Emma, 132, 172, 175, 177
  Emma Virginia (Dushane), 169
  Erskine Howard, 132, 164, 500
  Fortescue, 172
  Frances (Moore), 167
  Francis, 167
  George, 167
  George Ouchtred, 167
  Hamilton Howard, 170
  Hannah Maria (Weatherburn), 170
  Harriet Whitehorne, 169
  Harriet Whitehorne (Rathbone), 169
  Helen Martin, 132, 175, 177
  Henry, 132, 167, 168, 170, 172, 174, 177
  Henry Howard, 169
  Hercules, 168
  Hilda Doon, 170
  Isabella (Purviance), 168
  Isabel Stevenson (Clark), 132, 164, 500
  James, 171
  James Clark, 132, 164, 501
  Julia, 177
  Julia Christian, 132, 173
  Jane (Carlile), 171
  Jane (Rhames),172
  Jane Short, 174
  Jane Short (Butler), 132, 174, 177
  John, 166, 167, 168, 170, 171, 172
  John Henry, 172
  John Skinner, 170
  Jane, 171
  Katherine (St. Leger), 167
  Lewis Rogers, 132, 175, 177
  Marshall Howard, 170
  Maria Graham, 172
  Margaret, 171
  Margaret (Bonville), 166
  Margaret (Edgecombe), 167
  Mary, 170, 172
  Mary (———), 171
  Mary (Drury), 168
  Mary Isabella, 169

Courtenay—*Continued*
  Mary (Major), 170
  Peter, 166
  Philip, 166
  Robert, 171, 174
  Robert Graham, 132, 172, 173, 177
  Robert Martin, 132, 174, 177
  Sarah, 169
  Sarah (Drury), 168
  Sarah Jane, 171
  Sarah Mary, 168
  Thomas Anderson, 132, 174, 177
  Virginia Pleasants (Howard), 169
  William, 166, 167, 170
  William Ashmead, 172
  William Howard, 132, 164, 173, 175, 177, 178, 500
  William Major, 170
Cowen, Alpheus, 286
  Esther (Hewins), 286
Cowles, Marilla, 368
Cowman ———, 235, 240
  ——— (Hall), 235
  Henrietta, 340
  Henrietta (Harwood), 236
  Joseph, 235
  Thomas, 236
Cox, Amelia Georganna, (———), 230
  George Collins, 230
  Kate Cabell, 148
  Katherine Hamilton (Cabell) Claiborne, 149
  Mary Carolina (Hall), 230
  Robert Lawrence, 230
  William Ruffin, 149
Crabb, Elizabeth (Conoway) Booth, 293
  Thomas, 293
Craddock, Mary, 189
  Mary (Atchison), 189
  Mary McKinley, 189
  Samuel, 189
Craft, Abigail, 431
  Griffin, 431
  Hannah, 431
  Samuel, 431
Crag, Ann, 230
Cramphin, Elizabeth (Pottinger) Bowie, 92

Cramphin—*Continued*
  Mary (Jackson), 93
  Ruth, 93
  Thomas, 92, 93
Crane, Hannah, 314
  James, 242
  Joseph, 314
  Virginia (Hall), 242
Crankshaw, Hamilton, 456
  Margaret, 366, 456
  Mary Alice (Flinn), 456
Crapster, Bazil, 52
  Harriet (Dorsey), 52
Crawford, Elizabeth, 499
  Frank Vanderbilt, 450
  Helen, 496
  Joel, 266
  Julia (Lake), 450
  Robert Singleton, 450
  William Harris, 266
Creel, Mary Thompson, 139
Crépel, Antoine, 472
  Marie (Du Bois), 472
Crespel, Anthony, 472
Crewkern, Joan (Malet), 103
Crist, Henry, 220, 222
  Julia Franklin, 222
Crittenden, Elizabeth (Moss) Wilcox Ashley, 489
  Henry, 489
  John, 489
  John Jordan, 489, 491
  Judith (Harris), 489
  Lucy, 491, 507
  Maria Knox (Innes) Todd, 489
  Robert, 489
  Sallie (Lee), 490
  Sarah Lee, 489
  Sallie O. (Lee), 489
  Thomas T., 489
  William Logan, 489
Crocker, Adeline Chamberlain, 376
  Elizabeth, 461
  Hannah, 439
  Ruth (Hamblin), 439
  Samuel, 439
Cromwell, Frances, 442
  Elizabeth (Todd), 308
  Hannah, 61
  John, 308
  Oliver, 4

INDEX

Crosby, ——, 485
  Flo, 485
  Hannah, 332
  Theresa (Robergat), 485
Cross, Joseph, 256
  Mary, 379
  Sophia (Mulliken) Duckett, 256
Crow, Deborah, 33
Crowe, ——, 207
  Margaret (Cushing), 434
  Sarah (Fuller), 207
  Thomas, 434
Crowley, Joanna, 294
Crowninshield, Elizabeth, 184
Crupper, Anne, 105
Crusman, Cornelius, 154
  Nora, 154
Cruttenden, Ella Reed, 320
Culpeper, Mary, 103
Culver, Mabalo, 222
Cummings, Elizabeth, 285
  Ruth, 285
  Samuel, 285
  Susanna (Hood), 285
Cundall, Anna (Russell), 516
  Enoch, 516
Cunningham, Ephram May, 441
  Sarah Leavitt (Cushing), 441
Curtis, Annie M., 162
  Frederick Augustus, 162
  Harriette (Hooker), 162
  Mary, 431
  Thomas, 431
  William, 431
Cusak, ——, 310
  Ann (Brown), 310
Cushing, *Arms*, 433, 444
  Abel, 438, 439, 440
  Abigail, 439
  Adam, 438
  Agnes, 434, 435
  Alice, 434
  Alice (Cline), 435
  Ann, 442
  Ann (Mackenzie), 441
  Annabel, 434
  Anne, 436
  Barbara, 436
  Bridget, 436
  Catherine Jane (McClellan), 443

Cushing—*Continued*
  Catherine (Willard), 440
  Cecelia (Wilder), 440
  Charles Whiting, 440
  Christiana, 440
  Daniel, 437
  David, 441, 443, 438, 439
  Deborah, 437, 438, 439, 441
  Deborah Richmond (Jacobs), 440
  Edith, 443
  Edmund, 435
  Edward, 435
  Elizabeth, 436, 443
  Elizabeth (——) Wilkie, 437
  Elizabeth (Canz), 435
  Elizabeth (Jacob) Thaxter, 437
  Elizabeth Norris, 443
  Elizabeth Waters, 442
  Ella V. (Whitman), 442
  Elnathan, 440
  Elyne, 435
  Emily Grace (Marriott), 442
  Emma (——), 434
  Etheldreda, 435
  Etta (Whelan), 442
  Evelyn, 434
  Frances (Cromwell), 442
  Frances (Richards), 435
  Francis, 443
  Francis Cromwell, 443
  Galfridus, 434
  George Russell, 440
  Gertrude (Polly), 441
  Godey (——) Payne, 436
  Hannah, 441
  Hannah (Crocker), 439
  Hannah (Cushing), 441
  Hannah (Hawke), 437
  Hannah (Greenwood), 438
  Hannah (Loring), 438
  Hannah Russell (Hill), 440
  Hannah (Waterman), 438
  Henry Miller, 443
  Hosea, 440
  Isabel, 435
  Isabel (——), 434
  Jane, 440
  Jeremiah, 437, 438
  Jerusha, 440
  Joan (——), 434, 435

Cushing—*Continued*
  Joel (Jacob), 438
  John, 434, 435, 437, 442
  Jonathan, 439
  Joseph, 441, 442
  Joseph Mackenzie, 442
  Joseph Wiley, 442
  Josiah, 440
  Kate E. (Eadie), 443
  Katherine, 436
  Laban, 439, 441
  Lucy, 440
  Lydia, 439
  Lydia (Fearing), 438
  Lydia (Gilman), 437
  Mabel, 440
  Mabel (Gardner), 439
  Margaret, 434, 435
  Margaret E. (Folson), 443
  Margery, 435
  Margery (——), 436
  Mary, 438, 439, 443
  Mary (Jacob), 439
  Mary (Thaxter), 438
  Mary (Thomas), 440
  Matthew, 436, 437, 438
  Moses, 441
  Nancy, 440
  Nancy (Whitney), 441
  Nazareth (Pitcher), 436
  Nehemiah, 438
  Nicholas, 435
  Parnell, 434
  Peter, 435, 436, 437
  (Perez), 439
  Polly (Adams), 441
  Rachel, 438
  Rachel (Lewis), 438
  Rebecca Ann, 443
  Rebecca (Edmands), 441, 442
  Richard Cromwell, 443
  Robert, 434, 436
  Rose, 434, 435
  Ruth, 439
  Ruth (Cushing), 439
  Ruth (Lincoln), 439
  Sarah, 443
  Sarah (Hawke), 437
  Sarah (Jacob), 437
  Sarah Leavitt, 441
  Sarah (Leavitt), 441
  Sarah (Nichols), 438

INDEX

Cushing—*Continued*
  Sarah Pinkerton, 442
  Sarah (Simmons), 440
  Sarah (Wilder), 440
  Seth, 438
  Stephen, 435
  Susan (Hawes), 435
  Susannah, 441
  Theophilis, 436
  Theophilus, 438
  Thomas, 434, 435, 436
  Thomas Morris, 442
  Ursula, 435
  Wiley Edmands, 442
  William, 434, 435, 436
  William Whelan, 443
Cushman, Eunice (Osgood), 408
  Porter, 408
Custis, Ann, 77, 387, 390
  Daniel Park, 72
  Joan, 72
  Joane (———), 390
  John, 72, 390
  Martha (Dandridge), 72
Cutler ———, 26
  Penelope (Arnold) Goulding, 26
Cutt, John, 330

D

Dabney, Ann, 491
D'Abrincis, Adelicia (———), 165
  Hawise, 164
  Matilda (Avernell), 165
  Robert, 164, 165
  William, 165
Daggett, Annie, 448
Dale, Betty, 428
Dallas ———, 93
  Margaret, 92
Dana, Caleb, 64
  Edward, 448
  Frances Swan (Southgate), 448
Dane, Nathan, 424
  Sarah (Ballard), 64
Danforth, Nicholas, 331
Daniel, Elizabeth Hanna (Cabell), 147
  Joseph J., 218
  Maria Bassett (Smith), 218

Daniel—*Continued*
  Mary, 218
  William, 147
Darcy, Sarah, 60
Darden, Algernon Sidney, 386, 387
  Annie Jordan, 386
  Mary Allen, 386, 390, 391
  Mary Swepson (Allen), 386, 387
Darell ———, 346
Darley, Alice, 448
  Florence (Bradley), 448
  Henry, 4
  Henry Samuel, 448
Darnall, Eleanor, 113
  Eleanor (Brooke), 179
  Elenor (Hatton) Brooke, 179
  Henry, 179
  Phillip, 179
Darrah, William, 273
Dashiell, Amelia Eleanor (Marine), 350
  Eleanor Marine, 351
  Louisa Turpin (Wright), 351
  Marion, 191
  Mary Leeke, 349
  Miranda (Wheatley), 191
  Nicholas Leeke, 351
  William Winder, 191
Davenport, Effe, 343
  George Graham, 485
  Henry K., 484
  Jennie Brent, 485
  Jennie Brent (Graham), 484
  Richard Graham, 484
  Serena Hale (Gilman), 484
  Thomas Corbin, 485
Davidge, Dinah, 57
  Honor (Howard) Warfield, 52, 57
  John, 52, 57
Davidson ———, 477
  Eleanor (———), 258
  Empson, 258
  Fanta (Lena) Scrogin, 477
  Janet Clark, 497
  Janet (George), 497
  John, 258, 497
  Margaret, 258
  Mary (Bird), 258
  Robert, 497
  Samuel, 258

Davis ———, 144
  Abigail, 431
  Ann (Hammond), 58
  Anna (Fuller), 208
  Betsey Dale (Rockwood), 428
  Charles S., 428
  Elizabeth (Bowie), 93
  Elizabeth (Cabell), 144
  Ephraim, 93
  Francis, 58
  Hester Ann (Marine), 355
  Isaac, 378
  Jefferson, 117
  John, 431
  Kezia, 182
  Marie, 356
  Mary, 144
  Mary (Torrey), 431
  Mary Virginia (Ball), 41
  Moses, 207
  Olive Parlin, 377, 382
  Rosalia Ball, 41
  T. Carroll, 41
  Thomas, 93
  W. J., 355
D'Avranches, Robert, 165
Dawnay, Ann, 348
Dawney, Ellen, 197
Dawson, Eleanor, 221
  Elizabeth, 222
Day, ——— (Esom), 266
  Anne Emilla (Harris), 266
  Eliza (Proctor), 418
  Jerusha, 287
  John, 266
  Joseph, 418
  Lucy, 266
  Philena, 418
  Ralph, 289
  Sarah, 59
  William, 266
D'Ayncourt, Hawisa, 165
Dayton, Elizabeth (Todd), 198
  Isaac, 198
  Sarah, 198
Dean, Clarissa Maria (Wilbur), 511
  H. E., 299
  John, 289
  Mary, 509
  Nellie Kiser (Stewart), 299
  W. Harrison, 511

INDEX

Deane, Hannah, 403
  Lydia, 509
  Mehitable, 509
Deas, Allen, 311
Deatherage, Mary (Strother), 105
De Barrette, Barbara, 220
De Beauchamp, Ida, 102
  John, 102
De Bereford, Walter, 196
De Bohun, Alianore, 115
  Elizabeth (Plantagenet), 166
  Humphrey, 166
  Margaret, 166
Deboise, 503
De Brent, Clarissa (De La Ford), 102
  Elizabeth (Deneband), 102
  Hawise, 102
  Isabella (De Montacute), 101
  Jeffrey, 101
  John, 102
  Nicholas, 101
  Odo, 101
  Robert, 101, 102
De Broke, Edward Willoughby, 115
  Elizabeth Willoughby, 104, 115
  Margaret (De Neville), 115
Decatur, Stephen, 254
De Courtenai, Ermengarde (De Nevers), 165
  Hawisa (D'Ayncourt), 165
  Isabel (De Montlherry), 165
  Josceline, 165
  Milo, 165
  Reginol, 165
  Reginald, 165
De Courtenay, Agnes (St. John), 166
  Alianora (Despencer), 166
  Athon, 165
  Hawise (De Abrinces), 164
  Hugh, 166
  Isabel (De Vere), 165
  John, 165
  Margaret (De Bohun), 166
  Mary (De Redvers), 165
  Reginald, 164
  Robert, 164, 165
De Eton, Cicely, 319
  J. Nicholas, 319

De Forest, Jane Charlotte, 368
De France, Mattie Lee, 189
De Frankley, Emma, 70
  Simon, 70
De Graff, Nancy (Van Santvoord), 467
  William, 467
De Greene, William, 219
De Haydon, Isabel, 319
  William, 319
De Inglis, John, 196
  Phillip, 196
  Walter, 196
De La Ford, *Arms*, 102
  Adam, 102
  Clarissa, 102
De La Pierre, Estienne, 503
  Guillermine Martha, 503
  Marye (Vesian), 503
  Pierre, 503
  Prudence (Hierome), 503
Deleval, Frances, 16
De Luttleton, Thomas, 70
De Milliere ———, 503
Deming, Mary, 32
De Molis, Baldwin De Sap, 165
De Montacute, *Arms*, 101
  Isabella, 101
  Simon, 101
De Montlherry, Isabel, 165
  Milo, 165
De Motte, Margaret Field, 133
De Mowbray, Adelia, 319
  Roger, 319
Deneband, Elizabeth, 102
  Joan (De Brent), 102
  Thomas, 102
  William, 102
De Nevers, Ermengarde, 165
  Reginald Comte, 165
De Neville, Anne (Stafford), 115
  Margaret, 115
  Richard, 115
Denio, Emily Ware (Wilbur), 511
  I. Austin, 511
Denison, Edith (Brown), 154
  John, 154
  Mary, 154
Denne, Catherine, 77
Dennis, *Arms*, 181
  Annie Isabel (Smith), 181, 182

Dennis—*Continued*
  Arthur, 181
  Elizabeth (Robinson), 181
  Arthur Wellington, 181, 182
  Hope Ann, 181
  Hope Anne (Rhodes), 181, 182
  Joanna (Brown), 181
  John, 181
  John B., 199
  John Rhodes, 181
  John Robinson, 181, 182
  Sarah Maria (English), 199
Denslow ———, 207
  Jerusha (Fuller), 207
Densmore, H. B., 40
  Mary J. (Mather), 40
Dent, Barbara, 176, 179
  Margaret, 175, 180
  Rebecca (Wilkinson), 175, 176, 179, 180
  Thomas, 175, 179, 180
Denton, Ann (Brice), 61
  Vavhel, 61
De Popham, Hawise (De Brent), 102
De Port, Hugh, 319
  Joan, 319
De Quincey, Hawise, 165
  Saire, 165
De Redvers, Mary, 165
  William, 165
Derby, Bessie (Kidder), 183
  Charles, 184
  Clara Matteson (McGinness), 183
  Ebenezer, 184
  Elias Hasket, 184
  Elizabeth, 184
  Elizabeth (———), 183
  Elizabeth (Crowninshield), 184
  Elizabeth Crowninshield, 183
  Experience, 184
  George Horatio, 185
  George McClellan, 183, 185
  George Townsend, 183
  Hollis Hasket, 183
  John, 184
  John Barton, 184
  Lavina, 373
  Lucretia, 184
  Lucretia (Hinman), 183
  Margaret, 184

INDEX

Derby—*Continued*
  Martha, 184
  Martha (Hasket), 184
  Mary, 184
  Mary (Hodges), 184
  Mary (Townsend), 184
  Mary Angeline (Coons), 185
  Richard, 184
  Roger, 183, 184
  Roger Barton, 183
  Sallie (Barton), 184
  Samuel, 184
De Richmond, Alan, 401
  Elyas, 401
  Eudo, 401
  Hasculfus Musard, 401
  Roald, 401
  Roaldus, 401
  Roaldus Musard, 401
  Thomas, 401
  William, 402
De Ruggele, William, 429
De Savage, Thomas, 70
Deshler, David Wagner, 114
  Flora, 114
  Margaret (Nashee), 114
De Skegeton, Maud, 319
  Richard, 319
Desloge, Firmin René, 36
  Lucie Mary, 36
D'Espaigne, Marie Claudine, 330
Despencer, Alenor, 348
  Alianora, 166
De Townshend, Alice, 319
  Roger, 319
De Vere, Annie Clay, 41, 42
  Hawise (De Quincey), 165
  Isabel, 165
  John, 165
  Sarah (Jones), 41
  William, 41
De Verona, William, 165
Devotion, Edward, 431
  Martha, 431
De Warren, Adelia (De Mowlbray), 319
  Alice (De Townshend), 319
  Ann (———), 319
  Ciceley (De Eton), 319
  Edward, 319
  Elizabeth (———), 319
  Gundreda, 319

De Warren—*Continued*
  Isabel, 319
  Isabel (De Haydon), 319
  Isabel (Leigh), 319
  Isabel (Stanley), 319
  Joan (De Port), 319
  John, 319
  Lawrence, 319
  Margaret (Stafford), 319
  Margery (Bulkeley), 319
  Maud (De Skegeton), 319
  Reginald, 319
  William, 319
De Welles, Simon, 334
D'Ewes, Simon, 5
Dewey ———, 135
  Henrietta Massie (Bullitt), 135
  Margaret, 322
Dexter, Joseph, 418
  Sally (Thompson), 418
  Sarah Ann, 418
Dick, Frank M., 136
  John Julian, 136
  Julia Dunlap (Bullitt), 136
  Langhorne Bullitt, 136
Dickenson, Araziah, 446
  Sarah (Southgate), 446
Dickinson, Deborah, 465
  Joyce (Hance), 465
  Zebulon, 465
Diffenderfer, John, 308
  Sarah Ann (Todd), 308
Digges, Eleanor (Brooke) Darnall, 179
  Elinor (Brent), 109
  Francis, 109
  William, 179
Diggs, Catherine (Brent), 108
  George, 108
Dilgavson, Elizabeth (Howland), 225
  John, 225
Diller, Addie (Hughes), 366
  Barbara, 471
  Barbara (———), 478, 479
  Casper, 470, 478, 479
  Catherine (Hartley), 479
  Corinne, 366
  Corinne (Payne), 366
  Elizabeth (Abel), 478, 479
  Elizabeth (Ellmaker), 478, 479

Diller—*Continued*
  Ellen M., 478
  Isaac, 366
  Jane Louise, 366
  Jean (Han) Martin, 479
  Jeremiah, 478, 479
  Leonard, 478, 479
  Mary Magdalena (Hinkle), 478, 479
  Michael, 479
  Philip Adam, 470, 478, 479
  William, 366
  William Hughes, 366
Divoll, John, 407
  Ruth, 407
  Sarah (Osgood), 407
  William, 407
Dix, Avis M. (Wightman), 163
  George Lewis, 163
  Nettie E., 163
Dixon ———, 295
  Archibald, 137, 498
  Hannah (Hollingsworth), 295
  John, 295
  Julia Ballard, 498
  Kate, 137
  Margaret (Herndon), 498
  Mary, 500
  Minna (Logan), 137
  Sarah (Hollingsworth), 295
  Susan Peachy (Bullitt), 137
  Thomas Bullitt, 137
  William Bullitt, 137
Dobson, Abigail (Hollingsworth), 294
  Richard, 294
Dodington, John, 67
Donald, Graeme, 214
  Jane, 214
  Marian, 214
  Marian Otis (Gay) Burrage, 214
Doneghy, Alexander, 189
  Anna Belle (Coles), 189
  Ellen Peirce, 189
  Hanson Weitman, 189
  Herbert, 189
  Irvine, 189
  James, 188, 189
  Jessie (———) Murphy, 189
  John Templeman, 186, 189
  Kate Bradshaw (Campbell), 189

INDEX

Doneghy—*Continued*
 Lucy (Templeman) Moss, 188
 Lucy (Van Cleve), 189
 Martha Talbott (Preswitt), 189
 Mary, 189
 Mary McKinley (Craddock), 189
 Mattie Lee (De France), 189
 Media (Burton), 189
 Nannie Bertie (Wooldridge), 189
 Philip, 189
 Polly, 189
 Sarah, 189
Donnell, Andrew, 163
 Mary Bedford (Cooch), 163
 Rosa (Mathewson), 163
 Samuel M., 163
Donovan, Richard, 349
Doolittle, Abigail, 198
 Abraham, 198
 Isaac, 198
 Merribah, 418
 Sarah (Todd), 198
Doon, Caroline (Cathcart), 170
 Elizabeth Cathcart, 170
 John Glasgow, 170
Dorr, Caroline Louisa, 214
 Joseph, 214
Dorsey, *Arms*, 47, 61
 ——— (Elder), 42
 Achsah, 50, 60
 Amelia, 49
 Amelia (Gillis), 54
 Amelia (Green), 53, 57
 Amos, 50
 Angela, 53
 Ann, 49, 50, 52, 54, 58
 Ann (———), 49
 Ann (Dorsey), 49, 52
 Ann Elder, 52
 Ann Hanson (McKenney), 50, 53
 Ann (Owings), 53
 Ann (Poole), 52
 Ann (Ridgely), 48, 51
 Anna, 51
 Anne (Worthington), 61
 Ariand, 48, 49
 Azekiel, 54
 Bazil, 59

Dorsey—*Continued*
 Benedict, 48
 Benjamin, 48, 51, 56
 Benjamin Lawrence, 55
 Betty, 54
 Betty (Gillis), 54
 Caleb, 55, 57, 59, 308
 Catherine, 49, 52
 Catherine (Ridgely), 49
 Catherine (Thompson), 50
 Cecelia, 53
 Charles, 49, 51, 55, 58
 Clare, 53
 Clarissa, 54
 Comfort (Stimpson), 59
 Darius, 52
 Deborah, 59
 Dinah (Warfield), 57
 Edward, 47, 51, 52, 54, 55, 56, 58, 59, 60
 Edward Hill, 54
 Edwin, 50, 53
 Eleanor, 232, 308
 Elias, 55, 56
 Elinor (Warfield), 59
 Elizabeth, 42, 48, 49, 50, 52, 53, 54, 55, 57, 168
 Elizabeth (———), 59
 Elizabeth (Dorsey), 55
 Elizabeth (Hall), 48, 55
 Elizabeth Hall, 55
 Elizabeth Hall (Dorsey), 55
 Elizabeth (Worthington), 42, 50, 61
 Ella Loraine, 53
 Ellen (Warfield), 308
 Ely, 52
 Essex Ridley, 55
 Ezekiel John, 54
 Ezra, 57
 Flora (Fitzimmons), 59
 Florence, 53
 Frances (Watkins), 59
 Francis, 58
 George, 49
 Greenbury, 59
 Hannah, 56
 Harriet, 52, 54
 Harriet (Higgins), 257
 Henrietta, 49, 50, 53
 Henrietta (Dorsey), 50, 53
 Henrietta (Hammond), 50
 Henry, 48, 49, 54, 59

Dorsey—*Continued*
 Honor, 53, 56
 Honor (Elder), 51
 Honor Elder, 52
 Honor (Howard), 42, 50
 Honor (Howard) **Warfield** Davidge Wilkens, 52, 53, 57
 James, 54
 Jane, 51
 Jane (Dorsey), 51
 Janet (Kennedy), 49
 Jemima, 58
 Jemime, 53
 John, 47, 48, 49, 51, 52, 54, 58, 59, 60, 308
 John Hammond, 59
 Joshua, 47, 48, 49, 50, 51, 54, 55, 59, 246
 Julia Ann (Thomas), 54
 Katherine, 51
 Lacon, 58
 Lancelot Todd, 52
 Larkin, 58
 Laura (Worthington), 50
 Levin, 55
 Levin Lawrence, 55
 Lloyd, 50
 Lloyd Egbert, 50
 Lorenzo, 50, 53
 Louis, 53
 Lydia, 50
 Lydia Talbott, 52
 Mararet (Watkins), 48
 Margaret (Larkin), 47
 Marie, 55
 Martha (Hall), 246
 Mary, 50, 56
 Mary Ann, 55
 Mary (Belt), 59
 Mary (Dorsey), 50
 Mary (Glenn), 54
 Mary Hill, 54
 Mary (Lawrence), 56
 Mary Ridgeley, 48
 Mary Tasker (Bowie), 90, 245
 Mary (Warfield), 48
 Matilda, 54, 55, 56
 Matila (Dorsey), 50, 56
 Michael, 42, 50, 51, 52, 53, 57, 58
 Nathan, 53

INDEX

Dorsey—*Continued*
  Nathaniel, 53, 54
  Nicholas, 42, 48, 50, 51, 53, 61
  Nicholas Worthington, 50, 57
  Nimrod, 55, 56
  Noah, 50
  Noah Ernest, 90, 245
  Owen, 50, 53
  Patience, 51
  Patience Lucker, 55
  Philemon, 49, 52
  Phoebe (Todd), 58
  Plesance (Ely), 59, 60
  Priscilla, 54
  Rachel, 50
  Rachel (Lawrence), 49
  Rachel (Ridegly), 49
  Rachel (Warfield), 50, 57
  Rebecca, 48, 54
  Rebeckah (Maccubin), 54
  Rezin Hammond, 56
  Richard, 56, 60
  Robert, 54
  Ruth, 52, 55, 56, 58
  Ruth (Dorsey), 52, 55
  Ruth (Hill), 59, 60
  Ruth (Hill) Dorsey Greeniff, 60
  Ruth (Todd), 51, 52, 57
  Sally, 55
  Samuel, 5, 51, 54, 60
  Sarah, 42, 48, 49, 50, 51, 52, 53, 56, 59, 60
  Sarah (Dorsey), 48, 50, 59
  Sarah (Hammond), 55
  Sarah (Nelson), 55, 57
  Sarah (Richardson), 58
  Sarah (Todd,) 52, 55
  Sarah (Warfield), 52
  Sarah (Wyatt), 47
  Sophia, 60
  Sophia (———), 53
  Susanna, 58
  Susanna (Lawrence), 55, 56
  Susannah (Snowden), 56
  Thomas, 48
  Thomas Beale, 60, 61
  Tristram Shandy, 50
  Urith, 55
  Vachel, 49, 52, 54, 55, 57
  Venetia, 59
  Vincent, 59

Dorsey—*Continued*
  William Lafayette, 257
Doughty, Elias, 6
Douglas, Catherine (Brent), 108
  James, 108
Douglass, Eleanor (Howard), 176, 180
  John, 176, 180
  William, 329
Douradou, Marie, 115
Dowsett, Thomasine, 423
Doyne, Dorothy, 109
  Jane, 108
Drake, James, 15
  Sarah Ann, 15
Draper, Elizabeth (Avery), 32
  John, 32
Drew, James, 154
  Margaret, 154
Drinker, Ernesta, 136
Drowne, Henry Russell, 29
  Henry Thayer, 28
  Sarah Rhodes (Arnold), 28
Drury, Edward, 168
  John, 430
  Margery (Ruggles), 430
  Mary, 168
  Sarah, 168
  Sarah (Maugridge), 168
Du Bois, Abraham, 472
  Anne Marie, 471, 474
  Catherine (Blanshan), 471
  Chretien Maxmillian, 472
  Elizabet, 472
  Isaac, 472
  Jacob, 472
  Louis, 470, 471, 472, 473, 474
  Madalena, 472
  Marie, 472
  Mattys, 472
  Sara, 472, 373
  Sarah, 471
Du Bourg, Elizabeth Aglae, 115
  Louis, 116
  Pierre Francois, 115
  William, 115, 116
Duckett, Allen Bowie, 238
  Anne, 242
  Baruch, 239
  Basil, 256

Duckett—*Continued*
  Benjamin, 257
  Catherine E. W. (Goldsborough), 238
  Eleanor Howard, 239
  Elizabeth Howard, 239
  Elizabeth (Williams), 238, 242
  Elizabeth Howard (Duckett), 239
  Elizabeth M. (Waring), 239
  Estelle Bird (Israel), 239
  Katherine Bowie, 239
  Kitty, 239
  Kitty (Bowie) Clark, 239
  Kitty C., 239
  Kitty Howard, 239
  Lucy, 239
  Lucy (Sellman), 239
  Margaret (Howard), 238
  Margery Howard, 239
  Martha, 235, 256
  Martha Howard, 239
  Martha (Waring), 256
  Mary (Beans), 239
  Minnie (Hill), 239
  Oden Bowie, 239
  Richard, 91, 235, 238, 239, 242, 256, 257, 349
  Richard Battee, 239
  Sophia (Hall), 257
  Sophia (Mulliken), 256
  Thomas, 238, 239
  Thomas A., 239
  Thomas Allan, 239
Dudley, ———, 264
  ——— (Darell), 346
  Alfreda (———), 346
  Anne, 331
  Geoffrey, 346
  John, 346
  Joyce (Tiptoft), 346
  Louise Ludlow, 97
  Margaret, 346
  Thomas, 331
Duffy, John, 119
  Sarah Jane (Billings), 119
  Winifred, 119
Dula, Laura, 342
Dumaresq, Annie Margaretta, 214
  Philip, 214
Dummer, Stephen, 322

INDEX

Dumphy, Charlotte (Haskell), 367
Thomas, 367
Dunbar, Anstis (Champlin), 153
John, 153
Margaret, 347
Rhoda (Huntington), 317
Riley, 317
Dungan, Frances, 182
Dunham, Abigail (Wood), 416
Hannah, 416
John, 416
Dunlop, John, 495
Mary (Clark), 495
Dunn, Cecelia (Dorsey), 53
Daniel, 53
George, 95
Susanna Preston Lee (Breckinridge), 95
Dunton, Hepsibeth, 407
Dupignac, Ebenezer R., 33
Dupin, J. H., 222
Maria L. B. (Swearingen) Weathers, 222
Dupignac, Sarah Elizabeth (Avery), 34
Durand, Marie Frances, 115
Durant, Amy, 77
Durbeck, Lenore, 501
Dury, Elizabeth (Morris) Lewis, 359
Sarah, 359
William, 359
Dushane, Eliza (Patterson), 169
Emma Virginia, 169
Nathan Thomas, 169
Duval, Arabella, 313
Duvall, ——— (Willett), 244
Altizera, 254
Anna, 244
Anne (Fowler), 255
Cornelius, 229
Eliza (Hall), 244
Emma (Barron), 254
Jackson, 244
John, 255
John Mortimer, 229, 257
Maria Eleanor, 257
Mareen, 91, 229, 231, 349
Marsh Mareen, 255
Mary, 231, 242

Duvall—*Continued*
Richard I., 258
Richard M., 229
Samuel, 244
Sarah (Hall), 242, 255
Sophia, 255
Sue, 244
Susanna (———), 231
Thomas C., 254
Tobias, 244
Violetta, 229
Dwvelly, Jane (Cushing), 440
Lemuel, 440
Dwight, Hannah, 289
Hannah (———), 289
John, 289
Michael, 32
Rachel (Avery), 32

E

Eadie, Kate E., 443
Earle, Martha, 513
Mehitable, 517
Easley, Edward, 369
Frances, 369
James A., 369
Minnie Ada (Payne), 369
Eastin, Charles, 475
David, 475
Fanny, 475
George, 475
Lucy, 475
Mahala, 471, 475
Martin, 475
Philip, 471, 475
Rachel, 475
Rebecca, 475
Sarah, 475
Sarah (Smith), 471
Sarahanna (Smith), 475
William, 475
Eastman, ———, 53
Angela (Dorsey), 53
Roger, 203
Sarah, 203
Eaton, Ebenezer, 416
Elizabeth Richardson (French), 202
Francis Ormond, 202
Hannah (Rickard), 416
Herbert Edward, 202
Herbert Francis, 202

Eaton—*Continued*
Lydia (Gay), 212
Thomas, 212
Eaux, M. E. Villepont, 339
Echols, Betsey, 299
Eckley, Joseph, 327
Julia Ann (Jeffries), 326
Sarah (Jeffries), 327
Thomas Jeffries, 328
Eddy, Abigail, 79, 81, 84, 371
Ann (Jeffries), 327
Ezra, 86
Huldah Battey, 86
John, 327
Mary (Foster), 79
William, 79, 81
Eden, John, 454
Mary, 454
Edgarton, Erastus, 443
Mary (Cushing), 443
Edgecombe, Margaret, 107
Robert, 167
Edmands, John Wiley, 443
Rebecca, 441
Rebecca Ann (Cushing), 443
Edrington, Edmund, 216
Priscilla (Gordon), 216
Edwards, Ann, 76
Elizabeth, 73
John, 73
Mary, 197
Efell, Einion, 361
Effer, Elizabeth Ann (Tiffany), 462
Effner, William 462
Elder, ———, 42, 56
Charles, 58
Honor, 51
Honor (Dorsey), 56
Jemima (Dorsey) Hobbs, 58
John, 51, 56
Eldredge, Amos, 513
Rebecca (Wood), 513
Rhoda, 513
Elgood, Simon, 195
Eliot, Dorothea Dix, 508
Henrietta (Mack), 508
Jacob, 379
John, 379
Lydia, 379
Thomas Lamb, 508
Elkington, Ann, 70

INDEX

Ellegood, *Arms*, 191, 195
  Abigail (Mason), 192
  Ann (Riding), 192
  Ann Eliza, 193
  Ann Houston (Griffith), 193
  Anna, 193
  Anna Greenwood (Lambert), 194
  Catharine G., 193
  Claire Winder Dashiell, 191
  Elizabeth, 193
  Elizabeth (———), 191, 192
  Elizabeth (Cannon), 193
  George Robert, 194
  Hazell (Turner), 194
  Henry, 192
  Ida Horsey (Benney), 193
  Jacob, 192
  Jennie (Cobb), 194
  John, 192, 193
  Joshua, 193
  Joshua Atkinson, 191, 192, 193, 194
  Joshua Horsey, 194
  Margaret (Harmonson), 192
  Marion (Dashiell), 191
  Martha, 192
  Mary, 192
  Mary (Coulburn), 192
  Mary(Field), 191
  Mary Brent (Atkinson), 193
  Mary Jane, 193
  Matthew, 192
  Mazy, 192
  Peter Norley, 192
  Richard, 191, 195
  Robert, 192, 193
  Robert Griffith, 193
  Robert R., 194
  Robert Turner, 194
  Sarah, 192, 193
  Seth Griffith, 193, 194
  Thomas, 191, 193, 195
  William, 192, 193
  William A., 193
  William Thomas, 193
Ellery, Benjamine, 331
  William, 331
Ellingwood, Fanny, 424
Elliott, Benjamin, 326
  Elizabeth (Jeffries) Shepreve, 326
  Polly, 353
  Sabina, 311

Ellis, Asenath (Wilbur), 510
  Elizabeth, 216, 368
  Ellen (———), 476
  Ellen (Bryant) Brown, 17
  Joanna, 426
  Joana, 288
  Joseph, 289
  Mary (Wright), 288
  Patience, 513
  Rachel, 476
  Thomas, 288, 289, 471, 476
  William, 17
  Ziba, 510
Ellmaker, Elizabeth, 478, 479
  Leonard, 470, 478, 479
Elmer, Lewis Stewart, 355
  Martha Cooper (Cathcart), 355
Elmore, Julia Sparrow (Ruggles), 429
  William H., 429
Elting, Aaltje, 471, 473
  Aaltje (———), 473
  Cornelis, 474
  Cornelius, 471, 473, 474
  Eleanor, 474
  Geertje, 473
  Jacomyntje (Slecht), 471, 473
  Jan, 422, 471, 473
  Jans Roeloffsen, 470
  Rebecca (Van Meteren), 471, 473, 474
  Roeloff, 471, 473
  Sara, 471, 474
  William, 473
Elwell, Jane, 296
Ely, Plesance, 59, 60
Embree, Elizabeth (Lawrence), 14
  John, 14
Embry, George Washington (Swearingen), 223
  Mary, 223
Emerson, Daniel, 427
  Elizabeth (Bulkley), 427
  Hannah, 427
  Hannah (Emerson), 427
  Isaac, 202
  Joseph, 427
  Margaret, 202
  Mary, 427
  Mary (Moody), 427
  Ralph Waldo, 226, 427

Emerson—*Continued*
  Rebecca, 226
  Ruth (Haskins), 226
  William, 226, 427
Emmons, John A., 287
  Margaret, 137
Emott, James, 12
  Mary (Lawrence), 12
Enders, Nannie, 146
Engham, Mary, 178
  Thomas, 178
English, *Arms*, 196, 200
  Aaron, 198
  Abigail, 198
  Abigail (Doolittle), 196
  Adam, 196
  Albert John, 196, 200
  Benjamin, 197, 198
  Catherine, 199
  Catherine (Ross), 199
  Clement, 197, 198
  Cunnant, 197
  Devereux York, 200
  Edmond Franklin, 199
  Eli, 199
  Elisha, 475, 476
  Elisha G., 471
  Elisha Gale, 475
  Ellen (Dawney), 197
  Emily (Stocking), 199
  Emily Cobby (Hedgethorn), 199
  Franklin Edmond Stanton, 200
  Fred L., Lewis Chart No. 1
  Frederick Lewis, 342
  Grace (Yard), 197
  Hannah, 198
  Hannah Burdick (Stanton), 199
  Hannah Maria, 199
  Hannah Rebecca, 198
  Isaac, 198, 199
  Isabella, 197
  James, 196, 198, 476
  Jennie (Austin), 199
  John, 196
  John Todd, 198
  Joseph, 198
  Julia, 199
  Laura (Dula), 342
  Lewis W., 342
  Lillian (Harrington), 201
  Mahala (Eastin), 471, 475

INDEX

English—*Continued*
  Mardulia E. S. (Jackson), 471
  Mardulia Emma Sybil (Jackson), 476, 477
  Margaret (———), 476
  Mary, 196, 198
  Mary (———), 476
  Mary (Waters), 197
  Mary Spencer, 200
  Nancy (Griswold), 198
  Nathan Frederick, 199
  Nathaniel Spencer, 199
  Patrick, 196
  Pattie Marian (Lewis), 342
  Pattie Marian (Lewis), Lewis Chart No. 1
  Rebecca (Brown), 197
  Rosalind, 471, 476, 477, 478, 479
  Sarah, 198
  Sarah Abigail, 199
  Sarah (Dayton), 198
  Sarah (Haynes), 198
  Sarah Maria, 199
  Sarah (Ward), 197
  Sarah (Wharton), 475
  Thomas, 197, 476
  Waller, 476
  William, 197
  William Berney, 200
  William E., 471
  William Eastin, 476
  William Frederick, 199
  William Hayden, 471, 475, 477
  William Spencer, 199
Englissche, Richard, 196
Enoch, ———, 256
  Harry, 256
  Mary (Hall), 256
Enright, Mattie, 419
Ensor, Eleanor (Todd), 308
  John, 308
Eochaid, Heremon, 324
Eppison, Joyce, 297
Erskine, *Arms*, 493, 505
  Christian, 504
Esom, ———, 266
Estep, ———, 235
  Eleanor, 241
  Eleanor Maria, 240

Estep—*Continued*
  Elizabeth Gordon (Sudler), 241
  Harriet, 241
  Harriet Ann (Hall), 241
  Mary L., 241
  Rachel Hall, 241
  Rezen, 235
  Richard, 241
  Richard T., 241
  Sarah, 241
Estes, Eliza A., 458
  Ira, 458
Etheridge, Julia Crawford (Stewart), 298
  Robert, 298
Eustice, Mary, 350
Eustis, ———, 331
  Alexander Brooks, 330
  Aurora (Greland), 330
  Clemence, 330
  Emily Augusta, 331
  Frederick Augustus, 331
  Mary Ruth (Channing), 331
Evans, Ann, 92
  David, 304
  Ella (Warfield), 45
  Ethlyn, 45
  Florence, 45
  Florence (Kirkpatrick), 45
  Frank Garrettson, 45
  Gustavus Warfield, 45
  Gwen, 304
  Helen, 45
  Henry Gotheal, 45
  Henry Ridgeley, 45
  Jane, 361
  Margaret, 305
  Marion Dorsey, 45
  Mary, 162
  Mary Elizabeth (Garrettson), 45
  Mary Garrettson, 45
  Olivia Walter, 45
  Olivia Walter (Cook), 45
  Walter Dorsey, 45
Everingham, Dorothy, 348
Eyneham (———), 306
Eyre, John, 326
  Katherine, 326, 327
  Katherine (Brattle), 326
  Margaret, 348

F

Failing, Emily (Corbett), **149**
  Emily Corbett, 149
  Henry, 149
Fairbanks, Jonathan, 289
Fairchild, Sarah, 33
Fairfax, Francis, 348
Fanning, Charles Edward, 210
  Cornelia Spalding, 210
  Georgianna Frances (Walker), 210
Fanshaw, Martha M., 418
  Mary, 348
Farmer, Catherine, 14
Farnandis, ———, 54
Farnsworth, Lotta M., 394
Farnum, Mary, 380
Farrington, John, 289
  Nathaniel, 288
Farrow, Abraham, 477, 478
  Ann (Scott), 477, 478
  Isaac, 477, 478
  Mary, 477, 478
  Sybil, 478
  Sybil (———), 477
Farwell, Elizabeth, 508
Fassette, Almina Jane (Wilbur), 511
  Nelson, 511
Faulkner, Edmund, 406
Faunce, Joseph, 416
  Judith (Rickard), 416
Fay, Laura Gardinier (Lawrence), 13
  Theodore S., 13
Feake, Elizabeth, 464
  Robert, 464
Fearing, John, 438
  Lydia, 438
  Margaret (Hawke), 438
Felt, Mercy, 511
Fennard, ———, 502
Fenner, ———, 27
  Arthur, 339
  Elizabeth (Arnold), 27
  Julian Henry, 339
  Sarah, 339
  Thomas, 339
Fenwick, Dorothy (Plowden), 112
  George, 4

INDEX

Fenwick—*Continued*
  Henrietta Maria (Lancaster), 109
  James, 109, 112
  Maria, 109
  Teresa (Brent), 109
Ferguson, Mary, 10
Ferrell, Eugenia, 281
Ferris, John, 465
  Mary, 14, 465
  Mary (———), 465
Ffarington, Edmund, 6
Ffeeks, Tobias, 6
Ffield, Anthony, 6
  Benjamin, 6
  Robert, 6
Ffovbush, John, 6
Field, A. H., 222
  Catherine S. (Swearingen), 220, 223
  Charlotte (Martin), 262
  Christopher, 262
  Henry, 191
  Julia F. (Swearingen), 222
  Kate (Rodman), 280
  Katherine E., 220, 223
  Mary, 191
  Pattie Amelia, 262
  Richard H., 220, 223
  Seaman, 116
  William, 280
Fielding-Reid, Francis, 392
Fielding, Doris, 393
Fillis, Mary, 33
Finch, Priscilla (———), 92
  William, 92
Finnee ———, 513
  Elizabeth (Wood), 513
  Alexander, 483
  Elizabeth, 483
  Sarah, 482, 484
Fishburne, Rebecca, 339
Fisher ———, 283, 340
  Edith (Ridgely), 46
  Edward McCulloh, 340
  Gulielma Poultney (Lee), 340
  Hannah (Hewins), 283
  J. Harmanus, 340
  Joseph, 408
  Josephine McCulloh (———), 340
  Joshua, 288
  Julian Henry Lee, 340

Fisher—*Continued*
  Roberta, 43
  Sarah (Osgood), 408
  William, 46
  Thomas, 288
Fiske, Abigail (Poor), 423
  John, 423
  Mary Otis (Gay), 213
  Phebe, 423
  Phebe (Bragg), 423
  Robert T. P., 213
  Samuel, 423
  William, 423
Fitch, Adelaide, 65
Fitz-Alan, Eleanor, 197
  Richard, 197
Fitzherbert, John, 112
  Mary (Brent), 112
Fitz-Hugh, Mary, 107
Fitzhugh, Ann Eliza (Bullitt), 134
  Elizabeth Cole, 216
  Harriet (Bullitt), 134
  John, 134
  Lafayette, 134
Fitzimmons, Flora, 59
Fitzmaurice ———, 502
Fitzwater, Martha, 360
Fitz-William, Charles, 36
  Charles Bernard Raoul, 36
  Louise Delor (Walker), 36
  Lucie Delor, 36
  Marie Louise, 36
  Marie Zoé (Bain), 36
Flagg, Sarah W., 204
Flaidd, Ririd, 303
Fleming, Alexander, 344, 348
  Alexander, Lewis Chart No. 1
  Jane, 344, 348
  Jane, Lewis Chart No. 1
Fletcher, Deborah (Cushing), 441
  Grace, 353
  John, 353
  Josiah, 441
  Mary, 353
Flinn, Mary Alice, 456
Flint, Cornelius, 413
  Sarah Jane (Moulthrop), 413
Flowerdew, Anthony, 71, 72
  Edmund, 72
  Edward, 71, 72

Flowerdew—*Continued*
  Elizabeth (———), 72
  John, 72
  Martha (———), 72
  Mary, 72
  Temperance, 71, 72
  William, 72
Flynn, Catherine, 388
Folson, George S., 443
  Margaret E., 443
Fones, Elizabeth, 464
Foote, Elizabeth, 316
  Nancy Allyn, 160
  Sarah, 445
Forbes ———, 315
  Abigail, 12
  Abigail (Lawrence), 13
  Alexander, 13
  Mary (Huntington), 315
Ford ———, 48
  Eleanor Randall, 46
  James, 48
  Mary (Trimble), 48
  Mary (Warfield), 48
Foreman, Elizabeth (Smith), 74, 76
  Elizabeth Smith, 66
  Nehemiah, 76
Forester, Fanny, 405
Forman, Delia, 123
  Thomas M., 123
Fosten, Mary, 79
Foster, Hannah Capen, 285
  Sophia, 448
  Susan, 178
Foulke, *Arms*, 304, 306
  Cadwalader, 303, 304
  Catherine, 303, 304
  Edward, 303, 304
  Eleanor (Cadwalader), 303, 304
  Evan, 303, 304
  Grace, 303, 304
  Gwen, 303, 304
  Gwen (Evans), 304
  Hugh, 303, 304
  Jane, 303, 304
  Margaret, 303, 304
  Mary, 387
  Robert, 303
  Samuel, 304
  Thomas, 303, 304
Fowell, Elizabeth, 143

INDEX

Fowke, *Arms*, 141, 180
  Ann (Thoroughgood), Lewis Chart No. 1
  Francis, 348
  Gerard, 129, 173, 348
  Gerard, Lewis Chart No. 1
  John, 104, 348
  Margaret (Brent), 104
  Mary, 348
  Mary, Lewis Chart No. 1
  Roger, 348
Fowler, Anne, 255
Fox, Mary, 208
Frairy, John, 288
Francis, Marcia, 281
Frank, Andrew, 316
  Rachel (Huntington), 316
Franklin, Anthony, 14
  Deborah (Morris), 361
  John, 361
  Lydia (Lawrence), 14
Franks, Lettie, 297
Fraser, Susan, 92
Frederick, Mary L., 139
Freeman ———, 246
  John, 32
  Mary (Hall), 246
French, *Arms*, 201, 204
  Abigail, 203
  Abigail (Brown), 203
  Abigail (Philips), 403
  Amos Tuck, 201
  Ann, 203
  Ann (———), 202
  Anne (Richardson), 204
  Benjamin Brown, 204
  Daniel, 203, 204
  Diana (Wilbur), 510
  Dorothy (Whittier), 204
  Edward, 202, 203
  Edward Tuck, 201
  Eliza, 203
  Elizabeth (Richardson), 204
  Elizabeth Richardson, 202
  Ellen (Tuck), 201
  Elsie, 202
  Francis Ormond, 201, 204
  Gould, 204
  Hannah, 202, 203
  Henry Flagg, 204
  Hiram, 510
  James, 203
  John, 202

French—*Continued*
  Joseph, 202, 203
  Julia, 201
  Mary, 202
  Mary (Noyes), 202
  Mercy (Brown), 204
  Nicholas, 203
  Pauline (Le Roy), 201
  Pauline Le Roy, 201
  Philbrick, 203
  Samuel, 203
  Sarah (Eastman), 203
  Sarah (Gould), 203
  Sarah W. (Flagg) Bell, 204
  Simon, 203
  Stuyvesant Le Roy, 201
  Susanna (———), 203
  Timothy, 203
Frere, Bartle, 227
  Catherine (Arthur), 227
Fretwell, Angaline, 244
Frisby, Ariana (Vanderheyden), 61
  James, 61
  Sarah, 61
Frost ———, 56, 296
  Elizabeth, 56
  Mary (Dorsey), 56
Fry, Joshua, 129, 135
  Mildred Ann, 135
  Peacy (Walker), 135
Frye, John, 406
Fuller, *Arms*, 205, 209
  Ada C. (Schaeffer), 209
  Almon, 397
  Anna, 201, 207, 208
  Ann (———), 206
  Anna (Barrett), 208
  Anne, 206, 207
  Ann (Fuller), 206, 207
  Barnabas, 207
  Benjamin, 207
  Benjamin Chapman, 208
  Benjamin Franklin, 209
  Bethiah (———), 206
  Betsey, 511
  Caleb, 207, 208
  Caroline Matilda, 208
  Charles Francis, 209
  Clara Delia (Gould), 301
  Content, 207
  Content (Fuller), 207
  Cornelia, 208

Fuller—*Continued*
  Cornelia Annie, 209
  Cornelia Green, 208
  Cornelius, 207
  David, 207
  Desire, 207
  Edward, 205, 206, 301
  Elizabeth, 206
  Elizabeth (Young), 207
  Emily (Neville), 208
  Emma, 209
  Esther (Gould), 208
  Frances (———), 206
  Frances Allon, 301
  Frederick Augustus, 208
  George Milton, 209
  Hannah, 206, 207
  Hannah (Morton), 206
  Hannah (Weld), 208
  Henry Weld, 208
  Horace, 208
  Horace Frederick, 205, 209
  Horace Neville, 205
  James Edward, 301
  Jane (Lathrop), 206, 207
  Jean, 207
  Jerusha, 207
  Jerusha (Beebe), 207
  John, 206, 207, 211
  Jonathan, 207
  Joseph, 207
  Joshua, 207, 511
  Joshua Riley, 209
  Judith (Gay), 211
  Lydia, 207
  Margaret Emma, 209
  Margaret J. (Cathell), 209
  Marion Graham (Nimlet), 205
  Martha, 208
  Mary, 206, 208, 396
  Mary (———), 206
  Matthew, 206, 207
  Maude Louise (Knowlton), 301
  Melville Weston, 208
  Melville Whitaker, 205
  Mercy (Felt), 511
  Minnie J. (Jackson), 209
  Nicea, 209
  Nicea (Patterson), 208
  Patience (Chapell), 207
  Patience (Young), 207

INDEX

Fuller—*Continued*
  Rebecca (Parry), 207
  Robert, 206
  Rosina, 208
  Samuel, 206, 207, 301
  Sarah, 206, 207, 208
  Sarah Weld, 209
  Sophia, 208, 209
  Susannah Mary (McDermott), 209
  Sylvia Ann, 511
  Thankfull (Blossom), 207
  Thomas, 207, 289
  Thomas Weld, 208
  Virginia Weld, 205
  William, 208
  Wilson, 208
  Wilson Neville, 209
  Young, 207
Fulton, Elizabeth (Moulthrop), 413
  James, 413
Furnald, Almina Jane Wilbur (Fassette), 511
  Charles E., 511
Furness, Fairman Rodgers, 137
  Helen Kate, 137
  Helen Key (Bullitt), 137
  Walter, 137
Fürstenberg, Barbara (Rauh), 37
  Bernard C., 37
  John Bernard, 37
  Lucie Anne, 37
  Lucie Clara (Bain), 37
  Mary Barbara, 37
Furth, Jane, 140

G

Gage, Elizabeth Bishop, 62
  Elizabeth Bishop (Ballard), 62
  Margaret Ballard, 62
  Robert Thompson, 62
  Ruth Bulkeley, 62
Gager, John, 315
  Lydia, 315
Gaillard, Henriette, 339
Gaither, James E., 281
  Marcia (Francis), 281
  Nancy Martin (Kennedy), 281
  Nancy Rose, 281
  Thomas Richard, 281

Gallup, Sarah, 462
Gamble, Agnes Sarah Bell, 146
  Catharine (Grattan), 146
  Robert, 146
Gant, Elizabeth, 138
  John Stites, 138
  Joseph Rowlett, 138
  Mildred Bullitt (Stites), 138
Gantt ———— (Hilleary), 94
  Benjamin E., 258
  Harriet (Lowndes), 94
  Levi, 94
  Margaret Lowndes, 94
  Thomas, 90, 94
Gardiner, Jonathan, 126
  Lion, 4, 329
  Mary (Adams), 126
Gardner, Hannah, 152
  Henry, 152
  Hosea, 439
  Mabel, 439
  Mary (Whitney), 439
  Nannie, 366
Garfield, James R., 394
Garnett, D. D., 97
  Sarah (Tomkins), 97
Garrard, Frances (Bullitt), 131
  Mary (Smith), 477
  Sarah, 477
  William, 131, 477
Garrett, Godfrey, 72
  Martha (————) Flowerdew, 72
Garrettson, Eleanor (Ball), 45
  Florence, 45
  James Aquilla, 45
  Martha, 61
  Mary Elizabeth, 45
Garrison ————, 234
  Matthew, 6
Garritson, Amelia, 20
  Millicent (Tomlin), 20
  Washington, 20
Gaston, Anne, 237
Gates, Abigail, 373, 376
  Amos, 373
  Elizabeth (Clapton), 373
  Ellen M. (Huntington), 317
  Geoffrey, 373
  Hannah (Oldham), 373
  Isaac E., 317
Gathyp, Esther, 152
Gavan, ————, 45
  Georgie (Ridgely), 45

Gay, *Arms*, 210, 214
  Abby Frothingham, 213
  Abiel, 211
  Abigail, 212
  Anne, 214
  Annie Margaretta (Dumaresq), 214
  Arthur Otis, 214
  Benjamin, 212
  Calvin, 212
  Caroline Humphrey, 214
  Caroline Louisa (Dorr), 214
  Celia, 212, 213
  Charles William, 213
  Cornelia Spalding (Fanning), 210
  Dorothea Ellen, 214
  Eben Howard, 210, 214
  Ebenezer, 211, 212, 213, 214
  Eliezer, 211
  Elizabeth, 211
  Elizabeth Downs (Neal), 213
  Elizabeth Margaret, 213
  Ellen Blake (Blood), 214
  Frances, 213
  Frances Maria, 213
  Hannah, 211
  Harry Howard, 214
  Henry Pinckney, 213
  Hezekiah, 211
  Jerusha, 212
  Jerusha (Bradford), 212
  Joanna, 211, 212
  Joana (————) Baldwicke, 211
  John, 210, 211, 214, 289
  Jonathan, 211, 212
  Judith, 211
  Lucy, 448
  Lusher, 211, 212
  Lydia, 212
  Lydia (Lusher), 211
  Margaret (Allen), 213
  Marian Otis, 214
  Martin, 212, 213
  Mary, 212, 213, 289
  Mary Allyne (Otis), 213
  Mary Otis, 213
  Mary (Pinckney), 213
  Matilda (Travers), 214
  Nathaniel, 211, 212
  Persis, 212
  Philip Dumaresq, 214
  Pinckney, 213

INDEX

Gay—*Continued*
  Ruth (Atkins), 213
  Samuel, 211, 212, 213
  Sidney Howard, 213
  Sophie Margaretta, 214
  Walter, 214
  William Otis, 214
  Winckworth Allan, 213
Gebbings, Elizabeth (Bell), 67
  Thomas, 67
Gendron, Elizabeth, 310
  Philip, 310
George, Alonzo Phelps, 498
  Amabel (Lee), 340
  Amabel Lee, 340
  Amabel Lee (George), 340
  Ann Lee, 340
  Archibald, 340
  Henrietta Cowman, 341
  Henrietta (Cowman) Bowie, 340
  Isabella, 497
  James, 497
  Janet, 497
  Janet (Clark), 497
  John Cowman, 340
  Julia (Loving), 173, 497
  Julia Courtenay, 173, 497
  Lillian Independence (Kelley), 340
  Lizzie, 497
  May (Ankeny), 497
  Nannie, 498
  Nannie (Phelps), 497
  Peter, 497
  Robert, 173, 497
  Robert Clark, 173, 497
  Stephen Lee, 340
  William, 497
Geraghty, John, 201
  Julia (French), 201
Gerard, ——, 4
Germany, Mary C., 456
Gibbons, John, 113
  Sarah, 113
Gibson, Joseph, 63
  Dorothy (Ballard), 63
Giddings, George, 6
  Jane (Lawrence), 6
Gifford, Content, 516
  Edmund, 348
  Elizabeth, 348
  John, 348

Gifford—*Continued*
  Mary, 343
  Patience, 516
  Patience (Russell), 516
  William, 516
Giles, Elizabeth, 362
  Mary, 338
Gill, Helen Chenoweth (Stites), 138
  John Granville, 138
  Mildred Ann, 138
  Susan Barrett, 138
Gillette, Jerome, 398
Gillis, Agnes (Belt), 54
  Amelia, 54
  Betty, 54
  Ezekiel, 54
  Henry, 54
  Mary (Hill), 54
Gilman, Edward, 408, 437
  Hepsebeth Osgood, 408
  Lydia, 437
  Mary (Clark), 437
  Serena Hale, 484
Gilmour, Agnes (Anderson), 495
  John, 495
  Marian, 495
  Marian (Stirling), 495
  Thomas, 495
Gilpin, John, 273
  Mary A., 273
Gittings, Edith, 393
  Elizabeth (Macgill), 393
  James, 393
Glazier, Alice Brewer, 469
Gleason, Daniel, 412
  John, 68
  Laura (Moulthrop), 412
  Mary (Bell), 68
Gleaton, Francis Malinda (Stewart), 298
  George W., 298
  John S., 299
  Lucy, 299
  Sallie Fanny, 299
  Stephen, 299
Glen, Mourning, 266
Glenn, Mary, 54
Godard, Agnes, 348
Godfree, Francis, 196
  Mary (English), 196
Godfrey, Elizabeth, 343

Godman, ——, 243
  Anne, 242, 243
  Elizabeth, 242, 243
  Rachel (Hall), 243
  Rebecca, 242, 243
Goff, Louisa, 398
Goffe, Natalie, 44
Goldsborough, Catherine E. W., 238
Goldborough, Robert, 238
Goldsborough Sarah (Worthington), 238
  William, 238
Golightly ——, 310
Gooding, Abigail (Richmond), 403
  Mathew, 403
Goodrich, Bartlett, 24
  Isabell, 98
  Virginia, 24
Gookin, Amy (Durant), 77
  Arnold, 77
  Catherine (Denne), 77
  Daniel, 77
  John, 77
  Mary, 77, 78
  Mary (Byrd), 77
  Sarah (Offley), 77
  Sarah (Offley) Thoroughgood, 77
  Thomas, 77
Gordon, *Arms*, 215, 218
  ——, 257
  —— (Key), 216
  Alexander Tazewell, 217
  Ann (Sparke), 216
  Anne, 216
  Archibald, 134
  Archibald A., 134
  Armistead, 216
  Armistead Churchill, 215, 216, 218
  Betsey Pope, 514
  Charles Henry, 217
  Churchill, 188, 216
  Edith Churchill, 218
  Edward, 134
  Edward Clifford, 215
  Eleanor, 216, 388
  Eliza S., (Beale), 217
  Elizabeth, 216, 217, 348
  Elizabeth (Clayton), 216
  Elizabeth (Ellis), 216

INDEX

553

Gordon—*Continued*
  Elizabeth(Gordon), 216
  Elizabeth Cole (Fitzhugh), 216
  Elizabeth (Lindsay), 217
  Emily Adele (Slichter), 218
  Fannie, 134
  Frances Daniel, 218
  George, 215, 216
  Goerge Loyall, 215, 217
  Hannah, 216
  Hannah Elizabeth, 217
  Harriet, 134
  Harriett (Hart), 217
  Helen Martin, 134
  James, 215, 216
  James Lindsay, 215, 217, 218
  Jean (Campbell), 215
  John, 134, 216
  John Churchill, 216, 217
  Lavinia Battle, 218
  Louise (Bringier), 117
  Lucy, 216, 217
  Lucy (Churchill), 216
  Lucy (Gordon), 217
  Lucy Harrison, 216
  Lucy (Herndon), 216
  Margaret Douglas, 215
  Margaret (Hunter), 215
  Maria Breckinridge (Catlett), 215
  Maria Lindsay, 217
  Martha (Winston), 217
  Martin, 117
  Mary, 216
  Mary B. (Pegram), 217
  Mary (Beall), 217
  Mary (Daniel), 218
  Mary Daniel, 215
  Mary (Gordon), 216
  Mary (Harrison), 216
  Mary Long, 218
  Mary Read (Rootes), 217
  Mason, 217
  Nabby (Pope), 514
  Nancy (Morris), 217
  Nathaniel, 216
  Priscilla, 216
  Priscilla (Bullitt), 134
  Reuben Lindsay, 217
  Robert, 215, 251
  Samuel, 215, 216
  Sarah, 216

Gordon—*Continued*
  Sarah (Greenway), 215
  Thomas, 216
  Ursula (Peirce), 188
  William, 216, 217, 514
  William Fitzhugh, 216, 217
Gorsuch, Alice (Hall), 306
  Alice (Hillson), 306
  Ann, 306
  Anne (Lovelace), 306
  Danyell, 306
  Harriet, 251
  John, 306
  William, 306
Gotham, Desire (Howland), 225
  John, 225
Gough, Sophia (Dorsey), 60
  Thomas, 60
Gould, Anna, 285
  Charles M., 15
  Clara Delia, 301
  Esther, 208
  Henry, 429
  Lydia (Bell), 15
  Mary, 429
  Sarah, 203
Goulding, Penelope (Arnold), 26
  Roger, 26
Gower, Sarah (Peirce), 187
  Stanley, 187
Grabisch, Agatha Marshall (Bullitt), 140
  Joseph, 140
  Thomas Bullitt, 140
Graham, *Arms*, 219, 220
  ———, 187
  Asher Waterman, 219
  George, 484
  George Richard, 485
  Hamilton Field, 220, 223
  James Watson, 485
  Jane (Brent), 108
  Jane Love (Watson), 484
  Jennie (Brent), 484
  Jennie Brent, 484
  John, 348
  John Macdougall Atherton, 219
  Katherine E. (Field), 220, 223
  Kelley, 219, 220, 223

Graham—*Continued*
  Lillias, 348
  Lucien, 220, 223
  Lucien Dunavan, 220, 223
  Margaret (Peirce), 187
  Maria, 172
  Mary Valeria (Atherton), 219
  Richard, 108, 484
  Robert, 173, 348
Grandveaux, Edna, 44
Grassie, Annie, 384
Grattan, Catharine, 146
Gratz, Benjamin, 491
  Caroline Clifford (Bryan), 491
  Hermine, 491
Graves, Ann, 395
  Rose Victoria, 337
Gray, Benjamin F., 147
  Elizabeth Crittenden (Cabell), 147
  Jennie H., 455
Grayson, Alfred William, 96
  Benjamin, 347
  Benjamin, Lewis Chart No. 1
  Lettitia Preston (Breckinridge), 96
  Mary Elizabeth (Wagoner), 345
  Mary Elizabeth (Wagoner), Lewis Chart No. 1
  Spence, 345, 347
  Spence, Lewis Chart No. 1
  Susanna, 343, 345, 348
  Susanna M., Lewis Chart No. 1
  Susanna (Monroe), Lewis Chart No. 1
  Susanna Monroe, 347
Greeley, Caroline Ann, 425
Green, Amelia, 53, 57
  Ann Eliza (McCulloh), 445
  Anne, 236
  Betty (Hollingsworth), 294
  Elizabeth, 160
  Elizabeth Stockton, 445
  Ellen (Kennedy), 496
  Henry, 294
  Jacob, 445
  John, 496
  Leslie, 313
  Mary, 57

INDEX

Green—*Continued*
  Richard, 53, 57
  Ruth, 57
  Sarah, 27
  Sarah (Howard) Nelson, 53, 57
Greenburg, Cora Ester, 419
Greenbury, Katherine, 48
  Nicholas, 48
Greene, Ann (Bulkeley), 125
  Anna Lloyd, 329
  Catherine, 182
  Deborah, 182
  Deborah (Champlin), 153
  Elizabeth, 107
  Elizabeth (Arnold), 26
  Elizabeth (Marshall), 153
  Fones, 153
  Joan (Tattersalle), 182
  John, 26, 182, 329
  Kezia (Davis), 182
  Lydia, 182
  Martha (Russell), 516
  Mary, 308
  Peter, 26, 182
  Rufus, 516
  Samuel, 153
Greene, Thomas, 329
  William, 107, 125
  William Parkinson, 329
Greeniff, John, 59, 60
  Ruth (Hill) Dorsey, 59, 60
Greenleaf, Lucinda Maria, 373, 376
Greenman, Phoebe, 152
Greenway, Elinor (Matthews), 215
  Samuel, 215
  Sarah, 215
Greenwood, Hannah, 438
  Thomas, 438
Greer, Elizabeth (Courtenay), 172
  Thomas, 172
Gregg, Clara Louise, 37
  James Donald, 37
  Margaret (Campbell), 37
Gregory, Elizabeth (Moulthrop), 410
  Frances, 507
  John, 410
  Mildred (Washington), 507
  Roger, 507

Greland, Aurora, 330
  Jean Baptiste, 330
Gresham, Olive (Butt) Woodward, 76
  Thomas, 76
Greville, Elizabeth Willoughby (De Broke), 104, 115
  Fulke, 104, 115
  Katherine, 104, 115
Grey, Sarah, 303
  Sarah (Marine), 353
  Thomas, 353
Griffith, Ann, 232
  Ann Houston, 193
  Charles, 57
  Elizabeth (Nelson), 57
  Henry, 194, 232
  John, 161
  Mary Ella (Hall), 233
  Mollie, 248
  Robert, 233
  Ruth (Hammond), 232
  Sarah, 161
  Seth, 193
Griggs, Darthalow, 306
Grigsby, Elizabeth (Butler), 477, 478
  Elizabeth Butler, 471, 476, 477
  James Redmond, 477, 478
  Jane (King), 477
  Jane (Rosser), 471, 477, 478
  John, 471, 477, 478
  Nathaniel, 477, 478
  Susannah (———), 477, 478
  William, 477, 478
Griswold, Lydia, 316
  Marian, 378, 382
  Matthew, 378, 382
  Nancy, 198
  Ursula (Wolcott), 382
Groser, Antoinette A. (Bornard), 224
  Arthur, 227
  Bertha (Brown), 224
  Charlotte Lilian, 228
  Charlotte Sophia Philopena (Smith), 227, 228
  Courtney Brown, 224
  Dorothy Lola, 224
  Faith, 224
  Herbert Wilson, 228
  Kenneth Bedell, 224

Groser—*Continued*
  Lola M. (Waite), 224
  Marion, 224
  Mary Elizabeth (Haskins), 227, 228
  Mary Soren, 228
  Samuel Haskins, 224, 226, 228
  Thomas, 227, 228
  Thomas W., 228
  Thomas Wentworth, 227
  Wentworth, 228
Gross, A. Haller, 136
  Julia Dunlap (Bullitt) Dick, 136
  Maria Rives, 136
Grosvenor, Elizabeth, 124
  Randle, 124
Grover, Aurilly, 397
Guest, Alice (Bailyes), 359
  George, 359
  Phoebe, 359
Guffey ———, 340
  Elizabeth, 340
  Elizabeth Tyson (Lee), 339
  Henry Arthur, 339
  Nancy, 340
Guilarmine ———, 503
Guild, Mercy, 284
Gunnell, Virginia Blagden, 248
  William Hunter, 248
Gunning, Jane, 34
Gurovitz, Mary (Brent), 114
  Orin, 114
Guthrie, Benjamin Franklin, 19
  Frank, 19
  Keziah Jane (Pollard), 19
Gwathmey, Fanny Brooke, 392
  Frances Fielding (Lewis), 392
  Humphrey Brooke, 392
Gwynne, Alice Claypoole, 202

H

Habbot, Harriet, 425
Hackett, George, 403
  Lydia (Thomas), 403
  Sarah, 403
Hager, Elizabeth, 109
Haight, Titus, 465
Haines, Anne (Osgood), 408
  David, 408
  Mary, 160

INDEX

Hale, Abigail, 423
   Elizabeth (Strong), 424
   Joan (Kirby), 423
   Johanna (———), 424
   John, 424
   Joseph, 422, 424
   Mary (Hutchinson), 423
   Nathan, 424
   Rebecca, 422
   Rebekah, 420, 424
   Rebekah (Harris), 424
   Richard, 424
   Robert, 424
   Sarah (Noyes), 424
   Thomas, 423
   Thomasine (Dowsett), 423
Hales, John, 478
   Mary, 478
Haley, Leora B., 421
Hall, *Arms*, 229, 261
  ——— (Appold), 241
  ——— (Bowie), 232
  ——— (Boyd), 232
  ——— (Cowman), 235
  ——— (Estep), 235
  ——— (Garrison), 234
  ——— (Howard), 232
  ——— (Stevenson), 235, 236
   Addie T., 244
   Alexander, 235
   Alfred Sellman, 238
   Alice, 306
   Alice (Stewart), 240
   Alice Virginia (Homburg), 230
   Altizera (Duval), 254
   Andrew Jackson, 246
   Angaline (Fretwell), 244
   Ann, 247
   Ann (Crag), 230
   Ann (Griffith), 232
   Ann (Wells), 240
   Anna, 238, 259
   Anna May, 247
   Anna (Mohun), 249
   Anne, 233, 237, 239, 240, 245
   Anne (———), 255
   Anne D. (Mulliken), 258
   Anne (Duckett), 242, 243
   Anne Elizabeth, 241
   Anne (Gaston), 237
   Annie Leigh, 253
   Arthur Wallace, 260

Hall—*Continued*
   Augustus, 236
   Baruch, 245, 248
   Baruch Crittenden, 250
   Basil, 257
   Basil Duckett, 229, 257, 258, 260
   Benjamin, 91, 179, 231, 242, 243, 255, 349
   Bettie, 244
   Blake, 237
   Caroline, 257
   Catherine, 258
   Catherine Sandes, 241
   Charles William, 240
   Edward, 231, 232, 233, 235, 236, 242, 243, 246, 255, 259, 260
   Edward Grafton Washington, 246
   Eleanor Deborah, 240
   Eleanor Deborrah (Sellman), 240
   Eleanor (Dorsey), 232
   Eleanor (Estep), 241
   Eleanor Maria (Estep), 240
   Eleanor (Murdock), 242
   Eliza, 244
   Elizabeth, 48, 55, 232, 237, 240, 243, 248, 255, 256
   Elizabeth Ann, 237, 246
   Elizabeth Burnett, 260
   Elizabeth Claude (Stockett), 234, 237
   Elizabeth Hinkle (Rittenhouse), 250
   Elizabeth (Lansdale), 231, 235, 236
   Elizabeth (Meeks), 244
   Elizabeth (Perkins), 87, 243
   Elizabeth Sellman, 238
   Elizabeth Sellman (Welsh), 238
   Elizabeth (Watkins), 232, 233, 238, 239, 256
   Elsie, 252
   Emma Daingerfield (Tennant), 250
   Estep, 235
   Eva Spence, 260
   Eva Spence (Wallace), 259
   Evelyn, 253
   Florence Wode (Becker), 234

Hall—*Continued*
   Frances Stockett, 234
   Francis, 256
   Francis Asbury, 254
   Frances Barton Loney, 241
   Francis Chapman, 260
   Frank, 260
   Franklin Waters, 241
   Frederick, 236
   Grafton, 242, 246, 250, 254
   H. E., 244
   Harriet, 234, 258
   Harriet Ann, 241
   Harriet (Kent), 234
   Harriet Kent, 238
   Harriet Perkins, 252, 349
   Harriet (Sellman), 233
   Harry, 233, 237
   Harry Walton, 249
   Henrietta, 237
   Henrietta (Hall), 237
   Henrietta (Harwood) Cowman, 236
   Henrietta Kerr, 253
   Henrietta Kerr (Spalding), 253
   Henry, 48, 91, 230, 231, 232, 233, 235, 236, 238, 239, 240, 242, 256, 349
   Henry Stevenson, 230
   Isaac, 232, 235, 242, 250, 255
   Isabel (Hopkins), 244
   Isabella (Scott), 246
   Issabelle Frances (Allen), 241
   Jacob, 247
   Jacob Duckett, 245
   Jacob Thornton, 254
   James Williams, 253
   Jane Contee (Kent), 233
   John, 231, 235, 240, 242, 244, 255, 306
   John Edward, 244
   John Grafton, 251, 252
   John Henry, 255
   John Stephen, 232
   John T., 244
   John Thomas, 236
   John Washington, 233
   Joseph, 233
   Joseph Thomas, 234
   Julia, 233, 247
   Julius, 233, 234, 237

INDEX

Hall—*Continued*
- Katherine Gertrude (Robinson), 241
- Laura, 242
- Lola Anna, 250
- Louise (Hopkins), 253
- Lucy, 257
- Lucy (Carr), 260
- Lucy Orrick (Nicols), 260
- Magdelen, 231
- Margaret, 232, 233, 236, 237, 242, 256
- Margaret Augusta (Stubbs), 259
- Margaret (Davidson), 258
- Margaret Davidson, 259, 260
- Margaret Gassaway, 241
- Margaret Gassaway (Watkins), 240
- Margaret Hall (Harwood), 237
- Margaret (Harwood), 236
- Margaret Harwood, 234, 238
- Margaret (Howard), 233
- Margaret Jane, 247
- Margery, 233
- Maria, 237
- Maria Overton (Turner), 244
- Martha, 231, 232, 238, 240, 241, 242, 246, 256
- Martha (Bateman), 231, 232
- Martha (Duckett), 256
- Martha (Duckett) Odell, 235
- Martha Elizabeth Becker, 234
- Martha (Hall), 256
- Martha Sophia, 258
- Martha Thomas, 250
- Mary, 231, 232, 233, 241, 244, 246, 256, 261
- Mary (———), 240
- Mary Ann, 233, 244
- Mary Ann (Hall), 233
- Mary Ann (Hodges), 240
- Mary (Belt), 231
- Mary (Brooke), Bowling, 179
- Mary Carolina, 230
- Mary Davidson, 259
- Mary Dryden, 237
- Mary (Duvall), 231, 242
- Mary Eleanor (Cooper), 255
- Mary Ella, 233

Hall—*Continued*
- Mary Esther (Loney), 241
- Mary Etta (Waters), 234
- Mary Eugenia, 254
- Mary Jane, 248
- Mary Magdalen, 240
- Mary Priscilla, 234, 237
- Mary Rebecca, 251
- Mary Sophia, 240
- Mary Spalding, 253
- Mary Susannah, 253
- Mary (Watkins), 236
- Mordacai, 236
- Nancy, 256
- Nettie, 244
- Nicholas, 232
- Osborne Sprigg, 235
- Permelia Victoria (Iglehart), 258
- Phillip Dorsey, 260
- Rachel, 237, 243, 476
- Rachel Anne, 234
- Rachel Estep, 240
- Rachel (Harwood), 233
- Rachel Sophia, 241
- Rachel Sophia (Waters), 240
- Rachel Sprigg (Watkins), 237
- Rebecca Anne (Peach), 251
- Rebecca Frances, 252
- Rebecca (Magruder), 242
- Rebecca (Williams), 246, 250, 254
- Rebecca (Williams) Hall, 246
- Reuben Beauregard, 253
- Richard, 235, 236, 237, 251
- Richard Duckett, 87, 243, 251, 349
- Richard Henry, 234, 252, 256
- Richard Overton, 244
- Richard Watson, 244
- Rignal Duckett, 246, 250
- Rignal John Duckett, 242
- Robert, 230
- Robert Gibson, 230
- Robert Vinton, 253
- Rosa E., 249
- Ruth Adella (Beall), 251
- Ruth Anne, 250
- Ruth Anne Rebecca, 246
- Ruth (Jacob), 235
- Ruth Leeds, 253

Hall—*Continued*
- Ruth Williams, 253
- Sammie, 244
- Samuel Davidson, 258, 260
- Sarah, 87, 242, 243, 245, 255
- Sarah Beck (Williams) Parker, 246
- Sarah (Jacob), 233
- Sarah Ryland, 253
- Sophia, 233, 242, 256, 257
- Sophia (Welsh), 242
- Sue (Anderson), 246
- Summerfield Davis, 254
- Susan, 237
- Susannah, 243, 245
- Susannah (Perkins), 251, 349
- Thomas, 235, 236, 246
- Thomas Allen Waters, 241
- Thomas Harwood, 234
- Thomas Henry, 232
- Thomas Irving, 260
- Thomas John, 240, 241
- Thomas Sellman, 240
- Thomas Thornton, 254
- Thomas William, 229, 233, 257, 258, 260
- Tyler, 230
- Violetta (Duvall), 229
- Virginia, 242
- Virginia B. (Younger), 253
- Virginia Blagden (Gunnell), 248
- Wallace Kent, 234
- Watkins, 236
- William, 91, 231, 232, 234, 236, 241, 242, 243, 245, 255, 256
- William Henry, 237, 240
- William John, 237, 241
- William Osbourn, 237
- William Perkins, 244
- William Sprigg, 238
- William Thornton, 251
- William Turner, 253
- William (Williams), 250
- William Williams, 243, 251
- Williams A., 256
- Williams Edward Lucius Chapman, 260
- Wilson Iglehart, 259

Hallam, Amos, 152
- Phoebe (Greeman), 152
- Prudence, 152

INDEX

Hallett, William, 10
Halley, Alice Bell, 275
  Alice Hunter (Bell), 275
  Anne Hampton, 275
  Henry Simpson, 275
  James Helm, 275
  Katharine Anderson (Helm), 275
  Katherine Anderson Helm, 275
  Pattie Helm, 275
  Samuel Hampton, 275
Hallowell, Clara Lucie Vallé (Bain), 40
  John Edgar, 40
Hamblin, Ruth, 439
Hamilton, Alexander, 120
  Anne (Adams), 119
  Catherine, 148
  Flora (Brent), 114
  Flora Brent, 114
  Grace, 119
  Helen (McGill), 120
  Helen McGill, 120
  Jennie, 296
  John, 114
  John Worden, 114
  Silas Marland, 119
  Thomas, 93
  Thomas Benton, 114
  Winifred Lee, 114
Hammer, Margaret, 296
Hammond, ———, 258
  Ann, 58
  Ann (Dorsey), 58
  Augusta, 258
  Hannah Dorsey, 58
  Helen, 50
  Helen Heath, 60
  Henrietta, 50
  John, 58, 60
  Mary (Heath), 50, 60
  Mary (Howard), 60
  Philip, 61
  Rachel (Brice), 61
  Rezin, 55
  Ruth, 232
  Sarah, 55
  Thomas, 50, 60
  Washington, 238
Hampton, John Brewster, 33
  Ruth (Avery), 33
Hance, Joyce, 465

Hancock, *Arms*, 262, 265
  Anna, 264
  Ann (———), 263
  Arthur Boyd, 265
  Belle Clay, 262
  Belle Lyman (Clay), 262
  Benjamin, 263
  Charles Russell, 265
  Dorothy, 264
  Dorothy (———), 263, 264
  Durham, 263
  Eliza (———), 262
  Elizabeth Ann, 264
  Elizabeth Erskine, 269
  Elizabeth Hazelwood, 265
  Elizabeth (Hightower), 264
  Emma Lewis, 265
  Emma Louise, 269
  Emma V., 264
  Enoch, 264
  Gabriel, 264
  Harris, 262, 265
  Hector, 263
  Henry, 263
  Hull, 264
  James, 263
  James E., 264
  Jane Crawford, 265
  Joanna, 264
  John, 263
  John C., 264
  John Overton, 269
  Joseph, 263
  Magdalen, 264
  Marie Louise (Price), 269
  Mary, 263
  Noah, 264
  Richard, 266
  Richard Harris, 269
  Richard Johnson, 264, 265
  Richard Jordan, 265
  Roxanna, 264
  Ruth (Huggins), 264
  Sarah, 263
  Sarah (Ward), 263
  Thomas Benton, 264
  Thomas Hightower, 265, 269
  Thomasia Harris, 262
  Thomasia Overton, 265
  Thomasia Overton (Harris), 265, 266
  William, 262, 263, 264
  William Jordan, 264

Hancock—*Continued*
  Zebedee, 264
  Nathaniel, 263, 264, 330, 331
Handridge, Richard, 38
Handbridge, Sarah, 38
Handy, Henrietta (Ball), 46
  Levin, 46
  Love, 286
  Samuel, 194
Hankinson, Ann, 272
  Jemima (———), 272
  Thomas, 272
Hannah, Elizabeth (Stites), 138
  Ruth, 154
  William Morton, 138
Hard, Mary, 40
Hardigan, Olive (Butt) Woodward Gresham, 76
  William, 76
Hardin, Benjamin, 278
  Lucinda Barbour, 278
Harding, Asa, 285
  Ruth (Hewins), 285
Hardy, Elizabeth, 366
  John, 366
Hare, Elizabeth (Cabell), 145
  William B., 145
Harewell, Joan, 102
Harlakenden, Mabel, 329
Harlan, Aaron, 294
  Elizabeth, 294
  Elizabeth (Hollingsworth), 294
  Hannah, 294
  Samuel, 294
  Sarah (Hollingsworth), 294
Harmanson (———), 390
  Alicia, 69, 70, 387, 389, 391
  Anna (———), 69
  Elizabeth, 68, 69
  Elizabeth (———), 69
  Elizabeth (Yeardley), 69, 72, 387, 391
  George, 69, 72, 387, 391
  Gertrude (Bowman), 69
  Grace (———), 69
  Henry, 69
  Isabel, 69, 70
  John, 69
  John Kendall, 69
  Kendall, 69
  Susannah (Kendall), 69

INDEX

Harmanson—*Continued*
　Thomas, 69
　William, 69
Harmonson, Margaret, 192
Harnden, Elizabeth, 423
Harper, Agnes, 338
Harrington, Adams, 429
　Isabella (English), 197
　Jane Augusta (Ruggles), 429
　Lillian, 201
　Nycholas, 197
Harris, *Arms*, 265, 266
　Adria (Osborne), 265
　Amelia Gantt (Bowie), 94
　Ann, 489
　Ann Lewis, 266
　Anna Bowie, 94
　Anne Emilla, 266
　Arthur, 416
　Barbara Wingfield (Terrell), 266
　Charles Gantt, 94
　Charles M. B., 94
　Dwiggins Claude, 174
　Elizabeth, 488
　Emma Nan, 174
　Eusebia, 266
　Fred A. W., 22
　Frederick, 266
　H. V. Loving, 174
　Hannah (Stewart), 488
　Jemina, 266
　John, 266, 488, 489
　John Overton, 266
　Judith, 489
　Keziah, 266
　Laura (Loving), 174
　Marian B., 22
　Mary, 266, 363
　Mary (———), 424
　Mary (Claiborne) Rice, 265
　Mehitable (Rickard), 416
　Mourning (Glen), 266
　Obedience (Turpin), 489
　Overton, 266
　Rebekah, 424
　Robert, 265, 266
　Sallie, 266
　Susanna, 509
　Temperance, 266
　Temperance (Overton), 265
　Thomas, 265, 266
　Thomas Cadwallader, 94

Harris—*Continued*
　Thomas Henry, 265
　Thomasia Overton, 265, 266
　Walter, 424
　William, 265, 266
Harrison, *Arms*, 141, 180
　Elizabeth, 105, 130
　Frances (Whitgreaves), 112
　Hannah, 216
　Mary, 216, 361
　Mary Caile, 131
　Nathaniel, 216
　Thomas, 130
Hart, *Arms*, 270, 274
　Ann (Hankinson), 272
　Betsey A. (Howard), 466
　Byerly, 274
　Caroline, 466
　Catherine Louise (Badger), 273
　Charles Byerly, 270, 271, 274
　Elinor, 271
　Elinor (Wilson), 272
　Elizabeth, 271, 272
　Elizabeth (———), 271
　Elizabeth (Means), 272
　Ethel Hill, 270
　Francis, 273
　Harriett, 217
　Ida Virginia (Hill), 270
　Isabella (Long), 272
　James, 271, 272
　James Hankinson, 273
　Jane, 271, 272
　Jean (Means), 271
　John, 271, 272
　John Kirk, 273
　Joseph, 271, 272
　Lewis Justice, 270
　Margaret (Means), 271
　Margaret Newbold, 271
　Margaret Newbold (Smith), 270
　Mary, 271, 272
　Mary A. (Gilpin), 273
　Mary Elizabeth (Sperry), 273
　Mary Jane, 273
　Mary (McCalla), 272, 273
　Mary West (Horstman), 274
　Matilda (Maybin), 273
　Nancy, 273
　Nina Lewis (Justice), 270

Hart—*Continued*
　Rebecca A. (Reeves), 273
　Richard P., 466
　Samuel, 271, 272
　Sara (Byerly), 274
　Solomon, 272
　Temperance, 398
　Thomas, 270, 273, 274
　Virginia Justice, 270
　William, 271, 272
　William Bryan, 270, 273, 274
　William H., 271, 273
　William Henry, 274
Hartley, Catherine, 478, 479
　Ellen M. (Diller), 478
　John, 478
Harwood, Ann (Chapman), 236
　Anne Elizabeth, 236
　Anne (Green), 236
　Benjamin, 236, 237
　Elizabeth Anne, 236
　Elizabeth Anne (Harwood), 236
　Elizabeth (Lloyd), 236
　Henrietta, 236
　Henrietta Maria (Battee), 236
　Henry Hall, 236
　Joseph, 236
　Margaret, 236
　Margaret (Hall), 232, 236, 237
　Margaret Hall, 237
　Matilda (Sparrow), 236
　Mary, 236
　Mary (Harwood), 236
　Osbourn, 237
　Osbourn Sprigg, 236
　Rachel, 233
　Richard, 232, 236, 237
　Richard Hall, 236
　Thomas, 233, 236
　Thomas Noble, 236
Haskell, *Arms*, 366, 369
　——— (Stone), 366
　Abigail, 367
　Adeline (Hatch), 368
　Alexander Chevis, 480
　Alice (Van Yeveren) Alexander, 480
　Amy (Chandler), 368
　Betsey (Richards), 368
　Charlotte, 367

INDEX

Haskell—*Continued*
Charlotte Jane (De Forest), 368
Content, 368
Daniel, 367, 368
Diadama, 367
Diantha (Robinson), 367
Elijah, 367, 368
Elizabeth, 367
Elizabeth (Ellis), 368
Elizabeth (Hardy), 366
Frederika Christina, 480
Gideon, 368
Grace (Barnard), 368
Hannah, 367
Hannah (Baldwin), 368
Hannah (White), 368
Hannah (Woodbury), 367
Henry Louis Shafter, 368
Horace, 368
Jacob, 367
Jacob Reed, 368
John, 367, 368
Josiah, 367
Judith, 367
Lorenzo Cogswell, 368
Luctus, 368
Lucy Bates, 368
Mahitable (Barnard), 368
Mariett (Thrasher), 368
Marilla (Cowles), 368
Mark, 366, 367
Mary, 367
Mary (Spaulding), 368
Peres, 368
Robert, 366
Roger, 367, 368
Roswell, 368
Roxana Atilda, 368, 369
Sarah, 367
Sarah (Bants), 368
Sarah (Read), 367
Susan Atlantic, 368
William, 366, 367
Zenas, 368
Martha, 184
Haskins, *Arms*, 224, 228
David Greene, 226
Edward Soren, 227
George Shepherd, 227
Hannah, 227
Hannah (Upham), 226
John, 226

Haskins—*Continued*
Mary Ann (Soren), 227
Mary Elizabeth, 227, 228
Rebecca (Emerson), 226
Robert, 226
Ruth, 226
Sarah (Cook), 226
Sarah Emerson, 227
Thomas Waldo, 226, 227
Thomas Wilson, 227
Waldo Emerson, 227
Hasselrigg, Arthur, 4
Hastings, Isabel, 348
Hatch, Adeline, 368
Alonzo Parry, 89
Clara (McKinstry), 89
Florence, 245
Florence Clara, 89
Hathaway, Abraham, 509
Alice, 517
Rebekah (Wildbore), 509
Hathorne, William, 284
Hatton, Eleanor, 178
Henrietta, 250
Margaret (———), 178
Richard, 178
Thomas, 178
Haughton, Martha, 295
Haven, Catherine Matilda (Jeffries), 328
Charles Chauncey, 326
Havens, Charles, 462
Eleanor (Tiffany), 462
Hawes, Susan, 435
Hawke, Hannah, 437
Margaret, 438
Margaret (———), 437
Sarah, 437
Matthew, 437
Electa, 65
Hawkins, ———, 26
Elizabeth (Dorsey), 168
Elizabeth Dorsey, 168
Esther (Arnold), 26
John, 168
Hawley, Armelia (Wilbur), 510
Richard, 510
Hawthen, Elizabeth (Brent), 104
John, 104
Haynes, John, 329
Sarah, 198

Hays, Sara Hardin (Helm), 278
Thomas, 278
Hayward, Francis, 353
Gideon, 439
James, 378
Lydia (Cushing), 439
Mary, 353
Mary (Warren), 353
Hazard, E., 427
Elizabeth Breeze, 427
Hazeltine, Elizabeth, 333
Hazelwood, Elizabeth, 264
Hazen, Bernice Clayton, 399
Hazlewood, Annie Abbot (Rockwood), 421
Clarence, 421
Gordon Clarence, 421
Grace Burton, 421
Leora B. (Haley), 421
Lillian, 421
Ruth, 421
William Plumer, 421
Healey, Lydia, 32
Hearld, Elizabeth, 294
Heath, Helen, 60
Mary, 50, 60
Heckscher, Charles Hart, 270
Ethel Hart, 270
Ethel Hill (Hart), 270
Gustave Adolph, 270
Ida Virginia, 270
Johanna Barbara, 270
Ledyard, 270
Ledyard Hart, 270
Lucertia (Stevens), 270
Richard, 270
Hedgethorn, Emily Cobby, 199
James, 199
Heide, Ann, 162
Hele, Anne (Cabell), 143
John, 143
Helm, *Arms*, 275, 279
Benjamin Hardin, 278
Dorothy Crosby (Walker), 276
Elizabeth Barbour, 278
Elizabeth Pendleton (Barbour), 278
Elizabeth Tebbs (Nelson), 275
Emily P. (Todd), 278

INDEX

Helm—*Continued*
  Emily Palmer, 278
  George, 277, 278
  George Crosby, 276
  George Nelson, 275
  James Pendleton, 275, 276, 279, 281, 501
  Jane, 278
  Jean (Pope), 277
  John Larue, 277, 278, 279
  Kate Tebbs, 275
  Katharine Anderson, 275, 281
  Louisa, 278
  Lucinda Barbour, 278
  Lucinda Barbour (Hardin), 278
  Lucinda Hardin, 276, 281, 501
  Lucretia, 278
  Lucy A. (Washington), 279
  Mary, 278
  Melvina, 278
  Pattie Anderson, 275
  Pattie Anderson (Kennedy), 275, 281, 501
  Rebecca Jane, 278
  Rebecca (Larue), 277
  Sara Hardin, 278
  Squire, 278
  Thomas, 277, 278
  Thomas Kennedy, 275, 276, 281
  Thomas Preston Pope, 279
  William, 277, 279
Hemsdon, Ann (Rogers), 404
  John, 404
Henderson, Jacob, 231
Hendrick ———, 487
  Mary (Swigert), 487
Hendricksen, Maycken, 473
Hendrygken, Macyken, 471
Henneage, Katherine, 104
Henry, *Arms*, 141, 180
  Anne, 131
  Jane, 296
  John, 129, 173
  Patrick, 97, 129, 131, 483
Henslee, Hiram, 298
  Sarah Elizabeth (Stewart) Jones, 298
Herndon, Lucy, 216
  Margaret, 498

Hersey, Abigail (Cushing), 439
  Hannah, 286
  Jonathan, 439
  Thomas, 439
Heseltine, Delana (Wilbur), 510
  Seymour, 510
Hesketh, Florence (Breckinridge), 99
  Thomas Fermor, 99
Heustis, Alice Dunbar, 508
  James Farrington, 508
Hewins ——— (Ingraham), 285
  Agnes (Arden), 283
  Alice Emmons, 289
  Amasa, 285, 286
  Anna Fiske, 286
  Anna (Gould), 285
  Benjamin, 283, 284
  Bertha, 286
  Caroline L. (Chapin), 286
  Caroline Maria, 286
  Caroline T. (Brown), 286
  Catherine (Bird), 284
  Charles Amasa, 286
  Charles Carroll, 289
  Clara Carroll, 283, 289
  Eben Newell, 287
  Ebenezer, 284, 285
  Edith, 286
  Edward, 287
  Elijah, 285
  Elizabeth, 283
  Elizabeth (Alden), 286
  Elizabeth Alden, 289
  Elizabeth Allin, 287
  Elizabeth (Cummings), 285
  Elizabeth Fiske, 286
  Elkanah, 285
  Enoch, 284
  Esther, 286, 287
  Esther (Kollock), 285
  Florence, 287
  Florence Emmons, 287
  Frank Alden, 286
  George, 283, 287, 289
  George F., 287
  George Sanford, 289
  Gertrude Newell, 290
  Hannah, 283, 284
  Hannah Capen (Foster), 285
  Hannah (Hersey), 286

Hewins—*Continued*
  Hannah (Hewins), 284
  Harriet, 290
  Harriet Caryl, 290
  Harriet Whiting (Carroll), 283, 288, 289
  Harry William, 283, 290
  Hattie E., 287
  Increase, 284
  Irene (Balch), 285
  Jacob, 283, 284
  Jerusha (Day), 287
  John, 283, 284, 285
  Joseph, 283, 284, 285
  Josephine, 287, 289
  Judith (Porter), 284
  Lemuel D., 285, 286
  Lois (Whiting), 285
  Louise, 287
  Love (Handy), 286
  Lucy Chapin, 286
  Margaret, 283, 287
  Margaret (———), 286
  Martha (Trescott), 283
  Mary, 283
  Mary (———), 283
  Mary A., 287
  Mary Drake (Phelps), 290
  Mary Phelps, 290
  May (Phillips), 287
  Mehetable, 284
  Mehetable (Lyon), 284
  Mercy (Guild), 284
  Nathaniel Adams, 286
  Patty, 286
  Patty (Hewins), 286
  Phebe, 284
  Rebecca, 285
  Richard, 287
  Royall, 286
  Ruth, 285
  Ruth (Cummings), 285
  Ruth (Hewins), 285
  Samuel, 283
  Sarah, 284
  Sarah (———), 284
  Sarah (Hewins), 284
  Sarah (Seavey) Marden, 286
  Simon K., 286
  Thomas, 283
  William, 284, 285, 286
  William Alfred Samuel, 283
  Zebiah, 286

INDEX

Hewitt, Ann, 77
  William, 77
Heyburn, Alexander, 139
  Nancy Creel (Chenoweth), 139
Heydt, Abraham, 474
  Anne Marie (Du Bois), 471, 474
  Eleanor (Elting), 474
  Elizabeth, 474
Hedyt, Hans Joost, 474
Heydt, Isaac, 474
  Jacob, 474
  John, 474
  Joseph, 474
  Jost, 470
  Magdalena, 474
  Maria Susannah, 474
  Mary, 474
  Sara (Eltinge), 474
Heyer, Henry Yeatman, 66
  John C., 66
  Margaret (Johnston), 66
  Mary (Bell), 66, 74
  Mary Bell, 66, 69, 77
  Matthew Johnston, 66, 74
Hibbard, Eunice, 65
Hickman, Louisa F., 489
Hicks, Joshua, 184
  Martha (Derby), 184
  Rachel A., 15
  Willet, 15
Hierome, Anne, 502
  Jacques, 503
  Marthe (Le Roy), 503
  Prudence, 503
Higgins, Augusta (Hammond), 258
  Caroline (Hall), 257
  Dallas Hammond, 257
  Dallas Hammond (Higgins), 257
  Eleanor Ann, 257
  Elizabeth, 222
  Elizabeth (Dorsey) Adgate, 50, 53
  George William, 257, 258
  Harriet, 257
  James, 50, 53, 257
  Lackland, 258
  Lucretia, 257
  Maria Eleanor (Duvall), 257
  Richard Francis, 257

Higgins—*Continued*
  Richard Mortimer, 257
  Sallie, 257
  Susan (Mewburn), 258
Hightower, Elizabeth, 264
  Elizabeth (Hazelwood), 264
  Jordan, 264
Hill, Agnes (Brent), 104
  Augusta Bransford (Lewis), 342
  Charles Van Dyke, Lewis Chart No. 1
  Charles Van Dyke, 342
  Clement, 113
  Edward Lewis, 342
  Edward Lewis, Lewis Chart No. 1
  Eleanor (Brent), 113
  Elizabeth, 166
  Elizabeth Stockett, 234
  Ewing, 342
  George Washington, 270
  Giles, 104
  Hannah Russell, 440
  Harry W., 234
  Ida Virginia, 270
  Isaac, 440
  Joyce Mallory, 342
  Joyce Mallory, Lewis Chart No. 1
  Margaret Harwood (Hall), 234
  Mary, 54
  Minnie, 239
  Olive, 249
  Richard, 59, 60
  Ruth, 59, 60
  Sarah Jane (White), 370
Hilleary ———, 94
  Thomas, 349
Hilliard, William, 322
Hillman, James Frayer, 147
  Marguerite Cabell (Wright), 147
Hillson, Alice, 306
Hinckley, Mehitable, 31
  Sybil (Sparhawk), 31
  Thomas, 31
Hinckman, John, 6
Hines, John F., 97
  Mary Dudley (Breckinridge), 97
Hinkle, Mary Magdalena, 478

Hinman, Lucretia, 183
Hitchcock, Carrie Lillian, 169
Hite, Anne Marie (Du Bois), 474
  John, 471
  Jost, 470, 471, 474
  Rebecca, 471, 475
  Sara (Elting), 471
Hixon, John, 284
  Mehetable (Hewins), 284
Hoar, Ebenezer Rockwood, 427
  Ellen, 383
  Nathaniel, 509
  Samuel, 427
  Sarah (Wildbore), 509
  Sherman, 383
Hobart, Edmund, 322
  Mary Catherine, 30
Hobbs, Bazil Nicholas, 55
  Jemima (Dorsey), 58
  Joseph, 58
  Henrietta (Dorsey), 49
  Mary Ann (Dorsey), 55
  Samuel, 49
  William, 49
Hodges ——— (Sellman), 257
  Lucy (Duckett), 239
  Lucy (Hall), 257
  Mary, 184
  Mary Ann, 240
  Ramsay, 239, 257
  Thomas, 257
Hodgkin, Lucy (Brooke), 180
  Thomas, 180
Hoge, Mary Swift (Ballard), 65
  William J., 65
Holand, Aleanor, 346
  Thomas, 346
Holbrook, Margaret, 426
Holden, Catherine, 182
  Catherine (Greene), 182
  Charles, 182
  Elizabeth, 28
  Frances (Dungan), 182
  Randall, 182
Holladay Caroline Densmore (Huntington), 317
  E. Burke, 317
Holland, Albert, 248
  John, 399
  Marietta, 399
  Nannie (Woodward), 248

INDEX

Hollingsworth, *Arms*, 291, 300
——— (Frost), 296
Aaron, 297
Abigail, 294
Abraham, 295, 296, 297
Ann, 295, 296
Ann (Calvert), 292, 293
Ann (Maulden), 293, 363
Ann (Ree), 292
Ann (Robinson), 295
Ann, 295
Barbary (Shewin), 294
Betsie (Rogers), 297
Betsey (Echols), 299
Betty, 294
Betty (———), 294
Catharine, 294
Catharine (———), 292
Catherine (Cornish), 363
Catharine (Tyler), 295
Charles Armstrong, 300
Darthalow (Griggs), 300
Edna Earl, 291
Elizabeth, 294, 295
Elizabeth (Atkinson), 363
Elizabeth Ann Jane Carr (Rogers), 297
Elizabeth (Chandler), 295
Elizabeth (Harlam), 294
Elizabeth (Hearld), 294
Elizabeth (Jackson), 297
Elizabeth (Rogers), 297
Enoch, 294, 295
George, 294, 296, 297
Grace, 295
Grace (Cook), 295
Hannah, 295, 297
Hannah (Harlan), 294
Hannah (McCoy), 296
Hannah (Paschall), 363
Henry, 292, 293, 296, 363
Isaac, 295, 296
Jacob, 295
James, 294, 296, 297
James Edwin, 291, 300
Jane, 300
Jane (Elwell), 296
Jane (Henry), 296
Jemima, 296
Jennie, 297
Jennie (Hamilton), 296
Joanna (Crowley), 294
John, 291, 294, 295, 296, 297

Hollingsworth—*Continued*
Joseph, 295, 296, 297, 300
Joseph A., 300
Joseph Edwin, 291
Joyce (Eppison), 297
Judith (Lampley), 295
Julia Ann, 297
Julian, 300
Katharine (McKewen), 291
Letitia, 299
Levi, 293, 296, 299, 363
Lizzie, 300
Lucy H. (Moseley), 300
Lydia, 296
Lydia (Atkinson), 293
Margaret, 162, 296
Margaret (———), 295
Margaret (Hammer), 296
Margaret (Wright), 296
Martha, 297
Martha (Haughton), 295
Mary, 293, 294, 297, 363
Mary (———), 294
Mary Elizabeth, 300
Mary (Evans), 162
Mary (Reed), 294
Moses, 297
Nancy Johnson (Rogers), 295
Nathan, 296
Pamelia (McDowell), 297
Rachel, 294
Rachel (Parkins), 296
Rachel (Wright), 296
Rebecca (Bailey), 297
Richard, 297
Robert, 291, 296
Robert Emmett, 300
Roseannah, 299
Rosannah (Nichols), 297
Ruth, 293
Ruth (Rogers), 297
Samuel, 294
Sarah, 294, 295, 299
Sarah (Cook), 296
Sarah (Wright), 296
Stephen, 293
Susanna, 296
Susanna (Rice), 296
Susanna (Wright), 296
Thelma Elizabeth, 291
Thomas, 294, 295
Valentine, 292, 294, 363

Hollingsworth—*Continued*
William, 297
William Henry, 300
Zebulon, 162, 293, 363
Hollister, Mary, 334
Holloway, *Arms*, 301, 303
Abraham, 301, 305
Alexander, 302
Anne Harden (Ross), 302, 305
Catherine, 302
Charles Thomas, 301, 302, 303, 305, 306, 309
Edward, 302
Eleanor, 302
Eleanor Humphrey (Bowen), 301, 305
Ella Virginia (Houck), 302, 305, 309
Ellen Maria, 302
Fanny (Bayley), 302
Frances Allon (Fuller), 301
Grace, 302
John Merriman, 302
Mary Jane, 302
Rachel (———), 301, 305
Reuben Ross, 302, 305, 309
Robert, 301, 305
Virginia Leslie, 302, 305, 309
William Henry, 302
Hollyday, Sarah, 93
Holmes, Mary, 152
Mary (Rickard), 417
Nathaniel, 417
Holt, Catherine, 38
Edmund, 38
Henry, 63
James, 64
Nicholas, 406
Phebe (Ballard), 64
Sarah (Ballard), 63
Holyoke, Hannah, 451
Homburg, Alice Virginia, 230
George William Albert, 230
Hone, Catherine, 345, 348
Catherine, Lewis Chart No. 1
Judith (Aylmer), Lewis Chart No. 1
Theophilus, 345, 348
Theophilus, Lewis Chart No. 1
Thomas, Lewis Chart No. 1

INDEX

Hood, Susannah, 61, 285
  Zacharia, 229
Hooker, Harriette, 162
  Mary, 406
  Sarah, 425
Hooper, Eleanor (Holloway), 302
  George, 144
  James A., 302
  Rachel, 144
Hoops, Adam, 483
  David, 483
  Elizabeth (Finney), 483
  Isabel, 483
  Jane, 483
  Margaret, 483
  Mary, 483
  Robert, 483
  Sarah, 483
Hope ———, 294
  Rachel (Hollingsworth), 294
Hopkins ———(Gordon), 257
  ——— (Watkins), 239
  Abigail (English), 198
  Alexander Marshall, 257
  Anna, 257
  Arthur, 96, 145
  Augusta, 249
  Emanuel, 198
  Gordon, 257
  Isabel, 244
  J. Seth, 249
  Johns, 251, 256, 257, 258
  Louise, 253
  M. D., 208
  Mary, 96, 145
  Montgomery, 257
  Nancy (Hall), 256
  Samuel, 256
  Sophia (Fuller), 208
  Thomasin, 242
Horne, Rebecca (Rea) Stevens, 63
  Simon, 63
Horner, Harriet Love (Watson), 485
  John Scott, 485
Horowitz, Anna, 470
Horry, Elias, 310
  Margaret (Huger), 310
Horsey, Caroline, 109
  Joan (Brent), 102
  Thomas, 102

Horsley, Mary (Cabell), 144
  William, 144
Horstman, Sigmund H., 274
Horstmann, Mary West, 274
Horton, Frances Breckinridge (Steele), 99
  Jeter, 99
  Sarah, 157
Horwitz, Louisa Gross, 136
Hoskins, Elizabeth (Perkins) Hall, 243
  Martha Elizabeth, 218
  Nathan, 243
Hosmer, Abel, 377, 382
  Abner, 378
  Olive Parlin (Davis), 377, 382
  G. W., 378
  Joseph, 378
  Maria Davis, 377, 382
Houck, Bettie Trisler, 309
  Caroline Somerville, 309
  Ella Virginia, 302, 305, 309
  Hazeltine Howard, 309
  Howard (Hawkens), 309
  Jacob, 305
  Jacob Adae, 309
  Jacob Wever, 302, 305, 309
  John Mercer Porter, 309
  Mary George, 309
  Renthrope, 307
  Rose (Burmingham), 309
  Sudie Frances, 309
  Susannah Frances (Porter), 302, 305, 309
Houge, Mary, 455
Hough, Susan, 273
Houghton, Caroline (Sparhawk), 124
  Fannie Briggs, 124
  James Franklin, 124
  John, 407
  Mehitable (———), 407
  Myra, 418
  Phineas, 407
  Ruth (Osgood), 407
Houston, Robert, 194
Howard, *Arms*, 175
  ———, 232, 243
  Abner, 60
  Alexander Scott Bullitt, 132, 177
  Ann, 60

Howard—*Continued*
  Ann (Hall), 247
  Ann (Phillips), 176
  Ann (Sollers), 176
  Annie Christian, 132, 173, 177
  Annie Christian (Bullitt), 132, 177
  Baker, 176, 180
  Benjamin, 176
  Betsey A., 466
  Clara Hall, 247
  Cornelius, 47, 56, 60
  Edmund, 175, 176, 180
  Eleanor, 176, 180
  Elizabeth, 176, 180
  Elizabeth (———), 176
  Elizabeth (Hall), 243
  Ephraim, 56
  George, 176
  Hannah, 176
  Helen, 132, 177
  Henry, 52, 56, 169
  Honor, 42, 50, 52, 57
  Isaac, 247
  James, 51
  Jerusha (Gay), 212
  John, 47, 56, 59, 60, 132, 176, 177, 180
  John Beale, 56
  John Eager, 336
  Joseph, 56, 232, 233, 238
  Johsua, 57
  Linden Hall, 247
  Margaret, 233, 238
  Margaret (Chew), 336
  Margaret (Dent), 175, 180
  Maria (Strother), 132
  Martha (Hall), 232, 238
  Mary, 60
  Mary Elizabeth, 254
  Mary (Jones), 132, 177
  Mary (Latimer), 177
  Matthew, 56, 60
  Patience (Dorsey), 51
  Philip, 51
  Rachel, 57
  Rebecca, 176
  Rebecca (Brooke), 176, 180
  Ruth (Hill) Dorsey Greeniff, 59, 60
  Samuel, 51, 176
  Sarah, 53, 55, 57, 60, 455

INDEX

Howard—*Continued*
  Sarah (Briscoe) Truman, 176
  Sarah (Dorsey), 52, 56, 60
  Simeon, 212
  Sophia Catherine, 336
  Susannah, 59, 176
  Susannah (———), 60
  Thomas, 176, 180
  Vachel Denton, 56
  Virginia Pleasants, 169
  William Bullitt, 132, 177
  William Stevens, 176
  Ann (Lyne), 486
  Ann Bannister, 486
  Edward, 331, 409, 486, 490
Howell, Charles E., 350
  Martha (Jeffries), 350
  Marie St. Claire, 350
Howes, Abiel (Gay), 211
  Daniel, 211
Howland, Abigail, 516
  Abraham H., 517
  Benjamin Franklin, 517
  Bishop, 225
  Desire, 225
  Elizabeth, 225
  Elizabeth (Southworth), 225
  Elizabeth (Tilley), 225
  Hope, 225
  Isaac, 225
  Jabez, 225
  John, 224, 225, 228, 465
  Joseph, 225
  Judith, 516
  Lydia, 225
  Mary Ann (Russell), 517
  Mehitable Earle (Russell), 517
Hoyt, Nancy Hall, 83
Hubbard, Bethiah, 152
  William, 329
Hudson, Elizabeth, 361
  Jane (Evans), 361
  Mary (Richardson), 361
  William, 361
Huger, *Arms*, 310, 312
  ——— (Golightly), 310
  Allen (Deas), 311
  Ann (Brown) Cusak, 310
  Ann Elliott, 311
  Ann (Le Jan), 310
  Arthur Middleton, 311
  Benjamin, 310

Huger—*Continued*
  Caroline (Proctor), 311, 312
  Charlotte (Motte), 310
  Daniel, 310, 311
  Daniel Elliott, 311, 312
  Eliza Caroline Middleton, 311
  Elizabeth, 312
  Elizabeth (Chalmers), 310
  Elizabeth (Gendron), 310
  Elizabeth (Smith), 312
  Emma Middleton, 311
  Francis, 311
  Francis Kinloch, 311
  Isaac, 310
  Isabella Johannes (Middleton), 311
  Isabella Middleton, 312
  John, 310
  John Middleton, 311
  Joseph Alston, 311
  Joseph Proctor, 312
  Lydia (Johnson), 310
  Magdalen, 310
  Margaret, 310, 311
  Margaret Campbell (King), 311
  Margaret (Perdrian), 310
  Mary, 312
  Mary (Cordes), 310
  Mary Esther, 311
  Mary Esther (Huger), 311
  Mary (Kinloch), 310
  Mary Middleton, 311
  Paul, 311
  Richard Proctor, 312
  Sabina (Elliott), 311
  Sabina Elliott, 311
  Sarah Elliott, 311
  Stephen Proctor, 312
  William Elliott, 310, 311, 312
Huggerford, John, 104
  Katherine (Henneage), 104
  Mary, 104
Huggins, Luke, 264
  Ruth, 264
Hughart, Eva, 344
Hughes, Addie, 366
  Edward, 189
  Mary (Doneghy), 189
Huie, Helen Eleanor Grant (Bullitt), 131
  James, 131

Hume, Katherine, 503
  Thomas, 503
Humphrey, David, 305
  Elizabeth, 301, 305
  Elizabeth (Roberts), 305
  Margaret (Evans), 305
  Robert, 305
  Thomas, 350
Hungerford, Elizabeth, 166
  Walter, 166
Hunnewell, Richard, 371
Hunt, Anita Dunbar, 110
  Dunbar, 110
  Elizabeth, 334
  Hannah, 328
  Hester Ann (Benjamin), 80, 82, 84
  Leila Lawrence (Brent), 110
  Liddya (Lawrence), 14
  Meriam, 80, 82, 84
  Sarah Jane (Moulthrop), 413
  Stevanus, 14
  William, 328
  William B., 413
  William Washington, 80, 82, 84
Hunter, Margaret, 215
Huntington, Abigail (Bingham), 315
  Ann, 314
  Anna, 316
  Arabella (Duval), 313
  Caleb, 316
  Caroline Densmore, 317
  Christopher, 314
  Clara Leonora, 313
  Collis Potter, 317
  Daniel, 315, 316
  David, 36
  Elizabeth, 315, 316, 317
  Elizabeth (Foote), 316
  Elizabeth (Stoddard), 317
  Elizabeth Vincent, 313
  Ellen M., 317
  Eunice, 316
  George, 317
  Hannah (Crane), 314
  Hannah (Metcalf), 315
  Harriet, 317
  Harriet (Saunders), 317
  Henry, 347
  Henry Edwards, 313, 317
  Howard, 317

INDEX

Huntington—*Continued*
Howard Edward, 313
Isabel, 347
Israel, 316
John, 316
Joseph, 315, 316, 317
Leonora, 317
Leslie (Green), 313
Lucy, 316
Lucy (Metcalf), 316
Lydia (Gager), 315
Lydia (Griswold), 316
Margaret (Barrett), 314
Marian Prentice, 313
Mary, 315, 316
Mary Alice (Prentice), 313
Mary (Clark), 315
Mehitable (Metcalf), 316
Nathaniel, 315, 316
Phebe, 317
Rachel, 316
Rachel (Preston), 316
Rachel (Wolcott), 315
Rebecca, 316
Rebecca (Adgate), 315
Rhoda, 316, 317
Ruth (Rockwell), 314
Samuel, 315, 316
Sarah, 315, 316
Sarah (———), 316
Sarah (Clark), 315
Simon, 314, 315, 316
Solon, 316, 317
Susan, 317
Thomas, 314
Willard, 317
William, 316
Huppman, Ann Sedgewick, 337
Hurlbutt, George B., 126
Mary (Bulkeley), 126
Hutchinson, Alice (———), 423
Alice (Bosworth), 423
Bernard, 423
Emily Newbold (Bell), 15
Eunice, 384
Harry, 15
Mary, 423
Richard, 423
Thomas, 423
Hyerome, Rachel (———), 502
Hynson, Mary Elizabeth, 101

I

Iasigi, Amy Gore (Walker), 129
Nora, 129
Oscar, 129
Ide, Ann Daggett, 421
Edith Burton, 421
Elizabeth (Hewins), 283
Grace Burton (Hazlewood), 421
Grace Shirley, 421
Horton Francis, 421
Horton Gregory, 421
Melinda Rockwood, 421
Nicholas, 283
Iglehart, ——— (Watkins), 239
John Wilson, 258
Leonard, 239
Permelia Victoria, 258
Inglish, James, 196
Ingalls, Henry, 406
Mary (Osgood), 406
Ingersoll, Elinor Houghton (Bulkeley), 124
George, 320, 331
John Avery, 124
Susan, 136
Ingraham, ———, 285
Ingram, Anita, 173
Annie Courtenay (Loving), 173
Archer Wilmington, 24
Helen Courtenay, 173
Julia Courtenay, 173
Sophia Mary (Arnold), 24
William Foote, 173
Innes, *Arms*, 493
Ann (Harris) Shields, 489
Harry, 489
Maria Knox, 488, 489
Sally, 491, 507
Irby, Olive, 125
Irvine, Abraham, 189
Amelia (Moss), 189
Irving, Charlotte Jane, 171
Isaac, Jemina, 233
Isham, Mary, 127
Israel, Estelle Bird, 239
Izard, Allen Smith, 311
Emma Middleton (Huger), 311

J

Jackson, ——— (Kenney), 477, 478
Andrew, 485
Elizabeth, 297
Elizabeth Butler (Grigsby), 471, 476, 477
Ellenor (Ballard), 63
Francis, 477, 478
John, 63, 477, 478
John Farrow, 471, 476, 477, 478
Lydia, 321
Mardulia E. S., 471
Mardulia Emma Sybil, 476, 477
Mary, 93
Mary (Farrow), 477, 478
Minnie J., 209
Sally (Tyler), 477, 478
Samuel, 477, 478
Jacob, Charles Donald, 133
Edith (Bullitt), 133
Elizabeth, 437, 438
Hannah, 438
Hannah (Allen), 439
Jemina (Isaac), 233
Joel, 348
John, 348
Mary, 439
Mary (———), 437
Mary (Russell), 438
Mordacai, 235
Mordacci, 233
Nicholas, 437
Peter, 439
Ruth, 235
Ruth (Tyler), 235
Sarah, 333, 437
Jacobs, Deborah (Richmond), 440
Deborah Richmond, 440
James, 440
Mary (Robinson), 294
Thomas, 294
Jaffrey, George, 326, 327
Sarah, 327
Sarah (Jeffries), 326
James, *Arms*, 318
Albert E., 321
Ann Francis (Leavitt), 320, 322

INDEX

James—*Continued*
  Benjamin, 321
  Clara Leavitt, 320
  Donald Robertson, 318
  Elisha Benjamin Reynolds, 321, 323
  Ella Reed Cruttenden, 320
  Herbert Llewelyn, 320, 321, 322
  Howard Kellogg, 318, 320
  Martha (Meserole), 318
  Mary Ann (Thomas), 321, 323
  Mary Francis, 320
  Richard Leavitt, 318
  Sarah M., 321
Jans, Anneke, 10
Jansen, Katherine Johnson, 362
Jarvis, John, 330
Jaynes, Jennie, 344
Jefferies, Amelia M. (Smith), 303
  Ebenezer Arthur William, 302
  Ernest Smith, 302, 303, 306, 309
  John, 303
  Sarah (Grey), 303
  Virginia Leslie (Holloway), 302, 305, 309
  Virginia Lovelace, 303
Jefferson, Mary, 489
  Sarah (Ellegood), 193
  Thomas, 117, 489
  Warren, 193
Jeffries, *Arms*, 324, 331
  Almira (McBurney), 329
  Andrew Belcher, 327
  Ann, 327, 328
  Ann McLean, 329
  Anna Lloyd (Greene), 329
  Anne, 326
  Anne (Clarke), 326
  Anne Geyer (Amory), 328
  Benjamin Joy, 329
  Catherine Amory, 329
  Catherine Matilda, 328
  Charles Shimmin, 329
  Clemence Despaigne, 330
  Clemence (Eustis), 330
  Clementina Matilda (Wethered), 328

Jeffries—*Continued*
  David, 326, 327
  Deborah, 327
  Deborah (Lyde), 327
  Dorothy (Kinge), 326
  Edward, 328
  Edward Payson, 329
  Eleanor Gorsuch, 306
  Elizabeth, 326, 327
  Elizabeth (Usher), 326
  Emily Augusta (Eustis), 331
  Eyre Massey, 328
  Frances, 326
  George, 327
  George Jeffrey, 328, 329
  Hannah Hunt, 328
  Hannah (Winslow), 327
  Harriet Maria, 328
  Henry Upham, 329
  James Lloyd, 330
  Jane, 326
  John, 324, 326, 327, 328, 329, 331
  John Armory, 330
  Julia Ann, 328
  Katherine, 327
  Katherine (Eyre), 326
  Marian, 329
  Marian (Shimmin), 329
  Martha, 350
  Peter, 326
  Rebecca, 326
  Robinson Ardesoif, 328
  Sarah, 326, 327
  Sarah (———), Rhoads, 327
  Sarah Augusta, 328, 329
  Sarah (Jaffrey), 327
  Sarah (Rhoades), 328
  Virginia Lovelace, 306
  Walter Lloyd, 330
  William Augustus, 330
Jenks, Ann, 381
  Ebenezer, 381
  George Albert, 375
  Hattie, 375
Jensen, Lena Marie, 392
Jerome, Anne, 502
Jewett, Joseph, 441
  Leonard, 428
  Philomela, 333
  Sally (Rockwood), 428
  Susannah (Cushing), 441

Johns, Margaret Crabb, 93
  Sarah (Hollyday), 93
  Thomas, 93
Johnson, *Arms*, 332, 334
  ———, 49
  Arthur, 450
  Campbell Housman, 499
  Catherine Walker, 108
  Elizabeth, 332, 383
  Elizabeth (Kennedy), 49
  Emily (Welles), 333, 335
  Frances (Wicom), 332
  Francis Jewett, 332, 333, 335
  Georgia La Nauze, 499
  Hannah, 332
  Hannah (Crosby), 332
  Isaac, 332
  Jane, 398
  John, 332
  Lawrence, 363
  Louisa Macalester (Nevins), 332
  Lydia, 310
  Lydia (Bailey) Platts, 333
  Lydia (Ballard), 64
  Margaret, 465
  Margaret Annette (Clark), 499
  Mary Ella, 363
  Mary Stoddard, 450
  Moses, 333
  Obadiah, 64
  Otis Russell, 333, 335
  Philomela (Jewett), 333
  R. W., 98
  Rachel, 363
  Rachel (Boynton), 333
  Robert, 310
  Sally Frances, 98
  Samuel, 332, 333
  Susanna (Searle), 333
Johnston, Elizabeth (Hart), 272
  John, 272
  Margaret, 66
Jones, Alexis Smith (Ball), 43
  Ann (Gorsuch) Todd, 306
  Anne, 484
  David, 306
  Elizabeth Brierton, 145
  Ely, 347
  Honor (Dorsey), 53
  Joseph, 320

INDEX

Jones—*Continued*
Joshua, 53
Louisa, 418
Lydia, 397
Margaret, 247
Martha Alexis, 44
Mary, 132, 177, 358
Mary (Fuller), 206
Patience (Little), 320
Ralph, 206
Richard Andrew, 43, 44
Robert, 298
Sarah, 41, 320
Sarah Elizabeth (Stewart), 298
Spence Monroe, 347
Susannah, 343
William, 258
Jordan, Margaret, 144, 146
Paulina, 145
Samuel, 144, 145
Jorisse, Madelin, 471, 472
Joselyn, Thomas, 322
Joslyn, Sarah, 417
Joyes, Caroline Hancock Preston (Barr), 487
Morton Venable, 487
Juison, ———, 503
Jurdan, Mary, 42
Jurney, ———, 256
Elizabeth (Hall), 258
Justice, George Randolph, 270
Nina Lewis, 270
Sallie Fisher (Lewis), 270

K

Karraker, Ann Chenoweth, 138
Ann Lennox (Stites), 138
Charles William, 138
Kearney, Elizabeth, 360
Keeling, Adam, 77, 78
Alexander, 78
Ann, 73, 75, 77
Ann (———), 78
Ann (Keeling), 77
Ann (Martin), 78
Ann (Thoroughgood), 77, 78
Anne, 73, 78
Elizabeth, 73, 76
Frances, 73, 78
Grace (———), 78
John, 78
Lovey (Land), 74

Keeling—*Continued*
Thomas, 73, 74, 75, 78
William, 73, 77, 78
Keep, J. Lester, 34
Jay Lester, 35
John S. Bassett, 35
Marian Lavina, 35
Ogden Avery, 35
Sarah Coit (Avery), 34
Keith, Elizabeth, 348
James, 129
Kelley, ———, 340
Alta Maud, 400
Charles, 400
Charles William, 400
Edward, 400
Evelyn Rosette, 400
Ida Fern, 400
Independence, 340
Lillian Independence, 340
Mary Alice (Rhoades), 400
Robert Nelson, 400
Ruth Inez, 400
Kellogg, Edwin S., 248
Margaret (Woodward), 248
Kelsey, Mary Goodenow, 219
Kemp, Emily Page, 119
Louisa Richardson (Smith), 119
Perrin, 119
Kemper, Fontaine Llewellyn, 3
Helen Wilmer, 3
Sarah B. (Brown), 3
Kendall, John, 69
Rebecca (———), 372, 375
Susanna, 69
Susanna (Savage), 69
Tabitha, 372, 375
Thomas, 372, 375
Kennedy, *Arms*, 279, 281
——— (McDonald), 279
Alfred Worsley, 280
Ben Dudley, 280
Catharine M. (Anderson), 275
Catharine Martin (Anderson), 280, 282
Clarra, 280
Elizabeth, 49
Ellen, 496
Emily, 281
Eugenia (Ferrell), 281
Henry Clay, 280

Kennedy—*Continued*
Isabella, 496
James, 281
Jane (Buchanan), 279
Jane (Smith), 279
Janet, 49
Janet Gordon (Camp), 497
John, 279, 496
Katharine, 281
Laura, 280
Laura (Hall), 242
Lucy (Chapman), 280
Madge (Willard), 281
Margaret, 281
Margaret (Clark), 496
Mary, 279
Mary (Barret), 280
Matthew, 279
Matthew Woodford, 280
Minnie (Berthold), 280
Nancy Martin, 281
Nannie, 280
Orville, 281
Orville Anderson, 281
Pattie Anderson, 275, 281, 501
Rebecca, 280
Robert, 496
Samuel, 496
Samuel Smith, 280
Sidney Anderson, 280
Thomas Smith, 275, 280, 282
Thomas Willard, 281
Thomas Worsley, 281
Walter, 279
Walter Scott, 242
William, 496
William Buchanan, 279
William Thomson, 497
Kenner, Anne Guilhelmine Nanine (Bringier), 111
Duncan F., 117
Duncan Farrar, 111, 117
Frances Rosella, 111
George, 117
Nanine (Bringier), 117
Rosella, 117
Kenny, ———, 478
(———), 477
Kent, Harriet, 234
Jane Contee, 233
Joseph, 233, 234
Katherine, 109

INDEX

Kerr, *Arms*, 502
  Hugh, 495
  Janet, 495
  Mary (Wilson), 495
Kessler, Agnes Clare (Woodward), 254
  Clarence Summerfield, 254
  Lloyd Alexander, 254
  Mary Elizabeth (Howard), 254
Key, ———, 216
  Helen Scott (Bullitt) Massie Martin, 135
  Marshall, 135
Keys, Hannah, 333
  Ida, 366, 453, 456
  James, 366
  Nannie (Gardner), 366
Keyser, Betsey, 417
  Mary Hoke (Brent), 110
  Matilda Lawrence, 110
  Robert Brent, 110
  William, 110
Kibbe, ———, 323
Kidd, Isabella (Moulthrop), 413
  John D., 413
Kidder, Bessie, 183
  Bessie (Low), 183
  Greer, 183
King, Abraham, 23
  Charles, 46
  George Hales, 477, 478
  Hannah (Waterman), 23
  Isabella (Bragdon), 446
  Jane, 477
  John, 478
  Joseph, 298
  Katherine Bowie Duckett, 239
  Kitty Tennessee, 298
  Louisa (Ball), 46
  Mabel, 222
  Margaret Campbell, 311
  May, 446
  Mary (Hales), 478
  Mitchell, 311
  Patience (Ellis), 513
  Richard, 446
  Rufus, 446
  Sarah Ann, 46
  Sarah (Garrard), 477
  Thomson, 239

Kinge, Dorothy, 326
Kingsley, Eunice, 429
  Phineas, 429
Kinkle, Mary Magdalena, 479
Kinloch, Mary, 310
Kinney, Daniel, 417
  Lucy, 417
  Polly (Sprague), 417
Kirby, Joan, 423
Kirkham, Mary, 417
Kirkpatrick, Florence, 45
Kiser, Ida J., 299
Kitson, Margaret, 506
  Robert, 506
  Thomas, 506
Knapp, Charles W., 443
  Elizabeth Norris (Cushing), 443
Knight, Elizabeth (Champlin), 154
  Isaac, 424
  Jedediah, 154
  Rebecca (Abbot), 424
Knipe, Marie H., 418
Knollys, Anne, 74
  Francis, 74
  Katherine (Cary), 74
Knowles, Hester Eleanor, 355
  Ruth, 32
  William, 355
Knowlton, Daniel, 460
  Frank Allan, 301
  Lucy Jane (Stratton), 301
  Mary, 460
  Maude Louise, 301
  Thomas, 460
Kollock, Cornelius, 285
  Esther, 285
  Jacob, 285
  Jerusha (Billings), 285
  Royall, 285
Kynnersly, Isabel, 348
  John, 348

L

Lackey, Alta Maud (Kelley), 400
  Lawrence Henry, 400
La Core, Marjory, 461
La Favre, ———, 502
Laight, Ann Elliott (Huger), 311
  Edward, 311

Lake, Anna, 38
  Julia, 450
Lamar, Francés, 457
Lamb, Frances (Bulkeley), 127
  H. F., 127
  John, 126
  Lucy (Bulkeley), 126
  Lucy C. (———), 418
  Mary, 39
Lambert, Anna Greenwood, 194
Lamkin, Guy, 80, 82, 84
  Lois Noyes (Benjamin), 80, 82, 84
Lampley, Judith, 295
La Nauze, *Arms*, 502, 505
  ——— (Storey), 503
  Agnes Alicia, 504
  Alexander, 503
  Andrew, 503, 504
  Andrew George, 502
  Andrew Henry, 505
  Anne (Hierome), 502
  Anne Martha, 505
  Anne O'Reilly, 504
  Charles, 504
  Christiana (Parry), 164, 500, 504
  Francois, 504
  George, 164, 500, 503, 504
  George John, 504
  Georgina, 498, 505
  Guillermine Martha (De La Pierre), 503
  James, 502
  Jessie, 164, 276, 482, 500, 505
  John Paul, 503
  Martha, 503, 504
  Peter Marc Antony, 503
  Rachel, 503
  Richard, 504
  Robert, 503, 504
  St. Cyre, 503
  William Henry, 504
  Ysaac, 503
Lancaster, Henrietta Maria, 109
Lance, Lucy (Russell) Osgood, 408
  Robert, 408
Land, Ann (Woodhouse), 73, 75
  Anne Virginia, 66, 74, 76

INDEX

Land—*Continued*
  Edward, 73, 75
  Edward Cannon, 66, 74, 76
  Eliza, 74
  Eliza Woodhouse (Stone), 74
  Elizabeth (Edwards), 73
  Elizabeth (Keeling), 73, 76
  Elizabeth (Smith) Foreman, 74, 76
  Elizabeth Smith (Foreman), 66
  Frances (Keeling), 73, 78
  Frances (Langley), 73, 75
  Francis, 73
  Jeremiah, 73, 74, 75
  Littleton Waller Tazewell, 74
  Lovey, 74
  Mary Woodhouse, 74
  Mary Woodhouse (Land), 74
  Peter, 66, 73, 76
  Renatus, 73, 78
  Sarah, 74
  Thomas Stone, 74
  Walter Scott, 74
  William Keeling, 74
Lane, Dolly (Ballard), 64
  Elizabeth, 32
  George, 322
  Job, 32
  Jonas, 64
  Mary, 31
  Sarah, 32
  William, 322
Langhorne, Therese Caldwell 135
Langley, Frances, 73, 75
  James, 73, 75
  Joyce, 76
  Joyce (———), 75
  Margaret (Thelebal), 75, 76
  Nathan, 75
  Sarah (———), 75
  Sarah (Nicholson), 75
  William, 75, 76
Langman, Elizabeth (Brent), 107
  Thomas, 107
Lankford, Floyd, 241
  Sarah (Estep), 241
Lanman, James, 378, 381
  Marian Chandler, 381
  Marian (Penniman), 378

Lansdale, Elizabeth, 231, 235, 236
Lapham, John, 516
  Mary (Russell), 516
Larcom, Fanny (Ellingwood), 424
  Fanny Ellingwood, 424, 425
  Henry, 424
Larkin, Daniel, 153
  Eunice (Champlin), 153
  John, 47
  Margaret, 47
Larue, John, 277
  Mary (Brooks), 277
  Rebecca, 277
Lathrop, Jane, 206, 207
  John, 206
Latimer, Ann, 126
  Dorothy, 348
  Joan, 102
  Lydia (Bulkeley), 126
  Mary, 177
  Richard, 348
  Robert, 102, 126
Laurens, John, 7
Lawler, Cecilia Varonica, 400
Lawrence, *Arms*, 3, 16
  ———, 58
  Abigail, 13, 14
  Amy (Pearsall), 14
  Amy (Peyton), 4
  Ann (Burling), 14
  Ann (Pell), 14
  Anna (Townsend), 14
  Benjamin, 12, 55, 58
  Betsey (Talman), 14
  Caleb, 14
  Catherine, 18
  Catherine (Farmer), 14
  Catherine H., 15
  Charity (Clarke), 12
  Cornelius W., 15
  Daniel, 9, 10, 11
  Deborah (Smith), 12
  Edward, 5
  Edward N., 15
  Effingham, 14
  Elizabeth, 5, 11, 13, 14
  Elizabeth (Cornell), 12
  Elizabeth (Hager), 109
  Elizabeth (Smith), 11
  Emma (Ahles), 18
  Esther P., 15

Lawrence—*Continued*
  Eugene, 13
  Hannah, 13, 14
  Hannah (Bowne), 13
  Harriet, 15
  Harriet (Van Wyck), 14
  Henry, 4, 5, 14
  Ida Irene, 349
  James, 3, 12
  Jane, 6
  Joane, 6
  Joane (Anterbus), 6
  John, 4, 5, 6, 7, 8, 9, 10, 11, 12, 13, 14, 18
  Johnathan, 10, 11
  Joseph, 8, 12, 13, 14, 15
  Katerin (Beaumont), 5
  Laura Gardinier, 13
  Levin, 49, 58
  Liddya, 14
  Lydia, 14
  Lydia A., 15
  Lydia A. (Lawrence), 15
  Margaret (Robertes), 5
  Marie, 6, 11
  Maria C. (Prall), 15
  Marie (Wilkinson), 5
  Martha, 8
  Mary, 9, 12, 14, 56, 58
  Mary (Eustice), 350
  Mary (Ferguson), 10
  Mary (Townley), 12, 13
  Matilda, 109
  Matilda (Washington), 3
  Norris, 14
  Phebe, 14, 15
  Phoebe (Townsend), 14
  Rachel, 49
  Rachel A. (Hicks), 15
  Richard, 4, 5, 12, 13, 14, 15
  Robert, 3, 4
  Rosetta (Townsend), 15
  Ruth (Dorsey), 58
  Samuel, 12
  Sarah, 12, 13
  Sarah Ann (Drake), 15
  Sarah (Burling), 14
  Susanna (———), 8
  Susannah, 8, 55, 56, 58
  Susannah (Dorsey), 58
  Thomas, 5, 6, 8, 9, 10, 11, 12, 13
  Thomas Henry, 350

INDEX

Lawrence—*Continued*
  Upton, 109
  Urith (Randall) Owings, 58
  William, 4, 5, 6, 9, 10, 11, 12
  William C., 11
Laws, John, 194
Lawson, ———, 188
  Anthony, 75, 77
  Elizabeth, 92
  Ellen, 188
  Ellen (Peirce), 188
  Margaret, 75, 77
  Mary (Gookin), 77
  Mary (Gookin) Moseley, 77
  Thomas, 75
Lawton, Mary, 152
Layton, William, 107
Lea, Joan, 509
Leach, Azariah, 510
  Jacob, 510
  Joanna (Wilbore), 509
  Josiah, 509
  Lydia (Wilbore), 510
  Tabitha (Wilbore), 510
Leakin, Phil M., 258
Leavenworth, Helen, 120
Leavitt, *Arms*, 323
  Alice F., 322
  Ann Frances, 320, 322
  Caleb, 320, 322
  David, 322
  Delina (Robertson), 320, 322
  Elijah, 322
  Israel, 321
  John, 321, 322
  Lydia (Jackson), 321
  Martha S., 322
  Mary (Bate), 321
  Nancy, 322
  Nancy (Sewall), 320, 322
  Sarah, 441
  Sarah (———), 321
  Sarah (Beal), 320, 322
Le Ayre, John, 102
Le Despencer, Hugh, 166
Lee, *Arms*, 336, 341, 492
  Agnes (Harper), 338
  Amabel, 340
  Ann (Beekman), 338
  Ann (Theus), 338
  Ann Fenton, 113
  Arthur Fenner, 336

Lee—*Continued*
  Augusta Rose, 337
  Caroline, 339
  Dorothea (Smisea) Alison, 338
  Eliza, 339
  Elizabeth, 490
  Elizabeth (Bell), 490
  Elizabeth (Lawson), 92
  Elizabeth Tyson, 339
  Frances (Carter), 113
  Francis, 338
  Francis A., 339
  Francis Joseph, 338
  Gulielma Poultney, 340
  Hancock, 490
  Hannah, 92, 338
  Henrietta (Gaillard), 339
  Henry, 338
  Hilyard Cameron, 340
  Hutson, 339
  I. Allison, 339
  J. Martin, 339
  James Fenner, 336, 337, 339
  Jane Elizabeth (Martin), 339
  John, 489, 490
  John Eager Howard, 337
  Joseph, 338, 339
  Julia (Reynolds), 339
  Kendall, 216
  Lillian (Wathen), 337
  Lynch (Van Ryburne), 339
  M. C. Villepont (Eaux), 339
  Marie, 339
  Mary, 338
  Mary (———), 338
  Mary (Aylett), 113
  Mary Cornelia, 336
  Mary Cornelia (Read) Carroll, 336
  Mary Digges, 336
  Mary (Giles), 338
  Mary Hay (Thorme), 338
  Mary Sophia, 337
  Mary (Willis), 490
  P. Van Rhyne, 339
  Paul S. H., 338, 339
  Philip, 92
  Rachel, 338
  Rebecca, 338
  Rebecca (Fishburne), 339
  Robert, 338

Lee—*Continued*
  Sallie, 490
  Sallie O., 489
  Sarah Fenner, 336
  Sarah Fenner (Mallett), 339
  Sarah (Gordon), 216
  Sophia Howard, 337
  Stephen, 338
  Stephen States, 339, 340
  Susannah, 338
  Theodore B., 339
  Thomas, 338
  Thomas Ludwell, 113
  William, 338
  William States, 339
  Winifred Beale, 113
Le Engleis, Walter, 196
Le Engleys, John, 196
  Richard, 196
Le Englisshe, John, 196
Le Eyre, Joan, 102
Le Gos, Albreda, 165
  Richard, 165
Leigh, Dorothy, 109
  Dorothy (Doyne), 109
  Florence, 492
  Isabel, 319
  Robert, 319
  Sophia Kerr, 253
  William, 109
Leith, Hugh, 488
  Pauline (Brown), 488
Le Jan, Ann, 310
  Francis, 310
Leland, Hopestill, 288
Lena, Fanta, 471, 477
Lennox, ———, 13
Leonard, Ada Geraldine (Charruaud), 17
  Elizabeth, 509
  Horatio, 17
  Lucy, 159
  Mary, 509
  Tabitha, 510
Lerch, Augustus, 356
  Florence Louise, 356
  Florence Louise (Carter), 356
  Frank Thomas, 356
  Harry Miltenberger, 356
  Martha (Watkins), 356
  Martha Watkins, 356
  Mary Jane (Marine), 356

INDEX

Le Roy, Marthe, 503
  Pauline, 201
  Pauline W. (Bridge), 201
  Stuyvesant, 201
Leverett, John, 329
Levey, Alice E. (Tiffany)
  Cartwright, 463
  William, 463
Lewis ancestral Charts, between pp. 345 and 346
Lewis, *Arms*, 268, 342
  ——, 306
  —— (Brock), 267
  —— (Woodfolk), 267
  Ann, 267
  Augusta Bransford, 342
  Augustin, 267
  Augustus Bransford, Lewis Chart No. 1
  Betty, 267
  Betty (Washington), 268, 393
  Bransford, 344, 348
  Carroll Grayson, 344
  David, 440
  Edith, 463
  Edmund, 342
  Edward, 280, 343
  Edward A., 347, 348
  Edward A., Lewis Chart No. 1
  Edward Augustus, 343
  Edward McElhiney, 342
  Edward McElhiney, Lewis Chart No. 1
  Edward S., 347, 348
  Edward S., Lewis Chart No. 1
  Edward Simmons, 342, 343, 344, 345
  Effe (Davenport), 343
  Elijah, 440
  Elizabeth, 282
  Elizabeth (Godfrey), 343
  Elizabeth (Morris), 359
  Elizabeth (Whiton), 440
  Ellen Hackley (Pollard), 393
  Eugene Grayson, 344
  Eugene W., 348
  Eugene Washington, 344
  Eva (Hughart), 344
  Fielding, 267, 393
  Florence E., 348
  Florence Elizabeth, 344

Lewis—*Continued*
  Florence Parthenia, 344
  Frances Fielding, 392
  Francis D., 357
  George Chase, 344
  Grayson, 344
  Hannah, 440
  Hannah (Baker), 343
  Hannah (Lincoln), 438
  Helen (Carrick), 342
  Helen (Carrick), Lewis Chart No. 1
  Howell, 393
  James, 342
  Jane (Merriwether), 267
  Jennie (Jaynes), 344
  John, 267, 342, 343, 438
  John Zachary, 267
  Julia Peabody, 357
  Lucy (Cushing), 440
  Mamie (Carroll), 344
  Martha Elizabeth (Hoskins), 218
  Mary (——), 342
  Mary (Chandler), 357
  Mary (Gifford), 343
  Mary Long (Gordon), 218
  Merriwether, 268
  Mildred, 267
  Mildred (Lewis), 267
  Monimia (Chase), 344
  Nathanial, 343
  Nell Battle, 218
  Olive, 344
  P. Grayson, 348
  Parthenia (Bransford), 343, 347, 348
  Parthenia (Bransford), Lewis Chart No. 1
  Pattie (Cooke), 342
  Pattie (Cooke), Lewis Chart No. 1
  Pattie Marian, 342
  Pattie Marian, Lewis Chart No. 1
  Rachel, 438
  Richard Henry, 218
  Robert, 267, 268
  Sallie Fisher, 270
  Samuel, 343, 359
  Sarah, 438
  Susan J. (Washington), Lewis Chart No. 1

Lewis—*Continued*
  Susan Jean (Washington), 343, 345, 347, 348
  Susannah (Jones), 343
  Thomas, 342, 343
  Walter F., 348
  Walter Felix, 344
  Watson Cooke, 342
  Watson Cooke, Lewis Chart No. 1
Lidgett, Elizabeth, 326
Light, Elizabeth, 506
  Robert, 506
Lilly, Elizabeth, 130
Lincoln, Hannah, 438
  Jerusha, 510
  Lucinda, 510
  Ruth, 439
  Samuel, 439
  Sarah, 438
Lindell, T., 330
Lindsay, Elizabeth, 217
  Hannah (Tidwell), 217
  Reuben, 217
Lindsey, Joseph W., 489
  Maria Innes (Watson), 489
Linthicum, Catherine (Warfield), 49
  Lancelot, 49
  Lucretia (Higgins), 257
  Theodore, 257
Little, Ann (Warren), 32, 320
  Ephraim, 32
  Mary (Sturdevant), 32
  Patience, 320
  Ruth, 32
  Thomas, 32, 320
  Anne (Southey), 70, 389
  Edward, 389
  Elizabeth (Bowman), 70
  Esther, 70, 389
  Nathaniel, 70, 389
  Southey, 70
  Susanna (Water), 70
Livermore, Tabitha, 82
Livingston, Robert, 8
Lloyd, David, 303
  Edward, 56, 236
  Eleanor Burroughs (Morris), 364
  Elizabeth, 236
  James, 330

Lloyd—*Continued*
  Martha G., 222
  Stacy Barcroft, 364
Locke, Frances Sargent, 405
Lockwood, Caroline (Lee), 339
  Joshua, 338, 339
  Mary (Lee), 338
Logan, Agatha Madison (Marshall), 139
  Annie Priscilla, 139
  Caleb Wallace, 139
  Elizabeth (Green), 160
  Mary Josephine, 160
  Minna, 137
  William, 139
  William H., 160
Lohse, Emma Serena (Charruaud), 17
  John F., 17
Long, ———, 436
  Ann (French), 203
  Anna, 274
  Isabella, 272
  Katherine (Cushing), 436
  Launa Viola, 400
  Richard, 203
Loney, Elizabeth K. (———), 241
  Francis Barton, 241
  Mary Esther, 241
Longstreth, Elizabeth, 363
Loomis, Jane M., 458
Lord, Ichabod, 126
  Elaphas, 126
  Lucy (Bulkeley), 126
  Patience (Bulkeley), 126
Loring, Hannah, 438
  Hannah (Jacob), 438
  Thomas, 438
Lothrop, Abigail (Avery), 33
  Deborah, 33
  Deborah (Crow), 33
  Elisha, 33
  Samuel, 33
Lottier, Agnes Bell (Cabell), 147
  John D., 147
Louvaine, Hawyse, 348
  Matthew, 348
Love, Anne (Jones), 484
  Elizabeth Courts, 484
  John, 486
  Rebecca, 21
  Samuel, 484, 486

Lovejoy, Dorothy (Ballard), 64
  Henry, 420
  Jeremiah, 64
  Melinda (Wheeler), 420
  Persis Abbot, 420
Lovelace, ——— (Eyneham), 306
  ——— (Lewis), 306
  Anne, 306
  Anne (Barnes), 306
  Elizabeth (Aucher), 306
  Launcelot, 306
  Lova (Peckham), 306
  Richard, 306
  William, 306
Lovell, Robert, 188
  Ursula, 188
Loving, Anna Bella (Cassel), 174
  Anne Courtenay, 173
  Dorothy, 174
  Ellen Quigley, 173
  Emma, 174
  Hector, 174
  Hector V., 132, 177
  Hector Voltaire, 173
  Helen, 174
  Julia, 173, 497
  Julia Christian (Courtenay), 132, 173
  Julia (Courtenay), 177
  Katherine (McKenna) Brown, 174
  Laura, 174
  Mildred, 174
  Robert Courtenay, 174
  Virginia, 174
  William Voltaire, 174
Low, Bessie, 183
  Elizabeth (Holden), 28
  Phebe Ann, 28
  Samuel, 28
Lowell, Debach, 158
Lowen, Francis, 161
  Sarah, 161
Lowndes, Charles Tidyman, 311
  Christopher, 94
  Elizabeth (Tasker), 94
  Harriet, 94
  Sabina Elliott (Huger), 311
Lowry, ———, 134
  Annie Anderson, 376

Lowry—*Continued*
  David, 303
  Edward, 303
  Ellis, 303
  Helen (Bullitt), 134
  Robert, 303
Lucas, Clarra (Kennedy), 280
  Robert, 280
Luce, ———, 507
  Allen, 110
  Sarah Anne (Brent), 110
Ludlow, Mary, 103
Lund, Christopher, 344
  Elizabeth, 344
Lusher, Eleazor, 211
  Lydia, 211
Luttleton, Emma Frankley, 70
  Thomas, 70
Lyde, Deborah, 327
Lyles, ———, 258
  Catherine (Hall), 258
Lyman, Charles H., 511
  Clarissa Maria (Wilbur) Dean, 511
Lynch, Eleanor (Dorsey) Todd, 308
  William, 308
Lyne, *Arms*, 495
  Ann, 486
  Lucy Foster (Lyne), 486
  William, 486
Lynn, Gertrude, 133
Lyon, ———, 455
  Mary (Thomas), 455
  Mehetabel, 284
  Peter, 284
  Sarah (Ruggles), 431
  William, 431
Lyster, Henry F., 114
  Winifred Lee (Brent), 114
Lyttleton, Thomas, 70

M

Mable, Anne, 320
  Thomas, 320
Macaulay, Caroline Brown (Champlin), 155
  John Lansing, 155
McBurney, Almira, 329
McCalla, John, 273
  Mary, 272, 273
  Mary Matilda Stansell (Stewart), 299

INDEX

McCalla—*Continued*
  Rebecca (Darrah) Bryan, 273
  Walter Endox, 299
  William, 273
McCann, Daniel, 246
  Mary (Hall) Freeman, 246
McClellan, Catherine Jane, 443
McClenachan, Naomi, 363
MacCloskey, Josephine, 332
McClure, Amabel (Lee), 340
  Colbert Anderson, 340
McCormick, Anne, 243
McCowan, Margaret, 498
McCoy, Cora L., 399
  Hannah, 296
Maccubin, Rebeckah, 54
McCulloh, Ann Eliza, 445
McDermott, Edward J., 487
  Susan Rogers (Barr), 487
  Susannah Mary, 209
McDonald ———, 279
  John, 299
  Maude (Arnold), 253
  Sarah (Hollingsworth), 299
  Sarah Ryland (Hall), 253
  William Alexander, 253
  William Bartholow, 253
McDougall, Janet Clark (Davidson), 497
  William, 497
McDowell, Elise Rogers (Barr) 487
  John, 21
  Pamelia, 297
  William Wallace, 487
  Winifrede, 21
McDuffie, Angus, 17
  Sarah (Bryant), 17
McEwan, Eliza (Watson), 488
  Sallie Rodes, 488
  William, 488
McFarland, Betsey E., 510
McFerran, John B., 487
  Josephine Preston (Barr), 487
  Margaret, 487
Macgill, Elizabeth, 393
McGill, Helen, 120
  Helen (Leavenworth), 120
  John, 120
McGinness, Clara Matteson, 183

McGlaughlin, James, 271
  Mary (Hart), 271
MacGregor, Alexander, 497
  Janet Clark (Scott), 497
Mack, Henrietta, 508
McKenna, Katherine, 174
McKenney, Ann Hanson, 50, 53
Mackenzie *Arms*, 482
  Agnes (Campbell), 347
  Alex, 347
  Alexander Kenneth, 114
  Alexander William, 114
  Ann, 441
  Catherine, 347
  Colin, 441
  Jessie (Clark) Strater, 482
  Kenneth, 347
  Margaret Louise, 114
  R. Poyntz, 114
  Sarah (Pinkerton), 441
  Winifred Eleanor (Brent), 114
McKewen, Katharine, 291
  Martha Virginia (Stoddard), 291
  William, 291
McKim, Margaret (Emerson), 202
McKinstry, Clara, 89
McKnight, Reno, 398
Mackworth, Arthur, 329
MacLaren, Alice Austen, 445
  Donald, 445
  Elizabeth Stockton (Green), 445
McLaughlin, Laughlin, 279
  Rebecca (Clark), 279
  Robert, 279
  Tabitha, 279
McLellan, Abigail, 447
  Abigail (Browne), 447
  Hugh, 447
McNair, Annette de la Nauze (Williamson), 505
  Dorothy Mildred Trelawney, 505
  George Henderson Stanser, 505
  George Stanser, 505
  Hugh Noel de La Nauze, 505
  James Edward Parry Aust, 505

McNeale ———, 172
  Charlotte Mary (Courtenay) 172
McNutt, Mary Morton, 388
Macomber ———, 403
Maddox ———, 67
  Mary (Bell), 67
Magar, Grace (Moulthrop), 413
  William, 413
Magruder, James, 92
  Jane Beall, 251
  Mary (Bowie), 92
  Rebecca, 242
Mahew, Joseph, 471
Mahood, Frank, 247
  Julia White (Canter), 247
Maine, Dorcas, 323
Mainwaring, Mary, 178
  Roger, 178
Major, Lavina, 351
  Mary, 170
  Thomas, 352
Makeman, Agnes (———) Van Snyder, 358
Malet, Hugh, 103
  Joan, 103
  Margaret, 103
Malin, Hannah, 293
  Mary (Hollingsworth) Conoway, 293
  Rachel, 293
  Randall, 293
Mallett, David, 339
  Edward Jones, 339
  John, 339
  Peter, 339
  Sarah (Fenner), 339
  Sarah Fenner, 339
Mallott, Olive, 409
Malone, Sarah, 19
  Stephen, 19
Maltby, Anson, 100
  Elizabeth Marshall, 100
  Frances, 100
  Lees, 100
  Marion, 100
  Mary Breckinridge, 100
  Mary Desha (Breckinridge), 100
Manchester, Margaret (Wood), 513
  Thomas, 513

INDEX

Mandell, Caleb, 513
  Hannah (Wood), 513
Manigault, Arthur Middleton, 312
  Joseph, 311
  Mary (Huger), 312
  Mary Middleton (Huger), 311
Manley, Matilda Lawrence (Keyser), 110
  William Maurice, 110
Manly, Keyser, 110
Mann, Mary (Cushing), 439
  Joshua, 439
Manners, Elizabeth, 107
  Henry, 107
Manning, Louise, 344
Mansfield, Bethiah, 158
  Hannah, 158
  Margaret, 24
  Samuel, 24
Manton, Daniel, 469
  Dorcas, 468, 469
  Edward, 468
  John, 469
  Mary (Brown), 469
  Thomas, 468
Marden, Sarah (Seavey), 286
Mariel, Magdelon (———), 503
Marine, *Arms*, 349, 356
  Alexander, 351, 352
  Amelia Eleanor, 350
  Anna, 353
  Anna Barbara (Rupp), 355
  Anna (Robinson), 352
  Annie Eugenia, 355
  Charles, 352, 353
  David, 352
  Eliza (Robinson), 353
  Elizabeth (Charlescraft), 353
  Elizabeth Hester, 355
  Emma Hargis, 355
  Esther, 352, 353
  Fletcher, 353
  Fletcher Columbus, 356
  Fletcher Elliott, 354, 355
  Frances Elizabeth, 351
  Harriet Perkins, 350
  Harriett Perkins (Hall), 252, 349
  Hayward, 353
  Hester Ann, 355

Marine—*Continued*
  Hester Eleaner (Knowles), 355
  Ida Irene (Lawrence), 349
  James, 352, 353
  James Hargis, 355
  Janet, 352
  John, 352, 353
  John Fletcher, 355
  Jonathan, 352
  Kezia (———), 352
  Lavina (Major), 351
  Levisa, 353
  Louisa Emmalla, 355
  Lovey, 352
  Madison, 349
  Major, 352
  Margaret Ann (Levisa), 354
  Marie St. Claire (Howell), 350
  Martha Ann, 354
  Martha Jeffries, 350
  Mary, 353
  Mary (———), 352
  Mary (Fletcher), 353
  Mary (Hayward), 353
  Mary Jane, 356
  Mary Susannah, 351
  Matthew, 352, 353
  Matthew Harrison, 351
  Matthew Washington, 354
  Milleson, 351, 352
  Minnie Elizabeth, 355
  Molly (———), 353
  Nancy Elizabeth, 354
  Nancy Mezwick, 354
  Nancy (Rawlings), 354
  Polly (Elliott), 353
  Polly Mezwick, 354
  Rachel (Vaughan), 353
  Rhoda, 353
  Richard Elliott, 350
  Rachel (Victor), 352
  Sarah, 353
  Sarah Jane, 355
  Thomas, 352
  Thomas Price, 355
  Vashtie, 354
  Vashti (Charlescraft), 353
  William, 352, 353
  William John, 354
  William Matthew, 252, 349, 355

Marine—*Continued*
  Zorobabel, 352, 353
  Maris, Elizabeth, 161
  Markham, Elam, 208
    Rosina (Fuller), 208
Marriott, Emily Grace, 442
  Emily Palmer (Helm), 278
  Martin Hardin, 278
  Sophia Keyser (Boyd), 442
  William Haddon, 442
Marrs, Jessie La Nauze (Clark), 499
  Paul Rankin, 499
  William Rankin, 499
Marsh, Elizabeth, 320
Marshall, *Arms*, 141
  Agatha Madison, 139
  Elizabeth, 153
  Mary Graham, 46
  Sarah Ann (King), 46
  Thomas, 129
  Wm. T., 46
Marsham, Anne (Calvert) Brooke Brent, 106, 112
  Katherine (Brent), 112
  Richard, 106, 112
Marsiglia, Catherine Romano, 18
  Eliza H. (Ballantine) Charruaud, 17
  Gerlando, 17
  Gerlando Antonio, 18
Martin, Ann, 78
  Anne (Moorman), 282
  Bridget (Cabell), 143
  Catharine (Blanton), 282
  Charlotte, 262
  Charlotte (Haskell) Dumphy, 367
  Elizabeth (Fuller), 211
  Elizabeth (Lewis), 282
  George, 76
  Helen Scott (Bullitt) Massie, 135
  Jacob, 339
  Jane, 252
  Jane Elizabeth, 339
  John, 78, 282
  John Lewis, 135, 282
  Joshua, 367
  Mildred, 241
  Nancy Oliver, 282
Mason, Alice (———), 75

INDEX

Martin, Olive (Woodward) Smith, 76
  Rebecca (Murray), 339
  Richard, 211
  Thomas, 143, 282
Mason, Abigail, 192
  Albert Gardner, 214
  Anne, 477, 478
  Anne (Sewell), 76
  Caroline Humphrey (Gay), 214
  Elizabeth, 76
  Ellen (Washington), 506
  Francis, 75, 192
  George, 107
  George, Lewis Chart No. 1
  James, 506
  Lemuel, 76, 192
  Mary, Lewis Chart No. 1
  Mary, 348
  Mary (Fowke), Lewis Chart No. 1
  Sarah (Brent), 107
Massie, Helen Scott (Bullitt), 134
  Henry, 134
  Marie, 269
  Sarah (Upshaw), 269
  William, 269
Masterson, Richard, 512
  Sarah, 512
Maston, John, 6
Maulden, Ann, 293
Mather, *Arms*, 36, 40
  Amiel, 38
  Anna, 39
  Anna (Lake) Cotton, 38
  Atherton, 38
  Betsey N., 40
  Caroline M., 40
  Catherine, 39
  Catherine (Atherton), 38
  Catherine (Holt), 38
  Catherine L., 40
  Charles, 39, 40
  Clara C., 40
  Clarissac, 39
  Cotton, 39
  Cotton Smith, 39
  Eleazer, 38
  Eliakim, 39
  Elihu, 39
  Elisabeth, 39

Mather—*Continued*
  Elizabeth (Weeks), 38
  Hannah (Treat), 38
  Helen L., 40
  Henry William, 40
  Horace, 39
  Increase, 38
  Jerusha, 39
  John, 37, 39
  Joseph, 38
  Joshua, 39
  Lois, 39
  Lois (Burbank), 39
  Louise M., 40
  Lucinda, 39
  Marie (Cotton), 38
  Mary, 39
  Mary (Hard), 40
  Mary J., 40
  Mary (Lamb), 39
  Mary (Russell), 40
  Nathaniel, 38
  Philo, 39
  Rebecca (Stoughton), 39
  Richard, 37, 38, 39
  Sally, 40
  Samuel, 38
  Sarah, 39
  Sarah (Handbridge) Story Cotton, 38
  Solon Henry, 40
  Thersey, 39
  Thomas, 37, 39
  Timothy, 38
  William, 39, 40
  Zachariah, 39
  Zilpha, 40
Mathers, Samuel, 271
  Jane (Hart), 271
Mathews, R. Stockett, 233
  Sophia (Hall), 233
Mathewson, Rosa, 163
Mathis, Aminee C., 248
Matthews, Barbara (Brent), 103
  Clarence, 401
  Elinor, 215
  Eva May (Rhoades), 410
  George, 103
Maugridge, Sarah, 168
Maulden, Ann, 363
Maupin, Augusta, 43

Maxon, Joseph, 153
  Mary, 152
  Tacy (Burdick), 152
Maxwell, Elizabeth (Cooch), 161
  Ellen Peirce (Doneghy), 189
  J. C., 189
  Robert, 503
  Solomon, 161
May, Eliza Fitzhugh, 145
Maybin, John, 273
  Matilda, 273
Mayhew, Ann, 479
  Elizabeth (———), 479
  Joseph, 479
Maynard, Louise, 450
Mayo, Anne, 145
Mead, Mercy, 508
Means, Elizabeth, 271, 272
  James Howard, 329
  Jean, 271
  John, 271
  Margaret, 271
  Marian (Jeffries), 329
  Mary (———), 271
  William, 271
Mease, Isabel (Hoops), 483
  James, 483
Medairy, George, 44
  Henrietta Handy (Ball), 44
Medill, Jane, 171
Meeks, Elizabeth, 244
  Susannah (———), 244
  Wesley, 244
Melville, Elizabeth, 205
  Eunice Thruston, 153
Meredith, Margaret, 144
Meriwether, Mildred (Thornton), 483
  Nicholas, 483
Merriweather, Jane, 267
  Nicholas, 267
Merry, Joane (Rhoades), 396
  Ralph, 396
Merryman, Charles, 349
Meserole, Frost, 318
  Martha, 318
Metcalf, Elizabeth Vincent (Huntington), 313
  Hannah, 315
  John B., 313
  Leonard, 288
  Lucy, 316

INDEX

Metcalf—*Continued*
  Mehitable, 316
  Michael, 288
Meteren, Joost Jans (John), 470
Mewburn ——— (Hammond), 258
  Phillip, 258
  Susan, 258
Meyer, John, 77
Meyler, Josephine (Swearingen), 223
  R. J., 223
Mezwick, Leah (———), 354
  Luke, 354
  Mary, 354
  Molly, 354
Michael, Elizabeth (Thoroughgood), 72, 77, 391
  John, 72, 77, 391
  Sarah, 69, 72, 387, 391
Mickle, Hannah, 360
Middleton, Arthur, 311
  Isabella Johannes, 311
Midyette, Caroline, 247
Millard, Arthur, 134
  Fannie (Gordon), 134
Miller, Abraham, 20, 21
  Blanche F., 388
  Burton Rockwood, 420
  Catherine, 20, 479
  Elizabeth, 20
  Fanny Larcom (Rockwood), 420
  Florence Hall, 420
  Hannah (Birney), 21
  Helen, 383
  Jacob, 21
  James Cook, 420
  John, 21, 479
  Joseph, 20
  Louisa Abraham, 20, 21
  Louisa (Owen), 20, 21
  Salome, 20
  Tamar, 162
  Winifrede (McDowell), 21
Milleson ———, 351
Mills, Elizabeth, 267
  Frances (Pembroke), 371
  James, 454
  Jemima, 79, 82, 84, 371
  Samuel, 371
  Sarah, 25
  Susanna (Thomas), 454

Milnor, Eleanor De Vere, 41
  Eleanor De Vere (Ball), 41
  Howard Stabler, 41
  William Ball, 41
Minks, Elizabeth H. (———), 458
  Idella Gibson, 458
  William L., 458
Minor, Margaret Randolph, 140
Minter, Jeannetta Wilkins, 43
Mitchell, Anna Maria Parnham (Brent), 109
  Caroline, 364
  Caroline (Horsey), 109
  Joseph Thomas, 109
  Katherine (Kent), 109
  Louise, 109
  Robert Brent, 109
  Samuel Augustus, 364
Mohun, Anna, 249
  Clare (Dorsey), 53
  R. B., 53
Molyneux, Hanna, 12
  Hannah (Lawrence), 13
  Joseph, 13
  Mary, 13
  Moses, 13
Monroe, Andrew, 347
  Davidson Hall, 259
  Elinor (Spence), 347
  Frank Asbury, 259
  James, 347
  Margaret Davidson (Hall), 259
  Mary Eliza, 87
  Permelia Victoria, 259
  Spence, 347
  Susannah, 347
  Susanna, Lewis Chart No. 1
Monson, Emma, 419
Monteagle ———, 4
Montgomery, Janet (Muir), 495
  Matthew, 495
Monveille, Gabriel, 8
  Susanna (Lawrence), 8
Moody, Mary, 427
  Samuel, 427
Moore ———, 487
  Elizabeth Hester (Marine), 355
  Elizabeth (Watson), 487

Moore—*Continued*
  Frances, 167
  John, 353
  Mary (Marine), 353
  Robert M., 355
Moran, Mevoral, 454
  Nancy (Thomas), 454
More, Bridget (Cushing), 436
  George, 436
Morgan, Lydia Smith, 127
Morley, Ann, 348
Moorman, Anne, 282
Morrill, David C., 86
  Elizabeth Roberts, 86
  Isaac, 373
Morris, *Arms*, 365
  Adonijah, 411
  Agnes (———) Van Snyder Makeman Barr, 358
  Ann (Cheston), 363
  Ann (Pancoast), 362
  Ann (Willing), 361
  Anna (———), 411
  Annie Morris (Buckley), 364
  Anthony, 357, 358, 359, 360, 361, 362
  Benjamin, 360
  Benjamin Wistar, 362
  Caroline Mitchell, 364
  Caroline (Old), 363
  Caspar, 363
  Caspar Wistar, 362
  Catherine Wistar, 362
  Cornelia, 364
  Daniel Corrie, 364
  Deborah, 360, 361
  Effingham Buckley, 357, 364
  Eleanor Burroughs, 364
  Eleazer, 411
  Elizabeth, 359, 360
  Elizabeth (Giles), 362
  Elizabeth (Hudson), 361
  Elizabeth (Kearney), 360
  Elizabeth (Longstreth), 363
  Elizabeth Morris (Buckley), 362
  Elizabeth (Senior), 358
  Elizabeth (Watson), 358
  Ellen Douglas (Burroughs), 364
  Galloway Cheston, 364
  George, 360
  Hannah, 359, 363

INDEX

Morris—*Continued*
  Hannah A., 364
  Hannah Ann (Tyson), 363
  Hannah (Cadwalader), 360
  Hannah (Mickle), 360
  Hannah (Perot), 364
  Henry, 363
  Isaac, 359, 361
  Isaac Wistar, 362
  Israel, 359, 361, 363
  Israel Wistar, 362, 364
  James, 359, 360
  James Cheston, 363
  Jane, 363
  John, 359, 360
  Joseph, 359, 360
  Josephine Cushing, 442
  Julia Peabody (Lewis), 357
  Levi, 363
  Lewis, 7
  Luke, 359, 361
  Luke Wistar, 362
  Margaret (Cook), 359
  Martha (Fitzwater), 360
  Mary, 358, 360
  Mary (———) Coddington, 358
  Mary Ann C. (Cope), 363
  Mary Ella (Johnson) Stewart, 363
  Mary (Harris), 363
  Mary (Harrison), 361
  Mary (Hollingsworth), 363
  Mary Hollingsworth, 364
  Mary (Jones), 358
  Mary (Richards), 359
  Mary (Saunders), 361
  Mary (Sutton), 360
  Mary (Wells), 362
  Mary Smith (Pemberton), 362
  Nancy, 217
  Naomi (McClenachan), 363
  P. Pemberton, 364
  Phoebe, 360
  Phoebe (Guest), 359
  Rachel (Johnson), 363
  Rebecca (Cadwalader), 359
  Rebecca (Wistar), 362
  Rhoda Fuller, 364
  Richard, 7
  Samuel, 359, 360, 361, 362, 363

Morris—*Continued*
  Sarah, 359, 361, 362
  Sarah (Dury), 359
  Sarah (Moulthrop), 411
  Sarah (Paschall), 362
  Sarah Pinkerton (Cushing), 442
  Sarah (Powell), 361
  Sarah (Warder), 361
  Stephen P., 363
  Susanna, 358, 360
  Thomas, 361
  Thomas John, 442
  William, 359, 360
  William Hudson, 361
  Wistar, 363, 364
Morrison, Emily, 418
  Henry Ruffner, 95
  Mary Carson (Breckinridge), 95
Morse, Calvin, 508
  Charles Lewis, 35
  Clara Frances, 322
  Elizabeth (Penniman), 380
  Freeman H., 322
  Howard Leavitt, 322
  Joshua, 380
  Marian Lavina (Keep), 35
  Mercy Jane, 508
  Mercy (Mead), 508
  Nancy (Leavitt), 322
Mortimer, Elizabeth, 348
Morton, Elizabeth Hite (Smith), 475
  Hannah, 206
  Mercy, 416
  William, 475
Moseley, Anthony, 78
  Edward, 300
  Jane (Hollingsworth), 300
  Lucy H., 300
  Margaret Lawson, 78
  Mary, 464
  Mary (Gookin), 77, 78
  William, 77
Moss ———, 188
  Amelia, 189
  Elizabeth, 489
  Lucinda, 189
  Lucy (Templeman), 188
Mote ———, 296
  Susanna (Hollingsworth), 296

Mott, Dorothy, 451
  Dorothy (Smith), 451
  Margaret, 462
  Mark, 451
Motte, Charlotte, 310
Moulthrop, Abigail, 410, 411
  Abigail (Bradley), 410
  Adonijah, 411
  Agnes, 412
  Agnes (Newby), 412
  Alexander, 413
  Betsey (Wheeler), 411
  Christopher (Slee), 412
  Daniel, 411
  Delia (———), 412
  Elihu, 411
  Elizabeth, 410, 413
  Elizabeth (Betsey), 412
  Ellen, 413
  Esther, 412
  Gideon, 413
  Grace, 413
  Hannah, 410, 411
  Hannah (Belcher), 411
  Hannah Catherine (Wood), 413
  Hannah J. (Barlow), 413
  Hannah (Thompson), 410
  Isabella, 413
  Isabella Eliza (Newby), 413
  Israel, 411
  Jane, 412
  Jane (———), 410
  John, 410, 411, 413
  Joseph, 411
  Jude, 411, 412
  Keziah, 410
  Laura, 412
  Lucretia, 411
  Lucretia (Bradley), 411
  Lydia, 410
  Lydia (Page), 411
  Margaret Ellen (Stewart), 413
  Mary, 410, 411
  Mary Agnes, 394, 413, 414
  Mary (Whedon), 411
  Matthew, 410
  Nathan, 412
  Phoebe (Wood), 412
  Rhoda, 411
  Robert, 412, 413
  Samuel, 410

INDEX

Moulthrop—*Continued*
　Sarah, 411
　Sarah (Barnes), 410
　Sarah Jane, 413
　Sarah (Tuttle), 411
　Thomas Taylor, 413
　Timothy, 411
　Trueman, 412, 413
　William H., 413
Moylan, Isabel (Hoops)
　　Mease, 483
　Jasper, 483
　John, 483
　Mary Ricketts (Van Horne), 483
　Stephen, 483
Mudd, Jane, 107
Muir, Janet, 495
Mulliken, Anne, 245
　Anne D., 258
　Anne (Hall), 245
　Basil Duckett, 258
　Belt, 256
　Benjamin Hall, 256
　Charity (Belt), 256
　James, 91, 256
　Martha, 240, 256
　Mary, 91
　Sophia, 256
　Sophia (Hall), 242, 256
Mumford, Cornelius, 17
　Jonathan, 17
　Nancy (Bryant), 17
　Sarah, 23
Munford, Ann Mary (Rickard), 415
　Clarence, 415
　Evelyn, 415
　Walter, 415
Munro, Andrew, 347
　Catherine (Mackenzie), 347
　Catherine (Ross), 347
　Hector, 347
　Margaret (Dunbar), 347
　Robert, 347
Murdock, Abbie, 485
　Eleanor, 242
Murphy, (———), 99
　Catherine Sarah, 172
　Mary Ann, 80, 82, 84
Murray, A. Gordon, 134
　Anna, 134
　Archibald Gordon, 134

Murray—*Continued*
　Grace (Stanton), 134
　Harriet (Gordon), 134
　Henry M., 364
　Illa, 134
　Logan Crittenden, 134
　Mary Hollingsworth (Morris), 364
　Rebecca, 339
　Rosa, 134
Musam, Rebecca Vaughn, 222
Musgrave, John, 292
Muzer, Martha, 437

N

Nashee, Margaret, 114
Neal, Eliza, 447
　Elizabeth Downs, 213
　Emma, 369
　Hannah (Pray), 509
　Henry, 509
　James, 447
　Joanna, 509
　John, 67
　Mary, 67, 71
Neale, Abigail (Penniman), 380
　Elizabeth, 108
　Henry, 380
　Mary (Brent), 107
　Raphael, 107
　Roswell, 107
　Samuel, 380
　Susannah (Brent), 107
Neill, Lewis, 296
　Lydia (Hollingsworth), 296
Nelson, Benjamin, 57
　Burgess, 55, 57
　Elizabeth, 57
　Elizabeth Tebbs, 275
　George B., 275
　Hally Morrison, 388
　Henry, 57
　Kate (Tebbs), 275
　Rachel, 37
　Robert, 330
　Sarah, 55, 57
　Sarah (Howard), 55, 57
　William Pierrepont, 388
Nevill, George, 348
　Henry, 348
　Matilda, 348
Neville, Emily, 208

Neville—*Continued*
　Henry, 115
　Jane (Bourchier), 115
　Mary, 329
Nevins, Josephine (MacCloskey), 332
　Louisa Macalester, 332
　Richard, 332
Newbold, Margaret M., 270
　Rhoda Fuller (Morris) Brooke, 364
　Trenchard Emlen, 364
Newby, Agnes, 412
　Isabella (Atkinson), 412
　Isabella Eliza, 413
　Robert, 412
Newce, Mary, 348
　Mary, Lewis Chart No. 1
　William, Lewis Chart No. 1
Newell, Rebecca, 286
Newman, Florence A. L. (Tiffany Wickman, 463
　Levy, 409
　Mary Elizabeth (Osgood), 409
　Patience, 31
　Sarah, 396
　Sidney, 463
Newsome, Hellen, 106
Nichols, Elizabeth, 373, 376
　Nathaniel, 438
　Sarah, 438
　Sarah (Lincoln), 438
　Thomas, 322, 373
Nicholson, Alida, 512
　Marietta, 22
　Sarah, 75
Nicklin, Elizabeth (Calvert), 106
　Joseph, 106
Nickolson, Elizabeth Bruce (Ball), 43
　Elizabeth Ross, 43
　Marie Ball, 43
　Roberta Bruce, 43
　Ross, 43
　Thomas Ross, 43
Nicol, Agnes, 504
　Christian (Erskine), 504
　Robert, 504
Nicols, George Baynard, 260
　Lucy Orrick, 260
Nichols, Rosannah, 297

INDEX

Nimlet, Alexander, 205
  David, 205
  David Campbell, 205
  Elizabeth (Melville), 205
  Jean (Campbell), 205
  Marion Graham, 205
  Mary Ann (Whitaker), 205
  Virginia Campbell, 205
Nimmo, Annie Boyd (Ball), 41
  Ruth Natali, 41
  Waldern Carey, 41
Noble, Elizabeth (Ruggles), 432
  James, 432
  William, 6
Norcross, Nathaniel, 79, 81
  Richard, 81
  Susanna, 79, 81, 84
  Susanna (————), 79, 81
Norreys ————, 13
Norris, Elizabeth Waters (Cushing), 442
  Henry Latimer, 442
North, Emma Purner (Rawlings), 354
  Frances (Todd), 307
  Marie Rawlings, 354
  Robert, 307
  Samuel Maith, 354
Norton, Susan, 501
Norwood, John, 47
Nottley, Anne, 105
Noyes, Barbara (Wells), 154
  Barker, 154
  Elizabeth, 79, 80, 81, 82, 83, 84, 373
  James, 155, 424
  Joseph, 154, 202
  Margaret (Champlin), 154
  Mary, 202
  Nicholas, 82
  Sarah, 424
  William, 82
Nuhn, William, 399
  Winifred May (Rhoades), 399
Nutthall, John, 194, 349
Nuttall, Mary Brent, 193
Nutting, Elizabeth, 79, 82, 84
Nutwell, John, 112
  Mary (Brent), 112
Nye, Diadama (Haskell), 367
  Jonathan, 367

O

Odell, Martha (Duckett), 235
  Rignal, 235
Oden, Sarah Biggs, 455
Offley, Ann (Osborne), 76
  Robert, 76
  Sarah, 76, 77
Ogden, Ann (Robinson), 294
  Jonathan, 294
  Sarah, 34
O'Hagan ————, 13
Old, Caroline, 363
Oldham, Alice, 417
  Eva Mary (Rhoades) Matthews, 401
  George W., 401
  Hannah, 373
  Isaac, 417
  Ollie D., 401
  Palmer D., 401
Oliver, Juliatha, 298
  Rhoda, 280
O'Neil, Grace, 69
Opdyke, Jane (Hart), 272
  Samuel, 272
O'Reilly, Anne, 504
  John, 504
  Margaret, 504
  Margaret (O'Reilly), 504
  Myles, 504
Osborne, Adria, 265
  Ann, 76
  Ann (Hewitt), 77
  Anne, 67
  Edward, 77
  Peter, 67
  Thomas, 265
Osbourne, J. Alfred, 233
  Julia (Hall), 233
Osgodby, Adam de, 404
Osgood *Arms*, 405, 406
  Aaron, 407
  Abel, 407
  Abijah, 408
  Alphonso George, 409
  Amasa, 408
  Anne, 408
  Asahel, 407
  Benjamin, 405
  Charles Joshua, 409
  Clapa, 404
  Clarinda J., 409

Osgood—*Continued*
  Cytha, 404
  David, 407, 408
  Dorothy, 407
  Dorothy (Woodman), 406, 409
  Elijah, 408
  Elizabeth, 406, 407
  Ephraim, 407
  Esther P. (Lawrence) Port, 15
  Eunice, 408
  Frances Sargent (Locke), 405
  Francis Wright, 408
  Greenville P., 15
  Hannah, 406, 408
  Henry Elijah, 409
  Hepsebeth, 408
  Hepsibeth (Dunton), 407
  Hooker, 398, 406, 407, 409
  Jeanne Nicola, 15
  John, 398, 404, 405, 406, 408
  Jonathan, 407
  Joseph, 406
  Joshua, 398, 407, 408
  Joshua W., 408
  Lemuel, 407
  Levi, 408
  Lucy Eunice, 398, 409
  Lucy (Russell), 408
  Manasseh, 407
  Mary, 406, 408
  Mary Elizabeth, 409
  Mary Elizabeth (Russell), 408
  Mary (Hooker), 406
  Mary J. (Pannel), 408
  Moses, 407
  Robertus, 404
  Ruth, 407
  Ruth (Divoll), 407
  Samson, 408
  Samuel, 405
  Sarah, 406, 407, 408
  Sarah (Booth), 404
  Solomon W., 408
  Stephen, 398, 406
  Thomas, 405, 408
  William, 398, 407, 408
  Zenas, 407
Otis, James, 213
  Joseph, 213
  Mary Allyne, 213

INDEX

Overton, Harriet, 140
  Laura, 110
  Mary (Waters), 265
  Temperance, 265
  William, 265
Owen, John, 21
  Louisa, 20, 21
  Rebecca (Love), 21
Owens, Sophia Downing, 376
Owings ———, 55
  Ann, 53
  Arianna (Dorsey), 49
  Eliza, 55
  Richard, 57
  Ruth (Dorsey), 55
  Ruth (Warfield), 57
  Samuel, 49
  Thomas, 49
  Urith (Randall) Owings, 58
Oxford, Jane, 256

P

Pabodie, Elizabeth (Alden), 404
Packard, Annie May (Pearson), 376
  David Charles, 376
  Lester Earle, 376
Paddock, George, 416
  Sarah (Rickard), 416
Padelford, Elizabeth, 27
Paganell, Gervase, 346
Page, Lydia, 411
Paine, Ellen, 380
  Mary (Penniman), 380
  Robert Treat, 426
  Samuel, 380
  Sarah E., 511
Palmer, Emily, 65
  Hannah (Johnson), 332
  Potter, 47
  Thomas, 332
Pancoast, Ann, 362
Pannel, Mary J., 408
Paradise, Sarah Crow, 132
Parcell, Nicholas, 6
Pardee, Henry, 317
  Phebe (Huntington), 317
Pargiter, Amy, 506
  Robert, 506
Parigo ———, 397
  Judith (Richmond) Rhoades, 397

Park, Benjamin, 34
  Hannah Ann, 34
Parke, Eunice (Champlin), 153
  Thomas, 153
Parker ———, 455
  Catherine (Thomas), 455
  Helena Beulah, 433
  James, 13
  Jonathan, 32
  Joseph, 406
  Lucy, 418
  Nathan, 406
  Ruth Anne Williams, 246
  Ruth (Avery), 32
  Samuel R., 240
  Sarah Beck (Williams), 246
Parkhill, Charles Copeland, 98
  Letitia Porter (Breckinridge), 98
Parkins, Rachel, 296
Parkman, Marion Harriot, 329
Parmenter, Elizabeth, 380
  Joseph, 380
  Leah (———), 380
  Robert, 380
Parnham, Anna Maria, 108
Parry, Agnes (Nicol), 504
  Christiana, 164, 500, 504
  George, 504
  Rebecca, 207
  Hannah (Haskins), 227
Partridge, Catherine L. (Mather), 40
  Frank, 40
Paschall, Hannah, 363
  Sarah, 362
Patterson, Eleanor, 453
  Eliza, 169
  Eliza (Benson), 169
  Louise Parkhill, 138
  Nicea, 208
  Robert, 453
  William, 169
Patteson, Martha Louise, 146
Patton, Elizabeth, 96
Paul, Elizabeth, 395
Paulet, Elizabeth, 167
  John, 167
Pauncefoot, Maude, 103
  Walter, 103
Pawlett, Anne (Brent), 103
  Thomas, 103

Paxton, Harriette Sophia Newton (Whytlaw), 504
  William B., 504
Payne, Alida, 366
  Corinne, 366
  Edward Waldron, 366, 369, 453, 456
  Elizabeth, 384
  Elizabeth Waldron, 369
  Francis Edward, 369
  Godey (———), 436
  Ida (Keys), 366, 453, 456
  Julia Etta, 369
  Maryette (Waldron), 369
  Minnie Ada, 369
  Nanette, 366, 453, 456
  Richard J., 369
  Simon, 436
  William Morris, 369
Payton, Margaret, 222
Peabody, Ephraim, 423
  Rhoda (Abbot), 423
Peach, John Gibson, 251
  Rebecca Anne, 251
Peak, Christian, 182
Peake, Christian, 22
  Thomas, 22
Pearsall, Amy, 14
Pearson, Arms, 370, 373, 375, 376
  Abigail (Gates), 373, 376
  Adeline Chamberlain (Crocker), 376
  Alice (Barron), 373, 376
  Alice Le Barron, 376
  Amos, 373, 376
  Anne Anderson (Lowry), 376
  Annie May, 376
  Arthur E., 370
  Arthur Emmons, 80, 82, 85, 370, 373
  Edward, 375
  Edward Asher, 376
  Edward Lowry, 376
  Elizabeth (Nichols), 373, 376
  Ethel Bennett (Conant), 375
  Hepsibah (Swayne), 372, 375, 376
  Hiram, 373, 376
  Jame, 376
  James, 372, 373, 375
  John, 372, 375

INDEX

Pearson—*Continued*
  Jonathan, 373, 376
  Leonard, 375
  Lucinda Maria (Greenleaf) 373, 376
  Margaret Conant, 375
  Maudlin (Madeline), 372, 375
  Maxwell John, 375, 376
  Nancy Delia (Benjamin), 80, 82, 84, 370, 373
  Nella Jane, 370, 373
  Seth Greenleaf, 373
  Sophia Downing (Owens), 376
  Tabitha (Kendall), 372, 375
  William, 373, 376
  William Henry, 80, 82, 84, 370, 371, 373
Peckham, Lova, 306
Pegram, Mary B., 217
Peirce, *Arms*, 186, 189
  Elizabeth, 187, 188
  Ellen, 188
  Jane, 187, 188
  Jane (———), 186
  John, 187
  John Lovell, 188
  Joseph, 187, 188
  Margaret, 187, 188
  Mary, 187, 188
  Mary (———), 187
  Mary Ann (Berkley), 188
  Molly, 188
  Sarah, 187, 188
  Sarah (———), 187
  Sarah (Allaway) Ariss, 188
  Sarah Elliott (Ransdall), 187
  Sibella (Thompson), 187
  Thomas, 187
  Ursula, 188
  Ursula (Lovell), 188
  William, 186, 187, 188
Pelham, Comfort, 26
  Content, 26
  Edward, 26
  Freelove (Arnold), 26
  Joseph, 26
Pell, Ann, 14
  Caleb, 14
  Ellen, 333
  Mary (Ferris), 14
Pelow, Margaret, 415

Pemberton, James, 330
  Mary Smith, 362
Pembroke, Frances, 371
Pendarvis, Elizabeth, 123
  Josiah, 123
  Mary (Bedon), 123
Pendleton, Ann (Champlin), 153
  Ann Lewis (Harris), 266
  John O., 266
  Joseph, 153
  Sarah, 153
  Sarah (Champlin), 153
  Sarah (Worden), 153
  Sylvester, 153
Penhallow, Samuel, 330
Penniman, *Arms*, 377, 382
  Abigail, 380
  Ann, 380
  Ann (Jenks), 381
  Anson Whipper, 381
  Chiron, 381
  Deborah (———) Taft, 380
  Elias, 381
  Elizabeth, 380
  Elizabeth (Parmenter), 380
  Ellen (Paine), 380
  Hannah, 380
  Hannah (Billings), 379
  Huldah, 381
  Huldah (White), 380
  James, 379, 380, 381
  James Hosmer, 377, 378, 382
  James Lanman, 377, 382
  John, 379
  John Ritto, 381
  Jonathan, 380
  Joseph, 379, 380
  Josiah, 380
  Josiah Harmar, 377, 382
  Lydia, 379
  Lydia (Eliot), 379, 380
  Maria Davis (Hosmer), 377, 382
  Maria Hosmer, 377
  Marian (Chandler), 382
  Marian Chandler (Lanman), 381
  Mary, 101, 380, 381
  Mary (Cross), 379
  Mary (Farnum), 380
  Nathan, 380, 381
  Obadiah, 381, 382

Penniman—*Continued*
  Olive (Whipple), 381
  Peter, 380
  Phineas, 381
  Polly, 381
  Samuel, 379, 380, 381
  Sarah (Bass) Stone, 379
  Sarah (Gore) Bubgee Albee, 380
  Sarai (Sarah), 380
  Silence, 381
  Sylvanus Jenks, 381
  Waiting (Robinson), 379
  William, 381
Pennyman, William, 379
Pentz, Bettie Trisler (Houck), 309
  Trisler Simmons, 309
  William Fletcher, 309
Pepper, *Arms*, 383, 385
  Abigail (———), 384
  Anna (Youngman), 384
  Annie (Grassie), 384
  Benjamin, 383
  Charles Hovey, 383, 384
  Elizabeth, 383
  Elizabeth Hoar, 383
  Elizabeth (Johnson), 383
  Elizabeth (Payne), 384
  Ellen (Hoar), 383
  Eunice Gordon, 383
  Eunice (Hutchinson), 384
  Frances E. (Coburn), 383
  George Dana Boardman, 384
  Isaac, 384
  Jacob, 384
  John, 383, 384
  Joseph, 383, 384
  Mary, 383
  Robert, 383
  Sarah, 383
  Sarah (Simonds), 384
  Sherman Hoar, 383
  Stephen, 384
  Stephen Coburn, 383
Percy, Eleanor, 13
  Elizabeth, 348
Perdriau, Margaret, 310
  Orei, 310
Periam, William, 330
Perine, Addie (Slack), 234
  Lewis, 234
  Rachel Hall Slack, 235

INDEX

Perkins, Clara Leonora (Huntington), 313
  Elizabeth, 87, 243
  Gilbert B., 313
  Harriet (Gorsuch), 251
  John, 251
  Julia, 65
  Susannah, 251, 349
  Susannah (Clarke), 243
  William, 243
Perot, Hannah, 364
Perrins, Joan, 464
Peshell, John, 104
  Margaret, 104
Peter, John, 143
  Susannah, 143
Peters, Richard, 20
Petersilea, Carlisle, 280
  Nannie (Kennedy), 280
Pettes, Anne, 461
  Elizabeth (Crocker), 461
  Joshua, 461
Pevey, Hannah Holt, 425
Peyton, Alice, 106
  Amy, 4
  Edward, 4
  John, 106
  Marianne, 106, 112
Phelps, Edward, 63
  Elizabeth, 63
  Elizabeth (Adams), 63
  James H., 206
  John W., 206
  Mary Drake, 290
  Nannie, 497
  Ruth, 64
Philbrick, Philbrick (French) White, 203
  Thomas, 203
Phillips, Abigail, 403
  Ann, 176
  Ann (Lewis), 267
  Launcelot, 267
  Lewis, 267
  May, 287
  William, 267
  Sarah, 509
Phinney, Henry Frederick, 459
Phipps, David, 198
  Mary English), 198
  Pownall, 25
  Sophia Matilda (Arnold), 25

Pickett, Elizabeth, Lewis Chart No. 1
  John, Lewis Chart No. 1
Pidgeon, William, 6
Pike, John Nicholas, 62
  Lucy (Bishop), 62
  Lucy Bishop, 62
Pincham, Elizabeth, 146
Pinckney, Mary, 213
Pindell, ———, 240
  Ann (Hall), 240
Pinkney, ———, 338
  Susannah (Lee), 338
Pinkerton, Sarah, 441
Pitcher, Henry, 436
  Nazareth, 436
Pitts, Alice, 509
  Charles F., 232
  Sullivan, 232
Plant, Josephine A., 252
Plantagenet, Alianore (De Bohun), 115
  Anne, 115
  Edmund, 197
  Elizabeth, 166
  Thomas, 115
Platt, Hannah, 33
Platts, Abel, 333
  Lydia (Bailey), 333
Plowden, Dorothy, 112
  Edmund, 112
  George, 112
  Henrietta (Slye), 112
  Margaret (Brent), 112
  Winnifred, 112
Plumer, Charles Avery, 420
  Sarah Hale (Rockwood), 420
Plumpton, Agnes, 348
Pluyett, Sarah (English), 198
  William, 198
Poe, Eleanor (Brent), 114
  Orlando, 114
Pole, Isabel, 348
  John, 330
  William, 330
Pollard, Ellen Hackley, 393
  Keziah Jane, 19
Polly, Gertrude, 441
Pond, Daniel, 288
  Esther, 288
  Jabez, 212
  Mary (Gay), 212
Pool, Elizabeth, 403

Poole, Ann, 52
Poor, Abigail, 423
  Abigail (Hale), 423
  Alice Florence, 287
  Esther (Hewins), 287
  Henry, 423
  James Ridgway, 287
  John, 423
  Nathaniel C., 287
  Sarah (———), 423
Pope ——— (Luce), 507
  Ann, 507
  Elizabeth (Peirce) Bridges, 187
  Hester (———), 277
  Jean, 277
  Jane (Brown), 277
  Lucy (———), 277
  Mary (Sisson), 277
  Nabby, 514
  Nathaniel, 187, 277, 507
  Worden, 277
Poper, Elizabeth, 222
Popham, George, 330
  Hugh, 102
Porter ———, 162, 308
  Augusta (Maupin), 43
  Augusta Maupin, 43
  Elizabeth Frances (Todd), 308
  Elizabeth Prudence (Ball), 42
  George Frederick, 162
  George J., 162
  Gilbert Brackett, 162
  Hannah, 508
  Hunter Ball, 43
  Helen (Cooch), 162
  James, 308
  John Mercer, 308
  John Ridgely, 43
  John William Hunter, 42
  Judith, 284
  Letitia Preston (Breckinridge) Grayson, 96
  Mary George, 306
  Peter Buel, 96
  Robert, 308
  Sallie Macon, 43
  Susan (Huntington), 317
  Susannah (Buck), 308
  Susannah Frances, 302, 305, 308, 309
  William, 317

INDEX

Post, Catlyna, 467
  Esther P. (Lawrence), 15
  William, 15
Potter, Olive (Lewis), 344
  Bernard, 344
  Elizabeth, 445
  Nathaniel, 445
  Rebecca (———), 445
  Susanna, 27
Pottinger, Ann (Evans), 92
  Elizabeth, 92
  Rachel, 92
  Robert, 92
Potts, Hannah, 416
Powell, Abigail (Wilcox), 369
  Mary (Morris), 360
  Samuel, 360, 361
  Sarah, 361
Powys, Edward, 346
  Edward Cherleton, 346
  Hawyse, 346
  Joan (———), 346
  John, 346
  Joyce, 346
Prall, Abraham, 15
  Maria C., 15
Pratt, David, 65
  Joanna, 158
  Julia (Perkins), 65
  Julia Perkins, 65
Prather, Mary (Churchill), 131
Pray, Hannah, 509
Preeson, Susanna, 390
Prentice, Mary Alice, 313
  Patience, 126
Prentis, *Arms*, 386, 389
  Bernice (Cole), 388
  Daniel, 386
  Eleanor (Gordon), 388
  Eliza (Wrenn), 388, 389
  Elizabeth, 387
  Hally Morrison, 388
  Henning Webb, 388
  Janet Whitehead, 386
  John, 386
  John Brooks, 388, 389
  Joseph, 386, 387, 389, 390, 391
  Joseph Elliott, 388
  Katherine Lewis, 389
  Margaret Ann (Whitehead), 388, 390, 391
  Margaret (Bowdoin), 387, 389, 390, 391

Prentis—*Continued*
  Margaret Susan, 387, 390
  Margaret Whitehead, 388
  Martha (Alexander), 388
  Martha Josephine, 388
  Mary Allen (Darden), 386, 390, 391
  Mary (Brooke), 386
  Mary Hortense, 388
  Mary Morton (McNutt), 388
  Morton McNutt, 388
  Peter Bowdoin, 388, 390
  Robert Riddick, 386, 388, 390, 391
  Rose Hortense (Coster), 388
  Rose Marie, 388
  Sarah, 387
  Susan, 390
  Susan Caroline (Riddick), 387, 389, 390, 391
  Susan Josephine, 389
  William, 386, 387
Prescott, Benjamin M., 199
  Charles, 378
  Dorothy, 126
  Hannah Maria (English), 199
  John, 64
  Jonathan, 378
  Mary (Ballard), 64
Preston, Anna Sophonisba, 97
  Elizabeth (Patton), 96
  John, 96
  Josephine, 487
  Lettica, 96
  Rachel, 316
Prestwood, George, 143
  Mary, 143
Prevost ———, 97
  Frances C., 97
Prewitt, Martha Talbott, 189
Price, Amabel Lee, 341
  Curtis Ethelbert, 341
  Frances (Shaw), 341
  Henrietta Cowman (George), 341
  John Marshall, 341
  Marie Louise, 269
  Marshall Langton, 341
  Martha Elizabeth (Byrd), 269
  Roger, 303
  Sterling, 269
  Thomas Henry, 269
Prince ———, 32

Pringle, James S., 273
  Nancy (Hart), 273
Proctor, Caroline, 311
  Eliza, 418
Pryor, Isaac, 199
  Sarah Abigail (English), 199
Pullen, Marie, 450
Purviance, Catherine (Stewart), 168
  Elizabeth Isabella, 168
  Isabella, 168
  Samuel, 168
Putnam, Aaron, 33
  Elizabeth (Avery), 33
  Emma, 33

Q

Quigley, Corinne, 490
Quirk, Maude, 249

R

Rae ———, 162
Rafferty ———, 239
  Kitty Howard (Duckett), 239
Ralston, Clare Selby, 135
Ramsay, Margaret Whitehead (Prentis), 388
  Robert Lee, 388
Randall, Hannah (Beale), 58
  Thomas, 58
  Urith, 58
Randolph, *Arms*, 141
  William, 129
Raney, Mabel, 249
Rankin, Eli Shorter, 457
  Frances (Lamar), 457
  Jesse, 457
Rankin, Margaret, 457
  Margaret (Thomas), 457
Ransdall, Sarah Elliott, 187
Rapine, Daniel, 94
  Martha Magdalene, 94
  Mary, 94
Rathbone, Harriet Whitehorne, 169
Rauh, Barbara, 37
Rauterberg, Carl, 133
  Charles, 133
  Henry Bullitt, 133
  Julia (Bullitt), 133
  Julia Bullitt, 133
Rawlings, Cordelia Jane, 354
  Emma Purner, 354

INDEX

Rawlings—*Continued*
  Henry Flower, 354
  Hester, 354
  Jesse, 354
  John, 354
  Martha Ann (Marine), 354
  Mary C., 160
  Mary (Mezwick), 354
  Molly (Mezwick), 354
  Nancy, 354
  Nannie Leonard, 354
Ray, Sallie, 222
Rea, Joshua, 63
  Rebecca, 63
  Sarah (Waters), 63
Read, Mary Cornelia, 336
  Sarah, 367
  Sophia Catherine (Howard), 336
  William George, 336
Reade, George, 481
  Mildred, 507
Rector, Catherine, 462
  Mary, 462
Redlington, Sarah Collins, 375
Ree, Ann, 292
  Nichoias, 292
Reed, Allis (Rickard), 417
  Elizabeth, 104, 112, 115
  Giles, 104, 115
  Katherine (Greville), 115
  Mary, 294
  Mary (Richmond), 403
  Mercy, 460
  William, 403, 417
Reese, Chauncey B., 169
  Mary Isabella (Courtenay), 169
Reeves, Charles H., 444
  David, 273
  Elizabeth, 454
  Mary Buzby (Sloan), 444
  Rebecca A., 273
Reid, *Arms*, 392, 393
Reid ———, 54
  Andrew, 392
  Doris Fielding, 393
  Dorothy (Roher), 479
  Edith Gittings, 393
  Elizabeth (Taylor), 392
  Elizabeth Washington Fielding, 392
  Ernest Brooke Fielding, 392

Reid—*Continued*
  Fanny Brooke (Gwathmey), 392
  Francis Dorian Fielding, 392
  Francis Fielding, 392, 393
  George, 392
  Harry Fielding, 393
  John, 479
  Marie Magdalene (Svendsen), 392
  Priscilla (Dorsey), 54
  Susannah, 479
  William, 392
Remington, John, 330
  Jonathan, 331
Revel, Edward, 476
  John, 476
  Katherine (Scarborough), 476
  Rachel (Hall), 476
  Randall, 194, 470, 476
  Sarah, 476
  Sarah (Revel), 476
Revelle, Katherine (Scarborough), 477
  Randall, 477
Reynolds, Julia, 339
Rhames, Jane, 172
Rhoades, *Arms*, 394
  Abigail, 396
  Abigail (Coates), 396
  Alan, 400
  Almon (Fuller), 397
  Amphillis, 395
  Ann, 398
  Ann (Graves), 395
  Archie Lumnin, 399
  Aurilly (Grover), 397
  Axa, 398
  Bela, 398
  Benjamin, 396, 397, 398, 403, 404
  Benjamin D., 398
  Bernice Clayton (Hazen), 399
  Bertha Alice, 399
  Betsey, 397
  Cecil Peter, 400
  Cecillia Varonica (Lawler), 400
  Cora L. (McCoy), 399
  Deliverance, 397
  Edward James, 399, 400, 401

Rhoades—*Continued*
  Eleazer, 395, 396
  Eliakim, 397
  Elizabeth (Coates), 395
  Elizabeth (Eliza), 395
  Elizabeth (Paul), 395
  Elizabeth (White), 395
  Emily, 398
  Enid Frances, 400
  Ernest B., 398
  Ethel Grace, 401
  Eva May, 399, 401
  Ewell Nelson, 400
  Frances James (Brown), 394, 409, 414
  Frances Nell, 401
  Francis Marion, 399
  George, 395
  Hannah, 398
  Henry, 395, 398
  Ida May, 399
  Inez B., 400
  Invert D., 400
  James, 395
  Jane, 397
  Jane (Coates), 395
  Jane (Johnson), 398
  Jerome (Gillette), 398
  Joane, 396
  Joanna (Cady), 396
  John, 396, 397
  Jonathan, 395, 396
  Joseph, 395, 396
  Joshua, 395
  Josiah, 395
  Judith (Richmond), 397, 403, 404
  Lavisa, 398
  Lotta M. (Farnsworth), 394
  Louisa (Goff), 398
  Launa Viola (Long), 400
  Lucy Eunice (Osgood), 398, 409
  Lucy Maud, 399
  Lydia (Jones), 397
  Manetta (Holland), 399
  Martha, 396
  Mary Agnes, 400
  Mary Alice, 399, 400
  Mary (Fuller), 396
  Mary (Standberry), 397
  Minnie E., 399
  Nellie, 399

INDEX

Rhoades—*Continued*
  Nellie (Bishop), 398
  Nelson Carrier, 398, 409
  Nelson Osgood, 394, 399, 400, 409, 414
  Nora Juanita (Baker), 399
  Obadiah, 396, 397
  Rachel (Silsby), 396
  Ralph Benjamin, 399
  Ralph H., 398
  Rebecca (Stewart), 397
  Rena (McKnight), 398
  Roger Farnsworth, 400
  Samuel, 395, 396
  Sarah, 328, 396, 397
  Sarah (Baxter), 396
  Sarah (Newman), 396
  Serafina, 398
  Simeon B., 398
  Temperance (Hart), 398
  William Francis, 399
  Winifred May, 399
Rhoads, Henry, 327
  Sarah (———), 327
Rhodes, *Arms*, 182
  Ann Hope, 182
  Catherine (Holden), 182
  Charles, 181, 182
  Deborah (Greene), 182
  Elizabeth, 27
  Esther (Arnold), 182
  Hope Ann, 181
  James, 27
  Joanna (Arnold), 182
  Johannah, 323
  John, 182
  Nancy (Brown), 181, 182
  Peleg, 27
  Peter, 182
  Phebe, 28
  Sally (Arnold), 27
  Sarah (Arnold), 28
  Waite (Waterman), 182
  William, 28
  Zachariah, 182
Rhyddarch, Jane (———), 161
  John, 161
  Morgan, 161
Rice, Agnes (Van Santvoord), 466
  Mary (Claiborne), 265
  Susanna, 296
  William T., 466

Richards, Betsey, 368
  Flora Etta, 22
  Frances, 435
  Henry, 435
  Isaac Pratt, 22
  Josephine, 433
  Juliette, 159
  Marietta (Nicholson), 22
  Mary, 359
Richardson, Abigail (Ruggles), 431
  Anne, 204
  Elizabeth, 204
  Hally (Brown), 101
  Hally Brown, 101
  Lawrence, 58
  Mary, 361
  Samuel, 361
  Sarah, 58
  Thomas, 101, 431
  W. H., 204
Richmond, ——— (Macomber), 403
  Abigail, 403
  Abigail (Phillips) French, 403
  Abigail (Rogers), 402, 404
  Christopher, 397, 403
  Deborah, 440
  Ebenezer, 403
  Edmund, 402
  Edward, 402
  Eliakim, 397, 403
  Elizabeth, 403
  Elizabeth (Pool), 403
  Gersham, 403
  Hannah (Deane), 403
  Henry, 402, 403
  Joanna (Briggs), 403
  John, 397, 402, 403, 404
  Josiah, 403
  Joseph, 397, 402, 403
  Joshua Bailey, 397, 401
  Judith, 397, 403, 404
  Margaret, 403
  Mary, 402, 403
  Mary (Andrews), 403
  Mehitable (Caswell), 403
  Phebe, 403
  Phebe (Richmond), 403
  Phebe (Williams), 403
  Samuel, 402
  Sarah, 402, 403

Richmond—*Continued*
  Sarah (Hackett), 403
  Sarah (Thrasher), 403
  Susanna, 402
  Susanna (———) Barden, 403
  Thomas, 402
  William, 403
Rickard, *Arms*, 415, 419
  Abigail, 416
  Albert, 418
  Alice (Oldham), 417
  Allis, 417
  Alphus, 418
  Anna Mary, 415
  Barbara (Shong), 415
  Bertha (Conant), 416
  Bethiah, 416
  Betsey (Keyser), 417
  Blanch Sarah Anne, 419
  Charles, 418
  Cleo, 417
  Cora Ester (Greenburg), 419
  Daniel, 418
  Deborah, 417
  Eleazer, 416
  Elkanah, 416
  Emily (Morrison), 418
  Emma (Monson), 419
  Esther (Barnes), 416
  Fay Ebben, 415
  Francis, 419
  Frederick, 418
  Giles, 415, 416
  Grace Jesse, 419
  Hannah, 416, 417
  Hannah (———) Potts, 416
  Hannah (Dunham), 416
  Hannah (Snow), 416
  Harlow Ebben, 418
  Harvey Joseph, 419
  Helen M. (Coates), 418
  Henry, 416, 417
  Israel, 417
  Isaac, 417
  Jacob, 417
  Joan (Tilson), 415
  John, 416
  Joseph, 418
  Judith, 415, 416, 417
  Keturah (Bishop), 416
  Leonard, 417, 418
  Lester Earle, 415

586 INDEX

Rickard—*Continued*
  Lorenzo, 418
  Louisa (Jones), 418
  Lucy, 418
  Lucy C. (———) Lamb, 418
  Lucy (Kinney), 417
  Lucy (Parker), 418
  Marabah Charlotte, 418
  Marcellus Benjamin, 418
  Margaret (Cline), 418
  Marie H. (Knipe), 418
  Marion (Barnes), 417
  Martha C. (Carter), 418
  Martha M. (Fanshaw), 418
  Martha (Schwab), 415
  Mary, 416, 417
  Mary (Cook), 416
  Mary (Kirkham), 417
  Mattie (Enright), 419
  Maxin, 419
  Mehitable, 416
  Mercy, 416
  Mercy (Morton), 416
  Myra Adaline, 419
  Myra (Houghton), 418
  Myron, 418
  Orlin Luman, 415, 418
  Oscar Marcellus, 419
  Philena (Day), 418
  Polly, 418
  Rachel (Whiton), 416
  Rebecca, 416
  Rebecca (Snow), 416
  Rhoda (Russell), 418
  Samuel, 416, 417
  Sarah, 416, 417
  Sarah (———), 416
  Sarah Ann (Dexter), 418
  Sarah (Joslyn), 417
  Voadecia, 418
  Voadica, 418
  Voadica (Weston), 417
  Weston, 417
  Zeraviah (Bumpus), 417
Ricketson, Elizabeth, 515
  Rebecca, 515
Riddell, Annie (Daggett), 448
  Guy Crosby, 448
  Isabel Anderson (Southgate), 448
  Robert Hugh, 448
  Robert Southgate, 448

Riddick, Elizabeth (Riddick), 387
  Mary (Foulke), 387
  Robert Moor, 387
  Susan Caroline, 387, 389, 390, 391
  Willis, 387, 390, 391
Rideout, Nellie, 232
Ridgely, Ann, 48, 51
  Anna (Dorsey), 51
  Catherine, 49
  Charles, 59
  Deborah (Dorsey), 59
  Edith, 46
  Elizabeth, 48, 51
  Elizabeth (Dorsey), 49
  Elizabeth Dorsey, 45
  Florence, 46
  Frank, 46
  Georgie, 45
  Henry, 48, 49, 51
  John Randolphe, 45
  Katherine (Greenbury), 48
  Lisa, 15
  Mary Ball, 46
  Mary Louisa (Ball), 45
  Polly, 51
  Rachel, 49, 51
  Randolph, 45
  Rebeckah, 48, 49
  Rosa, 45
  William, 49, 59
Riding, Ann, 192
  Rose (Yeardley), 192
  Thomas, 192
Riecroft, Frances, 436
Riggs, Amelia (Dorsey), 49
  John, 49
  Samuel, 49
Riley, Lydia, 221
Risteau, Ann Boyd (Courtenay), 170
  Frances (Todd), 308
  George, 308
  Thomas Cradock, 170
Ritchie, Albert, 146
  Albert Cabell, 147
  Elizabeth Caskie (Cabell), 146
Rittenhouse, Elizabeth Hinkle, 250
  Smith Baker, 250

Roach, Abigail, 67
Roades, Amphillis, 506
  John, 506
Robb, Achsah (Ball), 46
  John, 46
Robergat, Theresa, 485
Robertes, Margaret, 5
Roberts, Eleanor, 305
  Elizabeth, 305
  Jane, 305, 482, 483
  Margaret (Foulke), 304
  Mary Daisy (Stewart), 298
  Nicholas, 304
  Walter F., 298
Robertson, Delina, 320, 322
  Hannah Elizabeth (Gordon), 217
  Patrick, 320
  William Joseph, 217
Robins, Arthur, 67
  Esther (Littleton), 389
  Grace, 389
  Grace (O'Neil) Waters, 69
  John, 389
  Mamie (Buck), 133
  Mary, 69, 70
  Obedience, 69, 70
  Vernon, 133
Robinson, ———, 244
  Alexander, 141
  Allen, 354
  Ann, 294, 295
  Anna, 352
  Anna (Duvall), 244
  Carrie Julia, 298
  Catherine, 345, 348
  Catherine, Lewis Chart No. 1
  Catherine (Beverley), 345
  Catherine (Beverley), Lewis Chart No. 1
  Catharine (Hollingsworth), 294
  Christopher, Lewis Chart No. 1
  Diantha, 367
  Eliza, 353
  Elizabeth, 181
  Elizabeth Bash (Sloan), 433
  Elizabeth (Booth), 294
  Elizabeth Conrad, 433
  Elijah, 367

INDEX

Robinson—*Continued*
  George, 294, 295
  George David Francis, 433
  James Hardwick, 298
  John, 345, 354, 432
  John, Lewis Chart No. 1
  Katherine Gertrude, 241
  Lucy, 432
  Martha (Webb), 298
  Mary, 294
  Nancy Elizabeth (Marine), 354
  Rhoda (———), 353
  Sallie (Allen), 354
  Thomas, 10
  Valentine, 294
  Virginia Cushing, 433
  Waiting, 379
Rockhold, Elizabeth, 52
  Mary, 52
Rockwell, Ruth, 314
Rockwood, Abby Ann (Abbot), 420, 422, 425
  Abigail, 426, 427
  Abigail (Conant), 427
  Agnes (Bicknell), 426
  Ann (———), 426
  Annie Abbot, 421
  Arthur Burton, 420
  Benjamin, 426
  Betsey, 427
  Betsey Dale, 428
  Daniel, 428
  Ebenezer, 422, 426, 427
  Edward Nelson, 420
  Elisha, 426, 427
  Elizabeth, 427
  Elizabeth (Adams), 426
  Elizabeth Breeze (Hazard), 427
  Elizabeth Davis, 421
  Fanny Larcom, 420
  Grace Burton, 421
  Hannah, 426, 428
  Henrietta, 420, 421
  Jane (Adams), 426
  Joanna (Ellis), 288, 426
  John, 426
  Joseph, 426, 427
  Josiah, 426
  Lubim, 422, 428
  Lubim Burton, 420, 422, 425, 428

Rockwood—*Continued*
  Lydia, 427
  Lydia (Burton), 422, 428
  Lydia Henrietta, 428
  Margaret, 426
  Margaret (Holbrook), 426
  Mary, 426
  Mary (Emerson), 427
  Mary Emerson, 428
  Matilda, 428
  Melinda Wheeler, 420
  Moses, 427
  Nathaniel, 288, 426
  Nicholas, 426
  Persis, 421
  Persis Abbot (Lovejoy), 420
  Polly, 428
  Richard, 288, 426
  Richard Burton, 421
  Sally, 428
  Samuel, 426, 427
  Sarah, 427
  Sarah Hale, 420
  Sibbel, 427
  Silence (———), 426
  Thomas, 426
  William Emerson, 420, 427
Rodes, Nellie (Bonsall), 488
  Sallie Ann, 487
  William, 487
Rodman, David Murray, 280
  Kate, 280
  Kennedy, 280
  Lee, 280
  Margharita (Welling), 280
  Pattie, 280
  Sidney Anderson (Kennedy), 280
Roelofs, Bertha, 181
Rogers, Abigail, 402, 404
  Andrew, 297
  Ann, 404
  Betsie, 297
  Eleazer, 404
  Elizabeth, 297
  Elizabeth (Alden) Pabodie, 404
  Elizabeth Ann Jane Carr, 297
  George, 297
  Hannah, 212
  J. Cecil, 25
  Jason, 487

Rogers—*Continued*
  John, 402, 404
  Joseph, 404
  Josephine (Preston), 487
  Lettie (Franks), 297
  Louisa Russell (Arnold), 25
  Margaret Stewart (Arnold), 25
  Martha (Hollingsworth), 297
  Mary, 404
  Mary (Hollingsworth), 297
  Nancy Johnson, 297
  Nathaniel, 297
  Robert H., 25
  Ruth, 297
  Susan Preston, 487
  Thomas, 397, 404
  Timothy, 404
Roher, Dorothy, 479
Rolfe, Jane (Peirce), 187
  John, 187
Rootes, Mary Read, 217
Roseboom, Hannah (Bryant), 17
  Jacob, 17
Ross, ———, 199
  Alexander, 305
  Anna Harden, 305
  Anne Harden, 302
  Catherine, 199, 347
  Reuben, 302, 305
  Sarah (———), 302, 305
Rossel ———, 503
Rosser, Jane, 471, 477, 478
Rossingham, Dyonis, 72
  Edmund, 72
  Mary (Flowerdew), 72
Rotch, Mary, 32
  William, 32
Rouse, Mabel (Cushing), 440
  William, 440
Rowe, Caroline (Burroughs), 351
  Frances Elizabeth (Marine), 351
  Perry Belmont, 351
  Walter Bosley, 351
  William Marine, 351
  Susan Anne, 433
Rowles, Susan Anne, 433
Rowley, Elizabeth (Fuller), 206
  Moses, 206

INDEX

Rowzie, Edward, 187
  Mary (Peirce), 187
Royall, Isaac, 285
Ruckman, James, 272
  Mary (Hart), 272
Ruddach, Alexander, 24
  Elizabeth Cecila, 24
Ruggles, *Arms*, 429, 432
  Abigail, 431, 432
  Abigail (Craft), 431
  Abigail (Davis) Williams, 431
  Ann, 430, 432
  Ann (Sumner), 432
  Benjamin, 432
  Ebenezer, 432
  Edmund Ingalls, 429
  Edward, 430, 431, 432
  Elizabeth, 430, 432
  Eunice (Kingsley), 429
  Florence, 430
  George, 429, 430
  George Fitch, 429
  Gershom Cheney, 429
  Hannah, 431, 432
  Hannah (Craft), 431
  Henry Bond, 429
  Jane Augusta, 429
  John, 429, 430, 431, 432
  John Gould, 429
  Julia Sparrow, 429
  Lucy (Robinson), 432
  Margery, 430
  Martha, 431
  Martha (Devotion), 431
  Mary, 430
  Mary (Curtis), 431
  Mary (Gould), 429
  Mary Gould, 429
  Nathaniel, 430
  Nicholas, 430
  Robert, 430
  Roger, 430
  Samuel, 430, 431, 432
  Sarah, 431
  Sarah (Beaman), 429
  Sarah Beaman, 429
  Thomas, 430, 431, 432
  William, 430
Ruggeley, Nicholas, 430
Rupp, Anna Barbara, 355
Rush, Mirah Logan (Bullitt), 140
  William Howard, 140

Rusk, Jeremiah, 398
Russell, Abigail, 516
  Abigail (Howland), 516
  Abraham, 516
  Alice (Hathaway), 517
  Anna, 516
  Anna Greene, 515, 517
  Anna (Tucker) Shearman, 517
  Asa, 517
  Benjamin, 418, 516
  Caleb, 514, 516, 517
  Charles, 18
  Charles Elmer, 289
  Clara (Ahles), 18
  Content (Gifford), 516
  Dinah (Allen), 516
  Dorothy, 515
  Dorothy (———), 515
  Elizabeth Alden (Hewins), 289
  Elizabeth (Ricketson), 515
  Gertrude, 289
  Hannah (Allen), 516
  Hannah (Moulthrop), 410
  Hozodiah (Smith), 515
  John, 68, 410, 451, 515, 516
  Jonathan, 515
  Joseph, 515, 516
  Joshua, 516
  Judith (Howland), 516
  Lucy, 408
  Martha, 516
  Mary, 40, 438, 515, 516
  Mary (———), 410
  Mary Ann, 517
  Mary Elizabeth, 408
  Mary (Talcott), 451
  Mary (Tucker), 516
  Mehitable (Earle), 517
  Mehitable Earle, 517
  Mehitable (Smith), 515
  Merribah (Doolittle), 418
  Peace, 516
  Philip Alden, 289
  Ralph, 410
  Rebecca, 516, 517
  Rebecca (Borden), 514
  Rebecca (Bordon), 516
  Rebecca (Ricketson), 515
  Reuben, 517
  Rhoda, 418
  Richard, 329

Russell—*Continued*
  Sarah, 411, 514, 516, 517
  Seth, 516
  Vertue (Smith), 517
  William, 516
Rutland, ———, 239
  Anne (Hall), 233, 239
  Thomas, 233, 239

S

St. Cyre, ———, 503
St. John, Agnes, 166
  John, 166
St. Leger, George, 167
  Katherine, 167
Salmon, Annie Eugenia (Marine), 355
  Barbara, 355
  David, 355
Saltonstall, Gordon, 9
  Mary (Whittinghame), 9
  Richard, 4
Salway, Joanna, 409
Sammis, Daniel, 316
  Mary (Huntington), 316
Sanders, Martin, 380
San Souci, Mildred, 43
Sappington, Polly (Ridgely), 51
  Thomas, 51
Sard, Sarah (Marine), 353
  William, 353
Sargent, John, 225
  Lydia, 225
  Lydia (Chipman), 225
Satterwaite, Mary Cabell (Breckinridge), 98
  T. P., 98
Saunders, Blanch Sarah Anne (Rickard), 419
  Elizabeth, 10, 11
  Elizabeth (Lawrence), 11
  Harriet, 317
  Harry, 419
  John, 11
  Mary, 361
Savage, ———, 168
  Alicia (Harmanson), 69, 70
  Ann (Elkington), 70
  Elizabeth, 68, 71
  Elizabeth (Bell), 70
  Esther (Littleton), 70
  Hannah (Tyng), 70

INDEX

Savage—*Continued*
  John, 69, 70
  Mary (Robins), 69, 70
  Thomas, 69, 70
Sawyer, Bertha, 30
  Elizabeth (Osgood), 407
  Thomas, 407
Say, ———, 4
Scarborough, Charles, 71, 476
  Edmond, 471
  Edmund, 68, 71, 194, 476, 477
  Hannah, 67, 68, 71, 471
  Hannah (———), 71, 476
  Katherine, 476, 477
  Katherine (West), 71
  Mary (Charleton), 71
  Tabitha, 67, 71
Schaeffer, Ada C., 209
Scheuch, Rebecca Maillard, 501
Schminke, Ann Eliza, 44
Schoolfield, Caroline (Cooch), 160
  Emily (Barnes), 160
  William M., 160
  William Smith, 160
Schwab, Julius, 415
  Louise (Troy), 415
  Martha, 415
Schwear, Cleland Nelson, 238
  Florence, 238
  Harriet Kent (Hall), 238
  Mary Walton, 238
  Phillip, 238
  William Hall, 238
Scott, Ann, 477, 478
  Antoinette (Tams), 142
  Charles, 497
  Charlotte, 497
  Elizabeth, 68, 445
  Ethel Hoyt, 142
  George B., 418
  Gwendolyn Garrettson, 45
  Helen, 131
  Helen (Evans), 45
  Helen Townsend, 45
  Isabella, 246
  James, 131, 142, 497
  Janet Clark, 497
  Lizzie (George), 497
  Marabah Charlotte (Rickard), 418

Scott—*Continued*
  Roseannah (Hollingsworth), 299
  Sarah (Brown), 131
  Sarah (Foote), 445
  Townsend, 45
  William, 299, 445, 497
Screven, Elizabeth (Pendarvis) Bryan, 123
  John, 123
Scrogin, Fanta (Lena), 477
  Jane (———), 477
  John, 477
  Joseph, 477
  Mary, 476, 477
  Sarah (Caldwell), 477
Searle, Susanna, 333
Seaton, Thomas, 24
Seaver, Anna Maria (Courtenay), 171
  Jeremiah, 171
Seavey, Sarah, 286
Seeley, Joanna (Archibald), 492
  Mary Gertrude, 492
  Thomas Melville, 492
Selby, Elizabeth, 135
Selden, Estelle (Stewart), 298
  George Kearsley, 298
Sele, ———, 4
Sellman, ———, 240, 257
  Alfred, 237
  Anne Elizabeth (Harwood), 236
  Eleanor Deborrah, 240
  Eleanor (Watkins), 237
  Harriet, 233
  John Stephen, 257
  Jonathan, 236
  Lucy, 239
  Mary Dryden (Hall), 237
  Richard, 237
  William, 233
Senior, Elizabeth, 358
Sessions, Abigail (Ruggles), 432
  Samuel, 432
Settle, Elizabeth (Pickett), Lewis Chart No. 1
  Joel, Lewis Chart No. 1
  Virginia, Lewis Chart No. 1
Sewall, Henry, 322
  Nancy, 320, 322
  Samuel, 322

Sewell, Anne, 76
  Henry, 76
  Jane, 179
  Jane Lowe, 107
  Mary, 107
  Nicholas, 179
  Susannah (Burgess), 179
Seymour, Clara Alden, 287
  David, 107
  Edward, 167
  Elizabeth, 167
  Elizabeth Allin (Hewins), 287
  Evelyn Hewins, 287
  Florentius, 107
  Gertrude Elizabeth, 287
  John W., 287
  Susannah, 107
Shackelford, Mildred (Martin), 241
  Rachel Hall (Estep), 241
  Richard Tillard, 241
  William Thomas, 241
Shattuck, Martin, 511
  Meribah Esther Hyde (Wilbur), 511
Shaw, ———, 513
  Content (Wood), 513
  Frances, 341
  Hannah, 513
  Lemuel, 428
  Rebecca (Wood), 513
Shearman, Anna (Tucker), 517
  David, 517
Shears, Frederick Charles Frazier, 259
  Permelia Victoria (Monroe), 259
Shelton, Abigail, 335
  Grace Jesse (Rickard), 419
  Hugh, 419
Shepardson, George W., 159
  Isadora, 159
Shephardson, Juliette (Richards), 159
Shepherd, Sarah (Eastman) French, 203
  Soloman, 203
Shepreve, Charles, 326
  Elizabeth (Jeffries), 326
Sherman, Mary (Russell), 516
  Philip, 516
Shewin, Barbary, 294

INDEX

Shields, Ann (Harris), 489
  Caroline (Hart), 466
  Caroline Hart, 466
  Hamilton Leroy, 466
  Virginia, 466
Shilton, Thomas, 72
Shimmin, Charles Franklin, 329
  Marian, 329
  Marion Harriot (Parkman), 329
Shippen, Edward, 24
  Margaret, 24
Shoemaker, Benjamin, 360
  Elizabeth (Morris), 360
Shong, Barbara, 415
  John Michael, 415
  Margaret (Pelow), 415
Shores, Maria, 342
  Maria A., Lewis Chart No. 1
  Patsy (Bransford), Lewis Chart No. 1
  Thomas, Lewis Chart No. 1
  Wilson, Lewis Chart No. 1
Shrine, Jane (Brent), 106
  Nathaniel, 106
Shure, Daniel Ferree, 302
  Grace (Holloway), 302
  William J., 302
Shute, Daniel, 439
  Mary (Cushing), 439
Sill ———, 24
  Sophia (Arnold), 24
Silsby, Rachel, 396
Sim, Mary (Brooke), 179
  Patrick, 179
Simmons, Cheston H., 450
  Eleanor (Howard), 176
  John Howard, 176
  Louise, 450
  Louise (Maynard), 450
  Sarah, 440
  Susannah (Howard), 176
Simonds, Sarah, 384
Simonton, Frances Elizabeth (Cooch) Armitage, 161
  John, 161
Simpill ———, 503
Simpson, George, 293
  Margaret, 495
  Ruth (Hollingsworth), 293
  William, 495
Sinclair, Marie, 491

Sisson ———, 513
  Mary, 277
  Mary (Wood), 513
Skinner (———), 91
  Anne, 450
  Content (Fuller) Fuller, 207
  Eleanor (Bowie) Brooke Clagett, 91
  Nathaniel, 207
  William, 450
Slack, Addie, 234
  Rachel Anne (Hall), 234
  William B., 234
  William Hall, 234
Slecht, Cornelis, 473
  Cornelis Barentise, 470, 471, 472
  Hendricus, 473
  Jacomyntje, 471, 473
  Mattys, 472, 473
  Petronella, 473
  Tryntje Tysse (Bos), 471, 472
Slee, Christopher, 412
Slichter, Emily Adele, 218
Sloan, Anne (Buzby), 443
  Elizabeth Bash, 433
  Elizabeth Burns, 443
  Elizabeth (Cushing), 443
  Fisher, 443
  Francis Burns, 433, 443
  Francis Eugene, 433
  Frank B., 433
  George F., 443
  George Frederick, 433
  Helene Buelah (Parker), 433
  Isabella Highland, 443
  Joseph Cushing, 443
  Josephine (Richards), 433
  Mary Buzby, 444
  Mildred Cushing, 433
  R. E. (Watt), 443
  Susan Luckett (Bash), 433
Slye, Henrietta, 112
Smiser, Dorothea, 338
Smith ———, 256
  Amelia M., 303
  Ann (———), 477
  Annie Isabel, 181, 182
  Benjamin, 26, 429, 451
  Bertha (Roelofs), 181
  Charles, 471, 475, 477
  Charlotte E., 488

Smith—*Continued*
  Charlotte Sophia Phillipena, 227, 228
  Deborah, 12
  Dorothy, 451
  Edward, 26
  Elisha, 26
  Eliza, 227
  Eliza Caroline Middleton (Huger), 311
  Elizabeth, 11, 26, 74, 76, 312
  Elizabeth Hite, 475
  Elizabeth R., 135
  Esther, 155
  George, 227
  George Williamson, 244
  Harry Hudson, 270
  Hozodiah, 515
  Hugh, 332
  Jane, 276, 279
  Jasper Keith, 298
  Jehiel, 33
  John, 76, 91, 471, 475
  John Frederick Sigismund, 227
  John Julius Pringle, 312
  Julian Ann Hollingsworth (Stewart), 298
  Kesia (Wood), 33
  Lebbeus Ensworth, 321
  Levisa (Marine), 353
  Louisa Richardson, 119
  Margaret (Bulkeley), 125
  Margaret (Hall), 256
  Margaret M. (Newbold), 270
  Margaret Newbold, 270
  Maria Bassett, 218
  Mary, 220, 232, 372, 376, 477
  Mary (Barker), 26
  Mary Gould (Ruggles), 429
  Matthew, 453
  Mehitable, 515
  Mitchell, 66, 74, 76
  Olive (Woodward), 76
  Phoebe (Arnold), 26
  Rebecca (Hite), 471, 475
  Richard, 11, 12
  Ruth, 33
  Samuel, 279
  Sarah, 26, 471
  Sarah F. (Whipple), 181
  Sarahanna, 475
  Simri, 181

INDEX

Smith—*Continued*
  Sue (Duvall), 244
  Susanna (Lawrence) Monviele, 9
  Thomas, 125
  Tabitha (McLaughlin), 279
  Vertue, 517
  William, 9, 10, 353
  William Mason, 311
  William Murray, 227
Smithson ———, 54
Snoddy, James, Lewis Chart No. 1
  John, Lewis Chart No. 1
  Nancy, Lewis Chart No. 1
Snow, Hannah, 416
  Rebecca, 416
  Rebecca (Brown), 416
  William, 416
Snowden, Ann (Ridgely), 51
  Susannah, 56
  Thomas, 51
Snowsell, Martha, 8
  Martha (Lawrence), 8
  Thomas, 8
Sollers, Ann, 176
Somery, Beatrix, 346
  John, 346
  Margaret, 346
  Rafe, 346
  Thomas, 346
Sommerland, Alice, 359
Soren, George, 227
  Mary (———), 227
  Mary Ann, 227
Soule, John, 417
Southey, Ann, 389
  Anne, 70
  Elizabeth, 70
  Elizabeth (———), 389
  Henry, 70
  Lewis, 389
Southgate, Abigail (Browne), 447
  Abigail (McLellan), 447
  Alice Austin (MacLaren), 445
  Alice (Darley), 448
  Amos, 446
  Arixene, 446
  Barbara Gay, 449
  Charles McLellan, 448
  Edward Payson, 447

Southgate—*Continued*
  Eliza (Neal), 447
  Elizabeth, 445, 446, 447
  Elizabeth (Bennett), 445
  Elizabeth MacLaren, 445
  Elizabeth (Potter), 445
  Elizabeth (Scott), 445
  Elizabeth (Steward), 445
  Elizabeth Virginia (Anderson), 448
  Ellen, 447
  Emily, 447
  Frances (Swan), 448
  Frederick 446, 447
  Frederick Chester, 448
  Hannah, 445
  Henry Martin, 447
  Horatio, 446, 447, 448
  Hugh MacLellan, 445, 448
  Isabel Anderson, 448
  Isabel Frances, 445
  Isabella, 446
  John, 445, 446
  John Barrett, 447
  Julia, 447
  Julia Abbey, 447
  Margaret, 446
  Mary, 445, 446
  Mary Frances (Swan), 448
  Mary (King), 446
  Mary King, 446, 447
  Mary (Webster), 447
  Mary Webster, 447
  Miranda, 446
  Moses, 446
  Octavia, 446
  Rebecca, 446
  Richard, 445, 447
  Robert, 446, 447, 448
  Robert Swan, 448
  Ruth, 446
  Sarah, 446
  Steward, 445, 446
  Stuart Leicester, 448
  William, 446
  William Scott, 447
Southworth, Elizabeth, 225
Spalding, Charles Clement, 253
  Hannah (Ballard), 63
  Henrietta Kerr, 253
  John, 63
  Sophia Kerr (Leigh), 253

Sparhawk, Caroline, 124
  Nathaniel, 31
  Patience (Newman), 31
  Sybil, 31
  Ann, 216
  Ellen, 16
Sparrow, Matilda, 236
  Rachel (Hall), 237
  Solomon, 237
Spaulding, Mary, 368
Spence, Elinor, 347
  Patrick, 347
Spencer, Abigail (English), 198
  Alice, 346
  Margaret (Johnson), 465
  Nathaniel, 198
  Nicholas, 188
  Ruth, 465
  William, 465
Sperry, Jacob, 273
  Mary Elizabeth, 273
Spiers, Elizabeth (Harmanson), 68
  Elizabeth Harmanson, 68, 69
  George, 68, 69
Spooner, Florence (Garrettson), 45
  Henry, 45
Sprague, Judith, 30
  Polly, 417
  Ralph, 330, 331
Sprigg, Elizabeth (———), 92
  Esther, 92
  Margaret, 92
  Osborne, 92
  Thomas, 349
Staats, Anna, 467
Stafford, Anne, 115
  Hugh, 348
  Joan, 348
  John, 319
  Margaret, 319, 348
Stanbury, Mary, 397
Standberry, Mary, 397
Standis ———, 502
Stanley, Isabel, 319
  John, 319
Stansbury, Emma Cornelia, 253
Stanton, Esther (Gathyp), 152
  Grace, 134
  Hannah Burdick, 199
  Joseph, 152

INDEX

Stanton—*Continued*
  Lois (Cobb), 152
  Mary (Champlin), 152
  Samuel, 152
  Susanna (Champlin), 152
  Thomas, 199
Staples, Patty, 510
Stapleton, Elizabeth, 348
Starling, Henry Lyne, 489
  Kate C. (Watson), 489
Stebbins ———, 461
  Sarah (Tiffany), 461
Steele, Anne VanderGraff, 99
  Caroline Dupre, 99
  Frances (Breckinridge), 99
  Frances Breckinridge, 99
  Helen, 99
  John Andrew, 99
  Kate, 134
Steenwyck, Cornelis, 7
Stephens ———, 403
  Mary (Richmond), 403
Stephenson, John, 25
  Georgiana Phipps (Arnold), 25
Stetson, Hannah, 153
Stevens ———, 38
  Angel (Aney), 352
  Caroline M. (Mather), 40
  Cordelia, 40
  Elizabeth, 409
  George, 40
  Lucertia, 270
  Mary, 63
  Rebecca (Rea), 63
  Samuel, 63
Stevenson ———, 235, 236
  Isabella, 496
  Margaret (Burns), 496
  Margaret (Cochrane), 496
Stewart, Abby Ballard, 299
  Abby Churchill (Ballard), 299
  Agnes, 252
  Alexander, 298
  Alice, 240
  Anita, 298
  Ann Eloise, 298
  Anna Briggs (Carter), 298
  Benjamin, 299
  Carrie Julia (Robinson), 298
  Catherine, 168
  Charles, 488

Stewart—*Continued*
  Corinne (Bickel), 298
  David, 233
  Elizabeth, 445
  Emma Lucille, 298
  Estelle, 298
  Eudox, 298
  Frances Malinda, 298
  Frances Josephine, 298
  Hammond, 240
  Hannah, 488
  Ida J. (Kiser), 299
  Isobel, 347
  Isobel Lamont, 119
  J. King, 298
  Jackson Benjamin Levi, 299
  James, 347
  James Hardwick Robinson, 298
  Jane (Rhoades), 397
  Jefferson Davis, 299
  John, 119
  John Archibald Bellah, 298
  John Lewis, 297
  Joseph Adger, 298
  Joseph Alexander, 298
  Josephine A. (Plant), 252
  Julia Ann (Hollingsworth), 297
  Julia Crawford, 298
  Julian Ann Hollingsworth, 298
  Juliatha (Oliver), 298
  Kitty Tennessee (King), 298
  Letitia (Hollingsworth), 299
  Margaret Ellen, 413
  Margery (Bruce), 347
  Martha Antoinette, 299
  Mary, 298
  Mary Amanda (Williamson), 119
  Mary Cliff, 299
  Mary Daisy, 298
  Mary (Hall), 233
  Mary Matilda Stansell, 299
  Nellie Kiser, 299
  Oliver, 397
  Rebecca, 397
  Sarah Elizabeth, 298
  Sarah (Striplin), 298
  Thomas, 409
  Thomas Dilworth, 299
  Walter, 347

Stewart—*Continued*
  William, 445
  William McClure, 252
Stimpson, Comfort, 59
  Rachel, 59
  Thomas, 59
  Charles Douglass, 140
  Dorothy Frances, 140
  Harriet (Overton), 140
Stirling, Marian, 495
Stites, Ann Lennox, 138
  Christiana Parry (Clark), 498
  Elizabeth, 138
  Francis Bell, 138
  Harry Pennington, 138
  Helen Chenoweth, 138
  James Walker, 139
  John, 138
  John Hunt, 138
  Louise Parkhill (Patterson), 138
  Mildred Ann (Chenoweth), 138
  Mildred Bullitt, 138
  Sarah Parkhill, 138
  Susie Barret, 138
  William Hopkins, 498
Stockett, Ann Sellman, 237
  Eleanor, 238
  Elizabeth Claude, 234, 237
  Ellen, 238
  Fannie, 237
  Francis H., 236
  Francis Henry, 234, 237
  Harriet Key, 238
  Margaret Harwood, 237
  Margery (Hall), 233
  Mary Priscilla, 237
  Mary Priscilla (Hall), 234, 237
  S. Richard Galen, 233
  Thomas, 349
Stocking, Emily, 199
Stockley, Susannah, 390
Stoddard, David Farnum, 41
  Eleanor De Vere, 41
  Elizabeth, 317
  Elizabeth Rogers (Ball), 41
  John C. Ten Eyck, 99
  Julia Ten Eyck, 99
  Martha Virginia, 291
  Mary Carlton, 41

INDEX

Stoddard—*Continued*
  Robert, 99
  William Bull, 41
Stone ———, 176, 180, 366
  Abbie, 28
  Abigail (———), 366
  Daniel, 28
  Eliza Woodhouse, 74
  Elizabeth, 105
  Elizabeth (Howard), 176, 180
  Harriet (Chase), 28
  John, 366
  Mary, 154
  Sarah (Bass), 379
  William, 105
Stoneburner, Austin C., 250
  Lola Anna (Hall), 250
Storey ———, 503
Story, John, 42
  Prudence Gough (Ball), 42
  Sarah (Handbridge), 38
  William, 38
Stoughton, Israel, 329
  Margaret (Barrett) Huntington, 314
  Rebecca, 39
  Thomas, 314
Stourton, Anne, 103
Strater, Edward La Nauze, 501
  Jessie (Clark), 482
  Jessie La Nauze (Clark), 501
  William Edward, 482, 501
Stratton, Lucy Jane, 301
Stretch, Aaron, 147
  Margaret Hodges, 147
Stringer ———, 49
  Alicia (Harmanson), 387, 389, 391
  Grace, 387, 389, 390, 391
  Grace (Robbins), 389
  Hilary, 387, 389, 391
Striplin, Sarah, 298
Strong, Elizabeth, 424
  Elizabeth (———), 424
  Hannah (Fuller), 207
  Joseph, 424
  Josiah, 207
  Thomas, 424
Strother, Alice, 345, 348
  Alice, Lewis Chart No. 1
  Benjamin, 345, 348
  Benjamin, Lewis Chart No. 1

Strother—*Continued*
  Margaret (Thornton), 348
  Maria, 132, 177
  Mary, 105
  Mary (Mason), 348
  Mary (Mason), Lewis Chart No. 1
  William, 348
Stroud ———, 295
  Elizabeth (Hollingsworth), 295
Strunsky, Anna (Horowitz), 470
  Anna Seraphine, 470
  Elias, 470
Stuart, Mary Ella (Johnson), 363
Stubbs, Francis, 259
  Margaret Augusta, 259
  Mary Elizabeth (Burnett), 259
Sturdevant, Mary, 32
Styles, Thomas, 6
Sudler, Elizabeth Gordon, 241
Sumner, Ann, 432
  Samuel, 432
Sunderland, John, 330
Sutherland, John, 107
  Susannah (Brent), 107
Sutton, Alice (Spencer), 346
  Constance (Blount), 346
  Elizabeth (Berkeley), 346
  John, 346, 348
  Margaret, 348
  Margaret (Somery), 346
  Mary, 360
  Richard, 346
Svendsen, Lena Marie (Jensen), 392
  Marie Magdalene, 392
  Olaf, 392
Swain, William, 314
Swan, Benjamin, 448
  Lucy (Gay), 448
  Mary Frances, 448
Swann, Edward, 454
  Jane (Thomas), 454
Swayne, Hepsibah, 372, 373, 375
  Jeremiah, 372, 376
  Mary (Smith), 372, 376
Swearingen, Catherine, 222
  Catherine S., 220, 223

Swearingen—*Continued*
  Charles, 221
  Daniel, 222
  Dorothy, 221
  Eleanor, 219
  Eleanor (Dawson), 221, 222
  Elimelech, 222
  Elizabeth, 221
  Elizabeth Crow (Brashiar), 222
  Elizabeth (Dawson), 222
  Elizabeth (Higgins), 222
  Elizabeth (Poper), 222
  Elizabeth (Walker), 221
  Fannie (Baker), 221, 222
  George Washington, 222, 223
  Henry Hodger, 222
  Hezekiah, 222
  Jane (———), 221
  John, 221, 222
  Joseph, 221
  Josephine, 223
  Josiah, 222
  Julia F., 222
  Julia Franklin (Crist), 222
  Lydia (Riley), 221
  Mabalo (Culver), 222
  Mabel (King), 222
  Margaret (Payton), 222
  Maria L. B., 222
  Martha (———), 221
  Martha (Bell), 222
  Martha G. (Lloyd), 222
  Mary (———), 221
  Mary E., 222
  Obed, 222
  Rebecca Vaughn (Musam), 222
  Sallie (Ray), 222
  Samuel, 221, 222
  Sarah, 222
  Theresa, 221
  Thomas, 221, 222
  Van, 221, 222
  William, 222
  William E. C., 223
  William Wallace, 222
  Zacharias, 221
Sweetser, Almira E. (———), 224
  Barbara, 224
  Converse Wentworth, 224
  Faith (Groser), 224

INDEX

Sweetser—*Continued*
  Warren C., 224
  William, 224
Swepson, Mary, 386
Swift, Charles, 286
  Mary, 65
  Zebiah (Hewins), 286
Swigert, Jane Love (Watson), 487
  Mary, 487
  Philip, 487
Swits, Abram, 467
  Eva, 467
Sylvester, Nathaniel, 329
Syme, John, 483
  Sarah (Hoops), 483

T

Taber, Amaziah, 514
  Thankful, 514
Taft, Deborah (———), 380
  William H., 206
Taintor, Sarah, 127
Talbott, Margaret, 135
Talcott, *Arms*, 452
  ——— (Wells), 450
  Anne (Skinner), 450
  Benjamin, 451, 452
  Dorothy (Mott), 451
  Elezur, 451
  Frank Vanderbilt (Crawford), 450
  Frederick Hooker, 450
  Hannah, 451
  Hannah (Holyoke), 451
  Helen (Wakeman), 451
  James, 450, 452
  James Frederick, 450, 452
  John, 450, 451
  Joseph, 451
  Julia Lake, 450
  Louise (Simmons), 450
  Marie (Pullen), 450
  Martha Eveleth, 450
  Mary, 451
  Mary (———), 451
  Mary Stoddard (Johnson), 450
  Nathaniel, 451
  Rachel, 451
  Rebecca, 126
  Samuel, 451, 452

Talcott—*Continued*
  Seth, 452
  Thomas, 450
Talliaferro, Mary, 483
Talmadge, John, 411
  Lucretia (Moulthrop), 411
Talman, Betsy, 14
Tams, Antoinette, 142
Tankersley, Sarah Marshall, 148
Tapping, Mary (Woodmansey), 31
Tapscott, John Sherman, 45
  Rosa (Ridgely), 45
Tarleton, Deborah (Cushing), 438
  Henry, 438
Tasker, Ann (Bladen), 94
  Benjamin, 94
  Elizabeth, 94
Tatham, Emilie, 136
Tattersalle, Joan, 182
Tayloe, John, 350
Taylor, *Arms*, 495
  ———, 484
  Adeline C., 490
  Andrew, 482
  Ann (Conoway), 293
  Anne Innes (Watson), 490
  Desire (Fuller), 207
  Dick, 117
  Edmund, B., 490
  Edmund H., 490
  Elizabeth, 392, 490
  Elizabeth (Can), 392
  Elizabeth (Fuller), 206
  Elizabeth (Lee), 490
  Hugh, 482
  James, 481, 482
  Jane, 482, 483, 484
  John, 207, 392
  Joseph, 206
  Mary Ellen, 151
  Myrthe (Bringier), 117
  Nancy, 454
  Philip, 293
  Sarah, 483
  Sarah Crittenden, 490
  Sarah (Finney), 482, 484
  Thomas H., 490
  Thomas Hart, 490
  Zachary, 117, 490
Tea, Tephi, 324

Tebbs, Kate, 275
Temple, John, 330
Templeman, Ellen (Peirce)
  Lawson, 188
  John, 188
  Lucy, 188
  Polly, 188
Templeton ———, 216
  Anne (Gordon), 216
Ten Eyck, Cabell Breckinridge, 99
  Hannah, 24
  John C., 98
  Julia, 99
  Laura Johnson (Breckinridge), 98
  Richard, 24
Tennant ———, 250
  Anne Eliza, 119
  David Brydon, 119
  Emma Daingerfield, 250
  Willie Anne (Buffington), 119
Tenney, Frank P., 280
  Laura (Kennedy), 280
Terrell, *Arms*, 267
  Ann (Lewis), 267
  Ann (Lewis), Phillips 267
  Barbara, 267
  Barbara Wingfield, 266
  Charles, 267
  Elizabeth (Mills), 267
  Joseph, 267
  Nicholas, 267
  Zachary, 267
Terry, Dorothy, 140
  Edward L., 140
  Jane (Furth), 140
  Robert, 6
Tevis, Lloyd, 99
  Louise, 99
Thaxter, Elizabeth, 437
  Elizabeth (Jacob), 437, 438
  John, 437, 438
  Mary, 438
Thelebal, Elizabeth (Mason), 76
  James, 76
  Margaret, 75, 76
Theus, Ann, 338
Thomas, *Arms*, 453, 457
  ——— (Kibbe), 323
  Allen, 117

INDEX

Thomas—*Continued*
Anna Mary, 454
Benjamin, 323
Breckinridge, 100
Caleb, 454
Catherine, 455
Catherine (———), 454
Charles, 456
Charles Crankshaw, 336, 453
Chester B., 399
Dorcas (Maine), 323
Edward Burroughs, 456
Edward Lloyd, 455
Elizabeth, 278, 454, 455
Elizabeth (———), 454
Elizabeth (Barton), 453
Elizabeth (Collins), 454
Elizabeth Covington (Wailes), 455
Elizabeth Eden, 454
Elizabeth Lee (Breckinridge), 100
Elizabeth (Reeves), 454
Ellen (Burroughs), 456
George, 454
Henry Philip, 455, 456
Henry Wailes, 366, 456
Hezekiah, 454
James, 453, 454, 455
James Lovick Albert, 456
Jane, 454
Jennie H. (Gray), 455
Johannah (Rhodes), 323
John, 453, 454, 455
Jonathan, 454
Joseph, 100
Julia Ann, 54
Leonard, 454
Lovick, 455
Lydia, 403
Margaret, 457
Margaret (Crankshaw), 366, 456
Martha, 455
Mary, 440, 455, 456
Mary Ann, 321, 323
Mary (Bruce), 455
Mary C. (Germany), 456
Mary (Cave), 454
Mary (Eden), 454
Mary (Houge), 455
Mary (Wilson), 454
Matilda, 109

Thomas—*Continued*
Nancy, 454
Nancy (———), 455
Nancy (Taylor), 454
Nanette (Payne), 366, 453, 456
Nathan, 455
Nathaniel, 455
Nellie (———), 455
Nellie (Rhoades), 399
Octavia (Bringer), 117
Payne, 366, 453
Philip, 455
Rebecca, 455
Rebecca (Avery), 455
Rowland G., 323
Susanna, 454
Susanna (———), 453
Teratia (———), 453
Thomas, 453, 454
Wesley, 455
William, 454, 455
Winfield Scott, 456
Zachary, 454
Thompson, Alfred Cookman, 309
Ann, 507
Ann (Hollingsworth), 295
Breckinridge, 95
Bridget, 152
Catherine, 50
Eleanor (———), 410
Ellen (Moulthrop), 413
Hannah, 410
Helen Kate (Furness), 137
Isaac, 152
James, 295
Jane, 107
John, 409, 410
Mary, 335
Mary Breckinridge, 95
Mary Carson (Breckinridge) Morrison, 95
Mary (Holmes), 152
Prudence, 152
Raymond Webb, 309
Richard Ryan, 95
Sally, 418
Samuel, 413
Sarah, 152
Sibella, 187
Sudie Frances (Houck), 309
Thomas, 187

Thompson—*Continued*
Wirt, 137
Wirt Furness, 137
Thorne, Mary Hay, 338
Thornton, *Arms*, 494
Ann (Thompson), 507
Elizabeth (Anderson), 491
Elizabeth Anderson, 491, 507
Frances (Gregory), 507
Francis, 348, 483, 491, 507
Francis, Lewis Chart No. 1
Harry Innes, 491, 507
James Dabney, 491, 507
John, 491
Lucy (Crittenden), 491, 507
Margaret, Lewis Chart No. 1
Margaret, 348
Mary (Talliafferro), 483
Mildred, 483
Robert, 348
Sally (Innes), 491, 507
Sarah Frances, 491, 507
Sarah Frances (Thornton), 491, 507
Sarah (Thruston), 491
William, 348
William Mynn, 491
Thoroughgood, Adam, 72, 76, 77, 391
Adam, Lewis Chart No. 1
Ann, 77, 78
Ann, Lewis Chart No. 1
Ann (Edwards), 76
Edward, 76
Elizabeth, 72, 77, 391
Frances (Yeardley), 72, 77
John, 75, 76, 77, 78
Margaret (Lawson), 75, 77
Pembroke, 75
Thrasher, Mariett, 368
Sarah, 403
Thoroughgood, Sarah (Offley), 76, 77
William, 76
Thruston, *Arms*, 493
Sarah, 491
Tidwell, Hannah, 217
Tiffany, *Arms*, 458, 463
Abigail, 460
Alanson, 461, 462
Alice E., 463
Almira, 461, 462

INDEX

Tiffany—*Continued*
  Amasa, 461
  Anna, 461
  Anne (Pettes), 461
  Annie, 460
  Bethyah, 460
  Calvin, 461, 462
  Caroline Martha (Cooper), 459
  Catherine (Rector), 462
  Clark, 461
  Consider, 459
  Ebenezer, 459
  Edith (Lewis), 463
  Edward, 460
  Eleanor, 462
  Eliezer, 459
  Eliza A. (Estes), 458
  Elizabeth, 462, 463
  Elizabeth (———), 459
  Elizabeth Ann, 462
  Ezekiel, 460, 461
  Ezra, 461
  Florence A., L., 463
  Frederick Trench, 460
  George, 458, 462, 463, 465
  George B., 458
  Hannah, 460
  Hannah (———), 459
  Harvey J., 462
  Humphrey, 459
  Idella Gibson (Minks), 458
  Isaiah, 459
  James, 458, 459
  Jane M. (Loomis), 458
  Jared, 461, 462
  Jonathan R., 462
  Joseph, 462
  Margaret (Mott), 462
  Marguerite, 458
  Marjory (La Core), 461
  Mary, 460, 461, 463
  Mary (Cornell), 462
  Mary (Knowlton), 460
  Mary (Rector), 462
  Mercy (Reed), 460
  Molly (Clark), 461
  Nathaniel, 460
  Orlando J., 463
  Pettes, 461
  Philena, 463
  Recompence, 459
  Ruth A., 463

Tiffany—*Continued*
  Ruth (Underhill), 463, 465
  Sally Ann (———), 462
  Sarah, 460, 461, 462
  Sarah (Gallup), 462
  Simeon, 460, 461
  Stephen, 460
  Submit (Brown), 461
  Thomas, 459, 460
  Washington, 462, 465
  Wealthy, 461, 462
  William, 461, 462
  William, H., 463
Tillard, Martha (Hall), 240
  William, 240
Tillett, James, 12
  Sarah (Lawrence), 12
Tilley, Elizabeth, 225
  John, 225
Tillinghast, Elizabeth (Champlin), 153
  William, 153
Tillotson, Ida M., 511
Tilson, Joan, 415
Tinkham, Cleo (Rickard), 417
  James, 417
Tiptoft, Elizabeth (Aspall), 346
  John, 346
  Joyce, 346, 348
  Joyce (Powys), 346
  Margaret (Badlesmere), 346
  Payne, 346
Tisdale, James, 31
  Mary (Avery), 31
Titus, Elizabeth (Haight), 465
  Elizabeth (Lawrence), 14
  Philena, 463, 465
  Richard, 465
  Silus, 14
Todd, Ann (Gorsuch), 306
  Anna, 307
  Annie, 307
  Averilla, 307
  Bernard, 308
  Christopher, 307, 308
  Eleanor, 308
  Eleanor (Dorsey), 308
  Elizabeth, 198, 308
  Elizabeth (———), 307
  Elizabeth Ann, 488
  Elizabeth Frances, 308
  Elizabeth (Harris), 488

Todd—*Continued*
  Elizabeth (Rockhold), 52
  Emily P., 278
  Frances, 307, 308
  George W., 308
  James, 307
  Joanna, 307
  John, 51
  John Harris, 488
  Lancelot, 51, 52
  Maria Knox (Innes), 488, 489
  Martha (Vicunes), 307
  Mary, 61, 308
  Mary (Greene), 308
  Mary (Trotten), 308
  Nathan, 308
  Philip, 307
  Phoebe, 58
  Richard, 307, 308
  Robert, 307
  Ruth, 51, 52, 57, 58
  Sarah, 52, 55, 198
  Sarah Ann, 308
  Thomas, 306, 307, 308, 488
  Thomas J., 308
  William, 305, 307, 308
Tolley, Mary, 61
Walter, 61
Tomkins, Christopher, 97
  Sarah, 97
Tomlin, Millicent, 20
Topping, Florence Adelaide, 30
  Henry J., 30
  Mary Catherine (Hobart), 30
Torrey, Mary, 431
Townley, Charles, 13
  Elizabeth (Smith) Lawrence Cartteret, 11
  John, 13
  Mary, 12, 13
  Nicholas, 11
  Richard, 7, 11, 12, 13
Townsend, Anna, 14
  Henry, 14
  John, 14
  Mary, 184, 344
  Mary, Lewis Chart No. 1
  Obadiah, 14
  Phoebe, 14
  Phebe (Lawrence), 14
  Richard, Lewis Chart No. 1

INDEX

Townsend—*Continued*
  Robert, 344
  Robert, Lewis Chart No. 1
  Rosetta, 15
  Samuel, 14
  Solomon, 14
  Thomas S., 15
Tracy, Sarah (Huntington), 315
  Solomon, 315
  Thomas, 315
Traill, Hannah (Howard), 176
  James, 176
Travers, Matilda, 214
Travis, Nicholas, 6
Treat, Catherine (Bulkeley), 126
  Dorothy (Bulkeley), 126
  Hannah, 38
  Richard, 126
  Robert, 38
  Thomas, 126
Trescott, Martha, 283
Tretheke, Joan (Brent) Horsey, 102
  Thomas, 102
Trimble, Mary, 48
  Robert, 48
Trimmingham, Catherine, 107, 484
Triplett, James, 188
  Jane (Peirce), 188
Trist, Hore Browse, 117
  Julian Bringier, 117
  Nicholas Browse, 117
  Nicholas Philip, 117
  Wilhelmine, 117
Trotten, Mary, 308
  Sarah Ann (Todd) Diffenderfer, 308
  Thomas, 308
Trotter, Edward Hough, 273
  Mary Jane (Hart), 273
  Nathan, 273
  Susan (Hough), 273
Troy, Louise, 415
Truax, Jacoba (Van Santvoord), 467
  Peter, 467
Truman, Sarah (Briscoe), 176
  Thomas, 176
Trumbull, John, 126
  Sarah (Bulkeley), 126

Tuck, Amos, 201
  Ellen, 201
Tucker, Abraham, 516
  Anna, 517
  Anne France Bland, 123
  Dorothy (Ballard), 65
  Edward, 65
  Joseph, 517
  Mary, 516
  Mary (Wing), 517
  St. George, 123
Tumey ———, 58
  Ruth (Dorsey) Lawrence, 58
Tureaued, Aglea (Bringier), 117
  Augustine, 116
  Benjamin, 117
  Stella, 116
Turgis, Susan (Cabell), 143
  Thomas, 143
Turner, Hazell, 194
  Helen Augusta, 80, 82, 83
  Jacob, 172
  Maria Overton, 244
  Mary, 23
  Mary (Courtenay), 172
  Nancy Hall (Hoyt), 83
  Samuel Williamson, 83
  Virginia, 248
Turpin, Mary (Jefferson), 489
  Obedience, 489
  Thomas, 489
Tuttle, Agnes, 411
  Arthur J., 200
  Bertmel, 198
  Hannah Rebecca (English), 198
  Mary Spencer (English), 200
  Philip English, 200
  Sarah, 411
  William, 409
Twiford, John B., 354
  Vashtie (Marine) Adams, 354
Twilley, Nancy (Walker), 355
  Robert, 355
  Sarah Jane (Marine), 355
  Thomas James, 355
Tyler, Caroline Atwood, 174
  Catharine, 275
  Charles, 477, 478
  Elizabeth Therese, 136

Tyler—*Continued*
  George Trotter, 136
  Gertrude (Lynn), 133
  Helen Bullitt (Cood), 133
  Henry Samuel, 174
  Jane Owen, 133
  Jane Short (Courtenay), 174
  John Cood, 133
  Levi, 174
  Owen, 133
  Ruth, 235
  Sallie, 478
  Sally, 477
  Therese Pauline (Coles), 136
  Thomas Courtenay, 174
Tyng, Hannah, 20
  William, 327
Tyron, Rhoda (Huntington), 316
  William, 316
Tyson, Hannah Ann, 363
  Hannah Ann (Wood), 363
  Isaac, 363
  Jesse, 51
  Rachel (Ridgely), 51

U

Udall, Philip, 6
Underhill, *Arms*, 463, 465
  Benjamin, 465
  D. Harris, 463
  Daniel, 463, 465
  Deborah (Dickinson) 465
  Edward, 463
  Elizabeth (Feake), 464
  Hannah (———), 465
  Henry, 465
  Joan (Perrins), 464
  John, 463, 464, 465
  John Edward, 464
  Mary (Ferris), 465
  Mary (Mosely), 464
  Nathaniel, 465
  Philena (Titus), 463, 465
  Ruth, 463, 465
  Ruth (Spencer), 465
  Timotheus, 463
Unfraville, Charles, 106
  Ursula (Brent), 106
Upham, Hannah, 226
  Hannah (Waite), 225
  Phineas, 225

INDEX

Upshaw, Sarah, 269
Urquhart, Judith (Sprague), 30
  Mary Magdalen (Hall), 240
  Mary Hepzebah, 30
  William, 30, 240
Usher, Elizabeth, 326
  Elizabeth (Lidgett), 326
  John, 326
Utter, Jebulon, 27
  Ruth, 27

V

Vallé, John Baptiste, 36
  Lucie Mary (Desloge), 36
  Mary, 36
Vallindenham, John Kell, 101
  Mary (Penniman) Carrington, 101
Van Bibber, Betty (Dorsey), 54
  James, 54
Vance ———, 483
Van Cleve, Lucy, 189
Vanderbilt, Alfred Gwynne, 202
  Alice Claypoole (Gwynne), 202
  Cornelius, 202
  Elsie (French), 202
  Geertje (Van Santvoord), 467
  Margaret (Emerson) McKim, 202
  Ryk, 467
Vanderheyden, Ariana, 61
Van Harlingen, Margaret, 468
Van Horne, Mary Ricketts, 483
  Philip, 483
Van Meter, John, 474
Van Meteren, Catherine, 473
  Geertje, 473
  Gysbert, 473
  Hendrix, 474
  Isaac, 474
  Jan, 474
  Jan Joosten, 470, 473
  John, 474
  Joost Jans, 472, 474
  Joost Janse, 471, 473
  Joosten, 471
  Lysbeth, 473, 474
  Maycken (Hendricksen), 473

Van Meteren—*Continued*
  Macyken (Hendrygken), 471
  Rebecca, 471, 473, 474
  Sarah (Du Bois), 471, 473
Van Metern, Isaac, 474
Van Noast, Jacob, 467
  Sarah (Van Santvoord), 467
Van Ryburne, Lynch, 339
Van Santvoord, *Arms*, 466, 469
  Abraham, 467
  Agnes, 466
  Alexander Seymour, 466
  Alice Brewer (Glazier), 469
  Anna (Staats), 467
  Anne, 467
  Ariantje (Bratt), 467
  Caroline Hart (Shields), 466
  Catlyna, 468
  Catlyna (Post), 467
  Cornelius, 467, 468
  Cornelius Zeger, 467
  Edith, 466
  Elizabeth (Van Schaack), 468
  Eugene, 468
  Eva (Swits), 467
  Frank, 469
  Geertje, 467
  Geertge (Bratt), 467
  George, 466, 467
  George Bancroft, 469
  Harold, 469
  Jacoba, 467
  John Griswold, 466
  Margaret, 469
  Margaret (Van Harlingen), 468
  Maria, 467
  Nancy, 467
  Richard Staats, 466
  Sarah, 467
  Seymour, 466, 469
  Staats, 467, 468
  Virginia, 466
  Virginia (Shields), 466
  Zeger, 467
Van Schaack, Dorcas (Manton), 468
  Elizabeth, 468
  Peter, 468
Van Snyder, Agnes (———), 358
  Herman, 358

Van Swearingen, Barbara (De Barrette), 220
  Geret, 220
  Mary (Smith), 220
Vantyne, Hiram, 418
  Voadecia (Rickard), 418
Van Wyck, Harriet, 14
Van Yeveren, Alice, 480
Varnum, Asive, 418
  Lucy (Rickard), 418
Vassal, Samuel, 330
  William, 330
Vaughan, Edward, 12
  Evan, 303
  Joseph, 353
  Mary (Lawrence) Emott, 12
  Rachel, 353
Venable, Margaret Read, 145
  Samuel Woodson, 145
Verney, Elizabeth (Brent), 103
  John, 103
Vesian, Marye, 503
Victor, Rachel, 352
Vicunes, Martha, 307
Vincent, Hannah, 197
Von Esbeck, Magdalene Therese Fredericke Feriin, 512
Von Geyer, Anne, 329
  Frederick William, 329
Von Harrach, Carolin Gräfin, 336
Von Huissenstamm, Agnes (Carroll), 336
  Alexander Gräf, 336
  Anton Otto Gräf, 336
  Caroline Gräfin (Von Harrach), 336
Von Kalkreuth, ———, 227
Von Kretschman, Clotilde Jenny Marie Therese, 512
  Magdalene Therese Fredericke Fürin (Von Esbeck), 512
  Oscar Karl Paul Theodor, 512

W

Waddell, James Gordon, 216
  Lucy (Gordon), 216
Wade, Elizabeth Storer, 172
Wagoner, Catherine (Robinson), 345

INDEX

Wagoner—*Continued*
  Catherine (Robinson), Lewis Chart No. 1
  Mary Elizabeth, 345, 348
  Mary Elizabeth, Lewis Chart No. 1
  Peter, 345
  Peter, Lewis Chart No. 1
Wagstaff, Pauline Le Roy (French), 201
  Samuel, 201
Wailes, Benjamin, 455
  Edward Lloyd, 455
  Elizabeth Covington, 455
  Levin, 455
  Sarah Biggs (Oden), 455
  Sarah (Howard), 455
Waite, Emmet E., 224
  Georgia (———), 224
  Hannah, 225
  Joseph, 225
  Lola M., 224
  Lydia (Sargent), 225
Wake, Anne, 166
  Thomas, 166
Wakeman, Helen, 451
Walcott, Lizzie (Hollingsworth), 300
  William W., 300
Waldron, Charles Henry, 369
  Emma (Neal), 369
  John G., 369
  Maryette, 369
  Roxana Atilda (Haskell), 369
  William J., 369
Walker, Amy Gore, 129
  Caroline, 252
  Dorothy Crosby, 276
  Edward, 18, 65
  Elizabeth, 221
  Elizabeth Whitney (Ballard), 65
  Fannie, 46
  George, 276
  Georgianna Frances, 210
  Jane (Smith), 276
  John Moselcy, 336
  Laura, 65
  Louise Delor, 36
  Margaret (Hoops), 483
  Mildred (Thornton) Meriwether, 483
  Nancy, 355

Walker—*Continued*
  Peacy, 135
  Sarah Fenner, 336
  Sarah Fenner (Lee), 336
  Sophia Howard, 336
  Thomas, 129, 483
  Zoe (Ahles), 18
Wall, Beverly, 298
  Mary (Stewart), 298
Wallace, Adam, 70
  Arthur, 259
  Eva Spence, 259
  Jean, 215
Waller, Amy, 476
  Lina (Watson), 489
  Robin Alexander, 489
Walling, *Arms*, 470, 480
  Ann (Mayhew), 479
  Anna Seraphine (Strunsky), 470
  Anna Strunsky, 470
  Cheves Thompson, 480
  Ellen M. (Diller), 478
  Frederika Christina (Haskell), 480
  Frederika Christina, 480
  George, 479
  George H., 478
  Georgia, 470
  Henry M. R., 478
  Henry Mesel Reid, 479
  John, 479
  Mardy Jackson, 471, 477, 480
  Rosalind (English), 471, 476, 477, 478, 479
  Rosamond, 470
  Sarah (Cake), 478, 479
  Susannah (Reid), 479
  William English, 470, 471, 477, 478, 479, 480
  William Hayden English, 470
  Willoughby, 471, 476, 477, 478, 479
  Willoughby George, 471, 477, 479
  Willoughby Haskell, 480
Walsh, Eliza, 108
Waltermeyer, John, 254
  Mary Gertrude (Woodward), 254
Walton, Elizabeth, 158
  William, 158

Ward, Enoch, 263
  George, 199
  Julia (English), 199
  Sarah, 197, 263
Warden, Elizabeth (Smith)
  Foreman Land, 76
  Malachi, 76
Warder, Sarah, 361
Ware, Joanna (Gay) Whiting, 211
  John, 211
Warfield, Alexander, 53, 57
  Allen, 49
  Ann (Dorsey), 49
  Ariana (Dorsey), 48
  Azel, 49
  Benjamin, 48, 49
  Catherine, 49
  Catherine (Dorsey), 49
  Charles, 52
  Charles Alexander, 51
  Davidge, 49
  Dinah, 57
  Dinah (Davidge), 57
  Edwin, 58
  Elinor, 59
  Elinor (Browne), 59
  Elisha, 48
  Elizabeth (Dorsey), 48, 50, 57
  Elizabeth (Ridgely), 51
  Ella, 45
  Ellen, 308
  Greenbury, 49
  Gustavus, 45
  Honor (Howard), 52, 57
  Jemime (Dorsey), 53
  John, 52
  Joseph, 50, 57
  Joshua, 48, 49, 57, 58
  Lloyd, 49
  Mary, 48
  Mary Jane, 262
  Philemon Dorsey, 49
  Rachel, 50, 57
  Rachel (Howard), 57
  Rebeckah (Ridgeley), 48, 49
  Rezin, 52, 57
  Richard, 59, 308
  Ruth, 57
  Sarah, 52, 57
  Sarah (Dorsey), 49
  Seth, 48
  Vachel, 49

INDEX

Warham, Esther, 38
  John, 38
Waring, Basil, 233
  Elizabeth (Hall), 233
  Elizabeth M., 239
  Jane (Oxford), 256
  John H., 239
  Julia Maria (Worthington), 239
  Martha, 256
  Thomas, 256
Warnard, Mary, 182
Warner, Augustine, 507
  Mary, 335
  Mildred, 507
  Mildred (Reade), 507
Warren, Ada, 347
  Alice (Webb), 320
  Ann, 32, 320
  Anne (Mable), 320
  Christopher, 320
  Elizabeth (Marsh), 320
  Gundred (———), 347
  John, 319
  Joseph, 373
  Mary, 353
  Richard, 32, 320
  William, 320, 347
Washburn, Joanna, 159
  Israel, 82
  Martha (Benjamin), 82
Washington, *Arms*, 506, 507
  ——— (Whittington), 506
  Agnes (Bateman), 506
  Alice (Strother), 345
  Alice (Strother), Lewis Chart No. 1
  Amphillis (Roades), 506
  Amy (Pargiter), 506
  Ann (Pope), 507
  Augustine, 346, 393
  Betty, 268, 393
  Elizabeth (Light), 506
  Elizabeth (Lund), 344
  Ellen, 506
  George, 3, 72, 199, 268, 346, 395
  Jane (Fleming), 344, 348
  Jane (Fleming), Lewis Chart No. 1
  John, 344, 346, 348, 506
  John, Lewis Chart No. 1

Washington—*Continued*
  Lawrence, 3, 344, 346, 348, 506, 507
  Lawrence, Lewis Chart No. 1
  Lucy A., 279
  Lund, 343, 345, 347, 348
  Lund, Lewis Chart No. 1
  Margaret (Butler), 346, 506
  Margaret (Kitson), 506
  Martha (Dandridge) Custis, 72
  Mary (Ball), 393
  Mary (Townsend), 344
  Mary (Townsend), Lewis Chart No. 1
  Matilda, 3
  Mildred, 507
  Mildred (Warner), 507
  Nathaniel, 277
  Robert, 199, 345, 348, 506
  Robert, Lewis Chart No. 1
  Susan J., Lewis Chart No. 1
  Susan Jean, 343, 345, 347, 348
  Susannah (Grayson), 343, 345
  Susanna M. (Grayson), 348
  Susanna M. (Grayson), Lewis Chart No. 1
  Susannah Monroe (Grayson), 347
  Thomas, 506
  Townsend, 344, 348
  Townsend, Lewis Chart No. 1
  Walter, 199
Waterman, Amy, 27
  Hannah, 23, 438
  Mercy (Williams), 182
  Resolved, 182
  Robert, 438
  Sarah (Lewis), 438
  Waite, 182
Waters, Arnold, 256
  Edward, 69
  Grace (O'Neil), 69
  Harriett, 241
  Isabel, (Harmanson), 69, 70
  Jacob 240, 256
  Martha (Mulliken), 240, 256
  Mary, 197, 265
  Mary Etta, 234
  Rachel Sophia, 240

Waters—*Continued*
  Richard, 197
  Sarah, 63
  Sarah (Prentis), 387
  Susanna, 70
  William, 69, 70, 387
Wathen, George Frank, 337
  Lillian, 337
  Rose Victoria (Graves), 337
Watkins ———, 232, 237, 239
  Alexander, 432
  Anne (Hall) Rutland, 233, 239
  Ariana (Worthington), 48
  Dinah (———), 240
  Edward, 110
  Eleanor, 237
  Elizabeth, 232, 233, 238, 239, 256
  Elizabeth (Hall), 233, 237
  Frances, 59
  Gassaway, 52, 240
  Hannah (Ruggles), 432
  John, 233, 239
  Mararet, 48
  Margaret Gassaway, 240
  Maria (Brent), 110
  Martha, 356
  Mary, 236
  Nicholas, 48
  Rachel Sprigg, 237
  Richard, 356
  Ruth (Dorsey), 52
Watrous, Daniel, 127
  Lydia Ann (Bulkeley), 127
Watson, *Arms*, 482, 492
  ———, 483
  ——— (Rutland), 239
  Abbie (Murdock), 485
  Adaline Crittenden, 488
  Alexander Mackenzie, 482, 492, 501, 507
  Andrew, 486
  Andrew Jackson, 485
  Ann Bannister (Howe), 486
  Ann Mary, 492
  Anne, 487
  Anne Innes, 490
  Belle Quigley, 490
  Charlotte, 488
  Charlotte E. (Smith), 488
  Christopher, 482

INDEX

Watson—*Continued*
  Clifford Bryan, 491
  Corinne (Quigley), 490
  David Loyall Farragut, 492
  Dudley, 488
  Edward Howe, 487, 489, 491
  Eleanor Quigley, 490
  Eliza, 488
  Elizabeth, 358, 403, 486, 487
  Elizabeth Anderson (Thornton), 491, 507
  Elizabeth Ann (Todd), 488
  Elizabeth Courts (Love), 484
  Elizabeth Love, 485
  Fanny, 485
  Flo (Crosby), 485
  Florence (Leigh), 492
  George C., 488
  George Crittenden, 490
  Harriet Love, 485
  Henry Howe, 488
  Hermine (Gratz), 491
  James, 484
  James Muir, 485
  James Thornton, 491
  Jane, 486, 488
  Jane Love, 484, 487
  Jane Swigert, 490
  Jane (Taylor), 482, 484
  Jessie La Nauze (Clark) Strater, 482, 501
  John, 485, 486, 487, 488
  John Crittenden, 490, 492, 507
  John Jordan Crittenden, 492
  John Love, 486
  Josiah, 482, 483, 485, 486
  Kate C., 489
  Lina, 489
  Louisa F. (Hickman), 489
  Lucy Crittenden, 492
  Luke, 358
  Margaret, 482, 483
  Margaret (Bourland), 482
  Maria Innes, 489
  Marie (Sinclair), 491
  Mary, 67
  Mary Eleanor, 485
  Mary Gertrude (Seeley), 492
  Olivia M., 485
  Pauline Clay, 487
  Pauline Green (Clay), 487
  Philip Swigert, 488

Watson—*Continued*
  Rebecca, 487, 488
  Robert, 67, 486
  Robert Walter, 490
  Sallie Ann (Rodes), 487
  Samuel, 484
  Sarah, 486
  Sarah (———), 358
  Sarah Lee (Crittenden), 489
  Sarah Thornton, 492
  Thomas Quigley, 490
  Warren Murdock, 486
  William Henry, 485, 486, 488
  William P., 490
  William Rodes, 488
  Zelie, 485
Watt, R. E., 443
Wattles, Caroline (Clagett), 88
  Elizabeth Taylor, 88, 245
  Henry Star, 88
Weatherburn, Hannah Maria 170
Weatherhead, Margaret, 24
  Samuel, 24
Weathers, Christopher, 222
  Maria L. B. (Swearingen), 222
Weaton, Charity, 86
Webb, Alice, 320
  Annie Jordan (Darden), 387
  Blanche F. (Miller), 388
  Edward, 160
  Joseph Prentis, 387
  Margaret Susan (Prentis), 387, 390
  Martha, 298
  Mary Evarts, 160
  Nancy Allyn (Foote), 160
  Robert Henning, 387, 388, 390
  Thomas, 320
  William (De Richmond), 402
Webber, Christopher, 432
  Lucy (Robinson) Ruggles, 432
Webster, Daniel, 353
  Grace (Fletcher), 353
  John W., 22
  Madeleine W., 22
  Mary, 447
  Noah, 447
Weeks, Amiel, 38
  Elizabeth, 38

Weld, Habijah, 208
  Hannah, 208
  Mary (Fox), 208
Welles, *Arms*, 335
  Emily, 333
Welling, Margharita, 280
Wells ———, 450
  Abigail (Shelton), 335
  Almira (Tiffany), 462
  Andrew Shelton, 335
  Ann, 240
  Barbara, 154
  David, 335
  Elizabeth, 154
  Elizabeth (Bourne), 334
  Elizabeth (Hunt), 334
  Emily, 335
  Giedeon, 462
  James, 154
  Johannah (Wilscoxson), 335
  John, 311, 334, 335
  Mary, 362
  Mary (Hollister), 334
  Mary (Thompson), 335
  Mary (Warner), 335
  Richard, 349
  Ruth (Hannah), 154
  Sabina Elliott (Huger), 311
  Thomas, 240, 334
Welsh, Elizabeth Sellman, 238
  Hannah Dorsey (Hammond), 58
  John, 58, 91, 242, 349
  Sarah, 161
  Sophia, 242
  Thomasin (Hopkins), 242
Wendell, Johannes E., 467
  Maria (VanSantvoord), 467
Wentworth, Ebenezer, 326
  Rebecca (Jeffries), 326
West ———, 33
  Ann, 71
  Anne (Knollys), 74
  Anthony, 71
  Charles, 71
  Francis, 72, 74
  John, 231
  Katherine, 71
  Martha (Hall), 231
  Mary (Avery), 33
  Onesipharus, 514
  Stephen, 231
  Temperance, 387, 390

INDEX

West—*Continued*
  Temperance (Flowerdew), 72
  Temperance (Yeardley), 74
  Thomas, 71, 74
  Zilpha (Wood), 514
Westcott, Damaris, 23
  Stukeley, 23
Weston, Frances, 135
  John, 417
  Voadica, 417
Wethered, Clementina Matilda, 328
Wharton, Henry, 108
  Jane (Doyne), 108
  Mary, 108
  Mary (Scrogin), 476
  Rachel (Ellis), 476
  Revel, 476
  Robert, 470, 476
  Sarah, 475, 476
  Thomas, 476
Wheatley, Miranda, 191
Wheaton, Elizabeth (Wood), 513
  John, 86
  Samuel, 513
Whedon, Mary, 411
Wheeler, Agnes (Tuttle), 411
  Betsey, 411
  Hannah (French), 203
  Jethro, 203
  Melinda, 420
  Obadiah, 411
  Thomas, 409
Whelan, Etta, 442
  William, 442
Whipple, Olive, 381
  Samuel, 381
  Sarah F., 181
Whitaker, 205
  Mary Ann, 205
  William, 205
Whitcomb, Dorothy (Osgood), 407
  Joseph, 368
  Josiah, 407
  Susan Atlantic (Haskell) Bowen, 368
White, Elizabeth, 31, 395
  Hannah, 368
  Huldah, 380
  John, 203, 368

White—*Continued*
  Marmaduke Goodhand, 354
  Nannie Leonard (Rawlings), 354
  Peregrine, 368
  Phebe, 509
  Philbrick (French), 203
  Sarah Jane, 270
Whitehead, Catherine (Flynn), 388
  Elliott, 388
  Margaret Ann, 388, 390, 391
Whitgreaves, Frances, 112
Whiting, Hannah (Dwight), 289
  Harriet, 288, 289
  Joanna (Gay), 211
  Judith, 289
  Lemuel, 289
  Lois, 285
  Mary (Gay), 289
  Nathaniel, 211, 289
  Sarah, 289
  Timothy, 289
  William, 289
Whitington, Ida (Woodward), 248
  William F., 248
Whitman, Ella V., 442
  Hannah (Rickard), 416
  Thaniel, 416
Whitney ———, 416
  Abigail (Rickard), 416
  Elizabeth, 64
  Hannah (Cushing), 441
  Jonathan, 64
  Mary, 439
  Mary (Wyman), 64
  Nancy, 441
  Silas, 441
Whiton, Elizabeth, 440
  Rachel, 416
Whittemore, Elizabeth (Rhoades), 395
  Margaret, 124
  Nathaniel, 395
Whittier, Dorothy, 204
Whittinghame, Mary, 9
  Mary (Lawrence), 9
  William, 8, 9
Whittington ———, 506
  Miles, 506

Whytlaw, Agnes Alicia (La Nauze), 504
  George La Nauze, 504
  Harriette Sophia Newton, 504
  John Newton, 504
Wickham, Florence A. L. (Tiffany), 463
  Harry E., 463
Wicom, Daniel, 332
  Frances, 332
  Mary (Smith), 332
Wight, Mary, 288
  Thomas, 288, 289
Wightman, Avis M., 163
Wilbore, Abiah, 509
  Abiathar (Witherell), 510
  Abijah, 509, 510
  Anna (———), 509
  Asenath, 510
  Bathsheba Witherell, 510
  David, 510
  Ebenezer, 509
  Elisha, 510
  Elizabeth (Leonard), 509
  Jacob, 509
  Jerusha (Lincoln), 510
  Joan (Lea), 509
  Joanna, 509
  Joanna (Neal), 509
  Joseph, 509
  Lois, 510
  Lucinda (Lincoln), 510
  Lydia, 510
  Lydia (Deane), 509
  Mary (Leonard), 509
  Meshach, 509
  Nathan, 510
  Patty (Staples), 510
  Phebe (White), 509
  Philip, 509, 510
  Rachel (Wittam), 510
  Shadrach, 509
  Solomon, 510
  Susanna (Harris), 509
  Tabitha, 510
  Tabitha (Britton), 510
  Theodora, 510
  Wealthy, 510
  William, 510
  Zilpath, 510
Wilbur, *Arms*, 508, 511
  Abigail, 25

INDEX

Wilbur—*Continued*
  Achsah, 510
  Alice Dunbar (Heustis), 508
  Almina Jane, 511
  Armelia, 510
  Asenath, 510
  Asenath (Wilbore), 510
  Betsey E. (McFarland), 510
  Betsey (Fuller), 511
  Clarissa, 510
  Clarissa Maria, 511
  David, 511
  Delana, 510
  Diana, 510
  Dorothea Dix (Eliot), 508
  Earl Morse, 508
  Elbridge, 511
  Elizabeth Fuller, 508
  Elizabeth Stocker, 511
  Emily Ware, 511
  George Washington, 510
  Gratia, 508
  Gratia Bragg, 511
  Ida M. (Tillotson), 511
  La Fayette, 508, 511
  Mercy Jane (Morse), 508
  Meribah Esther Hyde, 511
  Ralph William, 508
  Ruth Ann, 511
  Salina, 510
  Sarah E. Paine, 511
  Seymour, 511
  Sylvia Ann Fuller, 511
  Thomas Lamb Eliot, 508
  Viola (Bundy), 511
  William, 510, 511
  William Eliot, 508
Wilcox, Abigail, 361
  Anna Maria, 147
  Daniel P., 147
  Elizabeth (Moss), 489
  Sarah (Champlin), 153
  Stephen, 153
Wilcoxson, Johannah, 335
Wildbore, Alice (Pitts), 509
  Ann (Bradford), 508
  Benjamin, 509
  Eliezer, 509
  Elizabeth (Farwell), 508
  Hannah, 509
  Hannah (Porter), 508
  Jane (Bird), 509
  John, 509

Wildbore—*Continued*
  Joseph, 508, 509
  Mary, 509
  Mary (Dean), 509
  Mehitable (Deane), 509
  Rebekah, 509
  Samuel, 508
  Sarah, 509
  Sarah (Phillips), 509
  Shadrach, 508, 509
  William, 508
Wilder, Cecelia, 440
  Edward, 440
  Emma (Courtenay), 172
  Hannah (Lewis), 440
  Jabez, 440
  James B., 172
  Martha (Collman), 440
  Samuel, 64
  Sarah, 440
  Sarah (Ballard), 64
Wilkie, Elizabeth (———), 437
  John, 437
Wilkins, Eleanor Bedford, 160
  Honor (Howard) Warfield Davidge, 52, 57
  Jane, 113
  Joseph, 52, 57, 160, 162
  Mary C. (Bedford), 162
  Mary C. (Rawlings), 160
  Mary Hill (Dorsey), 54
  Rebecca, 55
  Sarah Conant, 162
Wilkinson, James W., 311
  Marie, 5
  Naomi (———), 179
  Rebecca, 175, 176, 179, 180
  Sarah Elliott (Huger), 311
  William, 173, 176, 179, 180
Willard, Catherine, 440
  Helen, 134
  Jacob, 440
  James E., 281
  Madge, 281
  Margaret (Brayton), 281
Willett ———, 244
  Abraham, 14
  Hannah (Lawrence), 14
  Harriet, 132
Willey, Achsah (Wilbur), 510
  Stephen, 510
Williams ———, 58, 397
  Abigail (Davis), 431

Williams—*Continued*
  Elizabeth, 238, 242
  Elizabeth (Bryant) Bonnell Ballantine, 17
  Elizabeth (Watson), 403
  Howell, 55
  Joseph, 206, 403, 431
  Lucile, 254
  Mary (Fuller), 206
  Mary (Standberry) Rhodes, 397
  Mary (Warnard), 182
  Mercy, 182
  Otho Holland, 58
  Phebe, 403
  Phoebe (Todd) Dorsey, 58
  Rebecca, 246, 250
  Rebecca (Wilkins), 55
  Roger, 182
  Samuel, 17
  Sarah Beck, 246
  William, 250
  Williams G., 257
Williamson, Anne Martha (La Nauze), 505
  Annette de (La Nauze), 505
  David, 505
  John, 122
  Mary, 122
  Mary Amanda, 119
  Mary (Bower), 122
  Robert Carter, 119
Willing, Ann, 361
Willis, *Arms*, 494
  Anne (Alexander), 490
  John, 490
  Mary, 490
  Nathaniel Parker, 227
Wilson ———, 503
  Anne Vander Graff (Steele), 99
  Bertha Alice (Rhoades), 399
  Content (Haskell), 368
  E. Waring, 99
  Elijah, 368
  Elinor, 272
  Ephraim, 212
  Frances Breckinridge, 99
  Hannah, 46
  Henry G., 399
  Joanna (Gay), 212
  John D., 46
  John Steele, 99

INDEX

Wilson—*Continued*
  Louisa, 46
  Marshall, 46
  Mary, 454, 495
  Mary Jane, 275
  Polly (Templeman), 188
  Samuel, 188
  Sarah Ann (Ball), 46
  Susanna Preston, 99
  William R., 46
Winchester, Alpheus, 510
  Benjamin, 510
  Theodora (Wilbore), 510
  Wealthy (Wilbore), 510
Wing ———, 514
  Abraham, 514
  Anstis (Wood), 514
  Content (Wood), 514
  Edward, 513
  Mary, 517
  Patience (Ellis), 513
Winslow, Abby Frothingham (Gay), 213
  Frances (Gay), 213
  Hannah, 327
  Isaac, 213
Winston, Martha, 217
Winthrop, Elizabeth (Fones), 464
  John, 4, 6
Wise, Barbara Robins, 67
  Hannah (Scarborough), 67, 68, 71
  Henry A., 68
  John, 67, 68, 71
  William, 68
Wistar, Anna Catharina (———), 362
  Caspar, 362
  Johannes Caspar, 362
  Katherine Johnson (Jansen) 362
  Rebecca, 362
  Sarah (Morris), 362
Witham, Henry, 179
  Mary (Brooke) Bowling Hall, 179
Witherell, Abiathar, 510
  Bathsheba, 510
Wittam, Rachel, 510
Wolcott, Rachel, 315
  Roger, 378, 382
  Ursula, 382

Wonn, Cecilia, 353
Wood, *Arms*, 512, 515
  Abby, 514
  Abigail, 416
  Albert, 514
  Alida (Nicholson), 512
  Anne Greene (Russell), 515, 517
  Anstis, 514
  Augustus, 515
  Benjamin, 454
  Betsey Gordon, 514
  Betsey Pope (Gordon), 514
  Caleb, 514
  Carl-Anton Oscar Henry, 512
  Clotilde Jenny Marie Therese (Von Kretschman), 512
  Content, 513, 514
  Deliverance, 513
  Desire, 513
  Edmund, 515
  Elizabeth, 456, 513
  Elizabeth Nelson, 487
  Elizabeth (Thomas), 454
  Ernst Friedrich Edmund Earle, 512
  George, 513, 514
  George Russell, 515
  Gideon, 514
  Hannah, 513
  Hannah Ann, 363
  Hannah Catherine, 413
  Hannah (Shaw), 513
  Henry, 512, 513, 515, 517
  Henry Russell Oscar Friedrich, 512
  Henry Taber, 514, 515, 517
  Jabez, 514
  John, 512, 513, 514, 516
  Jonathan, 456
  Joseph, 514
  Kesia, 33
  Margaret, 513
  Martha (Earle), 513
  Mary, 513
  Mary (———), 513
  Nathaniel, 189
  Patience (Ellis) Wing, 513
  Peter, 454
  Phebe, 514
  Phoebe, 412

Wood—*Continued*
  Rebecca, 513
  Rebecca (———), 513
  Rhoda (Eldredge), 513
  Richard, 514
  Robert, 117
  Russell, 514
  Sally, 514
  Sarah (Doneghy), 189
  Sarah (Masterson), 512
  Sarah (Russell), 514, 516
  Susanna, 513
  Taber, 514
  Thankfull, 514
  Thankfull (Taber), 514
  Thomas, 513, 514
  Walter, 513, 514, 515
  Wilhelmine (Trist), 117
  William, 513
  William Gordon, 514
  Zaruiah, 513
  Zilpha, 514
Woodbridge, Benjamin, 438
  Deborah (Cushing) Tarleton, 438
  John, 331, 406
Woodbury, Hannah, 367
  John, 367
  Mary, 158
Woodfolk ———, 267
Woodhouse, Ann, 73, 75
  Ann (Bacon), 75
  Anne (Keeling), 78
  Eliza (Land), 74
  Elizabeth (Calthrope), 74
  Henry, 74, 75, 78
  John J., 74
  John T., 74
  Jonathan, 73, 74, 75
  Mary, 73
  Mary (———), 75
  Pembroke (Thoroughgood), 75
  William, 74, 75
Woodman, Dorothy, 406, 409
  Edward, 409
  Elizabeth (Stevens), 409
  Joanna (Salway), 409
  Joshua, 409
  Olive (Mallot), 409
Woodmansey, Mary, 31
  Robert, 31

INDEX

Woodward, Abraham, 248
  Achsah (Dorsey), 60
  Agnes Clare, 254
  Alice Marie, 254
  Aminee C. (Mathis), 248
  Amos, 60
  Charles, 254
  Daniel Dodge, 248
  Frank Thornton, 254
  Ida, 248
  Jimmie Nellie, 248
  Laura Adina, 248
  Laura (Chandler), 248
  Lucile (Williams), 254
  Margaret, 248
  Martha (Anderson), 248
  Mary Eugenia (Hall), 254
  Mary Gertrude, 254
  Mary Jane (Hall), 248
  Mattie, 248
  Nannie, 248
  Neeta Hattie, 248
  Olive, 74, 76
  Olive (Butt), 76
  Olive (Smith), 74
  Rignal Duckett, 248
  Virginia (Anderson), 248
  William, 76, 254
  William Isaac, 248
Wooldridge, Nannie Bertie, 189
Worden, Mehitable (Hinckley), 31
  Samuel, 31
  Sarah, 153
Worrell, Catherine Penelope, 273
Worth, Elizabeth, 104
Worthington, ———, 127
  Ann (Dorsey), 50
  Anne, 61
  Ariana, 48
  Charles, 60, 61
  Elizabeth, 42, 48, 50, 61
  Elizabeth (Ball), 46
  Elizabeth (Ridgely), 48
  Hannah (Cromwell), 61
  Helen (Hammond), 50

Worthington—*Continued*
  Helen Heath (Hammond), 60
  John, 50, 60, 61, 308
  Julia, 127
  Julia Maria, 239
  Laura, 50
  Lloyd, 46
  Martha (Garrettson), 61
  Mary (Bulkeley), 127
  Mary (Todd), 61, 308
  Mary (Tolley), 61
  Nicholas, 239
  Samuel, 61
  Sarah, 61, 238
  Sarah (Howard), 60
  Susannah (Hood), 61
  Thomas, 48, 61
  Vachel, 60
  William, 60, 61
Wrenn, Eliza, 388, 390
Wright, Boykin, 147
  Boykin Cabell, 147
  Clara Louise, 29
  Constance Cabell, 147
  Hatfield, 353
  John, 296
  Louisa Turpin, 359
  Lydia (Eliot) Penniman, 379
  Margaret, 296
  Margaret Constance (Cabell), 147
  Marguerite Cabell, 147
  Mary (Marine), 353
  Rachel, 296
  Sarah, 296
  Susanna, 296
  Thomas, 379
Wyatt, Nicholas, 47
  Sarah, 47
  Susanna, 145
Wyllis, George, 329
Wyman, Mary, 64
Wymond, Adah, 147

Y

Yager, Elizabeth (Huntington), 317
  Hiram, 317

Yard, Grace, 197
Yate, George, 47
Yeardley, Ann (Custis), 72, 77, 387, 390
  Argall, 69, 72, 77, 387, 390, 391
  Elizabeth, 72, 387, 391
  Francis, 72, 77
  George, 71, 72, 77, 192, 387, 390
  Henry, 72
  Rose, 72, 192
  Sarah (Michael), 69, 72, 387, 391
  Sarah (Offley) Thoroughgood Gookin, 77
  Temperance, 74
  Temperance (Flowerdew), 71, 72
  Temperance (West), 77, 387, 390
Yearsley, John, 393
  Sarah (Conoway), 293
Yeatman ———, 143
  Elizabeth (Cabell), 143
Young, Clark, 498
  Elizabeth, 207
  Frances Anne (Breckinridge), 97
  George, 207
  Isabella, 498
  Isabella (Clark), 498
  J. C., 97
  James, 498
  John, 498
  Margaret, 498
  Margaret (McCowan), 498
  Marian, 498
  Mary, 108
  Patience, 207
  William, 498
Younger, Cecilia (Wonn), 253
  Richard B., 253
  Virginia B., 253
Youngman, Anna, 384

Z

Ziegler, Marie, 37

WITHDRAWN